D1715891

To Joyce Apsel
Thank you for your advice
and guidance

Anton Weiss-Wendt
01/01/09

MURDER WITHOUT HATRED

Religion, Theology, and the Holocaust
Steven T. Katz, *Series Editor*

MURDER WITHOUT HATRED

Estonians and the Holocaust

Anton Weiss-Wendt

SYRACUSE UNIVERSITY PRESS

This book was made possible in part with a generous grant
from The Lucius N. Littauer Foundation.

For a listing of books published and distributed by Syracuse University Press,
visit our Web site at SyracuseUniversityPress.syr.edu

ISBN-13: 978-0-8156-3228-3   ISBN-10: 0-8156-3228-2

Library of Congress Cataloging-in-Publication Data

Weiss-Wendt, Anton, 1973–
Murder without hatred : Estonians and the Holocaust / Anton Weiss-Wendt.
p. cm. — (Religion, theology, and the Holocaust)
Includes bibliographical references and index.
ISBN 978-0-8156-3228-3 (hardcover : alk. paper)
1. Jews—Persecutions—Estonia—History—20th century. 2. Holocaust, Jewish
(1939–1945)—Estonia. 3. Estonia—History—German occupation, 1941–1944.
4. World War, 1939–1945—Collaborationists—Estonia. 5. Estonia—Ethnic
relations—History—20th century. I. Title.
DS135.E73W45 2009
940.53'18094798—dc22
2009011131

To Helmut Weiss

ANTON WEISS-WENDT studied modern European history at Tartu University, Estonia. In 1999 he received his M.A. in Judaic studies from New York University. He earned a Ph.D. at Brandeis University. Dr. Weiss-Wendt has worked on comparative genocide studies and Stalin's terror. He has published in *Holocaust and Genocide Studies, Journal of Genocide Research, Yad Vashem Studies, East European Jewish Affairs,* and *The Journal of Baltic Studies.* Dr. Weiss-Wendt is currently affiliated with the Norwegian Holocaust Center.

CONTENTS

Appendixes

ILLUSTRATIONS AND GRAPH

MAPS

ACKNOWLEDGMENTS

This book greatly benefited from the support of numerous individuals and research foundations. Most of all, I am grateful to the Department of Near Eastern and Judaic Studies at Brandeis University, and personally to Jonathan Sarna, Mark Brettler, Eugene Sheppard, ChaeRan Freeze, and Anne Lawrence, who have created a great academic environment in which I thrived. Milton Kornfeld and the School of Arts and Science, Karin Grundler-Whitacre (currently at Harvard Divinity School) and the Center for German and European Studies, and Sylvia Fuks Fried and the Tauber Institute for the Study of European Jewry—all these individuals and institutes at Brandeis have recognized the potential contribution of my study to Holocaust scholarship by providing financial support for research and writing. I also want to thank the individual donors who have made my dream of pursuing graduate studies at Brandeis come true.

Another research institution that has played an enormous role in my personal growth as a scholar is the United States Holocaust Memorial Museum. I am privileged to have been associated with the museum for over a decade. The unsurpassed professional qualifications and personal qualities of the museum staff have made me feel always at home there. I want to acknowledge the following individuals at the Center for Advanced Holocaust Studies who have helped me to broaden significantly my perspective: Benton Arnovitz, Martin Dean, Paul Shapiro, Peter Black, Jürgen Matthäus, and Geoffrey Megargee. The person who probably contributes the most to the general atmosphere of collegiality at the Center is Gwendolyn Bowen-Sherman. I have received much personal attention and professional advice from the extremely professional and friendly staff at the museum's archives: Carl Modig, Vadim Altskan, Alexandra Borecka, and Michlean Amir. All that wonderful academic experience would have been impossible without the generous financial support of the Holocaust

Memorial Museum in the form of a Charles Revson Foundation Fellowship for Archival Research, which I was awarded in 2002. The eight-month stay at the Center for Advanced Holocaust Studies enabled me not only to conduct the bulk of archival research for my study but also to meet and exchange ideas with other Fellows.

I am indebted to Raul Hilberg, Ruth Bettina Birn, Christopher Browning, Severin Hochberg, and Alexander Prusin—historians who found time in their busy schedules to read and comment on the first draft of this book. Most of the criticism that the above scholars shared with me has been incorporated into the final draft. In addition, I want to extend my gratitude to historians who at one point or another shared their manuscripts with me: Elisabeth White, Andrew Ezergailis, Riho Västrik, Meelis Maripuu, Argo Kuusik, and Toomas Hiio. Andres Kasekamp was a big help in my navigation through the most recent Estonian scholarship. In consideration of a time-honored principle—about matters of truth, dispute if fruitful—I hope that none of the scholars whom I mention by name in the book would take my criticism personally.

Antony Polonsky and Michael Gelb are the two individuals who have influenced my thinking most profoundly. I feel lucky to have had Antony Polonsky as my academic adviser at Brandeis. Through his lectures, seminars, and personal insights I have learned the importance of contextualization. By personal example, Antony Polonsky has showed me how to use the professional skills of a historian effectively while remaining compassionate toward the people whom we study. Indeed, Antony Polonsky has taught me a lesson in humanity. The same can be said about Michael Gelb, who was the first scholar I met at the United States Holocaust Memorial Museum. I can truly regard Michael Gelb as my mentor; he literally opened up America to me. Personal conversations that I have had with Michael over the years were extremely stimulating. This book would not have been possible without the continual moral and academic support that I have enjoyed from these two great scholars and individuals.

The editing of the manuscript proved a learning experience thanks to Rebecca Adell, a good friend of mine who has invested a lot of her time and energy in the process. I derived much pleasure from working with Ellen Goodman, Mona Hamlin, and Lisa Kuerbis at Syracuse University Press, who displayed the highest professional and personal qualities. I am personally indebted to Steven Katz, who selected my manuscript for publication in the Holocaust Studies series of which he is the editor. It is an honor to be associated with the distinguished scholars who have published with Syracuse University Press.

Finally, I want to mention the following individuals who have helped me, if only indirectly, to stay true to my beliefs: Deborah A. Dyer, Tom Araya, Chuck Schuldiner, Lajon Witherspoon, and Mark Greenway.

INTRODUCTION

People in Germany often ask me about the subject of my research. When they learn that I write about the Holocaust in Estonia, their next question is: which particular aspect of the Holocaust? I am at a loss to answer that question. In my view, the Holocaust has just one aspect to it: mass murder. Tens of thousands of articles and books that have been published on the "Final Solution of the Jewish Question" struggle with the very same question: how can anybody commit such a heinous crime? In that sense, my study is not an exception. I, too, glare with astonishment at the number of victims. My question, however, is different. I look at mediators, the second tier of perpetrators and bystanders. Those people did not devise the Final Solution nor lobby for its implementation and yet they made a substantial contribution to the Nazi mass murder. In particular, what I want to know is what caused one particular people, the Estonians, to collaborate with Nazi Germany. A simple question that defies a simple answer.

A case study like the one I am attempting has its benefits and shortcomings. Of the three Baltic countries, Estonia has received the least attention from Holocaust scholars. Jews had settled in Estonia only recently and were few in number, which places Estonia among countries like Finland and Norway rather than Latvia and Lithuania. When it comes to death toll, three million Polish Jews make one thousand Estonian Jews look like a drop in the sea of sorrow. At the same time, the small size of the community makes it possible to account for each and every victim. In the case of Estonia, we are dealing with individuals rather than abstract numbers. The same can be said about perpetrators.

Nowadays we know as much about the history of writing about the Holocaust as we do about the Holocaust. By the 1980s scholars had split into two distinctive schools of thought, Intentionalist and Functionalist. In the United States during the 1990s the Intentionalist model of explanation of the Nazi genocide has regained ground, while Germany has remained a stronghold of Functionalism. The problem of collaboration, however, does not easily submit itself to theorizing. Local collaboration in the Holocaust is too emotional a topic to be subjected to cold analysis. Despite the fact that until very recently theoretical discourse on local collaboration in Eastern Europe was nearly nonexistent, researchers seem to gravitate toward the Intentionalist viewpoint. Standard narrative goes as follows: Nazis incited Poles, Ukrainians, Lithuanians, Latvians, and Estonians—who had become increasingly anti-Semitic during the year of Soviet rule—to lash out at Jews. That attitude implies a certain inevitability, as if we could not have expected anything but bloodletting. By accepting that argument, we obviously do not have to look any further than the Soviet invasion of June 1940 (in the case of Poland, September 1939). A short overview of the history of anti-Semitism in the region should then make the picture complete. I argue, however, that anti-Semitism alone cannot explain local collaboration in Nazi genocide of Jews—definitely not in Estonia. To substantiate my claim, I use a psychocultural approach.

Social structure of a society can help to explain the complexities of both individual and collective behavior. Twelve months of the Soviet rule could not possibly have transformed Estonian society beyond recognition, unless the changes had already begun to occur earlier. One way or another, the structure had apparently started disintegrating before 1940. The very foundation of the nation-state had cracks in it. Consequently, in order to be able to determine the causes of Estonian collaboration with the German occupier, I need to cast my net as widely as possible.

Most important I think is to understand how Estonians perceived themselves in relation to the larger world. For that matter, the dynamics of Estonian-Jewish relations are as important as those of Estonian-German or Estonian-Russian relations. What were the principles upon which the Estonian nation-state was built and did those principles change over time? Did it have any effect on Estonian political culture, and subsequently on the collective psyche? Those are the problems I address before I start looking at the events of the summer of 1941. Only at first glance can these questions seem unrelated to the study of the Holocaust.

The novelty of my approach is that I place local collaboration in the Holocaust within a larger phenomenon of collaboration. Involvement of some Estonians, Latvians, and Lithuanians in the Nazi genocide was just one aspect of their cooperation with the German occupation authorities. By looking at the

Holocaust in isolation, I argue, we overlook important cues that can enhance our understanding of the motives for collaboration. I am primarily interested in the Baltic perspective on the "Final Solution of the Jewish Question." Whenever possible, I try to compare the Estonian response to the Holocaust with that of Latvians and Lithuanians. To some extent, I also consider Finland. This comparison is probably the only way of explaining why the Estonian case was so different.

While attempting to place the Holocaust in Estonia into a theoretical framework, my study is strongly grounded in the historical method. My intention is, plain and simple, to tell the story. For the first time, I connect all three stages of the mass murder of the Jews in Estonia into one cohesive narrative. I try to avoid (as has been common in contemporary history-writing in Estonia) treating Jews who were citizens of Estonia separately from the Jews deported to Estonia from other European countries. By the same token, I look at other groups of victims such as Gypsies, the mentally ill, and Soviet POWs. This is why the death toll I calculated for Estonia is almost four times bigger than the officially accepted figure of 7,798. I decided to leave the theoretical discussion of collaboration for last. By so doing I put my theoretical discourse onto a firm empirical foundation rather than leave it to speculation.

ABBREVIATIONS AND ACRONYMS

AEL	*Arbeits- und Erziehungslager* (labor education camp)
AJDC	American Joint Distribution Committee
AKS	*Alte, körperlich schwache,* abbreviation Nazis used for prisoners subject to selection
AOK	*Armeeoberkommando* (army headquarters)
Baltöl	Baltische Öl GmbH (Baltic Oil Ltd.)
BdS	Befehlshaber der Sicherheitspolizei und des SD (Commander in Chief of the Security Police and SD)
Col.	Colonel
DSB	Deutsche Schutzbund (Grenz- und Auslandsdeutschtum) (German League for the Defense of Ethnic Germans Abroad)
Dulag	*Durchgangslager* (transit camp)
EG	Einsatzgruppe (mobile killing unit of the Sipo)
ERR	Einsatzstab Reichsleiter Rosenberg (Operations Staff Rosenberg)
ESTAG	Eesti Kiviõli (First Estonian Shale Oil Industry, Ltd.)
EWZ	Einwandererzentralstelle (Central Immigration Office)
Gen. Maj.	*Generalmajor:* brigadier general
GK	*Generalkommissar* (Reich commissioner)
HGr	*Heeresgruppe* (army group)
HptFw.	*Hauptfeldwebel* (first sergeant)
HSSPF	Höhere SS- und Polizeiführer (Higher SS and Police Commander)
I.A.	*Im Auftrag* (by order of)
KdS	Kommandeur der Sicherheitspolizei und des SD (Commander of the Security Police and SD)

KL	Kaitseliit (Estonian Home Guard)
Krim.-Komm.	*Kriminalkommissar* (detective inspector)
Lieut.	Lieutenant
Minölko	Mineralöl Kommando (Mineral Oil Commando)
NKGB	Narodnyi Komissariat Gosudarstvennoi Bezopasnosti, Temporary name for NKVD (February–June 1941)
NKVD	Narodnyi Komissariat Vnutrennikh Del (Soviet Security Police)
Obstlt.	*Oberstleutnant* (lieutenant colonel)
Obw.	*Oberwachtmeister* (sergeant)
OK	Omakaitse (Estonian Auxiliary Police) (Self-Defense)
OKH	Oberkommando des Heeres (Army High Command)
OT	Organisation Todt (Organization Todt)
Otrupf.	*Obertruppführer* (senior sergeant [RAD])
POW	prisoner of war
RAD	Reichsarbeitsdienst (Reich Labor Service)
Rbl.	*Rubl'*: Soviet currency
RFSS	Reichsführer SS (Head of the SS [Heinrich Himmler])
RKO	Reichskommissar für das Ostland (Reich Commissioner for the Ostland)
RM	*Reichsmark* (German currency)
RMO	Reichsminister für die besetzten Ostgebiete (Reich Minister for the Occupied Eastern Territories)
RSHA	Reichssicherheitshauptamt (Reich Security Main Office)
RuSHA	Rasse- und Siedlungshauptamt (Race and Settlement Main Office)
RVK	Reichsvereinigung Kohle (Reich Coal Union)
Schuma	*Schutzmannschaft* (auxiliary police)
Schupo	Schutzpolizei (German Municipal Police)
SD	Sicherheitsdienst (Security Service)
Sipo	Sicherheitspolizei (Security Police)
SK	Sonderkommando (special detachment of EG)
SS	Schutzstaffel (Nazi elite force)
SS-Brif.	*Brigadeführer* (brigadier general)
SS-Gruf.	*Gruppenführer* (major general)

SS-Hschaf.	*Hauptscharführer* (technical sergeant)
SS-Hstuf.	*Hauptsturmführer* (captain)
SS-Oberf.	*Oberführer* (between a brigadier general and a colonel)
SS-Ogruf.	*Obergruppenführer* (lieutenant general)
SS-Oschaf.	*Oberscharführer* (staff sergeant)
SS-Ostubaf.	*Obersturmbannführer* (lieutenant colonel)
SS-Ostuf.	*Obersturmführer* (first lieutenant)
SS-Rotf.	*Rottenführer* (corporal)
SS-Staf.	*Standartenführer* (colonel)
SS-Stubaf.	*Sturmbannführer* (major)
SS-Uscharf.	*Unterscharführer* (sergeant)
SS-Ustuf.	*Untersturmführer* (second lieutenant)
SSPF	SS- und Polizeiführer (SS and Police Commander)
Stalag	*Stammlager* (main camp)
TK	Teilkommando (partial detachment of SK)
TU	Tartu University
US FET	U.S. Forces European Theatre
Vabs	Vabadusvõitlejad (Estonian right-wing movement)
Valpo	Valtiollinen Poliisi (Finnish State Police)
VO	*Verbindungsoffizier* (liaison officer)
VoMi	Volksdeutsche Mittelstelle (Central Agency for Ethnic Germans)
WiIn	Wirtschaftsinspektion (Economic Inspectorate)
WiKo	Wirtschaftskommando (subunit of WiIn)
WVHA	Wirtschafts- und Vervaltungshauptamt (Economic and Administrative Main Office)
ZEV	Zentralstelle zur Erfassung der Verschleppten Esten (Deportee Registration Office)

MURDER WITHOUT HATRED

1 ESTONIANS AND THEIR STATE

In the context of East Central Europe, Estonia was a relatively homogeneous country during the interwar period. Minorities constituted slightly more than 10 percent of the total population of Estonia, as compared with the 30 percent average for Eastern Europe. Yet Estonia was the most reluctant of the three Baltic countries to sign the international treaty guaranteeing the rights of minorities. As a condition for membership in the League of Nations, the three Baltic countries were requested on December 15, 1920, to issue a declaration reaffirming ethnic minorities' rights. Estonia and Latvia refused to do so while referring to the fact that neither of the two countries owed its independence to the Versailles Peace Treaty or the Paris Peace Conference. Estonian officials contended that the assembly recommendation was already realized in the Estonian Constitution, which contained a minority clause.[1] In the end, following the example of Lithuania and Latvia, Estonia yielded to pressure and signed the Minorities Declaration, on September 17, 1923. The Minorities Declaration was similar to the Minorities Treaty, for both documents authorized the system of petitions that ethnic minorities could submit to the League of Nations Secretariat against their respective governments. Estonia, however, managed to insert a clause stipulating that no information regarding the violation of minority rights in Estonia could be submitted to the League of Nations from outside of the country. That clause mainly affected Germany, which was thus denied a legal channel for intervening on behalf of the ethnic Germans in Estonia.[2]

The Law on Cultural Autonomy, adopted in Estonia on February 12, 1925, and widely praised abroad, was as much a result of goodwill as of political compromise. Although the right to cultural autonomy was effectively extended to

1

all ethnic minorities, it was intended specifically for the Baltic Germans. The Baltic Germans were awarded cultural autonomy as compensation for both past grievances and anticipated detriment. Historically, ethnic Germans had owned most of the arable land in Estonia and Latvia. When the Estonian Republic was proclaimed in February 1918, up to 58 percent of all land still belonged to Baltic German landowners, whereas two-thirds of Estonian peasants (about 500,000) owned no land at all. The 1919 Land Reform stripped the ethnic Germans not only of their property but also of their high status, as it symbolized the destruction of the hated Baltic German domination in the region.[3] The land redistribution was carried out more radically in Estonia than in Latvia and Lithuania. Although not every estate affected by the Land Reform belonged to Baltic Germans, they sustained the greatest loss (86.5 percent). The Baltic Germans were never reconciled to the loss of the land. The humiliation experienced at the hands of the Estonians made the local German community appeal for redress to as high an authority as the League of Nations. Baltic German politicians accused the Estonian and Latvian governments of directly assaulting the German minority by means of the Land Reform. Some of them resorted to speculations about "strong Bolshevik leanings" among both the working class and the peasantry.

A sudden breakthrough in minority legislation occurred in the wake of the Communist putsch of December 1924 (I will discuss the putsch in more details below). The Law on Cultural Autonomy was adopted thanks to the unremitting lobbying of the German parliamentary faction. Local Germans thought of cultural autonomy not only as a means of preserving their ethnic identity but also as a way of keeping Estonia within the German/European cultural sphere.[4] As regards the impact of the autonomy law on the Jews, in the final analysis this group became the unintended beneficiaries of the tripartite relations between Estonians, Germans, and Russians.

Jewish history in Estonia began late and ended abruptly. The first Jewish congregations in Estonia came into existence in the mid-nineteenth century— that is, much later than in Latvia and Lithuania. Jewish immigration had been impossible because of the fact that Estonia lay outside the borders of the so-called "Jewish pale of settlement." In 1827 the Russian Tsar Nikolai I authorized the conscription of Jews into compulsory military service. Upon completing twenty-five years of service, Jewish servicemen—known as *Cantonists*—were allowed to settle outside of the pale. Tallinn, along with Pskov and Arkhangelsk, became a gathering place for Jewish soldiers. Often, the only way for them to stay was to convert to Christianity. Those Cantonists who remained true to their faith laid the foundation of the Tallinn Jewish congregation, in 1856. Within the next year a Jewish congregation was established in Tartu. Similar congregations came into existence in the mid-1860s in Narva, Viljandi, Pärnu, Võru, Valga, and Rakvere. Nevertheless, there were only 657 Jews registered in Estonia in 1867.[5]

On the eve of the First World War, the Estonian Jewish community reached its highest point with about 5,500 (exact numbers unavailable). Three-fifths of the Estonian Jews at that time lived in Tartu (2,027) and Tallinn (1,100).[6] The German occupation of Estonia, which lasted from February 1918 to November 1918, did not disrupt Jewish life in Estonia in any significant manner, but the following Bolshevik takeover did. Well-to-do Jews left for good and so did many community leaders. The hardship of war and the administrative acts of the new regime combined to bring Jewish social life in cities like Narva to a complete standstill. Of the prewar Jewish population of 523, only one-third stayed in Narva.[7] The Jewish population in Estonia decreased by another 3 percent between 1922 and 1934. By then, Jews constituted 0.4 percent of the total population of Estonia (4,434). Tallinn by far surpassed Tartu in importance, so that by the mid-1930s half of the Jews lived in the Estonian capital, as compared with only 920 in Tartu. Remarkably, by then only 79 Jews (1.7 percent) lived in the countryside, thus making Estonian Jewry the most urbanized in Eastern Europe. (See map 1.)

The Versailles Settlement placed Jews in most East European countries at a disadvantage. The Jewish minority found itself squeezed between two mutually opposing groups such as Ukrainians and Poles in Galicia, or Germans and Czechs in Bohemia. The situation of the Jews in Lithuania significantly differed from that in Latvia and Estonia: Lithuanians needed the support of the Jews against the Poles in Vilna. In the former Baltic provinces of the Russian Empire, where the number of constituents exceeded two, interethnic alliances were not so clearly defined. The titular nationality in these two countries sought to define themselves against their former oppressors, that is, Germans and Russians. The situation in Estonia was less about discriminating against ethnic minorities than about preventing ethnic Estonians from joining the mainstream Russian or German culture. Acculturated Estonians became an object of scorn for their alleged betrayal of the Estonian nation in the making.[8] It did not matter, therefore, whether the Jews allied themselves with the Germans or the Russians, so

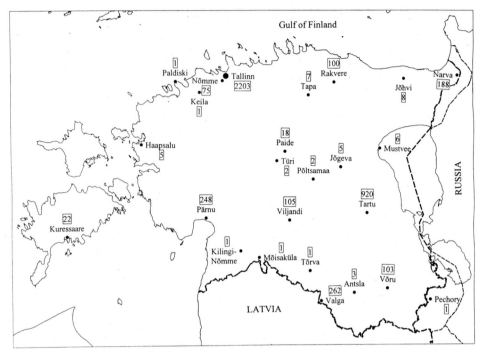

1. Distribution of Jews in Estonia; 1934 Census.

long as they remained out of the way of the country's majority population. That separation the Jews could indeed guarantee.

Jews had to deal with problems that other minorities in Estonia did not have. The most important issue was the recognition of Jews as an ethnic minority. Back in 1918, the Estonian provisional government had posed as a minority-friendly body, which recognized the Germans, Russians, Swedes, and Latvians as ethnic minorities. The 1920 constitution listed only three ethnicities that were *historically* connected to Estonia: the Germans, the Russians, and the Swedes.[9] The provisional naturalization law denied citizenship to a majority of the Jews in Estonia. Because of the fact that Estonia lay outside the pale of settlement, before 1917 Jews could not officially register as residents of Estonia, as specified by the naturalization law. In the absence of any provision dealing specifically with the Jewish case, Jews were relegated by default to the category of legal aliens. By the same token, no Jews were accepted into the ranks of the volunteer military organization Kaitseliit, created in November 1918. Lack of central organization prevented Jews from raising the issue directly with the Estonian interim government. Finally, the Tartu National Political Committee, which had represented the interests of the Estonian Jews since December 1918, succeeded in lifting the ban on conscription of Jews into the Estonian armed forces.[10]

The Law on Cultural Autonomy of February 1925 recognized as a minority any ethnic group of three thousand and more. Only Estonian citizens were to be counted, however. Interestingly enough, the U.S. consul in Estonia inferred from the document that only the Germans, Russians, and Swedes qualified as ethnic minorities. The consul was rather skeptical that the Estonian government would consider the request of the Jewish minority for cultural autonomy.[11] It took the Jews much longer than the Baltic Germans to implement cultural autonomy. On October 19, 1925, the Tallinn Jewish community announced in the name of the Estonian Jewry its desire to set up cultural self-government. A half-year delay was obviously caused by the provision that set the required number of members of the respective minority citizens of Estonia at three thousand. The Estonian Jews scraped together just enough citizens of Estonia (3,045) to qualify for an autonomous status. The rest of the community, some 1,500, claimed other than Estonian citizenship or no citizenship at all.[12] That lack of citizenship further strengthened the supposition that the drafters of the cultural autonomy law did not take Jews into account.[13] The government authorized elections to the Jewish Cultural Council in March 1926; the elections took place between May 23 and 25 of the same year.

Cultural autonomy came at a cost. By embracing autonomy, the Jewish and German minorities pledged adherence to the principle of separation of culture and politics. Cultural self-government precluded engagement in political activities.[14] All the benefits that Jews received from cultural autonomy were overshadowed by one particular aspect that had a long-lasting impact on the community—further isolation from other ethnic groups, first and foremost the Estonians. As Jews further coalesced into a tight-knit community, contacts with the Estonian population became less frequent.[15] The idea of Jews as loyal citizens of the Estonian State dominated the festivities held on the occasion of the tenth anniversary of cultural autonomy in 1936. Unfortunately, few Estonians were aware of the Jews' status as citizens.[16]

In comparison with the Latvian Jews, the Estonian Jewish community was rather poor. According to a report of the American Joint Distribution Committee

(AJDC) from the mid-1920s, most of the sixty-five Jewish families in Narva—the country's fifth largest Jewish community—lived in dire poverty. The heads of thirty-five families were artisans; the rest earned their livelihood by petty trade.[17] The economic potential of the Jews was inconsequential compared to that of the Baltic Germans. Estonian Jews controlled only 2.3 percent of trade and 0.6 percent of industry, although they did account for 2 percent of the country's weakly developed heavy industry. Almost all big Jewish-owned companies were located in Tallinn. At the same time, Jews were overrepresented in certain professions. Thus every tenth physician in Estonia was Jewish. According to the survey that the Jewish Cultural Council conducted in 1935, the occupational breakdown among Estonian Jews was as follows: trade—30 percent; small business—24 percent; artisans—15 percent; workers—14 percent; professionals—10 percent; big business—5 percent; landlords—1 percent; religious functionaries—1 percent.[18]

By the mid-1930s, only half of Jewish children in Estonia went to Jewish schools. Eighteen percent enrolled in German schools, 17 percent in Estonian, and another 10 percent in Russian, whereas in the previous decade 45 percent of Jewish children had attended Russian schools. The choice of school had to do with social class more than with anything else. Well-to-do parents sent their children to non-Jewish schools so that they could be better prepared for college, whereas the less fortunate ones had no other chance but to enroll their children in Jewish schools, which were free.[19] Parents themselves, however, routinely explained their choice as being on account of insufficient command of Estonian. Before 1930, the languages of instruction at the Tallinn Jewish high school were Russian and Hebrew, and thereafter Hebrew and Yiddish.

The numbers of Jewish students at Tartu University (TU) dropped from 188 in 1926 (4.0 percent of the total student body) to 69 in 1938 (2.1 percent). Some Jews claimed discrimination in the form of more vigorous entrance examinations.[20] Jewish students at TU were strongly influenced by Russian and Baltic German culture but not necessarily by Estonian or Latvian culture. Two-thirds of the members of the Academic Association for the Study of Jewish History and Culture had Russian high school diplomas. Another four Jewish academic associations at TU were the fraternities Limuwia and Hasmonea, and the sororities Ossidia and Hacfiro. All five associations promoted the Zionist Revisionist agenda and, with the exception of Limuwia and the Academic Association, rarely took an interest in student life in general.[21]

Zionism enjoyed universal support among the Estonian Jews. The main difference between Estonia and the other two Baltic countries was the conspicuous absence of the Jewish Orthodox politics represented by Agudes Yisroel. Otherwise, the Jewish political spectrum in Estonia was a cross-section of that found in Latvia and that found in Lithuania. Zionism was probably as strong in Estonia as it was in Lithuania. At the same time, a solid support base for Folkspartey (also known as Autonomists or Yyddishists) in Latvia was comparable with that in Estonia.[22] As regards participation in Estonia's political life generally, Jews took a rather passive stance. Except for a humble attempt in 1919 to ally themselves with one of the Estonian political parties, Jews essentially withdrew from the country's mainstream. In sharp contrast to Latvia, not a single Jewish deputy had been elected to the Estonian Parliament since its inception. In the parliamentary elections, Estonian Jews had consistently voted for the Socialists.[23]

Estonian folklore further attests to the lack of interaction between the Jewish minority and the Estonian majority. For example, Jews are mentioned in only nine proverbs out of 15,140 existing in Estonia.[24] Jewish themes entered Estonian folklore through Germany rather than Russia. Along with the Cantonists, a category of Jews that had left its mark on Estonian folklore was petty traders. Popular beliefs tied Jewish emigration to the United States in the 1880s to the traditional image of the wandering Jew, thus punished by some higher power. In the 1880s and 1890s the wandering Jew had allegedly been seen in all major Estonian cities. The idea was that sooner or later all Jews would leave Estonia for somewhere else. When Jews arrived in Rakvere for the first time, local Estonians wondered why the Jews did not have horns. In southern Estonia, people looked upon Jews as descendants of Judas or the devil. In Hiiu, parents used to admonish their children for misbehavior with the threat "Jews will kill children off," while in Pärnu a common saying was "Jews will take you away." The first half of a story recorded in 1922 in Keila talked about Gypsies; the story then continued, "but Jews were even worse." Throughout Estonia, people described murky business as "black like a Jew."[25] Surely Estonians' perception of Jews was more multifaceted than this. It would be fallacious to mistake folk beliefs for potential impulses to commit violence. What folklore does show, however, is that Estonians had few personal encounters with the Jews, whom they often perceived as the great unknown, the Bible people disconnected from reality.

The relations between the Estonian majority and the Jewish minority can be described as friendly yet largely superficial. When writing, rather infrequently, about the Jews, the newspapers tended to treat them as a somewhat exotic body, with no deep attachment to the Estonian soil. "What do we know about the life of Narva Jews?" was the title of an article that appeared in a local Estonian newspaper in 1930. "We know Jews as smart businessmen, and that is probably it," the opening sentence of the article read. The newspaper wrote that Narva Jews kept to their own, and sent their children without exception to Russian middle and high schools. It would be worthwhile for the local Jews to explain that phenomenon in public, the author of the article suggested. The article presented Narva Jews as through and through Zionists who continually collected funds for the benefit of Jewish settlement in Palestine. Some families had already moved to Palestine; others purchased plots of land there, ready to go in case the situation in Estonia turned for the worse.[26]

In comparison with other European countries, Estonia adopted a rather mild immigration policy in the late 1930s. Although Jewish immigration to Estonia was discouraged, all those who made it to the country could stay. There is no evidence that Jewish immigrants had ever been harassed in Estonia, as happened in France or Switzerland. In public and in private, however, Estonian officials often expressed their determination to prevent a massive influx of Jewish immigrants. Thus, in an interview in July 1938, the minister of welfare denied the existence of the so-called "Jewish Question" in Estonia, referring to the equality of Estonian citizens before the law. Then, however, he went on by saying that no more Jews would be allowed into the country.[27]

The Evian Conference, which convened in the same month, requested that Estonia accommodate a certain number of Jewish refugees. General Johan Laidoner, commander in chief of the Estonian army, refused to cooperate. The only exception was made in the case of two female Jewish consuls general who had represented Estonia in Frankfurt and Hamburg since the 1920s. Some Jews had entered Estonia from Latvia, taking advantage of the visa-free exchange between the two countries. The Estonian government raised its concern with its Latvian counterpart, but to no avail.[28] Governmental officials rebutted speculations about the wealth of the incoming Jews, who allegedly could generate additional revenues for the Estonian State, arguing correctly that those Jews who were forced to emigrate from Austria and Germany had previously been stripped of their belongings and capital.[29] Therefore, the admission of a larger number of Jews into Estonia was out of the question. One of the newspapers speculated that if a ship carrying Jewish refugees were to appear in Tallinn's harbor, Estonia should follow the example of countries like France, England, Switzerland, and Finland that closed their borders to the Jews.[30] The total number of Jewish refugees from Germany and Austria in Estonia could be estimated at one hundred.

The official position regarding Jewish immigration to Estonia, which was not unusual for 1930s Europe, displayed no particular hostility toward the Jews. Indeed, the level of anti-Semitism in interwar Estonia was lower than that in most countries of East Central Europe. The examples of anti-Jewish prejudice in Estonia fade in comparison with the extent of popular and political anti-Semitism in the other two Baltic States, in Lithuania in particular.

ANTI-SEMITISM

Earlier data suggest that Estonians distrusted Jews, whom they saw as newcomers to the country. The 1920s brought about such charges against the Jews as greed, deficient Estonian-language proficiency, and a propensity for Bolshevism. Some Estonians associated Communism with the Jews, just because several Bolshevik leaders happened to be Jewish. The leading Estonian newspaper *Postimees* (Tartu) published on average between ten and twelve anti-Semitic articles per year. In 1923, Estonian police arrested a group of individuals that had distributed anti-Semitic flyers. Mistrust on the part of the Estonians bred similar sentiment among the Jews toward the titular nationality.[31]

Anti-Semitic periodicals and pamphlets, which had been published in Estonia in the 1920s and 1930s, did not last because of a lack of devoted readership. The Estonian government interfered with the publication of an international anti-Semitic bestseller, *Juudi usu saladused* (secrets of Judaism), which was printed in Tartu in 1919, by removing the book from circulation three years later. A tabloid, *Juudid* (Jews), was launched in 1922 but only survived eight issues. Only two issues of *Kes on Juudid?* (Jews, who are they?) were published in 1925 and 1926, until this lampoon, too, ceased to exist. One other slanderous newspaper, *Kas Meie või Juudid?* (Us or the Jews?), lasted for eight issues until it was discontinued in 1929. *Valvur* (The guard) proved to be the most successful anti-Semitic periodical in Estonia. The quality of paper and layout of *Valvur* exceeded that of its predecessors. Published for several years in the early 1930s, *Valvur* presented itself as "the magazine that protects national culture/the anti-Jewish, anti-Socialist and anti-Communist magazine." *Juutide maailmavallutamise kava* (program of Jewish world domination) went out of print in 1934; this blatantly anti-Semitic pamphlet fell victim to the censorship that the new, authoritarian government of Estonia introduced in the same year.[32]

Cases of everyday anti-Semitism increased in Estonia following a November 1938 pogrom in Germany. On one occasion, a group of Jews were asked to leave the Kultas café in Tallinn, for they "disturbed the Estonian customers." At a local train station in Elva—a popular summer destination for the Jews—somebody changed the sign to "Jerusalem."[33] The reported instances of anti-Semitism sometimes had direct references to developments in Nazi Germany. One such case took place in a popular restaurant, Du Nord, in Tallinn on November 14, 1938. Following an international boxing competition in which Estonia defeated Germany, the hosts invited their guests for a dinner. A few Jewish customers at the restaurant made anti-German, or rather anti-Nazi, comments. The Estonian sportsmen intervened by throwing the Jews out of the restaurant. Two of the assaulted were subsequently taken to a hospital for treatment. Of all the Estonian newspapers, only the populist *Rahvaleht* reported the incident, even then in the form of a parody.[34] The story had a continuation when the owner of the restaurant published a rebuttal, in which he not only downplayed the entire incident but also threatened to take the newspaper to court. The fight at Du Nord opened up a public discussion, which demonstrated that, with the exception of a few liberal intellectuals, most Estonian nationalists welcomed the incident as a just response to Jewish arrogance. Other expressions of anti-Semitism were soon to follow: a Jewish doctor was injured in a nightclub; a Jewish jeweler was beaten and his car vandalized; the showcases of several Jewish businesses were broken. The police either did not report those cases at all, or else blamed them on drunkenness or theft rather than on anti-Semitism. For some people, that response might even sound plausible, considering that Estonian-owned stores had been vandalized from time to time too.[35]

Christian anti-Semitism had traditionally been strong in Catholic countries such as Lithuania. In Estonia, the principal denomination was Lutheranism, the religion associated with the German conquest and therefore not necessarily viewed as the *national* church. The religious factor was altogether muted in Estonian nationalism; Estonian society had already become increasingly secularized by the mid-nineteenth century.[36] In short, the Church did not have enough influence in the society to amass the support crucial for anti-Semitism. Neither was the Estonian military powerful enough to uphold a tradition of anti-Semitism independently. For one thing, Jewish officers were nonexistent in the Estonian army, as Jews were only found among the rank and file. During the war of national liberation of 1918–20 as many as 178 Jews (including 68 volunteers) fought on the Estonian side.[37] That did not prevent General Alexander Tõnisson, commander of the 1st Estonian Corps, from making a claim that there were only a handful of Jews on the Russian front in 1919. Another general, Johan Laidoner, said once to students at the Military Academy, "We should be glad that we have few Jews. We have acquired a good habit from tsarist Russia—to despise the Jews."[38]

The radical right in Estonia (the war veterans' movement, or the so-called Vabs)—in sharp contrast to similar organizations throughout Europe—had refrained from directly attacking minorities. Their political opponents attacked the Vabs by suggesting a link between the latter and the Baltic Germans. The Vabs vehemently denied the allegations and thus had to conceal their sympathy, if any, toward Nazi Germany. The radical press denied the validity of Nazi racial theory, at the same time emphasizing the importance of spirit and culture. The "Jewish Question" made inroads into Vabs's publications only after Hitler came to power in Germany. Otherwise, Jews rarely endured direct attacks from the Vabs. As far as anti-Semitism is concerned, the difference between the Estonian and the Latvian proto-Fascist movements could not be more striking. The Pērkonkrusts had unequivocally designated Jews—alongside Germans, Russians, and Poles—as enemies of independent Latvia; one of the first measures of the new organization was a boycott of Jewish shops.[39]

Nazi propaganda had very little to say about Jews in interwar Estonia. Take, for example, Peter-Heinz Seraphim and his anti-Semitic opus magnum, *Das Judentum im osteuropäischen Raum*. While Seraphim dealt extensively with the Latvian and Lithuanian Jewries, he failed to mention Estonian Jews even once in the 736 pages of his book. The section on minority rights omitted Estonia as well.[40] This and other examples indicate that the Nazis barely considered the "Jewish Question" in Estonia, while acknowledging its existence in Latvia and Lithuania. The *Mitteilungen über die Judenfrage*, an anti-Semitic publication based in Berlin, printed a lengthy article about the Jews in Latvia in the spring of 1938. The article, called "A Peasant Nation on Defense: Every Latvian Sets the Limits to the Jews," discussed the anti-Jewish measures introduced in Latvia, including their exclusion from professions and limitations imposed on their cultural activities. The article concluded that despite overall indifference toward the Jews, Latvians were eager to take over Jewish positions in industry and trade. However, the article argued, it could not be qualified as a genuine expression of anti-Semitism but rather as a "process of national, *völkisch* recovery."[41]

Nazis found no necessary prerequisites for the spread of anti-Semitism in Estonia. General studies of the late 1930s depicted Estonia's Jews as neither too wealthy nor too religious, and their share in media and mainstream culture as insignificant. According to one such work compiled by Hans Hinkel, Estonian Jews were on an acculturation track. Because of the unwillingness of the Estonians to accommodate Jews in their midst, however, the process of assimilation developed rather slowly. As proof, Hinkel referred to the low intermarriage rates in Estonia. The underground Communist Party had tried to expand its ranks by recruiting ethnic Estonians and Russians rather than Jews. Because Estonia had fewer Jews than Latvia and Lithuania, the study concluded, the local population was unable to comprehend the "Jewish threat."[42] Nazis complained that the Estonian government paid little, if any, attention to the "Jewish Question." Jews enjoyed full rights, which they used to their own advantage, particularly in the economy. Ordinary Estonians grew increasingly indignant toward the Jewish "parasites," but the country's leadership turned a deaf ear.[43]

Foreign Jewish commentators suggested several factors that kept the level of anti-Semitism in interwar Estonia relatively low: the pragmatic outlook of the Estonian people; meager numbers of Jews; and the relatively insignificant economic power of the Jewish community. That lack of significant economic power might have prevented the spread of popular jealousy and enmity, thus making Jews a rather unlikely scapegoat in times of potential crisis.[44] Actually, Estonia had experienced a continuous political crisis throughout its existence as an independent state.

ANTI-COMMUNISM

The Estonian State was born into a paradoxical relationship with Communism, which saw it mature and then collapse. Before the consistent attempts at cultural Russification of the early 1880s, Estonians remained positively disposed toward the tsarist government and Russians. The decisive spread of national consciousness among the Estonians did not ensue until the last decade of the nineteenth century. For the first time, "mass mobilization in the name of the nation" occurred in Estonia during the Russian Revolution of 1905, when the idea of cultural autonomy slowly gave way to that of political autonomy. Political nationalism largely came about as a reaction to Baltic German opposition to Estonian cultural nationalism.[45]

An independent Estonia would have been impossible without the Bolshevik takeover of Russia in 1917. At the same time Communism posed the greatest danger to its sovereignty. If Alexander Kerensky's provisional government had persevered, the Estonians would most likely have been confined to a far-reaching autonomy within the Russian state. The Bolshevik Revolution prompted calls for independence that Estonia would not have been able to negotiate otherwise. Estonian governing circles had observed its eastern neighbor with great suspicion. Any political development in Russia—whether the continual Bolshevik grip on power or potential right-wing/military dictatorship—set the future of the Estonian State in question. Germany to the contrary was considered incapable of harming Estonia's statehood.[46]

Estonia proclaimed independence on February 24, 1918. By that time German troops controlled most of the Estonian territory. Some Estonian officers followed the call to join the German-sponsored militia. However, frequent scuffles between Estonian and German soldiers led the occupation authorities to disband all auxiliary units within a month. The spear of German terror was aimed at Bolsheviks and members of other leftist parties, more than four hundred of whom had perished since the beginning of the occupation. Most arrests and executions took place on the basis of denunciations from Baltic German landowners. In some parts of the country, Estonians participated in the prosecution of Communists. In Viljandi, for example, two Estonian lawyers and a military officer joined Baltic Germans in a committee that sought information about Communist sympathizers, "who should be considered socially dangerous and who should be taken to court." Owing to an explicit policy promoting the interests of the Baltic German burghers and the landowner class, Wilhelmine Germany could not hold onto Estonia. Both Germans and Estonian Bolsheviks stumbled over the question of farmland redistribution. The German authorities guaranteed the Baltic German owners their estates, while the Bolsheviks, who in November and December 1918 seized the eastern part of Estonia, intended to convert them into collective farms.

Neither resolution found support among the Estonian peasants, who made up two-thirds of the country's population.[47]

From its earliest days, Estonia projected the image of an anti-Communist country. In the early 1920s, in pursuit of trusting relations with Estonia, the then weak Weimar Republic tried to assure the former that Communism would not affect German governmental affairs.[48] The American consul in charge in Reval (Tallinn) listed three reasons why the U.S. government should recognize Estonia: the distinctiveness of Estonians from the Russians; its conservative government; and the lack of Bolshevistic tendencies—a natural barrier against Bolshevism.[49] The Estonian Communist Party officially came into existence in 1920, following the signing of the Tartu Peace Treaty between Estonia and Russia. The underground Communist organization plotted the incorporation of the Estonian Republic into Soviet Russia. The Estonian government had persistently prosecuted Communists, charging them with conspiracy, sabotage, and other crimes.

The last vestiges of tolerance toward Communism in Estonia disappeared with the abortive putsch of December 1924. The Communist coup d'état was one of the last attempts of the Soviet Union to export revolution abroad. By attempting the overthrow of the Estonian government, the Soviets capitalized on the relative weaknesses of democratic institutions in Estonia. The Estonian section of the Comintern had its share in the decision-making too. The Estonian Communists pushed for action in order to prove their claims to the considerable subsidiaries that they had obtained from the main organization. The local Communists and their patrons in Moscow miscalculated on all accounts. The trial of 149 Communists in November 1924 did not create the anticipated revolutionary situation in Estonia. The conspirators failed to seize power because of the lack of popular support (even among the working class). Most of the ten thousand or so people who cast their votes for the Communist Party of Estonia (the United Front) in the 1923 elections were either Socialists or unionists. They did oppose the government but not to the extent of doing away with it.[50]

The 1924 Communist uprising had a long-term effect on Estonian political culture, and consequently on the Estonian mentality at large. The perception of a Communist threat led to the formation of a coalition government comprising representatives of all existing political parties in Estonia. For a short while, a sense of national unity had been forged in Estonia. The two biggest minority groups in the country—the Russians and the Baltic Germans—seemed to have buried the hatchet. The aftermath of the coup was marked with calls for a stronger presidency and a new constitution, which would then make emergency elections possible. The ruling Agrarian Party consolidated its power by establishing control over the country's defense. General Johan Laidoner, who was granted supreme military authority, introduced martial law. Among the other twenty or so decrees issued by Laidoner were the prohibition of public gatherings and the reporting of the whereabouts of visitors and travelers. Labor organizations were cleansed of Communist influences and a policy to outlaw the Communist Party of Estonia was set in motion. The concentration of power in the hands of several individuals appeared little short of a dictatorship. According to the U.S. consul in Tallinn, control was so strong that "even a thief could not practice his profession." Remarkably, there were no public complaints about Laidoner's dictatorial powers.[51]

Although Estonia was the last of the three Baltic countries to ban the Communist Party, it did so most resolutely. The Law on the Defense of State Order, which was passed in February 1925, forbade Communist activities and Communist propaganda in the country. It also introduced a series of new articles that imposed the death penalty for certain political crimes. Individuals charged with premeditated murder of top-ranking Estonian politicians, including the president, the army commander in chief, and the cabinet members, could be punished by death or forced labor without term. Capital punishment faced those who attempted to change the State order by violent means, to end the independence of the Estonian Republic, or to detach parts of its territory. Persons guilty of propaganda directed against Estonia's independence were to be imprisoned.[52] According to the new legislation, individuals suspected of subversive activities could be preemptively arrested. Those suspects who surrendered themselves voluntarily to the authorities under the provisions of the new law were given the option of leaving the country.[53] From this point forward, organizing a meeting required a police permit. Rental property owners were requested to watch out for suspicious individuals.[54] In spite of such harsh measures, the general population was nervous about the potential repetition of another and perhaps more serious situation like that faced by Estonia in December 1924. The successful attempt of the government to deprive the Communist Party of its legal status in Estonia did not alleviate the deep-seated fear based on the belief of omnipotent Communist propaganda in foreign countries.[55]

The abortive Communist uprising of 1924 defined the course of Estonian history for the next decade. By triggering the militarization of society and the renewed emphasis on conservative values, it marked a turn to the right in Estonian politics and culminated in authoritarian rule a decade later. During the twenty-two years of Estonian independence, martial law was in place for over ten years. In some provinces and cities, such as Tallinn, Narva, and Pechory, martial law remained almost permanent.[56] Even if not acknowledged at the time, the idea behind all those trends was to shield Estonia from the Communist danger. Characteristic of these efforts was the creation of a paramilitary organization—Kaitseliit (Defense Union or KL)—similar in its functions to the American Home Guard or the German Schutzkorps.

Since 1924 Kaitseliit has been probably the most important force in Estonia, cutting through the entire political and social spectrum. The structure and objectives of the KL reflected the political developments in interwar Estonia. From the very beginning, volunteers constituted the core of the organization. During the civil war of 1918–20, the KL became a target of criticism for various excesses against political opponents. In one particular case, a Viljandi military commandant threatened to execute hostages that had been arrested on Communist charges. The ensuing discussion regarding the founding principles of the KL suggested that its main objective was the suppression of a potential Communist uprising. The rank and file were to be selected on the basis of their political views. The former head of the KL, Admiral Johan Pitka, proposed to create special shock units consisting of war veterans, ready to fight against potential Russian aggression. This plan had been implemented following the unsuccessful Communist putsch in December 1924. The KL detachments in the southern Estonian cities of Tartu, Võru, and Valga appeared to be best prepared for such an emergency.[57]

The Kaitseliit was now officially proclaimed the "volunteer organization of loyal citizens." The KL was expected to be in a permanent state of preparedness to defend the security of the state and its citizens. The strongest emphasis, however, has been on Kaitseliit's role in nurturing Estonian nationalism. The KL was supposed in the first place to deepen the sense of national belonging among the Estonian population by means of lectures, concerts, exhibitions, sports competitions, and so forth. Finally, the KL was made responsible for general military training. In accordance with the Law on Military Service, which was introduced in March 1926, only those males who had done the obligatory military training could enter

state service. Military and KL officers received priority in acquiring administrative positions. The attempted Communist coup at once silenced the voice of
the opposition, which now could be blamed, when opportune, for undermining
the moral foundations of Estonian youth. The Socialists were the only political
party that opposed the introduction of obligatory military training in schools,
as well as the enrollment of high school students in the KL. In the KL, young
men not yet eligible for military service learned how to handle weapons. School
principals and teachers had welcomed the new regulations, which they thought
would strengthen discipline, make boys into men, and deepen their love for the
motherland. Remarkably, Estonia and Latvia were the only European democra-
cies with obligatory military training for middle and high school students—a
practice most extensively introduced in the Soviet Union.[58]

With time, Kaitseliit grew into the superstructure that helped to bridge the
social gap between the countryside and the cities. KL officers enjoyed the same status as the military but were treated as state employees. The KL spearheaded the
militarization of Estonian society by organizing numerous parades, fêtes, subscrip-
tions, and maneuvers, and by enlisting campaigns aimed at schoolboys and women.
The peace movement as promoted by the League of Nations did not inspire great
comment in the media. Instead, the local press quoted extensively from foreign
news reports of military conflicts or the prospects for new conflicts. KL maneuvers received exhaustive newspaper coverage, and whenever anything of a military
nature occurred, it was chronicled with enthusiasm.[59] By 1935, the membership of
the KL reached 34,000, 7 percent of the total male population. If we added to that
number women, boys, and girls in the auxiliary organizations, the total membership would soar to 53,000. As regards occupational distribution, the KL comprised
a cross-section of Estonian society: farmers—48 percent; workers—18 percent; civil
servants—17 percent; students—8 percent; the rest—8 percent. The strength of
the KL was growing while that of the Estonian Communist Party shrank. Of 2,000
members of the party in 1924, only 300 remained by 1934, and half of those were in
prison. Three years later, fewer than 100 Communists were still active.

AUTHORITARIANISM

The Estonian society of the 1920s and 1930s was profoundly conservative. The
agrarian nature of the state, low social mobility, and relatively high degree of

religious observance created a sense of security. Even though the elements of uncertainty and fear did not disappear, the peasantry's conservatism served as a shield against attempts at radical restructuring of society by either the radical left or the radical right. University students—including many war veterans among them—also shared conservative values. Fraternities, which commanded half of the student body, required service in the Kaitseliit of their members.[60]

In an attempt to prevent the Estonian radical right from coming to power, the conservative leadership carried out a bloodless coup d'état, thus joining the European family of authoritarian states. From March 1934 the country was virtually controlled by two men: Acting President Konstantin Päts and General Johan Laidoner. Päts replaced the multiple-party system with a state corporate system. All existing political parties and organizations were abolished in favor of the government-sponsored Patriotic League (Isamaaliit). Laidoner assumed the double position of commander in chief of the Estonian armed forces and minister of the interior, in which capacity he was authorized to ban strikes and meetings (both public and private). Freedom of speech was lost to censorship. Although the dual dictatorship of Päts-Laidoner presented the new political system as unprecedented, the corporate state principle introduced in Estonia closely resembled that of Mussolini's Italy.[61]

The relentless suppression of political unrest and promises to secure Estonia's international position won the authoritarian regime of Konstantin Päts the overwhelming support of the population. By chance, the beginning of the authoritarian period in 1934 coincided with economic recovery. After years of economic depression, Estonia now boasted a positive trade balance, industrial growth, a market for agricultural products, demand for consumer goods, and full employment. Most economic experts denied the new Estonian government credit for economic stabilization, except in the agricultural sector where the Päts regime stepped in with a number of protectionist measures.[62] As long as farmers saw their fortunes improving, a change of any kind in the existing political arrangement was rather unlikely.[63] An interesting feature of the Päts regime in Estonia was that popular support for the president had never been translated into anything like *Führerprinzip*. The government had continually stressed the "non-Estonian" nature of the cult of personality.[64] The Estonian radical right, which had made a case for a stronger presidency, could not claim a leader with unquestionable authority either. Nazi experts later explained this phenomenon in terms of the inherent individualism of the Estonians.

A sense of the biological weakness of the Estonian people, combined with growing fears of Communist danger, led some people to believe that the Estonian nation was on the brink of extinction. To combat those fears, the country's leadership launched a nationalistic campaign emphasizing the uniqueness of Estonian culture. Thus, following the suppression of the radical right in 1934, the authoritarian regime of Konstantin Päts initiated a systematic campaign of Estonianization. The establishment of an Estonian Bureau of Information and Propaganda later that year reflected the growing preoccupation with the "Estonian national idea." The chief of the Bureau was concerned that Estonian culture and language did not receive enough attention: there were too many Estonian children attending non-Estonian schools; other languages than Estonian were too often spoken; Estonians were employing too many non-Estonians; every Estonian should have an Estonian name.[65] From then on, everything—economy, politics, culture, lifestyle, or even music and fashion—had to be national and patriotic. The main idea behind the Estonianization campaign was to divert the masses' attention from politics. A decree of December 1934 forbade the media to criticize the government. In April 1938 another decree banned the publication of articles that could potentially damage Estonian foreign policy. In March 1936 the regime stripped Tartu University of its autonomous status.[66] The nationalist drive was also supposed to decrease the influence of German culture on the Estonian nation. All in all, the restrictive acts introduced between 1934 and 1940 were aimed as much at the majority population as at the minorities. Thus the Language Law of October 1934 forbade using other than Estonian (read: German) geographic and street names. It also commanded parents to send their children to state—that is, Estonian—schools, in the event that there were no schools with the children's native language as the language of instruction. This regulation mainly affected the Germans and the Jews.

The campaign of Estonianization illustrates the type of conservative nationalism practiced in Estonia in the second half of the 1930s. The propaganda espoused the virtues of national unity and patriotism, as opposed to destructive tendencies and class struggle. Estonian statesmen promoted the idea of the exclusiveness of Estonian culture, which prepared the ground for eventual cultural autarky. At the same time, Isamaaliit was nothing like the Nazi Party in Germany or the Fascist Party in Italy. The German observers made no mistake—National Socialism it was not.[67]

ESTONIAN-GERMAN RELATIONS

Estonia had been part of the German cultural world *(Kulturraum)* since the thirteenth century. Immigration from the German states to the Baltic region continued unabated until the mid-nineteenth century. The Baltic Germans offered the early model for the Estonian national movement. Thus the voluntary association movement was largely copied from its Baltic German original.[68] German cultural influences tended to be stronger than immediate political considerations: the foreign language Estonians knew best was German; when Estonians traveled abroad, they inevitably visited Germany. The nation-building process was still under way in Estonia in the 1920s and 1930s. The Estonians defined themselves against both the Russians and the Germans. However, it was almost impossible to completely separate themselves from the former ruling classes, particularly in the early years of the Estonian state. The language of instruction at Tartu University (founded by Swedes in 1632) was first German and then Russian. On the eve of the First World War, Estonians made up only 18 percent of the student body. In 1920, slightly more than 50 percent of the teaching appointments went to Estonians. In the first postwar semester, 53 percent of all classes at Tartu University were taught in Russian. Even though the numbers of non-Estonian faculty had eventually decreased, German professors continued to play an important role in Estonian academia.[69]

Ethnic Germans had played an even bigger role in the Estonian Lutheran Church. Lutheranism was a religion of the German ruling class in Estonia; throughout the nineteenth century the study and teaching of theology in Estonia was the prerogative of the Germans. In 1919 there were 74 German and 58 Estonian pastors. By 1939 this ratio had changed to 49 versus 173 in favor of Estonians.[70]

Relations between Estonia and Germany had improved by the late 1920s. Until then, the 1919 land reform had remained the main subject of contention between the two countries. The issue of compensation for the sequestered estates was one of the main reasons why the Estonian-German trade agreement was not signed until 1929. As Germany became stronger, Estonian statesmen began paying more attention to what they viewed in the immediate postwar years as a *quantité négligiable.*[71] There were three major aspects to Estonian-German relations: economic cooperation, political contacts, and the German minority.

Germany had increased its presence in Estonia first and foremost economically. By the second half of the 1930s Germany became Estonia's major trade partner, eventually leading to economic dependence on Germany. This tendency, however, had started in the previous decade. German imports to Estonia increased from 30 percent of the total in 1920 to 40 percent in 1922. Most of Estonian exports, 54.7 percent, went as well to Germany.[72] A mixture of political and economic calculations drew Estonia into the German sphere of influence. The authoritarian regime of Konstantin Päts resented the Soviet proposal to sign a unilateral guarantee pact. Simultaneously, the Estonian government intensified its economic ties with Nazi Germany.

Nazi Germany had its own reasons to encourage the economic and political rapprochement with Estonia and Latvia. First, Nazi Germany early on designated the Baltic States as part of its *Lebensraum,* which was supposed to help Hitler's regime to achieve autarky. Second, the two countries, Estonia in particular, were to play a role in converting the German economy into a war economy. In the case of a war against France and its allies, the Nazis wanted to ensure that they had enough raw materials and agricultural products to withstand a potential blockade. Last but not least, the Third Reich wanted to preempt rival countries from controlling the Baltic markets. The Estonian authorities were ready to overlook the far-reaching consequences of such economic dependence as long as they could export their surplus industrial and agricultural products and thus keep the populace content. Germany imposed the system of exchange clearings on East European countries, which gave the Reich easy access to various commodities. Estonia earned appreciation as a trade partner of Nazi Germany, given that the country still carried unpaid debts to the Weimar Republic. That meant that the initial balance was in favor of Berlin and that more goods flowed from Estonia to Germany than vice versa.[73] The Estonian shale oil industry was by far the most important for the German war machine in the making. I want to discuss the history of the Estonian mineral complex in more detail because of a role this economic factor came to play during the last phase of the Holocaust in Estonia.

Shale oil is Estonia's only mineral resource. The shale oil deposits are found in the northeastern part of the country, along the Tallinn-Narva railway line. The layers of shale oil vary between one and ten feet in thickness and are usually located only a few feet below the ground. The search for alternative sources of fuel in the last years of World War I made the Russian government consider the exploitation of the low-yielding shale oil. The independent Estonian State, however, lacked capital to take full advantage of those efforts. Thanks to foreign investments, the Estonian shale oil industry underwent rapid development in the 1930s.[74]

The Estonian oil reserves were estimated at one billion tons, as compared to four billion tons estimated for the United States. With the world consumption of oil amounting to 200 million tons annually, Estonia could thus satiate the market for a period of five years. The Estonian shale oil deposits were of very high quality: distillation yielded 20 percent crude oil, as compared with 10 percent in Scotland, and only 4–7 percent in Germany. That made the Estonian impregnating oil the best in the world. Among the most valuable products that could be obtained from crude oil were gasoline (25 percent yield), roof varnish, motor kerosene, diesel oil, asphalt iron varnish, coal tar, bitumen, pitch, and acetone. Shale oil was originally used in Estonia as a substitute for coal, which otherwise had to be imported from abroad. Thus it found use as a fuel for freight train engines, in cement manufacturing, and in the heating of buildings. By the mid-1920s, however, production shifted to oil extraction.[75]

On the eve of World War II, six companies, five plants, and eight mines had become involved in oil production in Estonia. The Scheel Bank pioneered the chemical industry in Estonia by having founded the First Estonian Shale Oil Industry, Ltd. (Eesti Kiviõli or ESTAG) in Kohtla-Järve. The Estonian State owned 59 percent of the share capital of the plant. The second biggest enterprise was the Estonian Oil Corporation, which was built in 1925 with Swedish capital. It owned mines in Viivikonna and a plant in Sillamäe. The largest enterprise was founded in 1932 with German capital and was owned by ESTAG. The plants and mines were situated near Sonda. British interests in Estonia were represented by the New Consolidated Gold Fields of South Africa, which ran a plant in Kohtla. The Estonian State greatly benefited from selling concessions to the foreign owners and charging them a special tax on oil products.[76] Private companies that operated in Estonia were primarily interested in crude oil (heating oil) and gasoline production.[77]

The Estonian shale oil industry had reached an unprecedented level of development in the second half of the 1930s thanks to profitable contracts with German companies. Until then, the main importers of Estonian shale oil were

Finland, Latvia, and Lithuania. From 1935 on, the German navy became the largest consumer of Estonian oil products. The domestic production of fuel could not keep pace with the rapid buildup of the German navy. In order to meet the growing demands, Nazi economic experts suggested substituting shale oil for coal. The low quality of the domestic ore opened up the Third Reich's markets to imports. ESTAG took full advantage of that opportunity, rebuilding its credit line that had been severely damaged by the German banking crisis of 1931. The negotiations regarding large-scale deliveries of oil products from Estonia commenced in the summer of 1934. The German navy intended to stake out a claim in Estonia before its competitors from the German air force did. The final document was signed in October 1935, with Mendelssohn and Co. Bank as a guarantor.[78] Following the "Aryanization" of the Mendelssohn Bank in December 1938, its shares in the Estonian shale oil industry were taken over by the Dresdner Bank and by I. G. Farben. Within the next year, the Dresdner Bank invested in the construction of yet another plant in Kohtla-Järve.[79]

The ESTAG case exemplifies the patterns of German economic penetration in Estonia. The contract signed between the Estonian State and the Scheel Bank on the one side and the German navy and the Mendelssohn Bank on the other

1. Oil distillery in Kohtla, owned and operated between 1941 and 1944 by Baltische Öl GmbH, 1930s; postcard.

was beneficial for all parties involved. The fact that the initiative came from the enterprise itself helped to keep the long-term political objectives of the Nazis in the background. Moreover, in its determination to rebuild Germany's military strength, the Nazi leadership was ready to overlook the immediate disadvantages of the deal. The Germans paid more but received less. According to the contract, ESTAG was to deliver 3,000 tons of crude oil a month, a supply not enough to fill the stoker of a single battle cruiser. To be operational, the German navy needed up to fifteen times more fuel. The first delivery to the German navy was shipped in March 1937. Subsequently, a number of similar treaties between the two countries were concluded, so that in 1939 alone Germany received from Estonia 105,000 tons of crude oil and 5,000 tons of gasoline.[80] Thanks to foreign—mainly German—credits, the output of crude oil and gasoline in Estonia tripled between 1935 and 1939.

The economic reliance on Nazi Germany could be easily translated into political dependency. The notion of "partnership" does not describe accurately the trade relations between the two countries. Germany sent to Estonia only such agricultural machines and manufacturing equipment that strengthened the branches of the economy that the Nazi war industry was interested in. In exchange, the Third Reich imported raw materials and agricultural produce such as flax, butter, beacon, eggs, and cheese. In 1939 Estonian phosphates were all but sold to Germany five years in advance.[81] By that time, foreign owners—predominantly German—controlled two-thirds of the private companies in Estonia.[82]

Mutual economic interests were a guarantee against infringements on minority rights in Estonia. Big Baltic German industrialists sat in the Estonian Trade and Industry Chamber (one of the most influential of them, Martin Luther, served as chairman of the Big Industry section), while General Laidoner was chairman of the ESTAG advisory board. As for the German Cultural Self-Government, the German Party, German-language schools, none of these institutions would have survived without financial support from Baltic German businesses.[83] It would be suicidal, therefore, for the Estonian government to kill the Law on Cultural Autonomy without risking alienating both Baltic German and Nazi German capital. As in 1925, when the Autonomy Law was promulgated, the Jews once again had very little involvement in the circumstances that enabled them to thrive in Estonia. Paradoxically, the safety of the Estonian Jews was guaranteed by the outcome of Estonian-German economic cooperation.

However, cooperation had a price tag attached to it: silencing news about the persecution of Jews in Nazi Germany.

The Soviet occupation and subsequent annexation of the Baltic States did not substantially hamper German economic interests in the region. During the first six months of 1940, Nazi Germany signed secret trade agreements with all three Baltic countries, by which 70 percent of their total exports went to the Third Reich. Being aware of the forthcoming Soviet expansion, the German Foreign Office nevertheless did not see reason to worry.[84] As before, the most important consideration for the Germans was to retain control over the Estonian shale oil. The head of the Reich Security Main Office (RSHA), Reinhard Heydrich, was concerned about the status of the industries in Latvia and Estonia vital for Nazi Germany. Number one on Heydrich's list was ESTAG, followed by the Luther plywood factory in Tallinn, several cellulose plants in Latvia and Estonia, textile manufacturers in Riga and Narva, and two banks— Libauer Bank in Riga and Scheel and Co. in Tallinn. Heydrich wanted those among the ethnic Germans who had worked in the abovementioned ventures to stay for at least another three months in the Baltics until they, too, could resettle to Germany.[85] Scheel Bank, anxious about nationalization, deposited its block of shares of ESTAG with the German Consulate in Tallinn. The shares were then transferred to the Netherlands, with the right of preemption reserved for the German navy. Immediately after the Soviet Union took over the Baltic States in the summer of 1941, the export of crude oil from Estonia declined abruptly, from 14,241 tons in July to 3,732 tons in August. During these two months, Germany imported a total of 450,000 tons of crude oil, mainly from Romania and the Soviet Union.[86] Notwithstanding the sharp disagreement between the Soviet and German sides, the latter haggled over a delivery of an additional 85,000 tons of crude oil from Estonia.[87] The Soviet Union continued honoring its obligations to its German ally; the only shale oil company in Estonia that was not nationalized by the government was ESTAG.[88]

The Nazi seizure of power in Germany was met with distrust in different quarters of Estonian society. The instinctive reaction to the news coming from Germany in the winter of 1933 was one of apprehension. The memories of the German occupation of Estonia during the final year of World War I were still fresh. What came to mind first was the *Drang nach dem Osten* idea, which the new, aggressive regime in Berlin might now want to revive. Political impotence, disguised behind nationalist slogans, made Estonian statesmen proceed very cautiously with regard to Nazi Germany. The Estonian government tried to maintain friendly relations with the Third Reich. No criticism of Nazism was voiced.[89] Former foreign minister Ants Piip outlined the following two commonalities between Nazi Germany and Estonia: authoritarian rule and the idea of the peasantry as the main pillar of the state. While Piip made his pronouncements in Berlin in June 1934, the leaders of the suppressed Veterans' movement stood trial in Tallinn. The Estonian press covered the latter event extensively but omitted the former.[90] Karl Tofer, the Estonian envoy in Berlin between 1936 and 1939, expressed his satisfaction with the level of Estonian-German relations; the German Foreign Office described the diplomat as a "sincere admirer of the *Führer* and National Socialism."[91]

The first signs of rapprochement with Nazi Germany appeared in the summer of 1934. Unmistakably, the turn in Estonian-German relations coincided with the beginning of the trade negotiations with the German navy. The Estonian public was still deeply anti-German, as illustrated by the overt hostility displayed toward the Baltic National Socialist Movement (Baltische nationalsozialistische Bewegung) headed by Victor von zur Mühlen. In November 1933, von zur Mühlen managed to take control of the Baltic German Party in Estonia, but was forced to resign. The Estonian press sounded the alarm about the coming of a Nazi state within the Estonian state and called for revision of the Cultural Autonomy Law. Von zur Mühlen was looking forward to forging an alliance with the Estonian right-wing Veterans' movement, which most resolutely rejected the offer, fearing to be associated with the Baltic Germans. In November 1934 leaders of the Baltic Nazi Movement stood trial, charged with running an illegal organization. However, contrary to general expectation, von zur Mühlen and his associates received relatively light sentences ranging from one month to a few weeks. The German Consulate in Tallinn believed that the judge proceeded upon a recommendation from the president and the government. Remarkably, the Estonian newspapers that had only recently bashed the Baltic German barons and their Nazi patrons in Germany now unanimously argued against any possible connections between von zur Mühlen's outfit and the Third Reich.[92]

By 1935, Estonia had irreversibly decided on its long-term political orientation toward Nazi Germany. General Laidoner announced in March 1935 that the Soviet Union was Estonia's only enemy and that Estonian soldiers had just one task at hand—to fight Bolshevism. The Latvian envoy in Tallinn speculated that the three Baltic States perceived Nazi Germany as a potential threat to their sovereignty in the following proportion: Lithuania 75 percent; Latvia 50 percent; Estonia 25 percent. The Estonian leadership based their assessment of the political situation on the experiences of the war of national liberation and the aborted Communist coup of 1924.[93] Hitler capitalized on Estonia's apprehension of its eastern neighbor when he suggested to the Estonian foreign minister, Friedrich Akel, in June 1936 to sign the bilateral nonaggression treaty with Nazi Germany. Hitler described the Baltic States as "glacis of the European anti-Bolshevik powers against Russia."[94] The German Intelligence Service, the Abwehr, was active in Estonia from 1935. Among its informants were such high-ranking Estonian military officers as Voldemar Rieberg, Emil Kursk, Villem Saarsen, and Alfons Rebane.[95]

Estonia failed to forge political alliances. Except with neighboring Latvia, Estonia was unsuccessful at signing guarantee treaties with Lithuania, Poland, and Finland, not to mention distant England and France, which let their influence in the Baltic States fade away. Germany thus remained the only power from whom they could seek support. From 1936 on, Estonia essentially had two foreign policies: an official policy of neutrality and an unofficial policy that advanced

2. Narva and Ivangorod fortresses, symbols of "civilized Europe" vs. "Asiatic East," 1930s; postcard.

Estonian-German relations. Pro-German policy manifested itself in overtly friendly statements and in coordination of Estonian foreign and defense policy with that of Berlin. For example, the head of the Estonian military staff, Nikolai Reek, insisted that Estonia would resist any attempt of the Soviet Union to pass through its territory. According to Reek, in the event of a Russo-German war, Estonia would mine the Gulf of Finland to upset the Baltic Fleet. To maintain good relations with Nazi Germany, the Estonian government effectively sabotaged efforts at cooperation within the Baltic region. Estonian military authorities ignored numerous warnings from their Latvian colleagues to stop buying arms from Nazi Germany, thus tying the Baltic defense policy to the latter. The Estonian side was afraid that in the event of a military conflict Latvia and Lithuania could request assistance from the Soviet Union against Nazi Germany. Latvia had a defense plan that accounted for a military invasion from both east and west; Estonia only expected aggression from the east. Estonian officials speculated that Nazi Germany agreed to guarantee sovereignty to Estonia, but not to Latvia or Lithuania. When listening to deputy foreign minister Oskar Öpik, one could get the impression that Latvia and Lithuania were small states compared to Estonia, which had certain political advantages over the other two Baltic countries. In short, Estonian politicians were convinced that Estonia struck a much better deal with Nazi Germany than had their neighbors to the south. The Estonian military believed that Hitler designated Estonia a bulwark against Communism. In a sense, Nazi Germany used Estonia as a bridgehead to spread its political influence over the Baltic States. In May 1939 the German envoy in Riga related to Berlin that Estonia's political and military leadership was Germanophile and viewed Nazi Germany as its sole savior from the imminent Soviet occupation.[96]

This is how the Estonian politicians saw their country in relation to Germany. The Nazis and their fellow travelers had their own idea of Estonia and Estonians. In 1927, the right-wing German League for the Defense of Ethnic Germans Abroad (Deutsche Schutzbund Grenz- und Auslandsdeutschtum, or DSB) submitted to the German Foreign Office a position paper entitled "The Estonians and Their Politics." The document is significant not only because of its length or scope but also because of its plain, "in-your-face" approach. What both the Foreign Office and the Nazi Party would have tried to keep for themselves, the DSB expressed directly. It is worthwhile summarizing main points discussed in the paper.

According to the DSB, Estonians were sober, practical people that lacked fantasy and genuine passion. In that respect Estonians were the direct opposite of Latvians. The idea of national independence had surfaced rather late among the Estonians. Until the very last moment, leaders of the national movement were content with the autonomous status of Estonia. It was only the Bolshevik terror that made a relatively small circle of Estonian politicians decide in favor of independence. Even nine years after, Estonians had not yet fully grasped the principle of national sovereignty. Hundreds of years of foreign rule had prevented Estonians from developing a sense of respect toward their governing institutions. The idea of a state personified by a strong leader was said to be alien to Estonians. The awareness of national independence in Estonia was related to Russia. The Estonians' capability to resist Communist Russia was considered high, whereas their chances to withstand a potentially democratic Russian state were minimal.[97]

Next the DSB paper addressed the issue of Estonian–Baltic German relations. It was not the Estonian peasants but the intelligentsia that felt animosity toward the Germans. Estonian media and literature were hotbeds of anti-German sentiment in the 1920s. Given the importance of public opinion in Estonia, even those few that expressed sympathy toward ethnic Germans in private berated them in public. Baltic Germans received the largest share of blame for the worsening of Estonian-German relations. When German troops first arrived in 1918, they were welcomed as liberators from the Bolshevik terror. However, premature talks about incorporation of Estonia into the German Empire alienated the local population. The 1919 land reform, which was aimed at German landowners, was an issue of prestige for the young Estonian state. Fear of pan-Germanism was another cause for animosity. Conscious of their low absolute numbers, Estonians felt vulnerable in the face of German power, which grew stronger and stronger. The Estonian leadership was said to have nurtured those fears to perpetuate the tensions between the titular population and the Baltic German minority.[98]

Finally, the DSB communicated its views on Estonian foreign policy to the German Foreign Office, with specific reference to the Soviet Union and Communism. From the perspective of Germany in the late 1920s, Russia had remained the biggest problem for Estonia. At the same time, the abortive coup of 1924, sponsored and orchestrated by Moscow, reduced support for Communists in Estonia to a minimum. The worst nightmare for Estonian politicians was the possibility of Germany and Russia deciding to join their forces at the expense of small states such as Estonia.[99] It is worth noting that the above interpretation of modern Estonian history was drafted before Hitler came to power in Germany.

The inhuman character of Hitler's regime aroused moral indignation among Estonian intellectuals. In response, however, members of the intellectual elite preached cultural escapism, which eventually turned into the endorsement of an authoritarian form of rule in Estonia. In any event, the majority of the population remained essentially unaffected by the strong criticism of the Nazi New Order articulated by some Estonian intellectuals.

In 1938, the Estonian Literature Association published a book that was meant to provide an objective assessment of the situation in Hitler's Germany. Eduard Laaman and Leonid Kahkra, two leftist lawyers, subjected the Nazi regime to harsh criticism. Laaman and Kahkra vehemently attacked racial theory; the two authors strongly opposed the onslaught against the Jews, leftists, and intellectuals; they rejected the policy of *Gleichschaltung* and false messianic claims. In their interpretation, Nazi anti-Semitism stemmed from an inferiority complex and primitive scapegoating. Laaman quoted from Friedrich Nietzsche to demonstrate that the brutality of the Nazi anti-Jewish policies was disproportionate to the alleged danger that the latter group might have posed to the purity of the German race. Laaman concluded that despite the fact that each and every state had the right to defend itself against the incursions of irredentist minorities, Jews posed no threat to Germany. Imagine the German reaction if the Estonian government had embarked on a course of persecution against the Baltic German minority, he wrote. The Nazi "iron fist" policy had long-term consequences for Estonia. Not only did it pull Estonia away from the fold of Scandinavia where it belonged, but it also sparked a near civil war. The general conclusion that Laaman and Kahkra drew in their book recapped the anxiety shared by many in Estonia: fear of German expansionism in the East.[100] The only way the Nazis could gain legitimacy in the eyes of the general Estonian population was to take a strong stance against what Oskar Loorits, a well-known Estonian linguist, described as "a 700-year domination" of Estonia by Baltic Germans. They pulled off this ruse by nominally dissociating themselves from the Baltic German tradition in Estonia.

Baltic Germans lost their political power in Estonia but not economic power. The land reform pushed even more Germans into industry and trade. By 1939 only 13 percent of Baltic Germans but 59 percent of Estonians were engaged in agriculture. At the same time the German minority was overrepresented in heavy industry, the insurance business, and banking. The Estonian economy benefited greatly from Baltic German investments. Mining, timber, and textiles were the three industries in which the local Germans tended to invest most. Baltic Germans, who constituted only 1.6 percent of the population, paid 14 percent of the total income tax and owned as much as a fifth of the state total wealth. The Estonian majority longed to undermine the economic status of the Baltic Germans but could not afford to intervene directly: any drastic measures would have spelled disaster for the Estonian economy. The Estonian State also did not want to risk another propagandistic war, in addition to one that the Baltic immigrants in Germany had waged against Estonia in the aftermath of the land reform of 1919.[101]

Germany took advantage of the Baltic Germans' stake in the Estonian economy to increase its influence in the country. The history of Scheel Bank, which I mentioned before, illustrates that trend most vividly. A native of Lübeck, George Johannes Scheel established a deposit bank in Reval (Tallinn) in 1884. By 1928, Scheel Bank was the largest private bank in Estonia. The bank's balance sheet of thirty million Estonian crowns comprised nearly one-third of the state budget; Scheel controlled 90 percent of the economic input of the Baltic Germans in Estonia. Scheel Bank suffered a hard blow as a result of the world economic crisis in October 1931. The Estonian State Bank refused a credit line to Scheel—ostensibly because of monetary considerations, but probably as part of a deliberate policy of financial strangulation. Help came unexpectedly from Mendelssohn and Co. Bank in Berlin, which extended a two-million *Reichsmark* (RM) credit to Scheel Bank. The German State served as a guarantor of the deal.[102]

The changes in German foreign policy had an immediate effect on the German minority in Estonia. Already, at the time of the Weimar Republic, Germany had made an important decision that helped to improve its relations with Estonia. It appeared increasingly counterproductive to maintain the distinction between the Reichsdeutsche and Baltendeutsche. By denying characteristics unique to the local German community, the authorities in Berlin attempted to create the impression that the 700-year page of German colonization in Eastern Europe was closed forever. From then on, German citizens received undeniable priority over their ethnic kin in the Baltics: German first and only then Baltic. Realistic in their assessment of the situation, German diplomats were largely influenced by German economic circles, which looked forward to expanding trade with the Baltic States and the Soviet Union. Thus they avoided expressing support for the "Baltic Barons" in order not to alienate their Estonian partners. The local German community had to comply with the new German policy vis-à-vis the borderlands. At that time, the only possible compensation for the downgrading of the status of the German minority in Eastern Europe was cultural autonomy.[103]

The Nazis from the very beginning distrusted Baltic Germans. Some of them even argued that the Baltic States would have been Germanized long before if it were not for the prejudices and conceit of the Baltic Germans. The head of the German police, Heinrich Himmler, had a personal aversion to the "Balts."[104] When Victor von zur Mühlen, leader of the pro-Nazi movement in Estonia, sought to establish a branch office of the Nazi Party in that country, he received a sharp rebuttal from Hitler.[105] In spite of their role in shaping Nazi ideology, after 1933 the Baltic Germans were deliberately repelled and their historical legitimacy questioned. The populist appeal of Nazi propaganda was hard to reconcile with the patrician worldview some Baltic Germans still held. Some members of the 1,500-strong Reichsdeutsche colony in Estonia complained about the Deutschbalten arrogance and their inflated sense of superiority even with regard to German citizens. The Nazi victory in Germany was said to have motivated the Reichsdeutsche in Estonia to close their ranks against the pretentious Deutschbalten.[106]

Estonians made a distinction between the Baltic Germans and the Germans in the Reich. From their perspective, not all Germans were Nazis but all Balts were Germans. Although Estonians knew that in a crisis situation Berlin would help its ethnics abroad, with time they came to perceive Baltic Germans as a separate body. This view may appear confusing yet could have been psychologically liberating. It meant that one could resent Germans and maintain normal relations with them at the same time. Unsophisticated minds judged Nazi Germany by its policy vis-à-vis Baltic Germans. Because Estonia was an important trade partner, Germany had no reasons to interfere in its domestic affairs or to assert any demands. The Central Agency for Ethnic Germans (Volksdeutsche Mittelstelle or VoMi), an organization that dealt with the German diaspora, expected Estonian Germans to remain passive and orderly. With the exception of a short period in 1938, when the pro-Nazi element within the local German community seemed to seize the initiative, VoMi managed to keep the situation under control until the fall of 1939.[107] Baltic Germans observed how Estonia had been growing closer to Nazi Germany in the late 1930s. For them, it seemed indeed inevitable. Bitter as they might be, some Baltic Germans interpreted the Estonians' friendliness toward Germany as compensation for mistreating the German minority at home.[108] Estonians had remained anti-German without any particular references to Nazism. The destructive Nazi ideology seemed to have no effect on their assessment of the Third Reich. Estonians perceived Hitler's New Order at most as a continuation of German imperialism. The difference between Germans and Baltic Germans was far more important for them than that between Germans and Nazis. To put it differently, Estonians did not have to be anti-Nazi to dislike ethnic Germans.

Paradoxically, the Estonians never stopped resenting the Germans. However, the peculiarity of Estonian history and a complex political gambit played by Germany confined the resentment to the Baltic Germans, their traditional adversary. The political gloom that descended over Europe by 1939 caught the Estonian nation off guard. Deafened by years of authoritarian rule, Estonians felt overconfident in their resolve to fight against potential Communist aggression. Unsurprisingly, that shaky ground did not hold when the country was put to a test.

2 THE BREAKDOWN, 1939–1941

THE RESETTLEMENT OF BALTIC GERMANS

The German invasion of Poland in September 1939 signaled the beginning of a radical program of ethnic restructuring of Europe. According to Nazi plans, the Polish population of the so-called Incorporated Territories was to be deported eastward in anticipation of the influx of ethnic Germans from Bessarabia, Bukovina, and the Baltic States. The resettlement program (German: *Umsiedlung*) had both practical and ideological underpinnings. The settlers were supposed to improve the racial composition of the Incorporated Territories while supplementing German labor, accounting for an additional 160,000 agricultural workers.[1] The resettlement process was set in motion by Hitler's speech in the Reichstag on October 6, 1939. As the most pressing task, Hitler indicated establishing a new ethnographic order, which he intended to achieve by removing the cause for potential conflict, that is, the minorities. The resettlement of the Baltic Germans, argued the Reich's representative in Estonia, would demarcate the ethnic borders and thus clarify the relationship between the states and the nations.[2]

Estonians had mixed reactions about the departure of Baltic Germans. The resettlement of Baltic Germans in the fall of 1939 was a watershed event in Estonian history. Popular opinion saw the Umsiedlung as the end of the 700-year domination of Estonia by the Germans. Although Estonians were glad to see the Baltic Germans leave, they felt anxious about the future. The old Estonia was gone, but how secure was the new one going to be? The Estonian politicians hid their fears behind the words of gratitude that they expressed to the leaders of the departing German community. As Kaarel Eenpalu told Baron Wilhelm Wrangel, "[T]his is the end of Estonia!" General Laidoner privately described the resettlement of ethnic Germans as an economic and cultural loss for Estonia. What they really meant was that the Baltic Germans were leaving Estonia in anticipation of the Soviet occupation and annexation.[3] Most people felt like the son of the Estonian admiral Johan Pitka, who conveyed to the British envoy in Tallinn in October 1939 that "Estonia is gone. Anyone who stays in Estonia will be murdered or deported."[4]

The fear of Bolshevism played a major role in the Baltic Germans' decision to migrate to the Reich. Some of them argued—apparently under the influence of Nazi propaganda—that they would prefer a meager existence in Germany to deportation to Siberia. The people who rushed to board the ships bound for Danzig, Stettin, and Posen felt frightened, and shared their apprehension with those who stayed. Sooner or later Estonia would be swallowed by the Soviet Union, they predicted. The outbreak of Soviet-Finnish war on November 30, 1939, convinced even the worst skeptics. The dilemma—to go or to stay—thus became a question of life and death.[5]

Ordinary Estonians felt even more confused. The sense of looming danger was pervasive. As the Baltic Germans were packing, Red Army units, in accordance with the Estonian-Soviet agreement, marched in. The connection between the two events was obvious, and caused panic among the population. The atrocities that the Bolsheviks had committed in Estonia in 1919 came once again to dominate popular discourse. The Estonians expected the worst was yet to come: the return of the Baltic Germans to their ethnic homeland meant that Europe had turned its back on the Baltic States.[6] And they may well have been right.

The Estonian and Latvian governments held different positions on the resettlement program. The difference in attitudes affected those ethnic Estonians and Latvians who wanted to join the Baltic German exodus. While Latvian propaganda scorned the renegades leaving the country, the Estonian media agreed with emigration. In the end, it boiled down to a simple question: who posed a larger danger—the Soviet Union or Nazi Germany? As of the fall of 1939, Latvians seemed to prefer Russians to Germans, whereas Estonians tended to make the opposite choice. As one Latvian writer speculated, Russians would have destroyed the Latvian intelligentsia but let the Latvian people live; Germans, if victorious, would have made Latvians into Germans.[7] As compared to the more withdrawn Estonians, Latvians expressed genuine joy for the departure of the Baltic Germans. The resettlement process in Latvia was accompanied by individual cases of anti-German violence. In Estonia, isolated excesses were recorded only in Tartu, a cradle of Estonian nationalism.

The Nazis envisaged the worst scenarios for the Umsiedlung, including spontaneous anti-German riots, in which case all ethnic Germans were to be evacuated immediately. The Baltic Germans in their turn were haunted by a vision of political commissars of the Red Army delivering them into the hands of local Communists. These fears proved unfounded, at least in the Estonian case. The Estonian government instructed the police (Kaitseliit) and the military to ensure the safety of the country's minorities. In his radio address, Minister of Economics Leo Sepp appealed to the population to treat the departing Baltic Germans cordially. Furthermore, some Estonian citizens inquired of leading Baltic German personalities about the possibility of resettling in the Third Reich. Most eager to emigrate were members of the disbanded Veterans' movement and former officers of the Russian army, fearful of potential Soviet repression. On October 5 the German Consulate in Tallinn received guidelines from Ernst von Weizsäcker to issue entry visas to those non-German individuals who were collaborating with the Nazi regime. According to the guidelines, the resettlement was to be carried out in a manner that would avoid provoking panic among both the Baltic Germans and the Estonians. The German press was likewise instructed to avoid using the terms "emigrants" or "refugees" with regard to the departing Baltic Germans. Nothing should suggest that the Third Reich was saving ethnic Germans from their doom and thus abandoning the rest of the Baltic people.[8]

A total of 13,700 ethnic Germans left Estonia for the Third Reich in 1939. The remaining 3,000 Baltic Germans were resettled in the fall of 1940. This delay caught the Nazis by surprise, for they had estimated that close to 99 percent of the Baltic Germans would resettle immediately.[9] This time around the Nazis were less inclined to intervene on behalf of local Germans, whom they considered the dregs of society. Apprehensive of Soviet infiltration, Himmler stipulated that only Baltic and Reich Germans were eligible to relocate to Germany, thus blocking the entry of ethnic Estonians and Latvians. Nevertheless, 2,055 Estonians and 1,821 Latvians still managed to emigrate to Germany during the final stage of resettlement in February and March 1941.[10]

The resettlement of ethnic Germans marked a psychologically important moment. With the Russian minority in check and the Germans all but departed, the nationalist idea of "Estonia" had never been so close to perfection. Finally, the Estonians were masters in their own home. The departure of Baltic Germans created an economic vacuum that only the state could fill. And indeed, in some branches of the economy ethnic Germans retained the highest positions until the very last days. In the Krenholm cotton mills in Narva (one of the biggest such companies in the former Russian empire), for example, the engineering staff was traditionally German, British, or Russian.[11] The Estonians now took over the positions vacated by the departing Germans. The Estonian daily *Päevaleht* carried a story on February 6, 1940, about a Põltsamaa businessman, Elias Brisk, who bought a farmstead from a departing Baltic German. The newspaper noted that it was the first time that a Jew purchased property from a resettled "Aryan." The author of the article suggested that the Estonian State should have intervened using the right of preemption.[12]

The Estonian government was in limbo. The Germans, whom it had been courting, seemed to abandon Estonia to its fate; the Soviets, whom it despised and feared at the same time, stood at Estonia's door waiting for a signal to break in. Rumors circulated as early as September 1939 about the division of the Baltic States between the Soviet and Nazi spheres of influence. Estonians were the last to learn about the deal. Dr. Helmuth Weiss, who was entrusted with the transfer of the Baltic Germans from Estonia, received unofficial information about the Molotov-Ribbentrop Pact during his trip to Berlin in September 1939.[13] The Päts regime was determined to prevent the Soviet takeover of Estonia. It did so by yielding to Soviet demands, all of them, one after another.

THE HUMILIATION OF 1940

Of the three Baltic countries, Estonia turned out to be the most compliant with Soviet demands. Unlike Latvia and Lithuania, let alone Finland, Estonia did not announce even partial mobilization. The Estonian leadership attempted by all means to avoid a military confrontation with the Soviet Union. Estonian Foreign Minister Karl Selter speculated in September 1939 about the Soviet plan to establish a protectorate over Estonia. Selter immediately accepted the Soviet demand to concede the right to build military bases in Estonia. While reassuring the Estonian people that they had nothing to fear, the authorities called upon the population to denounce those individuals who spread rumors about the imminent arrival of the Red Army. The Estonian government made no attempts to secure political or military support from other states. Instead, foreign diplomats were told that the Soviet Union allegedly had withdrawn its forces from the Estonian border.[14] The German Foreign Office worked hard to convince the Baltic States to surrender to the Soviet Union without mounting a military resistance.[15] Indeed, it seems that the summer 1941 scenario was in the making well before the Soviet Union put a stranglehold on Baltic independence.

Totally helpless, Estonian statesmen tried to shield their country from the looming Soviet aggression by invoking the issue of culture. Bound by the Molotov-Ribbentrop Pact, the Nazis ignored the Estonian president's appeal to keep Estonia within the German cultural sphere. In a desperate attempt to salvage the country from imminent disaster, Päts incorporated into his lexicon some elements of Nazi propaganda. In April 1940, for example, Päts asserted to the German consul in Tallinn that the Estonian people had never belonged to the Russian-Asiatic cultural milieu, which they always negated.[16]

The years of relative stability under the authoritarian rule of Konstantin Päts (1934–40) led Estonians to identify with the figure of the president. Half a decade of material prosperity had helped to shape popular belief in the political wisdom of the head of the state. As the political landscape in Eastern Europe turned from bad to worse, the Estonian population did not lose faith in their president. Indeed, Päts enjoyed overwhelming support among all strata of the population. Nobody questioned his qualities as a leader capable of navigating Estonia safely through rough waters.[17]

What Estonian politicians did in 1939 and 1940 contradicted what they had told Estonians for twenty years. The country's leaders had assured the Estonian population that the Russians would never again be able to cross their border. Thus, while touring the eastern part of the country in the spring of 1936, the commander in chief of the Estonian army, Johan Laidoner, stated that the Narva River would forever remain Estonia's border. It was not hard to guess what particular country Laidoner had in mind when he stressed that no matter where the enemy came from, it would be repelled at once.[18] The bravado betrayed subconscious fear of the Soviet Union. Remarkably, Estonians seemed to be fixated on the "Soviet danger" more than Latvians or Lithuanians were. In addition to a conventional military intervention, the Estonians dreaded the Russians' capability to physically exterminate the whole nation. In April 1939 Foreign Minister Selter told the German consul in Tallinn that Estonia would only march to the East.[19] The Estonian authorities continually promoted the idea of Finno-Ugrian unity. However, when in the winter of 1940 Estonians started volunteering en masse to fight alongside Finns against the Russians, the Päts government immediately prohibited such activity—all in the name of maintaining good relations with the Soviet Union. With a heavy heart, Estonians watched Soviet warplanes take off from an Estonian airfield for yet another bombing raid against the kindred nation of Finland.

The immediate reaction of Estonians to the Soviet occupation was that of humiliation. The humiliating character of the surrender offended Estonians the most. People were stunned by the meaning of a broadcast that cut through the air shortly before midnight on June 16, 1940: the Estonian president yielded to Soviet pressure by announcing the resignation of his government and an increase in the Soviet military presence in the country. Further details were to be elaborated in a meeting between General Laidoner and his Soviet counterpart, General Kiril Mereshkov, in the border town of Narva the following morning. As Laidoner rushed to the scheduled meeting in the early hours of June 17, he ran into Soviet infantry columns that had crossed the Estonian border without prior notice. A few days after Soviet troops occupied Estonia on June 16, 1941, the Estonian government still had a chance to tell its people and the world what was really happening. Instead, in his address to the country on June 18, Estonian Prime Minister Jüri Uluots emphasized the relationship of trust between the Soviet Union and Estonia. Estonian leaders argued that by accepting the Soviet ultimatum, they had saved the Estonian people.[20] The collective mood in the summer of 1940 could be at best described as confused. The defeat was indeed humiliating. As Saulius Sužiedėlis remarked in the case of Lithuania, the fatalistic attitude toward foreign intervention produced defeatism conductive to collaboration.[21]

The sense of humiliation was particularly strong within the Estonian military ranks. The Estonian high command did not share Päts's appeasement policy vis-à-vis the Soviet Union. The poor performance of the Red Army against the numerically smaller Finnish troops convinced the military of the possibility for resistance against the Soviets if the latter attempted to intervene in Estonia.[22] Ordinary Estonians, who had prided themselves on their country's past victories, were dismayed when the Soviets ordered the Estonian army to clear the barracks and the Kaitseliit (KL) to turn in their weapons. For many Estonians, the KL was more than just a paramilitary organization; it was the embodiment of a national ideal. In just a few days the KL ceased to exist. In Narva, the liquidation of the KL was

3. Pro-Soviet demonstration in Tartu, summer 1940; Herder Institute, Hintzer, 156429.

already completed by June 28, 1940.[23] The first, negative impression that the Estonian public got of the Soviet military personnel—its inadequate performance, worn-out uniforms, poor discipline—made them feel even worse.

SOVIET TERROR

The Soviet terror left an undeniable mark on the collective psyche of the Baltic peoples. What resonated was not only the scale of the terror but also the ways in which it was implemented. Estonians might have expected brutal force, but not in a form that ridiculed their statehood, which over time had acquired the quality of a secular religion.

The NKVD carried out arrests of leading Baltic politicians, industrialists, and military and police officers throughout 1940 and 1941. Close to one thousand people were arrested and tried before Soviet military tribunals in 1940. One-quarter of the arrested individuals received death sentences, while another quarter perished in detention during and after the war. It was, however, the summer 1941 deportation that shook the foundation of Estonian society. On the night of June 14–15, 1941, about 10,200 people of different social and political

4. Exhibition grounds in Tartu (the future site of a concentration camp), 1940; HI, Hintzer, 165198.

backgrounds were deported from Estonia into Russia proper. In Viljandi Province, for example, a rough breakdown of the deportees by social status looked as follows: well-to-do peasants—60 percent; police and governmental officials—15 percent; businessmen and free professionals—15 percent; political opponents—10 percent. Up to 80 percent of these people held membership in various paramilitary and political organizations, such as the KL, the Veterans' movement, and the Patriotic League (Isamaaliit.).[24] Reports from other provinces confirmed that mass deportation primarily targeted members of the KL and policemen.[25]

Although the 1941 mass operation was planned months in advance, it was the sense of political insecurity and military vulnerability that had triggered the deportation. The deportation reflected the NKVD's mistrust of the local population in the newly acquired territories.[26] In consideration of the aggressive plans of the Soviet Union, the decision to cleanse the borderlands of the potentially hostile categories of population may indeed have been preventive.[27] Not until half a year later did American diplomats inform their superiors in Washington about the Soviet purges. According to the U.S. Legation in Stockholm, the Soviet authorities decided to carry out the deportation as soon as they realized that war with Germany was inevitable. Owing to the time factor, Estonia reportedly suffered more than the other two Baltic countries. The first two categories targeted for deportation were Russian immigrants and Estonian functionaries. In the Estonian case, the Soviets achieved their objective of removing political leadership. A December 1941 report from Helsinki gave further details about the Soviet terror in Estonia, including the mass shooting of prisoners.[28] Hitler, in comparison, was personally briefed on the mass deportation two days after the fact, on June 17, 1941. German propaganda immediately picked up the story, announcing that the Soviets planned another, ten times larger, deportation in the Baltic States.[29]

The hastened evacuation and fear of sabotage prompted Soviet reprisals against the civilian population. The execution of detainees in several Estonian investigation prisons was probably the most extreme expression of the policy of repression. The three most notorious massacres occurred in Tallinn, Tartu, and Kuressaare. The announcement of war with Germany on June 22, 1941, caused a panic attack among the high-ranking Soviet officials in Tallinn. The next day, about fifty people were shot in the NKGB internal prison.[30] The Wehrmacht (German armed forces) troops were only two days away from Tartu when the head of the local NKVD gave the order to execute the remaining prisoners. One hundred ninety-two victims of the mass execution carried out on July 9 were buried in two trenches in Tartu prison's courtyard.[31] Saaremaa was one of the last Soviet strongholds in Estonia. Faced with imminent invasion from continental Estonia, the Baltic Navy Tribunal condemned to death all the inmates incarcerated in the island's capital, Kuressaare. The total of eighty-four people, including several Soviet soldiers and sailors, were executed through September 15 in the courtyard of a mediaeval fortress—the symbol of Kuressaare—and in the basement of a neighboring house.[32] In the summer and early fall of 1941 similar mass shootings took place throughout the western Soviet borderlands.

MILITARY CAMPAIGN IN ESTONIA IN THE SUMMER OF 1941

The German 18th Army crossed the border into Estonia at 7:10 P.M. on July 7, 1941. Considering the speed with which Lithuania and Latvia had fallen into the Germans' hands, the military high command did not anticipate any significant resistance in Estonia either. By the evening of the same day, German Army Group

North reported isolated fighting north of the Tartu-Viljandi-Pärnu line, predicting the instant end of the military campaign in Estonia. In preparation for a final battle over Leningrad, the Germans assigned particular value to airfields west of Tartu.[33] In effect, continental Estonia played a role in the German strategic plans only as a transit route to Russia. Additional considerations included control over the production of synthetic gasoline in northeastern Estonia, as well as military hegemony in the Baltic Sea region. The sooner the occupation of Estonia was completed, the more troops could be committed to the "Russian campaign." The Wehrmacht advanced in two directions: the 38th Army Corps set out to capture Pskov and the whole east shore of Lake Peipus, whereas the 26th Army Corps pushed toward Tallinn. This advance was meant to split the Soviet 8th Army defending Estonia into two, and eventually to prepare the ground for a concentrated attack against the key Russian city of Leningrad.

Initially, everything went as planned so that the southern part of Estonia was overtaken within a matter of days. The Wehrmacht captured Viljandi at the end of the second day of the campaign. The coastal city of Pärnu fell earlier that day too. On July 11 German troops entered the western suburbs of Tartu, Estonia's second largest city. Within the next two weeks, the commander in chief of the 18th Army, Georg von Küchler, brought another two small towns, Põltsamaa and Türi, under his control. After this, however, the pace slowed significantly. Aided by the weather conditions (heavy rainfall from mid-July on), the Soviet resistance intensified. The German high command underestimated the strength of the Soviet troops, which put up a more determined fight in Estonia than in the other two Baltic countries. The Soviet air force was still capable of inflicting substantial damage to the advancing Wehrmacht units. On July 30, Adolf Hitler expressed his concern about the military situation in Estonia to Field Marshal Wilhelm Keitel.[34] The early bravado about cleansing Estonia of Soviet troops in no time gave way to more thorough planning on the German part.

On July 27 the German 18th Army, reinforced by one additional division, launched a concerted attack along the entire front. Having captured several locations on both sides of Lake Peipus, the commanding staff announced the total destruction of the enemy forces in that area. On August 7 German troops reached the Gulf of Finland at Kunda; the Soviets faced the threat of encirclement. However, the imminent Soviet military defeat was postponed by the German decision to redirect several divisions eastward, with the purpose of securing a complex of shale oil processing plants in the area between Kiviõli and Sillamäe. By the evening of August 16 the shale oil region was in German hands. It took the 26th Army Corps ten days to reach the town of Narva on the border with Russia. From August 20 the German forces in Estonia concentrated their efforts on closing in on Tallinn.[35]

Of all Estonian cities, Tallinn played by far the most important role in Germany's military plans. A successful Blitzkrieg against the Soviet Union would allow Nazi Germany to mobilize its forces against Great Britain. In order to neutralize the British navy, the Germans needed to prevent the latter's access to seaports around Europe. The German high command considered Leningrad, Kronstadt, and Tallinn the three most important Soviet strongholds in the Baltics. The loss of Tallinn, a naval base with a shipyard, would significantly undermine Soviet military performance in the region. By capturing Tallinn the Germans would regain a safe supply route for their troops and secure strategically important deliveries from the Nordic countries. Lastly, Tallinn's capacity as a sea fortress would contribute to a final battle over the British Isles.[36]

The Soviets refused to surrender the Estonian capital without a battle. By early August preparations for the defense of the city were in full swing. The civilian population was mobilized for digging antitank ditches on the outskirts of Tallinn. By mid-August the three biggest industrial plants were evacuated by sea to Leningrad. The workers who stayed in Tallinn joined the rest of the population in building the fortification. This situation added to the general impression of Tallinn as emptied of civilians, with soldiers, marines, and members of paramilitary formations roaming the streets of the city.

A storm broke while the Wehrmacht was laying siege to Tallinn. By 1:40 P.M. on August 27 the German 254th Infantry Division seized the heights commanding Tallinn's port. In the early afternoon the 61st Infantry Division forced its way into the eastern suburbs of Tallinn, while the 217th Infantry Division slowly but steadily advanced through Nõmme. By 2:45 P.M. on August 28 downtown Tallinn was essentially under German control, yet the fighting in the harbor area continued. The hostilities subsided by that evening, when the 61st Division entered the historical quarters of the city. At 5:05 P.M. a swastika-adorned flag went up at the city hall building in the Old City. According to Army Group North war diaries, the attitude of the population toward the Wehrmacht troops was overtly positive.[37] Georg von Küchler, commanding general of the 18th Army, announced to his troops, "[Y]ou have liberated an old German city from the Bolshevik yoke." The German radio picked up on von Küchler's dictum, broadcasting on August 29 the following information: "Following heavy fighting, German troops captured the stronghold of the red Baltic navy, having thus recovered the old German Hanseatic city. German cultural landmarks in Reval are intact. The city is free of the red yoke. As elsewhere, the grateful population joyfully welcomed their liberator."[38]

The Soviet 8th Army fiercely resisted but could not fend off the attacks of the German war machine, which was superior in organization and weaponry. The Soviet high command had two infantry divisions at its disposal in Estonia. The Baltic navy and the air force, both subordinate to the 8th Army, provided additional support. The Germans had an important advantage over the Soviets—the support of the local population. With regard to the intensity of anti-Soviet resentment among the Estonians, the Germans could not have chosen a better time for the offensive. The horror of the Soviet repression turned even the regime's moderate supporters into its worst enemies. If it were not for the Soviet terror before and during the Nazi invasion, a German source affirmed, the population, particularly its more educated part, would not have been so positively disposed toward the invaders.[39]

The sight of German troops passing through Estonian towns and villages intensified the joy of liberation among the local population. Grateful villagers and city dwellers offered the Wehrmacht soldiers milk, cookies, and wine. German songs and exultant *Heils* filled the air. The crowds cheered the marching columns in Tallinn by showering them with flowers, candies, and cigarettes. A jubilant mood set in: women crying from joy, boys and youth gratefully shaking soldiers' hands, young girls marching along with the troops.[40] Bell chimes announced the arrival of the German army in Valga. In Elva, the locals erected two triumphal arches in honor of the Wehrmacht troops. In Otepää, also in the south, Estonians offered the Germans their best: a local male choir performed on a market square.[41] While watching the German army march in, the triumphant Estonian crowds took delight in seeing the latest military equipment of the Wehrmacht and its soldiers good-natured and friendly. In comparison, the Russian soldiers, "with their dull Asiatic faces, looked mistrustful, wild, and dispirited." This perception gave even more credibility to the Germans, to their bravery and trustfulness.[42] The notion that the German soldiers were the best (supposedly of

5. Showcase of *Postimees* bookstore in Tartu, displaying photograph of Soviet foreign minister Viacheslav Molotov, May 1, 1941; HI, Hintzer, 161939.

a higher moral standing than the Allied forces) persisted among Estonians even after World War II.[43]

The streets of Narva, Pärnu, Tartu, and Tallinn had not seen such an exuberant sentiment since late in the second decade of the twentieth century, when the Estonian Republic first came into existence. The emotions were genuine: for a short while Estonians sincerely supported the change of regime. The smiling faces and the cheering crowds did not, however, disguise underlying resentment and grief over the loss experienced during the year of Soviet dominance. Realized that grief, the new rulers skillfully used such sentiments to their own advantage.

The year of Soviet occupation left a mark on the Estonian psyche, both individual and collective.[44] The sense of betrayal, abandonment, and humiliation drove the population to expiate the shame and disgrace of 1940.[45] The immediate reading of the events of the summer of 1941 was that the Soviets targeted the Estonian nation for annihilation and that the Estonian people were only able to survive by engaging in a life-and-death struggle against Communism. The future leader of the Estonian puppet government, Dr. Hjalmar Mäe, for example, argued that the Soviets intended to deport the entire population so that they

6. Showcase in school supplies shop in Tartu, 1941–44; HI, Hintzer, 157881.

could resettle Estonia with "Asiatics."[46] (I will deal with Hjalmar Mäe and his administration in the next chapter.)

What was important was the presentation of repression. The German Security Police in Estonia came out with the number of deportees—61,168,[47] that is, 5.4 percent of the total population of Estonia. This was an aggregate figure of the citizens of Estonia who had been exiled, mobilized, and evacuated by the Soviets. Mäe had further rounded these numbers to 100,000—the figure he presented to Adolf Hitler on the occasion of the first anniversary of the "liberation" of the country.[48] All these people were deemed lost to the Estonian nation. The Nazis presented post-Soviet Estonia as an emaciated body dying of hemorrhage. It might take a long time, they predicted, before the Estonian people would recover from the blow inflicted by the Soviet terror. Mobilization affected the most potent (sexually) group of the population; taking into consideration the low birthrates in Estonia, the overall strength of the Estonian people was drastically undermined.[49]

According to wartime accounts, Estonians suffered twice as much as Latvians and three times more than Lithuanians. The deliberate distortion of statistical data cannot overshadow the fact that Estonia as a whole was devastated by war more than Latvia or Lithuania. More than half of the 13,054 buildings damaged were destroyed completely.[50] Only 10 percent of all power stations in Estonia remained operational, as compared to 90 percent in Latvia and Lithuania.[51] The urban population decreased on average by 13 percent. The biggest cities, such as Tallinn, Tartu, Narva, Pärnu, Rakvere, Võru, Haapsalu, and Kuressaare, reported losses between 11 and 19 percent. The smaller cities, such as Pechory, Valga, Elva, Otepää, Tõrva, Jõgeva, Mustvee, and Kunda, lost up to a quarter of their prewar population. Kallaste was reduced to two-thirds of its original size.[52]

The popular perception was that in spite of brute suppression, the Estonian nation had remained true to its traditions. Empowered with nationalist spirit, the Estonian people were capable of resisting the terror unleashed by the Russians, Jews, and Communists.[53] The idea of a conspiracy against the Estonian nation, and of the alleged role that the Jews played in that plot, rested upon the belief that the Jewish minority had experienced the Soviet occupation differently than the rest of the population. But to what extent was this notion grounded in reality?

JEWS UNDER SOVIET RULE

Stalin's regime struck the Estonian Jewish community hard, yet its effects were not deadly. The high level of assimilation among the Estonian Jews somewhat lessened the impact of the Soviet occupation on the community. Jewish cultural and welfare organizations were disbanded, individual businesses requisitioned, and assets seized.[54] It is reasonable to conclude that the Jews in Estonia suffered less under the Soviet regime than did their coreligionists in Latvia and Lithuania.[55]

Among the people deported from Estonia on June 15, 1941, there were 415 Jews, that is, about 10 percent of the country's total Jewish population. At least 110 heads of families were subject to arrest, whereas other family members were exiled. "Exploitation of paid labor" was the most common charge laid against deportees (in seventy-four cases). Another thirteen Jews received prison terms (in the case of Pinhas Katz a death sentence) as members of the Revisionist (Zionist) Movement. One-fourth of the Jewish deportees, or ninety-five people, died in exile.[56]

Although foreign nationals among the Jews were unscathed by the deportation, they rightly perceived it as a warning. As soon as Kurt and Edith Sekules learned that the Itskovitch family—Jewish businesspeople who had sponsored them into Estonia from Austria—was deported, they quickly bought a suitcase for themselves. A week later, Nazi Germany invaded the Soviet Union. The very next day, the NKVD arrested in one swipe all immigrants with German, Austrian, and Czechoslovakian passports. About 150 "enemy aliens" were brought to a detention facility at Harku, about ten miles west of Tallinn. Almost half of them were recent Jewish refugees from Germany and Austria. On July 3, a freight train holding the detainees left Estonia for Russia.[57]

During the months of July and August, two-thirds of the local Jewish community left Estonia voluntarily. Some Jews, however, decided to stay. When deciding whether or not to evacuate to Russia proper, Jews were often motivated by legitimate, if trivial, concerns: life conditions in the Soviet Union were poor. The following short conversation took place on a street in Tallinn some three weeks before the Germans captured the city. Upon the question of whether he wanted to go to Russia, Rachmiel Shadsunsky told his Estonian friend that there was not much there; his father had written to him from Russia that the people there were starving.[58] Religious concerns played a role as well. Observant Jews did not want to leave without their spiritual leader, Abe Gomer, supreme rabbi of Estonia since 1927. Gomer never left Tallinn and was subsequently murdered.[59] A majority of younger people, however, decided to leave Estonia for Russia, even though they felt apprehensive of the Soviet power. Among them were real estate owners, Zionists, and members of the Socialist Bund.[60]

Overall, evacuation from the areas still under Soviet control proceeded in an orderly manner. Owing to the geographic position of Estonia, those Jews who wanted to leave the country had enough time to do so—the precious time that their coreligionists in the rest of the Baltics and Ukraine did not have. Until early August one could obtain an evacuation permit fairly easily.[61] In Valga, on the border with Latvia, Jewish families were on the move as early as June 30. The city physician, as well as other Jewish doctors, left Valga for Pskov. A string of yellow Riga busses carrying Jewish refugees from Latvia passed through the area between July 1 and 7.[62] Quite a few Jews boarded the train that departed Tallinn for Russia on July 4.[63] The parents of Eduard Eitelberg found themselves among the refugees who left Tallinn by sea on July 6.[64] A week or so later, a train with the evacuated Jews was hit by a German warplane at Vaivara railway station not far from the Russian border; numerous passengers were killed or wounded.[65] This was a clear warning to Narva's Jews, most of whom cleared the city by July 17.

Some Jews, however, were only evacuated from Narva in August: Veterinarian David Burmistrovich, for instance, was truly lucky, joining a fire brigade that left the city on August 16.[66] On August 17 Narva fell. Apart from the 415 Jews who were deported in June, about 2,500 Jews fled to Russia proper. Thus, only one-quarter of the prewar Jewish population of Estonia stayed in their country—the smallest percentage anywhere in Europe. The thousand or so Jews who decided to stay in Estonia saw no reason for public animosity against them. They did not realize that they were all marked people.

JUDEO-BOLSHEVIK MYTH

Estonians and foreigners alike were amazed to see Jews in positions of authority in Soviet Estonia. Wolfgang A. Mommsen, who traveled to Estonia in November 1940 in the capacity of the head of the German Archival Commission, spotted recent Jewish immigrants from Nazi Germany on Tallinn's streets. Mommsen argued that up to 90 percent of the commissars appointed by the Soviet regime to nationalized businesses were Jewish, describing it as a "Semitic invasion."[67] These haphazard, and for the most part erroneous, observations later appeared in German Security Police reports on the "Jewish Question" in Estonia.

The perceived threat of a Russo-Jewish conspiracy stemmed from the popular belief that held Jews as quintessential Communists. In October 1941 Jüri Uluots, the most senior Estonian politician of the day, produced a twenty-four-page report entitled "On the Bolshevik Domination in Estonia, 1940–41." Under the heading "The Russians and the Jews," he noted the following. Immediately after the establishment of Bolshevik rule in Estonia, Russian officials and workers streamed into the country. The Russian presence became particularly strong in the cities. Together with the Russians came numerous Jews. The Jews acquired leading positions in various sectors of the economy, particularly in banking. Uluots then speculated about the degree of support for Communism in Estonia, which, according to his estimate, was between 3 and 5 percent. Even then, Uluots argued, it was mainly Jews and Russians and only a few Estonians who endorsed the Soviet regime.[68] According to the November 1941 report on the Bolshevik terror in Estonia, there existed a link between the number of Jews in the Soviet institutions and the number of victims of the Soviet deportation. Eleven Jewish employees in the head post office were thus set in direct opposition to about one hundred Estonian postal workers who had been deported.[69] Some people tended to believe that only Estonian workers had been deported, and not Jewish managers.[70]

The question is whether this narrative settled deeply into the minds of ordinary Estonians. Even if it did, the reaction was not always one of hatred or rage, but rather of disdain. First of all, the stories of encounters between Estonians and Jews during the year of Soviet occupation were rare. The following account comes from the annals of the Tartu Omakaitse (more on this organization in chapter 4) and describes the events of June 21, 1940. A Jewish youth ordered an older Estonian farmer to remove his hat during the performance of the *International* at a public gathering in Tartu. Following a rather comic exchange, the Estonian eventually refused to obey. While leaving the scene, the Jewish teenager threatened to inform on his Estonian interlocutor as a "saboteur." As for the Estonian public, "people around were laughing, more jokes were coming." Remarkably, this and not any other story made it into the Tartu Omakaitse chronicle, which was put in writing in 1942.[71]

The Estonian collective memory had deemed a Soviet paramilitary organization, the so-called shock battalions (sometimes translated as destruction battalions: *itsrebitel'nye bataliony*), the most dreadful body after the NKVD, responsible for terrorizing the Estonian population. Jews allegedly played a significant role in the shock battalion operations, often described as "terrorist" activities.[72] The belief that Jews were among the most zealous members of the shock battalions fueled anti-Semitism among the Estonian population.[73] Following the outbreak of the Russo-German war, the Soviet government embarked on a course of action against the saboteurs in the frontline areas. On June 26, 1941, the supreme military commander in Estonia, referring to an order from Lavrenti Beria, ordered the formation of shock battalions. A total of fourteen shock battalions were formed in Estonia (having endured heavy losses, the shock battalions were later regrouped and additional units formed). Ethnic Russians constituted over half of the 6,400 men enlisted in these units; nearly all commanding positions were filled by Soviet officers of Russian origin. However, Estonian wartime propaganda emphasized that between July 19 and August 24 the supreme command of the Estonian shock battalions was in the hands of Mikhail Pasternak, a Russian Jewish officer. A book published in Tallinn in November 1943 under the title *The Year of Suffering of the Estonian People* listed another eighty-nine names of Jewish members of shock battalions. According to the book, Jews constituted at least 8 percent of the total membership.[74] The actual number of Jews in these units was about 120, that is, less than 2 percent of the total strength. Among those who fell in battle were several veterans of the Spanish Civil War such as Victor Feigin.[75] Feigin, an active member of the Communist underground in Estonia, was appointed head of Tallinn Central prison. Half of the Jews who served in Estonian shock battalions were killed in action.[76]

German troops confronted a full-sized shock battalion for the first time on July 30, 1941, near the town of Kallaste on Lake Peipus. Aside from a general statement to the effect that Jews played a significant role in the shock battalions—like elsewhere in the Soviet Union—a German Security Police report provided no further details. Otherwise, 210 out of 250 members of this particular shock battalion were killed. The report identified forty female fighters, but failed to mention whether the shock battalion had any Jews among its ranks—a notable omission.[77] Glika Koblens, a seventeen-year-old from Jēkabpils, barely qualified as a "fighter." Although Koblens had managed to escape from Latvia, she ended up serving as a nurse in the shock battalion. Koblens was captured together with one other nurse, a seventeen-year-old Estonian. Despite the fact that both were Komsomol members, the Estonian woman received a three-month sentence whereas her Jewish colleague was executed.[78] Thirteen members of a Latvian shock battalion, including two Jews from Riga, were arrested near Viljandi. The tasks of this shock battalion included protecting the roads against the guerillas, arresting anti-Soviet activists, guarding the headquarters of the 125th Division, and assisting local militia.[79]

Among specifically Jewish organizations, Licht has been identified as a breeding ground for Communism in Estonia. The purpose of Licht, established by left-wing Jews in 1926, was to promote education. By the end of the 1930s, however, Communists took control of the organization. They created a youth section, which held discussions about the Soviet Union, Soviet literature, and so forth.[80] At least five active members of Licht were Communists. In 1936 they established permanent contacts with the underground Estonian Communist Party, helping the latter to disseminate propagandistic literature.[81] In retrospect, Licht caused more harm to Jews than to any other ethnic group in Estonia; its members drew up a list of Jewish associations and organizations to be dismantled by the Soviet authorities in July and August 1940.[82]

Unlike in Latvia and Lithuania, only a few Jewish names were directly associated with the Soviet terror in Estonia. Aside from Mikhail Pasternak, who held Soviet citizenship, Idel Jakobson was the most frequently cited Jewish name. Popular history recounts that Jakobson arrived from Latvia shortly after the war of national liberation with the sole purpose of overthrowing the legitimate Estonian government. A member of the underground Communist Party of Estonia, Jakobson was arrested in 1931 and sentenced to thirteen years of hard labor, but was granted amnesty in 1938 and subsequently deported to Latvia. Shortly after Estonia was occupied by the Soviet Union, Jakobson returned to Tallinn, where in September 1940 he was appointed deputy chief of the NKVD investigation department—the highest position in the Soviet Security Police a local Jew ever held. In the summer of the following year, Jakobson left for Russia.[83] A few more Jewish names were mentioned occasionally. One of them—Tallinn businessman and Communist Leonid Eisenstadt—helped to establish contacts between a handful of underground Communists within Estonia and their exiled comrades abroad.[84] According to an apocryphal story, it was Aaron Gutkin, the son of a Jewish textile wholesaler in Tallinn, who tore down the Estonian flag from the Long Hermann tower—a symbol of Estonia's statehood.[85]

Various statistical reports confirm that among the Communists there were indeed few Jews. As of January 1, 1941, the Estonian Communist Party had 1,169 full members, with an additional 867 people listed as "Candidates." Seventy-three percent of the party members were Estonians, 23 percent Russians, and 2 percent others. Even if one assumes that all the "others" were Jewish—they still numbered no more than forty, less than 1 percent of the total Jewish population. Although the number of Communists in Estonia increased to 3,751 by July 1941, about 1,000 of them had arrived from Russia proper. Many among the newcomers were ethnic Estonians as well as Russians. According to Soviet statistics, of the 3,751 Communists (information is available on 3,172), 1,479 managed to escape, 595 were mobilized into the Red Army, and 382 fell in combat. If these numbers are accurate, not more than 729 Communists must have fallen into the hands of the Nazis and their Estonian collaborators. Only 114 of them survived the war.[86] Thus the proportion of Estonian Jews in the Soviet apparatus fluctuated between 1 and 4 percent, regardless of which statistics one takes as a basis. One author, for example, calculated how many Jewish members of academic associations at Tartu University were in the NKVD, Communist Party, or shock battalions. Of the 373 members of two Jewish fraternities, a sorority, and an academic association, only nine collaborated with the Soviets, that is, 2.4 percent of the total.[87]

Some Estonians, however, continued to believe in a Judeo-Bolshevik conspiracy. Robert Raid, for example, included the following passage in his autobiographical book:

Tarmo smiled: let me name a few NKVD informers whom you probably remember from your times at the university. Then tell me whether you would have suspected them of being NKVD informers. All right: Kropmann, the lawyer who lived on Aia Street; the shoe-store owner Klompus; the textile merchants Mirvits, Bakscht, Kotkin; Pasternak, the owner of the large clothing store on Alexander Street; young Himmelhoch, whose parents owned the drugstore on Aia Street. Tarmo continued: do you have any idea who one of the "chiefs" of the NKVD is in Tartu? The photographer Schuras from Riia Street! Apparently he is the gray eminence of the NKVD. And do you know who is mayor of Võru? Max Judeikin, the son of the textile wholesaler? Yes! And one of the most active Communists in Võru is Leo Goldberg. Which Goldberg? The son of the leather goods wholesaler! He went to high school in Tartu, studied there, and was arrested for seducing minors.[88]

The Nazis claimed that the year of Soviet occupation dramatically changed Estonians' attitudes toward the Jews. Until then, the Jews had exhibited the utmost loyalty to their home country, but they immediately changed sides after the Soviets invaded Estonia. Communism had a particularly strong appeal to Jewish youth. Unable to provide any further details, Nazi reports once again mentioned the names of Gutkin and Feigin. Both were said to have been in the service of the NKVD. Tallinn Jews, who often disguised their identity behind Russian-sounding names, were allegedly overrepresented in the Soviet security apparatus. According to the German Security Police, "refined Jewish sadism" was widespread among the NKVD investigators in Tallinn. Without completely denying the suffering that Jews had endured at the hands of the new rulers, the Nazis presented them as beneficiaries of the Soviet regime. Although the Soviets had nationalized Jewish businesses, they continued employing the former owners in managerial positions. Among the top Soviet officials in Estonia were Minister of Trade Lazar Vseviev and Minister of Light Industry Leonid Eisenstadt, the son of the former head of the Jewish Cultural Council. The Nazis claimed that the Estonian population had become aware of the preferential treatment of the Jews by the Soviets, realizing that a Jew and Bolshevism were essentially the same.[89] According to a German Security Police report, Estonians had a subconscious racial instinct, which prepared them for an active engagement leading to the "final solution of the Jewish problem."[90]

The few anecdotes condensed in the above paragraph are essentially all that the Nazis wrote about anti-Semitism in Estonia on the eve of German invasion. This is remarkably little. Some scholars argue that the peoples of Eastern Europe, for example Latvians, collaborated in the murder of Jews under the impact of Nazi anti-Semitic propaganda.[91] There is no evidence, though, that the Nazis ever attempted to incite the Estonian population against the Jews either before or during the war. In Narva, on several occasions in August 1941, German planes dropped flyers that called upon Red Army soldiers to kill political commissars and Jews before surrendering. Printed in Russian, the flyers were meant specifically for the Red Army rank and file.[92] The fact that the first two movies shown to the public in Võru in August 1941 were *Traitor* and *Jud Süss* does not yet prove anything.[93]

During the war, the German Ministry of Education and Propaganda released tens if not hundreds of anti-Semitic posters. Neatly bound in a catalog, the posters were available in nearly all languages, including Estonian. Remarkably, only two such posters were meant for distribution in Estonia. One of them read: "The Jew is your mortal enemy! Stalin and the Jews are in one criminal gang!" A similar poster that called upon the onlookers—"The Jew does not belong amongst you! Throw him out!"—came in Russian, Ukrainian, Belorussian, Lithuanian, and Latvian, but not in Estonian. A poster that was expected to generate a particularly strong emotional response focused on the discovery of a mass grave, exhumed in the Ukrainian city of Vinnitsa in the spring of 1943.[94] The text of the poster, available in Lithuanian, Latvian, and Estonian, revived the memories of the Soviet terror in the Baltics. "Jewish Bolsheviks" were said to have carried out a mass execution of 12,000 Ukrainians. If it were not for the rapid advance of the German army, the poster claimed, all local peasants would have been victimized. The last line, predictably, called upon the population to engage in a life-and-death fight against Bolshevism.[95]

The lack of any substantial anti-Semitic indoctrination in Estonia can be explained in different ways. It is rather improbable that had the Nazis thought of

Estonians as ardent anti-Semites, they would have slowed down the flow of anti-Semitic propaganda. More likely, the Nazis invested little in anti-Semitic publications in Estonia because the "Jewish problem" was much less acute there than in the other parts of occupied Eastern Europe. As I will demonstrate in subsequent chapters, Estonians fought Communism relentlessly, so that no additional references to Judeo-Bolshevism were needed. There were simply not enough Jewish Communists in Estonia to sustain the Judeo-Bolshevik myth.

3

THE COLLECTIVE EXPERIENCE OF NAZI OCCUPATION

COOPERATION

If one were to use a weather forecast analogy to summarize Estonia's experience under German occupation it might sound as follows: mostly sunny, with scattered showers. Local German authorities struck the right tone by having chosen their language carefully. But they also chose the right people with whom to talk. By far the greatest asset in that regard was Hjalmar Mäe (born 1901), who was installed as the head of the Estonian Self-Government. The puppet government under Mäe was not directly involved in the Holocaust. In the context of collaboration, however, the Self-Government had one important function: to deflect criticism leveled at German agencies.

Hjalmar Mäe started working for the Reichssicherheitshauptamt (Reich Security Main Office or RSHA) in the winter of 1939–40. Mäe had mainly communicated with Sturmbannführer (SS-Stubaf. [major]) Hans Schindowski, an official in charge of Estonia in Department VI of the RSHA. In February 1941 Mäe managed to move to Germany. From Werneck Castle in Bavaria, where Mäe spent some time alongside two thousand other refugees from Latvia and Estonia, he was transferred to Berlin. Next, Mäe established contact with Peter Kleist and Herbert Petersen from Alfred Rosenberg's ministry.[1] On June 26 Mäe received an audience at Hitler's headquarters, where he was told about his assignment in Estonia. On that very day all the individuals handpicked to head the indigenous administration in the Baltic States, accompanied by Kleist's people from the Reich Ministry for the Occupied Eastern Territories (RMO), took a flight from Berlin to Königsberg, and then continued by car to the border city of Tilsit. Because of the reluctance of the military authority to let them go, Mäe spent more time in Tilsit than he had expected. Of the three leaders traveling to the Baltic region, Kleist only managed to get General Statys Raštikis to Kaunas.[2]

On July 15 Mäe was taken via Riga to Pärnu, which had just been captured by Wehrmacht troops. By the time Mäe reached the city, the leader of Sonderkommando (SK) 1a of the German Security Police, Dr. Martin Sandberger, was no longer there (more on Sandberger and SK 1a in the next chapter). The district commandant of Pärnu, reluctant to cede his authority to the indigenous administration, received Sandberger's protégé with hostility. Following Schindowski's advice, Mäe immediately returned to Riga. The slowdown of the German offensive prevented Mäe from reentering Estonia until August 18.[3] On his way to Tallinn Mäe made a short stop in Tartu, where he introduced himself to a German Security Police representative, Untersturmführer (SS-Ustuf. [second lieutenant]) Gert von Seefeld. While in Tartu, Mäe found time to visit a local concentration camp, which had been operational since mid-July.[4] Mäe finally met with Sandberger on August 30 in Tallinn. Sandberger had received instructions from Brigadeführer (SS-Brif. [brigadier general]) Walter Stahlecker, commander of Einsatzgruppe A (EG A) of the German Security Police, to take Mäe under his protection. When introducing Mäe to the commandant of Tallinn, Sandberger explained that the former was shortly to be appointed as the head of the Estonian civil administration, and that all questions concerning the staff of the Self-Government should from now on be addressed to him, Mäe, personally.[5] The military authorities approved Mäe's candidacy, thus eliminating the last obstacle in the way of Estonian-German cooperation. No difficulties were anticipated.[6] Experts in the Ostland Ministry argued that Mäe's appointment would preclude the power struggle in Estonia, as it had happened earlier in Latvia.[7]

The rest of the top officials in the Estonian civil administration lived up to Nazi expectations as well. Alexander Massakas (born 1905) joined the Vabs movement in 1933. Massakas was involved with the official Vabs publication *Võitlus*. Within a month of his appointment as minister of education in the Estonian Self-Government, Massakas married a citizen of the Reich.[8] It is worth noting that Commander of SK 1a Sandberger had sympathized with the Vabs movement, calling its former leader Artur Sirk a "genius." Sandberger expressed regret that the authorities in Berlin did not recognize the leadership abilities of those few Vabs personalities still around. Their positive attitude toward Germany and Nazi ideology on the one hand, and their opposition to the last Estonian government on the other—Sandberger argued—made those individuals a valuable resource for the occupying power.[9] Yet unmistakably, the Vabs's time was over. On August 2, 1942, a small group of followers met in the Tallinn Cathedral to hold a memorial service for Artur Sirk, who in 1937 had met a violent death. Among the dignitaries in attendance was Hjalmar Mäe. The public response was rather mixed. The Estonian nationalist circles showed little respect to the Vabs, labeling Sirk a "traitor." SS-Brif. Heinz Jost, commander of the German Security Police (Befehlshaber der Sicherheitspolizei und des SD or BdS) in the Ostland, warned the German civil administration against granting the Vabs too much trust, so as not to widen the gap between Estonians and Germans.[10]

Oskar Angelus, who was appointed minister of the interior, received recognition for his positive role in the resettlement of Baltic Germans in 1939. As a high-level official in the Estonian Ministry of the Interior, Angelus was said to have been very helpful to both ethnic Germans and his own countrymen trying to leave the country for good. Angelus took advantage of his position, and moved in early 1941 to Nazi Germany himself. Alfred Wendt (Vendt) too had a German connection. Wendt had received his Ph.D. from Kiel University and was working in the Estonian Ministry of Economics. His wife came from Germany as well. Wendt's last appointment, before his resettlement to Germany in March 1941, was at the Kiviõli shale oil–producing company. The Nazis were pleased to have Wendt as their liaison in a branch of industry so important for the German war economy. They could thus scarcely conceive of a better candidate for the position of minister of economics and finances.[11] Johannes Soodla, who had resettled in Germany as well, managed military affairs in the Self-Government. Soodla's wife was German, and by coincidence also a relative of Hjalmar Mäe's wife. While in Germany, Mäe negotiated with the Abwehr for Soodla to become his military adviser.[12] On October 28, 1941, Brigadier General Johannes Soodla was appointed inspector of the Estonian Security Police and the Self-Defense (Omakaitse), and in August 1943 as inspector of the Estonian Waffen-SS Division. Soodla had maintained close personal relations with the Reich commissioner and the military headquarters in Estonia. Soodla's son fought on the Eastern front as a German officer.[13]

The idea of indigenous self-administration was clear: The native leadership was to be led to believe that they could make independent decisions, without the right to object to any German policies. The better the Estonian officials did their job, the fewer German overseers were needed.[14] Indeed, Estonians heavily criticized First Director Mäe, while praising Commissar General (GK-Estland) Karl Litzmann, head of the German civil administration in Estonia.[15] Litzmann emphasized that "Mäe is a brave man. He is not afraid to take upon his shoulders what we do not want to carry."[16]

Officially, the German civil administration assumed control over Estonia on December 5, 1941. At the same time, Estonia remained within the jurisdiction of Army Group North (Heeresgruppe Nord or HGr North), or more specifically Security Division 207 (Sicherungsdivision).[17] As General Franz von Roques later explained, the above arrangement was made for two reasons: the importance of Estonia as a supply base for HGr North, and its proximity to the front line.[18] The area around Narva was allocated to the 18th Army. Since August 9, 1941, the headquarters of the Army Group North rear area had been in the southeastern Estonian city of Võru. In practical terms, the location meant that the military, under General von Roques, played a larger role in Estonia than in Latvia or Lithuania. In the long term, it had a rather positive effect on Estonia, for the considerable military presence smoothed somewhat the interoffice strife that plagued the other two Baltic States, Latvia in particular.

Von Roques praised the leaders of the Estonian Self-Government as loyal, clever, and farsighted individuals. The general did not fail to notice that the Mäe-Wendt-Angelus triumvirate spoke flawless German. As a matter of fact, they were German citizens.[19] Von Roques felt confident enough to grant the Estonian civil administration substantial autonomy.[20] The German military appreciated the effectiveness and promptness of the Estonian Self-Government, which stood in sharp contrast to the indigenous administrations in Latvia and Lithuania. The military authorities expressed their gratitude to the Estonian people for having delivered a significant amount of felt boots and furs to the Wehrmacht troops; analogous collection campaigns failed miserably in the two other Baltic countries. In the relevant period, Estonians collected twice as much iron scrap as Latvians.[21] Besides, military authorities tended to treat Estonians as equals, which ensured warm relations between the two. For example, in June 1943 the commandant of Tallinn, Generalmajor D. Scultetus, advised his subordinates to display true camaraderie with the members of the Estonian SS-Division, as well as to project the feeling of solidarity with the Estonian people generally. Germans and Estonians were bound by destiny *(Schicksalsgemeinschaft)* to achieve final victory, Scultetus wrote.[22] Indeed, ordinary people came to military headquarters without fear, ready to confide. Estonians had a particularly strong notion of Germans' fairness.[23]

From the outset, the Nazis encouraged mutual cooperation between German and Estonian agencies. Commissar General Litzmann conveyed the impression of a strict yet just ruler who respected the national consciousness of Estonians. In this respect, Litzmann differed significantly from his counterparts in Latvia and Lithuania. The fact that Litzmann was the son of a famous World War I general, and he himself a career military officer, set him apart from other Nazi officials. Litzmann's popularity with the population grew as he toured local factories, talking to people and showing his interest in their personal lives. Some people were pleasantly surprised that Litzmann, as they put it, had a "heart." With regard to Estonians Litzmann emphasized persuasion over force.[24] The extent of local collaboration enabled Litzmann to rule Estonia with only fifty-six Germans on staff.[25] Unlike Lithuanian or Latvian top bureaucrats, who were said to have been corrupt, leaders of the Estonian Self-Government were described as bearers of strong Nordic characteristics, free of corruption.[26] Even financially, the indigenous administration was on equal footing with its German overseers. While GK Litzmann received a salary of 24,000 RM and district commissars earned 14,000 RM, First Director Mäe took home 18,000 RM annually. A schoolteacher, at the same time, had to survive on 1,400 RM per year.[27]

People who worked under Litzmann in the Estonian Self-Government did not drag their feet. On the contrary, Mäe served as a mouthpiece for the German civil administration, drawing on his rhetorical skills. What few conflicts there were between German and Estonian officials were caused by one of the following: Germans at times displayed their feeling of superiority over Estonians; they shamelessly exploited the local economy; or they simply failed to consider fine psychological nuances when dealing with the local population.[28]

Mäe warned his Nazi patrons of mistakes that might cost them Estonian support. According to Mäe, partial German colonization of Estonia was possible as long as Nazis allowed the symbols of Estonian political culture to stay. What the Kaiser Wilhelm occupation force had failed to achieve in 1918 (by having banned the Estonian tricolor and the national anthem, and by treating Estonian POWs as Bolsheviks) could now be easily attained. To check on his political rivals,

Mäe suggested that his German masters send potentially unruly members of the former political parties to Russia proper, where they could provide valuable services to the Reich. Finally, Mäe expressed his disapproval of the Baltic German presence in Estonia.[29] This last point on Hjalmar Mäe's political program may sound contradictory, considering that his escape from Soviet-dominated Estonia in the winter of 1941 had only been possible within the framework of the Baltic German resettlement program. On balance, however, the anti–Baltic German stance of the leader of the Estonian puppet government appears to have been a well-calculated political move. Actually, by driving a wedge between Deutschbalten and Reichsdeutsche, Mäe was able to successfully manipulate Estonian popular opinion.

Mäe thus presented himself as an opponent of Baltic Germans. Whatever criticism the German and Estonian civil administrations received from the Estonian population, Mäe refocused the issue toward Baltic Germans, whose harmful influence he had continually stressed. That was indeed a smart move on Mäe's

7. First anniversary of the "liberation" of Tartu, July 1942. Dr. Martin Sandberger, commander of the German Security Police in Estonia, is second from left; Karl Keerdoja, Tartu's mayor, is third from left; and Dr. Hjalmar Mae, head of the Estonian civil administration, is fourth from left; HI, Hintzer, 162237.

part, considering that the Baltic Germans who made it back to Estonia were few in number. By mid-1942, there were barely two thousand ethnic Germans—former citizens of Estonia—in the country.[30] It did not escape the attention of the RSHA that the mere sight of Baltic Germans undermined the willingness of Estonian and Latvian agencies to cooperate. Mäe's strategy worked: the Estonian Security Police reported that the local population had maintained friendly relations with the Germans, while the attitude toward the Baltic Germans was worsening.[31] High-ranking German officials, including Himmler, hinted that Estonia's future depended upon the country's contribution to the victory over Bolshevism. Estonian intelligentsia interpreted Himmler's dictum to mean that the decision regarding independence had already been granted, but that it then was derailed at the last minute because of Baltic German opposition, spearheaded by Alfred Rosenberg, Reich minister for the Occupied Eastern Territories (Reichsminister für die besetzten Ostgebiete or RMO), and by Hinrich Lohse, Reich commissioner for the Ostland (Reichskommissar für das Ostland or RKO). The intellectuals held Mäe personally responsible for that mishap.[32]

The civil administration was established in Estonia rather late and therefore had no say in the implementation of anti-Jewish policies, except for the expropriation of Jewish property. The leaders of both German and Estonian civil administrations did not go beyond abstract allegations of international Judeo-Bolshevik conspiracy. In his public speeches, for instances, Litzmann had often referred to Jews as the source of capitalism, liberalism, and Bolshevism. The Reich commissioner presented Estonia as a bulwark of European culture against the Jewish-Asiatic subhuman of the Soviet Union. Litzmann had assured his listeners that Germans and Estonians could jointly defeat Judeo-Bolshevism. The Pärnu district commissar, Lothar Bombe, told the audience of one of the parishes that Estonia had joined other young European nations in the fight against international Jewish Bolshevism.[33]

Similarly, members of the Estonian civil administration did not shy away from holding "international Jewry" up to shame. When announcing a campaign for the collection of iron scrap, Minister of Education Alexander Massakas blamed the Jews in London and New York for having deprived Germany of copper.[34] Hjalmar Mäe had no difficulty incorporating the Judeo-Bolshevik theme into his public speeches. At a celebration of the first anniversary of the "liberation" of Estonia from Communism in October 1942, Mäe described Bolshevism as a tool of the international Jewry, designed to enslave all nations through NKVD terror.[35] When addressing the trade union bosses, Mäe said that the international Jewry had exploited the proletariat, yet the Estonian workers had not gone along with the Judeo-Bolshevik regime.[36] He also claimed that it was the Jews who had established trade unions in Independent Estonia.[37]

Hjalmar Mäe and other German underlings are not necessarily representative of the entire Estonian population. What is interesting, however, is that in spite of the general population's distrust of the leaders of the Self-Government, the population, by and large, shared the views expressed by Mäe and his colleagues.

POPULAR OPINION

Political reports coming from the Baltics confirmed the assumptions that Nazis had made before the Russo-German war. Most people remained uncertain about the political future of their country. The experience of the Soviet terror had buried the notion of self-reliance. The Estonian intelligentsia, decimated through deportation, was incapable of seizing the political initiative. In this context, almost any political resolution would pass muster with the lawmaking process.[38] These preconditions made the manipulation of public opinion an easy task for the German occupier. GK Litzmann candidly stated that there was no need to worry about the consequences of a price increase on the agricultural produce of Estonia. For the time being, Litzmann wrote, the farmers were so engrossed in grieving for their relatives and friends lost to the summer 1941 deportation, and so grateful to the Germans who had delivered them from evil, that nothing could shake their good faith.[39]

What Litzmann told Rosenberg in the fall of 1941 had remained true for the duration of the German occupation of Estonia: people's pressing everyday needs made political participation fade in relevance.[40] Ironically, with ideology assigned such an important role, its impact on the general population disappeared quickly. Taking refuge in the private sphere was not at all unusual. Sustaining one's physical and biological existence took precedence over everything else. In that respect, Estonians were not any different from the rest of the people in Nazi-occupied Europe, including the Germans themselves.[41] The year of Soviet rule had profoundly altered the Estonians' perceptions of political regimes. Most people (probably more so in the rural areas than in the cities) judged the

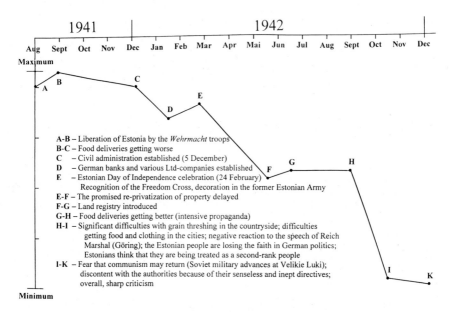

8. Shifts in Estonian popular opinion, August 1941–January 1943 (adapted from the original, 1943); NARA, T-454/36.

ideological tenets of a new regime by their personal well-being. There had been no attempts to confront Nazi ideology per se. Rather, Estonians expressed their dissatisfaction with the economic policy of the occupation regime by comparing it to Soviet practices. The years of Estonian independence did not seem a suitable yardstick in this regard. The twelve or so months of Soviet rule thus became the sole point of reference.

On certain issues the Nazis and the Estonians shared concerns. Elevating the Estonian nation to the status of a defender of Europe against the Bolshevik menace was one of them. In their speeches and writings, Estonian public figures often connected the ideas of shared culture, European heritage, and anti-Communism. According to Mäe, the Estonian war of liberation was a prerequisite for making Europe a safe haven against Communism. Uluots made similar remarks, arguing that Estonia's fight for independence had changed the course of Central European history. *Postimees* wrote in February 1943 that "[s]ince that time [1918] on, Lake Peipus has been the border of Europe, or more precisely, the border of the entire West-European culture. The Western world owes us a 'thank-you' for the defense of that border."[42] To bring that message to the masses, on March 26,

1942, a series of events was held in Tallinn commemorating the defense of the city against Ivan the Terrible's troops four hundred years earlier. Unsurprisingly, the theme of Soviet occupation of Estonia in 1940–41 dominated the festivities.[43]

Anti-Communism was the only common belief that all Estonians shared, irrespective of their political views. Estonians were preoccupied with the destruction of Bolshevism as a political and social force. Germany, as the only country capable of eliminating the danger of Communism, retained the confidence of the general population until the very last months of the war. Among ballots cast in Kuressaare in January 1943 there were quite a few paper slips with anti-Communist diatribes, but not a single reference to Germany or Germans. Not uncommon was the view that "regardless who rules over Europe, it is most important to see Communism annihilated and our autonomy recognized."[44] GK Litzmann was of the opinion that most people would be content if Estonia received a status similar to that of the Protectorate of Bohemia and Moravia or, for example, enjoyed the kind of rights that Bavaria had in the post-1870 German Reich.[45] Furthermore, Estonians saw themselves as having contributed more to the struggle against Communism than had their neighbors. Even after Nazi military successes became scarcer, and more and more people started turning their eyes to the West, Estonians remained continually preoccupied with danger from the East. Estonians hoped that "civilized states"—Germany, England, and America—would somehow reach an agreement regarding the future of the Baltic States and thus eliminate the threat of Bolshevism.[46] While the German army was in retreat and the city of Narva emptied of its population (in early February 1944), Estonians did reportedly behave in a dignified manner.[47]

In October 1943, the Estonian Security Police presented a list of the seven most common causes for anti-German feelings among Estonians. First on that list was the failure to eliminate the remnants of Bolshevism. But what would have happened if the enemy had prevailed? Estonians asked themselves whether the Germans would have been able to carry out a systematic evacuation of the civilian population.[48] Estonians distrusted the Germans, yet not to the degree of open confrontation; they distrusted the Russians even more.[49] A Finnish broadcaster in April 1943 summarized the situation in the following manner: "[I]t is obvious for Estonians who they are fighting against, but not necessarily, for what purpose."[50] As for the Germans, they did not care how the Estonians would resolve this dilemma, so long as the latter continued fighting the Russians.

This the Estonians did. Alexander Varma, the late Estonian ambassador to Finland, explained that "each and every Estonian will fly a German flag next to an Estonian one, yet not because he wants to give up Estonia's independence but in recognition of the German contribution to the fight against Bolshevism."[51] It was a classic love-hate relationship that Estonians had established with regard to the Germans. The Estonian people placed their hopes with the Germans because of their common opposition to Russia and Communism. While so doing, however, they did not stop hating Germans. It was a dysfunctional relationship that worked, but only for the Germans.

Estonians did not necessarily associate anti-Communism with Nazism. While the anti-Communist sentiment was genuine, an outgrowth of a specific historical context, Nazi ideology left Estonians unmoved. Extensive pro-Nazi propaganda never did take off in Estonia.[52] Estonians were said to be too reserved, too rational to believe the tenets of Nazi propaganda. The year of Soviet rule made Estonians even more skeptical regarding any kind of promises of distant happiness (such as ironic references to "Soviet paradise").[53] The popular rejection of the pompous ideological framework imposed by the Soviets did not automatically make Nazi ideological messages more attractive. It was almost impossible for the Nazis to convert Estonians to their creed, taking into account how disappointed the latter were with the capability of independence-era politicians to protect the vital interests of Estonia. Furthermore, the Estonians were also disillusioned with politics in general. The postwar Soviet trials of Nazi collaborators send a misleading message: in fact only a fraction of Estonians, Latvians, and Lithuanians shared Nazi views. In the case of Estonia, the occupation authorities did not even try to disseminate Nazi ideology through official channels.[54] Of all the strata of the Estonian population, workers were probably most receptive to Nazi promises. Karl Litzmann's speeches, like the one he delivered at the Luther plant in Tallinn in February 1942, found warm welcome among the workers.[55]

Unlike his colleagues in Latvia and Lithuania, GK Litzmann had actively promoted his Estonian subjects, emphasizing their distinctiveness among the peoples of the German East. For example, he opposed the introduction of a medal to be awarded to the "Eastern" peoples. Taking into consideration the high level of culture in Estonia, it would have been insulting to compare Estonians with the peoples inhabiting the Russian steppes. How could one forget that 80 percent of the Estonian population was declared fit for Germanization? Litzmann assured Lohse that the Wehrmach, the Security Police, and the Sicherheitsdienst (Security Service or SD) all shared his high opinion of the Estonians.[56] The results were quick to come: German-language courses had never been more popular in Estonia.

In April 1944, less than half a year before the German retreat from Estonia, the high command of HGr North came out with a lengthy study entitled "Characteristics of the Estonians: Dealing with Estonians." The study outlined the main features of the Estonian collective psyche and proposed how to use them for the Germans' advantage. For a military agency, the HGr North produced a surprisingly insightful document, which deserves a closer look.

Estonians prided themselves on their country's independence, the report said, and displayed great sensitivity about the cultural and political achievements of the Estonian nation. The so-called Freedom War lay at the heart of the Estonian national pride. Estonians grossly exaggerated its importance for the European continent. Estonian propaganda said that winning the war of national liberation was equivalent to "rescuing Europe from Bolshevism." Those who dared to doubt it were accused of having deliberately diminished a heroic epoch in Estonian history. In order to win the sympathy of the Estonian population, one needed only to familiarize himself with the events of the Freedom War. Proud of their countrymen's military capability, Estonian officers were particularly appreciative of such an interest. Because Estonians could never get over their loss of independence, it was recommended to avoid that subject altogether.[57]

As politicians, Estonians were materialists, not idealists. Estonians held a sober worldview, characteristic of peasants. What Estonians appreciated about Nazism was not the idea of national community (Volksgemeinschaft), but rather its social organization and social care. As regards Communism, Estonians rejected not so much its ideas of permanent revolution and class struggle, but rather took exception to the limitation of civic freedoms, nationalization of property, and first and foremost the atrocities committed against their people. Estonians were reluctant to acknowledge the influence of certain German intellectuals during the period of Estonian national awakening in the second half of the nineteenth century, as well as of German culture in general. Baltic Germans were particularly unwelcome. Ethnic Germans who had resettled in 1939 were said to have abandoned Estonia in a critical hour. Only after having drawn a clear line between Reich and Baltic Germans would Estonians cooperate with the Reich Germans.[58]

Estonian perspectives on Bolshevism are particularly illustrative. Taking into account the Estonians' practical way of thinking, it was of great opinion-forming value to base such a discussion on facts. When discussing the Bolshevik terror, Germans were instructed to play the role of attentive listener rather than express their own views and experiences. Estonians were of an opinion that they, unlike Germans, knew what Bolshevism was like. A common Estonian expression to Germans was, "You have not experienced anything like that!" Estonians perceived any German suggestions to the contrary as arrogance and a deliberate minimizing of their martyrdom. Estonians tended to exaggerate the extent of the brutalities committed against them, while overemphasizing the stance that the Estonian people had adopted in the face of terror.[59]

Both Estonian intelligentsia and farmers had an inferiority complex, which often resulted in political shortsightedness. Self-absorbed with their suffering, Estonians talked a lot about the tragedy of small nations. When having these conversations with Estonians, one should try to be very tactful, or else avoid these topics altogether. With respect to nationalism, this Estonian sensitivity became pathological. Estonians took any personal insult as an offense against their nation at large. Therefore, even those remarks that appeared harmless could be potentially damaging to a relationship. As long as the Estonians wanted to be acknowledged as a political force, under no circumstances must they be made to feel like a bargaining chip in a power play of the big nation-states. This idea should also be translated into personal relations with the Estonians. With clumsy handling, Estonians would feel themselves being used by the Germans. The concluding paragraph of the twelve-page document read as follows: "The Germans' attitude toward Estonians should be different from that of masters and slaves. Instead, Germans should treat Estonians like the older brother would treat his younger, weaker brother, having the latter's respect in return."[60]

Not only is the accuracy of the report striking, but also the degree of its operational implementation. One of the major problems of Nazi policy in occupied Eastern Europe was the reluctance to cede any autonomy to the vanquished peoples. Indeed, East Europeans, and Slavs in particular, were often treated as pariahs. It is a favored pastime of historians to speculate as to what would have happened if Hitler had reversed his rigid policy vis-à-vis the "Eastern" peoples. They would have been enthusiastic collaborators—just as the Estonians were! There was nothing that the German occupation authorities did in Estonia that would have impeded

9. Dismantled statues of Lenin and Peter the Great in the yard of the Gustav Peets factory in Tartu, summer 1941; HI, Hintzer, 162156.

their long-term objectives. An exception to the rule, the Nazis acted upon the guidelines summarized in the above paragraphs from the inception of the occupation, despite the fact that these guidelines were drafted four months before the end of the German occupation. A careful reader would also notice that Jews were nowhere mentioned in the study that examined Estonian mentality: the Germans, the Russians, the Communists were all, however, discussed. This silence is probably because the Jews had never made it into the Estonian collective consciousness as a monolithic group marked with certain features. Jews did matter only in relation to the abovementioned three ethnic/political groups. This relationship became crucial when it came to a decision over the life and death of individual Jews, a decision that the Germans turned over to the Estonians.

In a sense, Estonia became a Nazi showcase for the rest of occupied Europe. A relatively "good" racial composition, an experience of life under the Communist regime, and a careful preselection of the native governing body, all were factors that transformed Estonia into a model country under German rule. The example of Estonia should have showed other countries how small nations could benefit in the Nazi *New Europe*.[61]

10. Estonians debase Lenin's statue; HI, Hintzer, 162153.

NAZI COMPARISON OF ESTONIANS
WITH LATVIANS AND LITHUANIANS

The preconditions for collaboration were much better in Estonia than in the two other Baltic countries. The summer months of 1941 provided enough evidence for the Germans to start comparing Estonians and Latvians, always favoring the former. Latvians intended to rebuild their independence without any foreign—that is, German—help. They gave the impression of a people who were trying to get out of the Third Reich's orbit as soon as possible. General Franz von Roques apparently preferred Estonians to Latvians, as becomes clear from his postwar correspondence.[62] Hjalmar Mäe had an explanation as to why Estonians were so positively disposed toward Wehrmacht troops. Contrasted with the rise of chauvinistic sentiments in Latvia, Mäe related to one of his Estonian associates, Estonians took into account the existing political reality.[63] Germans took note of the different reception they were accorded in each of the three Baltic states. Lithuanians came forward, bringing the traditional gifts of bread and salt, and reportedly kissed the hands of German officers. Latvians, in contrast, at once put forward demands for reestablishing their independence. Estonians, however, had just one request: provide weapons with which to fight the common enemy. Outside observers noted that this request had been granted, thus ensuring relatively good relations between the Germans and Estonians—at least for the time being. It seemed altogether plausible that the Germans initially intended to grant Estonia special treatment.[64]

The Nazis treated each of the three Baltic peoples in accordance with the German perception of their respective racial value. The Estonians occupied the top position in that racial hierarchy. In the summer of 1942 Alfred Rosenberg came up with a list of twelve peoples that lived in the Ostland. Estonians and Livonians were ranked the highest, followed by Latvians and Ingermanland Finns. Lithuanians and Poles stood just above Russians and Ukrainians, whom Rosenberg considered of the lowest racial stock.[65] The Race and Settlement Main Office (Rasse- und Siedlungshauptamt or RuSHA) proclaimed the Estonians the best of all "Eastern" peoples.[66]

Germans had consistently described Estonians as the best racial stock in the Baltics and beyond. Sometimes racial appraisal was built into traditional stereotypes. Although the Waffen-SS uniform with the Latvian insignia was looked upon with a certain respect—as one travel report from October 1942 stated— Latvian soldiers and officers were trusted less than were their Estonian counterparts. From the racial point of view, the Latvian population did not make a very good impression. The report concluded that, keeping in mind the sadistic conduct of the Latvian Communists during and after the Bolshevik Revolution, the Latvians, taciturn and cunning, were definitely not the most pleasant people. It was a very different situation with the Estonians, who sported a good shot of Nordic blood, which they had inherited from their Finnish kin.[67] Racial scientists confirmed that the ratio between the Nordic and the East-Baltic racial type among Estonians was 26 percent to 28 percent, as compared to 18 percent to 33 percent in Latvia.[68] A Swedish delegation that visited Estonia in the spring of 1942 confirmed the previous reports, according to which Germans favored Estonians above other Baltic peoples. Lithuanians were regarded as the least sympathetic, partially because of the historical connections between Lithuania and Poland.[69] Occasional visitors argued that Estonia topped Latvia and Lithuania in all categories: racial composition, culture, economy, and governance. In that latter respect, Estonia was arguably at the same level as Finland and Sweden.[70]

From the Nazi point of view, the Estonians lived up to the image of a "cultural people" *(Kulturvolk)* better than did the Latvians. When it came to culture and race, Latvia was said to have exhibited more similarities with the "Slavic East." One other factor that depreciated the image of Latvia was the relatively strong Catholic influence and thus the exposure to Polish influence.[71] In spite of the strong sense of honor and self-consciousness of the Estonians, they were never hostile to the Germans, as for example were Czechs or Poles. Estonians treated the Wehrmacht soldiers much better than did Latvians. While the German army conquered Latvia in a matter of weeks, it did not occupy continental Estonia until two months later. Estonia also had endured more physical and property destruction than had Latvia. Therefore Estonians had more reasons to think of the Germans as liberators.[72] Commander of EG A Stahlecker noted as early as mid-July 1941 that the initial enthusiasm of the Baltic population toward the Germans would not last for very long. The attitude might change as soon as material hardship settled in, and even more so when the Baltic peoples realized that the Germans did not plan to restore their countries' independence. Stahlecker predicted that in Estonia the Germans could expect a warmer welcome than in the other two Baltic countries. Stahlecker argued that, in comparison with Latvians and Lithuanians, Estonians were better educated and stood altogether at a higher cultural level. Based on previous political experiences, the Estonians were to immediately comprehend that their survival was dependent on Germany. In recognition of Estonian goodwill, Stahlecker proposed to grant the country a political status similar to that of Slovakia or the Protectorate of Bohemia and Moravia.[73]

Estonians were also said to have been outspoken enemies of Bolshevism, to a greater degree than were Latvians or Lithuanians. The firm anti-Communist stance of the Estonians, already evident during the interwar period, came about because of good racial characteristics, a shared history with Germany, and a high level of culture. GK Litzmann listed the following three factors as proof of Estonians' anti-Communism: the interwar autonomy for the German minority, correct attitude toward the Third Reich, and anti-Communist leaning in general.[74] The Nazi and Soviet sources alike bestowed upon the Estonians the status of foremost anti-Communist nation in the Baltics. In July 1940, the Soviet authorities staged elections, whose outcome was predetermined. Whatever the degree of manipulation in those elections, the announced figures were different for the three countries. According to Soviet statistics, 96 percent of registered voters in Lithuania, 95 percent in Latvia, but only 82 percent in Estonia participated in the parliamentary elections. Approximately 99 percent of Lithuanians and 98 percent of Latvians cast their vote for the Communists. In Estonia, the corresponding percentage was 93.[75] Lithuanians may have been the most sincere in their choice, grateful for the reunification of the Vilna region with the rest of the country. In Latvia, Communism had a longer-lasting effect because of the painful experience of World War I.[76] Estonians, however, seemed to have been fixated on the attempted Communist coup of 1924.

Consider, for example, the Nazi plans to raise three Waffen-SS units in the Baltics, one for each country. On October 1, 1942, Hitler announced the formation of an Estonian Waffen-SS (Schutzstaffel) Volunteer Brigade (also known as SS Legion and, since February 1944, Waffen-SS Division). As a result of the general mobilization that Germans announced in the winter of 1944, with the approval of the Estonian opposition, 35,000 men showed up. The turnout in Latvia, which had twice the population of Estonia, was similar. In Lithuania, the mobilization campaign collapsed. Remarkably, the projected figures for Estonia, Latvia, and Lithuania were 15,000, 35,000, and 5,000 respectively.[77] Considering these figures, one cannot help arriving at the conclusion that after two and one-half years of occupation, a majority of Lithuanians had lost faith in the new regime. Support among the Latvian population remained more or less at the same level, but the Estonians exceeded all expectations of their German rulers. While Himmler rated the Latvian Waffen-SS Division as "very good," he said that the Estonian Battalion "Narva" (part of the Waffen-SS Division "Wiking") had fought excellently. Himmler praised the officers of the Estonian Waffen-SS Division undergoing training as "the best of all Germanic officers we have ever had."[78]

NO OPPOSITION

The way German occupation authorities treated Estonians approximated accommodation, which was a rather unfertile breeding ground for discontent and resistance. Indeed, Estonia was probably the only country in occupied Eastern Europe without armed anti-German resistance. Estonian laborers and farmers worked toward their quotas, and there were no acts of sabotage or killings of

German officials.[79] In comparison, in Lithuania the partisan movement (comprised predominantly of non-Lithuanians) was already in place in the winter of 1942. According to the HGr North report of January 1944, "bandits" stepped up their activities everywhere but in Estonia.[80] General von Roques confirmed that Estonia was free of partisans (partisanenfreieste).[81] The Self-Defense (Omakaitse or OK), with the help of the local population, had effectively apprehended the individual liaisons that the Soviets parachuted into Estonia.

One might well expect dissent within the German-sponsored Self-Government. The Germans dissolved the provisional government of Lithuania in August 1941, and its parent organization—the Lithuanian Activist Front—one and a half months later. The leader of the organization ended up in Dachau concentration camp.[82] The fact that many leaders of the Latvian Self-Government acquired their positions during the summer 1941 interregnum made them reluctant to subscribe to the more far-reaching goals of Nazi Germany.[83] Alfrēds Valdmanis, who served as minister of justice in the Self-Government he formed, was as much concerned about his career as was Hjalmar Mäe. Unlike the latter, however, Valdmanis had often criticized Nazi occupation policy, made contacts with the Latvian opposition, and in 1943 resigned from the Self-Government in an act of public defiance.[84] Nothing like that had ever happened in Estonia. Members of the Estonian Self-Government had been carefully selected in accordance with their disposition toward Nazi Germany. Head of the Estonian puppet government Mäe acknowledged after the war, "We were loyal."[85] In the Estonian case, it was not just conformity but a definite pro-German stance.

There had never been organized opposition in Estonia. Not even those citizens belonging to anti-German circles could overcome the trauma caused by Soviet repression to express their sentiment openly.[86] The Estonian national opposition movement was limited to a narrow circle of military officers and Tartu academics. Corroded by internal conflict, the Estonian intelligentsia was unable to forge unity even within its own ranks.[87] Colonel Victor Koern, commander of Viljandi anti-Soviet partisans, was probably the only individual capable of rallying the opposition. His activities in and around Pärnu during the first weeks of July 1941 attested to his leadership potential. (Koern fell in combat against regular Soviet troops on July 19).[88]

Attempts at regaining independence were nowhere to be seen in the fall of 1941. A flyer that circulated in Tallinn on June 30, 1942, made the first known call for passive resistance in Estonia,[89] yet to no avail. The academic elite came to embrace the idea that Estonia was too small a state to survive independently, and therefore should seek alliance with a more powerful state.[90] The political prospects for Estonia ranged from total independence to some kind of union between Estonia and Finland.[91] The proposals displayed naïveté, embedded in the experience of 1918. The self-styled leaders of the Estonian opposition conceived of alliances from Finland to Sweden, and even further afield to England—a country that had lost interest in that part of Europe since the early 1920s. Many believed that in the end the Western powers would deliver Estonia from the reign of tyrants.[92] In the spring of 1944 the German Security Police carried out several arrests of the Estonian intelligentsia. The cause for arrest was anglophile views, but never anti-German sentiment.[93] Estonians did criticize the lower echelons of German officialdom—decrying poor organization, laziness, and nepotism[94]—as they did with regard to native agencies. For example, in October 1943 workers at Krenholm cotton mills in Narva complained about the local German Economic Office (Wirtschaftskommando or WiKo), which they said first allowed them to grow cabbage but then forbade it.[95] This kind of petty concern, rather than issues of universal importance, sank the population's mood in Estonia.

Dr. Uluots, dean of the Law School at Tartu University, was the most recognizable figure among the Estonian intellectual elite. In German documents Uluots was described as leader of the opposition, and yet no action was taken against him. The truth is that neither Uluots nor any of his colleagues attempted in fact to challenge German authority, and he simply was not perceived as a danger. Uluots was in opposition to the Estonian Self-Government.[96] But that was exactly why Mäe and his like were installed in power—to parry blows aimed at the German rulers. In June 1944 GK Litzmann met Uluots to discuss the present political situation in Estonia, but also to probe the latter's links to anti-German opposition. According to Litzmann, it was possible to secure Uluots's cooperation.[97]

There were rumors about a thirty-man-strong band in southern Estonia, composed of nationalistic students and members of the OK. The band allegedly planned an armed uprising against the German rule in September 1942.[98] This kind of speculation had bred a broader rumor about the so-called "Green Legion," an anti-German clandestine organization. It turned out that the number of people who fled into the woods (most of whom were Communist sympathizers) did not exceed one hundred. The Estonian population denied support to this kind of marginal armed band, condemning the attempt to exploit the legacy of the summer of 1941 as the "forest brother" movement.[99]

A majority of the Estonian population backed the Germans until the very last days of occupation. Thousands of people took part in building the defense on the outskirts of Tallinn in 1944. According to the GK-Estland Office, "people were ready to make whatever sacrifice necessary in order to prevent the return of the Bolsheviks." Panic broke out when on September 18 the Germans unveiled an evacuation plan.[100] The Estonian civil administration remained loyal even then.[101] For the first and the only time, Estonians attempted to wrest power from the Germans as the latter were pulling out of the country in the second half of September 1944. The Germans, who effectively left Estonians to their fate, paid little or no attention at all to the events in Tallinn. A military report of September 21 summarized the developments in the Estonian capital in just one line: "For the first time ever, Estonian nationalists and Communists masterminded unrest in Tallinn."[102] An uprising of limited scope like the one in Tallinn had no impact whatsoever. A declaration released by the self-proclaimed Estonian government had very limited circulation. By then, escape from the advancing Soviet troops became a priority, and most refugees were unaware of the proclamation.[103]

German authorities had experienced much more pressure from Latvians and Lithuanians than they had from Estonians. The anti-German resistance movement in Latvia was quite substantial, even if split along ethnic and ideological lines. By the end of 1941 an underground group founded at the University of Latvia claimed three hundred fighters and branches in all major Latvian cities. In August 1943, four major political parties came together to establish the so-called Latvian Central Council. Less than a year later, members of the Council were arrested, and its leader, Konstantins Čakste, died in prison.[104] The level of resistance correlated with the degree of repression that the Germans applied in each of the three Baltic countries.

Estonians rarely experienced a deliberate German attack on their lives, as Lithuanians and Latvians sometimes did, and often Russians and Poles as well. In response to the murder of two officials from the Reich, four hundred hostages were executed in Lithuania on May 20, 1942. The commissar general in Kaunas described the victims as "Communists and saboteurs, mostly of Polish origin."[105] Following the debacle with the recruitment of Lithuanians into the Waffen-SS Legion in the spring of 1943, the Germans deported forty-six Lithuanian nationalists to the Stutthof concentration camp. A year later the Germans arrested General Povilas Plechavicius and sent him to a concentration camp for having disobeyed an order. In addition, they executed a number of soldiers from the Vilnius detachment as a deterrent to others.[106] In Latvia, the most widely publicized atrocity took place in the easternmost province of Latgale in early January 1942. Accused of having sheltered fugitive Communists and Red Army soldiers, thirty men from the village of Audriņi were executed on January 4, and the village itself was leveled to the ground. Another forty-seven people were executed in the village of Morduki two days later.[107] No such atrocities against the civilian population have been registered in Estonia. The village of Usadishche, where Sonderkommando 1a carried out a mass execution on March 8, 1942, was in fact situated southeast of Pskov and not in Estonia, as an EG report (and later the prosecution at Nuremberg) mistakenly identified it.[108] The only known case of a hostage shooting in Estonia took place in Kuressaare in November 1941. As an act of retribution for the death of a German soldier, a firing squad executed ten alleged Communists.[109]

Whatever the Nazis did or said, the way they positioned themselves vis-à-vis the Baltic peoples was to contribute to the former's foremost objective: establishing a new European order.

ESTONIANS IN HITLER'S "NEW EUROPE": A VISION

Of all German-occupied territories in Europe, the Baltic region had the most suitable qualities to become a testing ground for the Nazi "New Order." It was in Estonia, Latvia, and Lithuania, rather than in Poland, Ukraine, Belgium, Holland, or southern Europe, that ethnic restructuring met the least difficulties. Ironically, Nazi planners believed that the process of Germanization would have proceeded more swiftly if they had shifted the Estonians and Latvians eastward, instead of sending racially fit individuals from these two countries to the Reich. It seemed to the Nazis to be more beneficial to deploy Estonians and Latvians (but not Lithuanians) as middlemen in the Ukraine, Belorussia, and the Caucasus, thus pitting them against the "Eastern peoples."[110] While rendering valuable services to the Third Reich, the Estonians and Latvians—threatened by the vast and hostile East—would have instinctively sought German protection. Participation in the German program of colonization would have given the two nations equal status with the occupier. Nazi racial experts observed that neither Estonians nor Latvians objected to a deployment outside their home countries. By helping to govern the Ostland, Ukraine, and the Caucasus, the Estonians would have fulfilled their desire to be treated as equals. After twenty-odd years in German service, the Estonians would have dulled their sense of national belonging, thus availing themselves of complete Germanization.[111] The Baltic example should prove the success of the German population policy in Europe.

At a local level, however, nobody really knew the extent to which the program of Germanization should be carried out, and by what means. BdS-Ostland Stahlecker had complained about the lack of clarity on that matter. At the same time, he praised First Director Mäe, who used covert propaganda to pursue the policy of Germanization with respect to Estonians. Mäe and his associates proposed a twenty-year program of Germanization for Estonia, though without advertising it widely.[112] Ironically, that was the deadline that Himmler set up a few months later.[113] Mäe recalled the subject of a conversation between Himmler and himself during Himmler's official visit to Estonia at the end of 1941. According to Himmler, up to 70 percent of the Estonian population were pure *Germanen*, with the exception of their use of the Estonian language. Himmler acknowledged the achievements of the Estonian people and the Estonian State, suggesting that Mäe would remain for the foreseeable future the only Baltic leader with whom he would be willing to communicate.[114] Himmler had allegedly addressed Mäe as "prime minister" and never forgot to congratulate him on Estonian Independence Day. Mäe claimed that he had exercised a significant influence on the head of the German SS.[115]

The rumors that had circulated in Estonia throughout the war indicate certain awareness among the Estonian population regarding the future of their country. One rumor had it that once Leningrad was captured, Estonian officials would be assigned to various positions of authority in Russia, and the Baltic Germans would be moved back to Estonia. People also speculated about the plans to increase dramatically the population of Tallinn on account of ethnic Germans. It was the workers and not the intelligentsia who began to piece together the German strategy. By treating the Estonians well, the Germans were in fact trying to win them over to the Reich.[116] Indeed, in December 1941 the former owner

11. "West Battles the East," painting by Estonian artist Arthur Mihkelsoo (Michelson), Tartu, 1941–44; HI, Hintzer, 162183.

of Krenholm cotton mills in Narva, Andreas Baron von Knoop, was appointed general manager of the factory.[117] Similarly, in July 1942 the German civil administration (via Minister of Technology Arnold Radik) called upon the Estonian population to volunteer for service in Russia. The occupation authorities specifically targeted engineers—young unmarried men, preferably students of Tallinn Technical College. Those individuals were to sign a contract on the same terms as German employees.[118] A special detachment of the Estonian Security Police was supposed to assume duties in Leningrad. However, because the prolonged siege of the city failed, members of the detachment were assigned to Jägala concentration camp, some as guards and others as executioners.[119] (See chapter 8.)

Estonians wanted to believe that the Germans had good intentions. It seemed unlikely that Nazi Germany would ever consider Estonia part of its *Lebensraum*, given that Hitler had made no direct pronouncements to that regard. As a further proof, some individuals referred to the resettlement of the Baltic Germans in 1939–41. Considering the distance between the Reich and Estonia, it simply did not make sense for the Germans to look upon Estonia as their living space.[120] The occupation authorities had no misconceptions about the Estonians' willingness to become Germans: the Estonians willed that not.[121]

But that is precisely what Nazis had in stock for Estonia and Estonians. While observing Estonian officers in a training camp in Posen, Heinrich Himmler made general remarks regarding the future of the Estonian nation:

12. Arthur Mihkelsoo paints a mural in the Tartu district commissariat, 1941–43; HI, Hintzer, 158025.

> I am sure that once we start, we will be able to win them [the Estonians] over. They should understand that a 900[,]000-strong people such as the Estonians cannot vegetate in isolation in this world, but can instead join the Reich as a kindred people. In fact, the Estonians is one of the few races we can blend into the German nation without any difficulties, by eliminating just few fractions thereof. Inclusion by a means of ideology is as important because otherwise the Estonian people will simply die out.[122]

Not very often did Himmler say something like that about a particular nation. But when he did, then it was clearly for a reason. The Estonians had been described as "the most mature people in the Ostland both culturally and politically."[123] Whatever plans had been considered for the Ostland, the future of the Estonian nation was a decided matter: Germanization. With Latvia, in contrast, matters became more difficult, because the easternmost province of Latgale had to be cut off. The Lithuanians, because of their inadmissibly high proportion of Slavic blood, were simply written off.[124] Individuals conscripted into the Reich Labor Service (Reichsarbeitsdienst or RAD) were subject to racial selection: 30 percent of

Lithuanian conscripts were refused entry on racial grounds, 25 percent of Latvian conscripts, but only 15 percent of Estonian conscripts.[125] Estonian cities resembled East German cities, and the Estonian landscape resembled that of the North German coastal area. The absence of lice in Estonia, according to the Nazis, was also a German phenomenon. As for the national capital of the Estonians, Nazis considered it "the most beautiful city of the Great German North."[126]

From the Nazi perspective, anti-Communism was the only answer to the question of Estonia's future. Estonia had enjoyed independence for twenty-odd years but no longer. The shrinking population could not have sustained this geopolitically too important territory at the crossroads of the interests of great powers. Establishing a lasting foundation for the future Estonian entity would mean finding common political ground for both Estonia and Germany. Together with other East European countries (not directly incorporated into the Third Reich), Estonia was to become part of Nazi Germany's *cordon sanitaire*. As long as Communism posed a threat to the "New European Order," the Wehrmacht should stay in Estonia, ready to ward off potential aggression. In the absence of this military presence, it would be naïve to think that the Germany army would march into Estonia again to rescue the country from yet another Communist invasion.[127]

The concept of Germanization was far more complex than just colonization of the occupied territories by means of ethnic Germans. In the case of Estonia, it was a tradeoff between losing national identity and gaining respect and territory. GK-Estland Litzmann indicated as early as October 1941 that the Russian territory between Lakes Peipus and Ilmen would become part of Estonia.[128] The enlargement of the Estonian and Latvian commissariats general had several objectives. From the perspective of the local population, it would supposedly make the future German settlement in the region less painful. The territorial gain would foster the economic growth of the Estonian and Latvian economies, which were otherwise stagnating. It would also be beneficial for the erstwhile Russian areas. Most important, however, the very names "Estonia" and "Latvia" would disappear.[129] The historical nations of Estonia and Latvia would themselves dissolve into a far larger territorial entity.

In practical terms, the size of the population in both commissariats general would approximate that of Lithuania and Belorussia. Remarkably, Estonia's new border was to run along the Leningrad-Novgorod line, whereas Latvia was supposed to receive a much smaller chunk of land.[130] Hjalmar Mäe confirmed that the territory of Estonia was to grow at the expense of the Novgorod and Pskov regions. Mäe predicted that in ten years the Estonian population would increase by one million, and in fifteen years by one and one-half million. As he put it, "Estonians are used to eating chaffs, and they propagate like flies."[131]

For best results, it should appear as though the initiative for Germanization came from the Estonian rather than the German side. As was the case with other aspects of the Nazi occupation of Estonia, the German agencies tried to perform only supervisory functions. The Estonians were to internalize the idea that it was beneath their dignity to mix with other, non-Germanic groups residing in Estonia. The Nordic racial type was to be seen as responsible for all the positive features of the Estonian people, while contacts with the Russians brought to the fore all the negative ones. Ideally, the Estonians would themselves purge the unworthy racial element from their ethnonational body.

4 THE COMING OF TERROR

The policy of terror introduced in Estonia owed as much to individual actors as it did to the structure of the institutions that implemented it. In contrast to other occupied East European countries, local German authorities empowered the Estonian security apparatus instead of rigidly controlling it. Background research on the rank and file of the Estonian police force and militia—as far as the available sources allow for such analysis—reveals that a majority of the membership had reasons to collaborate with the Nazis, yet on their own terms. Most significantly, the local Nazi leadership made an effort to partially accommodate the Estonians' hopes and aspirations. Hypocrisy it was, but most Estonians bought into it. One individual who helped make it happen was Dr. Martin Sandberger.

DR. MARTIN SANDBERGER: A PERSON AND A NAZI

Martin Sandberger came to be the most powerful man in Nazi-occupied Estonia. No major political decision was made without Sandberger's consent. Sandberger was given the right to decide over the life and death of the Estonian Jewish community. He voted death. But he did not rush to implement his decision. In fact, he made others do it. By all means, Sandberger was better prepared for his mission in Estonia than many other high-ranking SS officials in occupied Eastern Europe.

Martin Sandberger was born into a businessman's family in Berlin in 1911. Between 1929 and 1933 Sandberger studied law at Munich, Cologne, Freiburg, and Tübingen universities, passing his bar exams shortly after the Nazis came to power. Sandberger had been paying his monthly dues as a member of the Nazi Party since November 1931 and was very upset when his membership card for some reason did not arrive in time. In August 1933 Sandberger became leader of the Nazi Student Association and in May 1935 joined the ranks of the SS. Yet at the age of twenty-five Sandberger had never been abroad and spoke no foreign languages. Together with his wife, also a Ph.D., Sandberger had three children, the youngest of whom was born in the fall of 1941.[1]

RSHA had favored Sandberger since his years at the German Security Police School in Berlin-Charlottenburg. Throughout his career Sandberger had received five decorations. Having started in the rank of major (SS-Stubaf.) in November 1942, Sandberger was promoted to lieutenant colonel (SS-Ostubaf.) and later to colonel (SS-Staf.). The description that RSHA Department VI gave of Sandberger in March 1944 provides valuable insight into Sandberger's personality:

> Dr. Sandberger is a talented SD Leader who has a very good spiritual and intel-
> lectual grasp. His oral skills make him a clever negotiating partner, logical, agile,
> and firm. Dr. Sandberger manages the powers of induction, which, combined
> with his innate inventiveness, make him devise large-scale, yet not always justi-
> fied plans. It is interesting to note though, that Dr. Sandberger is aware—even
> if only subconsciously—of this particular side of his personality and [is] trying
> to mold his thinking, trying to put it into a certain scheme. That also explains
> one other extreme he is prone to going into, that is, formalism. When properly
> guided, he is an extremely valuable employee who is soldier-like correct and
> spiritually disciplined. Dr. Sandberger applies his immense diligence and above
> average working capacity to whatever tasks he is entrusted with. As regards his
> personal attitudes, so far I was not able to find out anything inauspicious. We
> have received no complaints about him, neither on duty nor outside of work.
> When it comes to his worldview Dr. Sandberger is impeccable.[2]

People who met Sandberger during the war described him as a rational individual who would not pursue his goals at a breakneck speed. Sandberger gave
the impression of a person who always tried to avoid the worst. It was hard to
believe Sandberger could have ever "liquidated" anybody at all.[3] More important,
Sandberger received much respect from high-ranking Estonian officials, who
described him as "bright," "honest," "clever," and "daring." First Director Hjalmar Mäe, for example, got into the habit of discussing ongoing political issues
with Sandberger. The paternalistic tone of the leaders of the Estonian puppet government shows that they believed they could influence the youthful commander
of the Security Police and SD in Estonia (Kommandeur der Sicherheitspolizei
und des SD or KdS) and his decisions.[4] They could not have been more wrong.

Sandberger was rather different from his counterparts in Latvia and Lithuania. KdS-Litauen, SS-Staf. Karl Jäger, was a stereotypical soldier, a boorish guy who appreciated military discipline and despised politics. Like many other demobilized soldiers, Jäger had been unemployed for some time and had experienced poverty. On the top of that, Jäger went through a divorce that made him rely even more on alcohol. (He was fifty-one in 1941.) Jäger personally took part in the executions of Jews and forced other members of his commando to do the same.[5] SS-Stubaf. Rudolf Lange, a successful young lawyer who was appointed KdS-Lettland, had much in common with Sandberger. However, one particular feature set him apart from the latter: Lange was an ardent anti-Semite, arrogant and brutal.[6] Sandberger's personal attitude toward Jews, by contrast, is hard to pinpoint. Although an atavistic anti-Semite he probably was not, he showed Jews no mercy. Sandberger obviously took the so-called "Jewish Question" seriously. Otherwise he would not have ordered—more than a year after the last Estonian Jews had been murdered—Estonian members of the Security Police to produce proof of their non-Jewish origin.[7]

Sandberger had a better feel for his job in Estonia because of his previous experience with the population transfers in Poland in 1939–40. That was probably the first time Sandberger had come into contact with Baltic Germans. Himmler had arranged for the Baltic Germans from Riga, Tartu, and Tallinn to be resettled in the cities of Gotenhafen and Posen in the annexed Polish territories. To accommodate the incoming ethnic Germans, on October 8, 1939, Himmler ordered the creation of the Central Immigration Office (Einwandererzentralstelle or EWZ), under the responsibility of the chief of the German Security Police, Reinhard Heydrich. According to Heydrich, Gotenhafen alone could absorb about 90,000 Baltic Germans.[8] In his capacity as head of the EWZ, Sandberger was responsible for the resettlement of Baltic Germans in the Warthegau.[9] To make space for the incoming ethnic Germans, Sandberger was first to empty Posen and Gotenhafen of its Polish population, which had to be relocated to the Kielce-Radom region. What would happen to them there was of no concern to the Nazis; it was the rump Polish State that had to take care of its countrymen.

The first ship with Baltic Germans on board arrived in Danzig on October 18; the deportation of Poles commenced on October 17. The first wave of deportations was over by October 28, by which date six transports had moved more than 7,000 Poles from Gotenhafen.[10] To speed up the process, Sandberger negotiated with the military authorities for the establishment of a concentration camp that would temporarily accommodate the resettled Poles.[11] Himmler was satisfied with the work of Sandberger's agency, which he toured in mid-January 1940.[12] The next month Sandberger received a promotion and moved to the Personnel Department of the RSHA in Berlin. In April 1941, however, Sandberger received one other short assignment involving forced deportation. This time he was put in charge of the resettlement of the Slovenian intelligentsia from the Ljubljana region. (Out of the planned 100,000 people, only 20,000 were resettled.)[13] Following the establishment of the German Security Police headquarters in Tallinn in September 1941, Sandberger arranged for several of his former employees from the EWZ Office to come with him to Estonia.[14]

THE BLOODY TRAIL OF SONDERKOMMANDO 1A

Following the Polish campaign, the SS mobile killing units, the so-called Einsatzgruppen (EG), were about to be deployed against Great Britain. Since 1940, in preparation for the invasion of the British Isles, members of those commandos had been vigorously studying English at the Security Police School in Pretzsch. However, different winds began to blow in the spring of 1941. In early April, two of the commandos originally meant for Operation Sea Lion (*Seelöwe*) were dispatched to the Balkans. English language courses were then replaced by intensive Russian language training. Hitler thus went ahead with Plan *Barbarossa*.[15] By early spring 1941, the commanding officers of the Einsatzgruppen and all of their subdivisions had already been selected. Dr. Martin Sandberger, as leader of Sonderkommando 1a (SK 1a), was assigned to Estonia. Sandberger, who was the youngest of all SK/EK leaders, assumed the command following his arrival in Pretzsch from Berlin in early June. The formation of individual units began ten days before the attack on the Soviet Union.

The detachment under the command of SS-Stubaf. Sandberger was the smallest of the four Security Police commandos operational in the Baltics. Out of 105 members of SK 1a, 25 were SS-reservists. The rest of the personnel comprised 23 chauffeurs, 14 interpreters, 37 policemen, 2 radio operators, and 4 officials.[16] On June 23, SK 1a left Bad Schmiedeberg for Danzig via Landsberg-on-Warthe. Equipped with fifty vehicles, Sandberger's detachment reached Memel in East Prussia in just a few days. Before crossing the border into Lithuania, Sandberger divided SK 1a into three partial detachments (Teilkommandos or TK), headed by SS-Ostuf. Friedrich Reichelt, SS-Hstuf. (captain) Fritz Carsten, and himself.

Within the first days of the Russo-German war, the German Security Police joined forces with the Wehrmacht in making the areas on the East Prussian border "free of Jews." Between June 24 and 27, the police office in Tilsit organized massacres of Jews in Gargždai, Kretinga, and Palanga, with a total of 526 people killed. Although it was Stahlecker who gave the go-ahead for the cleansing operation, Sandberger was an accessory to the crime. As the most senior SS official after Stahlecker in that area, Sandberger instructed the head of the Tilsit police, SS-Stubaf. Werner Hersmann, to start executing local Jews en masse.[17] On June 25 Sandberger communicated from Memel his approval of this and similar operations within the twenty-five-kilometer zone along the former Soviet border.[18] On the same day, in accordance with Stahlecker's order, SK 1a joined the 18th German Army. Moving through Latvia, SK 1a carried out executions of Jews in Priekule, Šķēde, Grobiņa, Asīte, and Durbe.[19] Fifteen members of TK Reichelt, together with the men from one of the EK 2 partial detachments under the command of SS-Ostuf. (first lieutenant) Gerhard Grauel, carried out the first mass execution of Jews in the coastal city of Liepāja. They escorted Jews from a prison to an execution site located in a park next to the seashore.[20] At least forty-seven Jews and five Latvian "Communists" were executed in Liepāja on July 4.[21]

Together with fifteen members of his detachment and another twenty men from EK 2, Sandberger was among the first representatives of the German Security Police to reach, on June 27, the western suburbs of Riga.[22] Sandberger admitted that his detachment participated in an execution while at Riga, though on Stahlecker's order.[23] Before occupying the left bank of the Daugava, on June 29 Germans led all men under sixty into an open field. The following evening, a group of German policemen carried out a selection. First they picked out those of the assembled men that looked Jewish. Then they took the suspected group aside in order to check for circumcision. Those of the victims who were circumcised were murdered. Taking into account that at that time Sandberger was the most senior Security Police official in the area, it must have been his men that carried out the mass execution.[24] The fighting was almost over when Sandberger arrived in downtown Riga on July 1. Sandberger and his unit stayed in Riga for another three days.

THE COMING OF TERROR | 89

Sonderkommando 1a left Riga for Estonia in the early hours of July 5. The final destination for EG A was Leningrad and its vicinity.[25] Two days later Sandberger's men crossed into Estonia, moving in the direction of Viljandi. TK II under the command of SS-Ostuf. Johannes Feder advanced along with the 58th Infantry Division to Pskov and farther to Gdov and Narva. TK III marched on to Pärnu, which it entered on July 12 but was forced to leave shortly thereafter. On July 15 TK I, led by Sandberger, reached Tartu, the second largest city in Estonia. For the next ten days—as the Soviet resistance grew stronger—members of SK 1a assisted regular troops fighting the enemy in and around Tartu. In addition, the unit was engaged in routine security operations, which went particularly smoothly because of the timely establishment of the indigenous police and militia. The commander of SK 1a, with three vehicles, attempted to continue north but the Soviet counteroffensive forced him to return to Riga instead. Only at their second attempt did TK III—this time headed by Sandberger's deputy, SS-Hstuf. Fritz Carsten—manage to reestablish its presence in Pärnu.[26]

Sonderkommando 1a resumed its march on July 25. In two weeks the core of Sandberger's group reached the Baltic shore at Kunda. SK 1a then split into two groups, one of which headed east to meet TK Feder in Narva, while the other advanced west toward the capital city of Tallinn. Along the way, SK 1a established control over the shale oil area between Kiviõli and Sillamäe. Meanwhile, TK Feder, which advanced along the former Estonian-Soviet border north, finally reached Narva (Soviet partisans had tied up Feder's group for several weeks.) On the morning of August 28 Sandberger's detachment made its way into Tallinn. Over the next month, SK 1a established its presence in the rest of Estonia as well as in northwestern Russia: on September 2 in Haapsalu; on September 10 and 12 in Petergof and Krasnoe Selo; and on September 23 in Kuressaare.[27]

As they moved along, partial detachments carried out random executions. Latvian and Estonian anti-Soviet partisans assisted SK 1a in tracking and killing Communists and other "undesirables." Of the three partial detachments, only TK II left a paper trail (albeit rather short). In Rauna on the evening of July 8 members of the Feder unit shot thirteen men and one woman who were accused of collaborating with the Soviets in deporting Latvian nationals. The next day, Latvian partisans executed another twelve people. On June 10 TK II entered Estonia at Misso, where they executed five Estonian Communists. Another two people died at the hands of Estonian partisans. On July 11 a unit under the command of SS-Ostuf. Heinrich Cornelius shot fourteen more people in Vastse-liina.[28] Complicity in murder, however, was not the only contribution that Dr. Sandberger expected from the Estonian auxiliaries. Proving himself a skillful lawyer, Sandberger came up with a more complex scheme, which he now began implementing in Estonia.

SANDBERGER AND THE ESTONIANS

Sandberger identified as one of his priorities the establishment of a native police force, which was supposed to secure the rear of the Wehrmacht troops against Soviet shock battalions and to apprehend potential opponents of the new regime. Among other pressing tasks, Sandberger mentioned securing archives and cultural landmarks. The Jews, as an inimical category, were notoriously missing from Sandberger's list of priorities, being buried under the generic heading "urgent security measures" *(sicherheitspolizeiliche Sofortmassnahmen).* From the outset, the German Security Police was able to establish its presence in Estonia without offending the feelings of the Estonians. As Sonderkommando 1a moved from one locality to another, it left behind several Security Police officials, who then super-vised the formation of the Estonian Police and Self-Defense (Omakaitse or OK). Sandberger stressed that the limited strength of SK 1a made it dependent on local collaboration, which he said was abundant. For example, the German Security Police office in Tartu covered the entire southern part of Estonia but only had four SS officers on staff. From the very beginning, the Tartu office established good relations with the population, as well as with university circles.[29] There were enough volunteers among former police and military officers to render the Esto-nian Security Police an effective tool against Communists. Within half a year, the membership of the German Security Police in Estonia grew to 139, still a far cry from the 1,234 people enrolled in the Estonian branch of the police.

Thanks to Sandberger, relations between the German and Estonian branches of the Security Police developed in an atmosphere of mutual trust and friend-ship. As a result, a handful of Germans were able to exercise control over a much larger number of Estonians. Sandberger saw his role not only as the supreme police authority in Estonia but also as a person who understood the hopes and aspirations of the Estonian people. What in any other context would appear an obvious policy—to develop personal contacts with the Estonians, to acknowledge their achievements—became a distinctive approach to policy-making for the KdS-Estland. Extremely sensitive to nuances, Estonians became defensive every time they felt mistreated by the Germans. When treated as equals, however, they responded favorably. Sandberger believed that Estonians had several characteristics that placed them at the forefront of the Nazi struggle for the "New Europe." According to Sandberger, Estonians were a racially fit, pragmatic people with a strong work ethic ingrained in a conservative worldview.[30] Sandberger predicted, correctly, that Estonians would appreciate the trust invested in them. The more freedom of action Estonians had, the easier it became to manipulate them. Acts of discrimination, however, only bred nationalism.[31]

Sandberger's way of thinking can be traced back to the first comprehensive reports of the German Security Police from Estonia. Within three weeks of the military campaign, supposedly the Estonian population would have agreed to any political resolution. Sandberger sought to make full use of that situation even before the Germans assumed full control over Estonia, so as to avoid the kind of complications that arose in Lithuania and Latvia.[32] This approach to policy-making partially explains why the level of collaboration among the Estonians was substantially higher than that among the Latvians or Lithuanians. Estonia was the last of the three Baltic countries that Nazi Germany occupied. The Germans were constantly looking over their shoulders, trying to avoid the mistakes they made in the past. The Nazis realized that by suppressing national aspirations they were playing into the hands of the opposition. That was the last thing Sandberger wanted.

The first comprehensive report on the population's mood in Estonia was dated August 1, 1941. By that time the Wehrmacht had already occupied Tartu and Pärnu, but Narva and Tallinn still remained under Soviet control. The German Security Police was the first to relate to Berlin what it observed on the ground. Sandberger sympathized with the Estonians: however reserved, the majority of the population welcomed the Germans, and their physical appearance displayed strong Nordic characteristics. Sandberger also considered it a good sign that Estonians kept their houses and farms clean. Because Jewish numbers in Estonia were low, Sandberger did not consider the solution of the "Jewish Question" to be a problem. That was the only time Jews were mentioned in the report.[33]

Sandberger's plan of giving as much autonomy as possible to the Estonian police paid off. The Estonian Security Police was structured in accordance with

Independent Estonia's police. The 1925 provisions regulating the rights of the police were brought back: each of the fifteen provinces had a police prefecture; prefectures consisted of police districts covering a territory with anywhere between 15,000 and 60,000 people; the inspector's office supervised the activities of both the security and criminal divisions.[34] To win the trust of the population, Sandberger arranged for the Estonian Security Police and Omakaitse to become part of the Estonian puppet administration. In reality, however, the Estonian Security Police was a mirror image of its German counterpart, to which it reported directly. Each of the five departments within the Estonian Security Police (designated as BI through BV) corresponded to a counterpart in the German Security Police (designated as AI through AV). The two departments that carried out the policy of terror in Estonia were primarily the Security Police (AIV and BIV) and to some extent the Criminal Police (AV and BV).[35] The Estonian Security Police was authorized to conduct police investigations at its discretion, except in cases involving citizens of the Reich or ethnic Germans. The role of the German Security Police was to set the direction and on occasion to give advice. It reserved the right to intervene, but only if the Estonian counterpart failed expectations.[36] The only exception to the rule was the branch office in Kiviõli (established in January 1943). At Kiviõli, Estonian and German officers worked together, with no parallel structure in place.[37]

The modus operandi that Sandberger introduced in Estonia was unprecedented in the context of Nazi-occupied Eastern Europe. The degree of autonomy that the Estonian Security Police came to enjoy by far surpassed that of the native police forces in Latvia and Lithuania. EK 3 set up and closely supervised the Lithuanian Security Police. Like its Estonian counterpart, the Lithuanian Security Police did investigate individual cases. However, its authority did not extend to Jews.[38] At most, the police participated in the arrests and interrogations of those Jews who escaped from the ghettos.[39] In Latvia, the organization of the security police bore no resemblance to the parallel structure that Sandberger pioneered in Estonia. Indeed, by the end of 1943 the Latvian division within the Security Police had all but disappeared. The same was true of the KdS-Lettland branch offices outside of the Latvian borders.[40]

The SS and Police Commander (SSPF) Office, which was officially in charge of the native police force, played a much smaller role in Estonia than it did in Latvia or Lithuania. SSPF-Estland, SS-Staf. Hinrich Möller, essentially delegated his tasks to KdS-Estland Sandberger.[41] According to Möller, he only supervised Omakaitse and designated police prefects.[42] With regard to the "Jewish Question," confrontation between RKO Lohse and BdS-Ostland Stahlecker, which played out in Riga, barely made any waves in Tallinn. Moreover, when Lohse issued his guidelines regarding work-fit Jews in late July 1941, most of Estonia was still under Soviet control. Then and again, former members of the German Security Police in Estonia described Sandberger as a strong personality who firmly held the office in his hands. Not a single move could have happened without Sandberger's consent, they argued.[43]

Sandberger appeared to both his peers and subordinates as a rational individual standing for the interests of the Estonian people. He advocated a larger autonomy not just for the Estonian police, but also for the Estonian nation as a whole. Sandberger tried hard to maintain good relations with the local population. For example, as part of the celebration of Estonian independence in February 1942, a group of SS officers with Sandberger at the head attended a service in Tallinn Cathedral. Those who witnessed that most unusual appearance thought it might cost Sandberger his position. However, nothing happened. As Sandberger later confided to Mäe, it was a politically calculated move that he coordinated with his superiors. To the dinners that Sandberger often hosted in his apartment on the corner of Narva Avenue and Luha Street in Tallinn, he invited as many Estonians as Germans. There is a rare photograph of Sandberger attending a children's Christmas party in Tallinn in December 1942. Mäe was right when he argued that, owing to such attentive individuals as Sandberger and Litzmann, Estonia received probably the best treatment of all occupied East European countries.[44]

Sandberger's posture was just a façade. Only once or twice did he express his true beliefs, as for example in early August 1941 in the village of Gostitsy some twenty miles south of Narva. In an unusual display of comradeship, drinking with members of Feder's TK II with his shirt unbuttoned, Sandberger outlined the goals of Nazi politics:

We want to colonize the eastern territories. Therefore, the local intelligentsia must be exterminated in its entirety. It is better to shoot dead one more Russian than one less. It is better to install than not to install an Estonian officer—one of those that belong to our troop—in a position where he would most likely perish. The easier it would be for us to colonize and exploit those territories economically.[45]

General Litzmann unequivocally supported Sandberger and his methods. Litzmann did not rush to correct the mistake that many Estonians made, that of taking the limited autonomy they had for a promise of independence. Continued support from the local population was necessary for winning the war—still the main objective.[46] Litzmann's personal friendship with Himmler helped to get that idea across to senior offices in Berlin.[47] General Georg von Küchler, commander in chief of the German military in Estonia, did not have to convince Litzmann how important it was to grant the Estonian people limited political concessions; by doing so, the German authorities would be able to exploit the "cheerful and willing collaboration" *(freudigen und freiwilligen Mitarbeit)* of all strata of the Estonian population, in particular the auxiliary police and the workforce.[48] The two major agencies that carried out the policy of terror in Estonia under German supervision were the Omakaitse and the Estonian Security Police.

OMAKAITSE: TRADITIONAL NETWORKS

The "forest brother" movement, as it was known in Estonia, came about spontaneously. As soon as Nazi Germany invaded the Soviet Union, many Estonian men took to the woods, where they organized armed resistance groups. The mass deportation on June 14, 1941, also made people seek refuge in the woods. Otherwise, people joined the guerillas either out of conviction or out of necessity. The former group comprised Estonian nationalists and all those who resented the Soviet regime, while the latter was made up of men who either evaded mobilization or deserted the Red Army. Individual groups were organized on a territorial basis; among the chief organizers were former members of the Estonian Home Guard (KL) and the remnants of the military or police corps, which guaranteed discipline, minimal military training, and tactical capability. The groups, which ranged between five and five hundred men, operated from the hard-to-reach woods or swamps that covered most of the territory of Estonia. Estonians usually referred to anti-Soviet partisan bands as Self-Defense (OK).

A total of thirteen OK detachments operated in Estonia in the summer of 1941. In the six southern provinces the formation of the OK was completed between July 3 and 10. In the northern part of the country the foundation of the OK was not laid until after a month later. The OK was modeled after the former Estonian army and the KL. In the absence of distinctive uniforms, the rank and file sported white armbands, sometimes adorned with the Estonian tricolor. Until the end of the year the OK carried out a total of 5,033 round-ups, with the highest numbers recorded for August and September: 1,557 and 1,360 respectively. The Tartu Province OK proved the largest and most virulent organization, with 1,917 roundups. On 1,850 other occasions, the OK assisted the Wehrmacht and the Security Police in executing various tasks. For the first three months of the Russo-German war, the chain of command and respon-sibilities of the OK remained only vaguely defined. The German military and the German Security Police deployed the OK when necessary.[49] Commander in Chief of the German 18th Army Georg von Küchler named three categories of people he wanted to see within the ranks of the auxiliary police: former police-men, pro-German members of nationalist organizations, and former service-men.[50] The military authorities acknowledged the achievements of the OK, which they considered a security organization.[51] The participation of the OK in hostilities evoked the idea of Estonian-German brotherhood in arms, which the German side intended to use for its own advantage.[52] Through the summer of 1942, the OK performed traditional police tasks such as searches, arrests, and interrogations. Even past that date, the OK retained the right to handle "suspi-cious individuals," mainly partisans and POWs, independently.[53] The German Security Police used more explicit language: the OK was called into life for the purpose of carrying out executions.[54]

The best-organized partisan units operated in the southern provinces, which were relatively quickly overrun by German troops. Local commanders, selected from among the former members of KL and reserve officers, displayed a great deal of personal initiative. In Pärnu Province, the OK established itself on July 3, that is, five days before the German 291st Division captured the city of Pärnu. The guerillas had developed trusting relations with the German military, from whom they received weapons and access to radio in exchange for information of tactical and strategic importance. The Germans treated guerillas as "brothers in arms," which further cemented the mutual trust. The rank and file of the partisan unit was composed mainly of former KL servicemen, but also of high school and middle school students, and state and municipal officials. Some of the youngsters (sometimes not older than fifteen) performed guard duties alongside the adults. The head of the Pärnu OK, the legendary Estonian commander Victor Koern, appointed among others the commandant of a hastily established concentration camp.[55] Initially, the orders that individual OK units received were transmitted orally. That is probably why specific written orders for the arrest of Jews and other suspects in provincial cities were conspicuously missing.[56]

The level of organization of the Tartu OK set an example for the rest of Estonia. The formation of the Tartu OK on July 9 was the final link in the creation of a province-wide organization. Particularly active among the local commanders were Karl Talpak (former high school teacher) in Otepää, Friedrich Kurg (professional military officer) in Tartu, and Evald Mikson (former Political Police officer, famous soccer player) in Abja. OK membership in the province nearly tripled in a matter of weeks, from 2,334 in mid-July to 5,360 in early August, reaching 8,460 on September 1. Former members of the KL comprised up to 70 percent of the rank and file in the countryside, but a much smaller percentage in the cities. In Tartu, for example, it was mainly school youth, university students, reserve officers, and workers who joined the OK. Among the leaders of the OK there were predominantly younger KL officers, because their older peers had for the most part been deported by the Soviets. On July 13 the German military commandant of Tartu, Lieutenant Colonel Hans Gosebruch, proposed to Major Friedrich Kurg that he become OK commander in the German-controlled territory of Estonia; Kurg accepted the offer. The partisans' main task was to help the Wehrmacht in cleansing Estonia of Communists and their collaborators: "to cleanse the hinterland of the unclean elements, to deliver the Estonian people from the Jewish-Asiatic ghost."[57] Of all the OK detachments in Estonia, the Tartu OK was the only one that used anti-Semitic propaganda (other detachments did not reach a sufficient level of organization to wage propagandistic campaigns independently). On August 4 the Estonian OK command circulated the following leaflet, meant for distribution among the soldiers and commanders of the Red Army:

> Who has been ruling over your people for years? Your leaders have been Jewish! Who was Karl Marx, who was Lenin? They were Jewish! Do you really think Stalin is your leader? No, it is Beria and his gang that works behind the scene. A year ago, your Jewish gang treacherously, without a warning, burst into Estonia and began exterminating our people and devastating our land. You have neither faith nor God. That is why you act devilishly on the order from godless Jews . . . Surrender!

As of November 1, 1941, the Tartu OK had arrested 12,000 people and killed 4,812 "Bolsheviks"—more than in any other Estonian province.[58]

In Pechory, in the southeastern part of Estonia, the initiative for the formation of the OK came from the Wehrmacht. Between July 9 and November, the Pechory OK operated under the command of the local German headquarters. Until the end of the year, 761 OK men had conducted 172 roundups, which resulted in the arrest of 584 people and the violent deaths of another 116.[59] Of all the Estonian provinces, interethnic strife was most intense in Pechory, with its large Russian population. Feeling embattled by the hostile forces, the local OK and the police worked hand in hand. Almost 100 percent of the surviving members of KL now joined the ranks of the OK.[60]

The records of the Viljandi OK explain why former members of the KL were so prominent within the OK ranks. The KL servicemen belonged to the most diligent, well-to-do population group in the countryside. That made them a natural target of the Soviet repression. To survive, those men had to fight. After a year of Soviet occupation it was easy to identify the subject of hatred: Russians and Communists. Nationalistic youth were ready to start destroying anything that had the slightest reference to Bolshevism. By July 25 the OK net covered the entire territory of Viljandi Province. The effort at centralization, however, was thwarted by a rivalry between the local German headquarters in Viljandi and in Põltsamaa. When it came to the first military encounters with the hated enemy, the OK men, exalted by the smell of gunpowder, sought revenge against the Soviets.[61] On numerous occasions, members of the OK arrested and mistreated alleged Communists whose crimes in most cases they could not substantiate. At one time it was the property of the victims and another time personal revenge that prompted violence.[62]

A report from the Valga Province OK gives additional insight into the predominance of younger cohorts within the ranks of the organization. Members of the OK were all volunteers who over the period of several weeks received no pay for their service. Very soon, older men, particularly those who had to support their families, started leaving. In their stead came younger, more ambitious, ideologically driven men. The report contrasted the high spirits of the youth with the apathy that the older generation had displayed during the year of Soviet occupation. According to the report, many schools had underground cells, which sometimes competed with each other at committing acts of sabotage. Estonian

13. Members of Tartu Omakaitse check documents, July 1941; HI, Hintzer, 170382.

school youths were determined to turn the lives of individual Komsomol members, some of whom were Jewish, into hell. The Valga OK started rounding up political suspects—first and foremost Communists, real or imaginary—even before the Wehrmacht arrived. When German troops reached Valga on July 12, they discovered that the OK had already installed in power provincial and city administrations, as well as a chief of the police. The Germans confirmed the appointments made through the Valga OK.[63]

More revealing details about the formation of the OK come from the southernmost Estonian province of Võrumaa. Farmers had been presented as the crème de la crème of the Estonian nation, a group of people that constituted the core of the anti-Soviet resistance. In several counties, former members of the KL and other trustworthy men among the farmers were sent invitations to join the OK. Only in one county was the formation of an OK detachment carried out through "mobilization." As soon as the Wehrmacht overran Lasva County on July 9, a local Estonian military commander ordered all males to be assembled in the governmental office; members of the KL were to report in their uniforms, armed. In anticipation of roundups, the men who came from afar

14. Omakaitse review in Tartu, 1941–44; HI, Hintzer, 157831.

brought several-day food supplies with them. Most OK volunteers were affiliated with one of three organizations: the police, the military, or the KL. Among the guards at Võru POW camp there were thirty-six high school graduates. Those young men were said to have hated Russians, as all of the Estonian people allegedly had for centuries. Strong local identity among the farmers made Estonians in the countryside feel on the whole more nationalistic than their compatriots in the cities. Strong local identity worked for the benefit of the OK, whose territorial units displayed significant cohesion.[64] That cohesion explains why the OK was more successful in the southern, more rural Estonian provinces than in the industrial north. Military disposition played a role too: the Red Army rather quickly cleared southern Estonia, only to entrench itself for the next six weeks in the northern part of the country.

The passage of the German army through any given locality in Viru Province in northeastern Estonia was a signal for the creation of a guerilla band. The Vaivara County OK, in existence since August 16, received instructions from the German Security Police, which also appointed the head of the detachment. In some areas villagers began organizing resistance groups only after they received specific guidelines to that effect. The German backing boosted the population's morale. In Virumaa, the KL played a major role in putting the OK on the map. The KL had its own network, which ensured the cohesion of the units. Former members of the KL were automatically enrolled into the ranks of the OK, because no one doubted their loyalty to the Estonian national cause. At the same time, the very fact that the KL core had managed to survive the Soviet occupation raises certain questions. Indeed, some observers argued that the KL did survive only because it had pledged loyalty to the Bolshevik regime. Among the nonactive members of the KL were many opportunists who wanted nothing but to advance their careers. Denunciations and intrigues thus became the order of the day. Sometimes OK commanders posed as regents of sorts, whose power could only be curtailed by the German military authorities. However, taking into account that Germans were rather unwilling to interfere in local affairs, the OK continued to enjoy, particularly in the beginning, next to absolute power. In such cities as Kunda, Kiviõli, and Kohtla-Järve, where the Estonian civil administration was installed rather late, the OK had for some time remained the only executive organ alongside the local German headquarters. In Jõhvi, for example, the OK was entrusted by the Germans to assemble the municipal government and the police—a task that proved impossible because of the massive human loss during the year of Soviet occupation. The head of the Jõhvi OK had thus to deal with issues normally within the police's jurisdiction. In the absence of precise guidelines, the OK often made decisions on the spur of the moment. But the local population did not seem to mind, as long as the old Estonian administrative structure was in effect again. Whenever they had any problems, Estonian city dwellers routinely addressed the OK. Vaskoarva County, which encompassed the areas populated predominantly by Russians, remained essentially partisan-free.[65]

Similarly, in Narva the OK came into existence only after Wehrmacht troops entered the city on August 17. Recruitment began immediately among the jubilant crowd that gathered spontaneously in front of the city hall. By the end of the day 454 men and 80 women had joined the ranks of the Narva OK. Those individuals were described as Estonian patriots who wanted to help their country and their people, as well as to avenge the Estonian nation for all the suffering it had endured. All female members of the Narva OK had previously been part of the Women's Home Defense (Naiskodukaitse), a subsidiary organization of the Kaitseliit. Women performed auxiliary functions such as preparing food for the OK men who took part in the roundups. The Narva branch of the OK was established "because of the need to cleanse the city of hiding Communists and their collaborators." The fact that Narva was located next to the Russian border multiplied the assignments of the local OK: on several occasions the Narva OK took part in military operations against Soviet partisans in Russia proper. At the height of its activities in October 1941 the Narva OK had six hundred members. In addition to performing guard duties at bridges, plants, warehouses, and POW camps, the Narva OK temporarily took over for the Security Police. This arrangement persisted until the establishment of a police prefecture on September 28. Even then the Narva OK continued taking orders from both the Security Police and the German field headquarters (Feldkommandatur).[66]

In Järva Province as well, the Germans took the initiative. Upon arrival in any given locality, the military authorities summoned local members of the KL. Unsurprisingly, then, most of the people who joined the Järvamaa OK held KL membership. Officially, the Järvamaa OK was established on order from the German military commandant (Ortskommandant) on August 19. Among its activities the Järvamaa OK listed the following: fighting the Soviet troops; protecting the lives and property of the Estonians; and carrying out arrests of local Communists. By the end of the year, 3,346 members of the Järvamaa OK had conducted a total of 339 roundups.[67]

In Harju Province, guerilla bands came into existence in early July. On July 28 partisan commanders attended a meeting at which they decided to amalgamate into a larger unit under the name of Harju Militia. The unit commander immediately established contacts with the advancing German troops, which arrived in the area on August 9. In addition to engaging regular Soviet troops and shock battalions, partisans provided the Wehrmacht with military intelligence and even conducted joint military operations. By the time the Harjumaa OK was officially established on September 3, its membership had swelled to 4,772, and four months later to 8,582.

When it came to apprehending Communists, the OK usually acted on its own initiative.[68] On the Estonian west coast, the first partisan units came together as early as June 22. As elsewhere, former members of the police, military, and paramilitary formations played a major role in the establishment of the Läänemaa OK. In the absence of professionally trained officers, the KL servicemen assumed commanding positions in the detachment. Their weapons were acquired on the battlefield and later from the Wehrmacht.[69]

In Tallinn, Major Juhan Madise organized the first OK group on August 27. Two days later, one of the German division headquarters appointed Lt. Col. Alfred Luts commander of the Tallinn-Nõmme OK. Early on the morning of August 29, Madise and Luts met at the former KL headquarters at 4 Toompui-estee to work out logistics. An order went out to all detachments to work closely with the police in identifying and arresting subversive individuals. The Tallinn OK was officially under the Tallinn-Harju police prefecture. Up to 50 percent of the members of the Tallinn OK claimed membership in the defunct KL. On the eve of World War II, the local KL branch had boasted 5,000 male members, in addition to 750 women and 2,735 teenagers in auxiliary organizations. Between August 28 and 31 an OK unit under the command of Jaak Tavi arrested 48 "Jews-Communists," 182 members of Soviet shock battalions, and 150 general suspects. During the first days of occupation, at its busiest, the OK kept no lists of arrestees. The leading Estonian newspaper, *Eesti Sõna*, which had by then resumed circulation, provided an ideological foundation for the ensuing witch hunt: "a brutal Eastern conqueror deployed its best forces and its best preachers of 'Marxism-Leninism-Stalinism' to exterminate us . . . Now Western culture is

15. Members of Omakaitse escort Communist suspects along Estonia Boulevard in Tallinn, late August 1941, courtesy of Jeffrey Burds.

destroying Eastern barbarism."[70] As of September 2, Tallinn OK was fully operational, working under SK 1a supervision.[71]

The extensive authority granted to local OK branches led to abuses of power, particularly when it came to settling scores with the recent oppressors. The OK was supposed to deliver the arrested Communist suspects to the police for further investigation. In some cases, however, overzealous members of the OK executed high-ranking Communist activists on the spot. The Viru provincial government issued a memorandum on August 9 in which it pleaded for a recall of the unauthorized death sentences ordered by the OK. The head of the Tartumaa OK warned that military psychosis and lack of discipline could easily turn an armed crowd into a negative force.[72] As far as discipline was concerned, the OK failed miserably in comparison with its predecessor, the KL. The shortage of manpower made the local authorities lower the selection criteria for admission. While tainted behavior or unbalanced psyche would have prevented an individual from entering the KL, they were often overlooked when it came to joining the OK, so that "the old deeds became retouched." Younger volunteers with no military training lacked discipline altogether. Some people just appreciated the opportunity to bear and use weapons. The only thing that all these men had in common was the determination to fight Communism. There were always more candidates to participate in roundups than to perform guard duties. The OK leadership had difficulties convincing the rank and file of the necessity of the latter. Men who took part in the roundups experienced excitement comparable with that of a sporting competition. Being a camp guard, in contrast, was rather uneventful. Furthermore, guard duty involved more responsibilities and longer working hours but no pay. Later on, the German military authorities started paying guards on duty twelve rubles per day. Even then, it was only half of the average daily pay.[73]

On several occasions Estonian partisans reinforced Sonderkommando 1a, whose operational area soon covered the whole of Estonia and part of northwestern Russia. The OK provided the original cadre for the German Security Police outposts in Pskov, Gdov, Luga, Kingisepp, Krasnoe Selo, and Pushkin. That is what happened, for example, with the Viljandi OK. On August 12, a group of partisans under the command of Alexander Tilgre met near Türi with one of the SS partial detachments. OK men received an armband with the inscription "In the Service of the Security Police" *(Im Dienst der Sicherheitspolizei),* which made them nominally part of SK 1a. In a few days the group reached Rakvere, where

Sandberger personally received the oath of the Estonian officers. Everyone was given a choice of whether to join the ranks of SK 1a; nobody backed out. In less than a week, the Estonian members of SK 1a found themselves fighting against Russian troops near Luga. At the end of August and in early September they participated in cleansing operations in and around Tallinn, Paldiski, and Haapsalu until the unit was disbanded on September 10.[74]

The above description of OK activities in the summer of 1941 comes from the survey reports that each of the thirteen territorial units prepared on order from the Estonian civil administration later during the war. Those reports were meant to testify to the glory of the OK as a genuine people's organization. Eventually the requested information should have been reworked into a popular book. The fact that the data were entered retrospectively presents certain difficulties regarding its credibility. In other words, it may not be exactly what happened, but rather how the OK wanted to portray itself. The truth is that Jews were barely mentioned on 2,000-something pages of the OK reports. The reports spoke at length about Communists and Russians (often used interchangeably), but not about Jews, Gypsies, Poles, or any other minority. As for the reason why, mentioning them was probably considered unimportant or, more likely, of no benefit for self-promotion.

Estonian collective memory filed the anti-Soviet resistance of 1941 as "the summer war." The myth of the "forest brother" movement was thus born. Ironically, the Soviets contributed much to the myth-making. For example, a July 5 order from the Tartu military and Communist party leadership designated anyone who hid in the woods as "bandit accomplices,"[75] thus portraying all people in hiding as active fighters, no matter what the immediate reason for their going underground may have been. In light of the submissiveness that marked the preceding period (the late Estonian government's yielding to Soviet demands), the importance of the resistance-shaped consciousness is hard to overestimate. The glory of the immediate post–World War I years when the Estonians fought for their independence seemed to be back. The forest brothers erased the disgrace inflicted on the Estonian people, who were mistreated and humiliated at the hands of the Soviet "Asiatics." The stories of valor and courage conceived in the summer months of 1941 were to inspire future generations of Estonians.[76]

In some localities, forest brothers had become a formidable power. The partisan camp in Kautla (twenty-five miles southeast of Tallinn), for example, had separate male and female quarters accommodating up to 1,500 people. In the partisan-controlled areas (about 125 square miles), farms displayed Estonian flags, Central European Time was in effect, and the Soviet currency was abolished. The camp even had its own prison. Remarkably, in times when the principle of an "eye for an eye" was the order of the day, the Kautla camp had a trial chamber, with a former prosecutor from Tallinn presiding as judge and a former criminal police official conducting investigations.[77] Several other OK detachments had their own courts. The Võru OK field court alone meted out 265 death sentences. The case files as a rule were destroyed once the death penalty was carried out. For sure, most executions in the summer of 1941 were carried out without any formal trial. Once the German occupation became an established fact, however, the Estonian Security Police began conducting ex post facto investigations into the unwarranted killings, confirming the death sentences retrospectively.[78]

Contemporaneous observers emphasized the continuity between the KL and the OK. If it were not for the former, the latter would never have gotten off the ground. It was not unusual for local OK groups, for example those in Kabja and Otepää in Tartu Province, to call themselves "Kaitseliit." The importance of the KL was not only in its military capability but also in its educational appeal. The interwar KL was seen as a quintessential Estonian body, an overarching organization that held the nation together. The OK projected the value system articulated in Independent Estonia. Indeed, the OK picked up the torch lit in the war of national liberation of 1918–20. Many Estonians thought of the OK as a true representative of the people.[79] One of the largest Estonian newspapers, *Postimees*, wrote that "Janitor and teacher, worker and car driver, representatives of free professions, including physicians, all of them grabbed the guns! Pallas Art School students, a Venemuine Opera tenor, school children and university students. I got to know a lieutenant who used to be an academic from the Estonian Academy of Sciences, a professor of medicine, an older actor."[80] Close to 25 percent of the clergy and 8.5 percent of schoolteachers in Võru Province played a role in the creation and provision of leadership for the local OK.[81] Out of 270 members of the Torma OK, 174 were farmers, 60 farm laborers, 18 white-collar workers, 10 professionals, and 8 high school students. That equaled 29 percent of the parish's total male population.[82] The 5,820-man-strong Virumaa OK had fewer members of the KL among its ranks than other similar detachments—2,236. Among other professions the documents mentioned the military—91; policemen—30;

schoolteachers—57; priests—4, in addition to 448 female members.[83] On average, the level of education among the OK rank and file left much to be desired. One half of the servicemen had an elementary school education, while the other half had a middle school education. The officer corps as a rule had undergone formal military training. Half of the men could speak Russian, with another half capable of communicating in German.[84] Close to 9 percent of the total male population of Estonia volunteered for the OK. The percentage was much lower in cities, with the lowest in Tallinn—1.4 percent.[85] Intelligent, experienced, dedicated—that was the image that the OK nurtured among the larger strata of the Estonian population.

The OK formed the basis for all paramilitary organizations and combat units that were formed in Estonia during the three years of Nazi occupation. The OK supplied the bulk of recruits for both the Security Police and the police battalions. For example, of the original 1,438 members of the Saaremaa OK, 15 were employed with the Organization Todt (OT), 60 joined the Security Police, and yet another 200 later volunteered for Haapsalu Police Battalion 36.[86] The Security Police and the OK were sometimes described as "two branches of the same tree." Because the OK was essentially an Estonian organization, the Germans hastily established an indigenous police force so as to counterbalance it.

The RSHA planned all along to reorganize the indigenous paramilitaries according to certain standards. On July 25 RFSS Himmler advised his representatives in the East—Jeckeln, Prützmann, von Bach-Zelewski, and Globochnik—to begin hiring Ukrainians, Estonians, Latvians, Lithuanians, and Belorussians into the auxiliary police units. On July 31 all anti-Soviet partisan units that had formed spontaneously since the beginning of hostilities were officially disbanded, but recalled the next day under the name of *Schutzmannschaften*.[87] As regards the numerical strength of the OK, the 18th Army high command determined that in localities with more than 10,000 people the size of the auxiliary police force should not exceed 1 percent of the population, and in larger cities 0.5 percent.[88]

From then on the OK became subordinate to the newly created Estonian Security Police. In Viljandi, it happened earlier than anywhere else in Estonia—a week after the local OK detachment was created. Since July 16, the Viljandi OK had been functioning as an auxiliary police force with a rather limited membership. In the end, the Estonian side received the right to keep the size of the OK equal to that of the interwar KL. On September 5, somewhat larger and better structured, the Viljandi auxiliary police went back to its original name:

Omakaitse. In just one month, the number of fighters more than doubled, from 1,468 to 3,734. Like other similar units throughout the country, the Viljandi OK had mainly been involved with arrests of Communists and runaway Red Army soldiers. Later during the war it began supplying guards for Viljandi Dulag no. 375, one of the largest Soviet POW camps in Estonia. It was a local initiative to start rounding up Communist suspects, beginning in early July. The then commander of the Viljandi OK, P. Kutsar, issued an order that made the identification of suspects much easier. The order obliged landlords, homeowners, janitors, and tenants to report immediately to the OK headquarters all supporters of the Communist government and suspicious individuals in general.[89]

On paper, the OK was part of the Estonian Self-Government. On September 22, 1941, a new agency came into existence: the Police and OK Administration. The head of the newly created agency, Johannes Soodla, received orders from the German Order Police. The very next month, KdS-Estland Sandberger praised the Police and OK Administration, on whose collaboration he said he was dependent.[90] The ultimate authority over the OK was in the hands of General von Roques. In October 1942 von Roques initiated yet another reorganization of the OK: the mobile OK units went under military command, while the police took control over the local OK. In December of the same year the immobile OK units, based in each of the thirteen provinces, were transformed into five auxiliary police battalions (*Schutzmannschaftbataillonen* or Schuma) numbered from 29 through 33.[91] The stationary OK continued performing security tasks in Estonia, while the Schuma were redeployed against Soviet partisans in Russia proper. General von Küchler explained the effectiveness of the Estonian Schuma in antipartisan operations through their overall physical strength and strong hatred of Bolshevism.[92] By 1943 the OK membership had stabilized at 43,000. Of that number, the police battalions counted for 2,500. The Estonian police battalions participated in atrocities against the civilian population, including the Jews, in Poland and Belorussia.[93] This aspect of the Holocaust, however, is outside the scope of this study.

The OK performed mainly auxiliary functions. It was the Estonian Security Police that dealt with the individuals arrested by the OK. The machine of terror would not have worked as efficiently if it were not for the indigenous police force. Furthermore, OK had a weaker presence in the cities, where Estonian Jews traditionally settled.

ESTONIAN SECURITY POLICE:

A "MULTIPLE COLLABORATION" THESIS

The head of the Estonian Security Police was responsible for hiring new personnel, subject to approval by both Sandberger and Mäe.[94] According to the latter, the Pärnu police commissar, Alexander Tilgre, played a major role in the
creation of the Estonian Security Police.[95] The lack of linguistic skills alone made
the German Security Police dependent on its Estonian counterpart. That kind
of dependence would have been complete if it were not for a handful of Baltic
Germans in the service of the German Security Police who spoke Estonian.[96] The
formation of the Estonian police force was completed on June 10, 1942. That is
when Reich Commissioner for Estonia Litzmann prohibited hiring new personnel for the Estonian Security Police and the OK.[97]

The headquarters of the German and Estonian branches of the Security
Police were located on the same street, seven hundred yards from each other; a
two-story structure that housed the KdS-Estland Office overlooked the parliament building, whereas the Estonian police occupied a four-story building down
the hill, on the corner of Tõnismägi Street and Kaarli Boulevard. Cooperation
between the two police branches was not only on paper, though there was a lot of
that too: 80 percent of the incoming correspondence arriving daily at 16 Tõnismäe Street was from the Estonian BIV and BV departments.

Often people with no proper training were co-opted into the newly created
police force, for many professional policemen had been deported by the Soviets. During the first days of the Nazi occupation, the Estonian partisans arrested
thousands of people whom they believed to be dangerous Communists, subject
to liquidation. To deal effectively with the growing numbers of arrestees, the
so-called Punishment Planning Commission (Strafplannungskommission) was
established within the Estonian Security Police. This was a unique institution in
the context of Nazi-occupied Eastern Europe. The Commission, which was composed of three Estonian officers and, at times, lawyers, carried out investigations.
(The newly arrived officials of the German Security Police were surprised to find
in the ranks of the Estonian Security Police quite a few lawyers or even judges.)[98]
To create the outward appearance of a legal procedure, the presiding officers
called in the defendants, asking them several pro forma questions. The defendants left without knowing the decision in their case. But there was a decision,

and there was a punishment, handwritten on a standard form. Once the investigation was completed, the Commission translated the summary of a decision into German and submitted it to the commander of the German Security Police for review. The head of the Gestapo had the authority to halt the investigation if the political crime could not be substantiated. However, this rarely happened because of the personal philosophy of the KdS-Estland. Sandberger once said that he would prefer to lock up ten innocent people rather than set one offender free.[99] Before creating the Punishment Planning Commission, Sandberger was supposed to reach an understanding with BdS Stahlecker in Riga, yet the latter claimed to have known nothing about it.[100] Each police prefecture had its own Punishment Planning Commission. The Tallinn police prefecture, with its thirteen precincts, was the largest in Estonia. In Tallinn, the Commission held its sessions in the Tallinn Central prison. During the first three weeks of November, for example, the Estonian Security Police forwarded 282 draft decisions to the KdS-Estland. Of that number 79 people were sentenced to death, 154 were committed to concentration camps, and 49 were released.[101]

Estonians, including the police rank and file, believed that the Commission would avoid sentencing innocent people. The participation of Estonian lawyers in the work of the Punishment Planning Commission ought to have made justice prevail. Most people were confident that no punishment would be administered unless individual guilt was firmly established.[102] The Estonians were proud of their court system. A new generation of highly qualified lawyers had raised legal standards in Estonia. The trials of left and right radicals in the 1920s and 1930s had not shaken the Estonians' belief in due process. After a yearlong break of continuity caused by the Soviet occupation, the population was eager to restore the interwar court system.[103] The head of the Estonian Security Police, Julius Ennok (since April 1, 1943), echoed those sentiments when he urged his subordinates to administer severe but just punishment. There was no room for sentimentality and personal judgments, he said.[104]

The Estonian Security Police presented themselves as public servants. Estonian policeman were to execute orders in a way that the public would see as necessary. The police were to appear to be assisting the population and not intimidating it. Even then, the friendly, by all means correct behavior of the police officials did not spare them from the criticism of being laissez-faire. Ennok warned his subordinates that they must not lose the trust of the Estonian people. The police were to continue working in close cooperation with the commander of the German Security Police in Estonia, wherein each Estonian department head was to collaborate with his German counterpart. As long as the German side trusted the Estonian side, the latter should extend the same courtesy to the former, with no questions asked.[105]

Because ordinary people did indeed trust the police and their ways, the rumors about police brutality that suddenly leaked out caused an uproar among the public. On December 6, 1941, KdS-Estland Sandberger ordered the arrest of Jüri Pargas from the Tallinn prefecture of the Estonian Security Police. Pargas was charged with physical mistreatment of political prisoners, whom he had locked in unheated cells. The accused confessed that in fifteen or so cases he had ordered the prisoners to remove their shoes and then beat their soles with a rubber truncheon. This sadistic method allowed maximum pain but no visible marks of torture. Tallinn Prefect Evald Mikson was next to be arrested. Mikson (born in 1911) blamed Roland Lepik, head of the Estonian Security Police, saying that the latter had personally approved the method of forced confession. Lepik devised one torture called the "balls dance" (severing the prisoners' testicles). According to Mikson, Lepik intended to keep the German authorities in the dark about brutalities perpetrated by the Estonian police officials.[106]

Roland Lepik (born in 1910) served as the head of the Estonian Security Police from the end of October 1941. On December 8 Sandberger ordered the arrest of Lepik on the charges of corruption and excessive brutality. According to leaders of the Estonian Self-Government, Sandberger proceeded on their instigation. In order to avoid personal responsibility, Sandberger allegedly sent Lepik farther away, to Riga.[107] However, one may think of a more serious reason behind Lepik's removal. The dismissal of Lepik marked a new period in the development of the Estonian Police, which concurrently underwent several structural changes. The first wave of Communist persecution was over, but Lepik, as an unwanted witness, might have told much about the cooperation between the German and the Estonian branches of the Security Police. It was not in Sandberger's interests to let that disclosure happen;[108] neither did he want Lepik killed immediately. One of the two charges against the leaders of the Estonian Security Police was corruption. Sandberger could have been interested as well in the valuables that Lepik and Mikson had misappropriated from the arrested and the executed (rumor had it that Lepik owned about one hundred watches). One way or another, by replacing Lepik and Mikson, Sandberger seemingly restored justice and erased the blame weighing on his own office. In the meantime Sandberger continued to keep a close eye on Lepik and on Mikson, who remained in custody in Tallinn Central prison at least until November 1942. Sandberger finally authorized Mikson's release in July 1943; it was another half-year, though, before Mikson was actually released from prison.[109]

The Estonian Security Police received a new chief, Ain-Ervin Mere, who was officially appointed to that position on May 1, 1942. Nominally, Mere was subordinate to Hjalmar Mäe, the leader of the Estonian Self-Government.[110] The administrative changes did not affect the work of the Estonian Security Police, which as before received orders from KdS-Estland Sandberger. In April 1943 Julius Ennok replaced Mere as head of the Estonian Security Police. (Mere received a new assignment as battalion commander of an Estonian Waffen-SS regiment.)

The crimes within the jurisdiction of the Security Police were subdivided as follows: (1) political crimes; (2) crimes committed for political motives; (3) crimes against state authorities; (3) high treason; (4) crimes against a foreign state; (5) espionage and sabotage; (6) possession of explosives, weapons, and forbidden literature; (7) listening to forbidden radio broadcasts; (8) contacts with POWs, political prisoners, wanted political prisoners, and Jews; and (9) crossing the border clandestinely. Of all groups of the population, foreigners, Jews, and Gypsies became the subjects of police surveillance.[111]

It seems like an impossible task to draw a picture of an average official of the Estonian Security Police. In Narva, for example, he was a man with a middle school education and without professional police training, who showed no particular zeal in his work. Through the summer of 1943, the Narva police prefecture gathered information on 13,000 individuals; processed 2,350 case files; and placed another 1,000 people on the Wanted list.[112] The ethnic composition of the Estonian Security Police justified its name; in spite of the fact that Russians constituted 25 percent of Narva's population, the local security police employed just one ethnic Russian (out of fifty-six).[113]

The process of investigation was carried out with all sorts of violations. Notoriously, the Estonian Security Police carried on the ills associated with the Soviet NKVD. First of all, there were simply too many cases to handle at one time. Although the average was five investigations per day, police officials often had to process six, seven, or even eight investigations per day. Some of them, however, could not even meet the daily limit. This low output was not surprising considering the busy schedule of the Estonian policemen. Take, for example, Alexei Sarmuth, an official in the 2nd precinct of the Tallinn Security Police, who between March 8 and 14, 1942, accomplished the following: Sunday—forest work; Monday—interrogations; Tuesday—roundups and arrests; Thursday and Friday—office work.[114] Another reason for low output was the high turnover rate of personnel within any one police precinct.

The interrogation records had numerous shortcomings. Whether they were too wordy or too concise, in either case the incriminating evidence was usually missing. Thus a commanding officer once disciplined a subordinate who spent a total of ten hours interrogating two suspects. At the same time, in a typical Soviet manner, the police officials tried to investigate as many people as possible. Quality did not matter as long as the case files were processed in the quickest way possible. Nevertheless, the numbers for completed cases remained low.[115] The police officials cared little about the transcripts of investigations. While in some instances the investigation was carried out and sentence executed without much regard to evidence, in others numerous depositions were taken, irrelevant to any given case. Often they did not distinguish between hearsay and firsthand evidence.[116] The Communist charges were most problematic and involved the largest number of violations. Witnesses often accused one or another individual of Communism, without identifying the high-ranking Communists with whom the suspect had allegedly communicated. Subversive activities, criticism of the new regime, sympathy toward Communism, denunciations to the NKVD—most allegations could not be substantiated. Witnesses were time and again unable to provide adequate answers to the questions, thus revealing numerous gaps in their testimonies. Some cases had just one witness testifying. Yet other investigation files contained a corpus delicti without indicating the source of information. Whether the defendant joined a "criminal organization" (for example shock battalions) voluntarily or under duress played no role in the investigation; specific charges were usually missing; the difference between perpetrating and abetting crime was disregarded altogether. Incriminating evidence thus collected was obviously not enough to sentence an individual. Last but not least, Estonian police officials were never able to figure out what part of their work they were supposed to do in accordance with official guidelines as opposed to acting on their own initiative.[117]

One other problem was that Sandberger, or the respective head of the Security Police section, did not always read the exact translation of the summary prepared by the Punishment Planning Commission. Estonian and German texts varied,[118] potentially leading to abuse. The Estonian officials might have deliberately presented the cases in a way that guaranteed Sandberger's signature. And the truth is that Estonians had proposed harsher sentences than the Germans were willing to support.[119] When Ervin Viks, as head of Department BIV of the Estonian Security Police, disagreed with the ruling of his German counterpart, he usually returned the documents to the German Security Police for reconsideration.[120] Thus on October 27, 1942, the head of Department AIV, SS-Ostuf. Heinrich Bergmann, notified Viks of his decision in the case of Reet Türno (born Rose Tisch), whom he proposed to send to Jägala camp. Viks opposed that decision, arguing that it could potentially be damaging to dispatch a local Jew to the camp, where she might have spread all sorts of rumors. Bergmann accepted Viks's argument and ordered Türno executed.[121]

KdS-Estland Sandberger was satisfied with the performance of the Estonian police and the Estonians in general. As far as finding and prosecuting Communists was concerned, Sandberger related to Berlin, Estonians did not fail his expectations.[122]

The rank and file of the Estonian Security Police was composed of highly motivated, ideologically driven individuals (with some exceptions, as the example from Narva suggests). The Estonian Security Police School, which opened its doors in January 1942 in Tallinn, preferred male and female cadets who had suffered under the Bolshevik terror.[123] SS-Ustuf. Riho Sammalkivi was to become deputy director of the Police School. However, he was disqualified from the position because of his Jewish connections. During the time of Estonian independence Sammalkivi had invited Jews to meet and had received gifts from them.[124] For the same reason, half a year later the then head of the Estonian Security Police, Air-Ervin Mere, demoted Sammalkivi and sent him from Tallinn to Pskov.[125] In contrast, Narva Security Police welcomed an application from Ellen-Erika Allik. The nineteen-year-old factory employee expressed interest in the police service, saying that she wanted to take an active part in fighting Bolshevism. The background check on Allik confirmed that the young woman had never been part of a Communist organization and that she supported the present regime. Before Allik started her new job as a typist, she signed a standard form, which among other conditions cautioned her that criminal charges would be laid for sexual intercourse with Jews (the so-called *Rassenschande*) and individuals of the same sex.[126]

Some people wanted to join the Security Police to cover up their shady past. Some men were more successful than others, but on the whole the bad seed was weeded out. In Vilo County in Pechory Province, eleven people applied for the police service. For a number of reasons, three of them were rejected. Vasili Saarna (twenty-three) used to be a village elder under the Soviets and seemed to approve of Communism. Victor Saar (twenty-one) also could not be trusted; during the Soviet period Saar was known as a denouncer; his two brothers were convicted on criminal charges. Although Jacob Marjapuu (thirty-one) held correct political views, he was suspected of theft and used to become aggressive while drunk.[127]

It was not any different with the Omakaitse. Among the people who wanted to enlist in the ranks of the organization—as contemporaneous authors stressed—were all strata of Estonian society, including those involved with the Soviet regime. That is what Estonian partisans discovered when the German troops occupied Narva-Jõesuu on August 17. Among those coming to the assembly point was a former member of the Soviet militia, with his gun and a white armband.[128] The person that set up the Viljandi OK was actually the former head of the local committee for nationalization. As a former Soviet official, he soon received a vote of no confidence. All types of Communist activists, including Komsomol members, enrolled at once in the OK ranks. Unsurprisingly, those people were the most zealous.[129] Anti-Communism was the main selection criterion. In Pärnu, every potential member of the OK had to prove that he did not support Bolshevism. To verify this fact, one or several references were required from either military officers or high-ranking KL officials. After a while, the procedure became more elaborate: the head of OK was to personally approve the candidacy on the basis of a completed questionnaire. In Tallinn, an applicant had to swear that he had always been an enemy of Communism; that he was ready to fight against Communism; and that he had no Jewish blood in him. Even these strict measures could not prevent individuals who wanted "to wash off their former color" from joining the ranks of the organization. As a final resort, the Security Police was then asked to perform a political check on members of the OK.[130]

The Estonian Security Police was torn: how to check on individual members of the organization without exposing the latter as bogus? The police investigation indeed revealed numerous cases of multiple collaboration, subject to severe punishment up to a death sentence. Alfred Käblik was a member of Komsomol and allegedly had worked for the NKVD. To whitewash himself in the eyes of the new regime, Käblik joined the OK. As a member of the so-called People's Militia under the Soviets, Rudolf Kiin had participated in arrests. He was also accused of having torn down Estonian flags. Kiin bargained for pardon by joining the OK. Nikolai Kozakov was already known as a Communist during the period of Estonian independence. Among other deeds Kozakov was accused of having denounced his fellow citizens. Nevertheless, he volunteered for service in the OK, as did thousands of others. Manfred Brück, another alleged Communist, originally intended to join the Red Army. However, the abrupt change in the balance of power brought Brück into the ranks of the OK. As a member of the OK, Brück was caught red-handed misappropriating clothes and silverware belonging to victims of the new regime. Rudolf Mark headed one of the OK departments in Tallinn until his criminal past was uncovered. Mark turned out to be a recidivist, who stood trial six consecutive times. In addition, two witnesses stated that they saw Mark with the NKVD insignia. Otto Ridali had membership in the Vabs organization, but was later pressured to start working for the NKVD. In the fall of 1941, Ridali joined the Estonian Security Police in Tallinn; as an agent, he was said to have provided the police with falsely incriminating data on various individuals. A former police official, Aldis Saarepere joined the NKVD only to resume his responsibilities as a police constable shortly after the Soviet regime in Estonia collapsed. Once exposed, all of these individuals were executed.[131]

However, tens if not hundreds of members of the OK and the Security Police managed to conceal their often tainted past. Former Vabs member Alexander Viidik was one of those people. Viidik had been an officer with the Estonian Political Police but joined the NKVD service in the fall of 1940. On the order of the NKVD, Viidik stayed in Nazi-occupied Estonia with the intention of infiltrating the German Security Police. In August 1941, Viidik made personal contact with Commander of SK 1a Sandberger, who offered him a position with the Security Service (SD). Viidik was entrusted with hiring people for the SD; he did so by enlisting some hundred people whom he had known during the Soviet period. After 1945, Viidik continuously worked for the KGB.[132] The example of Elmar Ardla, a twenty-six-year-old from Tartu, is not atypical. In 1940–41 Ardla served as bailiff in a Soviet court. Feeling apprehensive about this particular episode in his biography, in the fall of 1941 Ardla joined what later became the 33rd Police Battalion, which among other responsibilities supplied guards for Tartu concentration camp. As platoon commander, Ardla assembled execution squads.[133]

Ervin Richard Adolf Viks also made his career in the police force. Viks joined the police force in 1920 at the age of twenty-three. Over the next twenty years, the service track took Viks to every big city in Estonia. By the time of the Soviet occupation, Viks was working as Political Police commissar in Kuressaare. According to the memoirs of a former Estonian priest, Viks was able to survive the Soviet occupation only because the NKVD needed his services.[134] Shortly after German troops entered Tartu in July 1941, Viks became deputy head of the Special Department at a local concentration camp. On October 29, 1941, SS-Ostuf. Viks was appointed head of Tallinn-Harju prefecture of the Estonian Security Police. Simultaneously he served as one of the three members of the Punishment Planning Commission in Tallinn. Viks's signature spelled death for hundreds of Jews and non-Jews whose files he considered. Viks treated his subordinates harshly yet correctly. When it came to work, Viks could be demanding.

The most notorious case of multiple collaboration was that of Ain Ervin Mere. In December 1941, SS-Stubaf. Mere (born in 1903) replaced Roland Lepik as head of Department BIV within the Estonian Security Police. On May 1, 1942, Mere took over the command of the Estonian Security Police, in which capacity he served until March 31, 1943. From then and until his escape to the Allied occupation zone, Mere served as a battalion commander in the Estonian SS Division. Mere would not have been promoted if his past had been exposed. In October 1940 the NKVD had recruited a new agent with the nickname "Müller." This agent was Ain Ervin Mere. The NKVD greatly appreciated agent Müller and his reports, which made it as far as Lavrenti Beria's desk. Mere submitted detailed reports about the follow-up resettlement of Baltic Germans (the so-called *Nachumsiedlung*), yet his biggest achievement was the exposure of an underground organization called the "Estonian Nazi Alliance." In recognition of his performance, Mere was appointed head of the special department of the Estonian Rifle Corps, which the Soviets hastily assembled in the summer of 1941. Shortly thereafter, Mere, along with many other Estonians, surrendered himself to the German troops. Luckily for Mere, his NKVD file was among those few that the Soviets managed to save. Later on, as the commander of the Estonian Security Police, Mere criticized NKVD methods of forcing confessions from prisoners,[135]

16. Major Ain Ervin Mere, head of the Estonian
Security Police in 1942–43; HI, Hintzer, 169609.

the methods he had learned firsthand. At the same time, Mere tried hard to curry
favor with his German supervisors—to some Estonian police officers' displeas-
ure. In his speeches Mere continually praised "Great Germany," its leader Adolf
Hitler, and the "New Europe" the latter was building. Most often, however, Mere
called upon his listeners to fight Bolshevism.[136] One can only speculate as to
what extremes people like Viidik, Viks, and Mere might have gone in order to
prove themselves true Estonian patriots, and thus by definition relentless anti-
Communists, in the eyes of their colleagues and superiors.

The new regime deliberately promoted people with low moral standards.
When hiring informers, the Estonian Security Police specifically targeted individuals who had either served terms in a concentration camp or had had their
sentence suspended. Naturally, those people were now trying to demonstrate
their loyalty or at least their anti-Communism. The Security Police instructed its
branch offices to use blackmail as a means of enlisting potential informers (for

example, blackmail of an individual who sympathized with the Soviet regime in Estonia but avoided punishment).[137] Indeed, that was the best human material available for the tasks expected of them. For example, people knew that Francis Viipsi had been a member of the Haapsalu shock battalion. The Estonian Security Police interrogated Viipsi twice, but released him upon a promise that he would join the OK and pursue Communists and supporters of the Soviet power in general. As a member of the OK, Viipsi indeed participated in the arrests and executions. Eight out of the twenty-seven members of the Haapsalu OK, who together with Francis Viipsi participated in the executions, had previously served in the Red Army.[138]

The swift transfer of ideological allegiances can be called the "phenomenon of multiple collaboration."[139] The Reich Security Main Office (RSHA) in Berlin expressed its concerns about the number of former Estonian Communists who crept into various institutions, including the police. Referring to a reliable source that they received, the RSHA officials claimed that oftentimes the Estonian Security Police or the OK refused to investigate Communist suspects within their ranks.[140] The situation was nothing short of a paradox: the Estonian population was engulfed with fear and rage against Communists, yet many Communists, out of fear of revenge, managed to get into the ranks of the police and the OK, the very organizations responsible for identifying and prosecuting Communists![141] However paranoid it may sound, this and similar reports reveal the dichotomy, which the Estonian institutions set up by the German occupier were never able to resolve. If they were to engage in all-out war against Communism, they should have purged their own ranks first. In addition to a substantial number of individuals who had worked, in various capacities, for the Soviet regime, compliance with the norms and regulations imposed in 1940–41 made pretty much everybody liable for collaboration charges. To avoid dealing with the complex issue of personal responsibility, the police and the OK, backed by the bureaucratic apparatus, initiated an anti-Communist hunt on an unprecedented scale. It did not matter that many, if not the majority, of those arrested and executed on Communist charges had very little to do with Communism, as long as the investigators and executioners themselves stayed out of the limelight. Unable to apprehend leading Communists—most of whom had escaped to Russia proper—the Estonian Security Police and the OK overcompensated by detaining thousands of other "offenders." Taking into account that policemen and OK servicemen, with a few exceptions, were all Estonians, it made it easier if potential suspects—particularly in the first round of persecution—were drawn from designated ethnic groups. In the Estonian case, those groups were the Jews and the Russians.[142] More and more, the situation in the summer and fall of 1941 resembled a scene from the theater of the absurd, except that the actors had real guns. But the actors, guided by emotions, were unlikely to have noticed any contradictions.

The phenomenon of multiple collaboration was rooted in the popular perception of justice. On the one hand Estonians wanted to see the Security Police and the OK as heirs of the interwar Estonian Political Police and the KL respectively. On the other hand, the Estonian Security Police and the OK were perceived as the antithesis of the Soviet Security Police and shock battalions. As true Estonian institutions, the Security Police and the OK were in gear now to face the international threat of Communism. In the vein of Marxist dialectics, some Estonians demanded that the Security Police become the successor of the NKVD, which they universally condemned. Sometimes Estonians drew a comparison between the German and the Soviet Security Police. Most people found the methods of the Gestapo milder and much more refined *(bedeutend kultureller)* than those of the NKVD.[143] The calls for harsh punishment of Communists and other "subversive elements" came from within the Estonian population. Consider the following complaint submitted to the Virumaa OK headquarters in September 1941. A suspicious individual was apprehended in Kabala. Because of his wounds, the arrestee was transported to Rakvere by train. The anonymous author wondered why the OK did not order such people instantly shot instead of treating them as decent citizens.[144] Arbitrary rule and score-settling plagued Estonian society in the wake of the German occupation. The police and the OK were incapable of reversing a practice that they had themselves abetted. All too often, the situation closely resembled that under the Soviet regime.[145]

Estonians professed anti-Communism to the same, or even larger, extent as the Nazis. The prestige of the occupation power among the Estonian population very much depended on the harshness of its policy vis-à-vis Communist suspects.[146] The Nazis sponsored an anti-Bolshevik drive without realizing the destructive capacity of the beast they released. Sandberger, for example, related to his superiors in Berlin that Bolshevism became obsolete in Estonia as soon as the leading Communist authorities fled from the country in the summer of 1941.[147] The reaction of the Estonians to an amnesty shows that the German occupation authorities might have underestimated the extent of anti-Communism among the local population. On December 20, 1941, GK-Estland Litzmann announced amnesty for minor offenders. Most of the people who were eligible for amnesty would have been released shortly anyway—those who came to embrace Communism either out of ignorance or under pressure. Through amnesty Litzmann wanted to demonstrate that despite the ferocity of the anti-Bolshevik struggle, the Third Reich was willing to extend its goodwill to anyone who had inadvertently embraced Communism.[148] The Ostland propaganda division was advised to take note of those people who were released from custody and who rejoined the workforce.[149] The Estonian population criticized the December 1941 amnesty, which they perceived as a softening of the German position vis-à-vis Communists. People expressed their indignation: amnesty was inconceivable, considering how badly Communists and their sympathizers had treated Estonians. Therefore the Estonian Security Police proceeded with caution while drawing a list of people to be released in August 1942. The local population was hostile toward individuals who were granted amnesty.[150] The Latvian population reacted similarly to the amnesty that the Germans announced in Riga in May 1942. The German Security Police in Latvia released some eighty people who had been detained on Communist charges. Contrary to expectations, the Latvians hated the thought that Communists were set free at a time when a group of nationalistic Latvians detained by the Germans was still languishing in prison. The negative effect caused by the first amnesty made KdS-Lettland Lange discontinue that practice altogether.[151]

Anti-Communism was permanently incorporated into the Nazi ideology.[152] However, as time went on the message lost its original appeal in the twists and turns of propaganda. Once Nazis touched the anti-Communist cord with the Estonians, Latvians, and other East-European peoples, they could not put the genie back into the bottle. Hatred against Communism and everything and everybody associated with it was impossible to control. Estonians settled for a complete elimination of Bolshevism, which had brought an end to their independence, by pulling into the net anyone even slightly tainted by pro-Soviet sentiment. People who were arrested on Communist charges were doomed. According to some reports, imprisoned Latvian nationalists received worse treatment than their fellow Communist inmates.[153] Statistics on executions show that in the case of doubt, Lithuanian auxiliaries tended to place their victims in the category "Jews," whereas Latvian auxiliaries in a similar situation branded the targeted individuals "Communists."[154] Doubt was not a problem for the members of the Estonian Security Police, who did not question the alleged Communist connection of the individuals in custody. The suspects were arrested and shot as Communists, even though in most cases they were not.

When it came to the murder of Jews, Estonia differed from the other two Baltic countries in one important aspect. The operational mode of the Estonian Security Police made unnecessary the creation of mobile death squads—staffed and sometimes managed by local auxiliaries—like those that existed in Latvia and Lithuania. The notorious Hamann commando in Lithuania and Arājs commando in Latvia committed numerous atrocities against the civilian population, first and foremost Jews. The structure and function of the unit led by Viktors Arājs, a thirty-one-year-old lawyer, closely resembled that of the German Einsatzgruppen. The commando came into existence specifically for the purpose of murdering Jews, Gypsies, and Communists; most of its activities occurred between July and September 1941. Three hundred members of Arājs commando were implicated in the death of at least 26,000 civilians.[155] Lithuanian auxiliaries constituted the core of the unit commanded by SS-Hstuf. Joachim Hamann that carried out mass executions throughout the country between July and October 1941. Moving from one locality to another, the Hamann commando murdered close to 77,000 Jews.[156]

The motives for collaboration and/or participation in the murder of Jews may not have been identical for Estonian, Latvian, and Lithuanian policemen. The difference had something to do with the nature of their assignments: The scope of atrocities committed by members of the Hamann and Arājs death squads made them a focus of the investigation of the Soviet, Lithuanian, and Latvians authorities, whereas the more subtle, bureaucratic mode of operation of the Estonian Security Police drew only limited attention of the Estonian KGB. Thus we are dealing here with two groups of perpetrators—actual executioners and the so-called desk murderers. Therefore, within the context of the Nazi occupation of the Baltic States, a comparative analysis of the motivation to commit violence can be carried out only to a certain extent.

According to Knut Stang, the majority of Lithuanians that joined the Hamann commando were anti-Semites, though probably not fanatic Jew-haters. In return for their collaboration, those individuals expected the Nazis to grant more concessions to Lithuania. Stang emphasized careerism and obedience to authority, which turned seemingly ordinary men, most of them under thirty, into mass murderers.[157] Strong Catholic tradition and a cult of personality, which had deeper roots in Lithuania than in Latvia or Estonia, made it easier to create and operate close-knit paramilitary communities. Those units, like the German SS, performed certain rituals to reinforce the notion of masculinity.[158]

Dzintars Ērglis analyzed one specific case of murder, in Krustpils, Latvia, and came to the conclusion that the individuals that joined the police force and/or Self-Defense sought power.[159] That archetype is identical with Theodor Adorno's "authoritarian personality." Remarkably, none of the five defendants whose files Ērglis perused collaborated at any time with the Soviets; at least one of them participated in the post-1944 anti-Soviet resistance movement. Rudīte Vīksne did an excellent quantitative study of 346 members of the Arājs commando. As far as their motives were concerned, there was a substantial difference between the men who joined the commando in 1941 and those who did so within the next two years. Most people from the 1941 cohort were relatively well-educated thirty-year-olds with military experience. Those individuals came of age in Independent Latvia: some of them served in the military or in the police force, while others pursued university studies and ran their own businesses. Unsurprisingly, then, they bitterly opposed the Soviet regime, seeking revenge for the injustice done to their country. In other words, the 1941 volunteers were ideologically driven, as opposed to their more opportunistic colleagues that enlisted in the Arājs commando in 1942 and 1943. Vīksne detected no outspoken anti-Semitism among the rank and file, which she claims was learned. To some extent, Vīksne contradicts her own thesis by suggesting that those Latvians who became members of the death squad had little idea about their tasks, that life under the Soviet occupation corrupted their value system, and that they fell under the spell of Nazi propaganda. In using trial records, one should be careful with the testimonies of the former policemen who claimed that they wanted to continue working in their profession or of the students who maintained that they joined the Arājs commando to be able to re-enroll in a university.[160]

5 "ESTLAND IST JUDENREIN!"

THE DECISION-MAKING PROCESS

Recent research has demonstrated the substantial involvement of the Wehrmacht in the murder of the Jews, in particular during the first months of the Russo-German war.[1] Because the Wehrmacht was the first among the German invaders to enter Estonia in the summer of 1941, it comes as no surprise that the first order to launch a large-scale cleansing operation behind the front line also came from the military. Battalion Friedrich of the German 18th Army was put in charge of these operations. Army Commander von Küchler gave the order to begin the operation on August 10. The 18th Army daily reports indicate that the main targets of the operation were the remnants of the Red Army and individual members of shock battalions. Whenever possible, Battalion Friedrich relied on the Omakaitse (OK) to carry out the cleansing. On one occasion, not far from Jõgeva, a group of OK members killed three German soldiers whom they mistook for Soviets.[2]

In preparation for the Russian campaign, German military intelligence provided the Wehrmacht with maps showing the distribution of Jews in Estonia, Latvia, Lithuania, and northern Poland.[3] As regards Estonian Jews specifically, the Wehrmacht acted upon guidelines issued before the invasion of Estonia. On July 4, Security Division 207 resolved to start immediately cleansing the woods of bands consisting of "commissars, Communists, and Jews." For the purpose of identifying such individuals, the division command recommended using Latvians and Lithuanians. All known Communists and male Jews were to be taken into custody as hostages. However, under no circumstances were these hostages to be handed over to the German Security Police. On July 5, Security Division 207 distributed complementary guidelines that prohibited mistreatment of the civilian population. Membership in the Communist Party and Jewish origin were insufficient grounds for carrying out an execution. Such people were to be arrested instead. At the same time, the guidelines made clear that it was not the Wehrmacht's responsibility to handle "politically and racially unreliable elements." In fact, responsibility lay with the organization specifically designated for this purpose: the German Security Police.[4] The 18th Army High Headquarters (Armeeoberkommando or AOK) confirmed earlier attempts to erase the Wehrmacht's criminal liability. On July 23, referring specifically to Estonia, AOK 18 mentioned a deal between the RSHA and Army High Command (Oberkommando des Heeres or OKH), according to which Einsatzgruppen could operate in the combat zone. Any interference with the special tasks carried out by the EG was prohibited.[5]

Field Marshal Wilhelm von Leeb, commander of HGr North, was the first to issue an order with regard to Jews, though not specifically Estonian Jews. On July 15, 1941, von Leeb released guidelines regulating the movement of civilians in the Baltic coastal zone. The document only mentioned Jews in passing: alongside foreign nationals, they were to leave the six-mile coastal zone within 48 hours.[6] Except for the Jews in Pärnu, this regulation had no practical implications until after Tallinn—the city with the largest concentration of Jews in Estonia—was captured six weeks later. On July 24, General Franz von Roques issued a decree that obliged the Jews to wear a yellow Star of David.[7] In spite of the Wehrmacht's contribution to the "Final Solution of the Jewish Question," the orders issued by military authorities in July and August 1941 clearly identify the German Security Police as the driving force behind the Holocaust. It was not any different in Estonia.

In the case of Estonia, there is a striking absence of two essential elements of the Holocaust as it had evolved in Eastern Europe: ghettos and pogroms. The Nazis decided that Jewish numbers in Estonia were too low to justify the creation of a ghetto. Subject to arrest and imprisonment like any other suspects, Jews were also to be investigated on a general basis. Apparently this policy was impossible in Latvia or Lithuania, both of which contained large Jewish populations. At his postwar trial, RKO Lohse insisted that the ghettos in the Baltics were established in order to protect the Jewish population from popular violence.[8] If what Lohse said was true, then the Jews must have felt totally secure in Estonia, where ghettos did not exist. Rather, Lohse lied, or exposed the hidden agenda of the German Security Police: to unleash seemingly spontaneous pogroms so that it could portray itself as the protector of law and order.[9] According to an EG report, a spontaneous uprising against the Jews did not take place in Estonia because of the lack of propaganda to that effect.[10] In fact, by the time German troops reached Tallinn, the RSHA had already instructed the EGs to prohibit gatherings of onlookers during mass executions.[11] This order essentially outlawed pogroms. Even then, I would argue that the German Security Police in Estonia made a conscious decision against inciting popular violence against Jews.

On September 10, 1941, Commander of SK 1a Sandberger issued the order that sealed the fate of the Estonian Jews. The order distinguished between male and female Jews. Police prefectures were obliged to compile lists indicating the age, sex, and working ability of the Jewish inhabitants. The lists, typewritten in German, were to be submitted by September 20. Meanwhile, the Jews were subjected to a standard set of limitations, including prohibition from certain professions, a freeze on mobility, restriction on access to public services and transport, and the unavoidable yellow star. The future location of a large Jewish camp had for sometime remained undetermined. The original choice was in Tartu Province, but was later changed in favor of a site closer to Tallinn, where the majority of Estonian Jews lived.[12] The regulations that came into effect in Estonia on September 10 resembled those introduced in Latvia on September 1.

Throughout September Jews had routinely been dispatched to Tallinn Central prison, in accordance with a standard decision that prescribed indefinite imprisonment in a concentration camp. Before that they were required to submit their valuables, money, and keys to the Tallinn-Harju police prefecture.[13] A passerby saw Jewish men in the courtyard of the German Security Police building on 16 Tõnismäe Street, which is where Jewish women went to plead for their spouses and sons.[14] SSPF-Estland Möller attempted ex post facto to divert attention from KdS-Estland Sandberger. Möller implied it was Heydrich who authorized the persecution of Jews in Estonia. According to Möller, within a week after he established his headquarters in Tallinn on September 2, he received RFSS Himmler in his office. Himmler arrived with a large delegation, including Heydrich. While in Tallinn, the latter convened a meeting with the members of SK 1a.[15] In fact, Himmler arrived in Tallinn on September 19, that is, ten days after Sandberger sanctioned the arrest of all Jews in Estonia.[16]

The document that Sandberger signed on September 10 provides no details about the ultimate fate of the Jews beyond their incarceration in a concentration

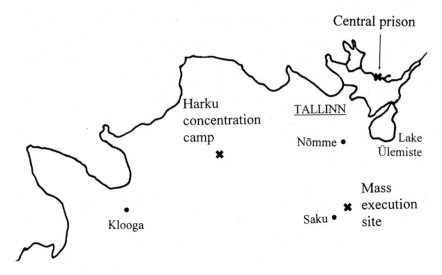

2. Sites of terror in and around Tallinn. Prepared by author.

camp. The EG reports were much more straightforward, though. All male Jews over sixteen years of age, except for physicians and appointed Jewish elders, were to be apprehended and subsequently shot. Within one month, the death toll reached 440, including 207 men from Tallinn.[17] Provincial cities were proclaimed *judenfrei* as early as October 12. The executions were carried out by the OK under the control of SK 1a. The estimated number of Jewish women and children who were still alive by mid-October was anywhere between 500 and 600. Two buildings in Tartu, including a former synagogue, served as impromptu prisons. Pärnu Jews were also incarcerated locally. Jews from Tallinn and the surrounding area were to be dispatched to a concentration camp at Harku, not far from the national capital. All Jewish women fit for work were to be engaged in pit cutting on the property belonging to the nearby Harku prison, a subsidiary of the Tallinn Central prison. This arrangement helped to solve the problems of nutrition and financing.[18] There was no hint in official German documents as to what would eventually happen to the Jewish women and children.

SANDBERGER'S LIE: THE PSKOV TRANSFER

On May 25, 1945, a German in civilian clothes in possession of an SS pay book and a passport in the name of Martin Sandberger presented himself at the headquarters of the 42nd U.S. Infantry Division in Kitzbühel in Austria. Three-day stubble and a tired appearance could not hide the obvious intellect of the man, who turned out to be the head of Department IVA of the RSHA in Berlin. An Intelligence check revealed that Dr. Sandberger was no. 39,931 on the Crowcass Wanted List: Sandberger, Martin. Description: height 5'9"; muscular build; black hair, thinning on forehead; gray eyes, oval face; large nose; speaks with North-German accent; married, three children. Sandberger requested to be taken to Intelligence in order to give valuable information with respect to the German Security Police and German Intelligence. When asked about the motive for this request, Sandberger stated that it was the natural desire of a German officer to offer his services to the victor in an honorable manner. When reminded that the Allied Powers did not recognize the existence of honor in the SS, Sandberger said that he hoped to be given the opportunity to prove his honorable intentions. Following a thorough interrogation at the U.S. Forces European Theatre (FET) Interrogation Center, Sandberger was transferred to Camp 020. He was detained as a possible war criminal or material witness to war crimes committed in 1941 in Pskov. The U.S. Military Intelligence officials observed that throughout his confinement at Camp 020, Sandberger exhibited the utmost politeness, correctness, and cooperation. Sandberger repeatedly volunteered information that convinced his captors that there was no willful reticence of any kind on his part. The only doubtful period in Sandberger's history appeared to be that between 1941 and 1943, when he was the KdS in Estonia.[19]

The hardest to believe was Sandberger's role in the murder of Estonian Jews. Sandberger related the following to U.S. Intelligence in the summer and fall of 1945. By the time his unit reached Estonia, there were about 450 Jews left in the country. Sandberger received the execution order but could not recall whether it emanated from the RSHA in Berlin or from Higher SS and Police Commander (HSSPF) Jeckeln in Riga. In any event, Sandberger claimed that he did not carry out this order but had the Jews interned in Estonian prisons. Later, in November 1941, he allegedly transferred the Jews to a camp near Pskov. Sandberger was worried that BdS-Ostland Stahlecker might have found out about the Jews had they remained in Estonia.

In Pskov, however, they remained outside of Stahlecker's jurisdiction. Sandberger claimed humanitarian concerns behind his decision. He also considered using Estonian Jews as slave laborers sometime in the future. Unfortunately, it so happened that Jeckeln learned about the Jews when he was touring Pskov in late 1941 or early 1942. Jeckeln immediately gave the order to execute the Jews, without Sandberger's knowing about it.[20] Sandberger repeated this story in a more elaborate form two years later at Nuremberg.

The honorable SS officer, as Sandberger portrayed himself, once again chose to be dishonest. The Pskov transfer is not mentioned anywhere in the records of the Security Police in Estonia. The railway administration had no relevant records either. The EG reports were silent about the purported deportation. Rebecca Sule was the only Jew whose file indicated that she "died" in December 1941 in Pskov.[21] Nevertheless, high-ranking officials in the Estonian puppet government, for example Minister of the Interior Angelus, talked about the Pskov transfer as an established fact.[22] Some scholars came to accept this version too.

Mark Dworzecki was probably the first to buy into Sandberger's rendition of the events. Dworzecki based his conclusions on a small number of documents produced by the Central Office of State Judicial Administration in Lüdwigsburg, Germany, deposited as copies at Yad Vashem in Israel. Most recently, Peter Longerich corroborated Dworzecki's findings, relying likewise on post-Nuremberg trial records.[23] To give Sandberger a "fair trial," next I will recount the final episode in the life of the Estonian Jewish community according to the KdS-Estland.

Sandberger implied that the personal ambitions of Commander of EG A Stahlecker (as of December 1941, BdS-Ostland) had made the latter resent the fact that several hundred Jews were still alive in Estonia. This ambition prevented Stahlecker from reporting to his superiors on the progress of the Final Solution in the Baltics. The RSHA officials in Berlin seemed equally puzzled as to why Sandberger had failed to fully implement the *Führerbefehl* in Estonia. Stahlecker ordered the execution of the remaining Jews in Estonia for the second time in October. Sandberger now faced a dilemma: although he did not want to damage his career by delaying the implementation of the order, he knew that the killing of helpless women and children might cause a negative reaction among the local population. As soon as a German civil administration was set up in Estonia, Sandberger speculated, his power as commander of the German Security Police in Estonia would be curtailed in favor of the SS and Police Commander. Finally Sandberger came up with the idea of sending the rest of the Estonian Jews outside of the country's borders to Pskov, a solution that should have satisfied everyone.

Stahlecker would have been able to pronounce the Estonian Commissariat General *judenrein,* and Sandberger would have saved face and relieved himself of any further responsibility at the same time. As long as Pskov lay within the authority of the KdS-Estland, Sandberger anticipated no difficulties in exercising control over the Jews in that city.[24]

Himmler was apparently dissatisfied with the pace of destruction of Jews in the Baltics. The new timetable laid down by Hitler made him decide to speed up the progress of the Final Solution in the Ostland. At the beginning of October Himmler toured Ukraine; some authors believe that it was during that trip that Himmler decided to replace SS-Ogruf. Hans-Adolf Prützmann, HSSPF-Ostland and North Russia, with SS-Ogruf. Friedrich Jeckeln, HSSPF-Ukraine and South Russia. On October 31 the two switched positions.[25] Upon his arrival in the Baltics, Jeckeln immediately began to implement his signature method of mass execution. Thus on November 30 and December 8, 1941, about 25,000 Latvian Jews were murdered at Rumbula near Riga. Jeckeln was known for his rigidity; he would have sacrificed his own family for the cause. That made Jeckeln a particularly efficient HSSPF in the eyes of Himmler. A quick-tempered man, Jeckeln often made decisions on the spot, without previously consulting either his immediate superiors or the actual experts. Sandberger and his subordinates who testified at the Nuremberg Military Tribunal argued that Jeckeln had a negative attitude toward the "soft-hearted" Sandberger. Indeed, Jeckeln continually demonstrated hostility toward him.[26] Shortly after the Rumbula massacre Jeckeln went on an inspection trip in the Ostland. While passing through Pskov, he allegedly discovered some four or five hundred Estonian Jews in a camp near the city. This discovery infuriated Jeckeln, considering that SSPF-Estland Möller had only recently reported that everything was in order in Estonia as far as the Jewish question was concerned.[27] According to one witness, Jeckeln shouted, "What! And they are still alive?"[28] In coarse language, Jeckeln ordered the immediate execution of the Jews. Jeckeln continued his trip but intended to return to Pskov a few days later. The executions were carried out by the German Municipal Police (Schutzpolizei or Schupo) under the supervision of the TK-Pskov led by SS-Ostuf. Otto Bleymehl, who reported directly to Sandberger. The Schupo consisted of policemen who had arrived in Pskov from Tilsit in the late fall of 1941. Because of the Christmas holidays, the total strength of the Schupo in Pskov did not exceed fifteen men. When the policemen and some ten to fifteen members of

Organization Todt (OT) arrived early in the morning at a killing site some 2.5 miles away from Pskov, a grave had already been dug. Policemen surrounded the Jews, who in the meantime were ordered to undress. As soon as the victims walked to the edge of the grave, Sergeant Gerhard Pieck and Obw. [?] Böttger opened fire. Witnesses claimed that Pieck, armed with a machine gun, did the entire job himself.[29]

The witnesses argued unanimously that it was Jeckeln who gave the order and that Jews were murdered in Pskov, but they disagreed on everything else. Sandberger's statement differed considerably from the testimony given by the Pskov policemen regarding the number of Jews and the date of their execution. One of the policemen who took part in the *Aktion* estimated the number to be sixty or seventy. His comrade spoke of several hundred people, but definitely fewer than five hundred. Considering the size of the grave (approximately 270 square feet) and the length of the operation (approximately four hours), the number of people killed could not have exceeded one or two hundred. Among the executed were both men and women but only a small number of children. According to Sandberger, the killing took place a few weeks before Stahlecker's death, in late January or early February 1942. Sandberger argued that because of the poor communication between Tallinn and Pskov, Bleymehl failed to immediately inform him of the execution. The policemen, however, insisted that the Jews were killed sometime between Christmas and the new year, probably on December 28, 1941. Last but not least, witnesses never said explicitly that the Jews who were murdered in Pskov came from Estonia.[30] Furthermore, Sandberger insisted that the Jews were executed by the Estonian camp personnel.[31]

The policemen had no reason to lie about the date of the execution, for it had no bearing on the credibility of their testimonies. The context in which the execution took place further supports their testimony. The Wannsee Conference, which was supposed to open on December 9, 1941, was rescheduled at the last moment for January 20, 1942. The conference timetable was affected by the Japanese attack on Pearl Harbor and the Soviet counteroffensive at Moscow. Heydrich, however, claimed that the event was postponed because one of the invited officials, SS-Stubaf. Rudolf Lange, could not attend. In his capacity as KdS-Lettland, Lange was busy supervising the execution of Jews in Riga.[32] However, not the least important factor was Stahlecker's yearning to pronounce the Ostland free of Jews. "Unfortunately," the Security Police failed to kill all the Jews in Latvia by the time the Wannsee Conference took place in January; some 3,500 Latvian Jews remained alive. Remarkably, Estonia was proclaimed judenrein, whereas Latvia was not. Such an announcement could not possibly have been made unless all (or almost all) Estonian Jews were already dead.

Sandberger's attempt to mislead the investigation is clear. His contradictory statements regarding the date of the execution attest to that deceit too. Sandberger played it safe, given that none of the major Nazi officials who could have revealed the truth about his tenure in Estonia was alive by the time of the so-called Einsatzgruppen Trial. BdS-Ostland Stahlecker died of wounds on March 23, 1942. Three months later, Czech partisans assassinated Chief of the RSHA Heydrich. GK-Estland Litzmann was killed in combat at the end of the war. Himmler was taken prisoner by the British but managed to kill himself by swallowing poison on March 23, 1945. HSSPF-Ostland Jeckeln was captured by the Soviets and, after a rather short trial, was hanged in Riga on February 2, 1946. Sandberger's deputy Carsten was said to have committed suicide in Tyrol after the war, and Bleymehl had been missing since February 1945. Perhaps the only high-ranking German official who could confront Sandberger was SSPF-Estland Möller. Möller, however, was not among the defendants at the Einsatzgruppen Trial. (On December 4, 1947, Möller received a death sentence for a murder he committed in 1934; he was released in 1955.) The leaders of the Estonian Self-Government certainly would have had much to say about the murder of Jews in Estonia. However, they owed their positions to Sandberger and therefore were not eager to tell the court the truth. In the absence of qualified witnesses, Sandberger was able to shift blame for his crimes without risking the possibility that his lies would ever come out.

Sandberger would not have been able to get away with his lies if the Nuremberg Military Tribunal had gained access to the archival records behind the Iron Curtain. The statistics provided by the Estonian Security Police rebuke Sandberger's claims. One only needs to tally the approximate numbers of Jews executed in each of the five largest police prefectures: Tallinn—666; Pärnu—137; Tartu—at least 50; Narva—32; Rakvere—22. Some 56 Jews executed in other cities bring the total to 963—the number presented by the German Security Police.[33] All the Jews were murdered in Estonia, not in Pskov. Jeckeln might have hastened the pace of the murders, which otherwise were initiated and supervised by Sandberger.

EXECUTIONS

The Jews who entered either Tallinn Central prison or Harku concentration camp were meticulously registered all the way through October 5, 1941. Then, on October 26, the Tallinn-Harju prefecture of the Estonian Security Police handed over a list of the executed Jews to the German Security Police.[34] By that time, all male Jews over sixteen years of age, with the exception of physicians, had already been executed by the OK under the supervision of the German Security Police. Female Jews in Tallinn and Pärnu were still alive, having been used as a source of slave labor.[35] In most cases executions were carried out by a special OK unit (among other cities, in Narva, Rakvere, Pechory, and Tallinn).[36] On occasion, it was a special unit of the Estonian Security Police that carried out the death sentences.[37]

Jews were treated differently from other prisoners, whether it was in a police precinct or later in Tallinn Central prison. Thus, by the evening of September 1, 1941, a detention cell in the 5th police precinct in Tallinn quickly filled with people. Among fifty-something arrestees there were also Jews, segregated in one corner of the cell. Within the following six days, one by one, the Jews were taken away, never to be seen again. It was no different at Tallinn Central prison: upon arrival, the Jews were separated from the non-Jews and placed into solitary confinement. Several days later other prisoners watched Jews boarding trucks in the prison courtyard.[38] The procedures at Tallinn Central prison were as follows. Upon receiving from the Estonian Security Police a list with the names of individuals sentenced to death, the prison commandant ordered the condemned into a special cell overnight. Simultaneously, the commandant notified senior guards about a forthcoming execution. Early the next morning, the guards once again checked the identity of the victims, stripped them to their underwear, tied their hands, and handed them over to a firing squad.[39]

Three or four trucks at a time took away between fifty and sixty people each. Germans from the Security Police, on two motorcycles, accompanied the convoy to an execution site (a Valdeku antitank ditch about eight miles south of Tallinn along Männiku Road). The firing squad was composed of members of the OK, who wore no distinctive clothes.[40] Between 1941 and 1944, about 2,500 inmates of Tallinn Central prison were executed in the Valdeku antitank ditch.[41] Jews and Gypsies were executed separately from the rest of the prisoners. By the same token, before execution, children were separated from their parents.[42] It is unclear whether *all* Tallinn Jews were executed at the antitank ditch. At one point, Sandberger mentioned a certain Jewish burial site near Harku.[43] However, there are reasons to believe that the KdS-Estland meant the Valdeku execution site, which was big enough to accommodate all the victims of the terror.

Executions were usually carried out early in the morning, as had been the custom in interwar Estonia.[44] The executed Jews were subsequently buried in secret. In each particular case, Commandant of Tallinn Central prison August Ilves requested permission for burial from the Security Police.[45] The German Security Police was concerned not to agitate the Estonian public unnecessarily. On one occasion the Estonian Security Police received a reprimand for allowing newspapers to publish obituaries for several individuals (non-Jews) who had been executed.[46] The German Security Police strove to implicate as many Estonian agencies as possible in the mass murder. For example, in February 1942, the Estonian Relief Agency was granted the right to collect the clothes of the executed. Sandberger discontinued this practice the following August in favor of the Estonian Security Police but then reenacted it in January 1943.[47] The Welfare Directorate did not object at any time. The Registry Office was another Estonian agency that actively cooperated with the Security Police. Upon request, the Registry Office provided a detailed record of any Jew whose identity could not be established. Usually, it was a copy of a birth certificate or a baptismal record. Upon reaching the Security Police, such a document became a death warrant for the person in question. Once the death sentence was carried out, Department BIV forwarded individual death certificates to the Registry Office. If the Registry Office was to reissue a death certificate to the relatives of an executed individual, it was obliged by an agreement with the Estonian Security Police to substitute the phrase "punished by death" for "died." In the case of Jews, only twenty-eight death certificates are available.

The secretive way in which Jewish people were executed and buried contrasted sharply with the publicity that the Nazis gave to the investigation of Soviet crimes. This publicity included compiling lists of the deportees, carrying out exhumations, and identifying the Soviets' victims, information that the Nazis used for propaganda purposes at home and abroad. Of the three Baltic countries, Estonia boasted the highest level of organization. Specifically for that purpose, an agency called the Deportee Registration Office (Zentralstelle zur Erfassung der verschleppten Esten or ZEV) came into existence in Tallinn.[48] The ZEV operated

17. Tartu region commissar Kurt Meenen unveiling a memorial plaque to the victims of Soviet terror in Tartu, summer 1942. Among other high-ranking officials who attended the ceremony were Sandberger and Mäe; HI, Hintzer, 162217.

within the Estonian Relief Agency. To document the Communist terror, the ZEV began collecting photos of victims and mass graves, archival records, and witness accounts—anything that illustrated the brutality of the Soviets.[49] The ZEV presented the following figures for Estonia: 7,204 persons arrested, of whom 1,818 were executed. According to the director of the ZEV, Elmar Tambek, by means of mass deportation the Soviets had intended to eliminate the Estonian leadership and the liberation war veterans.[50]

The ZEV was also put in charge of conducting exhumations and reburials, in which it collaborated closely with the police.[51] The first and largest exhumation in Estonia began in Tartu on July 15, 1941. In spite of the significant number of Jews among the deportees, they were deliberately denied the status of victims. From its inception in the fall of 1941, the ZEV entered the data on exiled Jews separately from those of the rest of the deportees.[52] Among 193 people executed by the Soviets in the Tartu prison in the summer of 1941, there was one Jew. However, when the memorial plaque was unveiled a year later, his name was omitted.[53] The Nazis deliberately promoted the idea that Jews could only be found among the

18. Reburial of the victims of Soviet terror in Tartu, St Paul Lutheran Church cemetery, March–April 1942; HI, Hintzer, 153848.

people who carried out arrests and deportations but not among those who were arrested and deported.[54]

Of the total number of people executed by December 1941, the Tallinn-Harju prefecture of the Estonian Security Police reported 610 Jews. Another thirty-five cases were under investigation. These numbers remained constant throughout the entire period of Nazi occupation. A statistical chart of August 1944 gave the figure of 666 executions.[55] Situational report no. 155 of January 14, 1942, proclaimed Estonia free of Jews. Six days later, that information was made public at the infamous Wannsee Conference in Berlin. Thus Estonia became the first country in Nazi-occupied Europe to be completely cleansed of Jews—a dubious fame it shared with Serbia.[56]

EXPROPRIATION OF JEWISH PROPERTY

Simultaneously with the destruction of the Estonian Jewish community, the Nazis and their indigenous collaborators attempted to seize property of the victims. They began with books. In August 1941 Tartu University assisted the German

Security Police in removing "Bolshevik" literature from circulation. President Edgar Kant, who was appointed to this position by Head of the OK Kurg on July 18, painstakingly counted the amount of gasoline that the university spent moving the books. By early November, the German Security Police began sorting the libraries previously confiscated from Jewish and Bolshevik owners. Kant suggested that the medical school staff pick up whatever books they might need for teaching and research purposes.[57] On December 9, Head of the Estonian civil administration Mäe signed the order that removed all banned literature, including that authored by Jews, from school libraries. It is worth noting, though, that not everybody obeyed the order; in Viljandi, librarians stored the books of the local Jewish community instead of turning them in.[58]

Judaica were objects of interest to two German agencies, the RSHA and the Operations Staff Rosenberg (Einsatzstab Reichsleiter Rosenberg or ERR). Frequently the two competed for the books from Jewish libraries. In Estonia, the bone of contention was the library that belonged to Jewish lawyer Dr. Julius Genss in Tartu. Known as an art collector and bibliophile, Genss had evacuated to Russia proper. By the time central Nazi agencies learned about the library, six thousand volumes listed in a catalog had already been distributed among various German and Estonian institutions. The Security Police in Tartu seized books on Judaica and Jewish art; their counterpart in Tallinn kept single editions of Russian and French classics; the Estonian Art Museum in Tallinn received some volumes as well. Through its representatives in Estonia, the ERR asked RSHA Department VII whether they could obtain copies of Soviet science and propaganda books, if available in multiple copies. The RSHA did not mind as long as they got to keep all the Judaica. KdS-Estland Sandberger suggested using local experts from the ERR to evaluate the holdings of the Genss library, but was rebuked by his superiors in the RSHA, who ordered the books to be sent to Berlin without allowing the Rosenberg men near them. The books were all packed and ready for delivery by the end of December 1941. However, because of an impasse between Himmler and ERR, the negotiations continued well into the spring of the following year. The trucks must have then taken the books to Berlin. In June 1942 the RSHA sent its own experts to Latvia and Estonia. As a result, Department VII obtained another eighty boxes of books and other materials in Estonia that had belonged to the Jewish community in Tartu and to several Jewish organizations in Tallinn. The former NKVD building in Riga was used as a temporary storage for some forty-five boxes containing the library and archives of the noted Russian-Jewish historian Simon Dubnov. The RSHA quickly made arrangements regarding the transfer of the scholar's collection.[59]

In the spring of the same year, Sandberger ordered the establishment of a new department within the Estonian Security Police. Based in Tartu, Department IVF was expected to do research on Bolshevism and Jews in Estonia, in cooperation with the Ministry of Education, the Central Archives, and the University Library. The new division could choose any books among those written by Communist and Jewish writers, which otherwise were singled out for destruction.[60] Around the same time, the Reich commissioner's office in Tallinn was putting together an art exhibition—"From Cranach to Gebhardt: Old Masters from Public and Private Collections"—to be opened at the History Museum on Kohtu Street. Some works on exhibit had previously been robbed from Jews.[61]

The Soviets authorities had seized Jewish businesses and real estate, so that the only property left for grabs was money, valuables, and household articles. In anticipation of their impending arrest, some Jews started selling their property. Ida Gelb, for example, managed to sell most of her belongings before she was arrested on September 24. The Estonian Security Police was interested in Jewish assets, and sometimes asked related questions of arrestees. Isaac Freidin said that he had not mixed with other members of the Jewish community and therefore did not know whether any of them had any valuables.[62] Sometimes the police initiated proceedings against individual Jews whose property they wanted to appropriate. Haim and Alexander Rubin happened to be rich, and that cost them their life. The circumstances of the Rubins's arrest resembled a cheap action-thriller.

Almost everyone in interwar Tallinn knew Alexander Rubin and his jewelry shop on fashionable Viru Street, probably the best in town. The people who, in September 1941, put on police uniforms knew him as well. Unsurprisingly, then, Alexander Rubin and his nephew Haim caught the attention of the Estonian Security Police. The police wanted to know where the two hid their property. Policeman Johan Parts named two people who were particularly interested in getting their hands on the Rubins's riches: Tallinn-Harju prefect Evald Mikson and Head of Department BIV Roland Lepik.[63] On September 25 the police interrogated Nikolai Rosenberg, who told the investigation the following. For the previous six years he had worked for the joint stock company J. Rubin. Shortly after the Red Army marched into Estonia, one of the shareholders, Haim Rubin, asked Rosenberg to bury a tin vessel in the latter's garage. Rosenberg obeyed but dug out the can, which was marked "no. 3," the following June. Nevertheless, he did not dare to open the can and instead put it back. A few days later, Rosenberg was mobilized into the Red Army, but managed to escape. When he checked again, the can was no longer there. Rosenberg threatened Alexander Rubin, another shareholder, that he would report the incident to the police, but Alexander bought his silence. Rosenberg assumed that the valuables must by then be in the possession of a particular individual with whom the Rubins seemed to be on friendly terms. The investigation records do not tell how much the police wanted the Rubins's diamonds and gold. Instead, Haim Rubin was labeled a Jewish person, who as a business owner had swindled his customers. That must be the reason why Rubin was put into the category of people "hostile to the German and the Estonian peoples."[64] Both Alexander and Haim Rubin appear on the list of Jews executed before October 6.

Ten days after the parents of fourteen-year-old Ruth Rubin were arrested, on September 25, the police came after her. Mikson, despite his high status, appeared personally at the scene. "I am going to shoot all of you if I do not find the diamonds!" shouted Mikson at everyone present. Ruth was pressured to reveal where her father kept his valuables. Eduard Paas, a police official at Tallinn-Nõmme prefecture, strictly followed the letter of the law when he began interrogating the fourteen-year-old. The girl told the policeman that for the last ten days she had stayed with a family friend—the only person she knew. Ruth swore that she did not participate in any Communist activities, did not personally know any Communists, and did not belong to Komsomol. On October 6, Ruth Rubin, together with four other Jewish women, was transferred to Harku concentration camp (on occasion designated a "ghetto"). Before sending Ruth Rubin to her death, Mikson allegedly raped the girl.[65] It seems to have been a routine case for Mikson, who regularly arrested Jews, occasionally beating them. It was not unusual for Mikson to check up to twenty-five Jewish homes and businesses a day.[66]

Generally, the dispossession of Estonian Jews was carried out on the basis of decrees that had earlier been implemented first in Lithuania and then in Latvia. Later in the fall of 1941 the police requested detailed lists of Jewish property, where exactly it was located, and how safely.[67] On September 11, *Postimees* published the announcement of the Tallinn commandant regarding the real estate of the Russians, Communists, and Jews who had left the country. Landlords or

"Aryan" neighbors were supposed to lock the respective houses and apartments and submit the keys to the commandant's office.[68] At least nine Jewish names appeared on the list of "Communist activists that fled" from Viljandi and whose property was confiscated.[69] The main concern was to prevent Jewish belongings and money from falling into the wrong hands. Hence, the former owners were prohibited from signing any property deals.[70]

The systematic inventory of Jewish property in Estonia did not begin in earnest until a year later. The process of expropriation involved several German agencies, most notoriously the civil administration, the Wehrmacht, and the Security Police, which all tried to get the biggest chunk for themselves. Estonian institutions and private citizens likewise took advantage of Jewish possessions. A conflict of interests was thus inevitable. In February 1942 the Estonian Self-Government requested that municipalities compile lists of all Jewish businesses that for one reason or another had avoided Soviet nationalization. In Põltsamaa, the only significant Jewish establishment was a department store that belonged to Elias Brisk. The business had been confiscated by the Soviet authorities and handed over to a local cooperative. Additionally, Elias and his brother possessed two pieces of farmland and agricultural tools, which at this point were deposited with the county administration.[71]

The property of the arrested Jews was temporarily deposited for safekeeping with their landlords. Personal effects either stayed in the apartment of the arrestee or were moved somewhere else in the house, usually to the basement.[72] In an attempt to preserve their property, some Jews signed beforehand an act of donation in favor of their non-Jewish friends, servants, or coworkers. The German civil administration annulled all contracts that involved a transfer of Jewish property to non-Jews after June 21, 1941. The Trusteeship (Treuhandverwaltung), which operated under the aegis of the Reich Commissioner's Office, obliged the military authorities to compile lists of Jewish property in their possession for the purpose of future redistribution. Effects had to be safely stored in designated places. In Tallinn, for example, the furniture that had belonged to Jews was taken to the Maakri Street synagogue, which was used for storage.[73]

Referring to the relevant orders from RKO Lohse and GK-Estland Litzmann, the Pärnu district commissar appealed to the population to submit any Jewish property, including real estate, personal belongings, valuables, and shares, that had been acquired after June 21, 1941. Noncompliance was to be punished with imprisonment and fines or—in severe cases of disobedience—with the death penalty.[74] Money and valuables were to go to the Reich Commissioner's Office in Tallinn, and gold coins forwarded directly to the Economic and Administrative Main Office in Berlin (Wirtschafts- und Vervaltungshauptamt).[75] When uncertain about the original ownership, the population was encouraged to declare the property nonetheless. Better one too many declarations than one too few, the Reich Commissioner's Office in Tallinn reasoned.[76]

All these decrees had little substance to them. Simply put, the German civil administration arrived too late to get their share of the loot. The military and the police had by then already picked up all the leftovers. Furniture formerly owned by Jews could be found in various offices and private apartments of police and military officers. When Trusteeship officials went to the Jews' apartments, they usually found empty rooms. Very little could be turned into money, to the disappointment of the main office in Riga.[77] For example: among the recipients of the Jewish property in the Narva district were the German Postal Service, the railway, and the gendarmerie, as well as the OK and private citizens. The biggest beneficiary, however, was the Wehrmacht, which for that matter refused to produce a list of Jewish property it had misappropriated. District Commissar Friedrich Jenetzky aspired to the image of an honest individual and reported a set of silverware, which he had used for representational purposes. Rakvere municipality distributed some Jewish possessions among the local population affected by war. The total monetary value of the Jewish property collected in the Narva district amounted to 9,000 RM.[78]

The German civil administration in Tartu encountered similar problems: the Security Police took over the property of executed Jews; the military appropriated everything else of value, furniture in particular. In the end, District Commissar Kurt Meenen accumulated approximately 10,000 RM from sold Jewish property, including but not limited to clothing, upholstery, peat, photo lab equipment, and watchmaker's tools. Not only individuals but also institutions acquired Jewish property. The Tartu University meteorological observatory, for example, paid 42 RM for a set of measuring instruments.[79] In Pechory, the property of two Jewish physicians such as medical books and tools was distributed between the local hospital and the Red Cross ambulance.[80] To get money flowing to its special "J" account, the Estonian Trusteeship Office settled for almost anything, including confiscation of property from Estonians who had been married to Jews. Thus a few items that Emma Tuch had brought into the family ended up in a storage facility on Sakala Street in Tartu.[81]

The German Security Police cemented friendly relations with its Estonian counterpart by magnanimously sharing with the latter whatever was left of Jewish property. In January 1944 KdS-Estland SS-Ostuf. Bernhard Baatz secured a few dozen leather gloves, mittens, suits, shoes, and curtains for his Estonian colleagues. These items, according to Baatz, should have boosted the enthusiasm for work *(Arbeitsfreudigkeit)* among Estonian police officials.[82] The robbing of Jewish property in Estonia even made it into the international news. The BBC German-language broadcast of June 26, 1943, accused top Nazi officials in occupied Estonia of personal enrichment. GK Litzmann was said to have illegally acquired property belonging to Estonian Jews. Whatever Litzmann got hold of, he sent back home to Germany. SSPF Möller was reportedly raising pigs for export at a farm he had seized. About Sandberger the radio said that he had confiscated General Laidoner's library, which he later shipped to the Reich.[83]

People who had acquired Jewish property in the summer and fall of 1941, by legal or illegal means, were reluctant to surrender it. To be able to keep what they thought lawfully belonged to them, some Estonians engaged in protracted correspondence with the civil and police authorities. Following an announcement by the local headquarters in Võru regarding a clearance sale of Jewish property, Rudolf Allikvee purchased a dresser drawer from Reiha Teitmann. In accordance with the established procedure, an Estonian police official verified the deal and received the money, 30 RM. The money thus collected was later transferred to the Security Police in Tartu. As far as Allikvee was concerned, he wanted the dresser drawer officially acknowledged as his property. Peeter Dorbek from Viljandi sought justice too. In July 1941 Dorbek bought a cupboard and a set of dishes to go along with it from a Jew. Dorbek was acting for purely selfish reasons: he purchased the cupboard for his daughter in Tallinn. Although officially Dorbek had received the abovementioned items for safekeeping, he treated them as his own. Dorbek was determined to fight till the last; his case was still under review in May 1944. That time around, Dorbek argued that he had to hand over the cupboard to his son-in-law, in the service of the German air force, whose entire property was lost during the Soviet bombing raid on Tallinn on March 9, 1944. Finally, Dorbek managed to get the cupboard to the countryside clandestinely—out of reach of the commander of the German Security Police in Viljandi, who wanted it for his office.

Gustav Kornel was not at all like the two individuals described above. He was educated. He was also a victim—a victim of war, that is. Dr. Kornel's apartment went up in flames as the Wehrmacht laid siege to Tartu. Dr. Kornel decided to start from scratch by making Nõmme his new home. Nõmme municipality acknowledged Dr. Kornel's sufferings at the hands of the Soviets by awarding him furniture formerly owned by a Jewish family. Very soon it also became common practice in Nõmme to distribute Jewish and Communist property among the war-affected people. Dr. Kornel pledged to handle the furniture with care and to follow regulations regarding its usage. The next thing Dr. Kornel knew, he was hired as an assistant professor at Tartu University. Because it was almost impossible to obtain household items in war-ravaged Tartu, Dr. Kornel took whatever he could with him, including furniture robbed from Jews. When asked to return the furniture, Dr. Kornel—as a law-abiding citizen—requested to buy it. It must have been a very good set of furniture, given that the Tartu University professor went all the way to GK-Estland Litzmann with his request. At least none of Dr. Kornel's relatives had died, as was the case with Helmi Ehajärv in Viljandi. Her husband, an anti-Soviet partisan, fell in combat and thus left the woman alone with a small daughter and stepmother to care for. On July 4, 1941, Ehajärv purchased a cupboard, four chairs, and a dining table from a local Jew, Jossel Blumberg, paying 150 Rbl. for everything. This was a real deal, because later these five items were estimated at 1,000 Rbl. The widow then wanted the purchase proclaimed legal so that she could keep the furniture, which was absolutely essential for her household, she said. Ehajärv once again evoked the memory of her fallen husband to save the movables. It was clear to her that she could not afford to buy furniture otherwise.[84] Sometimes Jewish property became the subject of blackmail. Thus, one of the tenants in the house owned by August Kapsi testified that the latter had misappropriated several pieces of furniture that belonged to Jewish renters.[85] In February 1943 alone, Estonian Security Police charged at least fifteen people with either hiding or trading Jewish property.[86]

The size of the Jewish community in Estonia and Latvia, and thus the amount of property it had owned, was not comparable. Naturally, then, Latvians benefited from stealing Jewish possessions more than did Estonians. When it came to acquiring utensils, bicycles, clothes, or even "stray chickens" that had formerly belonged to Jews, the city dwellers displayed a certain pragmatism. In one case, a Latvian sculptor asked whether he could buy gravestones from local Jewish cemeteries. Many of the Latvians who filed requests with the GK-Riga were poor (or so they claimed) and wanted to acquire things for free. As in Estonia, the petitioners often emphasized that they and their families were victims of the Soviet terror. Some Latvians made the case that they were entitled to Jewish property because they participated in the persecution of Jews. No such instances were recorded in the Estonian case. To generate revenues, the German civil administration sometimes auctioned Jewish property. In the fall of 1942 the very same authorities initiated a census of all Jewish property in private possession. To demonstrate that they were serious about it, at least two Latvians were executed for "robbing Jewish apartments"[87] and another Latvian woman sentenced to one year of labor.[88]

During the two months that the provisional Lithuanian government was in power, it took an active part in dispossessing Lithuanian Jews. The Lithuanian Academy of Science was entitled to get the books from Jewish libraries; the art museum was put in charge of art acquisitions; the Department of Culture was to receive musical instruments. Between October and December 1941, thousands of Lithuanians acquired Jewish property. As in Estonia, the most popular commodity was furniture, followed by bedcovers, clothes, and dishes. The price varied from a few pennies to hundreds of Reichsmarks. Those Lithuanians who received a share of Jewish property fell into the category of temporary owners. However, by the end of 1943 a majority of these people had paid in full for the right to keep indefinitely the things they liked.[89]

The synagogues in Estonia remained intact until the last months of occupation. Like elsewhere in occupied Eastern Europe, the Nazis used the largest buildings as POW camps. That was the original function of the Tallinn, Tartu, and Narva synagogues. At other times the synagogues were used as storage facilities. The synagogue on Maakri Street in Tallinn, for example, officially belonged to the headquarters of the Army Group North Rear Areas. That is where personal belongings of Leonhard Sammul (among others the Schröder piano) ended up in April 1942.[90] As of April 1943 the interior of the synagogue remained for the most part unchanged, except for a few broken benches and a missing chandelier.[91] The Tallinn synagogue was reduced to rubble by the massive Soviet air raid on March 9, 1944. The synagogue in Tartu was also damaged beyond repair.

THE GYPSIES

Jews were not the only victims of terror in Estonia. The Gypsies (Roma) often followed the Jews on the list of "undesirable elements." For lack of a comprehensive study of the *Parrajmos* (the Gypsy Holocaust) in the Baltics, I will summarize below the available data on the murder of the Gypsies in this part of occupied Europe.

In comparison with anti-Gypsy discrimination in the Weimar Republic, Gypsies lived in relative peace in Independent Estonia. Yet the Estonian criminal police kept a close eye on the Gypsies, employing means of surveillance similar to those in Germany. Haapsalu criminal police, for example, maintained a Gypsy database. The rest of the "albums" in the possession of the police listed criminals.[92] According to official statistics, as of December 1941 there were 743 Gypsies in Estonia; 399 of them lived in the cities and the rest in the countryside, mainly in southern provinces. Almost half of the Estonian Gypsies established themselves in Tartu Province, followed by Viru and Valga provinces.[93]

Unlike in Latvia, where the Einsatzgruppen and their auxiliaries immediately began executing the Gypsies, in Estonia the German Security Police took a rather wait-and-see attitude. Conflicting directives from central German agencies, which often discriminated between sedentary and itinerant Gypsies, prolonged the existence of the Gypsy community in Estonia. The head of the German Criminal Police in Estonia, SS-Ostuf. Heinrich Bergmann, who was in charge of the "Gypsy Question," eventually issued an execution order. Estonians' contribution to the decision-making process with regard to the Gypsies was negligible. The Gypsies were the only ethnosocial group in Estonia that did not have individual investigation files.[94] It was again the Wehrmacht that initiated the persecution of Gypsies in Estonia. On August 27, AOK 18 suggested to the Economic Commando Tallinn (Wirtschaftskommando or WiKo) to make all "loiterers" perform labor. Gypsies were to use their horses and wagons to help gather crops, if necessary under threat of punishment.[95] On order from General von Roques, on September 18 both sedentary and itinerant Gypsies were placed under police surveillance, with the purpose of forcing them to perform labor.[96] Viljandi prefect P. Kutsar, referring to a relevant order, instructed the police commissars to start arresting Gypsies and sending them to the Viljandi prison.[97] In reality, itinerant Gypsies were handed over to the German Security Police while sedentary Gypsies stayed under police surveillance.[98] Thus the local headquarters in Nõmme reported on October 26 that Jews and Gypsies were performing labor under close supervision.[99]

Even when arrested, work-fit Gypsies still had a chance to escape jail. For example, in November 1942 the German Security Police in Tartu contemplated the release of five Gypsies in its custody. These Gypsies had been arrested the previous May in Pechory Province. If not deemed liable for criminal or political offenses, these five Gypsies, as well as their relatives back home, were to be subjected to physical labor.[100] However, work provided only a temporary respite. In May and June 1942 Tallinn Central prison dispatched the Gypsy prisoners to the nearby Harku prison. All 243 imprisoned Gypsies, men and women, were murdered at Harku on October 27, 1942. The mass execution was carried out by the Estonian Security Police, most probably on an order from Bergmann.[101]

Gypsy teenagers had earlier been separated from their parents and dispatched to a children's colony in Laitse, southwest of Tallinn. According to a covering letter from the police, none of the sixty children had committed any crimes. They were locked up solely because of their ethnicity. The teenagers had spent about a year and a half in the colony when the Estonian Security Police claimed them. Sometime in late fall of 1943, two men with a bus arrived at Laitse. They claimed to have come to take the children to their parents. The request did not sound unusual, so the director of the colony arranged for each of the teenagers to receive a new school uniform. In accordance with the colony's regulations, the wards would be allowed to spend up to seven days at a time with their parents. However, they did not return after seven days; the bus took the teenagers to an execution site at Kalevi-Liiva (more about Kalevi-Liiva in chapter 9), about fifteen miles east of Tallinn.[102]

By the first week of February 1943, all Gypsies in Estonia, regardless of their status, were to be assembled in provincial centers for further transfer to Tallinn. The Security Police had just one concern—whether or not the arrested Gypsies could do physical work.[103] By the end of that month, more than five hundred Gypsies from all over Estonia had been herded into Tallinn Central prison.[104] Shortly thereafter, on three consecutive nights, close to two hundred Gypsy women with children were taken out of the prison. According to rumors, they were murdered.[105] The executions apparently took place at Kalevi-Liiva. There is evidence of at least forty Gypsies (twenty adults and twenty children) who were executed there in March. The murder was organized and carried out by Jägala camp commandant Alexander Laak. While Laak had no problems executing the adult Gypsies (with a single shot in the back of the head), he did not have the stomach for killing children, most of whom were between four and seven years of age. At this critical moment one of the camp guards, Jaan Viik, came to his superior's rescue, killing the children. As Viik later recalled, the children screamed, giving him creeps.[106] The remaining Estonian Gypsies—anywhere between 150 and 200 people—were transported in the summer of 1944 to Murru labor camp in Padise County (established as a prison in December 1941). Shortly after their arrival, the Gypsies were taken away and apparently executed.[107]

Unlike people in Germany or Austria, the local Estonian population had never appealed directly to the authorities to remove the Gypsies. Totally apolitical, Gypsies had nothing to do with the Soviet occupation and therefore escaped public attention. At the same time, no instances were recorded in which Estonians expressed their disapproval of deportations. Indeed, the February 1943 deportation of Gypsies was met with indifference bordering on public approval. The local police reported that the people were positive about the removal of "such elements."[108] Expectations of material gain, however minuscule, bred complicity. Village elders, for example, took over whatever animals Gypsies had left behind. Neighbors of Gypsies acquired household items, which they were entitled to use temporarily. The county administration received its share too.[109]

Most of Latvia's prewar Gypsy population of 3,839 were murdered.[110] The German Security Police proceeded immediately to execute Gypsies. Nearly all of 101 Gypsies from Liepāja were "evacuated" to Saldus, a city some forty-five miles to the east, where they were executed on December 5, 1941. A much larger execution took place in May 1942 near Bauska. Within several days, horse-driven carts transported between 200 and 250 Gypsies to one of the farmsteads in the area. A Latvian auxiliary police unit (Schutzmannschaft) guarded the perimeter.[111] About the same time, 173 Gypsies were shot in Ventspils, and another 19 in Aizpute. It is hard to say with certainty whether the Latvian contribution to the murder of Gypsies extended beyond guarding and convoying the condemned. One author argued that Latvian Rēzekne auxiliary police initiated the killing of Gypsies.[112] The question remains open, despite the revealing details about the execution that took place on January 6, 1942, in Ludza, a city east of Rēzekne. On that day, four or five Gypsy families (fifty people in total) were herded into trucks, taken to the nearby forest, and executed. Remarkably, until that very day Ludza Gypsies had been at large, allowed to stay in their homes. The local Gypsies apparently did not anticipate any trouble for themselves, but the surrounding population somehow sensed that the Gypsies were next to go after the Jews. The night before the execution, the Gypsies were locked up in the former "Jewish ghetto," recently emptied of its inhabitants. It must be around the same time (in any case shortly after the January 4 massacre at Audriņi) that twenty-five Gypsies from Zagorie village were murdered.[113] The execution took place in the Ančupāni Hills near Rēzekne and was carried out in all likelihood by the Latvians. In accordance with the order released on January 27, 1942, all but sedentary Gypsies in Latvia were to be imprisoned.[114] At least one Latvian was known to have saved Gypsies: Teodors Grīnbergs, archbishop of the Latvian Lutheran Church, intervened on behalf of the Gypsies as well as the Jews.[115]

One of the three Arājs commando units was dispatched in February 1942 to the Loknia-Nasva region, about thirty-five miles north of Velikie Luki. Although its priority was fighting Soviet partisans, the Latvian unit at times engaged in reprisals against civilians, including Gypsies. On one occasion, company leader Harijs Svīķeris ordered the execution of five Gypsy men, simply because they failed to provide personal information upon request.[116] It appears that the distinction between sedentary and itinerant Gypsies, as outlined in Lohse's decree of December 4, 1942, was not observed during these executions. Latvia was the only country in the Baltics where sterilization of the Gypsies was carried out. Thus the Liepāja police prefect reported that Lucia Strazdiņš was sterilized in a local hospital on January 9, 1942.[117]

Mass arrests and executions of Gypsies in Lithuania did not begin until summer 1942. A majority of Lithuania's 1,500 Gypsies were known as Polish Roma (which refers to their place of origin), held Lithuanian citizenship, and led a sedentary life. This may be the main reason why two-thirds of Lithuanian Gypsies survived the Nazi occupation. The German Security Police in Lithuania did carry out ad hoc executions of Gypsies, often citing a security threat as a pretext. Thus, following a partisan attack on a camp of the Organization Todt about thirty miles southeast of Vilnius, the local gendarmerie rounded up fifty Gypsies. Nine male Gypsies who managed to escape were allegedly the ones who fired the shots. On July 10, 1942, the gendarmerie commander ordered the execution of forty-one Gypsies in custody, including women and children. On November 18 of the same year, KdS-Litauen SS-Staf. Karl Jäger announced the order of HSSPF Jeckeln, according to which the itinerant Gypsies were to be treated like Jews. Deemed antisocial and politically unreliable, such Gypsies were to be locked in a family camp near Zapyškis where they were supposed to cut peat. Five days later, however, the restriction on mobility was somewhat softened, letting Gypsy property owners with steady employment stay free, if under continuous police surveillance. The arrested Gypsies as a rule ended up in Pravieniškės forced labor camp, where many of them were executed. According to survivors, the remaining Gypsies had been shipped to various sites in Germany and France where they were used as slave laborers.[118]

THE MENTALLY ILL

Shortly after coming to power in Germany, Nazis had enforced sterilization of the hereditary ill. A large-scale "euthanasia" program commenced in the winter of 1938–39 when the first mental patient, a physically deformed child, was killed. By the time the program was terminated in Germany proper in August 1941, anywhere between 70,000 and 93,000 mentally ill had lost their lives. The murder continued, however, in the occupied eastern territories.[119] The patterns of destruction of the mentally ill in the three Baltic countries were even more diverse than those of the Gypsies. Latvia and Lithuania were cleansed of mentally challenged individuals within the first eighteen months of Nazi occupation. In Estonia, however, mental institutions seem to have been left intact. Within the context of Nazi racial policy, that fact was truly unprecedented.

The killing of mentally ill people in Latvia began immediately. The murder was ordered, organized, and executed by the German Security Police with the help of the Latvian auxiliaries. On August 22, 1941, EK 2 in cooperation with the Latvian Self-Defense carried out the execution of 544 mentally ill people in Aglona, about twenty-five miles northeast of Daugavpils. The head of the institution, Dr. Bergs, sterilized the remaining ten patients, deemed "curable with defects." Within the following two weeks another 237 patients were murdered in Riga and Liepāja.[120] A particular individual associated with the extermination of the mentally ill in Latvia was Harry Marnitz. Himself a Baltic German, Marnitz was an expert on "racial issues," which he began implementing in various provincial cities in the spring of 1942. Using as a pretext the insufficient number of hospital beds available to the wounded Wehrmacht soldiers, in March Marnitz ordered "the removal" of some 500 patents from three mental institutions in Valmiera district. The Registry Office in Riga recorded data on 368 mentally ill people who "died" in that city in January 1942. Death owing to unidentified causes struck 243 mentally ill in April, and another 98 again in October.[121] Falsification of data belonged to the least grave offenses; Latvian personnel at the Riga psychiatric hospital were implicated in drawing lists of the wards and injecting sedatives before the patients' elimination. The staff lied to the relatives of the executed, denying any knowledge of what had happened to the wards.[122]

The notorious Arājs commando was involved in the murder of the mentally ill as well. The mentally ill were executed not far from Mežaparks, in the Biķernieki forest, one of the major killing grounds along with Rumbula. One such execution in June 1942 claimed the lives of 200 "imbeciles" from Riga. The Arājs men, on seven trucks, brought the patients to a pit where they assisted German policemen in the murder. All participants in the execution received their usual 17.5 ounces of spirits. In the Valmiera prison, a death squad executed the mentally ill, about sixty people in total, on two occasions in September and October 1942.[123] Altogether, the Arājs unit shot about 2,000 Gypsies and mentally ill people.[124] According to some estimates, a total of 2,232 mentally ill people were murdered in Latvia during the Nazi occupation.[125] In provincial hospitals, individuals suffering from a nervous disorder often shared the fate of the mentally ill; all those suffering from leprosy were likewise murdered.[126]

According to HSSPF Jeckeln, the murder campaign against the mentally ill had been completed in the Ostland by the fall of 1942.[127] The EG A consolidated report of January 31, 1942, provided the following numbers for mentally ill people executed in the Baltics: Lithuania—653; Latvia—693; Estonia—none.[128] To justify the murder of mental patients in Lithuania and northern Russia, the German Security Police presented them as a "security threat" (they had no guards, nurses, or food).[129] There is no documentary evidence regarding the murder of the mentally ill in Estonia such as we have for Latvia and Lithuania. According to official statistics from 1939, of the total of 3,358 mental patients registered in Estonia 1,184 were institutionalized at psychiatric hospitals. About one hundred patients of German origin had left Estonia in the course of the *Umsiedlung*. In December 1941, SSPF-Estland Möller received statistical data on mentally ill inmates in Estonian psychiatric hospitals. (To be more precise, the Estonian Ministry of Welfare calculated the number of occupied beds in the mental institutions.) Of 1,032 mentally ill in Estonia, 667 received treatment at Seewald in Tallinn; Jämejala in Viljandi had 240 patients; Pilguse in Saaremaa 48; and the university clinic at Tartu another 77.[130] There is no indication whether any further action was taken. In any event, statistics for Tallinn and its vicinity from the beginning of the occupation through August 1944 showed no executions of the mentally ill.[131] Indeed, it was forbidden to incarcerate the mentally ill.[132] Nor is there any evidence about sterilization and forced abortions in Nazi-occupied Estonia.

This does not tell the whole story, however. The mortality rates in Estonian psychiatric wards increased manyfold after the beginning of the German occupation. At Seewald hospital in Tallinn, for example, death rates among the patients in early 1942 were three times higher than they were in the spring of 1941. Thus, 67 out of 106 wards that had left the institution between January and March 1942 were proclaimed dead. During the same period a dramatic weight drop was registered for chronic male patients; most of the chronic patients at Tartu had died. As early as October 1941 Minister of Welfare Directorate Otto Leesment requested medical personnel to provide him with information on schizophrenics, "oligophrenics," epileptics, and maniacally depressed patients. The Estonian Self-Government encouraged hospitals to differentiate among the wards while the food rations were cut in half.[133] It is unlikely, though, that the practice of slow death was introduced locally. Although in August 1941 Hitler officially ended the "euthanasia" program, the mass murder of people with disabilities continued by other means. Asylum physicians subjected their patients to a starvation diet, meant to stamp out "useless eaters" and thus to save German taxpayers' money.[134] Despite the absence of written orders, there are reasons to believe that the policy of enforced starvation at Estonian psychiatric hospitals was deliberate. As the mental institutions closed one by one, the remaining wards were shifted from one hospital to another. Performing manual labor, agricultural work in particular, had ensured their survival.

The treatment that the mentally ill in Russia proper received from the Estonian members of Sonderkommando 1a was very different. Remarkably, the system of judicial inquiry that had previously been implemented in Estonia was now transplanted into Ingermanland where SK 1a operated in the fall and winter of 1941. On January 26, 1942, Hugo Raudsepp, a police official of Teilkommando-Ost, compiled the following summary in the case of Abutalip Abiasov. Twenty-year-old Abiasov was declared by the Soviets unfit for mobilization; he could not properly urinate and was mentally ill. And because Abiasov was a racial waste useless for the society, he had to be executed.[135] Several Jews among those murdered in Estonia were mentally ill. However, they were condemned to death because of their ethnicity rather than their psychiatric condition. Males and females, old and young, they were executed as Jews-Communists.[136]

Homosexuals in Estonia were by and large left in peace, probably because in Independent Estonia homosexual relations were only punishable if undertaken by force. As of the summer of 1942, no particular regulations with respect to homosexuals had yet been issued. However, the head of the German Criminal Police in Estonia, Bergmann, predicted that legislation with regard to homosexuals, similar to that in Germany, would soon be introduced in Estonia as well. Until then, he suggested starting to take homosexuals into preventive custody.[137] Following the introduction of labor education camps (*Arbeits- und Erziehungslager* or AEL) in Estonia in the summer of 1942, homosexuals, along with the work-shy, were listed as "asocials" who should be imprisoned for the benefit of society.[138] However limited, the discussion regarding the fate of homosexuals in Estonia is significant. Estonia might well be the only country in occupied Eastern Europe where the Nazis raised the issue of homosexuality. That fact implies that the Nazis might have been concerned with the purity of the Estonian nation, to the extent of playing with the idea of racial kinship.[139]

6 "JEWISH" FILES
TALLINN

The Estonian State Archives in Tallinn has a large collection of police investigation records. Among about four thousand case files slightly more than four hundred belong to Jews. Taking into account that the number of Jews who stayed in Estonia did not exceed one thousand, the available four hundred files comprise a fairly good sample. The investigation files contain attributes of a legitimate legal inquiry and include the following: warrants for arrest, protocols of interrogation, witness testimonies, decisions, and at times interoffice correspondence. Occasionally one finds warrants for search and search records, correspondence from relatives and rare intercessors, and in a few cases execution orders and death certificates. The case files vary in length between one and forty pages, with an average length of six pages. Usually, the only document in German in the case file is a summary of the decision. The bulk of the investigation files comes from the Tallinn-Harju police prefecture, in whose jurisdiction the majority of the Estonian Jews found themselves in August and September 1941.

The significance of the police investigation files is difficult to overestimate. The story of the Holocaust in Eastern Europe is usually told from the perspective of perpetrators or survivors. The very word *survivor* implies that the majority of those who were targeted perished. What is left of the millions of dead is often statistics—dates, figures, names—and sometimes not even that. There are few eyewitnesses apart from the perpetrators themselves who could tell how entire Jewish communities were turned into nameless victims. The Estonian Security Police investigation files may help us to convert abstract knowledge into a matter-of-fact narrative, to give mass death a human face. Some of the Jews who provided details about their arrest were executed the very next day. It is almost if dead men, women, and even children wanted us to know.

THE ARRESTS

It appears that in the beginning there was no uniform policy with regard to the Jews of Estonia. Sofia Isatchik, by way of example, was arrested on August 29 but released the same day. Local policemen made up their minds by 7:30 P.M., when Isatchik was brought back to the precinct.[1] The arrests were customarily carried out either by the Omakaitse (OK) or by the Estonian Security Police. The captors often had some sort of list of addresses. That was obviously the case with Jacob Epstein, a native of Tallinn, who on August 30 went to visit his siblings. Several members of the OK arrived and arrested Jacob and his brother David. Ephraim Olei was arrested on the same day under similar circumstances.[2] In Narva, the OK men went from house to house with a list of names—179 in total—prepared beforehand. On the margin, in handwriting, is indicated what happened to this or that particular Jew. While reading these notes, one can see that the majority of Narva Jews had fled from the city: "Has gone to the Soviet Union"; "not found in the house"; "tenants knew nothing"; "escaped with the whole family"; "empty room." Some of the older Jews, however, stayed: Olga Gorfinkel—"found"; Moses Hatzkelevich—"got him"; Fanny Usharov—"stayed here"; the Tsymbalov family—"janitor informed."[3] In Tallinn, the OK was looking for Rafael Goldmann. On October 15, an OK man made a sudden appearance at Goldmann's workplace. In a pocket of Goldmann's overalls he found a note indicating that its owner had evacuated to Russia proper.[4]

The names of the most noted Jewish Communists in Estonia were marked on a list that the RSHA had prepared before the invasion of the Soviet Union. More than a month before the decisive battle for Tallinn, the Gestapo compiled a list of individuals to be apprehended in the city. Seven people on the list were Jewish, including Leonid Aisenstadt and Victor Feigin, who were described as a "leading Estonian Jew" and a "Chief of NKVD in Tallinn" respectively.[5] All these individuals fled before the advancing German troops. Even later during the war, the Nazis and their Estonian collaborators did not give up hope of locating those individuals. Thus, in September 1942, the Estonian Security Police instructed its branch offices to start questioning ethnic Estonians arriving from Russia proper as to whether the latter had any information on certain Communists, former members of shock battalions, and Estonian Jews.[6]

Sometimes Jews were discovered accidentally, for example during routine police beats. At 2:00 P.M. on September 16, a constable of the 6th police precinct in Tallinn was checking on the tenants of a house at 5 Karja Street. In one of the apartments the police officer discovered Jossel Abramson, whom he brought to the precinct as "a Jew who was hostile to the present regime." Four days later, the same constable discovered yet another Jew, Gershon Herzenberg, who lived in a house on 12 Viru Street. While on duty, a constable of the 3rd police precinct spotted a passerby on Lembitu Street who looked Jewish to him. The constable asked the stranger, who went by the name of Meier Pevsner, to follow him.[7] Some people claimed to have seen posters calling on the population to report the location of Jews' apartments. One such flyer, for example, was seen in early September in downtown Tallinn, on the corner of Vabaduse Square and Harju Street. It remains unclear, though, which particular agency had distributed the posters.[8]

One of the most dramatic stories of arrest was that of Basse Majofis. One afternoon in mid-September, a woman in her fifties walked into the dining hall of a workshop in Tallinn. She inquired of a German SS officer about George Tsitovich, who was employed there as a locksmith and interpreter. When asked what she wanted and if she was Jewish, the woman attempted to leave. The officer ran after the woman and started interrogating her. First she denied her Jewish origin but then confessed: yes indeed, she was Jewish. Basse Majofis explained the nature of her request. Her younger son had been arrested by the Soviets in May; her older son and her husband were under arrest as well. She had learned that George Tsitovich and his father were released from jail and now wanted to ask him about the fate of her son. "Your son was executed," snubbed the officer and ordered the grief-stricken woman out. Basse Majofis was arrested in her home the next day. Remarkably, a few days before the arrest Basse Majofis sent a complaint to both local headquarters and the German Security Police about her confiscated property. She knew it was they—the officer that she encountered in the workshop and George Tsitovich—who had loaded her clothing and linens on a truck and drove away on September 4.[9] The Estonian Security Police knew well what happened to Basse Majofis's relatives. The arrest of Mordhe, her son, took place under most unusual circumstances. At 2:30 P.M. on August 31, a young man entered the 3rd police precinct in Tallinn and announced to the astounded constable that he was Jewish and therefore should be taken into police custody. The husband of Basse Majofis, Leib, apparently fell victim of a denunciation. Somebody told the police that Leib Majofis had been hiding in an apartment on 29 Lembitu Street. Next, constable Alexander Puppart decided to arrest Leib Majofis and dispatch him to Tallinn Central prison, where Mordhe Majofis had been incarcerated since September 1.[10]

Fifteen or so Jewish men fell into the hands of the Security Police because of particular circumstances. In a desperate attempt to get out, on August 21 and 22 the Soviets forced a large group of mobilized men onto a ship bound for Leningrad. However, a direct hit from a German bomber forced the ship, ironically called *Eestirand* (Estonian Coast), ashore. Upon disembarkation on Prangli Island, the recruits aboard the vessel were apprehended by the OK and taken back to Tallinn. Some of them, however, made it to Tallinn on their own. There they found themselves in an unfamiliar environment in a German-occupied city. Shapshe Permand, for example, could not think of anything better than rejoining a fire brigade. On September 9 Permand was arrested.[11] Among some 3,200 men on board *Eestirand* was Oskar Parvei; as an ethnic Estonian, Parvei was let go. To play down the fact of his mobilization into the Red Army, Parvei joined the Estonian Security Police in Nõmme, a wealthy suburb of Tallinn. In September and October 1941 Parvei personally arrested fifteen people, including a fifty-year-old Jewish woman—all of them on charges of Communism. The total number of Jews arrested in Nõmme during those two months was close to thirty.[12] Josef Izerovich was one of those arrested in that period. Izerovich was a pickpocket who was caught red-handed. Although the word *Jewish* was mentioned in his file, the investigation portrayed Izerovich first and foremost as a "habitual criminal." The execution order for Izerovich was carried out on October 5.[13]

As indicated, Estonian Jews had settled predominantly in the cities. Leo Klaus, however, had established his residence in a village near Paide. Klaus was serving as noncommissioned officer (NCO) at the commandant's office in Tallinn when the Communist uprising broke out in December 1924. The then twenty-one-year-old man was part of an execution squad that carried out death sentences. Three years later Klaus married a peasant woman and moved with her to Lehtse in central Estonia. There, Klaus earned a living as a butcher. In early October 1941 the Klaus family received an unexpected visitor, a local constable, who carefully catalogued all their belongings without specifying the purpose of that exercise. Approximately three weeks later the constable returned. Without a word, he counted the Klauses' belongings again, placed those belongings in a cupboard, and then sealed it. Only then did the constable announce that Klaus and his daughter were under arrest on the order of the Järvamaa District commandant. From Lehtse, the Klauses were sent first to Paide and then to Tallinn.[14]

Some Jews deliberately sought refuge in the countryside. Often it was a last-minute decision, as it was in the case of Koppel Koslovsky. He was able to flee thanks to the help of Estonians who had relatives and friends in the countryside. Before his appointment as the head of a department in the Ministry of State Control, Koslovsky used to work as a locksmith. During the last days of August he joined the workers' militia, which engaged the superior German forces on the outskirts of Tallinn. In the morning of August 31 Koslovsky came to the apartment of his girlfriend, Hilja Anderson, in Tallinn. He proposed leaving the city. The couple decided to bicycle south in the direction of Tori, where the woman's relatives lived. By the evening of September 1, Anderson and Koslovsky had reached Järvakandi County, just ten miles from their destination, only to be arrested as suspicious individuals by a vigilant OK patrol. The young man denied any affiliation with Communist organizations, but his girlfriend succumbed to the pressure, informing the interrogators that Koslovsky belonged to the Metal Workers trade union and held membership in the Komsomol.[15]

Two young Jewish women were saved by the action of their Gentile husbands. As soon as the German army entered Estonia, the Russian husband of Elena Iemelianova took her to the countryside. Iemelianova spent the next three years on an Estonian-owned farm near Keila-Joa. This refuge would have been impossible, however, unless her husband's friend at the Registry's Office had erased all references regarding her ethnicity from the relevant documents. Individual assistance and a bit of luck enabled Broche Rolaan to survive the war too. In the spring of 1941 Rolaan went on vacation to Lüganuse County, where her Estonian in-laws had a farm. The fact that only three elderly people lived in the village increased Rolaan's chances of survival. For the duration of the war she never left the house during the daytime. Even then, the story could have ended tragically. In August 1944, Bertram Neitsoff, a distant relative of the Rolaans who worked in the Kiviõli prefecture of the Estonian Security Police, notified Broche that somebody had betrayed her Jewish origin, but that he had destroyed the denunciation.[16] This is one of the few known cases of Estonians engaged in rescue efforts. The case of Uku Masing, professor of linguistics at Tartu University, and his wife, Eha, received greater publicity. The couple saved the life of Isidor Levin, who was one of Masing's students. Not only did they hide the young man, but also provided him with fake documents, thus preventing him from committing suicide.[17]

In the first three to five days following the seizure of Tallinn, the police force repeatedly referred to a Wehrmacht order that limited freedom of movement for male Jews. While processing the files of such individuals as Benjamin Patov, policemen sometimes added that, as a Jew, he constituted a threat to society and should therefore be isolated.[18] On September 14, military authorities reissued the Wehrmacht order, but now specified that *all* Jews must leave the coastal area within the next twenty-four hours. When it first came out, David Ginsburg and other affected Jews claimed that they were unaware of that regulation. This time, however, policemen went around telling the Jews to move beyond the ten-kilometer zone around Tallinn. Despite this order, Deborah Alperovich and Peter Abraham explained that they did not leave in time because they had heard that the deadline was extended. Other Jews, however, followed the order and left the city immediately.

Unfortunately, very few Jews knew people with whom they could stay in the countryside. The Aronovich-Jankel family—father, mother, and their two children—made their way to a farmstead in Tõdva County, where they stayed for a few weeks. Then the family moved to another farmstead, in Kiisalu, that belonged to Johannes Lepp. There the Aronovich-Jankels spent another two months, until they were finally arrested on December 8, 1941.[19] Altogether, some twenty people were arrested on the basis of the Wehrmacht order.

THE CHARGES

Warrants for arrest almost always contained the word *Jewish*. When it came to Jews, their ethnicity alone sufficed as a basis for arrest. However, only half of all judicial decisions bore reference to the ethnicity of the defendants. Jews were dispatched to jail as Communist sympathizers or, at the very least, as individuals subversive to the new regime. This incongruity between objectives and means is crucial to explaining the mindset of those who condemned the Jews to death. For such an explanation one need look no further than the protocols of interrogation and witness testimonies. What is striking about these criminal proceedings is that Germans were hardly mentioned. Upon reading the minutes of an interrogation, one gets the impression that Estonians and Jews were settling a dispute regarding Jews' allegiance to the Estonian State. Although all those later charged were indeed arrested as Jews, they had to prove they did not have malicious intent toward Estonians. Being part of the Soviet system was equivalent to pleading guilty. Therefore the investigators went to great lengths to establish the connection between Jews and the Soviet regime. The tragedy was that Jews did not know that they were doomed regardless, and therefore they made strenuous efforts to dissociate themselves from all things Communist, and sometimes even from those sharing their ethnoreligious affiliation.

Judging from the Jewish responses, investigators had devised a standard set of questions regarding alleged participation in Soviet organizations. By way of example, sixty-seven-year-old Jossel Abramson's response in September 1941 was nearly identical to thirty-two-year-old Bella Kletzky's response in April 1942:

> I did not participate in Communist propaganda, nor did I belong to any Bolshevik organizations. I did not denounce anybody; I did not participate in the deportation of Estonians to Russia. I was not a member of a shock battalion or workers' militia, nor was I an NKVD agent. Following the capture of Tallinn by German troops, I have not hidden any Communists; nor do I know anybody who did. I did not plan any acts of terror and/or sabotage. By the same token, Communists did not instruct me to carry out anti-German activities. I was not issued weapons, nor have I ever had one. I have nothing else to add.[20]

One other Communist suspect, Simon Rubinstein, was asked no questions at all. The eighty-four-year-old man was incapable of writing; indeed, he required medical assistance to be able to walk. That is what the police constable discovered when he came to arrest Rubinstein on September 19.[21] Even among the Jews under arrest, there were those who yielded to the Judeo-Bolshevik stereotype. Hannah Brin, a sixty-eight-year-old woman who earned her living by giving piano lessons, told the investigation that she did not approve of Communism, despite being Jewish herself. Esther Jakobson said exactly the same thing to her interrogator. Miron Brodsky stated that he had committed no wrong. Brodsky asserted pro-Estonian sentiments, despite being Jewish. Another arrestee, Isaac

Freidin, went so far as to confirm the belief in Russo-Jewish conspiracy that many Estonians held. Although he did not himself participate in deportations or arsons, Freidin said, he had heard that Russians and Jews were the ones to blame. Freidin was sentenced as a Communist anyway.[22]

Some Jews were rather naïve in their attempts to talk themselves out of the Soviet connection. Hain Herzfeldt, for instance, claimed that after the Soviet authorities had nationalized his business he deliberately refused to accept jobs, as a means of sabotage. Eli Haitin explained that his relatives had voluntarily left for Russia because they were afraid of small-arms fire. Jacob Bam argued, on the contrary, that he forbade his family to evacuate to Russia proper because he wanted to stay in Estonia. Bam failed to refute the original charge leveled against him: betrayal of the Estonian people. The only way for him to stay in Estonia, Rubin Racheltchik said, was to volunteer for the Red Army.[23]

There were many more cases in which alleged Jewish hostility toward the Estonians served as a basis for arrest. Against the name of Hirsh Ballak, for example, was written the following passage: "H. B. is Jewish, and because the people of Jewish origin are hostile to the Estonian people, he should be arrested too." Abram Abe Bass had allegedly committed a "crime of subversion" for he was engaged in "hostile activities with regard to the Estonian people." Markus Dubrovkin used to work as a musician in various places of dubious reputation. That was enough for the Security Police to accuse Dubrovkin of "betrayal of the Estonian people."[24] Jews contested their culpability by emphasizing the services they had rendered to the independent Estonian State. The fact that David Ginsburg was Jewish placed him automatically into the category of socially dangerous people. Ginsburg defended himself by saying that he did not deal with politics. Instead, he always had great esteem for the Estonian government and state laws. According to the protocol of interrogation, Moses Blechman did not and could not fight against the Germans as a member of the shock battalion—his old age saved Blechman from Soviet mobilization. The investigation established that he took part in the war of national liberation, had always respected the Estonian State, and back in 1918 had joined the Kaitseliit. Although Gershon Herzenberg was not a member of KL, he had regularly supported it financially. That fact alone, Herzenberg maintained, demonstrated his anti-Communist predisposition. Unable to comprehend what was going on, Elias Hoff suggested that the investigation team bring in witnesses, who would prove that he, Hoff, did voluntarily participate in the war of national liberation. Joseph Girskovits was arrested as a Jew who during the year of Soviet rule had displayed hostility toward the Estonian people. Girskovits contended that nobody had ever tried to enlist his support for the Communist cause. As further proof Girskovits mentioned a medal that he received as a Freedom War fighter. Gottfried Firk's case was even more eloquent as to his pro-Estonian stance. Not only did he fight on the Estonian side during the war of national liberation, but he also became a member of the radical right organization (the Vabs). In fact Firk was one of the first war veterans to do so, holding membership card no. 6. Schenny Katsev, a sixty-eight-year-old woman, had not been on the front, but she had carefully hidden the Estonian flag, which she then proudly put up as soon as the Soviet troops retreated.[25] Among the executed were at least fourteen Jews who had participated in the Estonian war of national liberation, 1918–20.

In several cases, the arrestees attempted to talk themselves out of suspicion by incriminating other Jews involved in Communist activities. Lazar Gershanovich mentioned the names of policeman Samuel Koslovsky, director of Estonian Silk Leo Epstein, and Epstein's brother, head of the NKVD maintenance department. Both parents of Harry Itskovich had been deported by the Soviets. Itskovich argued, as did several other Jews, that he was thrown out of the community because he wanted to marry an Estonian woman. He also claimed to have been anti-Communist. To give more weight to his words, Itskovich provided the police with the names of Jews who had served in shock battalions and the NKVD. During his interrogation, Moses Goldstein also revealed the names of two Jewish members of the Communist Party.[26] Gershanovich and Goldstein were both older men, whereas Valentine Klompus was only twenty-three when she got arrested. When Klompus told the Estonian Security Police that she knew only two Jewish Communists—Leonid Aisenstadt and the very same Epstein—she expected no rewards for herself. The next thing the courageous young woman told her examiner was, "as a Jew, I oppose Nazism and fascism for fascism promotes hatred against Jews."[27] This is the only known case of a Jewish prisoner, who was moreover a woman, daring to express her convictions directly to her captors.

It need not be qualified as betrayal when people placed in life-threatening situations chose to implicate other individuals as being involved in Communist activities. In the end, the names of Aisenstadt and Epstein, as well as their Communist affiliation, were widely known. Both individuals, along with other high-ranking Soviet officials, escaped to Russia and thus were out of reach of the Nazis and their Estonian collaborators. The Estonian Security Police failed to incriminate Jews not because it lacked evidence against them but simply because it had the wrong people in the dock. The search of the apartments of a soap factory owner, Bendet Glückmann, and a scholar, Julius Grünberg, revealed no political material.[28] In many cases the police were forced to modify the initial charges against the Jews for lack of incriminating evidence. For example, Salomon Epstein was arrested as a Jew who could be a potential threat to society if left at liberty. The investigation failed to establish Epstein's role in the Communist movement. Despite this, Epstein was imprisoned as a socially dangerous individual.[29] The efforts at forging the Judeo-Bolshevik connection could scarcely be more explicit than in the case of Anna Markushevich. Among the patients of a hospital in Narva was this twenty-year-old student from Leningrad. The woman had no documents and—in spite of what the Estonian police noted as her Jewish features—was listed as a Russian. The police officials insisted that Markushevich, a Jew, had allegedly encouraged other patients to celebrate the anniversary of the Bolshevik Revolution. No one else in the hospital was aware of this claim. Markushevich spent most of the day in bed sleeping, and had not had much interaction with the other patients. The hospital staff denied that any political manifestations had ever taken place in that particular ward, or in the hospital in general. Following her discharge from the hospital, Markushevich was thrown in jail, charged with subversive activities against the new regime.[30]

Among the hundreds of proceedings that the Estonian Security Police initiated against Jews, there were no more than four or five instances in which the "defendants" accepted, if not the charges themselves, then at least the fact of membership in any given Soviet organization. Even then, it was guilt by association. The atrocities, which popular opinion ascribed to Jews, were never mentioned in the investigation files. Hessel Aronovich, for example, was accused of serving in one of the notorious shock battalions. One of the witnesses, Juhan Elmest, testified that he saw Aronovich wearing a Soviet uniform and carrying a gun. Regardless of the precise outfit that Aronovich joined, whether a shock battalion or a workers' militia, the witness argued that Aronovich could not have gotten the uniform otherwise. At the same time, Elmest acknowledged that he did not know whether the defendant had participated in atrocities or not. Although Aronovich did confess to belonging to the 1st Tallinn workers' regiment, he argued that this affiliation was simply a means of evading general mobilization. The investigation protocol summarized the case as follows: "Aronovich voluntarily joined the workers' regiment, and he is an ethnic Jew." The twenty-two-year-old Hessel Aronovich was then charged with subversive activities and sent to Tallinn Central prison. Isaac Lopavok had also served in the workers' regiment. Unlike Aronovich, however, Lopavok had been forced to join the unit. Jacob Kolektor was another such individual whose arrest was based, at least in part, in reality. Since September 1940 Kolektor had been working as a policeman. Following the capture of Tallinn by German troops in August 1941, Kolektor hid for six days, until he was identified and arrested by the Nõmme OK on September 9. As in many other similar cases, the police had no evidence that the accused had ever abused his power. Engagement in armed struggle against the German army was the only official charge laid against Kolektor. Even if he did not mention his membership in a shock battalion, David Levin provided the investigation with enough information to condemn him as an inveterate Communist. Along with his direct responsibilities in the Kommunaar spinning factory in Tallinn, Levin had also performed guard duties (since mid-July). One of his assignments was to confiscate radios and weapons from the population. Levin and several of his colleagues ended up fighting regular German troops at Pärnu-Jaagupi in southern Estonia. As if that were not grave enough an offense, Levin was a member of Komsomol. Remarkably, Levin argued that he joined the ranks of the organization in order to get a better position at work. Rubin Rachelchik confessed that he was indeed an NKVD agent. According to Rachelchik, he had agreed to work for the NKVD under duress, and if he had ever denounced anybody, then only political commissars and Soviet military commanders. When unable to substantiate any political charges, the police attempted to pin criminal acts on Jews. Physician Aron Krenchinsky and his wife, Rosa, were accused of having broken into a drug store in Aegviidu. To recover the stolen goods, the Nõmme police conducted a search of the couple's apartment. Unsurprisingly, the search yielded no results.[31]

Among the people who had promoted the Soviet cause in Estonia there were only a handful of Jews. As follows from the previous paragraph, only small fry remained in Estonia. Most Jews, including those few who had reasons to fear for their life, had left for Russia in good time. Arkadii Lury put it plainly during his interrogation: "If I had anything against the current regime, I would have left."[32] In spite of the common knowledge about the low numbers of Jewish collaborators with the Soviet regime, the Estonian Security Police claimed the opposite. For example, the Security Police Office in Narva provided the following statistics regarding Communist activists in that city: Out of 3,424 people suspected of Communist activities, 55 were Jews (38 men and 17 women), that is, 1.6 percent of the total. It is a huge figure, considering that the entire Jewish population of Narva on the eve of World War II was only 173. At the same time, the Security Police reported thirty-two executions of Jews in Narva between August 1941 and July 1942.[33] One could thus surmise that *all* of the executed Jews were Communists.

At the bottom of all accusations was the belief that the Jews had placed themselves in opposition to the Estonian State and the Estonian people. In short, Jews had betrayed Estonia! If that was impossible to prove, Jews were branded subversive to the new regime. If that charge could not be substantiated either, Jewish origin automatically became a criminal offense. Otherwise, the Estonian Security Police had to eventually release people like Elias Elian. Following the promulgation of the order prescribing the arrest of all male Jews, Elian surrendered himself on September 15 to the police in Tallinn. Elian tried to convince the constable of the 4th police precinct that, owing to his old age he would not have been able to join any of the Communist organizations even if he had wanted to. And yet the decision read: Elian admitted he was Jewish, which made him a threat to the new regime.[34] Remarkably, the police investigation files bare no traces of racial ideology. Ephraim Olei was the only individual who was dispatched to prison as "non-Aryan, Jewish."[35]

LETTERS OF SUPPORT AND DENUNCIATIONS

Ironically, Estonians only got to know Jews during the year of Soviet occupation. Until then, encounters between the two communities were for the most part limited to business transactions: Estonian customers shopped in Jewish-owned stores, let Jewish tailors repair their garments, or at best went to see a Jewish dentist. Jews fit neatly within the stereotypes, which neither side cared to revise. That situation changed abruptly in the summer of 1940. Scholars who have written about the Jewish experience under Soviet rule have noted the increased visibility of Jews in positions of authority. Those Jews whose social status had changed for the worse, however, went unnoticed. With their businesses expropriated by the state, many Jews entered the general workforce for the first time. The most wide-spread but also least demanding type of organization at that time was the work-ers' cooperative, the so-called *artel*. It was in this forum that Jewish artisans, who until recently had had their own workshops, mingled with other laborers.

All but one petition submitted to the Estonian Security Police on behalf of the arrested Jews originated from their fellow workers. The colleagues of Abe Bass, Estonians and Russians alike, pleaded with the police authorities to allow him to return to their cooperative. If nothing else was possible—eleven cowork-ers of the Flora cooperative appealed to the Tallinn police prefect—perhaps Bass could resume his duties on parole. The undersigned said they were ready to take full responsibility. All records indicate that the petitioners were sincere in their desire to help out their coworker. The letters of support had been drafted within the first few days following his arrest. Practical considerations were mentioned only in passing, if at all. Abe Bass was said to have helped to raise the productiv-ity of the artel. Four men of the Lagermetall cooperative claimed that Mikhail Sheer was an indispensable specialist without whom they could not proceed. The artisans advanced three arguments in support of the detainee: he was through and through anti-Communist; he had helped Estonians evade Soviet repression; he had nothing to do with the rest of the Jews. Eighteen people signed the peti-tion on behalf of Salomon Epstein, a worker in their sewing cooperative. They knew that Epstein was arrested because of his ethnicity. Although he was Jew-ish, they wrote, Epstein was a loyal citizen. Furthermore, while Epstein hated Jews, he maintained good relations with the members of the cooperative—all of them Estonians. According to the petitioners, Epstein posed as an ardent anti-Communist who had impatiently waited for the Germans to arrive. Somewhat naïvely, Epstein's coworkers explained that he did not get along with the local Jews after having married a German woman. When the Soviets took over, those very Jews allegedly refused to take Epstein into their cooperative. Flora workers tried to convince the authorities that Bass had many friends in Germany, even within the Nazi Party. Bass refused to evacuate to Russia proper even though he knew that Jews were treated as "undesirable elements" in Germany. During the Bolshevik terror, Bass had helped Estonians by all means possible. Sheer had conducted himself similarly, arranging for the members of the Lagermetall to be relieved from the obligatory defense works in the summer of 1941. Further-more, he helped two of them evade mobilization. Fifteen architects, engineers, and craftsmen appealed on behalf of Abram Iliashev before the Security Police in Tallinn. Iliashev was always ready to help his fellow citizens. In particular, Iliashev was said to have hidden non-Jews from Soviet deportation. Apparently, there was nothing to illustrate the anti-Communist agenda of sixty-eight-year-old Iliashev, so his colleagues went on to say that he stayed away from politics altogether. The absolute record of petition cosigners was twenty-five—that is how many people appealed on behalf of Härmo Pant. They described Pant as an honest and accommodating person who had no Communist connections whatsoever.[36] In one case, a group of Tartu University scholars petitioned on behalf of Samuel Zlaff, assistant to renowned Estonian professor Ludvig Puusepp.[37]

However few the petitions on behalf of the Jews, the number of letters denouncing them was not significantly greater. In some cases, denunciation was implied. Several police reports began as follows: "In accordance with information received" or "it turned out that . . . " (However, it does not rule out a possibility that informants came from within the police and/or the OK.) The following report was filed on September 14 in Nõmme near Tallinn. A policeman notified his superiors that he had received information about a male Jew living on 38 Kadaka Boulevard. Once he got there, he indeed discovered someone called Israel Baskin. Baskin's ID revealed his Jewish origin ("ethnicity" was one of the entries in Estonian identification documents). Salomon Epstein believed that he knew by sight the OK man who arrested him. On the grounds that all Jews must be isolated, on September 2 a member of the OK brought Epstein from the latter's workplace at the Dvigatel plant.[38]

It was something other than moral inhibitions or fear of revenge that motivated the individuals who decided to stay anonymous in making their denunciations. If they so chose, the authorities could easily have established the identity of the unnamed informants. On October 11, 1941, one of the OK offices in Tallinn received an anonymous letter that read, "I'm drawing your attention to the fact that, on 122 Pärnu Ave., lives the Salome family (Polish Jews). They are extremely hostile to Germans and can become dangerous." The letter was forwarded first to a local police commissar and then to the head of the Estonian Security Police. Apparently the police had already received instructions with regard to denunciations; a handwritten note in the margins urged them to investigate and proceed in accordance with the guidelines.[39] Anna Kalmanson could have survived the war had it not been for a neighbor's denunciation. By March 1942, there were only a few Jews left in Estonia. The "Jewish Question" was not any longer on the agenda of the police force, which had more pressing tasks to perform. The postcard that the police constable of the Tallinn 6th precinct received on March 27 was obviously written by somebody from the lower social order. An anonymous addressee who signed only his or her initials, "J. K.," informed the police that Edla Linneberg had been hiding a Jew in her apartment. Written chaotically, in grammatically incorrect Estonian, the account betrayed the selfish interests of the author. Without a single comma, the anonymous author painstakingly listed all pieces of furniture and household items belonging to Kalmanson (who was mentally challenged) that Linneberg had allegedly appropriated. The informer ended her letter by saying that drinking orgies in Linneberg's apartment disrupted peace in the house. In all probability the author of the letter was Alma Helene Kolle, the landlady, whom the police questioned shortly after they received the denunciation.[40]

This and other similar cases call for a modification of the generic term "neighbors." Neighbors, or anyone else who knew Jews under arrest, were routinely summoned to the Security Police to testify. Some testimonies were positive, some negative. It was the landlords, however, who steadfastly denounced Jews living on their premises. Estonian Security Police encouraged the flow of denunciations by ordering landlords to compile lists of tenants for presentation in the police precincts.[41] Apparently some homeowners reported the Jews just to be on the safe side. As regards personal motives for making denunciations, greed overruled all other motives. Hatred is a strong emotion that galvanizes immediate action. Why, for instance, wait seven months before exposing a Jewish woman who had not even tried to hide? That is, however, exactly what "J. K." did with respect to Anna Kalmanson.

The services sector tended to generate more denunciations than any other occupation. While male artisans sometimes exhibited solidarity with their fellow Jewish workers, women in menial professions every so often evoked the ghost of Communism to get rid of their Jewish colleagues. Daisy Jaanimägi, an accountant in one of the state-owned stores in Tallinn, accused Ginda Rosenberg of subversive views. Jaanimägi informed the Estonian Security Police at Tallinn-Nõmme that she found the employment of a Jew as a cashier, that is, in a senior position, to be objectionable. State property should be protected against the Jews, who are discontent with our state order, she wrote. Another accountant in yet another Tallinn store blatantly accused Sonia Gasman of being a Communist. The denunciation led to the latter's arrest on August 29, 1941.[42] Almost all denunciations were authored by women, a persistent trend in Nazi-occupied Europe.[43] Salme Teder was one of those women reporting on Jews. Within days after the German army seized Tallinn, Teder notified the Estonian police of the whereabouts of Hanna Kronik. She insisted that Kronik, a Jew, stayed in contact with a member of a shock battalion.[44] There is no indication as to what motivated Gentile women to inform on Jewish women. I would suggest settling personal scores as one of the primary motives. However, anti-Communism might have played a role as well.

The practice of denunciation in Estonia displays both similarities and dissimilarities with the general trends that historians have observed elsewhere in Europe, including Nazi Germany. Only a nominal proportion of "Jewish" case files in Estonia can be traced back to a denunciation—5 percent versus 70 percent in Germany. The relatively low number of denunciations aiming specifically at Jews can be explained by two factors. Those Estonian Jews who stayed behind made a conscious choice and therefore did not intend to hide. With few exceptions, Jews could be easily located without help from the general population. A high level of organization in the Estonian Security Police and the OK enabled them to proceed instantaneously with the arrests of the Jews. The proficiency and dedication of individual members of these two agencies left little need for popular input in the apprehension of Jews. In contrast to the Gestapo in Germany, the Estonian police were active rather than reactive.[45] Furthermore, the German Security Police in Estonia was not keen on initiating proceedings based on denunciation alone. On January 10, 1942, Sandberger instructed his Estonian counterpart, Ain-Ervin Mere, to ensure that the arrests were carried out on the basis of solid evidence and not mere denunciation. Sandberger advised Mere to start prosecuting denouncers themselves.[46] Mere, however, argued that the police force under his command was totally transparent. Mere assured Sandberger that the private information that the police were gathering had been acquired by legal means, with the help of volunteer informers who came from all walks of life. Mere emphasized that the Estonian Security Police was defending the interests of the Estonian people.[47]

The rather limited number of denunciations of Jews may create a false impression about the extent of informing in general. The police were dismayed by the extent of mutual recrimination in Sonda in Virumaa Province. Most denunciations had no substance whatsoever, to the point that a special investigation commission set up for that purpose refused to consider them altogether. Even at that stage the documentation had exceeded all reasonable limits. Local police constables referred to the phenomenon as "denunciation fever" (kaebamistõbe). Usually, bigmouths among the local population appealed in writing, accusing one individual or another of all possible sins—in the first place of Bolshevism—and requesting their immediate arrest. In most cases, petitioners either referred to somebody else as their source of information or hid behind the indefinite "I have heard that . . . " Among the main causes of denunciation were unsettled court cases or protracted animosity, yet the first and foremost source of ill feeling was anti-Communism. Not infrequently, a certain fellow citizen was accused of partaking in robberies and murder allegedly perpetrated by the Russians. The investigation showed, however, that the suspected "monster" had himself been deported to Russia proper. The paradox was that the police—themselves at the forefront of the anti-Communist campaign in Estonia—objected to the arrests based on denunciations, thus breeding the rumor that the police were deliberately letting Bolsheviks go. The traditional perception of a healthy peasant society made the police conclude that informing was more widespread in urban, industrial centers.[48]

From a contemporary perspective, it is hard to imagine the extent and ferocity of the denunciatory practices in Nazi-occupied Estonia. Allegations of Communism at times pitched one family member against another. Anna Lind denounced her daughter-in-law as a Communist sympathizer. Following the arrest of his wife, the son verbally assaulted the mother. In response, Lind denounced him as well to the Estonian Security Police. According to Lind, her son had cursed Germans and threatened that Communists were soon to return.[49] Indeed, denunciations reached such alarming proportions that even officials at the highest level of administration acknowledged the problem. Estonian radio, on January 24, 1942, appealed to the population to stop reporting each other. Denunciations were deemed provocations whose objective was to cause trouble and unrest. The listeners were told that no citizen should report on another without a valid reason. The announcer named revenge and opportunism as the prime motives for informing. Next, however, he revealed that Estonians frequently reported on their fellow citizens—alleging support of Communist ideas—with the intention of diverting attention from themselves. In that respect, Nazi ideals were diametrically opposed to those of Communism, a program called "A Few Words to the People" concluded.[50]

WITNESS TESTIMONIES

Letters of support and denunciations mark the extreme poles of popular opinion with respect to Jews. Individual testimonies provide a more accurate overview of what ordinary Estonians thought of Jews. Unlike petitioners and informers, people who came to testify did so involuntarily and therefore had no personal stake in the outcome of the investigation. Estonian Security Police picked up random individuals who could provide information about Jews under arrest. Sometime it was the defendants who drew up a list of witnesses who could potentially testify on their behalf. Otherwise, the police questioned neighbors, landlords, colleagues, all those who knew the arrestee in question. Most, if not all, Jews were innocent and therefore steadfastly denied any wrongdoings on their part. Many of them did indeed believe that justice would prevail and that they would eventually be cleared on all charges. None of the arrested Jews anticipated his or her fate. It would be unrealistic then to expect that the Estonians who were summoned by the police to testify would know what was going to happen next to the Jews. Some of the witnesses chose their words carefully when they spoke about the Jews, while others did not. No matter what they said, the witnesses did not know that the prisoners' fate was already sealed. For the very same reason, the investigation saw no need to apply pressure to extract politically correct testimonies from the witnesses. All constituent parties of the investigation—the accused, the witnesses, and the accusers—sought justice. Their ideas of justice, however, differed significantly.

Some people made assumptions about the political affiliation of a particular Jew based on the personal traits of the latter. Marie Laande confessed that she would not be able to testify about the political outlook of Hessel Aronovich, simply because the latter had never talked about politics. Yet Laande believed that Aronovich did not support the Soviet Union. Otherwise, Aronovich appeared to the witness a decent individual. Hirsh Ballak, who since April 1941 had been working in a chemistry laboratory, appealed to the investigation team to call several witnesses who could supposedly corroborate his anti-Communist stance.

Ballak hastened to add that because his coreligionists stayed away from him, he had mixed mainly with Estonians. Alexander Villemsoo did not betray his Jewish associate's expectations, saying that Ballak did not approve of Communism, both before and during the Soviet occupation. As a reserved and slightly suspicious individual, Ballak did not deal with politics and at times used harsh language to describe Communists' conduct in Estonia.[51]

Other witnesses openly sympathized with the arrested Jews by extolling their human qualities and emphasizing their services in behalf of the Estonian people. Benjamin Nieländer said that, as a physician, Josell Abramson had performed his duties in an exemplary manner. It was commonly said, Nieländer continued, that Abramson had helped to exempt several Estonian men from mobilization by issuing them medical certificates. Abramson did not share Communist ideas, nor was he hostile to the Estonian people. Abram Saltsmann earned a similar description from Joosep Partes and Juuli Utto. A decent and quiet individual, Saltsmann had been working long hours at a paper mill. Saltsmann's neighbors confirmed that he did not get into politics, let alone have an affiliation with the Communist Party. In fact, Saltsmann was illiterate. Boris Niinemets owed his freedom to Leib Lipeles, and he did not forget it. Lipeles was aware of Niinemets's membership in the KL and yet took him into the cooperative. Later on, Lipeles warned Niinemets about the impending arrest, provided him with money, and made other necessary arrangements that guaranteed his safety. At one point Lipeles told Niinemets that he would rather go to a Nazi concentration camp than to Russia. Lipeles obviously did not have a clear idea about Germany, but had visited Russia as a tourist.[52]

The well-wishers among the witnesses tried to be helpful by dissociating a particular Jew they knew from the rest of the Jewry. That argument had as little effect on the Estonian Security Police as any other. The last time Maksim Kagan, a professional chemist, visited a synagogue was in 1910. Kagan had converted to Protestantism and had even purchased a burial ground in the biggest Estonian-Lutheran cemetery in Tallinn. Kagan got two well-known individuals to testify on his behalf. Bernhard Rostfeldt had known Kagan since 1921, when he was minister of agriculture of Independent Estonia. Villem Sepp also claimed twenty years of Kagan's acquaintance. Both men said in one voice that Kagan had communicated widely with all ethnic groups—Estonians, Germans, Russians—except Jews. In the absence of any incriminating evidence at all,

Kagan was charged with participation in subversive activities. In addition to twenty-five people who signed a petition on his behalf, Härmo Pant received support from two other men. A retired officer, Alexander Reinfeld, had known the accused since he was a child. According to Reinfeld, Pant had never participated in Communist activities of any sort, kept his distance from the local Jews, and last but not least was married to an Estonian woman. Jüri Pinding said that Pant belonged to a group of pro-Estonian Jews. Furthermore, he did not look Jewish. In the case of Gottfried Firk, witnesses seem to have come to an understanding before their testimony. Indeed, the testimonies of Arnold Friedrich Ernesaks, Nikolai Vaher, Vello Kasenurm, and Mart Margiste sounded suspiciously similar when praising Firk as a loyal citizen of Estonia. Appointed as the head of Soiuzutil (scrap collection), Firk had allegedly refused to fill positions with his fellow Jews, favoring Estonians instead. Firk claimed that Jews occupied 90 percent of all top positions in the Soviet Union, and therefore he wanted an Estonian as his deputy. According to all four witnesses, Firk had demonstrated the greatest reverence toward Estonia and Estonians, an attitude that had placed him in opposition to the rest of the Estonian Jews. A similar theme was present in the testimonies of Alexander Siimon and Eduard Ristmees on behalf of Gershon Herzenberg. Siimon thought highly of Herzenberg, arguing that the latter had behaved differently than the rest of the Jews, who had sought nothing but profit. Ristmees agreed that Herzenberg, unlike other Jews, was not hostile toward the Estonian people.[53]

Another way of presenting a particular Jew in a favorable light was to say that he or she had suffered under the Communist regime. Raul Simson began his testimony by saying that he had known Harry Itskovich for three years, but had mainly communicated with him in 1940. Simson portrayed Itskovich as an opponent of Communism whose parents had been deported and whose property had been confiscated. Simson conveyed his belief that Itskovich had not participated in any kind of anti-Estonian activities. Arnold Michelson used similar words to defend Salomon Epstein, who he said was an adversary of the Communist government. Epstein had lost his son to the Soviet deportation and had had his shop nationalized. Oskar Mõlts used to buy leather goods from Rachmiel Shadsunsky's workshop. The next time he met Shadsunsky, the former was working in a warehouse of the Unioon tannery. Mõlts had the following to say about Shadsunsky:

It seemed that he did not approve of the Soviet regime. Shadsunsky once told me that if he wanted to get rich, he could have gotten a better position for himself. That makes me think that he did not belong to the Communist Party. Shadsunsky told me that he did not want to go to Russia because he thought that the Germans would not do any harm to such a poor Jew as himself.[54]

The Estonians who testified against Jews sometimes placed their allegations into the context of the Russo-German war. Ella Brodsky, as a Jew, was accused of calling Germans "robbers" whom the Russians would soon dislodge from Estonia. The charges were based solely on the testimony of Helmi Jõõras. Brodsky dismissed the allegations as a lie. Her entire family stood opposed to Communism, Brodsky said. The woman swore that she had never said anything to anybody about the Germans. Nothing of what Ella Brodsky had said did in fact matter; she was sentenced as Jew-Communist.[55] A number of testimonies displayed xenophobia and prejudice. Olev Arens argued that all members of the Jewish fraternity Limuvia, including Eduard Eitelberg, were agents of the NKVD. At the same time, the witness acknowledged that he did not know Eitelberg by sight. He just thought Eitelberg was suspiciously active in the wake of the German attack on the Soviet Union. The same investigation file contains two testimonies in support of Eitelberg. Neither Elmar Velner nor Ervin Mägi noticed anything that would have betrayed Communist affiliations of their Jewish colleague. The very fact that Eitelberg was continually present at his workplace made his participation in a shock battalion or workers' militia unlikely.[56] Only a small fraction of the witness testimonies contained the traditional Judeo-Bolshevik discourse. From the perspective of those witnesses, Jewish visibility was a sufficient proof of Jews' pro-Communist stance. Marie Tiitsmaa was one of those who saw a logical nexus between the two. Since 1939, Abram Sachar-Schocher had been renting an apartment in the house where Tiitsmaa lived. Sachar-Schocher ran a dry-cleaning shop until the Soviets made him director of a store that sold car parts. According to Tiitsmaa, she realized right away Sachar-Schocher was a Communist sympathizer. He had always boasted of his high position, and he was Jewish. This one testimony was enough to send Sachar-Schocher to jail.[57]

In some testimonies, elements of Judeo-Bolshevism were interspersed with selfish motives—first and foremost greed. Of the hundreds of Jews who had been arrested in 1941, Rachelle Hanin was the only one charged with serving in the

NKVD. Born in Estonia, Hanin had spent ten years in Paris. Hanin was visiting her parents in Estonia when the war broke out. Unable to return to France, she moved into the house on 23 Viljandi Street in Tallinn that belonged to thirty-one-year-old Johannes Laugsoo. In the wake of the Soviet occupation, the NKVD arrested three of the tenants, two officers and a lawyer. At that time Hanin was dating a Jewish man called Elias Veinberg, who eventually moved into her apartment. According to Laugsoo, one day in July 1941 the following conversation took place between Veinberg and himself. Veinberg told the landlord that the garden attached to the house would soon belong to Hanin and himself. Upon being asked why that would be so, Veinberg allegedly answered that as NKVD employees they had priority. The investigators announced the charges against Rachelle Hanin without revealing their source. But Hanin immediately identified the personality of the accuser: Laugsoo had slandered her because he was greedy! As a landlord, Laugsoo had the keys to Hanin's apartment. According to the arrestee, the homeowner appropriated some of her belongings while she was away. When Hanin requested her property back, Laugsoo libeled her as an NKVD agent in order to get rid of her. To prove her innocence, Hanin suggested questioning two other individuals—Gershon Herzenberg and Josef Hirschhorn (both of whom were later arrested). Instead, the police summoned one of Hanin's neighbors, Ekaterina Käär, to testify. Käär ensured Hanin's execution. As it turned out, she had been closely watching every step of her Jewish neighbor's. Käär confirmed that Veinberg had frequented Hanin's apartment. Furthermore, she had seen him together with NKVD men. The witness proved her powers of observation when she told the police that, once in August, an NKVD car stopped in front of the house where Hanin and Veinberg lived. Another fifteen minutes had passed before they all drove away in the direction of downtown Tallinn. Käär noticed that the NKVD men treated the couple with respect, a sign that they were on friendly terms. About one hour later, the very same car brought Hanin and Veinberg back. Käär also knew that the deputy head of Tallinn Central prison, a Soviet Russian, was lodged in one of the rooms of Hanin's apartment. The witness chose to be precise even with respect to minor details: she did not know whether any Estonians had suffered as a result of Hanin and Veinberg's activities. Rachelle Hanin was sentenced on two counts—being Jewish and working for the NKVD.[58]

Decision forms bore one of two standard imprints—"Communist suspect" or "accused of subversive activities"—that served as the underlying guidelines of the Estonian Security Police. Only infrequently did a police officer strike out the official accusation and write "Jewish" above it. Estonians went first and foremost after Communists, real or imaginary. By doing so, they further contributed to the ideological discourse that had dominated the Estonian political landscape since the early 1920s. Raul Hilberg expressed a similar opinion as an expert witness in one of the denaturalization trials held in the United States in 1981. At present, I want to focus on the first part of Hilberg's conclusion, according to which Estonians had demonstrated high ideological commitment while apprehending Communists, but had largely followed German orders when it came to Jews.[59] The investigation file of Miriam Lepp illustrates that point most clearly. Everything was unusual about this case—the length, the dates, even the agency that instituted the proceedings.

On January 28, 1942, the head of Department BIV of the German Security Police sent a request to the Tallinn-Harju prefecture regarding one Miriam Lepp. Forty-five-year-old Miriam Lepp, Jewish, was married to a high-ranking Estonian police official, with whom she lived at Kurtna Manor in Harjumaa Province. It took the Estonian Security Police half a year to process the case. The contents of the thirty-four-page file explain this delay. First on the list of witnesses was Hans Vahtramäe, who told the police that the wife of Konstantin Lepp was a "person totally belonging to the Jewish faith." Referring to somebody he knew, the witness argued that Lepp, who claimed high-ranking patrons, had been spreading provocative rumors. It would be wise to eliminate Miriam Lepp, he said, for she did not know how to run the farmstead. The latter statement might even have been true, because after her husband was arrested by the Soviet authorities in September 1941, Miriam Lepp had to take over the household. The brother of Konstantin Lepp found it suspicious that Miriam had not been arrested along with her husband. It might have happened, Alexander Lepp speculated, because Miriam's brothers occupied important positions under the Soviets. One thing he knew for sure: Miriam Lepp was Jewish. It was rumored that Miriam Lepp had converted to Christianity. It was questionable, however—Alexander Lepp concluded in his testimony—whether this would really prevent her from being Jewish. To be sure on this issue, the police questioned a cleric, who confirmed that Miriam Lepp did indeed voluntarily abandon Judaism to become a Christian. In accordance with the order of April 24, 1942, Miriam Lepp was arrested and sent to Tallinn. Like thousands of others, Lepp was dispatched to Tallinn Central prison, charged with Communist activities.[60]

One can hardly imagine a person more pro-Estonian than Miriam Lepp (born Firk). Miriam grew up in the Estonian environment, speaking Estonian at home. Following her marriage to Konstantin Lepp in 1934, Miriam stopped communicating with her family altogether. Lepp went as far as to argue during the interrogation that she was a convinced anti-Semite. Lepp rejected as "absurd" the accusation that she had remained at freedom thanks to her Jewish brothers, who had allegedly worked for the Soviet regime. To further prove her allegiance to the Estonian cause, Lepp said that in the summer of 1941 she hid several policemen— among them Harry Männil—who had deserted from the Red Army. Lepp listed twelve individuals, all Estonians, who could have testified on her behalf. Over the next month Estonian Security Police questioned a total of eighteen witnesses, including the two policemen whose lives Lepp had saved. The police wanted to know three things: Miriam Lepp's attitude toward Jews; her political views; and what she did in 1940–41. One after another, the witnesses portrayed Miriam Lepp in the best possible light. For Lepp, her marriage had opened the doors to Estonian high society. She had a wide circle of acquaintances, exclusively Estonian. Witnesses agreed that Miriam Lepp was more than just loyal to the Estonian State; indeed she was an Estonian patriot. Lepp had cut off all relations with the Jewish community. Her attitude toward Bolshevism was extremely negative, hostile and bitter. In 1918, it had been the Germans that released Miriam Lepp from Riga's prison where the Communists had thrown her. One of the policemen who found refuge at Kurtna said that Lepp welcomed the German troops as liberators. Lepp found relief talking to other women whose husbands had been arrested by the Soviets. According to one of them, Miriam said that she was ashamed to have been born Jewish. Upon the question of what would have happened to the Jews if the Germans were to arrive in Estonia, Lepp allegedly answered that she did not care, and that Jews would have been justly punished for they had brought about Communism. Lepp reacted in a most unusual way when she learned about the persecution of Jews in Estonia: if she too ended up in a concentration camp, the Jewish inmates would most likely kill her there.[61]

The German Security Police became increasingly impatient with their Estonian counterparts, so that on July 3, 1942, the head of Department AIV, SS-Hstuf.

Paul Seyler, ordered Miriam Lepp's execution. From prison, on July 9 Lepp sent a desperate plea, trying one last time to prove her innocence:

> I grew up completely in the Estonian spirit. The first language I learned to speak was Estonian. In my home, we have always fulfilled our duties to our Homeland. Both my brothers volunteered in the Estonian War of Liberation. I have been interested in Estonian literature and history since I was a child. Konstantin Lepp, as a renowned public figure in Estonia, would never have married me if I did not bear in me the Estonian spirit. I have only moved in Estonian circles. Jews are alien to me; I have never had any contacts with them. I have always felt myself being Estonian and I will remain that forever. I had neither interest nor penchant for doing dirty business. My dream was to live in the countryside.
>
> The Reds arrested my husband on September 25, 1940. That is when my troubles began. I survived only because I hid myself. I risked my life hiding four police officials and several other Estonian men and women. Please call to testify on my behalf Director of the Interior Mr. Oskar Angelus and his deputy Mr. Johannes Raid . . .
>
> I beg your understanding of the unbearable situation in which I would find myself if I were to be sent to a camp amongst the people from whom I have become alienated due to my upbringing and my habits. But if the current situation will not give me an opportunity to live as a full member of the society, as a last resort, please intern me at my husband's farm under the control of the local administration. Please take into account my husband's situation and all the good that I have done to the Estonian people. I hope that my request will be considered.

Four days later Miriam Lepp was executed.[62]

Why drag her case on for so long when everyone in the Estonian Security Police knew that Lepp would be condemned to death anyway? At a time when the police personnel had a backlog of cases to clear,[63] they spent six months pursuing a Jewish woman whose fate was predetermined. First Miriam Lepp was a woman, and second she was completely integrated into the Estonian society. That might have had a certain effect on the police rank and file, which definitely did not want to appear as hardened killers. Yet in the case of such a strictly regulated body as the Security Police, individual motivation has to give way to structural explanation. To execute Miriam Lepp on the basis of her ethnicity alone, without first trying to tailor the accusation to fit the anti-Communist matrix, would have defied the purpose of the Estonian Security Police, which was originally set up as a guardian of tradition and order. That would be tantamount to confessing murderous contempt for justice, which it was indeed. There was a semantic nuance to it too: Department BIV of the Estonian Security Police (nearly identical to the Gestapo in Germany proper) was called in Estonian "Political Police" (*Poliitiline Politsei*). Thus the Estonian Security Police was trying hard to live up to its name. Members of the Estonian Security Police saw themselves as bearers of the Estonian national idea, but so did Miriam Lepp. The former had to murder the latter so as to prove its righteousness.

An examination of another case file reveals yet another preordained judgment. Rebecca Salome was exposed through a denunciation. The investigation into her case was opened on October 11, 1941, and ran through November of the next year. Salome, her Polish husband, and their two daughters were Polish citizens of the Lutheran faith who had moved to Estonia from the Soviet Union in 1929. The police had gathered the following information on the Salome family: Rebecca Salome's husband, Kazimierz, was sick and did not leave the house often; Rebecca Salome had established permanent contacts with the Soviet military personnel; she was seen in a car in the company of Red Army soldiers; Rebecca Salome was supposedly Jewish, which had yet to be proven. The police further established that the Salome family was hostile to the German people in general and the German military authorities in particular. Furthermore, one could see with the naked eye that they were Jewish. As usual, the Estonian Security Police then began interrogating witnesses. Jaan Neeser, who lived across the street, wondered about the Soviet military vehicles that had been parked in front of the Salome's house beginning in the fall of 1939 and all the way through the summer of 1941. Sometimes the Russians drove members of the Salome family around in their car. Salome herself often came into Neeser's office to use the telephone. He, Neeser, was curious about the conversations that Salome had on the phone, but was only able to overhear that she promised to be somewhere at a certain hour. Although Neeser did not know for sure whether Salome was Jewish, he insisted that she was of Jewish faith. Otherwise, judging by his answers, Neeser could not produce any incriminating evidence against Salome. Neither did Alexander Mugur, except that he too saw Salome in a car together with the Red Army soldiers. Although the Salomes appeared Jewish to him, he had no documents to prove it. Unlike the two men, Alfreda Sõjamägi had personal encounters with Rebecca Salome and therefore was able to tell the investigation that the latter was anything but a Communist sympathizer: She had never seen Salome in the company of Soviet soldiers. The landlord, Axel Vaal, explained away the mysterious appearance of Soviet official cars in front of his house. One of the tenants happened to be a Soviet navy officer. Whether Salome was Jewish or as to the nature of her political beliefs, the landlord did not know. However, it is true that he saw Rebecca Salome and her daughters going for a walk with Russian officers. While Karl Toomberg and Magda Sepp chose to be neutral in their description of the Salome family, one other neighbor, Richard Jürgenson, stated unequivocally that Rebecca and her daughters did indeed interact with Red Army soldiers.[64]

It was not until mid-April 1942 that Rebecca Salome and her two daughters were given a chance to defend themselves orally. Remarkably, Kazimierz Salome had never been interrogated once the police established that he was an ethnic Pole. Rebecca's younger daughter, Julia, was married to an Estonian, who was by then mobilized to active duty in the Red Army. The local Housing Department at a certain point decided that the floor space of Julia's apartment was big enough to accommodate one more person—the navy officer that the landlord mentioned in his testimony. From time to time the officer came to visit the rest of the Salome family, who lived in the same house. Yet Rebecca Salome denied that either she or her daughters had accepted rides from the Soviet officer, let alone having gone for a walk with him. Eugenia, the older daughter, was working at that time at the Tallinn municipality, which had an official car. Eugenia was on a demanding schedule and had to work extra hours. When Eugenia worked late into the night, the municipality provided her with a car and a driver to take her home and then back the next morning. Rather unusually, the interrogation protocols of Rebecca, Eugenia, and Julia Salome bore a postscript indicating that the police registry had no incriminating evidence against them. Eugenia's boss, Erich Moor, confirmed that Eugenia had worked under him as a typist and that in order to meet deadlines without violating the curfew he would sometimes dispatch the official car to fetch her from home. Moor and his colleagues were positive that Eugenia Salome had never expressed Communist views, nor had she been in touch with Red Army soldiers. Another four witnesses shared their experiences of work with Julia and Rebecca Salome. The two women were said to have been anti-Communist but also pro-Estonian and pro-German. Both Eugenia and Julia considered themselves Poles and so did others.[65]

The order was issued on September 22, 1942. The charges stayed the same: being Jewish, partaking in Communist activities. Two days later, Ervin Viks notified his German counterpart that Rebecca Salome had been executed. Predetermined judgments stemmed from anti-Communist paranoia. When suspicion turned into conviction, no further references to the corpus delicti were needed. Consider the description of Haja Jakobson as it appeared on the wanted list of the Estonian Security Police in Tartu:

Jakobson, Haja, daughter of Israel; born 21 April 1896; lived on 69 Adolf Hitler St.; Jewish. First worked in the NKVD as a typist; starting from 1 April 1941 worked in the cataloguing department, compiling some sorts of lists. Big intriguer and oppressor of Estonians. Nervous. Active Communist and member of Communist Party. Short, with crooked legs and bulging eyes.[66]

The same idea ran through the guidelines that Viljandi prefect P. Kutsar issued in July 1941. Kutsar wanted an update on the "events of general importance" such as criminal acts against the military, society, or individuals, committed by "Communists, Jews, and other terrorists."[67]

At the same time, I want to emphasize that the vicious anti-Communist witch-hunt affected Jews and non-Jews alike. For example, on November 31, 1941, Ervin Viks proposed the execution of seventy-three-year-old Miina Kuusik, an Estonian. The decision read as follows: "Kuusik was a supporter of Soviet power. If she were not as old, she would have definitely done something for the benefit of the Soviet Union. Her sons were Communists; she rejoiced at the sight of Tallinn burning; she distributed Communist literature."[68] During the first weeks of German occupation, anyone charged with Communist activities—even if identified by somebody on the street—could lose his or her life.[69] A majority of people suspected of political opposition and incarcerated in 1941 were minor functionaries in the Soviet system. Those people were found guilty by association and frequently executed. Estonian Security Police targeted specifically the following categories of "the enemies of the people": (1) members of the underclass, including farmhands, unskilled workers, and workers; (2) social misfits, including alcoholics and prostitutes; (3) habitual criminals; and (4) ethnic Russians.

Ruth Bettina Birn, who has analyzed the police investigation files, found the Estonian collective memory going as far back as the beginning of the twentieth century. For example, one Communist was alleged to have taken part in every Communist revolt from 1905 onward. That particular individual was executed even though he committed no wrongdoings in 1940–41. Another man allegedly hit a Baltic German landowner in 1917. Desecrations of national symbols, such as "dishonoring" the Estonian flag or the destruction of Freedom War memorials, were also often mentioned as grave offenses.[70]

WOMEN AND CHILDREN

What comes immediately to the fore in the cases of Miriam Lepp and Rebecca Salome is the late date of their arrest. Obviously the delay had something do with the fact that both women were married to Gentiles. However, perusal of investigation files reveals that Jewish women as a group were initially spared arrest. That fact runs counter to the generally accepted chronology of the Holocaust. Raul Hilberg, for example, divided the process of the destruction of the Jews in occupied Soviet territory into three distinct phases. In the Baltic area, according to Hilberg, the second sweep began in the fall of 1941.[71] Peter Longerich has modified that chronology by incorporating the experience of Jewish women and children in Lithuania in the summer of 1941. Longerich argued that the decision to extend the campaign of murder to women and children in late July and early August signified a cumulative leap in the policy of racial extermination, and thus constituted a transitional phase between the first two phases.[72] Yet Longerich fails to explain why the Einsatzgruppen and their auxiliaries did not start executing Jewish women and children immediately. Did it happen because of a restrictive order, or simply because no such order dealing specifically with Jewish women and children had ever been issued? The Estonian case suggests the latter. Until well into the second half of September or even early October, there seems to have been no uniform policy with regard to Jewish women. The timing, early October, corresponds with the date of Himmler's visit to the Ukraine, during which he supposedly sanctioned the killing of all Jews irrespective of sex and age.[73]

Even though the police were aware of the women's whereabouts, they did not rush to arrest them. In several cases, a woman was still free while her husband had already been incarcerated. As of September 15, the wives of Meier Pevsner,

Leib Majofis, Härmo Pant, Abram Sachar-Schocher, and Hirsh Harchat were still living at their permanent addresses. Eida Klompus and Rosa Krenchinsky even went to testify on their husbands' behalf on September 2 and 17 respectively. Many Jewish women in Tallinn were arrested within the last ten days of September, yet the largest number of female inmates arrived in Tallinn Central prison between October 8 and 11.[74] The Tallinn prefect, Evald Mikson, told a Finnish policeman visiting Tallinn about the execution of eighty elderly Jewish women in early October. According to Mikson, they were "useless."[75] As late as the first week of October, several Jewish women came to the Security Police headquarters on Tõnismäe Street, seeking contact with their husbands who had been arrested earlier.[76] The issue of gender was apparently irrelevant when Estonian Security Police made decisions in women's cases. Otherwise the policemen would have been able to see the irony in charging with Communist activities seventy-four-year-old Minoche Idelson, eighty-year-old Sarah Krenchinsky, eighty-year-old Jente Harchat, and eighty-four-year-old Ida Bruck. In one particular case, the KdS-Estland ordered a Jewish woman released. Sima Brashinsky, a well-to-do Latvian Jew, was released from Tallinn Central prison together with her two-year-old child on October 3, 1941. There is no indication as to why mother and son were allowed to return to their domicile.[77] Past the date in October, the police had apparently finished searching for Jews in Estonia as part of a deliberate policy. Subsequent arrests of individual Jews of both sexes had been conducted in an ad hoc manner.

The last Jewish women were apprehended in the spring of 1942. Each individual case is exceptional for its dramatic details. Gita Talaievsky had just celebrated her eighty-first birthday when she was arrested, on April 1, 1942. Born in Lithuania, Talaievsky had buried her husband in Odessa fifty-three years earlier. Talaievsky's child had died at birth. The widow came to Estonia via Kronstadt shortly before the 1924 Communist putsch. For the next twelve years, Talaievsky had lived with a so-called Nansen passport. She finally received Estonian citizenship in 1936. Gita Talaievsky had no relatives, no property, no anything. She signed the interrogation record in the language she understood best—Yiddish. Gita Talaievsky's life was extinguished on April 19, 1942. Anna Kalmanson, in contrast, had experienced no hardship. Her relatives took good care of Anna, who was mentally ill. All that time, thirty-six-year-old Anna and her two brothers had lived together. Lazar and Jehuda, who served as minor officials during the year of Soviet rule, evacuated in July 1941 to Russia proper. They would have definitely taken their sister with them, but Anna was denied entry. The brothers then decided to leave Anna with Edla Linneberg, who had for many years been employed in the Kalmanson family. The immediate cause for Kalmanson's arrest was an anonymous denunciation. The Criminal Police had already taken note of the sick woman. About two weeks before the arrest, a police official paid a visit to the landlady in whose house the Kalmansons lived. He promised to take the Jew away shortly, but failed to act on his promise. The same policeman, disguised as an employee of the social security department, also had a conversation with Anna's guardian. He promised Linneberg to relive her of Kalmanson sometime soon. When it did not happen, Linneberg requested additional information from the social security department, where she was told that none of their employees had ever visited her. The Security Police records indicate, however, that it was Linneberg herself who wanted to get rid of Anna Kalmanson. One way or another, on March 30, 1942, the constable of the 3rd police precinct in Tallinn, Endel Kõll, initiated proceedings against Anna Kalmanson for "the protocol had indications of an offense leading to public prosecution." Anna could neither read nor write and therefore signed the decision in her case by three big crosses. Given that it was impossible to interrogate Kalmanson properly, the police made an extra trip to the home of her former guardian, who then surrendered Anna's ID. Linneberg also provided the visitor from the Security Police with a medical certificate stating Anna Kalmanson's diagnosis. On May 2 Viks communicated Sandberger's decision with respect to Kalmanson: execution. But the poor woman did not live to see it. At 5:30 P.M. on April 30, 1942, Anna Kalmanson died in Tallinn Central prison of a heart attack.[78]

The most unusual case was that of Sarah Lipavsky. In the summer of 1941 Lipavsky evacuated from Estonia to Russia only to come back two years later. The reasons for her return remain unknown. On Adolf Hitler Avenue (formerly Narva Avenue) in Tallinn on August 14, 1943, Elisabeth Scheringer unexpectedly ran into Sarah Lipavsky. Scheringer immediately recognized Lipavsky as a person with whom she had had an argument in Tallinn customs in 1940. Next Scheringer asked a German soldier to apprehend the Jew, but he refused.[79] The Estonian Security Police did not refuse.

Jewish children as a rule followed their mothers first to Tallinn Central prison and then to Harku concentration camp. Leo Kletzky was only six in the spring of 1942. A Helsinki native, Bella Kletzky married a man from Tallinn and subsequently moved to Estonia in 1930. Her husband, Saveli, was conscripted into the Red Army in August 1941 but did not make it farther than Kuressaare, where he was executed on November 11. German Security Police classified Bella and her son Leo as pure Jews. On April 8, 1942, both were arrested and on the next day executed. Dr. Sandberger did not waste words to rationalize his decision: "it deals with Jews-Estonian nationals."[80]

Although the Estonian civil administration had not gone as far as the short-lived provisional Lithuanian government, which consented to the establishment of a Jewish concentration camp,[81] it did indirectly aid the "Final Solution." The input of Estonian bureaucrats in the decision-making process can be discerned from the case file of a Jewish girl, Beile Ratut. In November 1941, Virve Partkal, head of the center for imbecile children in Pärnu-Jaagupi, approached the Estonian Self-Government with the following request. Partkal wondered what should be done with a thirteen-year-old Jewish girl—whether Beile could stay or, in the opposite case, where should she be sent? The head of Welfare Ministry, Leesment, scribbled on the margins a note for Minister of the Interior Oskar Angelus: "How to get rid of the Jew?" In an official memo several days later Leesment was asking Angelus to express the latter's opinion in the Ratut case. A marginal note, which could as well have been written by Angelus, indicated that Beile Ratut, as a Jew, for obvious reasons could not stay where she was. The issue was then redirected to Roland Lepik and the Estonian Security Police, which ordered the girl dispatched to Central prison in Tallinn. During the interrogation, Beile only could state that her father, Haim (already executed by that time), had taken her to the institution for the mentally ill children the previous winter. The note below also explained why: "Beile Ratut, Jewish, is a degenerate (physically and mentally)." Nevertheless, the decision still bore the imprint that she was suspected of Communist activities.[82]

The story of the Pliner children is one of failing humanity. On November 26, 1941, Nõmme resident Elisabeth Letinkov sent to the local welfare department the following request. Jury Pliner had brought his three children to Letinkov's shortly before he was conscripted in late August. Upon the question as to why Pliner chose her of all people, Letinkov told that her mother used to babysit his children. There remained no other options because the former wife of Pliner had evacuated to Russia proper. Jury Pliner was among the men that were stranded on board the *Eestirand* and later arrested; Letinkov found herself taking care of fourteen-year-old Miriam and seven-year-old twins David and Siima. Letinkov insisted that she could not do that for very long for she was supporting her elderly mother and ten-year-old daughter. She pointed out that the Pliner children only had two suitcases with the most necessary clothes with them. And because Jury Pliner had not left any money, Letinkov asked whether the Jewish children could possibly be taken away. It turned out that Letinkov had been trying to get rid of the children for the past two months but always ended up being shuffled from one department to another. As a first step, the police acquired archival records on every individual the petitioner had mentioned, including herself. As Letinkov correctly wrote, Pliner divorced his wife in January 1941. What she did not mention, though, was that Pliner had married for the second time on August 20, and that his new wife's name was Elisabeth Letinkov! Head of Department AIV Seyler ordered Miriam, Siima, and David Pliner executed (their father was already dead by then) and Elisabeth Letinkov placed under police surveillance. On March 27, 1942, Leopold Jürgenson and Arthur Braun of the Estonian Security Police came to arrest the children, as well as to compile the list of items that belonged to Miriam, Siima, and David Pliner. Constable Braun meticulously recorded every garment in the two suitcases:

1. Suitcase, cardboard, beige	1
2. Suitcase, cardboard, brown	1
3. Children's underwear, various	85
4. Box with 5 Easter eggs	1
5. Embroidered white purse	1
6. Watch, of white metal, firma Kenisur, No. 875	1
7. Small scissors	1
8. Stockings, children's	12
9. Scarf, motley silk	1
10. Crayons, color	2
11. Scarves, wool	2
12. Jackets, wool, various	5
13. Pants, wool, of different color	3
14. Coat, brown	1
15. Blouses, various	8

16. Pants, various	5
17. Purse, white, with a zipper	1
18. Laundry soap	1
19. Pillows, with feathers	2
20. Bed linens, white	3
21. Blanket cover, white	1
22. Towels, white	5
23. Pillow cases, white	4
24. Sports dress, white	1
25. Children's boots, brown, old	3
26. Galoshes, little worn	2
27. Children's mittens, torn	2
28. Galoshes, torn	1
29. Slippers, made of fabric	3
30. Fluffy gray muffs	3
31. Hats with fluffy edging, torn	2
32. Coat, girl's, with fluffy collar	1
33. Boy's sailor jackets, blue	2
34. Winter coat, made of fluffy fabric, dark blue	1
35. Quilt, red, with orange edging	2
36. Pillows, big, of rose color	2
37. Pillow cases, dirty	2
38. Children's purse, made of leather, with postcards and similar meaningless children's items	1
39. Briefcase with meaningless children's toys	1
40. Suitcase with broken children's toys	2
41. Children's felt boots, torn	2
42. Umbrella, black, old	1

All listed items were deposited for safekeeping with Elisabeth Letinkov. A month later, German Security Police authorized the Estonian Relief to take over the children's possessions.[83] There is no way of knowing which particular Estonian child got to wear Miriam's coat, or who was the boy who tried on David's sailor suit, or whose parents rejoiced over the red quilt with orange edging that used to keep Siima warm during cold winter nights.

Taube Kuschner might well be the youngest person ever murdered in Estonia. The entries "profession" and "last occupation" had just one word written in them: baby. At the time of her execution in Pärnu in November 1941, the girl was five months and twenty-one days old. At least two more babies lost their lives. Marianne Schein gave birth in Harku concentration camp, while Lillian Sikk was eight months pregnant when she entered the gates of the Tartu concentration camp.[84]

The scheme of collaboration, as it was introduced in Estonia, made Estonian Security Police prosecute Jews exceptionally for political crimes. Arrested as "Jews," most victims were condemned to death on a charge of Communist activities. If that charge was impossible to prove, the Security Police labeled Jews "subversive to the present regime." The word *Jewish* appeared in the decision only if the police failed to present any incriminating evidence at all. With the Estonian policemen role-playing justice, the whole process of investigation was a hoax. Internal logic, as well as popular pressure, prescribed that the Estonian Security Police frame its activities as a counter-thesis to Communism. To admit that the Jews were murdered because of their origin and not because of their political beliefs would be equal to declaring nationalist ideology bankrupt, and thus to denying the very existence of the Estonian nation. The Estonians could not afford to undermine the principles upon which their state had been built.

Yehuda Bauer has recently refined the notion of dehumanization—one of the key concepts in the study of the Holocaust. To humiliate their Jewish victims, Bauer said, Nazis needed no particular orders or bureaucratic arrangements. Indeed, there was a consensus to that effect. At the same time, it was the tormentors themselves who lost their human characteristics while dehumanizing their victims.[85] In that sense, Estonian members of the Security Police were totally sane, perfectly human. Nobody in Estonia forced the Jews to scrub sidewalks or dance around the symbols of Soviet power. There is no evidence that the Jews under arrest had been mistreated in any humiliating way.[86] There was no torture applied, as had happened with ethnic Russian inmates, who sometimes were beaten for speaking Russian or merely for being one. Indeed, the Russian detainees had been treated considerably worse than the rest of the prison folks.[87] The Jews had been perceived as an ideological enemy and treated accordingly. Put on the same level as Communists, Estonian Jews were granted the benefit of dying decently.

The police investigation files revealed an array of popular views on Jews. While the overall number of denunciations, including indirect informing, exceeded that of petitions in behalf of Jews, supportive testimonies prevailed over damaging ones by a factor of three. It is pure arithmetic to conclude that close to 75 percent of the ordinary Estonians whose names had been mentioned in the investigation files were sympathetic to the Jewish plight. Among those who had betrayed Jews there were envious colleagues, xenophobic neighbors, and avaricious landlords. None of them knew much about Jews or had ever tried to understand them. Individuals who had interacted with Jews on an everyday basis, either at work or in personal settings, represented the opposite side of the spectrum. Finally, there were those who had received help from Jews and who now wanted to return the favor. However, not even the people who wished Jews well were able to see beyond traditionally held views. Still, they tried to vindicate a particular person they knew by contrasting him or her to the rest of the Jews. One or several such testimonies could not shake the belief of the police that they were on the right track in bringing action against the Jews.

7

THE END COMPLETE
JEWS IN PROVINCIAL CITIES

The speed of German conquest did not necessarily correlate with the pace of destruction in each of the major provincial Estonian cities. In some cities the last Jews were executed as late as December 1941. Pechory was one of the first Estonian provinces overrun by the Wehrmacht. It was on July 12, 1941, that Voldemar Kana, an officer of the former Estonian army, became head of the flying squad *(lendsalk)* of the Pechory Omakaitse. In the course of a year, his commando killed more than two hundred people in and around the city of Pechory. Among the victims was a Jewish family of five that was passing though Pechory on its way from Latvia. Kana, together with Leonhard Pindis, Osvald Pedask, and Rudolf Nüüd, executed the Jews behind the local Estonian Lutheran cemetery in late July 1941. The head of the family, whom Kana shot first, was said to have been a notorious Communist. The murderers appropriated whatever few effects the executed had; the OK local headquarters took their horse and the cart.[1]

In Paide, in central Estonia, the arrests of Jews commenced immediately after German troops entered the city on August 8. Rebecca Judelovich, for example, was charged with political opposition to the new regime. Judelovich and Selma Saadma had been students at a local German high school; Saadma described her former classmate as a person who could not stand Communists and who had socialized mainly with ethnic Germans. That was not enough, however, to crack open the Paide prison where Judelovich spent the next two months, until on October 6 she was transferred to the Tallinn-Harju police prefecture.[2] In one of his reports, Paide prefect V. Eelnurm described in detail how the local OK assisted the policemen in carrying out executions: each executioner was paired with a victim, whom he shot in the back of the head.[3]

The list of Jews arrested in the border city of Narva on the first day of the Nazi occupation (August 17) contained five names. Apprehended as "Jews," these five people were informed that they would be interned until the end of the war. However, on the following day four elderly people, aged between seventy-one and eighty-one, were released. Executions did not begin until September 9, when Jacob Kagan and Georg Laserson were condemned to death as Communist sympathizers. Executions were carried out by a special OK unit under the command of Johannes Ojavere. The Security Police office in Narva covered a large territory, extending as far as Jõhvi, about twenty miles to the west. Benjamin Beilinson, a Jewish dentist from Jõhvi, was arrested on September 20. Not only had he teamed up with a political commissar *(politruk)* and an NKVD agent but he also refused to part with his valuables. The death sentence for Beilinson was carried out on December 12.[4] In mid-October the Narva police commissar appointed Ester Toubin as a Jewish elder. Although Toubin had outlived all other Narva Jews, he did not survive either. The Estonian Security Police decided to postpone Toubin's execution, originally scheduled for mid-December, until after his Jewish origin had been established.[5] Olga Gorfinkel was one of the last remaining Jews in Narva. The seventy-one-year-old widow of a Narva rabbi died of natural causes in her apartment in the former synagogue on 12 Turu Street, which had by then been converted into a POW camp.[6] The total number of Jews and (itinerant) Gypsies executed in Narva was thirty-one and seventeen respectively.[7] Rakvere is the only city in Estonia for which the exact dates of execution of *all* local Jews are available. Four Jewish men were executed on August 18, that is, ten days after German troops captured Rakvere. The remaining eighteen people, both men and women, were shot on December 3.[8]

As elsewhere in Estonia, the population of Saaremaa Island welcomed the Germans jubilantly: the victorious troops received flowers and food; women put on their Sunday clothing; Estonian flags were raised. The grateful population shared information on Communists in hiding.[9] In Kuressaare, most Jews were executed between September 7 and 24, 1941. Several individuals were shot in October and November. The last Jewish victim on the island, a physician, Buras Lury, faced a firing squad on December 15. The Loode Forest, not far from the city, was chosen as the execution site. As in Tallinn, capital punishment was disguised as death due to natural causes. Notoriously, this deception only applied to Jews.[10] The Haapsalu Security Police carried out death sentences of Jews about the same time in September. As in Kuressaare, Jewish physicians were the last to go. A Haapsalu dentist, Jakob Weiner, "died" in Tallinn on October 14, 1942.[11] It might well be that Berra Smoliansky was the only Jew who lived on Hiiumaa Island. On October 31, a local police constable detained a woman who worked as a nurse in a Soviet military hospital. Johannes Peeba told the investigation that Smoliansky, unlike other Jews, did not rush to make a career but continued working in her profession after June 1940. Smoliansky was executed the following month.[12]

Pärnu boasted the fourth largest Jewish community in Estonia. Located on the Baltic coast in the southwestern corner of Estonia, Pärnu had already become a zone of operations in mid-July. As a result, only half of the Jewish population managed to flee from the city. Pärnu Jews were herded into the so-called Betty Barn (the Pärnu prison, officially designated—a concentration camp for political prisoners), which was administered by the local OK. The camp employed twenty-seven guards, in addition to fifty members of the OK. Mihkel Nõmm, deputy head of the Estonian Security Police in Pärnu, sanctioned the arrests, most of which took place in late July. The Jews were told that they would be released shortly after interrogation. None of them was prepared for a long-term imprisonment; prohibited to take any personal belongings with them, many Jews had nothing but summer clothes. As the nights became colder, the inmates, women with small children in particular, endured significant hardship. On September 5, fifteen Jewish women pleaded with the Pärnu police prefect to allow them to bring their warm clothes from home. The women had to address the police twice, for their first request was effectively ignored.

By then they already knew that their homes were all but cleared. "Crying, we beg for your kindness. We are all Estonian born, we are loyal citizens and love our homeland dearly," wrote the women to the inspector of penitentiaries. Unexpectedly, on September 25 local headquarters permitted a small delivery of shoes and warm clothes to the concentration camp. The problem of food was as acute. The daily ration for prisoners was 2.00 Rbl. per person, while the camp guards received 6.84 Rbl. worth of food. Ironically, it was the prisoners who prepared meals for the guards.[13] By September, all male Jews in Pärnu had already been executed: twenty men on July 13 and another twenty on July 26. An OK guard who shot Eide Matskin dead on October 4 pleaded self-defense. Otherwise, the murder of women and children did not commence until the last days of October, when they were taken from the camp to the local synagogue. Twenty-five women were then driven to the nearby Rae Forest and executed. Two days later, on November 2, the remaining sixty-two Jewish prisoners, all but fourteen of them children, were murdered right there in the synagogue.[14] All that remained were patches of women's clothes and family pictures, strewn near the dumpster.[15] Jewish women and children remained the last "political prisoners" in the Pärnu concentration camp when it was officially liquidated on October 30, 1941.[16]

The Estonian mayor of Pärnu later told Hermann Riecken, the newly appointed district commissar, what had happened to the local Jews: Estonian partisans killed the Jews out of revenge for their alleged role in the mass deportation. Following the Soviet retreat, the Jews lived in constant fear, feeling threatened by the Estonians.[17] We have only limited data on the perpetrators at Pärnu. Martin Jüris was twenty-six when he assumed the position of director of the Pärnu prison. Jüris was born in Pärnu, finished elementary and high school there. In 1939 he graduated from Tartu University Law School, and a year later cum laude from the Military College. During the Soviet occupation Jüris reportedly worked as an accountant.[18] Executions were carried out by a special OK squad under the command of Captain Villem Raid, the former head of the border guard at Mõisaküla. According to witnesses, Raid used to refer to executions as "playing soccer." The routine procedure began in the morning at OK headquarters, where the men from the firing squad received their weapons and ammunition. At some point, Captain August Orgussaar, head of the Estonian Security Police in Pärnu, and his German counterpart joined the group. From the Betty Barn, buses and trucks loaded with Jews went to the Rae Forest, about five miles away from the city. High-ranking officials usually followed the cavalcade in a car. Upon arrival Jews were lined up along the pit; the firing squad took position on the other side of the pit. The last image that the victims saw was the calming picture of a sea and slim pine trees graciously swaying in the breeze. The Estonians shot, while the Germans snapped pictures.[19]

Out of the 137 Jews executed in Pärnu, at least 18 came from Latvia. Another 12 Latvian Jews, including several members of a shock battalion, were executed elsewhere in southern Estonia in August and September.[20] The wanted list that the Estonian Security Police in Tartu distributed included the names of several Latvian Jews.[21]

JEWS IN TARTU

Random murder of Jews occurred in Tartu more frequently than anywhere else in Estonia during the summer months of 1941. As far as the morbid statistics

19. A university student, member of Omakaitse, guards a bridge in Tartu, summer–fall 1941; HI, Hintzer, 158675.

20. Soccer team of the Tartu office of the Estonian Security Police, 1943; HI, Hintzer, 157413.

of executed Jews were concerned, Tartu claimed the second largest number of victims in Estonia after Tallinn—probably as many as 158.[22] The first roundups were aimed at cleansing the city of suspected arsonists. Heavy shelling by Soviet cannons wrecked havoc on the wooden quarters of the city. It was estimated that about 12 percent of the housing in Tartu had thus been destroyed.[23] On July 13 the OK commander in South-Estonia, Maj. Friedrich Kurg, with the approval of Tartu commandant Obstlt. Hans Gosebruch, ordered all Tartu Jews confined to a just-established concentration camp. Unable to find any viable pretext for arrest, Kurg referred to "Jews-arsonists," including "children with Molotov-cocktail[s]."[24] That designation sat well with the German field headquarters, which had identi-fied the OK as a spearhead of the cleansing operations in the city of Tartu.[25]

Among the available files of the Estonian Security Police in Tartu, only twelve belonged to Jews. These twelve persons were executed between July 20 and August 16 on various counts. Four men were shot for either violating "disci-pline" or failing to report to work; four others were sentenced to death as a Com-munist, a member of a shock battalion, and NKVD agents respectively, while the rest had to die simply because of their ethnicity.[26] The charges against Isaac

Mogilkin meant a death sentence: collaboration with the NKVD and assistance in deporting an Estonian man. Mogilkin and Peeter Helk both owned clothing stores in a shopping strip on Fortuna Street. During his interrogation in the NKVD local headquarters back in 1940, Helk spotted Mogilkin in the same building. Described as an Estonian nationalist and anti-Communist, Helk had allegedly warned his wife that if he were ever to be arrested, it would be because of Mogilkin. The latter denied any association with the NKVD, except that he had as well been questioned on numerous occasions, mainly about his and other Jews' gold.[27] Late at night on August 1, 1941, a Tartu police constable received two visitors. Thirty-five-year-old OK member Eduard Hilpur brought seventy-seven-year-old Moses Kaplan to the prefecture. According to Hilpur, he had learned from somebody that one of the inhabitants at 10 Aida Street was a Jew, whom he then immediately apprehended. Hilpur took his civic duty seriously, as he locked Kaplan's apartment and delivered the keys to the police. Three days later, Kaplan was already in the Tartu concentration camp, where Captain Juhan Jüriste assigned him to the so-called "Special Department." Kaplan was executed one day later.[28] From time to time the Germans conducted arrests as well. For example, on August 9 Wehrmacht soldiers arrested a tannery owner, Susman Trapido, at his home. Sixty-eight-year-old Trapido only got to live two more days after that. As of September 19, 1941, the total number of those executed in Tartu reached 405, including 50 Jews. According to the German Security Police, by that date there were no more Jews under arrest in Tartu.[29] All local Jews at one point or another had gone through the Tartu concentration camp.

The Tartu concentration camp was established on the former exhibition grounds on Näituse Street. The exhibition grounds had served as an original assembly point for Estonian partisans. That is where the Tartu Omakaitse was born. Four large 200-by-65-foot pavilions that used to exhibit the best of Estonian produce now housed prisoners. Men and women, criminal and "political" offenders, were kept in separate barracks. Each barracks individually and the camp territory as a whole were enclosed with a barbed-wire fence. Former storage barracks (popularly known as *barak smertnikov* or *Lepiku parakk*) served as the last stop for those condemned to death. The doomed were denied basic human rights such as regular meals and sleep. Once they left the barracks, they never came back again.[30]

21. Celebration of the second anniversary of the "liberation" of Tartu, at Tamme Stadium, where Major Friedrich Kurg receives an Iron Cross, July 1943; HI, Hintzer, 158452.

The two small houses within the perimeter of the camp were occupied by camp administration and the "Special Department of the Omakaitse Commandant's Office," or simply Special Department. The head of the Special Department was Roland Lepik, a guerilla fighter from Ahja. Together with Lepik in the Special Department worked several former police officers, including Ervin Viks, Evald Mikson, Valentine Keder, and Alexander Koolmeister. The function of the Special Department was to investigate the details of individual offenders. Sometimes the Special Department received guests from the Estonian Security Police, who also participated in the interrogations. During the interrogations, department officials often abused prisoners both verbally and physically. No formal records of investigation were kept; the death penalty and indeterminate imprisonment were the only two verdicts the Special Department ever pronounced.[31] Like the Estonian Security Police branch offices throughout the country, the Special Department at Tartu forwarded summaries of decisions to the German Security Police. A proposal of capital punishment, which often accompanied the list of prisoners, was customarily approved.[32]

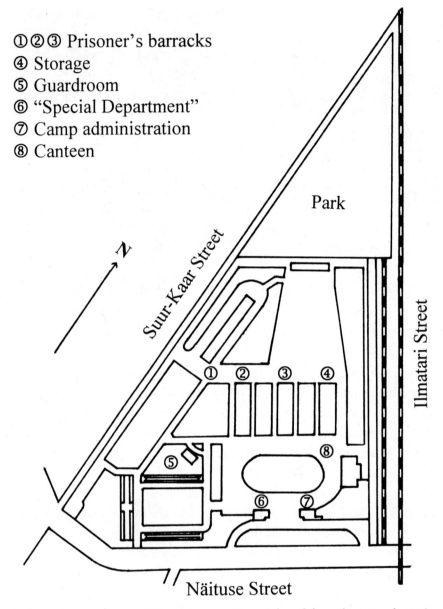

① ② ③ Prisoner's barracks
④ Storage
⑤ Guardroom
⑥ "Special Department"
⑦ Camp administration
⑧ Canteen

3. Concentration camp on Näituse Street in Tartu (adapted from the original, 1961); USHMM, RG-06.026.11.

One of the Tartu concentration camp top officials was Juhan Jüriste. As did tens of thousands of other Estonians, Jüriste had his German last name changed into an Estonian-sounding one. Jüriste was a professional military officer, having served first in the Tsarist army, then in the Estonian army, and finally in the Red Army. Jüriste held a membership in the veterans' organization (Vabs), which he left in March 1934. Jüriste had been removed earlier from the list of active members of the Home Guard (Kaitseliit) for not paying his membership fee. On January 1, 1941, Jüriste was transferred to the reserve. For a while he worked in a hydroelectric power station, until he received a job in Tartu municipality. Jüriste became a typical Soviet bureaucrat, working in the department responsible for the allocation of living space. During the July interregnum, Major Kurg approached Jüriste on the matter of joining the OK. Jüriste accepted the offer, thus replacing TU professor Julius Mark as commander of one of the two original OK companies in Tartu. Yet the prospect of fighting at the front did not excite Jüriste, who managed to stay in the city while pleading indisposition. On July 16 Kurg appointed Jüriste commandant of the Tartu concentration camp, which had come into existence a few days before at the initiative of Estonian partisans. Kurg explained to Jüriste that the people he was about to see in the camp had been arrested on political charges, that is, those who sided with the Soviets.[33] Jüriste assumed his responsibilities as camp commandant on July 21, while the Soviet troops were still holding onto their positions on the right bank of the Emajõgi River.

Jüriste was neither intellectually gifted nor well educated. Although Jüriste could at times be rude to his subordinates, sadist he definitely was not. Guards tried to stay away from Jüriste, particularly when he was drunk. As a former officer, he expected the guards to obey their commander as well as the service regulations of the Estonian army. Indeed, Jüriste valued discipline above all; he frequently checked the posts around the camp several times a night. This and other initiatives of Jüriste took a toll on his health; because of his bad foot, Jüriste used a cane. Even then, one could see his military bearing.[34] It was his military background that made Jüriste believe that by accepting the position of a camp commandant, he was fulfilling his obligation to the homeland. Among his subordinates, Jüriste had the reputation of being a haughty, hot-tempered, vicious individual.[35] Sometime in the late fall of 1941 Jüriste and his wife received a new apartment on 23 Õnne Street. Quite "new" it was not: the apartment belonged to a Jewish couple who had been executed.[36] About the same time, one of Jüriste's subordinates delivered two suitcases with personal effects of the murdered Jews to his apartment.[37]

Jüriste had under his command sixty guards and three officers on duty: Karl Linnas, Elmar Ardla, and Alexander Laak. The number of guards correlated with that of prisoners, at one point reaching one hundred. The guards were hired on a voluntary basis. Those who wished to become camp guards came for an interview with Jüriste. If Jüriste found the candidate suitable for the job, he recommended that man to Lepik, who then made the final decision. As the main criterion for selection Jüriste identified formal military training.[38] On August 1, Lepik replaced Jüriste as camp commandant, while continuing to serve as head of the Special Department. Lepik's superiors expressed their appreciation of his work at Tartu by promoting him to the position of head of Department BIV of the Estonian Security Police in Tallinn. Upon Lepik's recommendation, Linnas became the next commandant of the Tartu concentration camp. Linnas served in this position from September 1941 to May 1942. Jüriste, meanwhile, switched to supervising the guards.

In late fall 1941 an OK detachment that had been guarding Tartu concentration camp was incorporated into the 33rd Police Battalion. Most men cited material benefits as the main reason for joining the camp guard. It was either salary or extra food rations; none of the former guards evoked ideology as a prime incentive. Some people chose to work at a concentration camp to avoid going to the front. Sometimes the decision to join the camp personnel came out of the desire to prevent unnecessary questions about one's past or even potential blackmailing. That was a concern to Osvald Mets, whose brother had been sentenced to death for participating in the abortive Communist putsch of 1924.[39] News about the employment opportunity spread by word of mouth. It also happened that a commanding officer sometimes brought in the people he knew. More often, however, a guard who had already been hired recommended his friend for a job. The criterion for selection was past service in the police, the military, or the Kaitseliit. On August 27 the camp was moved to a new location, to the former military barracks known as Kuperianov Barracks. These barracks had been built during World War I as a military hospital. The reason for the move was simple: the pavilions on the exhibition grounds had no heat and therefore could not be used during the winter. The new camp was located essentially on the same street, close to

22. Kuperianov Barracks, Tartu concentration camp, 1941; HI, Hintzer, 158684.

downtown Tartu and the train station (postal address: 175 Kastani Street). Partially built by prisoners themselves, the camp had the same layout as the old one, that is, two barracks for the inmates and one for the Special Department. The bigger of the two barracks accommodated less dangerous offenders—women on one side and men on the other. A guard post outside the barracks was supposed to dissuade the prisoners from peeping through the windows, which had barbed wire instead of glass. A kitchen and a room for First Sergeant Fritz

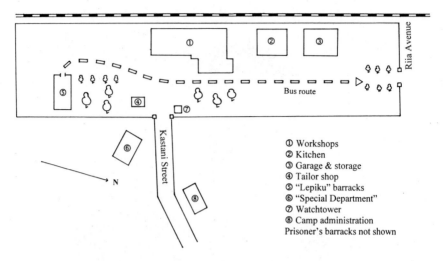

Bus route

① Workshops
② Kitchen
③ Garage & storage
④ Tailor shop
⑤ "Lepiku" barracks
⑥ "Special Department"
⑦ Watchtower
⑧ Camp administration
Prisoner's barracks not shown

Kastani Street

Riia Avenue

N

4. Concentration camp on Kastani Street in Tartu (adapted from the original, 1961); USHMM, RG-06.026.11.

Giesen (the field headquarters commissioner who regularly came for inspections) flanked the building. The barracks for individuals condemned to death not only had a different name—Barracks no. 5—but also a different interior. Originally built as a lockup for insubordinate soldiers, Barracks no. 5 was ideal for its purposes: individual cells; guard posts inside and outside the building; impenetrable barbed-wire fence along the perimeter. Next to the barracks was located storage for personal belongings. Because of a lack of space, the Special Department was later relocated to Kastani Street, about fifty yards away from the camp. A combination of a wooden fence and barbed wire was used to separate the Kuperianov Barracks from the outside world. Here and there watchtowers were installed, equipped with machine guns. Jüriste and Linnas supervised the construction and the subsequent move.[40] At different times, the Tartu concentration camp had between 400 and 800 prisoners (at the height of its activity 1,500).

The camp, originally under the field headquarters' command, was later taken over by the German Security Police (which was located only a few blocks away on 85 Riia Avenue). On a daily basis, however, it was essentially the Estonian Security Police and Tartu prefect Victor Roovere that ran the camp. According to Rosalie Eres, who worked as an interpreter in the Tartu concentration camp, the bulk of paperwork in the camp was in Estonian. Only infrequently did the camp

23. Tartu concentration camp guards escort prisoners to work, 1941; HI, Hintzer, 158673.

administration receive guidelines from the German Security Police, Eres insist-ed.[41] The Germans whom the prisoners encountered while performing labor out-side of the camp territory usually stressed that they had nothing to do with the Tartu concentration camp, meaning the Estonians took control into their own hands.[42] Except for Giesen, no Germans were present at executions. All the thou-sands of people who perished in Tartu died at the hands of the Estonians.

EXECUTIONS AT THE TARTU CONCENTRATION CAMP

Prisoners arrived in the concentration camp from different locations: the prison, the police department, or outside of Tartu. The guards that delivered prisoners brought a covering letter that identified the barracks in which the latter should be committed. In the case of Jews, it was usually the Germans that brought them. Initially, Jews had been assigned to the barracks for nonpolitical prisoners. Very soon, however, Lepik ordered Jews locked in the barracks for the condemned-to-death. Officials of the Special Department, who wore civilian clothes, had regularly fetched prisoners from that barracks for investigation. Anyone who went through that procedure was a sure candidate for execution.[43] Particularly in the beginning, a prisoner who arrived in the morning was often executed in the evening, and by night one of the guards was already wearing his clothes.

Executions were usually carried out during the evening hours. At any single time, between fifteen and twenty-five prisoners lost their lives. One could anticipate an execution every time the commanding staff made their appearance on the camp grounds. (In a futile attempt to stamp out awareness of what was going on, before each execution, prisoners in the barracks were ordered to lie down on the floor.) Commandant Linnas; Lieutenant Harry Koppel, his deputy; Valentine Keder, head of the investigation unit of the Special Department; and Giesen, the field headquarters commissioner, usually supervised executions. Otherwise, every officer at the Tartu concentration camp, particularly those from the Special Department, at one time or another participated in the executions. Two trucks would stop in front of Barracks no. 5. As Lepik (when he was commandant) was reading aloud the names off the list, a guard went inside the barracks to fetch the victims. Those individuals condemned to death, in pairs, were stripped of their clothes down to their underwear, and their hands were tied behind their backs. (Following the escape of a prisoner, all the condemned were customarily tied with rope to each other.) Each prisoner was assigned a guard, and then all climbed into the first truck. Members of the OK, who were to be posted around the execution site, boarded the second truck. Sometimes guards were already drunk before the execution. Former prisoners recalled the eerie sound of the songs that the drunken guards bawled while leaving for the execution site. The guards that stayed in the camp did not miss their chance to misappropriate at least some of the clothes that the condemned left behind. Trying to snatch the best items inevitably led to fights among the guards.[44]

After a short while, buses replaced trucks as a means of transportation of the condemned to the execution site. There were two such buses—a small REO and a big GMC—both bright red. Those were unusual buses; without seats but with benches along the sides, they had previously been used for transporting fish. Elmar Kink drove the REO, while Herbert Tamm was the GMC bus driver.[45] On occasion, the Tartu concentration camp made requests to the local bus depot. The buses headed to the so-called Jalaka Line, an antitank ditch about three miles southwest of Tartu. Following the outbreak of the Russo-German war, Soviet military authorities ordered the local population to build a defense against the advancing German troops. They chose the village of Lemmatsi as the site for a

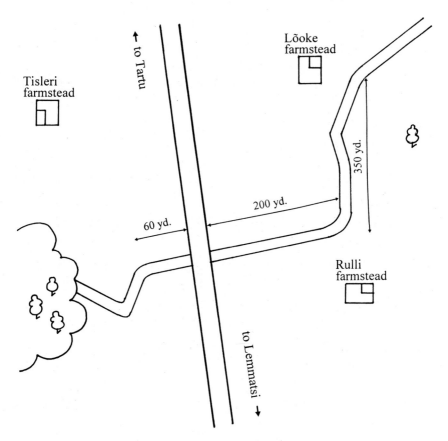

5. Mass execution site—the so-called "Jalaka Line"—near Tartu (adapted from the original, 1961); USHMM, RG-06.026.11.

giant, one-mile-long antitank ditch. The trench, which ran across the Tartu-Riga highway, was surrounded by farmsteads, some of them as close as fifty yards. Farmers knew all too well what was going on at the trench at night. Prohibited from leaving their homes during the executions, farmers got used to the sound of gunshots, which were often interrupted by screams of terror. Sometimes they heard guards singing popular Estonian songs such as "Eestimaa, mu isamaa" (Estonia, my homeland) and "Metsa läksid sa ja metsa läksin ma" (you went to the forest and so did I).[46]

There were no fixed days for executions, which were carried out as often as twice a day in July and August, and twice a week thereafter. Generally, Barracks no.

5 was emptied as quickly as it was filled. While the concentration camp was still at the exhibition grounds, it was either Lepik or Alexander Koolmeister who assembled a firing squad. Later, at the Kuperianov Barracks, this responsibility fell on Elmar Ardla, one of the three officers on duty. Ardla commanded the platoon from which executioners were drawn. At roll call, Ardla customarily enquired if anybody wanted to volunteer for execution duty. The volunteers were then assembled in a special firing squad.[47] They were usually off-duty guards. Sometimes there were more volunteers than needed, which ruled out the possibility that anyone was forced to participate in an execution against his will.[48] Thus Jüriste honored the request of one of the guards, who asked to be relieved because of heart disease. "Alright," the guard commander said, "if you are such a coward, I will not assign you to the firing squad."[49] As one of the executioners, Hans Laats, later explained, "only those participated in executions who wanted to. Those who did not express such a desire were not even asked to participate." Among the volunteers were several eighteen-year-olds.[50] Some of the guards became almost permanent members of the firing squad, volunteering whenever they had time. The guards were further induced to participate on the promise of the meager possessions of the executed as well as additional vodka allowances.[51] Fritz Giesen made sure that executioners had enough alcohol, of which he consumed a substantial amount himself. The guards appreciated Giesen's bringing milk-cans with spirits and beer into the camp. During his visits to the camp, Giesen behaved as if he were the boss, making the rounds and punching prisoners. Reportedly, Giesen lived in a four-bedroom apartment lavishly decorated with furniture confiscated from Jews.[52]

The list of executioners at Tartu concentration camp is long:

Arnold Eelmets | Karl Laurits
Evald Eelmets | Agu Leetmaa
Herman Ehrlich | Olav Linde
Karl Elk | Herbert Luha
Voldemar Jakobson | Johannes Luhasaar
Johannes Käärik | Endel Mark
Osvald Kahur | Endel Matto
Victor Kaur | Johannes Pennar
Valter Kerro | Herbert Ratnik
Nikolai Kiima | Elmar Robert

Arvo Kivijarv

Alfred Kolberg

Aleksander Kroon

August-Feliks Kroon

Jaan Kübar

Alfred Kukk

Alfons Külaots

Udo Kupper

Ilmar Kütt

Edgar Laabent

Hans Laats

Alexander Sägi

Paul Sepp

Enn Sügis

Ernst Suits

Villem Talvik

Robert Taska

Alfred Tõnismaa

Elmar Trossek

Elmar Unt

Alexander Vaht[53]

Prisoners were forced to kneel facing the trench. Immediately before the execution, Leppik (and later Linnas) announced the verdict: On account of crimes committed against the regime, the arrestees were being sentenced to death. Each victim was paired with an executioner who took position directly behind him or her. Koolmeister, and on occasion Jüriste, usually gave the firing order. Inevitably, there were several misses. One of the officers—Linnas, Laats, Koolmeister, Ardla, Jüriste, Koppel, or Giesen—then came to the edge of the pit and delivered "mercy" shots. Koppel, Aardla, and Linnas belonged to the same fraternity and thus were referred to as the "Viroonia trio." The camp guards buried the bodies, received their share of alcohol, and left.[54]

For the majority of Tartu Jews, the concentration camp was only a short stop on their way to death. Initially, Jews were herded into the synagogue on Turu Street. Then, however, the military authorities decided to start using the synagogue as a makeshift POW camp. Jews in their turn were moved into two different buildings on Alexandri and Pargi Streets (a detention facility on 9 Pargi Street came to be known as the "Jewish camp"). From there, one family after another, Jews were taken to the concentration camp. It was a matter of days before they were all executed. Upon the question of what was going to happen to them next, Jews received a prompt answer: they were about to be taken to Riga. The only difference between the execution of Jewish and non-Jewish prisoners was that in the former case no lists were drawn up. Harry Koppel supervised more executions of Jews than anybody else, not the least because he was eager to get their valuables.[55]

The first known mass execution of Jews took place on July 15 or 16 and claimed the lives of fifty men, women, and children.[56] In late October another group of Jews was delivered to the Tartu concentration camp. There were between twenty and thirty people in that group, mainly women of different ages, as well as three children. The execution order was in place within a few days. Under the pretext of taking the Jews to a bath, the guards forced the women and children out of Barracks no. 5 and ordered them to undress. Those who refused were stripped by force. In the beginning the prisoners remained calm, but once they realized what was going on they started crying (including the children). Their reaction did not affect the guards, who were busy tying the victims' hands with rope. Once finished, they shoved the Jews into a bus with curtained windows; the condemned crouched on the floor while the guards sat. Two of the three guards climbed onto the roof of the bus. Linnas, Koppel, Laats, Ardla, and Giesen—all the officers—followed the bus in a car, all the way along Riia Avenue, then left. The bus stopped next to the Jalaka ditch. Harry Koppel was in charge. He ordered the women off the bus, some of whom obeyed while others were violently thrown to the ground. One of the women, twenty-eight-year-old Tartu native Golde S., was completely naked; one of the guards, Udo Kuppar, raped her on the way to the execution site. On their knees, facing the trench, the victims heard Koppel's announcement that as Jews they were to be exterminated and hence the execution. Once the firing squad did its job, Koppel finished off those women who showed signs of life.[57] Karl Elk personally knew the Mirvitz family, who ran a china shop in downtown Tartu. And here he was, sitting on a bus next to twelve-year-old David, eleven-year-old Eugene, and eight-year-old Lilian, while their mother, Mia Mirvitz, walked to her death. Because Mia Mirvitz was an ethnic German, she was given a choice to leave her children and thus survive, but she refused. It was their turn now: Endel Mark led the children by hand to the edge of the pit. Lilian became unruly, constantly asking about her mother. "Here," Mark showed the girl the corpse of her mother in the bottom of the pit. Next, from a short distance, he shot Lilian in the head.[58] One of the Jews among the executed wore a distinctive gray overcoat; a guard later asked the camp tailor to alter that coat to fit his figure.[59]

The snow was already on the ground when Elmar Puusepp, a prisoner at the Tartu concentration camp, received his next assignment—to saw firewood for one of the homeowners on Alexandri Street. While doing his work, Puusepp saw

a red bus pulling in front of the former Jewish school across the street. Karl Linnas, the then Tartu concentration camp commandant, addressed men, women,
and children as they were leaving the school building. Linnas explained to the
Jews that they were going to Riga and therefore had to take all their belongings
with them. Linnas said the same thing to a little girl with a life-size doll, whom
he helped onto the bus. Having finished his work, Puusepp returned to the camp.
The bus he had seen in the morning was already there, yet empty; one of the
guards had the doll.[60] Oskar Art was the bus driver who took those Jews—twenty
adults and five children—first to the concentration camp and then to the Jalaka
ditch. The adults, their hands tied with rope, were executed first, followed by the
children.[61] Sometimes small children were executed separately from their parents. Hans Laats recalled one such case when up to ten children between three
and fifteen years of age were murdered. According to Laats, Koppel shot the
youngest of the children in the head while holding them by the leg. What was
left of the tiny bodies, Koppel threw into the pit.[62] This time the guards received
beer instead of vodka. To conceal the extent of the murder, later during the war
the Germans started exhuming and burning the bodies of the victims executed
during the first years of the occupation. In 1943 the RSHA created the so-called
Sonderkommando 1005 (also known as Blobel Commando) especially for that
purpose. The actual exhumation was done by Jewish prisoners.[63] In November
1943, between seventy-five and eighty Jews arrived at the Tartu concentration
camp from Tallinn Central prison. The Jews looked miserable: emaciated, they
had been denied baths for months. The exhumations commenced in December
and lasted until April of the next year. Although the gruesome works at the Jalaka
antitank ditch were an open secret, the Germans tried, at least symbolically, to
prevent the public from learning about the scope of the operation. As Jewish
prisoners moved along the pit, they enclosed the immediate work area with a tall
fence. The Germans filmed them working. The suffocating smoke of the burning
flesh clogged the air for weeks, disturbing city dwellers. "The Communists are
burning," one of the guards, Karl Eelmets, explained to the camp inmates. Over
a period of four months, most of the Jewish workers perished. Tied to each other
with rope, suffering from cold and malnutrition, only twenty-two people were
still alive in April. As the last corpses went up in flames, the German guards from
SK 1005 herded the remaining Jews into a nearby sauna, sealed the door and the
windows, and then set it on fire. Local Estonian farmers were the only ones to

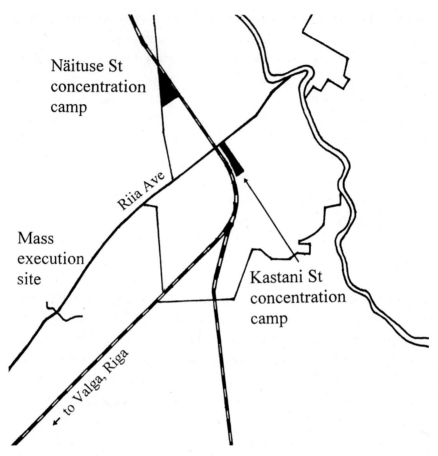

Näituse St
concentration
camp

Riia Ave

Mass
execution
site

Kastani St
concentration
camp

to Valga, Riga

6. Sites of terror in and around Tartu. Prepared by author.

tell the story.[64] Only ashes remained of more than 3,500 people who had been executed in Tartu between 1941 and 1944.[65]

JEWS OF MIXED ORIGIN

Whatever difficulties the Estonian Security Police had had when pinning crimes on what the Nazis called "full-blooded Jews," it turned out to be even harder in the case of Jews from mixed families. Several Jews among those executed had non-Jewish wives. The fact that somebody's partner was Estonian or German did not safeguard against arrest. At most, it could postpone it for a few days, as happened to Arkadii Lury. When conducting a search in Dr. Salomon Lury's apartment on September 1, the OK refrained from detaining his son, Arkadii, simply because he had an Estonian wife. However, they came back two days later, this time seeking him. There was nothing that could save Salomon Epstein from imminent death. However, the concerted effort by his colleagues and his German wife made the Estonian Security Police change the execution order for Epstein to one of internment in a concentration camp for an indefinite period. Born in East Prussia, Helene Epstein (Tomantat) made a good impression on the German Security Police: she ran one of the best male fashion stores in Tallinn; two of her brothers served in the Wehrmacht; her son had been deported to Russia. Helene Epstein said she pleaded on behalf of Salomon Epstein because he was her husband and because he helped her family greatly. At one point, the police arrested the entire family of Josef Rubanovich, including his Russian wife, Vera, and their daughter, Kira. Vera's sister appealed to Minister of the Interior Angelus to have her released from Harku prison because "she was not Jewish and had no other faults."[66] Apparently Vera Rubanovich was released, because on April 28, 1944, she was arrested again. The cause for arrest was formulated as follows: "an ethnic Russian who was married to a Jew." Simultaneously with Vera Rubanovich, her daughter, Kira, was also arrested. The charges were the same, except that Kira had divorced her Jewish husband in 1938.[67]

"Aryan" wives now and then sought information about their Jewish husbands. Some women tried to find comfort in their loved one's death, while the others sought to go on with their life. Two German women—Anna Bertha Kliachko (Lüdtke) and Margaret Mirwitz (Krones)—were issued the death certificates of their husbands, who "died" in Tallinn Central prison and the Harku concentration camp respectively. In both cases the word "executed" was crossed out and "died" written above it. The circumstances of Konstantin Mirwitz's "death" involved dark irony. The fact that Mirwitz was a Lutheran and also a member of the German Cultural Council left the police with only one option: to evoke his Jewishness. Having established that Mirwitz was born Jewish, the police dispatched him to prison so that "he would not be able to evade trial and punishment." Notoriously, the German Security Police cared much less about nuances than their Estonian counterpart and tended to reveal the true cause of death to the relatives of the murdered Jews. Elias Elian was executed on September 19, 1941. Five days later, Elian's wife, Elisabeth (apparently German), requested from KdS-Estland Sandberger information about her husband. She wanted to know if her husband was Jewish and whether he was still alive. Elisabeth Elian explained that she needed that data to file for divorce. The Estonian Security Police intended to write off Elias Elian's case as death from "natural causes," but was overruled by Sandberger, who urged the police to tell the woman that her husband had been executed for being a full Jew. With Anna Scher, the Estonian Security Police interacted without any mediation: the woman was told that her husband Mikhail had "died." Meta Ulrike Katz (Kirnmann) was Estonian and therefore approached the BIV Department. The nature of Meta Katz's request was similar to that of Elisabeth Elian: she wanted a divorce from her husband, Salomon Katz, in case he was still alive. She might even have been able to do so because Salomon Katz was not executed until a week later, on October 4. Elfrieda Rogovsky waited until the following June to inquire whether her Jewish husband had "by any chance" died by then, so that she could divorce him posthumously. It did not seem to be a problem given that Aron Rogovsky had been executed on September 5, 1941.[68]

The Jewish women from mixed marriages, like female Jews in general, survived the first few months of Nazi occupation. The wife and son of Victor Alaots were arrested in Tartu on November 11. Following the arrest of his wife, Victor Alaots received a summons to report to the local Security Police office. A police official strongly recommended to Alaots that he divorce his wife, as well as refrain from any subversive activities against the new regime. For a month or so, Riva Alaots and her child were locked in a Jewish school on Alexandri Street. Throughout that time the head of the family regularly visited the school, bringing milk for his son. He saw Jewish women and children in the school but not men, who by that time had already been executed. In December, Victor Alaots was reunited with his son, who did not qualify as a "thoroughbred" Jew. Riva Alaots never returned.[69]

Jews of mixed origin, the so-called *Mischlinge*, had never been numerous in Estonia and, therefore—according to RKO Lohse—did not require special legislation. By mid-1942 there were about 250 such people in Latvia and between 10 and 20 in Estonia. Lohse recommended treating those Jews as Mischlinge of the first grade, in accordance with the classification adopted in Nazi Germany. Lohse had previously been impelled by BdS-Ostland Jost to issue an order prohibiting the employment of Mischlinge in the local administration.[70] In the Estonian case the order was totally unnecessary. Tamara Köhler was born in 1924 into a mixed family. Her Jewish mother evacuated to Russia proper but her Estonian father stayed in Narva. Tamara herself was registered as "German," which seemed to be all right with the Estonian Security Police.[71] Another senseless formality: in November 1943 the German Security Police in the Ostland ordered all Jews stripped of their identity documents. As everybody knew, by then all Jews in Estonia had already been locked up in camps. Nevertheless, the regulation regarding IDs also applied to half-Jews and three-quarter-Jews. For the first time ever, the document mentioned members of the Karaite sect of Judiasm, who were not to be treated as Jews.[72] Isaac Babadzhan was the only Karaite registered in Tallinn throughout the war.[73]

Among the victims were several foreign Jews who had moved to Estonia shortly before the war. Among the first German Jews who arrived in Estonia (in 1936) was Maria Anna Hoefer. As a Lutheran, Hoefer did not attract much attention, until in August 1942 one of her neighbors denounced her. Magda Beek claimed that thirty-seven-year-old Hoefer of all things wanted to rape her. Leopold Silberstein emigrated in 1933 from Germany to Prague. Four years later, Silberstein received an appointment at Tartu University as a professor of Czech language and literature. In the fall semester of 1940, Silberstein switched to teaching the Russian language. Apprehensive of potential anti-Jewish violence, on July 13, 1941, Silberstein left Tartu for the countryside. The following day, Silberstein was arrested by the OK, which explained to him the reason for his arrest: Silberstein was Jewish. It did not matter that Dina Michelson, one of Silberstein's colleagues at TU, was a Latvian citizen, for she too was murdered for being a Jew. Leopold Levanovich came to Estonia directly from Germany in 1938. Levanovich had spent two-thirds of his life working as a physician and a dentist in Berlin. From June 1941 until his arrest on September 22 of the same year, Levanovich worked in a neurological hospital in Tallinn. Levanovich received the same treatment from the police as the local Jews: he was charged with Communist activities. On October 8, the director of the Harku prison received an order to transfer Levanovich immediately to Tallinn Central prison, the site of his execution three days later.[74]

Rochelle Riva Brenner arrived in Estonia in 1938. Brenner was born out of wedlock to a Swiss mother and a Jewish father. She emigrated from Germany to Austria, only to seek refuge in Estonia a couple of years later. The Estonian

Security Police listed Brenner as Jewish, even though the woman herself claimed Swiss ethnicity. Upon her arrest on October 10, 1941, Brenner "confessed" to being Jewish. An older couple, Mihkel and Tiina Piirikiri, who lived across from Brenner's apartment on 29 Harju Street in Tallinn, testified that she had mingled with Jews, as well as with a Russian political commissar who allegedly brought her packages of various sorts. The witnesses claimed that Brenner extolled the Soviet order, and now she was making friends among the German military. Brenner denied the charges, saying that she had never interacted with Communists and their collaborators or assisted in the deportation of Estonians. Her execution was carried out on November 7. Dora Ratner was eighteen when she arrived in Tallinn from Berlin in December 1930. Neither political nor racial grounds played a role in her decision to immigrate; love brought Dora Ratner to Estonia. She married a man who owned a candy factory in Tallinn, and who subsequently was arrested by the NKVD. Dora Ratner must have been so happily in love that she did not notice what was happening in Europe. The woman asked the investigation to ascertain from any of her relatives in Germany and Austria that she was not a Communist.[75]

Remarkably, Jews with passports issued by foreign countries (unoccupied by Nazi Germany) escaped death and even were later released from detention. For the first time, the Nazis encountered the problem of Jewish foreign nationals following the conquest of France in June 1940. American Jews faired the best: in the fall of 1941, the German Foreign Office convinced Adolf Eichmann to exempt U.S. citizens from deportations so as to avoid acts of discrimination against ethnic Germans in the United States.[76] In Tallinn, thirty-four-year-old U.S. citizen Elias Dreyer was arrested on December 16, but was released on January 30 on the order of the German Security Police. Dreyer and his four-year-old son could stay free but were required to register in a police precinct daily. On February 1, 1942, new guidelines went out to all police departments to spare Jewish foreign citizens.[77] Apparently the order did not cover the Jews in the occupied East European countries, who were all doomed.

JEWS—POWS

Nobody thought of the Jews who were taken off the *Eestirand* as prisoners of war. Indeed, they were arrested as Jews. The issue of Jewish inmates came to the fore as soon as the first POW camps were established in Estonia in the summer and early fall of 1941. In addition to Jews who found themselves in POW camps in Estonia, the Security Police in Tallinn also received Jewish POWs from Finland. Each Jewish POW had a story to tell. Ezra Pressman was mobilized in his native Slutsk in Ukraine on June 23, 1941. In September, near Leningrad, German troops surrounded his 204th Infantry regiment; Pressman was first transferred from the Volosovo POW camp to the main camp (*Stammlager* or Stalag) 381 at Tapa, and on January 29, 1942, to Tallinn Central prison. The German Security Police ordered Pressman's execution on February 23, 1942. Mikhail Kissis was another person executed on that day. Twenty-year-old Kissis came from Ukraine too. The 47th Engineering Battalion to which he belonged had been building military barracks on Saaremaa Island. On September 29, 1941, Kissis was dispatched to Tallinn Central prison as a "POW-Jew." On February 18, 1942, the abovementioned Stalag 381 at Tapa delivered eight Jews to the Security Police in Tallinn. Three of them admitted they were Jewish, whereas the other five did not. The latter had been identified as "Jews" by their fellow POWs, an identification later confirmed by a German physician who checked them for circumcision.[78] Undoubtedly all eight faced a firing squad.

The Punishment Planning Commission of the Estonian Security Police also recommended capital punishment for David Katz. It was in 1940 in Odessa that Katz had become a Communist Party member. As a political commissar, Katz was to expect no mercy when he fell prisoner in June 1942 near Volkhov. His execution took place in Tallinn on January 14, 1943. Miron Birmann had been at Tapa since May 1942, not as a POW but as a camp physician. Birmann had been born into a mixed family; his mother was an ethnic German from Kuressaare. This fact of his biography protected Birmann for some time, until in December 1942 the camp administration accused Birmann of having assisted several prisoners to escape. On February 5, 1943, KdS-Estland Sandberger ordered Birmann's execution. Abram Maisel had a similar experience, except that he was one of the few Estonian Jews who did indeed collaborate with the Soviet power. A native of Viljandi, Maisel was sentenced in 1938 to forced labor for espionage. Thanks to the Soviet takeover in June 1940, Maisel was not only released from prison but in fact became its director. Maisel had barely served for two months in the Red Army before he was taken prisoner in late October. Unexpectedly to himself, Maisel became part of the Wehrmacht, first as an interpreter and then as a physician. Another two months passed before Maisel's Jewish identity was exposed. He was shot in Pärnu on April 1, 1942.[79]

A group of Soviet POWs, among them three Jews, was shipped to Estonia from Finland on January 2, 1942. Moses and Boris Levi came from Estonia, while Alter Meyer Kopel was originally a refugee from Lithuania. All three were mobilized into the Red Army and taken to the Soviet naval base on Hanko Island. In late November, the 124th Engineering Battalion to which they belonged was dispatched to another island, Russaari, and later surrendered to Finnish forces. Isaac Schatz went through several POW camps until he too ended up in Tallinn Central prison. As soon as Head of Department BIV Viks learned that among the Soviet POWs there were Jews and a Communist, he passed that information to the German Security Police. On the order of KdS-Estland Sandberger, all four individuals were executed on January 14, 1942.[80]

On one occasion, the Finnish State Police (*Valtiollinen Poliisi* or Valpo) handed over several Jews to the German Security Police in Estonia. In accordance with an agreement between KdS-Estland Sandberger and the head of the Valpo, Arno Anthoni, the Finnish side could ship illegal immigrants to Estonia. On August 28, 1942, the Valpo deported twenty-six Estonians and Russians to Tallinn. The deportation list from November 6 had twenty-six names on it: eighteen POWs of Russian and Estonian origin, and eight Jews. Among the Jewish prisoners there were two children: six-month-old Franz Kollmann and eleven-year-old Kurt Huppert. With the exception of Elias Kopelovsky, who was a Latvian citizen, the rest originally came from Germany and Austria. Valpo had plans to ship to Estonia at least thirty-five foreign-born Jews, but failed to implement the plan because of the outcry in the Finnish public. The November deportation came about as a result of negotiations with the Valpo and remained the only case in which the Finnish authorities yielded to Nazi pressure to surrender Finland's Jews.[81] Until today scholars have believed that the Jews who were deported from Helsinki on November 6, 1942, were later murdered at Auschwitz-Birkenau. In fact, they were executed shortly after their arrival in Tallinn. Head of Department IVA Bergmann went to Tallinn harbor to meet the German freighter with the prisoners on board. The Jews were immediately dispatched to Tallinn Central prison. On December 8 Anthoni requested information from Sandberger on Elias Kopelovsky. According to rumors emanating from Stockholm, Kopelovsky had been executed. Anthoni, however, believed that Kopelovsky ended up in a labor camp. Sandberger assured Anthony that Kopelovsky, along with other Jews, had been transferred to Berlin, where he was indeed confined to a labor camp. The rumors regarding Kopelovsky's execution were false, he said.[82] Sandberger was lying, again. On November 10, 1942, on the order of the KdS-Estland, Head of Department IVE SS-Ustuf. Gert von Seefeld arranged for a summary execution of Finnish Jews.[83] According to a Finnish source, the youngest of the prisoners, Franz Kollmann, was poisoned while in Tallinn Central prison.[84] Of the eight Jews, only Georg Kollmann (born in 1912) miraculously survived.[85]

INFORMATION ABOUT THE HOLOCAUST AT HOME AND ABROAD

The fact that information about the November 1942 deportation from Finland had reached Sweden prompts a larger question: what was known abroad about the plight of the Jews in the Baltics? That would include awareness of the Holocaust generally as well as specific knowledge about local collaboration in the Nazi murder of Jews. So what did Estonians say or think about the Jews, if anything at all?

All sources indicate that the majority of Estonians attached little importance to the "Jewish Question" both before and during the war. An Estonian police official wrote in 1943 that Jewish numbers were so low in Estonia that Estonians barely noticed Jews. Unlike in Nazi Germany, the "Jewish Question" had never been a priority in Estonia. Jews were not a problem. In short, people did not care.[86] The Estonian public paid no attention to the plight of the Jews. The Warsaw ghetto uprising was the only related occurrence that was mentioned in conversation. Even then, the rendering of those April–May 1943 events was rather incomplete. People spoke of the fighting that erupted in Warsaw between the Poles and the Jews on the one side and the Germans on the other. The local population was up in arms against the Germans, who had created unbearable conditions in the city.[87] The Estonian anti-German opposition barely commented on the Nazi policy of extermination. A flyer entitled *Võitlev Eestlane* (fighting Estonian), of August 28, 1943, contained a vague reference to Jewish genocide. When discussing the Nazi terror, the flyer mentioned that "we should add to that Jewish concentration camps."[88] One month earlier, GK-Estland Litzmann received an anonymous letter that extolled Russia and severely criticized Germany. Judging by the contents, the author of the letter was an Estonian Communist. Among other accusations, the anonymous author wrote the following: "They [the Germans] murder the Jews, rob the nations, and then live off their labor."[89]

Many passionate battles have been fought over the question of what exactly the Allies knew about the Holocaust and what prevented them from intervening. It would be naïve to think that the West would have intervened on behalf of a handful of Estonian Jews. And the Allies knew indeed that only a small number of Jews were left in Estonia at the end of 1941. The anti-Hitler coalition (remarkably, the Americans) possessed fairly accurate information about the genesis of the "Final Solution of the Jewish Question" in Estonia. The hub of information was the U.S. Legation in Stockholm. Swedish neutrality enabled extensive data collection. Trade with Nazi Germany on the one hand and the influx of refugees from the former Baltic States on the other placed Stockholm at the foreground of intelligence gathering.

Informants within Estonia passed on the information to the U.S. Legation in Stockholm, which had sections responsible for each of the three Baltic countries. Thus, by late December 1941 American diplomats knew that most of the Estonian Jews had left the country for Russia proper. Just as correct was the information that the remaining Estonian Jews were interned at Harku (described as a correction house for boys) not far from Tallinn. About thirty Jews were supposedly interned at Tartu.[90] Of the three Baltic nations, the Latvian exiles in the United States appeared to be the best informed about the situation back home. An extensive report that the Latvian Legation in Washington, D.C., prepared in 1943 also mentioned Estonia. The report provided a detailed account of the destruction of both the Estonian Jews and the Czech Jews from the Theresienstadt transport. Shortly after the Germans' arrival, Jews were compelled to wear distinctive marks on their clothes. From the assembly point in Harku some male Jews were sent "farther away." The remaining Jewish women, children, and old men soon followed the men into the camp. No further information was available, except that no more Jews were seen in Tallinn and that the Harku camp "appeared to be empty." The supposition was that the Jews either died of privation or were executed. Latvian diplomats were aware as well of a mass execution of Czech Jews in October 1942. A thirty-car train with prisoners arrived at Raasiku station. From Raasiku, Jews were transported to a special camp at Jägala. The locals who saw the prisoners at the station believed that they were Czechs and not Jews—well-dressed men, women, and children. Nobody heard about that camp afterward. However, according to the report, soon thereafter Estonian villagers came across a ravine filled up with fresh earth . . . [91]

Information about Jewish forced labor camps in Estonia barely leaked out of the country. There is a reference to the American initiative to ransom the remaining four thousand Jews still engaged in synthetic oil production at the end of June 1944.[92] It is rather unlikely that the scheme, which originated in Stockholm, had received any further consideration in Washington. On June 29, 1944, Peter Kleist of the Ostland Ministry offered to release at least two thousand Latvian Jews to the U.S. War Refugee Board in exchange for a cash payment. A few days later, Kleist came out with a more staggering plan: he suggested evacuating the remaining Jews from the Baltic countries in exchange for medical supplies. This proposal, too, fell through. As regards the Baltics, the only achievement of the War Refugee Board was evacuating in the fall of 1944 about 1,200 people from Estonia, Latvia, and Lithuania. None of them was Jewish.[93] Ironically, the evacuation was carried out shortly after the Nazis killed off the Jews at Klooga; among the evacuees there might also have been individuals who helped to bring about the "Final Solution of the Jewish Question."

American Jewry struggled to get information about the fate of their brethren in Eastern Europe. Because of the lack of reliable sources of information, much less was known about the situation of the Jews in the Baltic States than, for instance, in Poland. Although Nazi anti-Semitic propaganda had only a minor effect on the Baltic peoples—as *The American Jewish Year Book* reported in 1942—certain segments of the population participated in pogroms. In October 1942, the *Manchester Guardian* wrote that out of fifty thousand Jewish residents of Riga, only four thousand were still alive. In Lithuania, the Nazis and "Lithuanian Quislings" were said to have executed most of the Jewish population. There were rumors that the Estonian Jews had either been gassed or deported to an unknown destination. Referring to an article in the February 1943 issue of *Deutsche Zeitung im Ostland,* the Jewish press carried the news that Estonia had become "free of Jews." Using the same source, *The American Jewish Year Book* announced that the Estonians had been forced to proclaim October 26 an annual national holiday to mark the departure of the last Jew.[94] The fact of local collaboration in the extermination of Jews was generally known, though disputed. There was little credibility attached to the reports that originated with individual refugees who managed to get out of the occupied Baltic countries. For example, a woman described as a "recent visitor from Riga" told American diplomats in Stockholm that a total of 26,000 Jews had been killed in Latvia. She claimed that it was the Latvians who murdered those Jews, while the Poles and Lithuanians refused to shoot. The informant assumed that the fancy clothes that the people of the lower classes began to wear were evidently taken from the Jews whom they shot.[95] Interestingly enough, when *Ny Dag* (an organ of the Swedish Communist Party) printed a story about the Nazi occupation of Latvia, it identified the Germans as solely responsible for the extermination of the Jews.[96] It is all the more remarkable because the author of the article was Andrejs Jablonskis, a Latvian Communist who was appointed minister of justice of Soviet Latvia; of all people, he must have known about the extent of local collaboration in Latvia. Indeed, the article illustrates the trend introduced by the Soviets in the aftermath of the Second World War, namely to downplay indigenous collaboration in the Holocaust.

Lithuanian émigrés also claimed ignorance about local collaboration in the extermination of the Jews. In July 1943, the Swedish magazine *NU* published an article by Ignas Scheynius, in which he argued that the Lithuanians refused to assist the Germans in killing Jews.[97] At times, denial digressed into brazen lies. The same author claimed later that the Germans recruited ethnic Ukrainians and Kyrgyz for the police service in Lithuania. Those individuals had proper Communist training and therefore were fit to perform dirty tasks. It was allegedly they who carried out the destruction of the Lithuanian Jewish community. This and similar insinuations were disseminated from the highest tribunes, notoriously before the Foreign Political Club of the Swedish Parliament.[98] The atrocities committed against the Jews in Lithuania became another source of contention between the Lithuanians and the Poles. The animosity between the two communities was played out in various settings, including international media. A BBC radio broadcast in the Lithuanian language on December 8, 1942, warned Lithuanians in Lithuania against persecuting Poles, Jews, and other minorities. The broadcast was based on information that the Polish Embassy received from its Legation in Stockholm. The Polish lobby obviously wanted in this way to pressure the "Lithuanian Quislings" to abandon their discriminatory practices against the Polish minority. Thus Jews were mentioned only pro forma. The BBC originally planned to produce a series of similar broadcasts, but dropped the idea under pressure from the British Foreign Office, which wanted to avoid further straining relations between Polish and Lithuanian émigrés.[99] However, the war of words continued unabated and was soon transplanted to North America. Thus the Lithuanian Social Democrat newspaper *Maujienos* (Chicago) blasted the Poles for their malicious anti-Lithuanian propaganda. "They tried to spread news that Lithuanians were assisting the Nazis in liquidating Jews," the newspaper wrote, "whereas it was well known that next to Germans the worst antisemites in Europe were the Poles."[100] The conflicting reports confused the analysts at the U.S. Legation in Stockholm, who could no longer tell who was murdering Jews and why. In the case of Lithuania, for example, the Americans came to think that the Germans were killing Jews with the purpose of taking over their commerce, industry, and real estate. The occupiers were eliminating Jews because they wanted to Germanize the Lithuanian cities.[101] The Estonians' role in the murder of Jews was not specifically discussed at the Stockholm Legation.

8

JEWISH TRANSPORTS FROM CZECHOSLOVAKIA AND GERMANY, FALL 1942

Circumstantial evidence indicates that the rerouting of two Jewish transports from Germany and the Protectorate to Estonia was largely accidental. Between August 15 and October 3, 1942, a total of seven trains departed from Berlin and Theresienstadt for the East, all but two heading to Riga. Train no. Da404 that left Theresienstadt on September 1 was on the road for fully four days. On September 5 the train went back to the Protectorate. It is unclear, though, whether one or two Jewish transports arrived in Raasiku from Germany. According to survivors, there was one such transport. However, when it came to the arrival date of the German transport, former prisoners mentioned either mid-September or early October. Estonian railway personnel complicated the matter even further, arguing that the total number of Jewish transports that had arrived in Estonia in the fall of 1942 could be as high as five. Two different lists assembled in Berlin and Frankfurt-on-Main tell two different stories. Confusion arose because the destination of one of the transports was marked "Riga" and not "Raasiku." What might also have caused a mistake was that one of the listed transports originated in Berlin, while the other was assembled in Frankfurt-on-Main but stopped in Berlin to collect more human cargo. Train no. Da405 that left Berlin at 7:50 P.M. on September 10 arrived in Raasiku at 12:15 P.M. on September 13. One other train, listed as Da406, departed Berlin on September 26, supposedly bound for Riga. That was the information the Frankfurt authorities had on record.[1] The list of Jewish transports compiled in Berlin, however, indicated clearly that the train went instead to Tallinn (Raasiku).[2] With the benefit of hindsight, I would argue that Da405 most likely ended its journey in Riga, while Da406 continued all the way to Estonia.

Raasiku, a small train station fifteen miles east of Tallinn, was the first stop for more than two thousand Jews who arrived in Estonia in September 1942. In preparation for the deportations, in August construction began on a new concentration camp. The camp, which was located in Jägala, five miles north of Raasiku, had an all-Estonian staff. The camp administration was composed of five people: commandant Alexander Laak, his deputy Ralf Gerrets, senior guard Jaan Viik, bookkeeper Jaan Vilkes, and supply officer Kristian Rääk. In addition, the camp employed a driver, Arnold Madar, and seventeen guards. All these people were on the payroll of the Estonian Security Police.

Ralf Gerrets was born in 1905, the year of revolution that was marked with unprecedented anti-German violence in the then Baltic provinces. The name "Gerrets" was of Swedish origin. Gerrets's father was Estonian, spoke excellent German, and appreciated all things German. After Gerrets Senior remarried, this time a Baltic German, German became the language of everyday use in the family. In 1915 the Gerrets moved to St. Petersburg, where the head of the family got a bookkeeping job in an English trading company. In the wake of the Bolshevik Revolution, the Gerrets family returned to Estonia. In 1925 Ralf Gerrets graduated from a German school and began serving his term in the Estonian army. Gerrets had failed to find a job, which forced him to pursue a military career. As a consequence of hard living conditions, Gerrets contracted tuberculosis, which he had fought ever since.[3]

From his early years, Gerrets had a split personality. He was brought up German; his ethnicity was marked as "German." In a word, Gerrets belonged to the category of outcasts dubbed *kadaka sakslased* (juniper Germans)—a derogatory name for Germanized Estonians. This label caused great discomfort for Gerrets, who in 1930 officially changed his ethnicity to "Estonian." The identity problem continued haunting Gerrets later at Jägala. Former camp guards remembered Gerrets as a Baltic German. According to survivors, Gerrets insisted he was a Baltic German.[4] Following the 1940 occupation of Estonia, Gerrets was automatically transferred into the Soviet 22nd Army Corps. In March 1941, however, Gerrets came down with pneumonia aggravated by tuberculosis and was discharged from the military. In the same month, Gerrets's parents resettled in the Third Reich. While German troops were conquering one Estonian city after another, Gerrets found himself in a sanatorium in Tallinn-Nõmme, treating kidney tuberculosis. In October 1941 Gerrets moved to Haapsalu, where he joined the Omakaitse. However, his kidneys continued bothering him so that in the summer of the next year Gerrets admitted himself to another sanatorium, this time in Tartu.[5]

Having regained his health, at least for the time being, Gerrets joined the Estonian Security Police. Gerrets was appointed deputy commandant of the Jägala concentration camp. He received that position through his colleague from the OK, Alexander Laak, who became commandant of that camp. Laak coaxed Gerrets to join the Jägala staff by saying that it was going to be a short-term assignment in a naturally beautiful place—not work but simply pleasure. The pace of German military advances made him indeed believe that the job would only last four months. In addition, Gerrets, who was suffering from latent tuberculosis, capitalized on Laak's promise to provide him with health coverage for the whole year. Otherwise, Laak simply needed a man with a good command of German.[6] As regards Laak (who at one point changed his name from the Russian-sounding Krainev), he joined the Estonian Security Police to avenge his brother who had been killed by the Soviets. According to survivors, Laak did not come across as an anti-Semite. Laak once told a female prisoner that he looked upon them, the Jews, as nationals of a small country under foreign rule.[7]

Gerrets learned in just a few days why knowledge of German was so important. Before Gerrets and Laak assumed their duties at the Jägala camp, the two went on a business trip to Riga. Accompanied by SS-Oschaf. Karl Gehse and another officer from the German Security Police in Tallinn, they arrived at the Jewish ghetto in the Maskavas district of Riga. There, the guests from Estonia received a two-day-long introduction to mass murder. While touring the ghetto, they observed trucks loaded with the clothes of executed Jews. On the following day the Estonian delegation had a hands-on experience: they were taken to an execution site several miles from Riga. During the four hours that they spent at the pit, Gehse, Gerrets, and Laak witnessed the execution of four busloads of Jews. Gerrets recalled the most gruesome details of the murder. According to Gerrets, at one point Laak requested to "try his hand" on the Jews. Permission was granted; Laak murdered between thirty and forty people. In the evening of the same day they returned to Tallinn. Laak explained what the trip was all about: a Jewish transport was about to arrive in Jägala.[8]

The Estonian delegation's host in Riga was SS-Ostuf. Kurt Krause, the ghetto commandant. Over a hearty breakfast with wine Krause explained to his Estonian guests how the "Final Solution of the Jewish Question" worked in practice. Krause announced that Hitler had ordered all Jews around the world exterminated. However, it was impossible to murder all the Jews in the Nazi-controlled territories immediately. To ensure the success of the "mass operations," Jews were first to be concentrated in ghettos and special camps in their home countries. From those camps Jews were to be taken by trains to other countries for execution. In that way, Krause added, entire trainloads of Jews had disappeared without attracting much public attention. Krause then went into the specifics. He only had as many inmates in his ghetto, Krause told his Estonian colleagues, as necessary for sorting and repairing the clothes of the Jews that were executed on a daily basis. In short, the Riga ghetto functioned as a kind of factory for the extermination of the Jews and for supplying the German State with clothing from the executed. Finally, Krause said something about the two categories of Jewish transports that had arrived in the ghetto. The difference between the two was that the Jews were either immediately murdered or exploited as slave laborers. However, once the need for a workforce decreased, Jewish laborers were to be executed too.[9]

Work at Jägala commenced immediately after Laak and Gerrets returned from Riga; there was not that much time left before the arrival of the transport. The construction work was completed in two weeks. Prisoners from Tallinn Central prison erected a barbed-wire fence around the existing barracks and built six watchtowers. During the interwar period the barracks had been used by the Estonian army as a summer training camp and had neither running water nor electricity. The camp was divided by barbed wire into three zones: women's barracks, men's barracks, and warehouses. Next to the river there was a cluster of summerhouses used by camp administration. Potentially, the Jägala camp could accommodate up to nine hundred people.[10] Ten days after the beginning of construction, the camp personnel—twenty men—arrived. They were from the Estonian Security Police—fresh graduates from the Fürstenberg Police School near Berlin. Some of the guards had previously collaborated with the Soviets. Friedrich Anijalg, for example, joined the Komsomol in 1940 and worked in the *Kommunist* printing-house in Tallinn.[11]

The next step was to find a proper execution site. Laak and Bergmann, then head of Department AIV, found one quickly: the Kalevi-Liiva dunes in the vicinity of Kaberneeme village. (Before 1940, the site was used as an artillery range.) They came across an excellent location: a 100-by-50-foot hollow, hard to spot from the road. At the very last moment, Bergmann notified the camp leadership that they were to expect two Jewish transports instead of one. Because of the camp's limited capacity, Bergmann ordered the immediate execution of the Jews.[12] Once again, Tallinn Central prison dispatched a group of prisoners condemned to death to dig a big hole at Kalevi-Liiva. Laak, Mere, and Gerrets (whom prisoners mistook for a German) from time to time came to the site to see how the work was progressing. Laak was obviously drunk when he arrived at the pit one day. "Do not be afraid, work faster," Laak told the prisoners. "I will not bury you in that hole. It is meant for others to rot here." The prisoners then understood it was a mass grave they were digging.[13] Everything and everybody was ready for the arrival of Jews.

In the first days of September, Commandant Laak convened a meeting of the camp guards. In the presence of the head of the Estonian Security Police, Ain Ervin, Mere, Laak announced that camp personnel were about to carry out Hitler's fundamental order. Laak explained that Jews should be exterminated as a racially inferior element. Next, Major Mere took the floor. Mere began by saying that he was an ardent opponent of Communism. To make it sound more convincing, Mere demonstrated a scar on his forehead, which he said he received while fighting Bolsheviks between 1918 and 1920. (Guards rumored, though, that Mere earned his scar in a drunken brawl.) Mere presented Hitler's order to exterminate the Jews as an "honorable" obligation. Mere urged the guards to have no pity on Jews, whom he called "subhuman bacilli."[14]

THE THERESIENSTADT TRANSPORT

Rumors about further deportations had circulated in Theresienstadt ghetto for quite some time. By means of mass deportations from Theresienstadt ghetto, the Nazis sought to create space for about forty thousand elderly Jews from Germany who were expected to arrive between June and September 1942.[15] On August 28, 1942, the ghetto administration announced that one thousand Jews were to be dispatched to Riga. Many Jews joined the transport voluntarily so as not to be separated from their families. Among the deportees were also a few "Aryans."[16] Escorted by the municipal police, the train left Theresienstadt on September 1. The transport was deemed a "labor commando," which prevented underaged children and the elderly from joining it. There were 1,002 people on the train— 558 women and 444 men. The prisoners traveled in passenger coaches and were allowed to take some of their personal belongings with them. More important, families could stay together. The Germans explained to the passengers that it was altogether an "elite" transport. Upon arrival at their destination, the Jews were told that they would be staying in small houses, each family having a room of its own. After traveling through Dresden, Posen, Bromberg, Marienburg, and Tilsit, the transport arrived in Riga, where it was then moved back and forth at the train station for a few hours. Finally, passengers got word: Riga could not accommodate them. From what they understood, typhus had laid waste the local camp, which was filled to capacity anyway. Some Jews reassured themselves with the thought that perhaps they would survive in the end. Why else why would the Nazis want to take them so far away if they were doomed? The trip continued farther north, until on September 5 the train stopped at a platform in the midst of the forest. The passengers had no idea where they were, why they had come there, and what was going to happen to them next. The sign on the railway station read "Raasiku."[17]

The first thing the passengers who got off the train saw were several blue buses parked near the railway station. The shining chrome of the buses had a sedative effect on the Jews: things seemed not to be that bad after all![18] Indeed, in September and October 1942 the Security Police in Tallinn had three buses at their disposal: Volvo, Dodge, and Scania. The last bus on the list was newly delivered from Tartu.[19] Next to the buses stood six men in SS uniform, speaking with each other in German. Martha Brichta picked up one line: "Here come the Jewish whores, the Jewish pigs!"[20] The selection of prisoners at the Raasiku train station and the subsequent execution at Kalevi-Liiva were carried out under the supervision of higher officials from the Estonian and German Security Police. Among those present were the head of Department AIV, SS-Ostuf. Heinrich Bergmann; the head of the "Jewish" desk, SS-Oschaf. Karl Gehse; and the commander of the Estonian Security Police, SS-Stubaf. Ain-Ervin Mere.[21] The majority of the Jews were directed toward the buses, while 155 young, healthy persons (75 women and 80 men) were ordered to get back to the platform to help

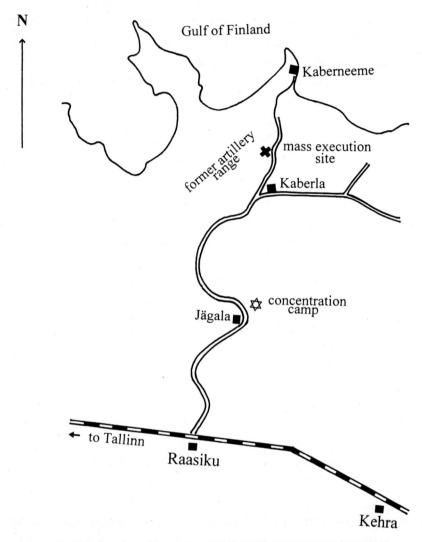

7. Area around Jägala (adapted from the original, 1960); USHMM, RG-06.026.12.

unload the luggage. Although Mere had the highest rank, the survivors thought of Bergmann as the top Nazi official for he personally selected people to join either of the two groups. Laak and Gerrets followed Bergmann yet did not take any active part in the selection. All commands were given in German. The first Estonian word the Jews from Czechoslovakia learned was *kurat* (damn it!), the curse the guards that cordoned off the Raasiku railway station used most often.

Despite attempts to introduce order, the scene at the train station was chaotic: hundreds of people on both sides of the train, screams, barking dogs. Women were still carrying suitcases from the pile of luggage to the trucks as the first bus pulled out. Bergmann assured the worried women that the buses were there to ensure a comfortable ride for their parents, whom they were to join in a camp shortly. An Estonian officer, who turned out to be Alexander Laak, added that it would be improper to make the elderly persons ride in a truck, from which they could unintentionally fall off.[22]

Hanna Klenkova boarded one of the trucks with eight other women. The guards who sat between them were Estonians but the driver was German. Otherwise, the bus and truck drivers were mainly Estonians: Georg Leemet, Conrad Bergstein, Georgi Vies, Rudolf Jürimaa, Herbert Vahur, and Voldemar Eigi [Jõgi?]. Pretty much all of them got a few items that belonged to Jews. For a while, a bus with elderly passengers followed the truck on which Klenkova rode. Then, however, the truck turned right while the bus went straight. That was strange because the women were told they were going to the same place. As the women became unruly, guards started cursing at them and firing in the air.[23] The people who rode the bus, however, seemed to be unaware of what awaited them: children could not help waving to local farmers they saw from the window.

Buses stopped some forty yards before the trench. The firing squad, which had arrived on the morning of September 5, took position inside the trench. There were eight of them, armed with light machine guns. The executioners belonged to a special detachment of the Estonian Security Police based in Tallinn. The entire camp guard, except for a cook, participated in the operation. Some of the Jägala camp guards joined the firing squad, while the others took part in the selection at the Raasiku railway station.[24] As Jews got off the buses, Laak told them to undress. Gerrets explained to the victims that they were going to take a bath (a lie he had learned in Riga). Next Gerrets collected from the Jews—who were already naked by then—rings, earrings, and watches. Finally, the Jews ran a gauntlet composed of policemen. As he had done in Riga, Laak grabbed an automatic gun and jumped into the trench, thus joining the rest of the executioners.[25]

Members of the firing squad had apparently decided that they deserved more than just money or alcohol for their work. They singled out the prisoners with gold teeth and, before murdering them, extracted the teeth with pliers. It took some time before German officials from the Security Police, who observed the executions from afar, realized what was going on and put an end to the torture. They were concerned that the screams coming from the ditch might cause commotion among the Jews heading toward the mass grave. Several days later the Germans even ordered an investigation, yet Laak was able to report that the perpetrators came from Tallinn and not from Jägala.[26] The executioners worked nonstop, fortifying themselves from time to time with vodka and snacks (buses arrived every fifteen minutes). The camp guards, who were posted along the perimeter, drank as well, even before the executions. They scooped vodka from a milk can in which alcohol had been delivered to the execution site. Once they finished for the day, the guards drove back to the camp, where they had a drinking bout.[27]

Despite all the preparations, the murderers miscalculated the number of victims in relation to the size of the trench. There were too many of them. The heap of corpses towered above the mass grave, so that even after it was covered with soil, here and there limbs were visible. Furthermore, from the grave one could still hear the voices of wounded people. To appease their consciences, several guards fired in the direction the voices were coming from, yet to no avail.[28] It was already dark, but camp guards were still wandering around the mass grave looking for valuables. During the execution they saw the firing squad men hiding in the sand the better items they found on Jews. The executioners intended to claim them later but did not have time.[29] The Jägala guards for the most part did not participate in the mass execution. It was not because they were so radically different from the guards at the Tartu concentration camp, but because Commandant Laak was a compassionate man in his own peculiar way. As a father of two teenage sons, Laak found it atrocious for eighteen-year-olds to shoot people. He would rather do it himself, and he did indeed, executing defenseless prisoners one after another.[30] The execution was over by eight in the evening. All in all, about 850 Jews from the Theresienstadt transport, including 100 children, were murdered at Kalevi-Liiva on September 5, 1942. When everything was over, trucks took the clothes of the executed to Jägala.

The mass execution took place on Saturday. Throughout the day, Estonians whose farmsteads were located nearby could hear screams and gunshots. In the evening, the local youth at Kaberla—a village half a mile away from Kalevi-Liiva—came together to dance; the wind carried the sound of shooting as far as Kaberla.[31] Days later, several Estonian farmers from the area made their way

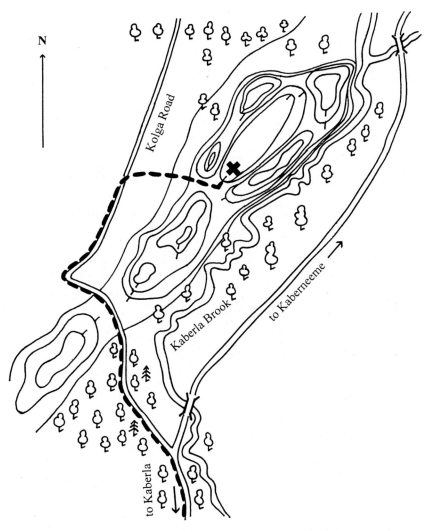

8. Mass execution site at Kalevi-Liiva (adapted from the original, 1960); USHMM, RG-06.026.12.

to the execution site. What they saw was shocking: a mass grave barely covered with sand, two or three corpses, and teeth, many teeth, actually a heap of teeth. Hundreds of different objects lay on the ground, objects so frightfully normal: buttons, laces, cups, razors, forks, coins, hairpins, glass beads, artificial limbs. The farmers found several wooden clubs and whips made of metallic wires; some of these implements had pieces of human skin stuck to them.[32]

FEASTING ON BLOOD: PERSONAL BELONGINGS

In less than half an hour, the women who had driven from Raasiku station on trucks stood in front of a camp, which looked rather uninhabited. First, guards forced the women to strip naked and searched them, misappropriating jewelry and watches. The search was carried out under the guidance of Alexander Laak, with no Germans in sight. In the end, the women were told to do "gymnastics" so that if they had anything hidden in their vaginas it would fall out.[33] After this humiliating procedure, the women were ordered to bring the suitcases into storage. By the time they finished it was already dark. Finally, the Czech Jews from Theresienstadt were distributed between the three barracks, where they spent the next three days without food or drink.[34]

Several days after, two individuals among the male and female prisoners were designated as "Jewish elder" *(Oberjude)* and "police" *(Polizei)* respectively. There is very little information about the male Jews who arrived in Estonia from Czechoslovakia. These Jews were locked in the male prisoners' zone of the camp. The only opportunity for the women to meet the men from their transport was at the Jägala River, from where the men brought water into the camp. Whenever possible, women tried to hand over to the men some food that they had received from local Estonian farmers in exchange for clothes. If caught, they were most surely punished. While neither Laak nor Gerrets physically abused Jewish women, they took revenge on Jewish men. Women observed how the two forced the men to crawl in the mud or to stand half-naked in the snow.[35]

When reflecting on their arrival in Raasiku—the railway station, the luggage—some women realized what their function was going to be. Their job at Jägala was sorting personal effects of the Jews from the Theresienstadt transport. The storage, a 120-by-30-foot barracks, was located in the administrative quarters. The barracks was filled with stuff: toiletries, sewing kits, shaving equipment, cameras, glasses, medicine, clothes, textiles, shoes, kitchenware, tools, toys, foodstuff, all kinds of suitcases, purses, bags—anything that the deportees could fit within the hundred-pound quota. First the women had to arrange the clothing by type of fabric and then by its quality. The Jews had taken their best items with them when they came to Theresienstadt ghetto and later to Estonia. Bergmann, Laak, Gerrets, and other voracious souls realized this too. From time to time, all three individuals made their way into storage, where they picked up a few things for themselves. When Gerrets went home on vacation, the women who worked in the storage facility presented him with something for his wife. Gerrets was also a passionate coin collector, so the female prisoners knew how to please him. For his birthday Gerrets received a few shirts and a pack of cards. Sometimes Laak received requests from his superiors in Tallinn, in which case he arrived with a wish list and sizes marked on it. The police officials were particularly interested in fine bed linens, scarce in Estonia at that time. They claimed the best quality linen sets—"like those a bride gets." Everyone got at least something. For Christmas, each camp guard received a suit, a shirt, a tie, and a pair of shoes. The rest went to hospitals and children's homes across Estonia.[36] Books, documents, passports, anything made of paper were routinely destroyed.

The best items traveled to a depot on 11 Toomkooli Street in Tallinn where members of the German Security Police could purchase them, if semilegally, for a reasonable price. The first truckload that arrived from Jägala contained raincoats; the next truck brought suitcases, then lady's shoes, suits, and so on. A long line of policemen wanted to buy cheap, good-quality watches. They paid cash to SS-Rotf. Otto Sievers, who was in charge of the depot. Both the seller and the buyers knew where the watches and jewelry came from. SS-Hstuf. Wilhelm Suttor, for example, paid 3.50 RM for a watch, while Kriminalkommissar (Detective Inspector, Krim.-Komm.) Josef Schmid became the lucky owner of a miniature Minox camera.[37] Female employees of the Security Police inquired about when a new delivery from Jägala was to arrive; once they had the chance to purchase lovely umbrellas. Wives of the leading Estonian police officials, for example the wife of Ervin Viks, also made their way to the depot looking for bargains. Some of them tried on garments right in the depot, unsure of whether it was worth buying coats and suits tainted with blood. Once the depot staff hosted Alexander Kreek, a famous Estonian athlete (who won a gold medal in shot put in 1938). Kreek presented a document that entitled him to a suit. Because of his large size, Kreek was only able to get a jacket.[38]

Although the Jews suspected that their loved ones were all dead, they could not reconcile themselves with the idea. The women kept asking Laak and Gerrets what had happened to the people who boarded the blue buses upon their arrival at Raasiku. "You do not have to worry," the answer was—"those people were doing fine, they did not even have to work anymore!" But what about their luggage, which they were not allowed to take with them? Gerrets anticipated that question too: "Some of the clothes you guys are sorting will go to your relatives!"

Laak invented a whole story about a "winter camp" where most of the elderly Jews were allegedly staying. If somebody tried to escape, Laak threatened the women, their loved ones in the "winter camp" would be shot.[39]

Four weeks after their arrival in the camp, Hanna Klenkova and thirty other women were dispatched from Jägala to Kostivere, where they spent another three weeks harvesting potatoes, beets, and cabbage. At Kostivere, which was located less than three miles from Jägala, Jewish women worked along with Estonian and Ukrainian prisoners. Kostivere, along with two other estates, was the property of the German Security Police in the Ostland. The SS took over the 700-acre estate on January 10, 1942.[40] The estate manager, SS-Uschaf. Andresen, did not mistreat the women, as SS-Oschaf. Baron Balthasar von Buxhöveden, the Security Police official in charge of Kostivere, often did. In their own words, Jewish women were expected to work as hard as the horse-driven machine that dug out potatoes. Baron Buxhöveden used his whip every time any one woman could not keep pace with the horse. They were only allowed to rest when the horse was tired; at night the women were locked in a stable. Once the crop was in, women returned to Jägala.[41] Since they had left the Jägala camp, its prison population had nearly doubled. The newcomers were Jews from Germany.

THE FRANKFURT-ON-MAIN/BERLIN TRANSPORT

At the time of the first deportation from Frankfurt on Main on October 19, 1941, there were about ten thousand Jews living in that city. Within a year, all but one thousand Jews had been deported to ghettos such as Łódź, Minsk, Kaunas, Izbica, and Theresienstadt. The tenth and last deportation from Frankfurt took place in September 1942. By that time, the only Jews left in Frankfurt were a few hundred young people—nurses, physicians, and artisans—who had been helping with the liquidation of Jewish institutions.[42] On September 22, 1942, the Frankfurt Gestapo herded more than 200 Jews into the former Jewish old people's home on Börne Street. The Gestapo announced that all of them were subject to deportation. Two days later, buses took the Jews to the railway station, where a passenger train with six coaches was already waiting for them. Craftsmen and blue-collar workers and their families constituted the majority of the deportees. (The transport was designated a *Handwerkertransport,* that is, a skilled workman's transport.) In addition to 50 RM in cash, Jews were allowed to take with them clothes, blankets, and food supplies for eight days. The train with 236 Jews left Frankfurt Ostbahnhof on September 24, 1942. In Berlin, the Frankfurt municipal police handed the train over to a police transport commando. It was also in Berlin that the deportees received water for the first time.[43]

Meanwhile, Hilda Levy found herself among the Jews who on September 25 were crammed into the synagogue on Levetzow Street in Berlin. On the next day, Levy along with other 810 Jews was escorted to the goods depot on Putlitz Street. More Jews arrived from a collection camp on Grosse Hamburger Street, as well as from police detention facilities. The Frankfurt transport, which now contained several more coaches, had steam up. However, the journey did not begin until later at night, after the Berlin Jewish community distributed soup among the deportees. Coaches were locked and windows sealed. The train pulled out of the railway station close to midnight on September 26.[44] By then the transport had 1,049 Jews on board—354 men and 895 women.[45] It was not the first time that Berlin Jews were sent to the Baltics to their death: thousands of Jews had been deported from Berlin to Riga and Kaunas. Throughout the duration of the war, 63 transports left Berlin for the East in addition to 117 transports that went to Theresienstadt, bringing the grand total to 50,535 people. The highest German officials in Berlin directly involved in the deportation of Jews to Estonia were municipal councilor SS-Ostubaf. Otto Bovensiepen and his deputy SS-Stubaf. Kurt Venter.[46]

Inside the coach, Helga Verleger (Drexler) discovered a cross-section of German Jewish society: young and old, men and women, pious men with beards, and so forth. Verleger felt hot wearing the five dresses she had put on one atop another in order to circumvent the hundred-pound quota on luggage that deportees had to comply with. For the duration of the trip, the Jews had to subsist on their own food; water was provided during the short stops along the way. After a journey of several days the train stopped in Riga, which many believed was the final destination of the Da406. When it turned out that it was only an overnight stopover, passengers sank into despair; some of them even had a premonition of mass execution.[47]

The journey lasted approximately five days. What happened to these German Jews in Estonia was a repeat of the scenario described earlier. As soon as the train passed the railway junction at Tapa, Bergmann telephoned Laak. Laak then immediately ordered buses to the Raasiku station. Bergmann and his men arrived shortly thereafter. At the train station, the Jews were divided into two groups: the larger group, consisting of mainly elderly people, was ordered onto the buses, whereas seventy or so younger women boarded the trucks loaded with luggage. It was again the buses that captured prisoners' imagination; several referred to the buses as "elegant" and "nice." Selma Sundheimer did not yet know how lucky she was to be separated from her aunt, who got on the bus: the two never saw each other again.[48]

There were proportionally more male survivors from the Berlin transport than were from the Theresienstadt transport. The SS confronted each of the men on the platform with the question "What are you?" Ninety-six healthy men, who let themselves be listed as craftsmen or workers, remained on one side of the train (without being able to see what was happening on the other side) and thus survived. They were taken to Jägala, yet not to the camp itself. In a forest behind the camp men had to exchange their civilian clothes for prisoner's uniforms. By the time they came back to the train station, nobody else was there. The men boarded the same train that brought them to Estonia; however, instead of Germany they ended up in Jaunjelgava in Latvia.[49]

There was no consensus among the witnesses so as to who did the actual killing. Ralf Gerrets argued that the firing squad, as before, was composed of members of the Estonian Security Police special commando, while at least two other witnesses (Jaan Viik and Friedrich Anijalg) insisted that this time around the camp guards did the job themselves. Commandant Laak once again participated in the execution; Laak alone arguably handled at least four busloads of Jews. The victims, in groups of four or five, descended into the trench where they were forced to lie down next to each other. The next group of Jews had to lie on the corpses of those who were murdered before them. (In Nazi jargon this type of execution was called a "sardine tin.") As the execution went on, the heap of corpses became higher and higher until it reached the edge of the trench. By the end of the day, the executioners were shooting while standing on the dead bodies. The organizers and perpetrators of the murder, however, had just one concern: to fit as many people into the mass grave as possible.[50] At least 800 German Jews lost their lives at Kalevi-Liiva.[51]

THE JÄGALA CAMP

In the camp, German Jews encountered their coreligionists from Czechoslovakia, who told them they were in Jägala, Estonia. But a hearty welcome it was not:

the Czech Jews despised everything German. "You are Hitler, you are Germans," they said to them. The initial alienation between the two groups of prisoners at Jägala was similar to that between "indigenous" Latvian Jews and German Jews in the Riga ghetto.[52] Ironically, Jägala became a microcosm of an imaginary society in which Estonians were the masters, Czech Jews (installed as camp police and bloc elders) constituted the middle echelon, and German Jews (associated with Germany and Germans) came to occupy the lowest hierarchical position.

In official documents Jägala appeared as a "labor education camp" (*Arbeits-und Erziehungslager* or AEL). Jägala was one of the few labor camps in Estonia that was staffed and operated entirely by Estonians. Although Jägala was located only a thirty- to forty-five-minute drive from Tallinn, officials from the German Security Police rarely visited the camp, thus essentially ceding the reins of government to their Estonian colleagues. Commandant Laak received instructions from the Head of Department AIV Bergmann and his Estonian counterpart Mere. At least once a week either of the two telephoned Laak. Other than that, Laak was relatively independent in his actions, and at least once gave the order to execute several diseased prisoners at Jägala. Mere visited Jägala for the first time in late fall 1942. Mere's visit was prompted by particular circumstances. One of the guards, [?] Uibo, told a female prisoner, with whom he had an affair, about the murder of her mother. Uibo was on the brink of mental breakdown and thus revealed to the rest of the guards what he said to his lover. Laak was concerned that the news could spread among the inmates and asked Mere for advice. Mere told Laak that if prisoners were agitated beyond reason, all of them should be murdered immediately. Fortunately for the prisoners, most of them were simply incapable of grasping the truth about mass murder. The Jews were allowed to live, but not the guard Uibo, whom Laak shot personally.[53] Beside Bergmann and Mere, Sandberger was the highest Security Police official who at least on one occasion visited Jägala. Unfortunately, no further details of Sandberger's visit are available.[54]

Ralf Gerrets was in charge of the camp's bookkeeping; he compiled lists of prisoners—alive and dead alike—and interpreted for Laak, who spoke poor German. Each morning Gerrets, whom the prisoners called *stonostka* (centipede), came into the women's barracks with a list of daily assignments. He announced the names and the kind of work that female prisoners were supposed to do. At times Gerrets decided that one or another woman did not have to perform

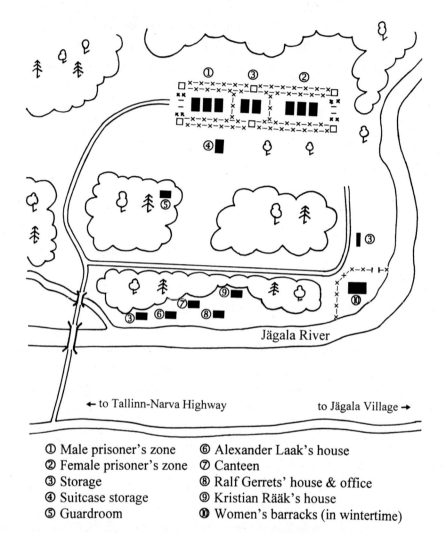

9. Jägala camp (adapted from the original, 1960); USHMM, RG-06.026.12.

① Male prisoner's zone   ⑥ Alexander Laak's house
② Female prisoner's zone   ⑦ Canteen
③ Storage   ⑧ Ralf Gerrets' house & office
④ Suitcase storage   ⑨ Kristian Rääk's house
⑤ Guardroom   ⑩ Women's barracks (in wintertime)

physical labor; when the rest of the barracks inmates came back from work at night, those women were not any longer there.[55] Some guards claimed that they saw Gerrets and Laak coming into the women's barracks at night and leaving in the morning.[56] Thus, one time Gerrets came into the barracks "looking for that doll" *(wo ist diese Puppe?).*[57] Sometime in August 1943, Gerrets dispatched Anka Dubova and one other young woman, both professional nurses, to entertain Laak and his guest Mere, whose dog allegedly needed medical treatment. A few days later, Laak took Dubova and three other women from the Theresienstadt transport to Kalevi-Liiva, where he shot them. One of the executed women was Laak's personal sex slave. Small executions like this one were not even reported to the Security Police in Tallinn.[58]

This information raises the question of how many Jews were there at the Jägala camp and what happened to them next. In mid-November 1942, the German Security Police in Riga requested information from Sandberger regarding the number of Jews and their deployment in Estonia. The KdS-Estland reported 338 Jews in three different camps: Jägala—53 men and 150 women; Tartu AEL—40 men; and Tallinn AEL—105 men and 60 women. Of those Jews, 135 were felling trees in the forest or working in the fields under the supervision of the Estonian Security Police.[59] Originally, Jägala's lifespan was determined at four months. However, it took much longer to process the clothes and other effects left behind by victims. The camp remained in operation, but its population was to be drastically reduced. The available data on individual executions at Jägala (that is, Kalevi-Liiva) are at most scarce and often contradictory; survivors and perpetrators suggested different dates and numbers.

The biggest selection at the Jägala camp took place in late fall 1942. In November Gerrets handed over to the Jewish elder a list containing fifteen names of prisoners who had to be "hospitalized." Instead of the hospital, those fifteen received a bullet at Kalevi-Liiva.[60] Ailing Jews were also taken away from the camp later; former inmates did not know whereto but surmised the worst. To ensure their own survival, prisoners who had bandages usually took them off before the roll call.[61] Young women felt no safer than any other inmates at Jägala. All that survivors knew was that one day Anka Dubova disappeared, and so did two young women from Pilsen who worked in the storage facility, and yet another five or six pretty women whom Laak and Gerrets had subjected to sexual harassment.[62] In June 1943, sixteen Jewish women who had until then been working in the Security Police storage depot in Tallinn returned to Jägala. Laak, who single-handedly shot the prisoners, allegedly scoffed at one of the women who refused to undress before the execution: "Saint Peter will admit you into the next world even naked!"[63]

And yet, in consideration of what was to follow, the conditions at Jägala were still bearable. The barracks lacked light, latrines, and, most important, heat. Therefore, in early December 1942 the remaining female prisoners were taken to another, heated barracks next to the river.[64] The women were allowed to pick berries and mushrooms, as well as to grow vegetables. In spite of the threat of corporal punishment, prisoners engaged, rather successfully, in barter trade with the camp guards. Fanny Lederer was able to make an arrangement: one day she worked from eight in the morning till eight in the evening and then had the next day off.[65] In the summer, women went swimming in the Jägala River.

Despite the fact that Jägala had watchtowers and a barbed-wire fence, the camp guards did not take their responsibilities seriously, thus giving prisoners a chance to escape. However, no attempts at escape were registered. This was the case for two reasons. First, the camp administration by and large succeeded in deceiving the prisoners, who continued to believe in the existence of a fictitious camp where their friends and relatives had allegedly been taken. Second, Czech and German Jews did not know the Estonian language and thus were unable to establish lasting contacts with the surrounding population.[66] Occasionally Jewish prisoners came into contact with local farmers, mainly women. Former prisoners later recalled getting milk, vegetables, and other produce from the Estonians. One of the women that prisoners met in the forest turned out to be a teacher whose husband had fled to Finland. The teacher revealed to the young women that their relatives had been executed and that they were doomed too.[67]

The Jägala camp had a short lifespan. More than half of the prisoners (ninety-six women and forty-six men) were transferred to Tallinn Central prison as early as mid-December 1942.[68] The last group of Jewish prisoners left Jägala in the summer of 1943. According to the records of Tallinn Central prison, two groups of Jewish men and women—twenty-four people in each—arrived on June 26 and August 19 respectively.[69] Another eleven women arrived on August 21. By September 1, 1943, the Jägala camp was no more. It was the prisoners themselves who had to dismantle the camp installations: to remove the barbed wire, to take down the watchtowers, to disassemble the barracks.[70]

The total number of Jews murdered at Kalevi-Liiva was at least 1,700 (but probably 1,754). Among other victims who lay buried in the dunes were forty Gypsies and scores of "political prisoners" of mainly Estonian and Russian origin.[71] In the spring of 1944, Sonderkommando 1005 began burning the corpses of the prisoners executed at Kalevi-Liiva in 1942 and 1943. Local farmers remembered the nauseous smoke of the burning flesh that seemed to permeate everything. The freshly planted pine trees could not conceal the traces of mass murder:

the surrounding area was covered with tiny pieces of human bones. The rumors that Blobel Commando had used a special machine for grinding bones were false; all that the Germans had at their disposal was a stone-crusher.

TALLINN CENTRAL PRISON

Tallinn Central prison was located within walking distance of the harbor, less than 100 feet from the Baltic Sea. The prison was (and still is) popularly known as the "Battery," which comes from the street name, Suur Patarei (big battery).[72] The prison was built during the Tsarist period and ranked the third worst prison in Europe (outside of Russia), after such notorious institutions as the Cherche Midi in Paris and the Moabit in Berlin.[73] The Tallinn concentration camp, under the name Tallinn Central prison, became operational on August 28, 1941, that is, on the first day of German occupation. On July 1, 1942, the Estonian Security Police took over the prison, which now was officially designated as the Tallinn labor education camp (AEL). Henceforth, Tallinn Central prison and two other institutions at Tartu and Murru received two categories of prisoners: protective-custody prisoners *(Schutz-häftlinge)* and the so-called police prisoners *(Polizeihäftlinge)*. As of January 1943, the former barely formed 15 percent of the prisoner population.[74]

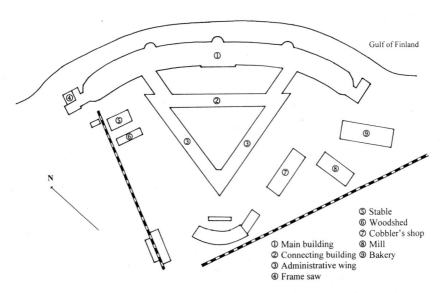

10. Tallinn Central prison (adapted from the original, 1943); USHMM, 1999. A.0153/2.

Tallinn Central prison was comprised of two wings: women stayed in the old wing while men occupied the new wing. The guards were Estonians, either elderly men or youths. One former prisoner observed that the guards were sycophantic toward their German superiors: they treated prisoners roughly and became even more violent when a German was at hand.[75] The prison had room for six thousand and was always overcrowded. According to Sandberger, as of January 1943 there were no foreign nationals held at Tallinn Central prison.[76] Obviously, Jews were excluded from that category, because five months later the KdS-Estland reported 228 Jews—Czechoslovakian and German nationals—incarcerated there.[77]

The Frankfurt engineering company Philipp Holzmann received a contract for rebuilding the shipyard in Tallinn. The company was assigned 140 Jewish women, who reported to work immediately, starting on January 2, 1943. As it later was revealed in conversation, of those 140 women 60 were from Czechoslovakia, 40 from Berlin, and the rest from Frankfurt. And there were conversations, and more. Bella Strauss and other women soon learned that one of Holzmann's foremen, Friedrich Hohmann, came from the same city as they did. Hohmann was kind enough to let the women use his wife's address in Frankfurt to which they could send letters to their relatives and friends in Germany. In a matter of months, Hohmann started receiving correspondence, which he then forwarded to the Jewish women who worked at Tallinn harbor. One time he received as many as four small packages in one day. Inspired by the news from home, the women worked better than before, plastering, laying bricks, casting concrete, or laying cable. At a certain point the German Security Police in Tallinn became interested in the personality of Hohmann, who had been interrogated at least four times with regard to his contacts with Jews. The then head of Department AIV, Bergmann, often came to the worksite at the harbor to check on the Jews. He once picked out ten of the youngest and prettiest women, who from then on, every Saturday, had to come to clean the Security Police rooms in downtown Tallinn. The cleaning was obviously not all that was expected from those young women.[78]

Ninety-eight of them worked at Tallinn harbor in the summer of 1943. The women, who wore civilian clothes with no distinctive armbands, were escorted daily from Tallinn Central prison and back. People on the streets were sympathetic toward the prisoners. Indeed, they were all pretty young women who could hardly be identified as Jewish.[79] Their guards were Volksdeutsche from Poland, armed yet dressed in civilian clothes. In the end, it was only a ten-minute walk to

the harbor. At the harbor, the Jews cleaned rubble and unloaded goods. Accord-
ing to survivors, some Estonian workers at the shipyard shared food with them.
Among the people who helped them, the female prisoners mentioned the names of
Victor Makarov, Elmar Preimut, Alexander Kaur, and Juku Rannamets. Relations
with the Ukrainian and Russian POWs, on the contrary, left much to be desired.
These sometimes stole the food that Estonian workers left for the Jewish women.
The latter viewed POWs as rude and primitive.[80] Of the German foremen who
supervised them at work, the women remembered Otto Gutzeit. They said Gutzeit
provided them with additional food and altogether treated them as humans.[81]

Jewish women complained that they had to sleep on the bare floor, but the
prison officials assured Sandberger that the Czech and German Jews lived com-
fortably—six or seven people per cell, had plank beds and even straw mattresses.[82]
In reality, ten women shared six available bunk beds. It was hard to sleep at night
because of cold, heavy odor, or frequent air-raid warnings. Jaundice was so wide-
spread among the prisoners that it was not even considered a real disease. Jewish and Gypsy women had cells on the same first floor of the prison. There were
between seventy and a hundred female Gypsy prisoners at Tallinn Central prison,
before they all disappeared one day. An Estonian female guard explained what happened to those women with a telling gesture, passing her hand across her neck.[83]
When Estonian prisoners got sick, they could get treatment at a prison hospital.
Jews, however, had to stay in their cells no matter how serious their illness was. Jewish women did not interact with the rest of the prison population. They were subject
to a separate roll call, carried out by the German SS. According to the survivors,
they experienced mistreatment at Tallinn Central prison but no selections or executions.[84] For example, Bergmann once bloodied Anka Kraus and Erna Frischmann,
who refused to reveal the name of an Estonian who gave them a piece of bacon.[85]
Prisoners had to forage for food, unless they were ready to settle for meager prison
portions that left them hungry. For "breakfast," the women received a piece of dry
bread, fish leftovers, and a cup of brownish water, meant to be coffee. At 11:00 A.M.
everyone got half a liter of cabbage soup with a few pieces of meat in it; it was hard
to get used to the taste of horsemeat and baking soda (used as a salt substitute).
Finally, at 6:00 P.M. prisoners were rewarded for their hard work with a few potatoes, a piece of bread, and a drink with a fishy aftertaste.[86]

In October 1943, the German Security Police replaced the 120 Jews who until
then had been working at the Tallinn shipyard.[87] For the women from Germany

and Czechoslovakia, December 11 became their last day in Tallinn. Shortly after evening roll call, the female Jewish prisoners, with their backpacks and straw mattresses, were escorted to the train station. Although rumors had circulated for quite some time that the Holzmann company was about to redeploy some of their workers to Vaivara, the prisoners refused to believe them. Never again would they find as good a physical and social environment as they had during that year in Tallinn. The change was quick to follow. Members of the Estonian SS, some of them drunk, escorted the train all the way from Tallinn to the shale oil region in northeastern Estonia. One of the guards made the female prisoners curtsy, while another had fun throwing cigarette butts at them. An Estonian officer claimed one of the prettiest young women, whom he took into his compartment. Finally, the train stopped at Kohtla railway station. While it was still the Estonian guards who accompanied Jews on their several-hour march to Ereda, the person who ordered them around was the German SS-Uschaf. Heinz Drohsin.[88]

Out of 2,051 Jews who were deported to Estonia in the fall of 1942, only 74 survived: 48 from Theresienstadt, 19 from Berlin, and 7 from Frankfurt. Most of the survivors were on board the ship that arrived in Stutthof from Tallinn on August 23, 1944.[89]

CALLOUS THEY WERE

Alexander Laak, the former commandant of Jägala, arrived in Tallinn together with the last group of Jewish prisoners. In Tallinn, Laak was appointed commandant of Tallinn Central prison, which position he held through September 1944. As he did once before, Laak helped Gerrets out by finding him a position at Tallinn Central prison. Failing health, however, made Gerrets change his plans. (One time Gerrets went from the execution site at Kalevi-Liiva straight to the doctor's office in Tallinn to get shots.) The winter and spring of 1944 he spent again in the tuberculosis hospital in Tartu.

What made members of Tartu Omakaitse and policemen from Tallinn participate in mass executions of Jews at Jalaka and Kalevi-Liiva respectively? The situation had changed considerably from that of the frantic summer months of 1941. The initial battle frenzy, the rage against anything and anybody associated with the Soviet regime, had subsided somewhat. The victims were mainly women and children who did not quite fit into the collective image of a Soviet aggressor.

The commanding officers sometimes displayed hostility toward Jews, but the actual executioners for the most part did not. The patterns of behavior evident in the fall of 1941 at Tartu and a year later at Jägala closely resemble those emanating from the classical psychology experiments conducted by Stanley Milgram and Philip Zimbardo in the 1960s and 1970s.[90] Both camps existed as miniature societies isolated from the rest of the world and rather loosely supervised by Germans. That isolation increased the sense of empowerment among the camp staff and made arbitrary rule an order of the day. Jägala commandant Alexander Laak, for example, used to berate the camp guards who failed his expectations: "For you, I am god, king, and devil. I can shoot any of you and nobody would care a damn!"[91] German supervisory agencies, which were also corrupt, promoted brutality, most likely deliberately. Brutalization rather than hatred was the single most potent factor that led Estonian policemen and paramilitaries to abuse and kill defenseless Jewish women and children.

Defendants in the postwar trials claimed—for what it is worth—that they did not harbor any particular hatred against Jews or Gypsies. One gets a similar impression when reading the interrogation records. Oftentimes, defendants referred to victims as "Czechs" or "Germans," and not as "Jews." They said that the prisoners, many of whom were blond, wore nice clothing, looked intelligent, and obviously came from rich families. In fact, the prisoners too presented themselves as "Czechs" and "Germans" rather than "Jews." There was nothing political about those Jews, who had nothing to do with the Estonian State and its collapse. The hatred and rage narratives simply do not apply here.

Brutalization was born of the nearly unlimited authority that Estonians exercised at the Tartu and Jägala concentration camps. Deputy commandant Ralf Gerrets was cruel toward prisoners but fun to share company with. Gerrets had developed a habit: before entering the prisoner's zone in the Jägala camp, he got himself a whip. Senior guard Jaan Viik, in his broken German, constantly rushed Jewish women *arbitten*. One of the guards recalled an episode in the men's barracks at the Tartu concentration camp sometime in September 1941. The guard commander, Juhan Jüriste, clearly intoxicated, spotted a Gypsy, whom he mistook for a Jew. "What is that," he exclaimed, "one goddamn Jew is still alive?" However, once Jüriste realized his mistake, he let the unfortunate prisoner be.[92] Among other crimes, Jüriste was implicated in the murder and rape of nineteen-year-old Vera S., who definitely was not his only victim.[93] A senior guard of the women's barracks was Endla Taska, the wife of another camp guard at Tartu. Camp inmates remembered Taska as a cruel individual who beat female prisoners with a rubber stick. Several times during the winter, Taska forced Luisa Frei to wet her own hair, which immediately froze in the cold. Taska did that because she envied the prisoner's beautiful hair.[94]

The Jägala concentration camp was built to accommodate specifically Jews, but the Tartu one was not. Indeed, Jews constituted a small proportion of all victims in Tartu. When it came to actual executions, there is no evidence that the guards differentiated between Jewish and non-Jewish victims. Those who repeatedly volunteered for a firing squad had a lust for blood in general. According to several testimonies, some executioners took pride in killing people, which they called a "real job." When intoxicated, the guards told the camp inmates they even had a kind of competition as to who would kill more people.[95] It seems as if they took pleasure in such conversations, as if they enjoyed seeing the frightened look in the prisoners' eyes. Some of the guards, for example Robert Taska, had a propensity for sadism. One time Taska came to the women's barracks and said literally the following: "It feels so good to kill Jews with a knife, in particular the pregnant women and small children! As if it were a downy pillow you are stabbing!" Hilda Jalakas was one of the nine pregnant women who heard these words. At another time, guards forced women, old and young alike, first to run around the courtyard and then to lie down in the mud. The guards seemed to enjoy the spectacle, which they called a "drill." First they derided the women, then started beating them. As a result of this torture, several elderly women remained lying motionless in the mud.[96] This treatment was not very different from when Endel Mark related to prisoners the gruesome details of the executions of small children, which had earned him the nickname "children's killer." Karl Eelmets called it "killing young cockerels"; fresh bloodstains on Eelmets's greatcoat proved that he was deadly serious about that.[97] To kill was to cross a certain boundary, the boundary that transformed killers into superhumans. Those who killed—the "real men," in their own words—scorned those who did not.[98] Guards exchanged laughs and were altogether in a good mood as they walked back to the bus after having carried out yet another execution.[99]

The next question is how that violent behavior translated into Estonian-German relations. It was one thing for KdS-Estland Sandberger to call upon his subordinates to treat the members of the Estonian Security Police with respect, but what did Estonian policemen think of their German colleagues? Friendship it probably was not, but deference certainly. Jägala commandant Laak did not feel insulted when the German Security Police officers asked him to get them whatever they wanted from the clothes left behind by the murdered Jews. For his deputy, Gerrets, the names of Gehse and Bergmann sounded as familiar or as distant as those of Viks and Mere. Once Jewish possessions reached the Security Police vaults in Tallinn, everyone took part in the loot: Germans and Estonians, men and women. They were indeed equals, equals in crime. At the same time, the Estonians became enraged when they felt that the Germans tramped on their national pride. The very same Laak who had no problem following German orders to kill people by the hundreds was very upset about the conversation he had with Bergmann sometime in the fall of 1942. Laak was furious: "Some lousy German dares to shout at me, an Estonian officer!"[100] That attitude is what Sandberger tried to prevent, for the most part successfully.

According to one hypothesis, Jewish deportees from Czechoslovakia and Germany were brought to Estonia possibly to erect a big concentration camp that HSSPF Jeckeln had planned for the area near Tallinn. This would explain why the second trainload of Jews was marked as a skilled workman's transport. The camp was never built, however, thus erasing the need for manpower.[101] Nonetheless, the decision to reroute the Theresienstadt and Berlin transports to Estonia was most likely spontaneous. That decision paralleled the recruitment campaign on behalf of the Estonian shale oil industry. While two thousand Czech and German Jews were about to arrive in Estonia, the local police were snatching Lithuanians off Kaunas and Vilnius streets for a subsequent labor assignment in Estonia. If there was a coordinated effort, the Jews could also be used as slave laborers. Apparently, by the fall of 1942 nobody had yet considered the exploitation of cheap Jewish labor, probably because the very possibility of Jewish deportations to Estonia was ruled out as unattainable.

9
JEWISH SLAVE LABOR FOR THE BALTÖL EMPIRE

BALTIC OIL LTD. AND THE PRODUCTION
OF SYNTHETIC OIL IN ESTONIA

The head of the Office of the Four-Year Plan, Hermann Göring, recognized synthetic oil production in Estonia as the most essential industry in the Baltics.[1] In doing so, Göring drew upon Hitler's order of October 12, 1942, that called for rebuilding the oil refineries of Estonia.[2] The decision regarding the future political status of Estonia was dependant to a great extent on the future of the shale oil industry.[3] For one thing, the Estonian shale oil industry played an important role in defining the course of warfare on the Eastern Front during the first nine months of 1944.

Originally, the German navy intended to start processing Estonian shale oil in Hamburg. Göring, however, was inclined to use existing facilities in Estonia. There was more at stake than just profit. Göring realized early on that disregard for nationalist sentiment might be counterproductive for the German effort at maintaining political stability in Estonia. Otherwise, the Estonians would have immediately started drawing a parallel between Soviet and German conduct.[4] The Soviets had little time on their hands to destroy the Estonian shale oil industry completely. The Mineral Oil Commando North (Mineralölkommando Nord or Minölko North) was expected to join the German 26th Army Corps heading for Estonia. Minölko North laid claim to oil refineries even before Wehrmacht troops captured the northeastern region of Estonia. As soon as the German army established control over the shale oil area, Minölko North scrutinized the refineries in Kiviõli, Kohtla-Järve, and Sillamäe. The Kiviõli refinery had incurred the least damage and therefore was designated the first to be rebuilt. Production at Kiv[[õ]]li began as early as August 26, 1941, with daily output of some two hundred tons.[5] In less than a year, the Germans were able to rebuild all six refineries. Yet output remained low compared with that of the prewar years. Twenty thousand tons of shale oil produced in November 1941, or fifty thousand tons in May 1942, fell short of the annual output in Independent Estonia amounting to 1.8 million tons. The lack of manpower undermined efforts to raise production to its prewar level.[6]

It took the Germans some time to recognize the importance of shale oil production in Estonia. During the 1941 summer campaign, AOK 18 inquired of the navy whether the latter would prefer it to capture the shale oil region first and then turn to Tallinn or vice versa. The reply was that the shale oil region was not important enough and that the refineries in all probability had already been demolished.[7] The fortunes of Estonia's shale oil region had significantly improved by the fall of 1942 as the Germans withdrew from the Caucasus. The Soviets had frustrated German attempts to capture the oilfields in the Crimea and North Caucasus. At the initial stages of preparation for the implementation of Plan Barbarossa, the German navy revealed its plans to start using Soviet crude oil reserves. However, when Wehrmacht troops reached the Crimean peninsula in December 1941, they found all the refineries destroyed and equipment removed. Frustration was high: Hitler reacted by issuing an order designating the production of synthetic fuel a top priority.[8] Among the major problems that the Germans encountered in Russia were transportation and the attendant difficulties of rebuilding the oil refineries. Without fuel, however, the prospects of the occupying power looked grim. Not only did lack of fuel hamper the exploitation of natural resources in the already occupied territories of the Soviet Union, but it also put additional stress on the German military and its combat capabilities.[9]

On March 27, 1941, a new joint-stock company, Continental Oil (Kontinentale Öl A.G.), was established in Berlin. Officially, the company was supposed to represent the interests of the German oil industry abroad. In practice, however, it received a monopoly (for ninety-nine years) for the exploitation of oil deposits in occupied Eastern Europe.[10] Baltic Oil Ltd. (Baltische Öl GmbH or Baltöl) was officially established as a branch company of Continental Oil on October 1, 1942. Baltöl received large concessions for exploiting shale oil, petroleum, and natural gas resources in the Ostland and neighboring territories. The German navy was identified as the sole recipient of the abovementioned minerals.[11] While Organization Todt (Organisation Todt or OT) was charged with constructing new refineries and rebuilding old ones, the Estonian Mineral Oil Commando (Mineralölkommando Estland or Minölko Estonia) in Kiviõli was brought to life with the purpose of helping Baltöl overcome any potential difficulties. The Kiviõli directorate reported to the main office in Tallinn.[12] Within a year, Baltöl had developed into a huge enterprise: in 1943 alone the company received 82 million RM in credit.[13]

In September 1943, Baltöl negotiated a fifteen-year contract with the navy. Deliveries of crude oil were to increase from 100,000 tons in 1943 to 425,000 tons in 1946.[14] The Reich minister for armaments and war production, Albert Speer, outlined the plans for expansion of the shale oil industry during his visit to Estonia on December 22, 1943. Major reconstruction of the railway system would enable the German war machine to receive up to forty trainloads of shale oil derivates daily. An additional 30 percent increase in deliveries could be achieved by making full use of a sea route from Paldiski.[15] *Revaler Zeitung* announced ecstatically that Estonian oil reserves would be enough to cover Germany's needs for the next 150 years.[16] The golden age of the Estonian shale oil industry was about to begin, as the Germans were dismantling equipment from the oil-producing facilities in Kherson and Slantsy and shipping it to Kiviõli and Kohtla-Järve. The situation in Romania, a major oil supplier to Nazi Germany, was deteriorating and so were the supply routes in southern Europe. The more the territory under German control shrank, the more important Estonia became to the Nazi war economy.

By the end of 1943, all five refineries—Kiviõli, Kohtla-Järve, Sillamäe, Kohtla, and Jõhvi—had for the most part been rebuilt and worked at top capacity. In addition to these refineries, Baltöl operated seven quarries and mines, some of them eighty yards deep.[17] The amount of crude oil produced in 1943—about 107,000 tons, or 66 percent of the prewar output—was expected to double in 1944, and then again in 1945. Fuel for the German navy constituted 85 percent of the total Baltöl production. Because of its qualities, crude shale oil turned out to be excellent fuel for submarines: it was heavier than water and therefore did not rise to the surface if a submarine got hit, thus increasing its chances of escaping from the enemy.[18] The engineering staff was close to starting to produce fuel for warplanes. Two new refineries that were planned for Vaivara and Ereda were never built because of deterioration of the military situation.[19]

An acute shortage of manpower plagued the shale oil industry all the way through 1943. The Baltöl had at its disposal merely one-fourth of the workforce employed in the 1930s. There was no hope of bridging the gap with local workers; the shale oil region was sparsely populated. The Labor Office in Tallinn announced early on its inability to supply the company with manpower. Furthermore, the police authorities did not yield to the request to release miners and industrial workers from active service in the police battalions and the Omakaitse. Failure to meet the challenge endangered the deliveries of crude oil crucial for the German navy.[20] Because of the strategic importance of shale oil production, Baltöl was given priority with regard to the workforce: no other industry in Estonia could claim workers until the company's needs were satisfied. In the fall of 1942, the industry giant began hiring farmers, but with little success. To fill the shortage, the management needed at least 2,250 workers but was only able to secure 300. So dire became the situation with respect to manpower that the Germans halted the program that sent (often against their will) able-bodied men from Estonia to Germany.[21] This is why the number of Estonians in the Reich Labor Service (Reichsarbeitsdienst or RAD) remained minuscule compared with that of Latvians and Lithuanians. By October 1942, at most 860 Estonians had departed for the Reich. Later on, conscription into the RAD in Estonia (the so-called *Sauckel-Aktion*) was stopped altogether, thus creating a precedent. (In comparison, over 100,000 Lithuanians worked in the Third Reich.)

As of November 1942, Baltöl was short nine thousand workers. Yet all requests for additional workforce had been refused. The attempt in June 1942 to bring some five hundred construction workers from Königsberg failed. In September and October 1942, Baltöl tried its luck in Lithuania. The employment offices in Kaunas and Vilnius scrambled to deliver 500 workers to Jõhvi and Kohtla-Järve. The police went ahead with roundups after only a few dozen men showed up at an assembly point. With delay, two transports departed for Estonia on October 23 and 26 respectively.[22] In May 1943, news spread about a possible transfer of 2,400 British POWs captured in Italy to Estonia. Despite threats to cut off deliveries of crude oil to the Italian navy, nothing came of this proposal either.[23] In January 1943, Baltöl reported a total of 7,300 workers: 3,200 Estonian civilians; 2,000 Soviet POWs; 900 Lithuanian and Latvian forced laborers; 800 personnel (including 70 Germans); and 400 Ukrainians. Another group of Ukrainians (500 men) provided security for the factory buildings.[24] They called it "ethnic mixture." To maintain a considerable number of German employees at Baltöl turned out to be costly and therefore the number of German employees was reduced to 1 percent. The management was unable to match salaries and the standard of living with those in the Reich. Another option would be to start hiring Baltic Germans who had previously resettled in the Reich and who could often be found on the staff of such companies as I. G. Farben.[25]

Soviet prisoners of war constituted the main source of labor for Baltöl. Specifically for that purpose, Army Group North established a transit camp (Dulag 377) in the shale oil region. With its main camp in Kiviõli, Dulag 377 had five subcamps: Kohtla, Kütte-Jõu, Ahtme, Käva, and Kukruse.[26] In accordance with the agreement that Baltöl signed with the Wehrmacht, the company had to provide accommodation for POWs, while the military took care of food supplies and supervised the guards. The commandant of Dulag 377 received guidelines from the leader of the Estonian Mineral Oil Commando.[27] The first two hundred POWs were delivered as early as the fall of 1941. Henceforth, Baltöl tried to bring the POWs completely under its control. To guard its POW workers, through September 1943 Baltöl employed the Omakaitse (OK) and an internal plant security force *(Werkschutz)*. Only one-third of the 650 Estonian and Ukrainian members of the plant security force had weapons. In contrast, a regiment-strong OK (three to four thousand) was fully equipped with guns, which servicemen kept at home. Both the OK and Baltöl Security received orders from HSSPF-Ostland Jeckeln;[28] Army Group Narva provided logistics support. The military training of the OK, according to their German superiors, left much to be desired.

As of December 1943, Baltöl employed 17,133 workers, in addition to 11,645 workers in the service of OT.[29] The 24 percent increase in the workforce after June 1943 occurred mainly on account of Jewish slave laborers.

JEWISH SLAVES UP FOR THE BIDDING

From January 1943, GK Litzmann's office in Tallinn held regular meetings at which the future of the shale oil region was discussed. The German Security Police was one of the permanent participants in the consultations. During the first half of 1943, the Germans experienced a series of setbacks. As the military situation was deteriorating, the OKH had to lift the siege of Leningrad. The shale oil industry in Estonia, essential for the German war machine, urgently needed manpower. To help the situation, on June 21, 1943, Himmler ordered the liquidation of the remaining Jewish ghettos in the Ostland. The work-fit ghetto inmates were to be transferred to Estonia, and the rest "evacuated to the East," that is, murdered. In Estonia, Jews were to be locked in concentration camps.[30] Deportations of Jews to Estonia should have balanced the planned withdrawal of 25,000 POWs from the Ostland. That decision went back to a July 1942 meeting at which Albert Speer announced that from then on, Soviet POWs were the only workers to be used in mines in Germany. In the spring of the following year, the Reich Coal Union (Reichsvereinigung Kohle or RVK) decided to transport up to 200,000 POWs to Germany proper, mainly to the Ruhr area. The first POW transports were expected to arrive in July and August 1943.[31]

Jeckeln received Himmler's order on July 19. Jeckeln communicated the order to Sandberger, who then forwarded it to the liaison SS officer at Baltöl. The following week, Himmler's order went down to the Economic Inspectorate Ostland (Wirtschaftinspektion or WiIn), which began discussing its implementation with its subdivision, the so-called economic detachment (Wirtschaftskommando or WiKo). In order to prevent contact between Jews and the local population, the Inspectorate recommended that concentration camps be built at the refineries or in their immediate vicinity. In anticipation of the influx of Jewish slave labor, Fritz Sauckel, plenipotentiary general for labor mobilization, paid a visit to Mineral Oil Commando Kiviõli on July 17, and again, on July 25, toured the oil refinery at Kiviõli.[32]

As the date of deportation approached, more and more German agencies in Estonia put forward requests for Jewish workers. One of the major players in the field was Organization Todt. OT officially began its operations in Estonia in December 1941. From June 1, 1943, OT dramatically increased its presence in Estonia. Some commentators saw this expansion as nothing less than an attempt at creating an "OT Empire" in Estonia.[33] In Estonia, OT employed people of sixteen different nationalities. The largest groups of foreign workers came from Germany, Belorussia, Latvia, Croatia, Georgia, Belgium, Lithuania, Poland, France, Spain, and Ukraine.[34] OT maintained four branch offices in the shale oil region: in Kiviõli, Jõhvi, Kohtla, and Kunda. In October 1943, OT launched a barracks construction program, which mainly relied on a Jewish workforce. OT was expected to deliver a total of sixty-three wooden barracks for existing and new labor camps.[35] However, that was not the main reason why OT needed Jewish workers.

The closer the front drew to the borders of Estonia, the more acute became the need to protect the Baltic region in general and the shale oil industry in particular. On August 12, 1943, Hitler ordered the construction of the so-called Eastern Wall (Ostwall), a colossal fortification stretching from the Black Sea in the south all the way to the Baltic Sea in the north.[36] Field Marshal von Küchler notified Hitler early of the plans for retreat. Hitler first objected but then conceded on the condition that all necessary preparations for the retreat had been made. Building upon Hitler's dictum, in mid-September Army Group North unveiled plans for the defense along the Narva-Peipus line under the code name "Panther Line." The Wehrmacht was expected to pull back to the new positions by late winter–early spring of 1944.[37] To conceal the extent of the building project, the Panther Line was sometimes referred to as an "anti-bandit stronghold." For Estonia, an additional defense, called the Tannenberg fortification, was planned. It was to be built parallel to the Panther Line, some five miles west of the coastal village of Mummassaare, to Auvere.

The importance of the Tannenberg fortification, also known as the Narva Position (Narwa-Stellung), was hard to overestimate. The line of defense in mainland Estonia, augmented by a mine barrier at sea, was supposed to ensure German control over the Baltic Sea. By breaking through the defense, the Soviets would have effectively cut the Wehrmacht supply routes, as well as hindered iron ore deliveries from Sweden, essential for the German armaments industry. As for the Allies, breaking through the defense would also mean an advantage over Germany at sea. Last but not least, as long as the front stayed in Estonia, there was a chance that Finland would remain in a state of war with the Soviet Union.[38] While trying to secure whatever workforce was available for building the Eastern Wall, OT cast its eyes upon Jews. The shape of the Narva River required building a bridgehead immediately east of the city of Narva. This project alone required about twenty thousand workers. In order to have at least part of the job done before winter, military contractors were urged to "improvise."[39] Vaivara, as the site of one of the two planned refineries, was located next to the combat zone; although the Baltöl management was unhappy with the prospect of ceding some of its workforce to the construction of the defense, it had no choice but to agree to deliver the workers—predominantly Jewish. According to the estimates provided by OT, at the initial stage of construction 2,300 people would be enough.[40]

To discuss the forthcoming deployment of Jews in more detail, on July 20 Sandberger met with the Baltöl director, Wilhelm Mathy. The first 2,800 Jews were to arrive sometime before September. Of that number, 1,000 were to work in mines, with the rest assigned to building the defense. Six hundred Jews would go to Kohtla; 400 to Viivikonna; 800 to Slantsy; and 200 to Kiviõli. In addition, Baltöl sought 100 Jewish craftsmen (mainly shoemakers and tailors). The people were to arrive by October. Armaments factories were promised 300 Jewish workers. Another 250 Jews were assigned to a glass factory at Järvakandi, the biggest of its kind in the Baltics.[41] Three other bidders—Tallinn Harbor, Estonian Phosphates, and Port-Kunda—jointly placed a request for five hundred workers.[42] OT, meanwhile, hiked its demand to six thousand workers. Estonian police battalions were supposed to provide guards: one guard for every ten prisoners. The first 150 guards were to report for duty immediately.[43] Baltöl reacted by placing an order for an additional sixty wooden barracks. On August 7, WiIn received information about the start of deportations of work-fit Jews from the ghettos in Lithuania. According to the original timetable, the deportations would be over by the end of the month. Himmler determined October 15 as the deadline past which Jews could not perform labor outside of concentration camps.[44] According to the Economic Commando in Tallinn, by the early fall of 1943 up to ten thousand Jews were to arrive in Estonia.[45]

JEWISH DEPORTATIONS FROM VILNA AND KOVNO GHETTOS

According to rough estimates, as of September 1943 about 54,000 Jews remained in the Baltics. Forty thousand of them were deemed fit for work.[46]

The Nazis first started looking at places closest to Estonia, such as Daugavpils, which at that time still contained about 450 Jews. The plans to bring in Jews from Daugavpils, however, failed because of opposition on the part of the local German civil administration.[47] In the search for slave labor, one need not have looked any farther than Lithuania.

By the summer of 1943 there were about twenty thousand Jews left in Vilna (Vilnius) ghetto and another seventeen thousand in Kovno (Kaunas) ghetto.

Deportations from Vilna ghetto to Estonia commenced on August 6. Because the ghetto inhabitants had been fooled by the Germans so many times before, they no longer believed the latter's assurances of a safe environment for deported Jews. Because of armed resistance, the auxiliary police were only able to round up one thousand Jews for deportation to Estonia. Jacob Gens, head of the Jewish ghetto administration, assured the deportees that they were about to be sent to Estonia to work, not to die. As proof, Gens promised that the foremen from that transport would soon return to the ghetto. To everybody's surprise, that turned out to be true: on August 11, one of the foremen was distributing letters from people who had gone with him to Estonia. The Nazis figured that if the ghetto inhabitants would not believe the foremen, they would be more trustful of their friends and relatives. Therefore, Jews from the first transport were encouraged to write to their brethren in Lithuania in order to convince the latter to join them in Estonia.[48] One particular line in those letters made them look genuine. Some writers hinted that labor camps in Estonia were close to the frontline, thus making escape and eventual liberation a possibility.[49] One individual, for example, wrote that "the uncle with mustache works 80 km away," while the other asked to send him "bucks, so he could go see uncle Joseph."[50]

On August 19, the SS began herding the Jews for deportation to Estonia. Leaders of the German administration who made an appearance in the ghetto on the morning of August 23 announced that the remaining ghetto population was to be distributed between Kaunas, Latvia, and Estonia. Gens volunteered to provide the lists of deportees, which included family members of the people from the first "Estonian" transport, the unemployed, and those who had arrived in the ghetto only recently. A thirty-five-car train with 1,200 Jews departed Vilna for Vaivara on August 25. A few days later an SS courier brought back to the ghetto a bunch of letters from the workers from the second transport, who wrote that they were indeed performing labor and that the food was good.[51] Most ghetto inhabitants, however, put little trust in those letters, considering them a Gestapo trick. Truthful information about the conditions in Jewish labor camps in Estonia did spread by word of mouth: people slept on bunks in huge unheated barracks; of private property, one was only allowed to keep a bowl and a spoon; the food was awful; the average workday lasted fourteen hours; the guards beat prisoners mercilessly; because of the hard work, poor nutrition, cold, and diseases, people dropped like flies.[52]

Gens exhorted the ghetto population to be patient. Even though the German quota of five thousand was not met, he announced an end to deportations to Estonia. On September 1, however, the Germans renewed their demands. The only concession that Gens managed to get from the German Security Police was that the required number of people would be assembled by the Jewish ghetto police, without any interference from the Estonian and German police. Gens further succeeded in convincing the wives of the men who had already been deported to Estonia to volunteer for the journey. Thus, on September 4 a transport carrying 1,400 male and 2,200 female Jews pulled out of the Vilna railway station.[53]

The fourth and the last transport bound for Estonia left the Vilna ghetto on September 24. There were about 1,600 male Jews on that train that traveled through Daugavpils, Riga, and Tartu to Vaivara. The same number of female Jews was dispatched to the Kaiserwald (Mežaparks) concentration camp near Riga. The rest of the Jews were executed at Paneriai and Majdanek. The Vilna ghetto was no more. According to Yitzhak Arad's calculations, anywhere between 7,300 and 9,130 Jews were deported from the Vilna ghetto to Estonia.[54] The German Security Police in Vilnius came up with the figure 14,000.[55]

With the destruction of the Vilna ghetto, Kovno and Shavli (Šiauliai) remained the only two ghettos in Lithuania. On July 11, 1943, the Kovno ghetto received an unexpected guest—the commander of the German Security Police in Estonia, Dr. Sandberger. Nobody knew what to make of this visit. Jews at Kovno used every bit of information to learn what was happening to their coreligionists at the Vilna ghetto. The news they received was alarming: the ghetto inhabitants learned about the deportations from the Vilna ghetto to Estonia in August and early September. It was not all that unpredictable, therefore, that a transport with three thousand Jews departed Kovno for Vaivara on September 15. However, upon arrival in Estonia three days later, only 1,800 able-bodied people ended up staying; the rest were taken back to Tauragė in Lithuania. The next deportation to Estonia, the so-called *Estlandaktion,* took place one month later. With the quota set at 3,000, the Ukrainian and Lithuanian police managed to collect 2,709 Jews. The train left Kaunas-Aleksotas on October 26.[56] The final large-scale deportation to Estonia took place in late November 1943, when a transport with five hundred male Jews arrived from Kaiserwald.[57]

24. Jews in the Kovno ghetto boarding trucks for deportation to Estonia; USHMM, 81079.

THE VAIVARA CAMP SYSTEM

The geographic distribution of identified reserves of shale oil in Estonia determined the location for the future Jewish forced labor camps. Major deposits of
shale oil were to be found in the triangle—Rakvere-Vaivara–Lake Peipus—and
that is where all but a few Jewish forced labor camps were built. There were nineteen major camps in Estonia (going from east to west): Narva, Narva-Jõesuu,
Auvere, Putke, Vaivara, Viivikonna, Soska, Kuremäe, Jõhvi, Ereda, Kohtla, Saka,
Kiviõli, Sonda, Aseri, Kunda, Jägala, Lagedi, and Klooga. Some of these camps
were supposed to last only for a few weeks but remained operational for months.
Jägala and Lagedi were not, strictly speaking, "labor camps." Lagedi only existed
for one and a half months in August and September 1944 and was meant to be a
transit camp for the Jews bound for the Stutthof concentration camp in Poland.
Larger camps such as Viivikonna, Kiviõli, and Ereda were effectively subdivided
into two sections, hence the disparity in numbers of Jewish camps in Estonia as
they appear in various accounts. In addition, the Germans operated five small

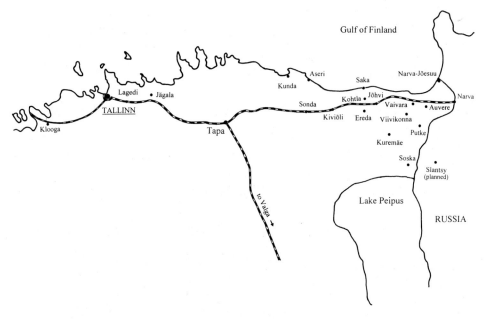

11. Jewish forced labor camps in Estonia, 1943–44. Prepared by author.

camps in northwestern Russia, southern Estonia, and northern Latvia. The Soviet advance in the fall of 1943 interfered with the German plan to establish a midsize camp in Slantsy, located just east of the Estonian border. For the same reason, the camp in the Russian village of Kerstovo near Kingisepp was evacuated within a month after its creation in October 1943. The four camps established outside of the shale oil region in late fall 1943 and early winter 1944—Panikovichi, Üle-nurme, Pechory, and Kūdupe—were in existence for only a brief period of time. Thus we are talking about twenty-five different camps. The SS camp administration had its seat in Vaivara, some fifteen miles west of Narva.

Officially, the Vaivara concentration camp was established on Himmler's order of September 15, 1943.[58] A few weeks later Vaivara received a field post number: 58,969. Vaivara was designated as the main camp (*Stammlager* or Sta-lag), which commanded numerous subcamps *(Aussenlager)* or labor camps *(Arbe-itslager)*. "Vaivara" was often used as a generic name for all Jewish labor camps in Estonia. All Jewish prisoners who arrived in Estonia passed through Vaivara, which justifies calling it a transit camp (*Durchgangslager* or Dulag). In accordance with the official Nazi classification, none of the Jewish labor camps in Estonia can be called a "concentration camp," for it was not the SS Economic and Admin-istrative Main Office that established them.[59] As any other concentration camp, though, Vaivara had five departments: commandant's office; chief of administration; protective custody camp leader; camp physician; and political department, that is, Gestapo. SS-Hstuf. Otto Brenneis served as chief of admin-istration at Vaivara, whereas the position of protective custody camp leader remained vacant throughout the existence of the camp. The Gestapo was only formally part of the camp system for the camp received instructions directly from the RSHA in Berlin.[60] Altogether the German camp personnel in Estonia did not exceed fifty people, including four female guards (three of them in the Klooga camp).[61]

The highest authority in each labor camp was the commandant, usually at the rank of sergeant. In fact, it was the prisoners who called the head of the camp the "commandant" (officially, only the main camp at Vaivara had a com-mandant). However, the nature of the assignment made individual camp lead-ers more independent in their decisions, effectively raising them to the status of a commandant.[62] Several companies of the Estonian 287th Police Battalion in Rakvere and one company of the 290th Police Battalion in Tartu provided guards for the Jewish slave labor camps. The total number of guards stood at about 300, that is, almost seven times fewer than originally planned. (By May 1944, though, that number had increased to 396.) The guards had no right to enter the camp territory. Internal camp life was regulated by Jewish elders, who together with the Jewish police (the so-called *Kapos*) were responsible among other things for assigning prisoners to labor details. That system made it possible to cut the number of German personnel, who in some cases were limited to a comman-dant and an SS medical orderly. The latter was supposed to brief the former on the health conditions in a camp using prisoners' medical records. Quite often, the SS personnel from one camp came for a visit to another camp, where they sometimes partook in brutalities.[63] This fact explains why survivors who were in different camps sometimes mentioned the same names of their torturers.

SS-Hstuf. Hans Aumeier was appointed head of the Vaivara camp complex. Before his arrival in Estonia, Aumeier already had an impressive service record. Aumeier was one of the first SS officers to receive appointment at Dachau, in 1934; his next stop was Buchenwald. In 1939 Aumeier became commandant of Flos-senbürg camp and in February 1942 the deputy of Rudolf Höss at Auschwitz-

Birkenau. The latter described him as an individual who was "restless, easily influenced, good-hearted, eager to serve, and willing to follow any order." At the same time, Aumeier did not think of the consequences of his actions, was reluctant to take responsibility, and lacked initiative. That was pretty much how Himmler described Aumeier, whom he had known since 1928. Höss was dissatisfied with Aumeier's performance at Auschwitz and felt relieved when the latter left for Estonia on August 16, 1943. He could not ruin anything there, Höss noted contemptuously, because it was off the beaten track and Himmler never went there.[64]

But Aumeier did not fail as Höss predicted. On the contrary, Aumeier's superiors praised his ability to establish and successfully run the camp complex in Estonia. Under the most primitive conditions, and with only a few German personnel, Aumeier was said to have built from scratch a system of Jewish labor camps with more than nine thousand inmates. In the wake of the German withdrawal from Estonia in the fall of 1944, Aumeier went to Dachau—another tacit acknowledgment of his "achievements."[65] During his tenure in Germany and Poland, Aumeier became known for his brutality. His signature torture was the exhausting roll calls: one at Flossenbürg in the summer of 1941 lasted forty hours and took the life of one hundred Polish prisoners! Aumeier was involved in the construction of the first gas chamber at Auschwitz-Birkenau and later participated in the selection of Jews for gassing. He also selected female inmates for medical experiments. The overall number of victims—Jews, Poles, and Soviet POWs—for whose death Aumeier was at least partially responsible runs into the tens of thousands.[66]

The second most influential individual in the Vaivara camp system was SS-Ostuf. Dr. Baron Franz von Bodman, who as the camp chief physician exercised significant authority. In this capacity, von Bodman played a major role in the so-called selections, that is, picking out prisoners for execution. Work-unfit Jews were customarily transferred to Ereda, where they were subsequently murdered. In Nazi jargon, it was called "being sent to Riga." According to survivors, in July 1944 von Bodman signed the order authorizing the execution of 10 percent of the remaining Jewish population in each of the camps.[67] Before arriving in Estonia, von Bodman had served in the commandant's office at Auschwitz. At the time of his assignment in Estonia, von Bodman was thirty-four years old.

Jews were constantly moved from one camp to another, depending on the amount of work to be done. The total number of Jews in slave labor camps in Estonia increased from 3,300 in September to 9,207 in November. By May 1944, however, that number was reduced to 6,565.[68] Jewish prisoners worked under the supervision of OT on various assignments such as construction, cutting trees, and building roads and railway tracks. Their principal economic activity, however, was mining shale oil and building fortifications. Prisoners were expected to crush 2.6 cubic yards of oil-bearing rock per day, which would produce 88 quarts of oil. Jews were convoyed daily from camp to a worksite and back. In fact, OT came to Estonia even before the Jewish prisoners did: the OT assignment at Vaivara officially began on June 1, 1943.[69]

High officials from Tallinn who visited the Sillamäe refinery in late November established that Jewish camps at Vaivara, Viivikonna, and Ereda were unprepared for harsh winter conditions.[70] Prisoners wore the same clothes they had worn when they first arrived in Estonia. Jews had to use blankets or sacks to patch their clothes. However little warmth it provided, many inmates put newspapers or paper sacks between their shirt and coat.

Upon arrival in a camp, prisoners received a pair of clogs. These "shoes" were locally produced and never fit properly. Before putting their feet into the clogs, prisoners wrapped them in rags so as to make it less painful. The single most popular topic of conversation among the prisoners was food. Jews subsisted on bread and soup (water mixed with flour and occasional pieces of potatoes, beet, or cabbage that were often rotten).[71]

The explanation for the relatively high survival rate among these Jewish prisoners can be found in a February 19, 1944, communication of BdS-Ostland SS-Oberf. Friedrich Panziger. Referring to an order from Jeckeln, Panziger unequivocally forbade executions of prisoners. Panziger said that prisoners constituted an important share of the workforce; furthermore, one could not have mass graves so close to the combat zone.[72] With the exception of individual cases of murder, until July 1944 no mass executions of Jews took place in the labor camps in Estonia. None of the camps had a crematorium; corpses were burnt on pyres outside of the camp territory.

In the summer of 1944, the SS carried out the so-called "10-Prozent-Aktionen," which did indeed decimate the camp population by one-tenth or more. Some survivors perceived those executions as an act of revenge for the failed assassination of Hitler in July 1944.[73] Among the victims were mainly people incapable of performing physical labor, that is, the elderly, the sick, and a few remaining children. Executions were carried out by the German SS, without much input on the part of the Estonian policemen who guarded the camps. In the case of large-scale executions the camp personnel received assistance from the local branches of the German Security Police.

JEWISH WORKERS AND THE GERMAN WAR INDUSTRY IN ESTONIA

Besides production of synthetic oil, Estonia and Tallinn became an important industrial hub, serving the needs of the German navy. Half a dozen factories in the Estonian capital produced, among other items, cable, flashlight batteries, generators, motor parts, radio and sound devices, oxygen, and acetylene. Of thirty-five factories in the Baltics that produced goods exclusively for the German military and navy, thirteen were in Estonia and nineteen in Latvia. Nearly as many people were employed in Estonia as in neighboring Latvia (50,000 and 54,000 respectively). In the largest of the three Baltic countries, Lithuania, the workforce stood at 19,000. To exploit Estonian industry to the fullest, an additional 50,000 laborers were needed.[74] As if seeking to prove the numbers, in January 1944 Baltöl ordered 50,000 pairs of straw shoes from Pskov for its Jewish, Belorussian, and POW workers.[75]

It appears that at least in the beginning, Jewish slave laborers were enough to satisfy the growing needs of the "mammoth concern," as the Germans dubbed Continental Oil Ltd. By November 1943, Estonia reported the lowest demand for workers in the Baltics. Most people were needed in construction and agriculture; Baltöl and Estonian Phosphates, however, only placed a request for 760 people.[76] The higher the number of Jewish, POW, and "Eastern" slave laborers (Ostarbeiter) in the Baltic industry, the more Estonians and Latvians could be relieved of work duty and subsequently sent to the front to fight the Soviets. In Estonia, the number of slave laborers gave the green light for mass conscription into the Waffen-SS Division.[77]

September 1943 statistics mentioned Jews for the first time. Between July 1 and September 30, the number of workers at Baltöl and its OT contractor increased from 25,351 to 32,028. Of 7,000 new workers about 4,000 were Jewish.[78] The second transport from the Vilna ghetto, which arrived in Estonia on September 3, brought 1,127 Jews: Baltöl in Viivikonna received 301 people, and OT in Vaivara another 826. On September 5, OT in Vaivara received another shipment of 1,571 Jews.[79] After a short stopover at Vaivara, prisoners were distributed among different labor camps. Although the Baltöl management was looking forward to expanding its workforce, it was unsure about the capability of the Jews to perform physical labor. The Baltöl directorate predicted that the average output would drop on account of the new workers.[80] Indeed, among the four groups of workers, Jews had the lowest efficiency rate: 1.33. In the case of "Eastern" workers, the estimated efficiency rate was 3.02; in the case of POWs 3.03; and the highest in the case of Estonians at 3.94. Obviously, undernourished, feeble-bodied Jews had the least strength, let alone experience, to work in shale-oil mines and refineries. However, as early as October their average yield increased to 1.42, and then again to 1.50 in November, hitting 1.81 in January. The Baltöl management argued that the increase was owing to a bonus system, introduced in the last two months of 1943.[81] Understandably, then, employers preferred non-Jewish workers to Jews. Thus the proposition of Baltöl to replace six skilled workers at the Volta-Hansa factory with fifty Jews was declined. The Jews were said to lack the skills necessary for working on the navy program (the Tallinn factory employed 250 workers to produce electric motors).[82] Baltöl management also expressed skepticism with regard to Jewish workers, who could only perform limited tasks and required a substantial number of guards. Estonian policemen were rather few in number, whereas Baltöl's security force was overstretched protecting the Slantsy plant from Soviet partisan attacks. Moreover, among the Jews there were many women and children.[83] In the final analysis, however, the Economic Inspectorate positively evaluated the Jews' overall work capacity. When working under proper supervision, Jews were said to be diligent and reliable laborers.[84]

After all, only a few Baltöl plants directly employed Jewish workers: 447 people at Kivioli; 697 at Sillamäe; and 76 at Ereda. A total of 850 Jewish men and 360 women made up 7.5 percent of the manpower.[85] In comparison, POWs, Estonians, and the "Eastern" workers constituted 40, 32, and 11.5 percent respectively. If the Germans had called off the Jews who worked in the mines, the output would have fallen 5 percent. A similar move involving Soviet POWs would have sunk the production by 61 percent. By all accounts, OT and Baltöl preferred POWs to Jews. OT disputed the decision to hand over five thousand POW workers to Army Group North. They argued that Jews could not substitute for Soviet POWs, many of whom were skilled workers. Production would most likely go down too.[86] This attitude partly contributed to a relatively high survival rate among the Jews deported to Estonia in 1943. Whereas the Baltöl management fought for each POW worker, it was ready to let Jews go. Thus the chief executive officer, engineer Ewald Schön, explained in March 1944 that Baltöl would have been able to survive without the three thousand Jews just evacuated from Narva, but insisted that all of the POWs should stay.[87]

As might be clear from the preceding paragraphs, OT and Baltöl constantly moved their Jews around. In October 1943, one hundred Jews on loan from OT Ereda camp unloaded a freight train that brought dismantled equipment from Slantsy. Once finished, the Jews returned from Kohtla to Ereda. Simultaneously, OT was building barracks for the Kiviõli and Kohtla-Järve forced labor camps (which held six hundred women and children each). In order to speed up the process, Baltöl conceded seven hundred Jews to OT: three hundred for Kiviõli and the rest for Kohtla-Järve.[88] In February 1944, Baltöl negotiated with OT for the deployment of Jews on construction sites at Ereda and Kohtla-Järve. The deployment would have happened earlier if it were not for the long distance between the work sites and the Jewish camps and the low working capacity of the Jewish prisoners. Otherwise, Jews were to replace the work-unfit POWs and Belorussians.[89] According to Baltöl statistics, OT managed a total of 3,319 Jewish workers, who were distributed among five different sites: Kiviõli (981); Kohtla-Järve (1,163); Jõhvi (202); Ereda (115); and Kohtla (858).[90]

EVACUATION

Jewish forced labor camps in Estonia had a much shorter lifespan than was initially planned. Steady Soviet advances made the Germans contemplate discontinuing synthetic oil production in Estonia. Whatever was happening to Baltöl also affected the Jews. Oil was nothing short of blood: running out of options, the Germans decided to hold onto Estonia as long as possible. The agony lasted for a good half-year. On January 20, 1944, the German army began the retreat via Narva. In February 1944, Army Group North implemented the New-Year Vacation plan. By February 27, the 16th Army had completed the withdrawal to the Panther Line position.[91]

The Soviet offensive forced the Germans to make hard choices: should they stay to the last, securing the oil production so essential for the overall military performance, or should they pull out, having previously dismantled the equipment and thus saved it? By February 1, 1944, a demolition plan (Sprengplan) was in place for Sillamäe, Kohtla-Järve, Kohtla, Kivioli, Püssi, and Jõhvi-Ahtme. In the case of Sillamäe, an alert level I was implemented and OK units withdrawn.[92] Nevertheless, the OKH decided to take risks. On February 5, General Field Marshal Wilhelm Keitel communicated Hitler's order to continue works at Kivioli, Kohtla-Järve, and Jõhvi. Hitler prohibited indefinitely the evacuation of the above-mentioned installations; all previous deadlines remained.[93] Minölko Estonia also stepped in by halting the transfer of workers from either Baltöl or its OT contractor. The columns of workers already on the march were to be returned immediately.[94] In the meantime, the exposed leaks in the foundation of Baltöl were turning into a flood, endangering its very existence. OT then and again had to use scores of workers to patch the holes in the German defenses. Thus Baltöl never received the promised POW and Jewish workers evacuated from Narva on February 1.[95] The building of defenses against Soviet air and sea raids pulled an increasing number of workers away from the Baltöl production lines. The loss of a power station in Narva adversely affected the oil output. At the same time, thousands of tons of construction materials were on their way to Estonia from the Reich.

By mid-February, Soviet troops, advancing from the south, were poised to cut the railway line at Vaivara. Simultaneously, the Soviets attempted a landing at Mereküla, just a few miles away to the north. The threat posed by the attack made the OKH order the Viivikonna mine and the Sillamäe refinery cleared.[96] Over the next two weeks the entire area within fifteen miles of the former Estonian border was evacuated. About fifty freight cars loaded with materials and equipment were expected to arrive from Sillamäe alone. The order arrived on February 13 to start immediately evacuating the Estonian population from Sillamäe and Viivikonna. POWs and Jews were also to be removed from Viivikonna. During the night of February 13–14, 150 POWs, 700 Jews, and a group of Estonian civilians were taken, partly on trucks and partly on foot, from Viivikonna to Ereda.[97] According to the war diaries of Minölko Estonia, there existed plans to transfer 700 Jews from Viivikonna to Breda in the Netherlands. To make space for the incoming Jews from Estonia, 800 sick Jews languishing in a tent camp at Breda were then to be taken to Riga.[98] Needless to say, these fantastic plans never materialized.

The decision to remove *all* Jews from the shale oil region was made during the visit of Speer's representative, Dr. Böning, to Kivioli on February 23. Six days later Böning discussed the plan of transfer with the Vaivara camp administration. Minölko Estonia went so far as to draw evacuation routes for the entire Baltöl and

OT workforce, including POWs and Jews. Two Jewish columns—2,500 people in each—were supposed to start marching across Estonia into Latvia. Using country roads, in fourteen days the Jews would cover about 150 miles. Along the way to Riga, they were to pass through Ereda, Kohtla, Kiviõli, Kabala, Väike-Maarja, Võhma, Suure-Jaani, Tori, Sindi, Häädemeeste, Salacgrīva, and Dunte.[99] However detailed, those plans were shelved too.

The negotiations continued in March, though without much success. OT announced that it would continue using Jews on defense works until a replacement was found. OT would only let Jews go in exchange for 2,800 workers, preferably POWs. Meanwhile, KdS-Estland Baatz requested that the Estonian police battalion that guarded the Jewish camps stay in place. As of March 19, Himmler had not yet granted permission to withdraw. On the very same day, and in violation of all previous agreements, OT sent another 300 Jews to build a fortification at Saka. The presence of SS-Ogruf. Oswald Pohl, head of the SS Economic and Administrative Main Office, at a meeting in Riga the following week did not produce the desired effect either.[100] By March the entire shale oil region was engulfed by war. On March 18, the first known transport of 863 male prisoners departed Estonia for the Stutthof concentration camp; the prisoners were probably from Tallinn Central prison and most likely non-Jewish.[101] The news that finally arrived from Riga on April 24 was rather discouraging: Berlin had reconsidered the earlier plans to assign five thousand POWs to the Baltöl program. Jews were to stay, if only temporarily.[102]

In spite of the initial setback, the Germans managed to put oil production in Estonia back on track. Indeed, except for a temporary drawback in February, oil output remained stable or even increased slightly over the spring and summer months of 1944.[103] According to estimates, in 1944 Baltöl needed at least twelve thousand workers to effectively manage all its mines and refineries. An earlier attempt to get several thousand Soviet POWs from Riga had failed. In a desperate attempt to secure any workers at all, in late May 1944 Baltöl inquired about the Russian refugees-cum-forced-laborers who had not yet been shipped to the Reich. By the end of the spring, references to Jews as a likely source of manpower had become rarer.[104] As late as July 15, the OKH forbade the withdrawal of POWs from Estonia so as to ensure that Baltöl's work be uninterrupted.[105]

By early summer 1944, the situation with regard to manpower had become desperate. Instead of proceeding with the evacuation of Jews, Baltöl and OT were told—if worse came to worst and no other workforce was available—to seek out more Jews. Operation "total war effort" *(Totaler Kriegseinsatz)* was in effect. As a result of the tripartite discussion between Vaivara, Baltöl, and OT in early June, the interested parties came out with the figure six thousand. That is how many Jews were needed to keep the oil tap open. SS-Hstuf. Aumeier promised to find the required number of Jewish slave laborers in the shortest time possible. Following the meeting, the parties went in search of manpower, anybody at all they could lay their hands on.[106] Aumeier cast his eyes on Hungary and its Jews, who had been rounded up and deported since May. A small proportion of the Hungarian Jews were inadvertently saved through OT, which had been deploying them since February 1943.[107]

Aumeier kept his word. For the first time, a Jewish transport from Hungary came under consideration on June 6. Two days later, it was not yet clear whether the new arrivals would be POWs, Jews, or "Eastern" workers. On June 11, however, a train with 500 Hungarian Jews onboard was already at the Kiviõli station. Among other prisoners on that train was Lea Meiri from Kassa on the Slovakian border. She and other Jewish women had barely escaped death at Auschwitz, from which they were taken to Latvia. Half of the Jews stayed in Riga while the second half were sent farther north to Estonia.[108] Baltöl received information that the rest of the 3,500 Jews bound to arrive from Hungary would be women as well. This was not exactly the kind of people Baltöl was looking for: it wanted miners, craftsmen, and metal workers.[109] The affair lasted less than two weeks. The SS kindly offered to bring more Jews from Hungary, but the Estonian Mineral Oil Commando declined the offer because of the low output of women and inadequate supervision. Moreover, the Office of General Plenipotentiary for Labor Allocation had just "found" an additional three thousand POWs for Estonia. The second transport from Beszterce, which was supposed to arrive in Estonia on June 24, went to Latvia instead.[110] As regards the Jews from the first transport, Baltöl quickly discharged the women, who ended up cutting trees in the forest.[111]

Hungarian Jews were not the only foreign Jews who ended up in Estonia in the late spring and summer of 1944. As of March 24, 1944, there were 2,867 prisoners in Tallinn Central prison, among them 61 Jews. By the beginning of the summer, however, the numbers soared to 3,997 and 240 respectively.[112] The number of Jewish prisoners increased on account of French Jews who arrived in Tallinn via Kaunas on May 19. Transport no. 73 with 878 Jewish men on board

left Paris-Drancy for Kaunas on May 15. One hundred and sixty Jews were murdered upon arrival in Kaunas and Praveniškės three days later. In Estonia, 60 out
of more than 200 French Jews were executed within a matter of days. The rest
of the group were assigned to repair the landing strip at Lasnamäe airport. Two
other executions, which took place on July 14 and August 14 respectively, cut
the number of survivors from the Paris transport down to 34.[113] Tallinn Central
prison's records allude to the presence of a limited number of Jewish prisoners
from France in Estonia: on August 23, thirteen male Jews—most of whom had
French first names—were transferred from Lasnamäe labor camp (prison) to
Tallinn Central prison.[114] Eventually, the remaining French Jews were deported
to Stutthof; only fifteen of them survived.

By mid-July there were still 3,744 Jews at four construction sites in Kiviõli,
Kohtla-Järve, Ereda, and Kohtla. In fact, because of the relocation or complete
withdrawal of POWs, the proportion of Jewish workers had even increased. Baltöl
could no longer pursue the building program at Kohtla-Järve, for the workforce
there was up to 60 percent Jewish. Taking into account that Jews made up 47 percent of the remaining workforce, whereas their productivity was 50 percent lower
than the average, the management pronounced the Estonian shale oil industry
extinct.[115] All non-Estonian workers, including Jews, were viewed as unreliable.
Those who were reliable (that is, Estonians and Germans), however, made up
only 10 percent of the workforce.[116] In the last days of July, Army Group North
ordered five thousand Baltöl workers to dig antitank ditches on a five-mile stretch
between Jõhvi and the seashore. Minölko Estonia agreed to release the workers on the condition that 2,400 Jews from Kiviõli camp remain. Then, however,
Baltöl came out with an alternative proposal: the company would send two thousand Jews to East Prussia in exchange for one thousand POWs.[117]

Negotiations regarding the replacement of the remaining 4,500 Jews by
POWs started by May.[118] By early August, Baltöl was ready to shift the Jews to
East Prussia, yet was waiting for a personal go-ahead from Hitler. About 2,050
Jews had already been moved to an area near Tallinn where they awaited the next
available ship to take them to Stutthof. The remaining 2,500 Jews were expected
to arrive from the shale oil region shortly.[119] By this time, however, chaos was
already settling in. The following few days saw the arrival of several mutually
exclusive orders. On August 4, Speer sanctioned the redistribution of 14,000
Baltöl workers among Army Group North, OT in East Prussia, and the so-called

Geilenberg Program.[120] On August 9, Army Group North received Hitler's order halting the evacuation of the 4,500 Jews from Baltöl. At 11:30 A.M., however, Aumeier ordered the withdrawal of all Jews from the Baltöl installations by noon of the same day. Two days later, that is, on August 11, OT received confirmation that Hitler approved the removal of Jewish workers.[121] Indeed, by August 10 all remaining Jews in the shale oil region were concentrated in Kiviõli for the subsequent transfer to Tallinn, from which they were expected to carry on to East Prussia. However, in the midst of preparations for the final deportation, on August 13, Economic Staff East communicated Hitler's order that brought the entire operation to a halt.[122]

Taking into account that Romania was about to fall to the Soviets, one can understand why Hitler was reluctant to surrender yet another fuel-producing area. In order to increase its fuel supplies, Nazi Germany had to rely on synthetic oil production in Estonia.[123] It is clear, however, that by the last week of August 1944, Hitler made a final decision to terminate the oil program in Estonia.[124] The decision was carved in stone: all 4,150 Jews from the shale oil region were to be shipped to the Reich. One of the largest transports carrying Jews and Soviet POWs departed from Tallinn on August 18. Five days later, all 4,408 prisoners reached their destination: Stutthof concentration camp near Danzig.[125] By that time, however, some Jews had already decided to take their life into their own hands by fleeing from the camps. In the first weeks of September, the gendarmerie in cooperation with local headquarters carried out a series of roundups in the Kohtla area. As a result of these raids, at least six Jews were shot and another ten handed over to the German Security Police—an apparent death sentence. All the apprehended individuals were charged with having partisan links.[126] One of the factory buildings in Tallinn was designated a temporary shelter for those two thousand Jews who were expected to arrive from the shale oil region in the second week of September.[127] The statistical report that OT sent to Baltöl on September 12, 1944, listed 8,114 workers, none of them Jewish.[128]

INTERACTION BETWEEN JEWISH PRISONERS AND THE LOCAL POPULATION

Despite the fact that forced labor camps in Estonia only existed for about a year, Jews had many opportunities to interact with the local Estonian population, whether it was with camp guards, civilian workers, or local farmers. Members of the 287th Police Battalion guarded the perimeter of the camps and rarely physically abused prisoners, even though some Jews had grave memories of individual atrocities committed by Estonian guards during their deportation from the Vilna ghetto. The first people whom Lithuanian Jews encountered in Estonia were SS-Oschaf. Helmut Schnabel and the battalion rank and file. Schnabel got into the habit of whipping some of the prisoners as soon as they arrived at the Vaivara railway station. He was the only one who did so.[129] Nevertheless, over the course of a year, Estonian guards shot a number of Jews who attempted to escape or left their labor detail to beg for food. There were several cases when the guards knocked Jews unconscious for walking or working too slowly.[130]

Jews, naturally, sought contacts with the local population. The purpose of those contacts was threefold: to get in touch with Jewish prisoners from other camps; to find food; and to get through to the pro-Soviet underground movement. Unfortunately, the Jews did not know that the partisan movement was essentially nonexistent in Estonia. Jews rarely escaped from the camps for they were afraid of the Estonian guards, some of whom brutalized Vilna ghetto inmates during the September 4 deportation. Those who attempted to flee were often caught in the woods by Estonian farmers and handed over to the Security Police. Jews differentiated between Estonians who knew some Russian and those who spoke no Russian at all. According to survivors, the former were better disposed toward them than the latter. By the same token, former prisoners juxtaposed the unkindness of the Estonian policemen with the friendlier attitude of ordinary people. In similar situations, different people reacted differently. Sonia Katz, for example, remembered being treated by a forty-year-old Estonian surgeon in Kunda. Following a brutal operation on the woman's face that the surgeon performed without any anesthesia, he told her in Russian, "Jews and dogs feel no pain!" An Estonian nurse who assisted the surgeon, however, felt compassionate toward the female prisoner and let her rest after the painful operation.[131]

Twenty-three-year-old Molly Ingster managed to bribe an Estonian guard at Vaivara, who let her and her son escape. Unfortunately, Ingster did not have another 15,000 rubles to pay to the Estonian farmers who refused her shelter.[132] Boris Kacel managed to save a few gold coins, but he had something even better to offer. As an electrician at Vaivara, Kacel was able to explore the area outside of the camp territory. Kacel thus established contact with one of the local farmers, who in exchange for wires promised to provide the former with produce. Kacel visited the farmer on several occasions and received generous amounts of food from him. This food prolonged Kacel's and his father's lives. Other farmers, who got annoyed with frequent visits of hungry camp inmates, sometimes gave nothing.[133]

Estonian farmers who helped Jews in one way or another usually expected something in return. Ironically, the Germans learned about the typhus epidemics that broke out in the Vaivara forced labor camp on December 4, 1943, by identifying two carriers of disease, both Estonians. An engine driver and another woman from Viivikonna came into contact with Vaivara Jews with whom they had been illegally trading.[134] Fifteen years after the war, farmers in the Vaivara area still had items that previously belonged to Jews: clothes, rags, household items, and so forth.[135] One other commodity was illegal medical treatment that local farmers sometimes received from Jewish camp physicians (reportedly in Ereda and Kuremäe). In return, some Estonians promised to help establish contacts with the nonexistent underground movement, as, for example, did an Estonian druggist whom Dr. Mark Dworzecki met in Kuremäe. When Dworzecki arrived at the drugstore to meet with the "partisans," however, the Estonian Security Police were waiting for him.[136]

Often enough, farmers were willing to share food with Jews who helped them on the land. Karin J., whose parents had a farm not far from Vaivara, remembered several Jewish women helping them to gather the harvest sometime in September 1943. It was Karin's brother, a member of the local OK and food supplier for the local forced labor camps, who brought the Jews to the farm.[137] Farmers were enticed to use slave labor. In accordance with the existing regulations, farmers only had to provide food and shelter for those POWs who worked for them; no additional payments were required.[138] Farmers looked forward to using Jewish labor for the same reasons they welcomed POWs who escaped from the camps. Farmers tended to hide the POWs who worked for them, essentially preventing the military authorities from taking the prisoners back to the camps.[139] Even under the threat of punishment, farmers continually employed POWs whom the OK or they personally apprehended. They did so because of the shortage of farm laborers.[140]

Between September 1943 and July 1944, the Estonian Security Police sentenced several dozen individuals to prison terms for trading with Jews from Klooga. The individuals engaged in illicit business with the Jews were mainly local

Estonian farmers but also some Russian civilians employed at the Klooga camp. The charges included illegal trading and possession of Jewish property. Fedor Panin, who worked as a carpenter in the camp, bought linens and clothes from Jews. A search revealed that another camp worker, Boris Timofeiev, purchased a coat, a suit, and a jacket. Among those arrested was only one individual, coincidentally also a Russian, who helped the Jews gratis. Tatiana Kukharsky received a six-month sentence after she threw a loaf of bread to a group of Jews returning to camp from work. The woman told the investigation that she felt sorry for those Jews. Remarkably, of all people charged with illicit contacts with Jews, Kukharsky was the only one with a high school diploma.[141] Nobody investigated Mihkel Raudsepp, a camp guard. Raudsepp used to buy from Jews rings, watches, gold coins, and so forth, which he later sold for profit at a market in Tallinn.[142]

Barter trade with Jewish inmates of Klooga camp continued nonstop—during the day in the workplaces, at night over the fence. By firing a shot in the dead of night, an Estonian guard signaled to the Jews to come over to the fence. On the other side of the fence, Estonians from near and far waited with bread, herring, meat, and so forth. Estonians who sold food to Jews often demanded payment in gold. Sometimes the sellers did not honor their commitments. Without that little extra food, however, Jewish prisoners faced starvation. One could often see camp inmates picking scraps from the garbage, eating potato peels and coffee beans instead of food.[143]

These and similar scenes made some Estonians help the Jews without asking anything in return. Benjamin Weintraub, for example, established contact with a certain Karl Koppel in Keila, a town seven miles east of Klooga. From Koppel he not only received bread, butter, cheese, and other foodstuff, but also a couple of guns and a few rounds of ammunition.[144] The Soosaar family was one of the few that stayed in Klooga village during the winter. Their house was located on the road that Jews walked daily to and from work. Whatever they had themselves (mainly bread and bacon) the Soosaars shared with the Jews. In the winter they left food in a birdhouse so that prisoners did not have to wander through the snowdrifts to get to the house. Upon request from one of the prisoners, Hans Soosaar got him a map of Estonia.[145] Another Klooga resident, Elviine Hinsberg, helped Jews with food until one of her countrymen denounced her.[146]

Still, material gain was the single most compelling factor that prompted Estonians to assist Jews. Thus, following the Germans' withdrawal from Klooga on

September 20, 1944, a group of villagers with a sack of bread made their appearance on the camp grounds. For a few dozen Jewish survivors it was the only food they were to get before the arrival of Soviet troops several days later. Yet the Jews had to pay for the bread: clothes, jewelry, watches, American dollars, all kinds of payment were accepted. It is true, though, that those Jews who had absolutely nothing to give in exchange received food free of charge.[147]

In contrast, former prisoners universally praised Dutch OT workers for their "human, warm, and good" attitude toward Jews. At Aseri, Vaivara, Jõhvi, Ereda, and Kiviõli, the Dutch often shared bread and preserves with Jews, even though they often did not have enough food themselves. By tacit agreement, the Dutch overseers at Aseri paid no attention if the Jewish workers failed to fulfill the quota. Those Dutch who worked as truck drivers at Jõhvi shared information with Jews about other forced labor camps. According to Mark Dworzecki, a joint Dutch-Jewish underground cell had for some time been operational at the Vaivara camp.

Jews at Klooga received an additional boost of enthusiasm when they learned from the Dutch that the Red Army was approaching. Indeed, Klooga Jews insisted that the Dutch treated them "as their brothers."[148] Hanna Panyrkova, one of the few survivors from the Theresienstadt transport, had sweet memories of Christmas 1943 at Ereda. One of the Dutch workers who took part in the Christmas celebration at the commandant's office stole a roasted hen, which he brought to the women's barracks so as to help them fight both hunger and the gray reality of camp existence.[149] No such stories about the Estonians were preserved; it would not occur to Jews to call Estonians "brothers."

10 JEWISH FORCED LABOR CAMPS, 1943–1944

THE ARRIVAL: VAIVARA, VIIVIKONNA

Sources on Jewish forced labor camps in Estonia are rather limited and by no means complete. Except for a few statistical reports, there are basically no German documents that talk about life in the camps. Work statistics are only available in the case of Narva and Klooga camps. Monthly reports compiled by chief physician Dr. Baron Franz von Bodman constitute the most valuable source for the study of the camps. For many years these reports were considered lost but they then resurfaced in the late 1990s. As regards the numbers of camp inmates and the dates within which camps were operational, von Bodman's communications to the SS Economic and Administrative Headquarters in Berlin can be trusted. When it comes to the number of deaths in each particular camp, however, the reports tend to be a much less reliable source. Von Bodman, who was mainly concerned with sanitary conditions in the camps, tended to downplay the mortality rate among the Jews. Thus selections and killings were nowhere mentioned in his reports.[1] That leaves us essentially with one notoriously unreliable source: postwar trial records. Survivors, whose depositions were featured prominently in West German war crime trials, used the opportunity to speak out, whereas the defendants in those trials tried to reveal as little as possible. As a result, we have an array of conflicting testimonies that cite different names, dates, and figures. To blend those bits and pieces into one coherent narrative at times seems an impossible task.

No matter what camp Jews were assigned to, all of them first arrived in Vaivara. The camp was built in an open field, one mile from the Vaivara train station. Farther south was massive woodland. In addition to living quarters, Vaivara had a bathhouse, storage, a kitchen, workshops, the office, and a room for the Jewish elders' use. The camp administration and the SS occupied two barracks outside of the camp territory. Nearby were located Dutch workers' barracks, the so-called "Dutch camp."[2] The Vaivara camp was built on farmland. In fact, several Estonian farmers found themselves living on the camp grounds, surrounded by barbed wire. Following the construction of the first ten camps in Estonia, both Vaivara and Viivikonna II were supposed to be dissolved. That, however, did not happen.

As of October 25, 1943, there were 907 Jews at Vaivara. Over the next month, the number of inmates increased to 1,237.[3] The increase occurred on account of the decision to turn Vaivara into a collecting point for sick Jews from other camps. The German administration made this decision in the wake of a typhus outbreak in several Jewish labor camps. Suffering from typhus, dysentery, and

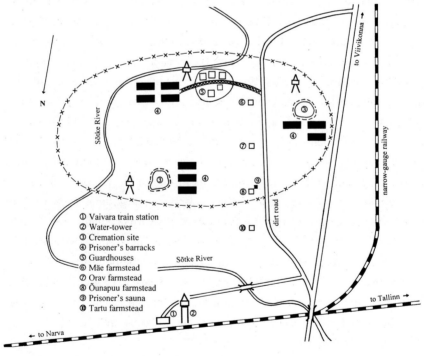

① Vaivara train station
② Water-tower
③ Cremation site
④ Prisoner's barracks
⑤ Guardhouses
⑥ Mäe farmstead
⑦ Orav farmstead
⑧ Õunapuu farmstead
⑨ Prisoner's sauna
⑩ Tartu farmstead

12. Vaivara camp (adapted from the original sketch of Boris Lipkin, early 1990s). Prepared by author.

other infectious diseases, those Jews who ended up in Vaivara could only await death.[4] The epidemic of spotted fever that broke out at the Vaivara camp at the beginning of December peaked by Christmas. By that time, 264 sick Jews, or 20 percent of the total camp population, were registered in Vaivara. According to survivors, the camp had a special section for children. Indeed, chief physician Dr. von Bodman in his first report to Berlin mentioned about 460 children staying at Vaivara. Although von Bodman continued calling the presence of children, whose number was reduced in half by November, "a burden," he was not yet ready to order their summary execution. The children's camp was run by a Jewish physician from Kaunas, who commanded a group of Jewish nurses. Up to 200 children were supposedly taken by train to Riga during the camp evacuation in February 1944.[5]

Vaivara commandant SS-Oschaf. Helmut Schnabel had been part of the Nazi camp administration since 1934, first at Sulza in Thuringia and then at Buchenwald. His first assignment was at Viivikonna. For a week or so in December 1943 Schnabel substituted for SS-Hschaf. Kurt Pannicke in Narva. Schnabel spent his last months in Estonia commanding a labor camp at Ereda. In July 1944, Schnabel brought the camp inmates first to Tallinn and then to Stutthof.[6] Every time a new transport arrived in Vaivara, Schnabel ordered Jews to form two rows in a roll call area. He then demanded that the newcomers submit their valuables. One or several camp inmates who accompanied Schnabel went along to collect the valuables. At random, Schnabel ordered one Jew or another to undress and then personally searched him. Once he shot a prisoner on the spot for failing to report his valuables.[7]

Upon arrival, Boris Kacel, along with other prisoners from the Kaiserwald transport, was led into a long, dimly lit barracks. A 150-foot-long and 50-foot-wide barracks had continuous rows of two-tier bunks on each side and a few long tables and benches in the middle. There was no way the two small cast-iron stoves with chimneys through the roof could heat such a large space. Two small windows at each end of the room gave very little natural light, so the electric lights were switched on at all times. As happened earlier at the Jägala camp, Latvian and German Jews felt unwelcome among the Lithuanian Jews who had arrived in Vaivara one month earlier. The latter derided the newcomers as a "fine and gentle class of Jews," who retorted by calling their coreligionists from the Vilna ghetto ill-mannered and rough.[8]

While some Jews were engaged in building a narrow-gauge railway and digging antitank ditches, the majority of Vaivara camp inmates worked in a quarry and in the Sillamäe oil refinery about two miles north of the camp. Jews also built barracks for a construction company from Ulm called Ludwig Truchsäss. Women had a somewhat better lot than men: some of them cleaned the German living quarters immediately next to the camp.[9] A prisoner's daily ration consisted of 4.5 ounces of bread, a cup of soup, tea without sugar, 0.7 ounce of margarine, and 0.7 ounce of jam. Because of poor nutrition, the most common causes of death in the camp were dysentery, exhaustion, and starvation. The number of deaths exceeded fifteen per week or seventy per month. Dead bodies were burnt in a nearby forest twice a week.[10] At first, prisoners felt uneasy seeing the enormous bonfire of a makeshift crematorium, but with time got used to it. Vaivara had a special crew that took care of the corpses, which they placed on specially designed wooden platforms before setting them afire with gasoline.[11]

According to different estimates, two big and between fifteen and twenty small selections took place at Vaivara camp within one year of its existence. The first large-scale selection was carried out shortly after the camp became operational in August–September 1943, whereas the second one occurred immediately before it was dismantled. Meanwhile, the SS camp administration wore the prisoners down with small yet nonetheless deadly purges. Many witnesses identified Schnabel as a driving force behind the dreaded selections at Vaivara. Gita Grilches named at least five elderly prisoners whom Schnabel helped into a truck bound for a nearby forest. Those five seemed to have believed Schnabel when he told them they were about to be assigned an easier job. "To peel potatoes," Riva Raichel overheard Schnabel saying. The selections usually took place during the evening roll call. Overnight, the doomed were locked in a special barracks, from which they were removed in the morning, shortly after the labor details had left the camp. All that remained were the clothes of the executed, which the trucks later brought back to the camp. And because Schnabel was an economical individual, he ordered those garments made into prisoners' caps.[12] Sometimes Schnabel suddenly appeared in a barracks or in the bathhouse, with the same intention—to identify and remove the work-unfit. At one time, for example, he told the prisoners that in preparation for evacuation the camp administration wanted to know the names of those who were unable to walk. Schnabel carefully wrote down the names of the Jews who volunteered the information. He explained that they did not have to perform labor anymore. As soon as the labor details left the camp following the next morning's roll call, all twenty-five people on the list were taken away. Schnabel by all means deserved the nickname Vaivara prisoners gave him: "death's head" *(Totenkopf)*.[13]

Among other names of their torturers, the Jews mentioned two: SS-Hschaf. Kurt Pannicke and SS-Oschaf. Heinrich Šatkus (Schattkus). As commandant of Narva camp, Pannicke often came to Vaivara, where he sometimes partook in the selections. Among his numerous victims was a former member of Vilna ghetto Jewish Council, whom Pannicke forced to repeatedly get up and down before killing him.[14] Although he was not even a German but rather a Lithuanian, Šatkus remained in the prisoners' memory as a cruel individual like his boss, Dr. von Bodman (both arrived in Vaivara on September 22, 1943). It is unclear how Šatkus made it from a mattress dealer in Šiauliai to an orderly in Vaivara. One witness claimed that he administered a deadly carbon injection to two prisoners, a woman and a teenager infected with typhus.[15] According to survivors, the trucks with the condemned traveled to the forest as often as twice a month. The total number of victims at Vaivara could be anywhere between 200 and 500.[16] On February 2, 1944, a freight train took 605 sick and feeble adults and 185 children to Ereda. Šatkus, who accompanied the transport, saw those Jews delivered to the section of the Ereda camp designated for the sick and the elderly. While only one person from the February 2 transport died along the way, out of the remaining 2,466 Jews who set out on march from Vaivara three days later, 44 did not make it to the destination. Among the SS personnel who accompanied the Jews to Kiviõli, Ereda, Jõhvi, and Kohtla (and who were ultimately responsible for their deaths) were SS-Uschaf. Karl Theiner, SS-Uschaf. Theodor Schmitz, SS-Uschaf. Ernst Runde, and SS-Stubaf. Heinrich Helmlinger.[17]

The Jewish slave labor camp closest to Vaivara was just a few miles away, in a worker's hamlet called Viivikonna. In fact, there were two different camps— Viivikonna I and Viivikonna II—that had different reputations among the prisoners. The barracks in Viivikonna II were built on wet ground, while those in Viivikonna I were on sand. The first Jewish prisoners arrived in Viivikonna II from Vaivara sometime between September 6 and 10. There were 901 of them: 544 men, 240 women, and 117 children. Jews relieved the hundred or so POWs who had hitherto been working in the mines and auxiliary facilities. To prevent contacts between the two groups, the miners were divided into two shifts: a Jewish shift and a POW shift.[18] Some Jews worked in quarries, using dynamite to break shale oil rocks; big chunks were transported to Kohtla-Järve for fuel extraction, while crushed stones were used to heat the ovens.[19]

Upon arrival, Jews had to surrender their clothes in exchange for striped prisoner robes, which were delivered from Riga. To facilitate the capture of prisoners who might attempt an escape, women had their heads shaved completely, while men only partially. Male and female prisoners lived in separate barracks. Women were mainly engaged in building defenses.[20] Viivikonna II, commanded by Schnabel, was built on a swamp, ankle deep in water. At the beginning, Jews had to live in so-called Nissen huts or *Tonnenzelte* (prefabricated shelters, semi-cylindrical in shape, made of canvas stretched over a metallic framework), without having a chance to properly dry their robes. Bunia Perelstein recalled that one night her hair froze to the tarpaulin wall of the hut, so that she hastily cut her hair off in order to make it in time for the morning roll call. Work began at six in the morning and lasted until seven in the evening, with a roll call scheduled at 5:00 P.M. Food rations were inadequate: a half-pound of bread, 0.3 ounce of margarine, and watery pearl-barley soup.[21]

Schnabel left grim memories at Viivikonna. At a roll call on the day after the arrival of Jewish prisoners in Viivikonna II, Schnabel ordered some ten to twenty elderly men to lie down on the muddy ground. He then kicked them with his boots and strangled to death one of the victims. In Vaivara, eleven-year-old Mordechai Rosenberg fell unconscious under the blows of Schnabel's whip. One other survivor barely escaped blindness when Schnabel hit her in the face with a rubber club. During his time in Ereda, Schnabel was said to have beaten anyone whose face he disliked. Even the slightest "misbehavior," such as asking for more food or not taking off one's hat quickly enough, was punished. One thing all survivors remembered clearly was a dog whip that Schnabel always carried with him, frequently using it on prisoners. Isaac Narkunski recalled removing bloodstains from Schnabel's whip. At the time of the crime Schnabel was thirty-one years of age.[22] Yet Schnabel was definitely not the only higher SS official who authorized and personally participated in murder. Jews in Viivikonna I felt as unsafe as their coreligionists did in Viivikonna II. Commandant of Viivikonna I SS-Oschaf. [?] Bock selected children for execution (the so-called *Kinderaktion*) as early as September 1943.[23]

On February 4, Viivikonna I camp was shut down and its 872 Jewish prisoners escorted to Vaivara. On the night of February 14, 150 POWs and 700 Jews set out on the march from the Viivikonna II camp to Ereda. While the POWs and Estonian civilians rode on trucks, the Jews had to travel on foot.[24] Following the dissolution of Vaivara and Viivikonna camps, the central camp administration moved to Saka, about seventeen miles to the west. A Jewish forced labor camp was built in Saka sometime in the fall of 1943, just north of the existing POW camp. This time, antiaircraft defense played a major role in choosing the location for the camp.[25] During the summer 1944 selection at the Saka camp, Dr. von Bodman singled out about one hundred work-unfit Jews for execution. Among the individuals who carried out the execution were camp commandant Pannicke and SS-Hschaf. Max Dahlmann, who occupied the position of treasurer in the main office.[26]

CAMPS THAT DID NOT LAST: FROM NARVA TO JÕHVI

Most of the Jewish forced labor camps located in the area between Narva and Jõhvi operated for less than half a year. The Soviet winter offensive forced the Germans to start evacuating the easternmost camps in January 1944. One of those camps, Slantsy, only existed on paper. The facility in Slantsy, about five miles west of the Estonian border, belonged to Baltöl. Located on a railway line between Pskov and Veimarn, Slantsy had a rather large shale oil mine built in 1933. According to estimates, the mine could produce up to 300,000 tons of shale oil per year. The entire Soviet personnel of the mine had been evacuated; to make the mine operational required between three thousand and four thousand workers.[27] Baltöl formally acquired ownership of the Slantsy mine in September 1942. Army Group North began negotiating for the creation of a concentration camp in Slantsy as early as July 1942. The German Security Police rejected the proposal on the grounds that civilian workers and POWs would require a substantial number of guards, who at the time were unavailable. The economic profitability of the Slantsy mine was yet another question.[28]

At one point Jews were considered as a potential workforce for the Slantsy mine. In late September 1943, the field headquarters in Gdov prevented the transfer of five hundred Jewish workers to Slantsy, referring to the threat posed by Soviet partisans. Minölko Estonia was quite upset by this decision, arguing that Jews from Belorussia were not only the most reliable workers but also had an above-average working capacity. Within the following few days, Minölko Estonia managed to convince Army Group North headquarters to lift a ban on the movement of Jews *(die Judensperre aufzuheben)*. Next, however, the sides failed to agree on the number of guards necessary for ensuring the safety of Jewish workers. Minölko Estonia talked about a forty-man-strong internal plant security force, whereas the office in Slantsy suggested bringing in at least two hundred German soldiers. As civilian workers deserted en masse, POWs escaped in ever increasing numbers, and partisans roamed around the Slantsy mine, only regular troops could make a difference, argued Economic Commando (Wirtschaftskommando or WiKo) Gdov and its office in Slantsy. As of October 2, plans were still under consideration to bring five hundred Jews to Slantsy. Two days later, however, military authorities canceled the transfer once and for all. Less than a month later, the mining equipment was dismantled and shipped to Estonia.[29]

The military situation north of Slantsy was only slightly better, which was enough for the Germans to bring approximately 350 Jews to the village of Kerstovo, about twenty miles east of Narva, in late October 1943. Prisoners in the Kerstovo camp lived in Nissen huts in the most deplorable conditions. Despite the growing number of Jews wounded by Soviet shells, the German camp administration intended to run the camp until after the demolition work in which prisoners were engaged was finished. So confident were the authorities that they did not even have a guard unit at Kerstovo. At the end of November, the camp was dissolved and its inmates transferred first to Narva and then to Putke. Putke was located on the left bank of the Narva River and used to house Soviet POWs before it became a Jewish slave labor camp. The camp guards were from OT. Built on marshland, the Nissen huts were connected together by duckboards—the only way to move around the camp. In January 1944, 200 Jews from the Narva camp joined the original 150 inmates at Putke. The number of deaths, at the same time, dropped from twelve to seven. Work at the camp continued until February 4, when OT personnel pulled out without prior notice, ahead of the approaching Soviet infantry. SS orderly [?] Rabl took 334 prisoners on a ruthless march through forest and swamp to Vaivara.[30]

At one point, the SS camp administration decided to transfer several hundred Jews from the Klooga camp to southern Estonia. On November 9, 1943, a transport with 250 prisoners arrived in Panikovichi, a village about thirty miles west of Pskov (formerly part of Estonia). The camp was built on dry ground and, because of the distance from the shale oil region, was loosely supervised. Dr. von Bodman's report from January 1944, however, no longer mentioned the Paniko-vichi camp. Within the same time period, three other camps were established. The one in Ülenurme, immediately south of Tartu, housed 127 Jews; the camp in Pechory held 98 prisoners; and finally, Kūdupe, a Latvian village next to the Estonian border, had to accommodate 299 more prisoners. Starting on February 10, the person in charge of all three camps was SS-Uschaf. Karl Theiner. The Jews locked in the Ülenurme and Pechory camps most likely were transferred there from Panikovichi. Within the first two months of their existence, twenty inmates in those two camps died. According to Dr. von Bodman, by mid-March, prisoners from Ülenurme, Pechory, and Kūdupe were transferred to Riga.[31] This fact, however, cannot be confirmed.

At the end of October 1943, two hundred male Jews were dispatched from Ereda to a distant village on the left bank of the Narva River. Located right across from Slantsy, the Soska camp fared only slightly better than the latter camp. On the first day of the new year, 1944, the Jews had to relocate to Kuremäe, where they stayed until February.[32] The highest number of prisoners at Soska was regis-tered in November: 495.[33] Camp inmates worked in a shale oil mine and loaded goods in Gorodenka, a village on the Narva River. To transport the mined ore to the Kohtla-Järve and Kiviõli refineries, the Jews started building a narrow-gauge railway. Living and working conditions at Soska made prisoners believe that they were being deliberately starved to death.[34] The camp was located on swampland. The only road that connected Soska with the outside world became impassable after rain; the camp could then only be reached by boat. Drinking water was available from a spring about 550 yards from the camp, and food supplies were trucked from a location about thirteen miles away. The barracks had no floors and only thin walls. Among the prisoners were many old, frail, and sick people with chronic illnesses such as diabetes and asthma. In spite of the quarantine in effect in the Soska area, prisoners were continually driven to work. Hard labor and disease claimed the lives of thirty-one Jews at Soska.[35] The OT foremen occa-sionally beat Jewish workers, yet no cases of murder were registered at Soska.[36]

The camp commandant, SS-Oschaf. Arno Reissig, came down with spotted fever shortly before Christmas 1943, and was replaced by SS orderly Wilhelm

Genth. This was a rather unexpected turn for Genth, who otherwise was trained as a musician. In 1943 Genth did a crash course in medicine, which made him qualified for an assignment at Majdanek death camp. A thirty-man-strong Estonian detachment had a more complex task than simply guarding the camp: because of the combat zone's proximity and the distance from major urban centers, Soviet partisans had been actively infiltrating the area around Soska from beyond the Narva River. Once Wehrmacht units started rolling past Soska on their way west, it became clear that the camp would not survive for much longer.[37] The rushed evacuation of the Soska camp showed the urgency of the situation that the Wehrmacht faced in Estonia in the winter of 1944. By early morning on February 3, the Red Army reached the Narva River, setting the village of Permisküla ablaze. At this point, the Jews at Soska, who were known to have previously exchanged messages with Soviet troops, were only three miles from the front line. When Genth received the evacuation order, German artillery was taking position four hundred yards behind the camp, while German infantry was digging in two miles in front of the camp. At 2:45 P.M., 437 Jews set off for a six-hour nonstop march to Kuremäe. Twenty-three sick prisoners had the luxury of traveling on horse-drawn sledges. The rest had to travel on foot. As a result, several older Jews died of heart failure and pneumonia.[38]

Kuremäe is known for its Russian Orthodox convent, which was built during the closing decade of the nineteenth century. Located south of the Tallinn-Narva railway, Kuremäe was not more than a village when it became the site of a Jewish labor camp. The first 150 inmates who arrived in Kuremäe in late October 1943 stayed in the former community center, a place for folk gatherings and theater performances. In the beginning, the only other building in the camp was an infirmary barracks, built by prisoners. In the first month or so, Jews did not even have to wear prisoner's uniforms. They worked on the railway, cut trees in the forest, and performed other manual tasks.[39] Those Jews who arrived in Kuremäe from the Kovno ghetto found the living conditions in the former much worse than in the latter.[40] By November, the number of prisoners increased threefold, reaching 850 three months later (on account of the Jews evacuated from Soska). To accommodate the incoming workforce, five Nissen huts were built. Dr. von Bodman complained about the high percentage of people at Kuremäe unfit for work. Von Bodman did not specify how the camp administration managed to "reduce" the number of inmates so labeled.[41]

More than eighty Jews, mainly those who could not perform physical labor, lost their lives in numerous selections at Kuremäe. These people were executed and their bodies burnt on a pyre outside of the camp. According to witnesses, the worst atrocity at Kuremäe was perpetrated by camp orderly SS-Uschaf. Erich Scharfetter. It was hard to mistake Scharfetter for anybody else: slim, six feet tall, he spoke with a Saxon accent. Once, in late February 1944, camp commandant SS-Uschaf. Alfred Engst asked Dr. Mark Dworzecki, a Jewish physician from Vilna who worked in the camp infirmary, to make a list of the so-called AKS prisoners (*alte, körperlich schwache:* old and feeble). As Dworzecki continued to insist there were no such prisoners at Kuremäe, Engst single-handedly selected twenty-two elderly men.[42] Scharfetter led the men one by one into a barracks, forced them to kneel, and then murdered them with an ax. As if that were not enough, he then sliced the victims' throats with a knife. Following the execution, Harry Kagan and three other prisoners were ordered into the barracks to clean up the mess. Scharfetter kindly handed over his knife to Kagan to cut off the prisoner's number from the clothing of the executed. The knife's handle was sticky with fresh blood. The ax was lying right there, on the barracks' floor. A horse-drawn cart borrowed from a local farmer took the bodies to the pyre.[43] From that moment forward, Jewish prisoners all over Estonia started calling Scharfetter "Ax Man" (*Kirkenik),* a name whose mere mention stirred fear. The camp guards, members of the Estonian 290th Police Battalion, came from Tartu. Platoon commander Vladimir Umberg established a good rapport with Scharfetter, who soon became his drinking buddy.[44]

At least twice during the month of February, Soviet warplanes fired at the camp, wounding several prisoners. At that point, the German infantry position was no more than ten miles from Kuremäe. On March 1, Engst, Genth, and Estonian and Ukrainian guards escorted the Jews from Kuremäe to Kohtla.[45] Twelve people died or were shot on the march.[46]

One other camp in which orderly Scharfetter left behind a bloody trail was Jõhvi. The camp was conveniently located near the Jõhvi train station on the Narva-Tallinn railway line. One hundred and seventy Jewish prisoners lived in two solid barracks, one for men and another for women. The third barracks was used as a kitchen. A tiny room in that barracks served as an "office" for the Jewish camp elder. The camp, which originally housed Soviet POWs, was surrounded by barbed wire. Estonian, and occasionally Lithuanian, guards took positions at the two entrances on each side of the camp. Jews and Soviet POWs were building a big military hospital in Jõhvi—the main purpose for the creation of a labor camp in that city. Some prisoners also worked at a sawmill right outside the camp.[47] The hospital was being built by a construction company from Ulm, Ludwig Truchsäss. The company employed Jews, who could be easily identified by the yellow star that they were obliged to wear. Several Jewish women also worked as maids, cleaning the offices and living quarters of German workers. The latter asked no questions of their Jewish servants, who they said looked pale and were scantily dressed. One day, the women did not report to work, nor did they come the day after. Soviet POWs replaced the Jewish workers, and Polish women took over the cleaning duty.[48]

The situation in the camp had still been bearable during the period when Jõhvi camp had been operated by OT in cooperation with the Jewish camp administration. (One of the former prisoners recalled a local OT leader removing and burning a portrait of Hitler, whom he cursed vehemently.) It changed abruptly after Scharfetter assumed the position of camp commandant. It was once again Scharfetter whom former prisoners identified as the most notorious killer at Jõhvi camp. The first murder at Jõhvi occurred shortly after his arrival in the camp in late October. Scharfetter injected two sick prisoners with a substance that caused their imminent death. During the last weeks of 1943, Scharfetter shot another two Jews who had caught typhus.[49] When typhus epidemics broke out in December, a group of prisoners from Jõhvi was transferred to Vaivara. The camp itself was dismantled in mid-January 1944.[50]

Traveling by rail from Jõhvi toward the Estonian border, one would hit Auvere, a small train station between Vaivara and Narva. The first Jews—150 men and 20 women—arrived in Auvere on September 15, 1943. They initially stayed in a school building but then were moved to the so-called Tonnenzelte. By November the number of prisoners increased to 571. The prisoners mainly worked on the railway, hauling materials from the narrow-gauge rail to the normal-gauge one and vice versa. Those building the railway had to stand all day long up to their ankles in ice-cold water. Among the Jews were many elderly people who could barely handle the hardship of the work. As a result, within three months at least eighty-two prisoners died.[51] In the case of Auvere, we have a detailed description of torture administered in essentially all Jewish labor camps in Estonia. A routine punishment at Auvere looked as follows. Prisoners were forced to lie face down on a bench, with their hands tied underneath it. One German held tight the victim's head and another one the feet. The instrument of torment was a whip made of ox tendons with a metallic wire in the middle; the victim had to count the blows and if the unfortunate person failed to count properly the torture was repeated, up to fifty lashes. Nobody can tell with certainty how many dozens of prisoners died from this torture in Estonia. Other means of breaking people included tying them, naked, to a pole for several hours or denying them food.[52]

At the end of November, a typhus epidemic broke out in the camp. To halt the spread of the disease, the German administration arranged a hot-water bath for the prisoners. Following the bath, however, SS-Oschaf. Wiesner ordered the Jews to stand outside naked for fifteen minutes. As a result, several Jews died of pneumonia. Those who contracted typhus had to subsist on five ounces of bread and water (the last delivery of potatoes to the camp was in mid-December 1943) while lying on the barren floor of the barracks. The camp shut down for a month and the prisoners' food rations were cut in half. Dr. von Bodman and a group of higher military and civilian officials who came to Auvere for inspection were only interested in preventing contact between the infected on the one hand and Germans and Estonians on the other.[53] On January 29, 1944, a truckload of sick Jews was taken from Auvere to Vaivara, only to be followed by 487 Jews who set out on the march on February 4. SS-Uschaf. Ernst Runde took 200 Jews to Kiviõli while the rest of the group stayed at Vaivara. One of the older prisoners who could not walk fast enough, Shmuel Segalowicz, met his death in the Baltic Sea where an SS-man threw him from a high cliff, while one other Jew was shot.[54]

The seashore in that part of Estonia is particularly picturesque: mounting limestone abruptly turns into a several-miles-long beach. For three months in the fall and winter of 1943, Narva-Jõesuu, an internationally known beach resort, was home to a Jewish forced labor camp. The three hundred Jews who arrived in Narva-Jõesuu in early November had been transferred from the Narva camp. SS-Uschaf. Scharfetter served as the commander of the new facility, which was considered a subsidiary of the Narva camp.[55] In Narva-Jõesuu, Jews performed two kinds of work: cutting trees and building barracks for the military. The work-site was located on the other side of the Narva River where prisoners were taken daily by boat.[56] Originally, the camp was located in the former city sauna on 26 Koidu Street. However, at noon on November 10, 1943, the building went up in flames. There were fewer than a dozen sick Jews in the camp when the fire broke out. Although a police report indicated no victims among the Jewish prisoners, on the very same day the body of a Jew was cremated on a pyre in downtown Narva-Jõesuu.[57] The prisoners were then moved to a former Waffen-SS convalescent home. As of December 29, 1943, the camp had 261 prisoners, 68 of them suffering from spotted fever. In that month alone, 33 Jews died at Narva-Jõesuu, mainly from diarrhea. In January 1944, the remaining prisoner population was evacuated from Narva-Jõesuu to Vaivara.[58]

One of the biggest Jewish forced labor camps was located in the border city of Narva. Narva was different from other Jewish labor camps in Estonia for its inmates lived not in wooden huts or temporary tarpaulin tents but in a solid two-story brick building. In addition, there was a hospital with forty beds. The barracks belonged to a canvas mill that was owned and operated by the Krenholm Company. In fact, the camp was located on the grounds of the factory in Ivangorod, on the right bank of the Narva River.[59] Next to the camp there was a canal, built in the previous century for the purpose of generating power. Prisoners washed themselves in the canal until a washing barracks was constructed. Jews were building defense on the outskirts of the city. The work was supervised by several German companies: Lenz was in charge of digging antitank ditches, Schröder of building roads, and Filzer of floating timber. Camp guards, ethnic Estonians and Latvians, stayed in private homes outside the factory grounds.[60]

The camp population at Narva consisted of Jews from the second and the fourth Vilna transports. Herman Kruk was part of a group of some eight hundred men who arrived in Narva via Viivikonna on October 7, 1943.[61] Sima Skurkowicz was among the eighty female and three hundred male Jews who arrived in Narva in November.[62] While at worksites outside the camp, Jewish prisoners often went begging for food. The city dwellers sometimes gave them bread,[63] but apparently not everybody did. On one occasion in mid-December, nineteen-year-old Isaac Zukermann failed to return with his group back to the camp and hid in a barn instead. However, the next morning a local farmer discovered him and then delivered him to the gendarmerie, describing him as a person without proper identification; Zukermann was thus escorted back to the camp.[64] Those who attempted to escape and were eventually caught had their clothes marked with a big red dot. At a later stage, and not only in Narva, the marked people, along with the sick and feeble, became the first candidates for execution.[65] Prisoners also died from starvation and grueling work. The dead bodies were customarily incinerated in a

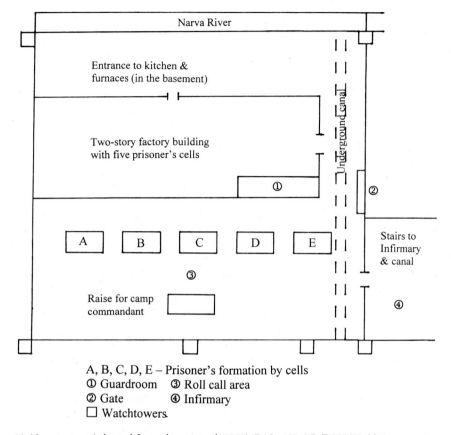

A, B, C, D, E – Prisoner's formation by cells
① Guardroom   ③ Roll call area
② Gate   ④ Infirmary
☐ Watchtowers

13. Narva camp (adapted from the original, 1962); BAL, 408 AR-Z 233/59, V11.

factory furnace; Yitzhak Drabkin and his son were put in charge.[66] In the absence
of proper medical assistance, typhus claimed many victims among the Jewish
prisoners. The typhus epidemic, as well as individual cases of cholera, ravaged
the Narva camp in November, December, and January. In December 1943, the
mortality rate reached 10 percent: 125 out of 1,290 Jewish prisoners died in that
month alone.[67] According to Herman Kruk's estimates, about 400 people died in
Narva camp.[68]

Shortly before the new year, camp commandant Pannicke ordered the sick
and work-unfit to assemble before him. All of them, about thirty people, were
searched and then taken by truck to Ereda where they were later executed.[69] The
remaining prisoners received grim evidence of the crime: several days after a

Jewish lawyer, Brauder, from Vilnius disappeared, a leather jacket that he had owned was seen in the hands of the commandant. The latter gave it as a gift to one of his darlings in the camp. Pannicke used to entertain himself by watching Jewish prisoners very quickly taking their hats off and putting them back on ("like a shot from a machine gun!") upon his command. Those who could not keep up with the pace received a punch in the face from the commandant.[70] For these reasons, prisoners called Pannicke "Tormentor" (Peiniger). One of his favorite lines was "My Jews I shoot myself!" (meine Juden erschiesse ich selber!) In December 1943 Pannicke suddenly fell ill; for one week, Schnabel substituted for Pannicke as Narva camp commandant. The most notorious atrocity at Narva camp took place on Christmas Eve in the presence and with the active participation of Schnabel. Prisoners lined up for the evening roll call, captivated by an unlikely view of a gigantic Christmas tree towering above the courtyard. Schnabel and SS orderly Ernst Runde, who often addressed camp inmates as "gentlemen!" (meine Herren), made the prisoners stand for long hours in the cold. The roll call continued well into early morning. At one point Schnabel ordered five prisoners delivered from the infirmary. Brought on stretchers, the sick cried in pain, but were cut short by Schnabel's "shut up." Schnabel used his feet and a club to do away with the unfortunate five. Following the murder, the bodies of the victims were dumped into the canal and on the next day burnt in the factory furnace.[71] The rest of Narva continued celebrating Christmas.

On January 20, 1944, the German army began its retreat via Narva. The evacuation of the civilian population from Narva began on January 25 and lasted until February 3. On January 29 and 30, trucks moved 210 sick and feeble Jews to Vaivara. In the evening of January 31, the Panther Line came under Soviet fire, which forced the Germans to withdraw the remaining 733 Jews from Narva. For twenty long hours, prisoners under the command of Schnabel marched through swamps in the direction of Vaivara, being occasionally attacked by low-flying Soviet warplanes. On the march Schnabel reportedly shot three feeble Jews—a number confirmed by Dr. von Bodman.[72] Unsurprisingly, Schnabel denied the charges, insisting that he deliberately forbid the Estonian guards to shoot without his command.[73] Another five to ten Jews were murdered during the overnight stay at Vaivara. Yitzhak Zohar recounted the story. Zohar and other Jews who worked for the Lenz Company were able to take their tools with them, which they loaded on a few sledges. Not everybody could make it from Narva to Vaivara in the dead of winter; those with the sledges helped to carry the unfortunate people who could no longer walk. As the column of prisoners reached the Vaivara camp at dusk, SS-Uschaf. Oskar Helbig was waiting for them at the gate. The newcomers did not know who he was, but were warned by their coreligionists to stay away from Helbig, the "death angel" *(malach hamoves)*. First, Helbig ordered the exhausted people who were resting on the sledges to be left in an empty barracks. There they remained, in the cold, without food. The next morning, as the prisoners from Narva were about to leave the camp, they inquired of the local Jews about the feeble persons left in the barracks. "Their bodies would be burnt soon," the prisoners gloomily reported.[74] The rest of the group, about eight hundred men, arrived in Kiviõli on February 7. Former commandant Kurt Pannicke was assigned to Kuremäe, and when that camp ceased to exist a month later, to Aseri.

THE INDUSTRIAL HUB: KIVIÕLI, KOHTLA, EREDA

The center of shale oil production in Estonia was located in Kiviõli, which thus had the largest concentration of forced labor camps in the whole of Estonia. The first Jews—358 men and 89 women—arrived in Kiviõli on September 28, 1943.[75] With the arrival of the second transport the number of prisoners increased to 600.[76] The camp was located next to the Kiviõli workers' hamlet and, like the one in Viivikonna, was subdivided into two sections. Kiviõli I—headed by SS-Uschaf. Wilhelm Werle—was considered the main camp, and Kiviõli II—under the command of SS-Rotf. [?] Wirker—its subsidiary. A Baltöl refinery marked the border between the two camps. The usual barbed-wire fence and watchtowers made the picture complete. The Kiviõli I camp had between six and eight living barracks, in addition to a kitchen, a bathhouse, and an infirmary. Workshops, a garage, storage, and military barracks were all located outside of the camp grounds. OT employed ten German and Estonian workers, and fifteen Jewish prisoners to repair the hundred or so vehicles towed to the garage. The majority of Jews, however, were mining shale oil for the Baltöl Company.[77] Prisoners, assembled in fifteen labor details, received daily work assignments from the camp commandant. On the opposite side of the road from the Jewish camp was an OT camp. Every day, ten OT foremen escorted four hundred male and two hundred female prisoners to work, which consisted of cutting trees in the forest. Apparently, attempts at escape were rare so that twenty members of an Estonian police battalion were enough to guard the Jews at work.[78] The guards received food coupons, which they could use in the Baltöl Company canteen. One can be sure that the guards were served other than oil-contaminated water, which the prisoners had to drink. Under no circumstances were Jews allowed to communicate with other workers, with the POWs in particular. Within four months, the prisoner population had tripled. Dr. von Bodman reported the following figures for October, November, and February: 448, 698, and 1,300 respectively.[79] In comparison with other Jewish camps, the mortality rate among the Kiviõli prisoners was relatively low. The numbers of dead rose, however, when a typhus epidemic broke out at Kiviõli on December 7, 1943.

The Soviet winter offensive stalled the construction works at Jõhvi and Kohtla. By March 1944, Kiviõli remained the only oil producing facility that was expanding. The heaviest burden lay on Soviet POWs, who constituted close to half of the 3,308 construction workers. Another 901 workers were Jewish.[80] By late March, POWs were expected to replace all 1,400 Jews at Kiviõli.[81] Within the Jewish camp itself, no further construction was allowed past August 1, 1944. Yet there is no indication that the Kiviõli camp was at any time overcrowded beyond its capacity. Each barracks' room accommodated forty people, who slept on two-tier bunks. In the middle of the room was an iron stove, heated by shale oil. Those rooms saw much suffering, including murder. In February 1944, commandant Wirker caught one of the Jewish prisoners, Isaiah Schuster, baking on a stove a few potatoes he had brought from work. Wirker whipped Schuster until the latter collapsed. Finally he stepped on the victim's neck; the inmates who witnessed the crime were then ordered to dispose of the dead body.[82]

As a whole, however, the situation in the camp turned worse only after the arrival of SS-Uschaf. Runde and SS-Uschaf. Helbig in Kiviõli in February and March 1943 respectively. In comparison with these two, even commandant Werle appeared a relatively polite person. Prisoners described Helbig as young and handsome; on his very first day at Kiviõli, Helbig organized a gruesome "exercise" for prisoners, who had to carry heavy stones from one corner of the camp to another. One time in February, Helbig deliberately created conditions that led to the death of a young man from Vilnius, Shimon Rit. Around the same time, Helbig oversaw a selection among the sick, forty of whom he in the most brutal way threw onto trucks ready to leave for a nearby forest.[83] "Our killer" is how prisoners referred to Helbig in conversation. According to von Bodman's report of February 20, 1944, in that month 104 Jews (the sick, elderly, and feeble) were allegedly sent to the Riga concentration camp. The problem with this statement is that there was no concentration camp in Riga at that time. The Kaiserwald camp in a suburb of Riga was essentially a registration center, from which Jews were reassigned to other camps and worksites. Thus there was no rationale for dispatching a hundred or so frail Jews to worksites more than two hundred miles away. In all likelihood, these Jews were executed on the spot. There were speculations about the existence of up to three gas chambers, allegedly built somewhere in the forest close to the Kiviõli camp.[84] None of the survivors' testimonies corroborated that rumor, however.

The selections at Kiviõli—four or five in total—were carried out in a routine, bureaucratic manner. An SS orderly compiled lists of names of older prisoners, who then were taken aside during the roll call, usually on Sundays. Each selection claimed the lives of thirty to forty Jews.[85] The last selection took place about two weeks before the camp ceased to exist in September 1944. SS officers Werle, Runde, von Bodman, and sometimes Aumeier were usually present at roll calls. While von Bodman was selecting Jews for execution, Schnabel, Runde, Werle, and others made sure no prisoner attempted to escape. Dr. von Bodman walked along the rows of prisoners, occasionally pointing out with his finger clad in a white glove one Jew or another. "This one will have to come too," he pronounced now and again. The victims thus selected were immediately escorted onto a truck, followed by a full complement of SS personnel.[86] Joseph Levin, who worked as a car mechanic, made a terrifying discovery that erased any doubts about the fate of the prisoners removed. One side of a truck he repaired was covered with blood; scribbled on the back was "we, from this camp, will be shot." The truck later returned with a heap of bloodied clothing and shoes. Nora Levin found another short note that read, "Schnabel and Runde shoot." When asked what really happened, the driver only answered, "Do not ask, you know it yourself!" Moshe Levin would never forget because he had cleaned Werle's coat soaked in blood. (Before the war Werle worked as a wine trader.)[87] After one such selection, camp dentist SS-Oschaf. Franz Mang packed his tools and disappeared for a while—as he put it, "went to the front." Soon after, Fanny Pitum, who worked as Mang's assistant, was seen with a mess tin filled to the top with gold teeth and teeth with gold fillings.[88]

The so-called "10 percent selection" was supposedly the most thorough of all and therefore involved a certain degree of preparation. The Nazis needed an execution site large enough to accommodate hundreds of victims from the remaining Jewish camps in the shale oil region. On August 2, 1944, seventeen members of the German SS were summoned to Aumeier's headquarters in Saka. On a truck loaded with various kinds of firearms, including heavy machine guns, the entire group departed for a forest west of Saka. Aumeier ordered them to dig four eighty-by-fifteen-foot trenches; the sheer size of the trenches suggested that they could not have been used for military purposes. It took about eight days to complete the work. Once ready, the trenches were covered with a layer of fresh-cut trees. Another three days passed before Aumeier appeared again at the site, glanced at the trenches, said, "well done," and then left. The next day, a truck arrived with three barrels of gasoline and one barrel of petroleum. That must have been August 14.[89]

The mass execution commenced on August 15. Four trucks with trailers must have brought the total of three or four hundred Jews to the trenches that day. Aumeier, Brennais, and von Bodman arrived in time to see a heavily armed Waffen-SS unit taking position near the site. The German SS formed the cordon, while the Estonian SS was instructed to keep the local population away from the execution site. Jews from the first truck were ordered to take off their clothes and lie face down. As a demonstration, Aumeier, Brennais, and von Bodman each picked up one prisoner, took them to the edge of the trench, and then shot them in the back of the head. Following Aumeier's departure, Pannicke became leader of the operation. Seven or eight people at a time, the Jews were forced to approach the trench. When the number of corpses reached seventy or so, the executioners poured gasoline over them and set them on fire. Once the trenches became filled to capacity, they were covered with soil, and later trees were planted on top of them so as to ensure that nobody would ever find out about the murder.[90]

In the afternoon, another Jewish transport of four hundred arrived. The executions continued until the end of August. Jews from the Sonda and Kohtla camps shortly followed those from Kiviõli to the mass execution site. The total number of Jews murdered at this particular site (as cited by one of the witnesses)—3,500—seems to be inflated.[91] As regards specifically the Kiviõli camp, the vital statistics looked roughly as follows: 2,500 Jews moved to Stutthof and 400 executed.[92]

The construction of a camp at Ereda began in mid-November; the builders were prisoners themselves. Ereda was located deep in the woods, in a swampy area south of the Narva-Tallinn railway line. The camp was divided into the so-called Upper and Lower Ereda, connected with each other by a road that ran across a 200-yard open field. Lower Ereda, which had a number of semicircular cardboard barracks built on piles, was established first. As the name implies, Upper Ereda was built on more solid ground: the wooden barracks were still under construction as of December 1943. Upper Ereda also housed a medical facility, commandant's office, and the ever-present roll call area, whereas the kitchen was located in Lower Ereda. Once Upper Ereda was completed, Lower Ereda (which prisoners used to call the "live grave" or even the "Estonian Auschwitz") became a dumping ground for the sick and children. The Ereda camp, partially enclosed by a barbed-wire fence, was guarded by members of an Estonian police battalion clad in distinctive green uniforms. The detachment was stationed outside of the camp, and so was the site for the disposal of corpses.[93]

The area around Ereda was crammed with all kinds of camps. The road that ran along Upper Ereda led to Kohtla, the nearest railway station. Some sixty yards away from the camp, OT barracks were located, seven miles farther a Soviet POW camp, and, in the distance, a Waffen-SS vocational camp.[94] From the camp grounds one could see the barracks of the C. Deilmann Company (a mining company based in Dortmund), which employed Russian forced laborers to construct shafts for mining shale oil. Until November 1943, the company was building a mine at Slantsy. At Ereda, C. Deilmann employed nine German foremen, who had about twenty-five Russian forced laborers under their command. When completed, the mines were to become part of the Krupp Concern.[95]

The majority of the Jews at Ereda arrived from Vilna. Upon arrival in Vaivara on September 5, the prisoners made a fifteen-mile journey to Ereda. Most of the one thousand prisoners, including three hundred women, worked for the C. Deilmann Company.[96] Living conditions in the camp were deplorable: the clothes prisoners wore were nothing more than rags; they had to report to work at 4:00 A.M. seven days a week. The barracks had neither doors nor floors but only broken windows. Prisoners suffered terribly from cold: their bodies sometimes froze to the ground at night. Any minor offense was punishable. Everyone, including camp commandant Drohsin, whipped prisoners, so that pieces

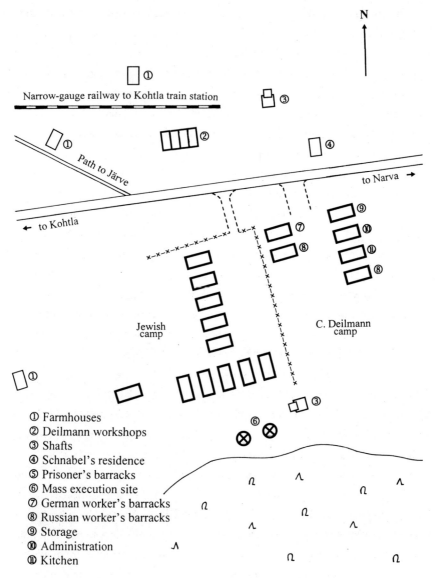

N

Narrow-gauge railway to Kohtla train station

Path to Järve

to Narva →

← to Kohtla

Jewish
camp

C. Deilmann
camp

① Farmhouses
② Deilmann workshops
③ Shafts
④ Schnabel's residence
⑤ Prisoner's barracks
⑥ Mass execution site
⑦ German worker's barracks
⑧ Russian worker's barracks
⑨ Storage
⑩ Administration
⑪ Kitchen

14. Ereda camp (adapted from the original, 1963); BAL, 408 AR-Z 233/59, V11.

of flesh fell off their buttocks. Two or three people at Ereda died every day of "natural" causes.[97]

The first commandant of Ereda, SS-Uschaf. Heinz Drohsin, died on February 21, 1944, under unique circumstances. Drohsin had an affair with a Jewish prisoner from Czechoslovakia, Ingeborg Sylten. Catching her in an attempt to escape, Drohsin first shot his partner and then committed suicide. Helmut Schnabel arrived in Ereda with the agenda to strengthen discipline in the camp. Schnabel oversaw the liquidation of the Ereda camp at the end of July 1944. Following the incident with Drohsin, Aumeier imposed a new rule that made camp administrators live outside the camp territory. Sexual intercourse with Jewish women was strictly forbidden, but many German civil employees ignored the rule. Those who were caught red-handed were usually suspended from work. And so Schnabel rented a room in a farmer's house within walking distance of the camp. Twice a day, before prisoners went to work and after they returned, Schnabel conducted roll calls in Upper Ereda. Wherever he went, Schnabel carried a revolver and a dog whip with him.[98] Another German in the camp was SS orderly Scharfetter, who arrived in Ereda in January 1944 "to ensure the proper implementation of medical orders."

For several months Ereda served as a destination for Jewish prisoners from the dissolved camps in northeastern Estonia. In February alone, about four hundred Jews arrived in Ereda. From the direction of Jõhvi came, on foot, a group of some 250 people. Considering that most of the newcomers were women and men in their fifties, one can only imagine how hard it was for those people to move in deep snow. And indeed, three prisoners remained lying in the snow; Schnabel ordered them shot.[99] The prisoner population at Ereda swelled from 752 in December to 1,600 in February and 1,907 in March. The mortality over the same period increased tenfold: 11, 109, and 161 people respectively.[100]

Schnabel was extremely inventive when it came to separating healthy Jews from the less fortunate ones. On February 13, 1944, the workers returning to the camp met face to face with Schnabel, who was waiting for them at the gates. Schnabel ordered the prisoners to roll up their pants and then hit their thighs with a stick. Those with swollen feet he put on a list. The next morning, all of those—probably as many as 350—were taken away.[101] Chief physician von Bodman covered up mass executions at Ereda by reporting to his authorities in Berlin that in February 1944 a total of 896 Jews, including 184 children, were dispatched by train to the Riga concentration camp. Another 500 sick Jews, according to von Bodman, were taken to Riga in April.[102] There is no evidence that would support either of the two statements. Most likely they were a lie, for it is hard to imagine how the sick and the children could have been put to work in Riga. Scharfetter became known at Ereda for having shot three young Jews. Scharfetter could not overlook the offense those three had committed: suffering from typhus, the prisoners could not make it to the latrine and relieved themselves between the barracks.[103] According to one witness, between twenty and thirty sick Jews were murdered on the march from Ereda to Kiviõli. They were reportedly pushed off a cliff into the sea. Among the individuals implicated in that crime were Schnabel and one other SS orderly, Runde.[104] By contrast, survivors did not recall any such atrocities perpetrated by the Estonian guards. Those were mainly young men who had not completely lost their sense of decency. In the winter, some guards stepped into the women's barracks to get warm.[105]

Along with Kiviõli, Lagedi, and Klooga, Ereda preserved a detailed account of the summer 1944 mass execution. The following description is based on the testimony of a C. Deilmann employee, Franz Leichter. A sense of imminent disaster settled in Ereda as early as July 22 when trucks brought back the Jews who three weeks earlier had boarded a train supposedly bound for East Prussia. Agitation among the prisoners increased when on the next day they were ordered first to collect firewood in the forest and then to dig two big holes. Between 30 and 40 feet in diameter and 2.5 feet deep, the two pits had a soil embankment around them. Schnabel personally supervised the work. In the afternoon several trucks loaded with gasoline parked in the camp. Nobody knew where the drivers came from, except that they wore the SS uniform. On July 24 (which fell on a Saturday) the Jews were not driven to work as usual but remained locked in the barracks. Not less alarming was to see so many SS men present at Ereda at one time—six, including Commandant Schnabel. Estonian guards had already been removed by that time. The first shots were fired about 6 P.M., followed by thick smoke coming from the southern part of the camp behind the barracks. While three people under Schnabel's command were busy shooting at the pits, the remaining SS men from time to time went back to the barracks to fetch another group of victims. The slaughter resumed on Sunday morning, lasted the whole day on Monday, and only subsided by Tuesday afternoon, July 27. Throughout the entire time of execution there were only two attempts at escape. In both cases, the Jews were killed on the spot.[106]

Before the mass execution, the Germans forbade the local population from approaching the camp grounds. Farmers were ordered to keep the windows and doors of their houses shut.[107] Leichter and his colleague from C. Deilmann—under the pretext that they had to check the level of water in the mine, which was located next to the pits—managed to get very close to the execution site. There they saw a horrible picture. The pits were burning red. The Jews stood on the edge of the pit. A shot in the back of the head brought them down. The flames immediately consumed the bodies. A group of some 100 or 150 Jews were waiting for their turn to come. Within the half-hour that the two men, benumbed, spent at the pits, they counted 75 dead. The stench of burning flesh became unbearable. It took a bottle of vodka to bring Leichter and his coworker to their senses when they returned to the camp. On Sunday morning, one could see intoxicated SS men roaming around the camp grounds. One wonders whether they could aim at all; some victims, no doubt, were burned and buried alive. The pace of execution then slowed down.[108]

The C. Deilmann Company was ready to leave Ereda on August 22. Those who were left behind were many: according to Franz Leichter, up to 1,400 Jews were executed in those three days in July. He said it was common knowledge in the camp at that time.[109] Yet that number seems too high, for we know that at least some Jews were on a train that left Ereda for Lagedi on July 28. According to a former inmate, Shlomo Baranovski, the number of sick and feeble Jews left behind amounted to a few dozen.[110]

Next to the giant camps in Kiviõli, Ereda, and Kohtla, there existed three small Jewish forced labor camps in the area—Kunda, Aseri, and Sonda. The first two were located on the Baltic seashore, northwest of the industrial core, while the third was on the railway line between Kiviõli and Rakvere. Life in Kunda revolved around a cement plant. Built in 1871 (the third oldest in the Tsarist Empire), the plant was run by a Danish company. The director of the plant, engineer Theodor Hansen, who simultaneously served as Danish and Icelandic vice consul to Estonia, had occupied this position since the 1930s. The Jews who arrived in Kunda in October 1943 worked in the plant and in a quarry. Men crushed oil-bearing rock, while women loaded it onto trucks. Kunda was apparently the smallest Jewish camp in Estonia: from Vilnius came ten female and thirty male Jews, while Kaunas was the home city of another twenty women and thirty men. Within the next eight months the camp population fluctuated between 200 and 232. To reach the camp, which was located deep in the forest, one needed to take a railway trolley and then continue on foot for several miles. In the camp, Jews lived in three wooden buildings that had tiny rooms on each of their two floors. The buildings were solid, but also bug-ridden. Nevertheless, Dr. von Bodman was proud of the Kunda camp: not only did it have a delousing facility and a sauna with running hot and cold water but also a toilet with "seating facility."[111]

Prisoners described the first commandant of Kunda, Adolf Kley, as a "sadist," but acknowledged that SS-Uschaf. Hans Becker (a pharmacist by profession), who replaced Kley, retained some vestiges of humanity. At one point, the commandant (not clear which one) ordered the prisoners to compose a song praising the camp and his leadership. The first two verses of the song, which the Jews had to sing every time they went to and from work, went as follows:

Wir sind in Lager dort geschickt/Die Arbeit will uns macht frei
Und trotzdem was die Arbeit schwer/Gutmütig und freulich darf man sein
Wir sind im Lager, wir haben ein Bad/Die Suppe nach der Arbeit schmeckt uns gut
Wir sind zufrieden mit unser Lagerführer/Welcher macht für uns gut!

We were sent to this camp/the work will make us free
And despite the fact that work is hard/one should be good-natured and cheerful
We are in the camp, we have a bath/the soup tastes good after the work
We are happy with our head of the camp/who is good to us!

Instead of "welcher macht für uns gut," some prisoners used to sing "welkher zakt fun unds das blut" (who sucks our blood). While having fun drinking with local women, the commandant often ordered a Jew to play the violin. Other prisoners were supposed to sing, sometimes naked.[112] Despite all the humiliation that Jews experienced at Kunda, only one death was recorded in the camp, in February 1944. The Estonian camp guards did not take their job seriously, often failing to report for duty, especially at night.[113] Prisoners from Kunda, alongside those from Sonda, Putke, and Kiviõli, were evacuated to Stutthof in late August 1944.

The camp at Aseri became operational on May 8, 1944. As in Kunda, two hundred Jews at Aseri worked in a quarry.[114] Between May and August 1944, the commandant of Aseri was Kurt Pannicke. As a result of the selection that Pannicke carried out at Aseri in July, between forty-two and fifty prisoners lost their lives. Pannicke, with a submachine gun, hopped on one of the three trucks that transported the condemned—women, children, and the elderly. As had happened often before, the Jews were executed outside the camp grounds but their clothes were later brought back to the camp.[115] According to one of the former inmates, Alan Weiler, all eight guards who convoyed the victims to the execution site were Estonians.[116] As Pannicke returned from the execution site (near Ereda), he stopped by a laundry. "Here it is": Pannicke threw his bloodstained shirt to Sima Skurkowicz to wash. Skurkowicz asked Pannicke why his shirt had blood all over it. "I fought a duel with Jews," Pannicke said, grinning.[117] In late July 1944, the remaining Jews were transferred first to Kohtla and then to Riga. Like the rest of the Jews in Estonia, former Aseri inmates ended up in Stutthof.[118]

Those Jews who passed through Sonda considered it one of the most agreeable labor camps in Estonia. The Sonda camp had existed for less than half a year and provided relatively good living conditions. Sonda commandant SS-Oschaf. Arno Reissig was one of those rare Nazi officials in Estonia who displayed correct behavior toward Jewish prisoners.[119] The camp officially opened on February 22, 1944; prisoners at Sonda were building wooden barracks for the military. Sometime in March 1944, the Germans transferred to Sonda 200 able-bodied Jews from Vaivara, thus bringing the number of prisoners to 296. The men, who were lured by work at a sawmill, ended up cutting trees in the forest. In comparison with Vaivara, the regime at Sonda was less severe, work lighter, barracks cleaner and less crowded. Best of all, however, the Jewish camp elder, a butcher from Vilna, established good rapport with the camp commandant. Owing to the special relationship between the two, a local slaughterhouse occasionally delivered leftover meat to the camp. However few small pieces of meat prisoners found in their daily soup, it helped them to carry on. At the end of August 1944, the camp inmates were transported by rail to Stutthof. Before then, however, several high-ranking German SS officers, accompanied by German SS soldiers armed with machine guns, carried out a notorious 10 percent selection.[120] These victims should be added to the list of twenty-eight Jews who perished at Sonda between March and June 1944.

The camp at Kohtla was usually referred to as "Goldfields" (named after the company that used to own the refinery). The camp was established rather late, in January 1944, and served as an assembly point for the Jews evacuated from other camps. For three weeks, Jewish prisoners made a daily six-mile trip from Ereda and back to build barracks in Kohtla. Among those who built the Kohtla camp and who eventually became its first inmates were fifty women from the

Theresienstadt and Berlin transports. The rest of the camp population—to use the lexicon of the Jews from Central Europe—were *Ostjuden*.[121]

Kohtla rated much higher among the prisoners than did Ereda, particularly during the first months of its existence when the camp was under the command of Otrupf. Anton Gross from OT: bunks instead of bare floor; instant heating in the barracks; soup that one could eat without being afraid of potential consequences. On the negative side, a swampy area around Kohtla where Jews were building a road had an adverse effect on their physical health. The prisoners' feet became wet even before they began their daily work, and that was in the winter![122] Within a few weeks, however, hundreds of Jewish prisoners began arriving from the dissolved camps at Vaivara and Auvere, and with them the German SS administration. Along with the name of camp commandant SS-Oschaf. Fred Stiebitz, two other names were mentioned: SS-Schaf. Alfred Engst and SS-Uschaf. Erwin Bahr. One of those three, according to survivors, was a pederast who always had with him a fourteen-year-old Jewish boy, who for that matter was spared physical labor.[123] The food at once became worse, the roll calls longer and more exhausting. Sometimes the camp personnel entertained themselves by forcing Jews to fistfight each other.[124] As a result of the transfer of Jews from Kuremäe in early March 1944, the camp population at Kohtla increased from 1,200 to 1,543.

In early September, the prisoners set out on a march to Tallinn. The evacuation began in the dead of night when about fifty SS men arrived in the camp. Schnabel and Pannicke followed the prisoner convoy in a staff car. The Jews had no idea about the final destination, which could have been an execution site. Yet Pannicke assured the prisoners that they were to be taken to Tallinn and from there to a labor camp in Germany. But then the unexpected happened: the driver of the first truck took a wrong road. As soon as the Jews saw all six trucks getting off the Narva-Tallinn highway—which they had traveled several times before—visions of violent death returned. It was still dark as the prisoners began jumping off the trucks and running into a potato field. It is not clear whether it was Schnabel or Pannicke who gave the order to shoot at those fleeing. At least five people were left lying motionless. The rest of the group carried on to Tallinn, which they reached in the late afternoon of the same day. The name of the ship that took the Jews from Kohtla to Danzig was *Mar de Platte*.[125] Six days after, they stood in front of the gate of the Stutthof concentration camp.

11 KLOOGA

Of all Jewish forced labor camps in Estonia, Klooga has received the most attention in the literature. (I will explain why at the end of this chapter.) In direct translation, *Klooga aedlinn* means "Klooga garden town"[1]—a tiny place next to the Baltic Sea. Klooga is literally built on sand: if you dig your shovel deep, a stream of water spurts. A beautiful pine forest and gorgeous white sand beach, as well as the short distance from Tallinn, made Klooga a popular destination for city dwellers. To be precise, Klooga is located twenty-four miles west of Tallinn, not far from the seaport of Paldiski. That is where Edith Sekules's family first moved when they arrived in Estonia from Austria in 1938. The Nazi occupation turned this peaceful coastal village into hell on earth for thousands of prisoners who were brought there.

Klooga was a camp site even before the arrival of Jewish prisoners in September 1943. It is just a few miles away from Paldiski where the Red Army established a military base in 1939. Brick buildings and the surrounding area were originally built as military barracks and training grounds respectively. The first inmates arrived in Klooga in the summer of 1942: one hundred Soviet POWs who worked in construction under the supervision of OT. By late August 1943, Klooga still accommodated Finnish refugees from Ingermanland. Several transports of Russian refugees-cum-slave-laborers were to arrive shortly. As of September 14, Klooga and Põllküla camps held a total of 9,227 people from Russia proper.[2] Back then, the camp still made a relatively good impression: barracks were clean and food rations satisfactory.[3] Chief physician von Bodman claimed that of all the Jewish camps, Klooga boasted the best sanitary conditions.

For some time Klooga was called "OT camp," yet officially it was a Waffen-SS labor camp. The first Jewish transport, which arrived on September 7, 1943, brought to Klooga 650 women and 50 men. Another 748 Jews who arrived on the 29th of the same month were all males.[4] Unlike the first two transports from Vilna, the third one from Kovno consisted of 500 women.[5] Benjamin Weintraub, along with other Jews from Vilna ghetto, arrived in Klooga on September 29, 1943. As the prisoners made it to the camp grounds, they discovered signs denoting various professions stuck in the sandy soil in front of a barracks. For good or bad, Weintraub declared himself a carpenter. Next, the twenty-three-year-old experienced a barber's scissors running a straight naked line in the middle of his head—to prevent escape. The prisoners were then given unmistakable striped blue shirts and jackets. A cloth label on the shirt had the personal number of the prisoner and a Star of David.[6] Not unusual for Nazi penitentiaries, the prisoners' first assignment was to build a barbed-wire fence around the camp.

The number of Jews at Klooga increased from 1,453 in October to 1,842 in February;[7] 84 inmates were in fact children. As of June 1944, there were 2,168 Jews and 150 Soviet POWs at Klooga.[8] According to the official statistics from the summer of 1944, most of the prisoners were women—1,239. Of that number, 671 came from Vilna and 439 from Kovno. Women were on average five years

25. A warning sign in German, Russian, and Estonian posted at the entrance to the Klooga concentration camp that reads "Stop! You will be shot without warning!"; USHMM, 98896.

younger than men, twenty-seven vs. thirty-two. Of 916 men, 719 came from Vilna, 59 from Kovno, and 14 from Warsaw. The great majority of the Jews, both men and women, were blue-collar.[9]

Men and women lived in separate barracks surrounded by barbed wire, about 150 yards apart. SS guards were stationed between these two barracks; another barracks in the middle housed OT employees. A building outside the fence, to the right of the main gate, housed camp administration; another building, to the left, provided accommodation for the Estonian guards. Klooga was connected with the outside world by railway, which ran just north of the camp. Klooga was the largest and the best-organized Jewish camp in Estonia. It had its own laundry, two baths, two disinfection stations, two hospitals, a tailor shop, a carpenter shop, and a barbershop.[10] The Germans even allowed dental care in the camp, though they tended to knock out more prisoners' teeth than got treated.[11] Until noon, prisoners had to live on a single cup of chestnut coffee. During the lunch break they received an unvarying bowl of soup and then in the evening a few slices of bread and one ounce of margarine. The margarine stank so that many were unable to eat it.[12]

As of May 1944, Klooga employed 1,735 prisoner-workers, 1,077 of whom were women. Camp inmates were engaged in building barracks and bunkers. Timber, cement, gravel, and concrete were the materials Jews worked with. The camp also had a sawmill, a joinery, and a clog workshop—about a hundred workers in each. Occasionally Jews were dispatched to the nearby port of Paldiski to move freight. Yet the main type of production at Klooga was underwater concrete signal mines, manufactured only in this camp. (Each mine weighed one ton.) The Jews produced concrete for an Estonian company, A.I.K. The director of the company, Evald Selart, was an Estonian, and so were the foremen. Initially, each prisoner was supposed to produce fifteen concrete blocks, one hundred pounds each, to fulfill the daily norm. Later the quota was raised to nineteen, then to twenty-five, thirty, thirty-five—all the way to forty blocks per day.[13] Work in reinforced concrete was considered to be the hardest at Klooga—penal hard labor even for the Klooga inmates, as Herman Kruk wrote. Female prisoners twisted wires, while male prisoners pounded concrete. Concrete produced by Jewish slave laborers was used to build bunkers.[14] A group of prisoners loaded the camp's products into boxcars on a siding about half a mile from Klooga. Work proceeded in three overlapping shifts: from 5:30 A.M. to 6:30 P.M.; from 3:00 A.M. to 12:00

P.M.; and from 12:00 P.M. to 9:00 P.M. As of early August 1944, Klooga still worked at full capacity. Close to 50,000 concrete blocks, with 3,000 more produced every day, were ready for delivery. Since the fall of Narva in July, building materials had been used for building the defenses around Tallinn.[15]

Prisoners worked under the supervision of an OT special commando, which consisted of some eighty civilians and thirty-six mine experts from the navy. All of them lived in a barracks outside of the camp grounds. Only a few SS guards were employed at Klooga: six, plus two or three female SS overseers.[16] When it came to brutalities, female SS guards were on a par with their male counterparts, except that they targeted women. One of them, Agnes "Anni" Gastren, related to prisoners that before she came to Klooga she had spent time in a brothel.[17] According to survivors, the OT administration treated them badly. The head of Klooga OT, Kurt Stache, was said to have been particularly cruel. Stache used to whip Jewish workers, but more often unleashed his dog on them; he did not intervene until after the dog had almost killed the victim.[18] Prisoners felt relieved when the younger, crueler OT guards were sent to the front and in their stead came older OT guards. The older guards were more compassionate toward Jews and allowed them to beg for food.[19] OT people—or *Dotniks,* as prisoners called them—were on the spot during the last day of Klooga's existence, on September 19, 1944, beating the squatting prisoners who awaited execution. At the same time, witnesses refrained from indiscriminately blaming the OT, saying that some of its personnel—remarkably those at Vaivara, Ereda, Jõhvi—behaved correctly toward Jews.[20]

The 3rd company of the Estonian 287th Police Battalion guarded the camp from outside, as well as escorted prisoners to and from work. The battalion manned five posts in two shifts, about twenty-five guards at a time. The guards (110 in total) were not allowed on the camp grounds, which were the German SS's domain. Commander of the unit Lieut. Alfred Hendrikson received orders directly from the Klooga commandant. Among other responsibilities, the guards were supposed to prevent contacts between the prisoners and the local population. Hendrikson ordered his men to shoot without warning at any Jew who left work. And they certainly did leave, in search of food. Some prisoners went begging for food from Estonian farmers, while others looked for leftovers at a dump near the officers' barracks. Whenever they found out, the guards beat the Jews, sometimes with a ramrod but more often with their fists. At least one prisoner was shot in an attempt to leave his workplace.[21] Of all the Estonian guards, prisoners identified August Sinipalu as one of the cruelest. The word Sinipalu used most frequently— *kurat* (damn it!)—stuck to him as a proper name. At first glance, Sinipalu might appear a decent individual, as he allowed Jews to acquire food from the local farmers. When they came back, however, as fifteen-year-old Peisah Rubanovich once did, Sinipalu seized bread, potatoes—whatever they brought—and sold it to another prisoner, whom he later robbed as well. Gun butt, ramrod, anything at all Sinipalu tried on camp inmates, including children.[22] Platoon commander Mihkel Raudsepp was another individual said to have punched camp inmates.[23] In October 1943, a Jewish prisoner died at the hand of Alfred Kuklane; in January of the next year, Alfred Karu shot a Jewish woman who refused to hand over her gold ring.[24]

Relations between the Estonian guards and the German OT personnel left much to be desired, as is predictable considering that the German commanding staff at Klooga changed eight times over a period of eleven months. In one case, for example, a drunken German serviceman shot at an Estonian guard. Food speculation was a major source of mutual incriminations. One time an OT truck sped through the Estonian checkpoint into the camp; the truck was loaded with foodstuffs to be sold to Jewish inmates. On another occasion, a Jewish prisoner was caught with a stolen sheet of leather, which was probably delivered to the camp by German OT employees. More than once, several Jews left the camp without permission. Once apprehended, the Jews claimed that "Estonians did not allow us to go, but Germans did." When cigarettes and money, both in large quantities, were found on Jews, suspicion fell on ethnic Russian members of the guard company. Because ethnic Russian guards could communicate with Jewish prisoners in Russian, they were subsequently removed from Klooga. The police battalion command was altogether determined to prevent communication between Jewish inmates and Soviet POWs.[25] One may conclude that the Estonians tended to be tougher than the Germans or Russians toward the Jews at the Klooga camp.

Klooga prisoners suffered from such diseases as influenza, bronchitis, dystrophy, and heart disease.[26] The mortality rate sometimes reached 10 percent per month. On March 25, 1944, chief physician Dr. von Bodman reported that "the health conditions in the camp are deteriorating. An increase in the number of deaths is conditioned mainly by injuries and unsatisfied hygiene." Only those with a body temperature over 40 degrees Centigrade were accepted into the camp infirmary. By an unspoken rule, the number of patients admitted to the infirmary at one time could not exceed eight. Some survivors claimed that the rest of the patients were routinely murdered by drug injection.[27] In his capacity as head of the infirmary, SS-Uschaf. Wilhelm Genth, who arrived in Klooga in August 1944, regularly mistreated the sick Jews. "Those who could not walk had to depart for the next world," Genth used to say; Genth was often seen drunk. On August 15, 1944, SS-Uschaf. Werle replaced SS-Oschaf. Bock as Klooga commandant. Before leaving Klooga, Bock sent to his home address in Germany a box with valuables robbed from Jews such as rings, watches, and gold teeth.[28] About the same time in August, the entire German camp administration relocated from Saka to Klooga. Dr. von Bodman arrived in Klooga on September 3. Two days later, prisoners spotted the dreaded Vaivara commandant, SS-Hstuf. Aumeier—or *Vaivarchik* or *Sortovshchik* (Selectioner), as they called him.[29] By September, the then defunct Vaivara camp complex still had about fifteen people on staff.[30] The prisoners' situation turned worse, as the high-ranking SS officials attempted to outdo each other in nastiness with regard to Jews.[31]

DEATH AT KLOOGA

According to survivors, Klooga was weighed down by selections, which claimed about five hundred lives by early 1944. One of the largest selections took place at the end of December 1943 when about one hundred Jews were shot in response to three successful attempts at escape from the camp.[32] Even those few who risked their life attempting to escape from the camp very soon gave up their hope. Once caught, the fugitives disappeared without a trace. The Germans used to say that the escapees "had gone to Riga." A whisper went around the camp about the existence of a gas chamber and crematorium at Riga. The phrase "going to Riga" thus became synonymous with death. As ominous as the word "Riga" was the number "25"—that is how many lashes one got at Klooga, the severity of the committed offense notwithstanding.[33] Anything, from not greeting a German properly to owning a second shirt, was considered an offense. Another way of torturing prisoners was to leave them either for two days without food or, during the winter, for two to three hours in subzero temperatures.[34] The corpses of the dead were routinely burned. The relatives of the departed were forbidden on pain of death to collect the ashes. Thus a woman who managed to keep a bit of what used to be her father was executed. To give birth in the camp was prohibited as well. When it happened nevertheless (in February 1944), the two babies were instantly killed. Another birth was recorded in May. These tiny bodies were also reduced to ashes. Survivors implicated SS orderly Erwin Bahr in the murder.[35]

The ultimate fate of the Jewish prisoners at Klooga was closely linked with a makeshift concentration camp in Lagedi, about thirteen miles west of Tallinn. The transport that arrived from Ereda on July 29, 1944, was sidetracked because the Wehrmacht had seized the ship that was supposed to take the Jews farther, to Stutthof. All 2,050 prisoners were instead unloaded in Lagedi. To facilitate the deployment of the Jews, OT provided them with the tools for digging antitank trenches.[36] There were no barracks or tents at Lagedi: prisoners slept in the open air (luckily, over the six-week period of the camp's existence it did not rain even once).[37] The deplorable conditions translated into an ironic rhyme: "Lagedi-tragedy."[38]

Commandant of Lagedi SS-Schaf. Engst was among the few commanding SS officers whom Jewish prisoners praised. According to Nissan Anolik, Engst was more human than other German personnel, allowing Jews to wash themselves once a week in the Baltic Sea. Despite the hard work and poor-quality food, Lagedi was considered one of the better camps.[39] Yet Jews felt it necessary to bribe camp officials and guards, on whose whim they were dependent. Jews collected money to buy eggs, hens, geese, and other produce from local Estonian farmers and then presented it to the camp administration.[40] Prisoners and captors alike realized that the end was near. The Royal British Air Force considered bombing the shale oil region of Estonia as early as October 1942.[41] In the summer of 1944, the Soviet air force intensified aerial raids against various targets in Estonia. On several occasions, Jewish slave labor camps were hit. In places like Lagedi there were also victims.[42] However, the aerial raids did not scare the Jews. On the contrary, some of them started praising God as the bombs exploded.[43]

On August 22, the Germans transferred 500 Jews from Klooga (250 men and 250 women) to Lagedi. By that time all but 11 Jews from Lagedi had already been shipped to Stutthof.[44] The train passengers had a full view of the Jewish camp, which was located across from the Lagedi railway station. On August 19, however, all that the commuters could see was hundreds of suitcases strewn across the field. The camp guards and OT men were seen going through the piles of clothes looking for things, silk underwear in particular. The passengers speculated that the Jews had been either murdered or drowned in the Baltic Sea.[45] This time they were wrong, and so were the new arrivals from Klooga. The prisoners erred when they thought it was the end; they were allowed to live for one more month. The Estonian SS guards at Lagedi were newcomers from the Eastern front and tended to treat prisoners better than had their peers at Klooga.[46] Yet that improvement did not prevent the guards from shooting two Jews whom they caught stealing potatoes from a field.[47] In the new camp Jews were expected to build defenses from concrete blocks manufactured at Klooga. When unloading the blocks from boxcars, Benjamin Anolik found several letters sent to him by a female friend who stayed at Klooga. She wrote that the vicinity of the camp was filled with SS men who had fled before the advancing Red Army. Beatings, as well as the workload, had increased. As a token compensation, the food rations had increased too: the soup became thicker and the bread more nutritious.[48]

In the afternoon of September 18, thirty trucks operated by the German Security Police arrived at the gates of the Lagedi camp. There they waited for two hours until the prisoners, who were building antitank bunkers around Tallinn, came back from work. This time, the Jews were not marched into the camp as usual but were lined up in groups of thirty on the road next to the trucks. Truck drivers and guards formed a big circle around the vehicles, forcing the prisoners to step inside. SS-Hstuf. Brenneis announced to the prisoners that they were being transferred to Germany and that each of them was to receive a loaf of bread, margarine, jam, and sugar. All but two trucks reached their destination. Nissan and Benjamin Anolik were on the truck that arrived in an unidentified location somewhere in the forest shortly after eight in the evening. The brothers Anolik overheard somebody telling the guards in German that they had come too late and that everybody was already gone. The last truck left Lagedi at 9:00 P.M. but did not get very far either: along the way it broke down. Although the driver eventually fixed the problem, the guard was at a loss as to what they should do next. Following the advice of an officer they met along the road, the crew drove the truck to Tallinn Central prison. The prisoners on the two trucks (thirty-four men and forty women) reached Tallinn in the early morning hours of September 19. The Jews only got to sleep a few hours before they were bundled off to Klooga.[49]

These seventy-four people did not know that this little mishap saved their lives—for just one more day. Uriah Simanovich was one of the only two survivors who could tell what happened to the rest of the prisoners. The truck Simanovich was on stopped in a forest about four miles from Jägala. Something immediately caught his attention—big piles covered with tarpaulins. Simanovich only realized what it was when SS guards forced him to lie down on top of the heap: he was lying on the corpses of the people taken away before he was. There must have been at least four layers below him, and probably as many more fell atop him, hit by bullets. Suddenly Simanovich felt on his face a sticky liquid that smelled like oil. Wounded but still conscious, Simanovich collected all his strength, removed himself from the pyre, and ran away. The Germans used hand grenades to ignite the pyres.[50] SS-Uschaf. Oskar Helbig was in charge of the mass execution, which claimed the lives of 426 Jews.[51]

A mass execution of Jews at Lagedi and Klooga was not inevitable. Rather, the Nazis resorted to murder when they realized that the inmates of these two camps could no longer be evacuated to Germany. Indeed, of all groups, Jews had the lowest priority. The OKH developed a plan of evacuation for Estonia, originally called *Königsberg* and later changed to *Aster*. Around September 15, the navy commando at Klooga received the order to start packing their personal belongings so as to be ready for departure.[52] As of September 4, there was still space available on the ships bound for the Reich.[53] But the work at Baltöl and all its subsidiaries had to continue.[54]

A deadly circle was slowly but steadily closing in on the Jews who remained in Estonia. On September 10, KdS-Estland SS-Ostuf. Baatz authorized the SS special commandos, in extraordinary cases, to carry out executions of prisoners without prior notice. One of the three commandos was designated *Buchner*.[55] By mid-September the front at Tartu collapsed. In order to avoid encirclement, Army Group Narva decided to retreat in the direction of Pärnu and eventually into Latvia, thus exposing Tallinn to an enemy attack. That was the end. On September 17, what until then had been an evacuation plan became an order. Estonia was to be cleared within the next two days, that is, by September 19. Baltöl said it needed up to three days to complete the withdrawal; however, there was no time left for bargaining. Army Group Narva provided Baltöl with nine trains, which then transferred the remaining eight thousand workers from the shale oil region. An agency in Tallinn, specifically designed for that purpose, began stockpiling explosives to implement the demolition plan.[56] Early in the morning of September 18, the OKH issued the order that put all means of transportation, first and foremost ships, at its disposal. A few hours later, Tallinn was sealed off by the military. The last-minute rush could have been prevented, yet the Germans did not want to upset the Latvian and Estonian troops by announcing, early on, a large-scale evacuation.[57] By the evening of September 18, the Germans finished the demolition of the Kiviõli oil refinery. In Tallinn, German officials hastily began to burn documents; the work continued deep into the night.

What had until then worked for Jews now turned against them. Baltöl regarded Soviet POWs as better workers and therefore had no regrets letting the Jews go. When it became clear, however, that not everything and everybody could be saved from the sinking vessel called Estonia, the Germans went after the more valuable source of slave labor: the POWs. During the month of September, the Germans managed to evacuate nearly all the POWs employed at Baltöl. A total of 22,500 POWs were driven from the mainland to the Estonian islands.[58] Up to 30,000 Estonians, German soldiers, and civilian personnel—masses of people— streamed to the Tallinn harbor in a desperate attempt to get out of the country before it was too late. The Red Army was only a few days away from the Estonian capital. By that time, Jews ceased to be a concern for anyone. In fact, they were expendable. The German navy reported on September 21 that it had success- fully evacuated all its personnel—close to twenty thousand people—via Estonian ports, in the first place Tallinn. At 10:09 P.M. on September 23, 1944, the last ship with German troops on board pulled out of Tallinn harbor. Reports on the evacuation did not mention the Jews at Klooga.[59]

Another factor that caused delays in the evacuation of Jews from Klooga, as mentioned earlier, was the importance of Estonia for the German war economy. Tallinn dockers did small-scale repairs on German warships, while numerous plants in and around the city manufactured a number of essential components for the navy in general. The work had to continue no matter what. For obvi- ous reasons, Klooga provided a much safer working environment than Tallinn, which was prone to Soviet air raids. Indeed, in August some production lines were moved from Tallinn to Klooga.[60] The military was altogether more success- ful in carrying out the evacuation than Baltöl, which lay outside of HGr North jurisdiction.[61]

The signs of impending evacuation made Jewish prisoners hopeful about their future. As individual Wehrmacht and OT units started leaving, some Ger- mans made peace with Jews. "Soon you will liberated," they told the inmates, "but our lot is bad." Jews understood well what the Germans meant by saying, "*that* is out of the question" (in other words, a mass execution). Jews who had been tensely awaiting deliverance often greeted each other with "may we be liberated as soon as possible!" The failed assassination of Hitler, cities captured by the victorious Red Army, the sound of bomb explosions—daily news raised tensions to an unprecedented level. Jews started counting the days, if not the hours, until they would walk out free men.[62]

Sometime after midnight on September 19, Dr. von Bodman arrived in the German Security Police headquarters in Tallinn to discuss the Klooga issue. Evidently Aumeier was also present at that meeting. It did not take long to assess the situation: because of the transportation system breakdown and the rapid Soviet advance, it had become impossible to evacuate the Jews from Klooga. The decision was then made to execute them. The execution order was to be implemented by a special SS commando, which immediately set out for Klooga.[63]

At five o'clock in the morning Klooga prisoners formed for a routine roll call. Instead of the usual four guards, this time the area in front of the women's barracks teemed with armed men, posted as close as twelve feet from each other. Klooga commandant Werle showed up in the company of five other high-ranking German officials.[64] The prisoners were all waiting for that: Werle announced that the entire camp was being evacuated by sea to Germany. Therefore, nobody had to report to work outside the camp that day. To dispel the prisoners' doubts, head of the camp office SS-Hstuf. Walter Schwarze added that he was going to accompany the camp inmates all the way to East Prussia.[65]

Benjamin Weintraub was on the last truck that arrived in Klooga from Tallinn. He saw an alarming sight: all two thousand–something prisoners gathered behind a barbed-wire fence next to the women's barracks. When he asked what was going on, a guard told him that prisoners were being taken to Riga and to Germany. RIGA![66] About 7:00 A.M., Schwarze selected 301 healthy strong men among the Jews; ten Estonian guards took them in the direction of the railway line. The men were told that they had to finish the job they had started the day before, which was a lie. Instead they had to unload the boxcars that were to allegedly transport all the prisoners to Germany. From a distance, one could see these men carrying logs from the cars and into the forest. In the meantime, the rest of the prisoners were ordered to squat, in which position they remained for several hours.[67] The 301 men were ordered to construct peculiar platforms. First they laid four heavy logs in a square. Then they filled in the square with pine boughs, scattering small kindling wood among them. Next they put long cross-pieces across the square, and across these they laid shorter logs, thus creating a kind of floor. In the center they put up four poles in a square about a foot square, which they kept free of sticks and boughs. After they finished, there were four such platforms, each about thirty feet square.[68]

Wilhelm Föhles worked as a cook in the kitchen inside the camp. Föhles reported to work at 6:00 A.M. to have meals ready for some 120 SS and OT personnel at Klooga. Usually several Jewish women helped him with cooking. Strangely enough, on September 19 the Jewish assistants did not show up as usual in the

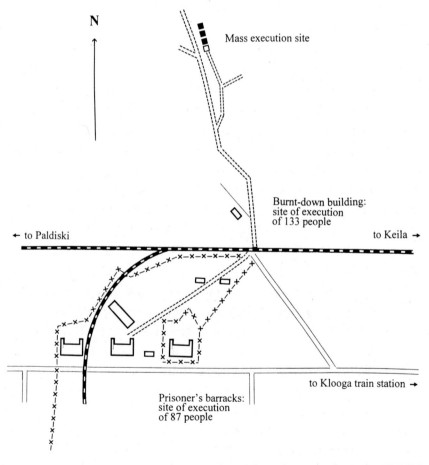

15. Mass execution sites at Klooga camp (adapted from the original, 1944); USHMM, RG-22.002M/25.

morning. Instead, the chef was assigned two local Estonian women. So the three of them were cooking until 8:00 or 9:00 A.M. What was also strange was the eerie quiet in the camp; no Jewish labor details passed by the kitchen on their way to work. When Föhles looked out the kitchen window he saw the entire Jewish camp population—men, women, and children—lining up in front of the women's barracks. In front of them prisoners stacked blankets, coats, whatever few possessions they had. Next Föhles received an order from the camp administration to cook meals for twenty-five more people. Although Föhles did not know who those people were, word of mouth spread that it was a "special commando" or "death squad." At 11:00 A.M., they all came to the dining hall to eat their lunch. Death squad it appeared to be: the men wore peaked caps, boots, and the same collars as the SS people at Klooga. They behaved coarsely. The men ate quickly and then left.[69]

At noon, the prompt Germans fed the prisoners in the enclosure. The people, who had received no food since the night before, began eagerly eating their meal, which was particularly filling on that day. Even a pig was slaughtered on that occasion, allegedly to provide prisoners with meat to take with them on the road. But something was still wrong: the 301 workers did not come back for lunch. What was holding them up? And again, a guard answered: perhaps it had been decided to take them straight to Riga without first coming back here![70] Yet some prisoners were relieved when they learned about 301 helpings that were put aside: the workers were obviously to join them soon! Jews who had just finished eating their lunch were ordered to gather in groups, one hundred people in each, men and women separately.[71] At one point, one of the men carrying logs dropped his load and ran back to the camp shouting, "Jews, run for your life! We are going to be murdered!" (Yidn, ratevet sikh, men hareget unds ois!) The prisoner was shot on the spot and his desperate cry hung in mid-air before the rest of the Jews were able to grasp its meaning.[72]

Meanwhile, the men at the platforms were divided into groups of thirty. The first three groups were ordered to climb onto the platforms where they were to lie down on their stomachs. Next, SS men with pistols stepped up and shot them one by one in the back of the head. Those who attempted either to resist or to run away were shot in the face or stomach. Immediately afterward, the rest of the group was forced to build another layer on top of the bodies of their coworkers, even though some of them still showed signs of life. While doing so, they were told to be careful so as not to block the central square with sticks and boughs, which was to serve as a chimney, giving draft to the fire. Once the second tier was ready, three more groups went onto the platforms.[73]

Two-thirty P.M. The sound was unmistakable and it came from where the workers had gone in the morning. The first thing that came to prisoners' minds was that the front was nearing Klooga. Only after the second salvo did people in the enclosure realize what awaited them. The sound of shots caused a commotion among the men; women began screaming. The guards, who walked back and forth in front of the two large groups of prisoners, had difficulty controlling the panic-stricken crowd. The nearest door of the U-shaped barracks was about sixty feet away, and that is where about one hundred Jews ran for their lives. Once inside, people tried to hide wherever they could: they threw themselves under bunks, crept into corners, climbed onto upper bunks. A few dozen Jews made it to the attic. One of the prisoners cut the electric wires, causing a short circuit. The barracks plunged into darkness. For a moment, silence broke out. The guards did not want to risk their lives and called for reinforcement. Two SS men entered the room on the first floor, spraying it with bullets. Eighty-seven people were killed in that one room alone.[74] Luckily for the prisoners who hid in the attic of the women's barracks, the murderers did not go upstairs.

At about 4:00 P.M., Schwarze picked up six prisoners, who helped to load two barrels of gasoline on a truck and then drove away. Another hour passed before the guards began dispatching groups of male Jews, fifty to one hundred people in each, into the forest. Shortly thereafter shots rang out.[75] Women endured the most horror. Unlikely to become unruly, Jewish women had to wait until nine in the evening to be escorted to their deaths. About thirty of them were taken to one of the wooden barracks and executed.[76] The last group to be murdered were the sick and the hospital personnel who took care of them. All these Jews were taken to the pyres by truck. Prisoners could hear Schwarze asking the guards whether there were any more men left in the camp.[77] The cordon was lifted at two in the morning on September 20.

Once the pile of bodies grew eight to ten layers high, the Germans poured gasoline over the corpses and set them on fire. The bonfire burned for the next two and a half days. Afraid of being cut off by the Red Army, the Germans left the killing site before the smoke settled down. The fourth pyre was only half

26. Clothes of the Jews who were murdered in the Klooga concentration camp on September 19, 1944; USHMM, 47621.

as tall as the other three when the SS went back to the camp to finish off the remaining prisoners. One of the barracks became a giant cemetery. There, one by one, the SS escorted prisoners, whom they ordered to lie down on the floor and then shot. Very soon, all eight rooms of the barracks were filled with dead bodies. Next, the building was set ablaze. At least 133 people were murdered in this particular building.[78]

The individual who supervised the mass execution at Klooga was the head of Department IV of the German Security Police in Tallinn, SS-Hstuf. Georg Buchner.[79] Buchner was one of the original members of Sonderkommando 1a that entered Estonia in July 1941. Shortly before the mass execution, a twenty-five-man-strong SS commando arrived in Klooga with the purpose of strengthening the camp personnel.[80] Altogether, about eighty Germans were present in the camp on September 19. Among the main organizers of the execution, survivors named Schwarze: he provided instructions to the SS personnel, gave orders to bring Jews to the pyres, and finally told them to set the bodies on fire.[81] Most

27. Burned corpses lie on the grounds of the Klooga concentration camp; USHMM, 47627.

of the German camp administration in Estonia were present at Klooga at the time of the execution: Aumeier, Brenneis, Pannicke, Engst, Dahlmann, Helbig, Scharfetter, Genth, and von Bodman.[82] That made them directly responsible for the massacre.

The most contested issue remains the Estonians' role in the September 19 execution. According to survivors, Estonians guarded the perimeter, while Germans did the shooting.[83] Isaac Ratner, for example, overheard the SS men who were killing the prisoners on the first floor of the barracks he was hiding in saying to each other that they should move quickly before the escape route to Riga was cut off. Obviously they spoke German and not Estonian for Ratner to understand it.[84] The night before the mass execution, the commander of the 3rd Company that guarded Klooga informed his men about the forthcoming evacuation of the camp to Germany. The guards were supposed to escort the Jewish prisoners. The next morning, the company, with its full complement, surrounded the camp. One of the guards, August Sinipalu, saw the German Security Police commando taking prisoners in small groups into the forest. To get a better view, Sinipalu came closer to the execution site, but left shortly after to eat his dinner. Yet something pulled Sinipalu back to the railway tracks where he joined his comrades, watching. "Have they already started taking women?" he asked his fellow servicemen. No, they had not, so Sinipalu went back to his barracks. He would have probably called it a day, until one of his colleagues summoned him to go "to listen to Jews' screams." They made it just in time to witness one of the buildings going up in flames. Some of the Jews trapped inside were obviously still alive—they were calling for help. Their screams did not die out even after half an hour, as Sinipalu was walking back home. On the next day, that is, September 20, Sinipalu and his company left Klooga by rail, first to Keila and then to Tallinn. There were no Germans in sight, only the thick black smoke from the still burning pyres.[85]

Survivors recalled seeing in situ an Estonian SS unit they had not seen before—"Estonians from afar," they called them (*fremde:* a German translation of the Russian *chuzhye* or Polish *cudzy*). These people wore the same uniform as the German SS but spoke Estonian to each other. Armed with automatic weapons, the unit cordoned off the camp from outside. Estonian soldiers were also seen guarding the immediate execution site. The Estonians had the blood of at least eighteen Jews on their hands. Those Jews were shot as they attempted to flee, either from the pyres or from the roll call area.[86] The Estonians whom the survivors were talking about were from the SS training and replacement unit no. 20 (Estonian no. 1), which came into existence just a few months before the massacre and which was located next door to the Jewish camp at Klooga. The unit was composed of about two thousand recruits undergoing military training before being sent to the front. Following his early-morning visit to Tallinn, Aumeier made a surprise appearance in the Estonian SS training camp. Commander of the unit SS-Stubaf. Georg Ahlemann yielded to Aumeier's request to dispatch about seventy of his men to help cordon off the Jewish camp. At 8:00 A.M., the Estonian SS assumed their positions around the camp.[87] Even if they did not kill, they could not resist taking advantage of the massacre; the next morning, from the attic window, frightened survivors watched members of the Estonian police battalion going through the clothes and belongings of the murdered Jews in the roll call area.[88] Among the foraging soldiers was Mihkel Raudsepp, who appropriated two quilts, a few bedsheets, and a fur coat.[89]

The Jews who took refuge in one of the barracks' attic were able to see from the window gigantic flames and smoke rising above the forest. Afraid of leaving their hideout, the survivors spent the next three days in the barracks, lying on the floor between the broken window frames. Only at night did they dare to go out foraging for food. When the Red Army entered Klooga on September 24, 1944, only 108 survivors came to greet them.[90] From the attic window, they saw soldiers down in the courtyard. The soldiers spoke Russian. That meant liberation, at last! Evidence of murder was everywhere: dead bodies lay scattered all over the camp grounds. An investigation commission (the so-called Extraordinary Commission) discovered the remnants of the three big pyres filled with the burnt human remains. Another heap of corpses designated the site of a barracks where more than one hundred Jews were executed. One other barracks was still standing but the people inside were all dead. The Commission was only able to identify 491 bodies. The final report estimated the number of people murdered at Klooga on September 19 at anywhere between 1,800 and 2,000. Survivors, however, spoke of 1,500 or 1,700 Jews who were executed on that day.[91] According to my calculations, the number of victims, including 150 POWs, could not be lower than 1,784.

As this chapter attests, Klooga was not the only Jewish forced labor camp in Estonia whose inmates were murdered. Small-scale executions took place in almost all camps. The number of victims at Kiviõli and Ereda was comparable to that in Klooga. Neither was the technique of murder that the Germans used at Klooga unique: dead bodies went up in flames in downtown Narva-Jõesuu, in factory furnaces in Narva, and at numerous other camp sites. In spite of that, until now we have had as much information about Klooga as about all the other Jewish camps in Estonia combined. Beside the hastily assembled records of the Extraordinary Commission, which interviewed some survivors in September and October 1945, Soviet judicial authorities displayed no interest in the plight of Jewish deportees from Lithuania. No criminal investigation of the atrocities committed in Jewish slave labor camps in 1943 and 1944 has ever taken place. Such an investigation, however, was feasible in the immediate postwar years when many bystanders were still alive. If it were not for local enthusiasts such as Boris Lipkin in Sillamäe, the public would know next to nothing about individual Jewish camps in Estonia.[92] Whenever one talks about the Holocaust in Estonia, the name "Klooga" is universally mentioned. Why is such disproportionate attention paid to one particular camp? This attention happened for two reasons, one emotional and another political.

When the Red Army entered the Klooga camp grounds, the pyres were still hot and smoking. The gruesome images of half-burnt bodies distorted in agony were shocking even to Soviet soldiers who had been hardened by years of brutal warfare. They had not seen anything like that before: photos from Klooga showed soldiers staring in disbelief at what used to be human beings. In short, Klooga was news for the Soviets. By the same token, Klooga was one of the first Jewish camps of any kind that made the American press. The first war-crimes trial ever, held in the city of Krasnodar in July 1943, revealed to the world the truth about Nazi gas vans. A year later, the Red Army entered the Majdanek death camp, airing shocking images of brutalities committed there. However, until the September massacre at Klooga, the Western public saw the Jewish genocide through Soviet eyes. At Klooga, Western writers and journalists for the first time encountered the Holocaust face to face. But it happened by coincidence.

28. Soviet soldiers view human remains near the pyres in the Klooga concentration camp; USHMM, 98894.

While congratulating Joseph Stalin on the Soviet takeover of Tallinn on September 22, 1944, Winston Churchill requested permission for the British navy attaché in Moscow to visit the Estonian capital. The attaché was eager to see a German acoustic torpedo, which the Red Army had captured in Tallinn harbor. Permission was granted and so the British navy attaché, accompanied by a group of famed writers and journalists, traveled to Tallinn. The delegation consisted of Harrison Salisbury, who later became associate editor of the *New York Times;* well-known playwright Lillian Hellman, who at the time served as cultural adviser to the U.S. ambassador in Moscow; Nobel Prize laureate Graham Greene; Australian-British writer James Aldridge; and Alexander Werth, a correspondent for the *London Sunday Times* and the BBC (in 1964 Werth published one of the most stunning accounts of Russia's experience in World War II). Before they got to see anything else, they saw Klooga.[93]

One other individual who visited the Klooga camp in September 1944 was John Hersey. During World War II, Hersey wrote for the *New Yorker* and *Life.* Hersey's best-selling book reflecting his experience as a war journalist won him the Pulitzer Prize in 1945. Hersey was one of the first Western journalists to land in Hiroshima after the atom bomb explosion on August 6, 1945. Back in October 1944, Hersey published in *Life* a nine-page article entitled "Prisoner 339, Klooga: Pole Who Escaped Labor Camp Tells How the Nazis Tortured, Butchered and Burned Their Captives." The article, written in an engaging, emotional style, was essentially the life story of one particular survivor, Benjamin Weintraub. The Extraordinary Commission had also questioned Weintraub, among others. Some of his experiences at Klooga became part of the official narrative later published in Soviet newspapers. The stories that the Soviet and American press told were essentially identical, except that Hersey's article related more personal details, whereas the articles in Soviet-Estonian newspapers focused on the perpetrators of the crime. In short, *Life* was more about journalism, whereas *Sovetskaia Estonia* sought to mobilize support for the ongoing war effort against Nazi Germany. In December of the same year, the Soviets produced a newspaper-size poster called "Klooga Calls for Revenge!" *(Klooga kutsub kättemaksule!)* Using graphic images of atrocities committed in the Klooga forced labor camp, the poster called on the local population to "bring to book the German executioners and their collaborators—Estonian bourgeois nationalists." This is how the Soviet power wanted to present the Holocaust to the outside world.

TRAGIC STATISTICS

The deadly assault on human life at Klooga and numerous other places through-out the country raises the question about the total number of Jews murdered in Estonia during the Nazi occupation, 1941–44. We have fairly accurate figures for the period preceding the 1943 mass deportations: 963 Estonian Jews; 30 Latvian Jews; 7 Finnish Jews; 16 Jews-POWs; and 1,754 Czech and German Jews. The problem with the later period is that we still do not know the exact number of Jews deported to Estonia from Lithuania and Latvia in the summer and fall of 1943. The number that was consistently mentioned in popular literature, based largely on survivors' testimonies, is 20,000. By adding the numbers of Jews in each of the seven transports—four from Vilna, two from Kovno, and one from Kaiserwald—we arrive at an aggregate number as low as 12,309 and as high as 19,009. Baltöl, as indicated earlier, expected the arrival of 10,000 or 12,000 Jews. The head of the Vaivara camp administration, Aumeier, had on file a similar fig-ure: 8,900 (the number of Jews–slave laborers in Estonia in February 1944).[94] Of

29. Group portrait of survivors of the Klooga concentration camp in front of a barracks; USHMM, 98909.

all high-ranking German officials in Estonia at that time, Vaivara chief physician von Bodman likely had the most precise data. The highest number of Jewish prisoners appeared in his report of November 1943: 9,207. To that number one should add at least 200 French and 500 Hungarian Jews who were deported to Estonia in May and June 1944 respectively. Probably all the Hungarian Jews, but only fifteen French Jews, were evacuated to the Stutthof concentration camp. The ship that left Tallinn for Stutthof on August 18, 1944, had about 4,150 Jews on board. It was in von Bodman's interest to downplay the number of deaths in Jewish forced labor camps in Estonia, and that is what he did. The ten reports that von Bodman complied between November 1943 and June 1944 displayed obvious inconsistencies: while the aggregate figure for Estonia stood at 1,423, statistics of individual Jewish camps added up to 1,711 (indicating that the WVHA authorities in Berlin did not read von Bodman's reports carefully). Even more incredible is the information about 1,500 Jews who were allegedly shipped from Kiviõli and Ereda to Riga in February and April 1944. In the unlikely event that the sick and the children were indeed deported to Latvia, they did not have a chance to survive the war in any case. A conservative estimate of the number of deaths in Jewish forced labor camps in Estonia would thus be 5,572. That brings the total number of Jews who were murdered in Estonia to 8,614, with a death rate of 63 percent.

12 CONCLUSIONS
EXPLAINING COLLABORATION

Almost every author who has written on the Holocaust attempts to analyze the phenomenon of collaboration. Many of these attempts, however, are only partially successful. Scholars sometimes go from one extreme to another when dealing with the problem of collaboration. Very elaborate, almost scientific, theories compete with simple, if not simplistic, explanations. For the benefit of analysis, I adhere to a more straightforward definition of collaboration. I believe that the definition proposed almost fifty years ago by John Armstrong captures the idea of collaboration most precisely: "cooperation between elements of the population of a defeated state and the representatives of the victorious power."[1] What makes the Baltic case so special is that there were two victorious powers rather than one and that Lithuania, Latvia, and Estonia were defeated not once but twice. However, when the Nazi dictatorship overcame the Soviet regime in the summer of 1941, the majority of the population hailed it as a victory and not a defeat. When trying to rationalize their own collective behavior, the Baltic peoples were ready to reconsider the very idea of collaboration.

More often than not, authors ask legitimate questions but fail to address them consistently. For example: Dov Levin correctly identifies frustration as one of the major responses of the Baltic peoples to the Soviet occupation. It may be true that ethnic antagonism—as Levin emphasizes—was growing, contained only though the Soviet repression. Then, however, Levin slips into a conventional track, explaining the wave of pogroms through the aggressive urge of the Baltic populations, whom the Germans enabled to vent it.[2] Yet we know there were no pogroms in Estonia; the only conclusion one can derive from Levin's analysis is that Estonians, in contrast to Lithuanians and Latvians, were a peace-loving nation. What is important is comparison. However, comparison only works when a scholar chooses legitimate subjects for comparison. By comparing the level of anti-Semitism in interwar Lithuania with that in Hungary, Romania, and Nazi Germany, Saulius Sužiedėlis, predictably, found it not to be alarmingly high.[3] Sužiedėlis would have been compelled to draw a different conclusion had he decided to compare Lithuania with Estonia, Finland, or even Latvia. Like Sužiedėlis, Andrew Ezergailis recognized the importance of a comparative method, yet he too made an odd selection of case studies for comparison. The question is how much insight one can get by comparing Latvia and Denmark or Latvia and Vichy France, whereas a more natural comparison would be that between Latvia and two other Baltic States, or perhaps Ukraine or Bessarabia.[4]

One other methodological fallacy is to reject the very notion of "Estonian," "Latvian," "Lithuanian," or "Ukrainian" collaboration on the grounds that none of the four nations existed as independent political entities under the conditions of German occupation. First of all, ethnic identification is inevitable. Ethnic Estonians comprised close to 100 percent of the Estonian Security Police rank and file. The proportion of ethnic Russians in the Omakaitse was slightly higher, yet negligible in absolute terms. Those were for all intents and purposes Estonian agencies. That was not the case, for example, in Belorussia: with regard to ethnicity, the local auxiliary police force roughly corresponded to the overall population in any given area (that is, was comprised of Belorussians, Ukrainians, Russians, and even Tartars).[5] Perhaps even more important is what Estonians themselves thought of the Estonian Security Police and the OK. There can be no doubt that the individuals who enrolled in these two organizations in the summer and fall of 1941 perceived them as essentially Estonian. Very often, without any formal procedure, anti-Soviet partisans simply put on the insignia that identified them as the bearers of power. Although the name was new, the police and the OK effectively reconnected with the interwar Estonian Political Police and the Home Guard. The majority of the population viewed their countrymen in uniform as legitimate representatives of the Estonian people. The sense of national belonging became even more acute after a year of Soviet occupation, during which nationalism had been suppressed. As long as we deal with individual complicity in murder, ethnicity will stay on the record. If we want to understand what makes people partake in crime, we simply cannot ignore social and cultural contexts. In other words, those individuals who falsely accused Jews or those who pulled the trigger did so as self-conscious Estonians rather than as German marionettes.

Sometimes scholars deliberately avoid dealing with the problem of complicity in murder by mixing together various forms of collaboration. Thus Ezergailis lumps together political, military, and criminal collaboration only to arrive at a preconceived conclusion that Nazis rejected the Latvian offer of collaboration.[6] Gerhard Bassler, while arguing against simple formulas, tends to excuse collaboration altogether. According to Bassler, collaboration was often the only effective form of resistance. Alternatively, collaboration turned into resistance when it did not achieve the desired objective. Bassler draws his conclusions from a case study of Alfrēds Valdmanis on the Latvian civil administration.[7]

Some authors dismiss the problem of local collaboration by questioning the idea of voluntarism. The Germans incited Lithuanians to participate in pogroms, scholars such as Ezergailis say. Baltic nationals did not join the police battalions voluntarily but were in fact drafted.[8] As regards Estonia, one author argues that members of the police and the OK were essentially soldiers, and soldiers are used to following orders. Having been granted the right to bear arms, such people felt bold and unrestrained, capable of killing almost anybody.[9] This view posits obedience to criminal orders as the main cause of aberration. Stanley Milgram described that pattern of behavior decades ago. According to Milgram, an ordinary person who makes his victim suffer does so out of a sense of obligation, a conception of his duties as a subject and not from any particularly aggressive tendencies.[10] Christopher Browning, who studied the collective and individual behavior of the members of one German unit, points out the significance of peer pressure in turning a random group of individuals into habitual killers.[11] While obedience is indeed an important force, it is not the true motive for mass killing or human destructiveness in general. Ervin Staub, for instance, argues that by overemphasizing the power of authority, Milgram in fact slowed the development of a psychology of genocide.[12] In either case—thugs or paramilitaries—we are dealing with groups. Not quite so in the case of Estonia. Policemen who investigated "Jewish" cases did so on an individual basis. Investigators did not personally choose victims: the defendant might be Jewish, Russian, or Estonian. There were never more than three people who served on a Punishment Planning

Commission at one time. The only German input at that point was to approve or overrule decisions passed by the Commission. The absence of coercion in any form makes obedience to authority irrelevant as a factor.

Within the context of the Nazi-occupied Baltic States, there have been no consistent attempts made to explain what led individuals to become accomplices to murder. Christoph Dieckmann found a new generation of young radical nationalists rising in Lithuania in late 1938. Those Lithuanians embraced nationalism and anti-Semitism as essential components of nation building.[13] The problem with this explanation is that the individuals involved in the Holocaust in Estonia were neither extremely young nor radically nationalistic. Indeed, many of them had substantial work experience. More important, most of the perpetrators also continued in their careers during the Soviet occupation. Those who did not—for example, the leaders of the Estonian Self-Government—were overtly pro-German. (Their contribution to the "Final Solution of the Jewish Question" was limited, too.) When asked to speculate as to what caused Latvians from the notorious Arājs death squad to participate in the murder of Jews, Ezergailis at one point exclaimed, "They did so for a bottle of *Schnapps!*"[14] This is probably why Ezergailis in his heavily documented monograph was unable to make any definite conclusions about the participation of Latvians in the Holocaust.[15]

The attempts to place collaboration with the German occupier in the Baltic States within a more rigorous methodological discourse do not fair any better. Knut Stang, for example, incorporates the theory of colonialism into his study of indigenous collaboration in Lithuania. Stang does indeed provide a viable analysis of the causes of collaboration, none of which, however, could be derived from the colonial model, which he drops halfway through his article anyway.[16] Michael MacQueen offers a different model, which he calls "White Terror"—a regime of terror instituted as a temporary means of controlling of a population in a period of counterrevolution.[17] Novel as it may sound, that theory begs more questions than it provides answers. First of all, the very notion of revolution/counterrevolution has little to do with the reality of the military occupation that the Baltic countries experienced in 1940 and 1941. Neither was it a situation of civil war involving two or more warring factions. The purpose of the White Terror remains unclear, given that there was no anti-German or anti-Lithuanian resistance that must then have been broken (MacQueen's contention that terror facilitated the ghettoization of the Jews is questionable). Finally, the White

Terror model fails to explain motivations to commit violence against particular ethnic groups.

Eric Haberer was the first to offer a regional perspective on local collaboration in the Baltic States. Unfortunately, when developing his otherwise sophisticated analysis, Haberer fell into the deterministic trap. Haberer speculates that the extent of collaboration that the Nazis received in Estonia, Latvia, and Lithuania made the region a testing ground for genocide—a "flashpoint of genocide," as he calls it. To begin with, Haberer is mistaken when he talks about "Omakaitse commandos" in Estonia as being equivalent to the Arājs commando in Latvia or the Hamman commando in Lithuania. The first two groups carried out individual "sentences" passed by sham tribunals, whereas the latter operated as mobile killing units. The factor of demoralization and a human propensity for greed and sadism did indeed play a role in the Baltics, but probably not as big a role as Haberer suggests. Interethnic violence, from the time of the 1905 Russian Revolution forward, was not unique to the Baltic region and therefore could not have made Estonians, Latvians, and Lithuanians into bearers of a political culture that legitimized the resolution of conflicts by force. Neither was discrimination against ethnic minorities universal. In short, Haberer argues that destructive social forces in the Baltic States had been in the making for decades. Only in the final pages of his essay does Haberer address the psychological causes of collaboration, in particular social disorientation and economic dislocation prompted by Soviet occupation. Finally, Haberer discusses the "turncoat phenomenon," which helps to explain the zeal of ex-Communist collaborators, some of whom later joined outspoken nationalists in hunting down and murdering Jews. This thesis, however, undermines Haberer's argument regarding the culture of violence.[18]

A PSYCHOCULTURAL EXPLANATION: PETERSEN, STAUB, HERMAN

The most innovative and penetrating analyses of violence come not from historians but from political scientists, sociologists, or even psychiatrists. Next I will discuss the findings of Roger Petersen, Ervin Staub, and Judith Herman, who in my opinion have made lasting contributions to the study of collaboration. I will start with the most recent work by Roger Petersen, who looked at emotional mechanisms of violence. Petersen identified three major emotional responses—Fear, Hatred, and Resentment (using capital letters so as to distinguish his constructs from emotions in general)—which most likely triggered ethnic violence in the Baltics in the summer of 1941. The Baltic States, which switched political realms three times within a very short period, thus make a perfect case study. With each change, power and status relations among groups shifted, thereby overturning a well-established ethnic hierarchy. If the element of Fear is present, Petersen argues, then the group that poses the biggest threat will be the target of ethnic violence. Hatred makes the target of ethnic violence the group that has traditionally been attacked with similar justification. If Resentment is the dominant emotion, then the ethnic target will be the group perceived as farthest up the ethnic status hierarchy. These emotions occur in relation to a structural change.[19]

According to Petersen, "resentment is the feeling of being *politically* dominated by a group that has no right to be in a superior position." Violence most likely occurs when a subordinate group has risen in status. Exercise of public violence can effectively eliminate the root feelings of Resentment. In short, Resentment is the desire to reestablish the former hierarchy. To test his theory, Petersen uses a case study of Lithuania. Petersen believes that neither Fear nor Hatred, but Resentment, could have been the cause of anti-Jewish violence in Lithuania in the summer of 1941. (Lithuanians did not feel threatened by Jews, and Lithuanian-Jewish relations were "decent by regional standards.")[20]

Petersen's analysis works well with Lithuania (the case he knows the best) and with western Ukraine/eastern Poland, but much less so with Latvia and not at all with Estonia. In the case of Estonia, Petersen remarks that the Jewish minority was so small that it did not register on the ethnic hierarchy.[21] What bedevils Petersen was the absence of pogroms, that is, disorganized yet centrally tolerated, short-lived outbursts of violence. The problem is that Petersen deals essentially with mob violence but not with institutionalized violence. As experience shows, and as the Nazis learned firsthand, the pogrom type of violence could sustain itself for only a very short time. Of all the emotions that Petersen considered, only Hatred—which he for the most part discards—could explain the long-term use of violence. The emotion-based theory that Petersen advances does not go beyond the initial phase of violence. To ordinary people, nothing suggested that the Jews were a subordinate group in interwar Estonia. To the contrary, Jews appear to have enjoyed the same rights as other Estonian citizens. In addition, their minority status entitled them to special privileges. Although the Soviet occupation did change some collective perceptions, Estonians hardly believed that Jews dominated them politically—a key element in Petersen's definition of Resentment. By the same token, Petersen ignores the disparity between an emotional response generated by a group and that displayed by individual members. If it was Resentment, as Petersen suggests, we should have been able to see its traces in the deliberations of the policemen, the civil servants, or the ordinary people. Instead, Estonians' attitudes toward Jews tended to be rather pragmatic, with no extreme emotions recorded. This attitude implies that either the set of emotions that Petersen listed is incomplete, or his interpretation of those emotions is inadequate.

Estonians felt betrayed when they started seeing individual Jews in positions of power. The reasoning went as follows: we left the Jews in peace and also helped them to preserve their culture. The Jews, however, did not appreciate our generosity and sold out to the Soviets! The common sentiment was that Jews had led too comfortable a life in Independent Estonia. Frustration and rage, which Petersen has considered in his study as well, seemed to be the dominant emotional response to the onset of Soviet occupation. Unwilling to concede the fundamental flaws within their respective states, which surrendered to the Soviet power without a single shot fired, Lithuanians, Latvians, and Estonians shifted the blame for their misfortunes onto others. The fact that those "others" happened to be Jews implies latent anti-Semitism. The slogan of "Judeo-Bolshevism" helped to rationalize the choice of a culprit.[22] The projection of a feeling of frustration onto other groups is just an effect. What causes the frustration, however, is the failure to fulfill goals. Frustration is closely connected with another condition that prompts aggression: a real or perceived threat to the physical and psychological self. In his book *The Roots of Evil,* Ervin Staub eloquently explains the psychological mechanisms that lead to violence.

Staub maintains that life-threatening situations give rise to the powerful self-protective motive to defend one's physical well-being as well as one's worldview. Disruption in customary ways of life can change people's assumptions about the world and their comprehension of reality. The need to protect the collective psychological self has to do with the cultural self-concept of a people. A sense of superiority and collective self-doubt can significantly strengthen this need. In combination, these two trends effectively fuel nationalism (in other words, the desire to enhance the status, power, or influence of one's country). Throughout the interwar period, Estonians felt vulnerable to Communist aggression, which they thought might reduce their numerically weak nation to permanent slavery or even destroy it. At the same time, Estonians considered their country to be a bulwark against Bolshevism, an outpost of Europe facing the barbarian East. As Staub notes, high self-evaluation often masks self-doubt, and a weak self-esteem can enhance threat.[23]

Soviet terror and the frustration caused by the demise of a national state prompted hostility. The appropriate targets of this hostility, however, could not be easily identified, for Communist and Soviet cadres had enough time to flee from Estonia. The hostility, augmented by a sense of injustice committed, was therefore displaced and directed toward substitute targets. Finding a scapegoat (in this case Jews) made people believe that they were in control of the situation. It also erased one's own responsibility for any of the past mistakes and thus eliminated the sense of guilt. Aggression is an effective self-defense mechanism that reestablishes self-esteem and public esteem. What we observe here is not actual justice, but the perception of justice. Whoever is held responsible for the injustice committed, he or she will often be perceived as evil and deserving of punishment. Generally, nationalism tends to grow stronger in the experiences of shared trauma, suffering, and humiliation, which are sources of self-doubt. A wound inflicted on the collective feelings of a society strengthens the sense of belonging.[24] Similarly to individuals, a nation can be deeply affected by "shell shock." Psychiatrists refer to this neurosis as *posttraumatic stress disorder*. Roger Petersen and Ervin Staub explain what causes posttraumatic stress disorder and describe its symptoms. Judith Herman, herself a psychiatrist, is more interested in the healing process. She deals specifically with the victims of rape, trapped within the triangle of perpetrator-victim-therapist. Herman's discussion of a victim-therapist relationship brings us closer to understanding what made the majority of Estonians collaborate with the Germans and why the extent of collaboration in Estonia was larger than in any other Nazi-occupied country in Eastern Europe.

Rape is intentionally designed to produce psychological trauma: The purpose of the rapist is to terrorize, dominate, and humiliate his victim. The victim, overwhelmed by force, has intense feelings of fear and anger. The sense of danger persists even after the actual danger is over. The victim remains on the alert for new threats, anywhere up to six months but not less than three. Traumatic events produce profound and lasting changes in emotion and cognition.

The victim tends to have inaccurate perceptions and to show false judgments. Traumatic symptoms tend to become disconnected from their source. Aggressive impulses become disorganized and unrelated to the situation at hand. In her humiliated fury, the victim imagines that she can only regain her psychological balance through revenge. At the same time, she is intolerant of aggression in any form.[25] That is when the community and the therapist can step in to help the victim of rape.

Most survivors need assurance of safety and protection. In the immediate aftermath of the trauma, rebuilding of trust is essential. The criminal justice system can formally address issues of recognition and restitution. Indeed, above all the survivor desires to bring offenders to justice. The victim recognizes the importance of justice not only for her personal well-being but for the health of the larger society. The survivor also gains recognition from the public exercise of power. By scoring a symbolic victory over the perpetrator, the victim erases the humiliation of the trauma. However, as statistics show, only 1 percent of rapes are ultimately resolved by arrest and conviction of the offender. At the same time, uncontrolled outbursts of aggression are counterproductive, because they eventually increase the victim's burden of guilt and shame.[26]

A community can create an environment conductive to the healing process. However, communal support alone cannot guarantee full recovery. Only a professional therapist knows how to rehabilitate a victim of rape. The core experience of psychological trauma is disempowerment. Recovery, therefore, is based upon the principle of restoring control to the traumatized person. The patient who enters the therapeutic relationship is vulnerable to exploitation. Thus therapy requires a collaborative working relationship built upon persuasion and mutuality rather than on coercion and authoritarian control. The therapist acknowledges the victim's pain and seeks a resolution that restores some sense of justice. The therapist identifies not only with the victim's helplessness but also with the victim's rage. The patient may adamantly insist that she has no psychological problems. In that situation, the therapist may want to reframe accepting help as an act of courage. The principle of respecting the patient's autonomy is of great importance in the therapeutic relationship. An inexperienced therapist, however, tends to take on an advocacy role for the patient, implying that the latter is incapable of acting for herself. The more helpless, dependent, and incompetent the patient feels, the worse her symptoms become.[27]

What Judith Herman determined clinically was enacted in the Baltic States in the summer of 1941. It appears as if her rape-narrative has been drawn from the experience of the Estonians, Latvians, and Lithuanians under Soviet and Nazi rule. The Estonian people, as a collective, sought redress for both the unfulfilled promise of nation-state and the near-death experience of Soviet terror. Dr. Martin Sandberger, head of the German Security Police in Estonia, carefully led the traumatized nation through the stages of recovery and into the brighter future of Hitler's "New Europe." Like a skillful but corrupted therapist, Sandberger granted the Estonians as much autonomy as was possible under the conditions of occupation. He gave power to the Estonian Security Police, which then opened a quasi-legal investigation into the crimes committed against the Estonian people. Although a mockery of justice, it appeared as a genuine attempt to bring offenders to account. It occurred differently in Latvia and Lithuania, whose peoples the occupation regime subjected to tight control, thus aggravating the feeling of humiliation they had experienced under Soviet occupation. By unleashing bloody pogroms and organizing death squads, the Nazis quenched the resentment felt by many Latvians and Lithuanians. In the long run, however, it had the opposite effect on the collective psyche of these two peoples, who now started comparing Nazi policies with those of the Soviets. One response was anti-German resistance, which the Nazis managed to avoid altogether in Estonia.

NATIONAL HISTORY REVISITED

What I have discussed on more than three hundred pages comes down to two propositions: (1) one cannot discern the motivation to commit violence without first overhauling national history (in this case Estonian history); and (2) it is impossible to explain collaboration in the Holocaust outside of the general framework of collaboration. How many times one hears the following cliché: Participation in the Holocaust was a shameful page in the history of Estonia (Latvia, Lithuania, Ukraine, and so forth). Local collaboration in the Nazi murder of Jews was not inevitable, but neither did it come as a total shock. The way Estonian society functioned—the principles it was built upon, the values it had promoted, the perceptions it generated—opened a window of opportunity for the Nazis. The latter were able to fit the integral nationalism of East-European casting into the ideological mold of exterminationist racism.

It is one thing to say that it was Estonian, Latvian, or Lithuanian "national-ists" who collaborated in the Nazi murder of Jews, but what do we really mean by that? What about those individuals who first helped the Soviets to establish control over Estonia and then changed sides—do they fit the profile? Or those city dwellers who denounced Jews to the Security Police—were they nationalists too? The sad irony is that beneath the multiple motives that prompted private individuals to take steps that eventually led to the physical destruction of the Baltic Jews, omnipresent was the desire to see their country free and independent again. Jews as such were unimportant, hatred generated against them was cir-cumstantial, and yet it would supposedly benefit Estonia if, under the conditions of Nazi occupation, Jews were no more.

The year of Soviet rule played a significant role in turning certain segments of the Estonian population against Jews. However, the importance of the Soviet occupation should not be overestimated. Émigré authors have embraced a rather simplistic vendetta theory to explain the upsurge of anti-Semitic violence in the Baltics in the summer of 1941. Simply put, they reason that while some of "them" did it to "us," some of "us" did it to "them." The fact of retaliation was unfortu-nate, yet not inevitable.[28] It is hard to believe that the twelve months of Soviet domination had such an adverse effect on Estonian society that the latter imme-diately started purging its ranks of all those who did not fit the ideal image of an Estonian national.[29] Rather, the Soviets subjected Estonian nationalism to a test, sowing chaos in the minds of those who carried its banner. For twenty-odd years

30. Anti-Semitic cartoon by an Estonian artist; *Deutsche Zeitung im Ostland,* January 4, 1942.

Estonians tried to define themselves as a nation. By the late 1930s, the nationalist enterprise seemed to be just one step away from being proclaimed a success story. But then something unpredictable happened: the Baltic Germans left Estonia once and forever. The resettlement of Baltic Germans created more opportunities for titular ethnicity. At the same time, it made Estonians' perception of Germany and Germans further removed from reality. Without a clear understanding of the tenets of Nazism—which was essentially impossible in the sanitized environment of the authoritarian Estonian state—Estonians now completely lost track of the goals and means of the Third Reich. There was no consensus in the society as to whether the Germans, the Nazis, and the Baltic Germans were one and the same people and whether they wished Estonia well or wanted to harm it. The Soviet occupation occurred at the all-time highest point for the Estonian national idea. When Baltic Germans were all but gone, the state came crashing down. The magnitude of the setback is hard to overestimate. It looked like a Barbarians revolt, and the Jews—the very people who were in check and seemingly content—joined the uprising.

As Staub emphasizes, the degree of opposition and conformity to a new social order depends on the nature of the preceding society. When it comes to understanding the roots of mass violence, cultural continuity is particularly important.[30] The Estonian State collapsed so quickly partially because of its internal weaknesses. The breakdown of the carefully constructed idea of nationhood disoriented some people and consequently drew them into the Soviet orbit. Others chose to cooperate with the Soviet regime to ensure their personal safety. The collective response to the Nazi occupation, as has often been underscored, was founded on the preceding experience of Soviet occupation. And that is where the notion of multiple collaboration comes in. The year of Soviet occupation in Estonia was a relatively peaceful period. Unlike in Lithuania,[31] no significant anti-Soviet resistance was experienced in Estonia. The lack of a coordinated effort to overthrow the Communist regime was as damaging to Estonian national pride as was the Soviet takeover itself. The fact is that, however grudgingly, a majority of the population acquiesced to Soviet rule. Essentially, their acquiescence was nothing more than an instinct for survival and as such not subject to moral judgment. Estonians, however, resolved to pronounce that judgment at the first opportunity. They felt that they had to, because the twenty-two years of independence were at stake, because the national idea ought to be reinstated in all its past glory. What followed was a mockery of justice, but nobody seemed to care. The state of confusion assumed countrywide proportions.

The Estonian State, or at least the idea thereof, ought to be restored. The question was, however, what exactly had to be rebuilt? The Silent Era of the late 1930s had lost its appeal. President Päts and his entourage were discredited (popular opinion reports barely mentioned the names of the late Estonian statesmen). The former head of the State borrowed some of his authoritarian methods from the Estonian radical right. Those, however, as the Security Police reported, no longer commanded the support of the population. The shaky democracy of the 1920s was discarded as nonsense. But what other defining periods or moments in Estonian history could then be elevated to the status of a model? Nothing can be more consoling in a defeat than the memories of great victories. Humiliated and denigrated, Estonians looked back at times when they came together to repel an enemy. Owing to circumstances, Germany and the Germans came to be seen as saviors. The Communists—they were the incarnation of evil! The Estonians hardened as a nation while fighting back the Communists in the early 1920s. To wash off the shame of defeat and to ascertain one's existence, one thus decided to declare an all-out war against Communism. Complicity in murder was the most effective clearance method. Given that, conviction must have played the least significant role in the large-scale campaign against Communists, real or imaginary.

COLLABORATION AS A BROADER PHENOMENON

That discussion leads to my second point, namely, how collaboration in the Nazi murder of Jews fits within the broader phenomenon of collaboration. The destruction of the Jews, as we now know, marked the first stage in the Nazi plans of racial restructuring of Eastern Europe.[32] By radically changing the demographic map of the continent, Nazi racial experts wanted to fix structural problems of Europe once and for all.[33] In the wake of the German colonization of the Baltic States, Nazi racial ideology identified Jews as the first ethnic group to be cleansed.[34] By the same token, partaking in the murder of Jews was one of many different forms of collaboration with Nazi Germany, and probably not even the most central one. The fact that some Lithuanians, Latvians, and Estonians participated in atrocities against Jews had little bearing on how the Nazis regarded the three Baltic peoples. Otherwise they would have probably chosen Lithuanians over Estonians.

The Nazis observed Lithuanians molesting Jews at Lietūkis garage in Kaunas, torturing them at Rainiai, and killing them en masse in Belorussia and Ukraine. Fewer than 5 percent of Lithuanian Jews survived the war—the lowest percentage anywhere in Europe. What could be more satisfying a sight for the Nazis than that? In reality, however, the German authorities were consistently dismissive of Lithuanians, complaining about their low racial value, limited contribution to the war effort, and political unrest. In Estonia, persecution of Jews was confined to investigation cells of the police prefectures. No pogroms, no beatings, no humiliation, just the dead letter of the case files. But the Nazis were pleased nonetheless. So what exactly did Estonians do (or not do, or do differently from others) to earn the appreciation of the new rulers?

The first question one needs to ask is: collaboration with whom, or alternatively, opposition against whom? In both cases, the answer was Nazi Germany. It was the Germans who kept the record of their failures and achievements vis-à-vis the conquered populations. In the case of Estonia, Nazi bookkeepers were unanimous in their opinion: it had one of the highest levels of collaboration—even by West European standards—and one of the lowest levels of resistance. The closest parallel can be drawn with the puppet state of Slovakia, a country that was mentioned in contemporaneous documents more often than others. Estonians might have believed that the Estonian Security Police and the Estonian SS Division were contributing to their country's independence and that a few Estonian intellectuals who rallied around anti-German slogans could change the balance of power, the belief the occupation authorities nurtured. So little were the Germans troubled by the voice of dissent that, according to Hjalmar Mäe, anyone who entered a café in Nazi-occupied Estonia would have found the same heated discussions as those before 1940, as if there was no war at all. Talking to a journalist in 1958, the head of the former Self-Government argued that freedom of speech in Estonia was not violated at all. In that sense, Estonia enjoyed special treatment; Mäe invited his interlocutor to show him any other country in occupied Europe where this would have been possible.[35] Estonia was probably the only country in Nazi-occupied Europe without an organized armed resistance. Insignificant in numbers and divided, the political opposition was incapable of generating mass support. The true believers would be seriously disappointed if they got a chance to peruse Nazi wartime records, which tell us that the German authorities were by and large satisfied with the Estonians' overall performance throughout the period of occupation.

In many respects the Estonian case was different from those of the rest of occupied Eastern Europe. Throughout the 1930s, and particularly after 1935, Estonia maintained close relations with Nazi Germany. What first began as economic cooperation quickly turned into the coordination of Estonia's defense and foreign policy with that of the Third Reich. The Nazis designated Estonians as a better human stock than many, if not all, "Eastern" peoples. Estonians were said to be emotionally more mature, racially better developed, and politically more in tune with the Nazi anti-Communist ideology than were Latvians or Lithuanians. The northernmost of the three Baltic countries, Estonia was the last to be occupied. This delay gave the Germans time to reconsider some of their policies that had backfired in Latvia and Lithuania. Coincidentally or not, the highest German authorities in Estonia managed the art of politics much better than most of their colleagues in occupied Eastern Europe. Karl Litzmann, Martin Sandberger, and Franz von Roques, who were in charge of the civil administration, the security police, and the military respectively, established trusting relationships with their Estonian counterparts. Furthermore, they worked in close cooperation with each other, thus avoiding the exhausting interoffice strife that bedeviled occupation administration elsewhere. As a result, Estonians enjoyed broader autonomy than did Latvians and Lithuanians. Estonia was spared the reprisals that the Nazis occasionally carried out in Latvia and Lithuania.

The Estonian puppet government enjoyed much less support from the population than did the police or the OK. Individuals such as Hjalmar Mäe and Oskar Angelus failed to project a sense of continuity with Independent Estonia and therefore lacked the confidence of the people. The Estonian Security Police and the Omakaitse, on the contrary, came together spontaneously in the summer of 1941 when morale was at its highest. Many in the police and OK claimed membership in various interwar organizations, which attested to their legitimacy. It was not the civil administration but the OK that the Estonians used as a platform for the realization of their political ideas.[36] The first leader of the OK, Friedrich Kurg, expressed the sentiment that many in Estonia shared: by joining the battle against Communism, Estonian partisans attempted to wipe away the shame and humiliation caused by the Soviet takeover of 1940.[37]

At first glance, the principle of reciprocity does not seem to work: Estonians contributed to the "Final Solution of the Jewish Question," fought against the Red Army, and, not least important, made no efforts to rise against the German rule.

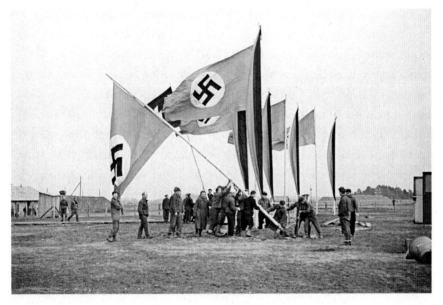

31. Estonian deserters from the Red Army in the Viljandi POW camp, March 28, 1943; HI, Hintzer, 153313.

In short, they did all of these without receiving anything in return. That is what made Ezergailis propose his thesis of collaboration, which he claims was offered by the Latvians but rejected by the Germans. In fact, the Estonians, and to a lesser degree the Latvians, gained more than they bargained for. The biggest gain was emotional and as such can be neither measured nor displayed. The Nazis restored the Estonians' sense of national pride: they gave new meaning to the notions of culture, ethnic identity, and the struggle for survival. In short, the Nazis pushed all the right buttons to ignite Estonian nationalism, which the Soviets had unsuccessfully tried to extinguish. Let me illustrate with one example. Following the success of the spring 1942 exhibition called "Europe's Vital Struggle in the East," the Nazis gave the go-ahead to another exhibit: "The Vital Struggle of the Estonian People." Permission was granted on the grounds that Estonian national sentiment had grown considerably. In any other country in occupied Eastern Europe, such an acknowledgment would have inevitably brought about repression, but not in Estonia. Despite numerous problems that local Nazi officials found with the exhibit, it opened in 1943.[38]

32. Mere, Mäe, Sandberger, and Litzmann review ethnic Estonian soldiers who deserted the Red Army at Nevel in 1943. Following the review, the soldiers were released from the camp; HI, Hintzer, 153323.

The Nazis enabled Estonians to speak about their nation and culture in superlatives. While omitting all references to the long-term program of Germanization, the Nazis hinted that Estonians and Latvians would be rewarded with high-status positions in the East and that their countries would expand at the expense of Russia. But the promise of autonomy trumped it all. Having experienced independence for the first time in their history, the Estonians wanted above all to restore their country's sovereignty. To do so, they were willing to sacrifice not only their own lives but also the lives of others. The Estonians anticipated better treatment than that accorded to Latvians and Lithuanians, and therefore took great trouble to prove their goodwill.[39] The Estonians literally competed with the Latvians and Lithuanians in trying to collect more scrap metal, more felt boots, more of everything for the Wehrmacht troops. There was essentially no cooperation between the Estonian and Latvian civil authorities, mainly because the Estonian side did not want to compromise their privileged position vis-à-vis the Germans.[40] However contradictory it may appear, the Estonians continued supporting the German occupier even after their hopes of gaining autonomy were dashed. They did so for the following three reasons: fear of

Russian Communism, distrust of the Western powers, and the lasting belief that the offer of collaboration would produce fruit in the form of autonomy, even if in the distant future. Many in Estonia internalized the idea that it was the Nazis who could bring back the Estonian State. Estonians sought to use the Nazis as a tool, but instead became one. And dire consequences resulted.

Taking pride in their high culture, the Estonians wanted to be treated as equals to Germans. Thus the occupation authorities were constantly reminded that Estonians stood on the same level with the Germans. In one particular respect, the Estonians took more credit than did their German peers: Estonia supposedly rendered Europe an unredeemable service by having halted the Communist tide in 1918 and 1919. In private, Estonians emphasized that they "also had something to contribute."[41] They strove for recognition, and recognition they received (partly because it was a favorite line of Nazi propaganda). This is why the Estonian Security Police attributed to Jews the crimes that they allegedly committed against the Estonian and German peoples, as if Estonian policemen and members of the OK were auditioning for the role of a savior of pan-European proportions. The first editorial in the first issue of the first Estonian newspaper published after the retreat of the Red Army in the summer of 1941 was entitled "Estonia Is Back in Europe." Thus August Oinas wrote in *Postimees* on July 13, 1941,

> The past experiences attest deep conviction that Estonia is in Europe. With our lifestyle and culture, our spiritual and material civilization, our concept of human rights and values, our idea of law and order, we belong to and will always be part of the family of European nations. Those who want to inculcate into us Asiatic customs and habits will fail.[42]

Contrary to what some authors have argued, it was not the paradigmatic opportunist Hjalmar Mäe who "tried to instill in Estonians the ideology of the European mission of Nazism."[43] Rather, Mäe expressed the sentiment shared by many Estonians.

The Estonians, as a collective, were fooled. Yet the delusion was equally theirs. By evaluating the Nazis and Nazism from a narrow nationalistic perspective, the Estonians could never see the forest for the trees. They perceived Hitler as Kaiser Wilhelm and the German Security Police as the *Reichswehr,* only better, because the Nazis scolded the Baltic Germans—the traditional adversary of the Estonians and Latvians. As for the Germans, by acknowledging the Estonian nation, its past achievements and its present contribution to the war effort, they strove to achieve just one objective: to prepare the grounds for subsequent Germanization.[44] As Saulius Sužiedėlis once wrote, "befriending one devil to fight another is one thing; to be seduced into seeing the world through the devil's eyes, another."[45] Indeed, Estonians' worldview, which they considered to be uniquely theirs, originated with the power they had accepted as the lesser of two evils. The Nazi policy of mass murder remained an abstract matter for the great majority of Estonians. This is probably why, once the Estonian Jews were all gone, the "Jewish Question" instantly disappeared from public discourse. Not once after the fall of 1941 did police reports on the population's mood mention Jews.

MURDER IN THE NAME OF . . . INDEPENDENCE

Those Estonians who took part in the persecution of Jews were motivated by a set of confusing, potentially flammable ideas. They came to embrace the Nazi slogans that promised Estonia a position in Hitler's New Europe equal to that of other countries. At no point in time, neither before nor during the war, did Estonians subscribe to Nazi racial ideology. Whatever Estonians said or did, their terminal goal was to rehabilitate the Estonian State, which had collapsed like a house of cards in 1940. The perception was that in order to be successful at fighting Russian Communism, which robbed Estonia of its independence, one ought to demonstrate the superiority of Estonian culture over that of the "Asiatics."

Estonians sought to demonstrate to the new rulers that they were different, that they had higher standards than their Communist oppressors or even their Baltic neighbors, and therefore should be treated as equals by the Nazis. One way of doing so was by substituting for lynch justice a form of justice that could be accepted by the majority of the population as legitimate. Thus the Estonian Security Police was given the right to investigate cases on an individual basis. Police investigation files had all the elements of a legal inquiry, purporting impartiality and due process. Mobile killing squads like those composed of ethnic Latvians and Lithuanians did not exist in Estonia. The Omakaitse carried out executions of individuals condemned to death by pseudo-courts (or rather by three-man tribunals). In the wake of the Soviet mass deportation, the quest for justice in Estonia was genuine, but the execution thereof fundamentally iniquitous. The

Estonian Security Police borrowed its methods from the Soviet NKVD. A certain percentage of the police and the OK rank and file had previously collaborated with Soviet authorities. And what could be a better way of proving one's dedication to the nationalist cause than by punishing its enemies, real or imaginary? And so Jewish citizens of Estonia were arrested as "Jews" but condemned to death as "Communists" or at the very least as "individuals subversive to the current regime." The Jewish victims' profile—over half of whom were women, children, and the elderly—alone demonstrates the absurdity of those allegations.

The Estonian case makes us rethink one of the major concepts in the study of genocide: dehumanization. Killing a fellow human almost always causes psychological trauma. To ease one's conscience, a killer-to-be needs to find a justification. By presenting the victim as intrinsically substandard, subhuman, actually vermin, the executioner kills him or her not once but twice. This way of rationalizing crime was rare in Estonia. On the contrary, Estonian policemen elevated their victims to a higher status, attributed superhuman qualities to them. Thus, before fourteen-year-old Ruth Rubin and eighty-four-year-old Ida Bruck were murdered, they were turned into "Communists," at least on paper. As Kurt Pannicke, the notorious German commandant of the Narva camp, once put it, "I fought a duel with Jews." That is, a duel: members of the Estonian Security Police were engaged in a life and death fight with the powerful enemy, not with some kind of scum! From the perspective of perpetrators, making helpless victims look menacing worked much better than depreciating them. It could potentially increase the murderer's sense of self-worth, make the deed more meaningful to the larger society, and render a service to the country: He was not any longer squishing a meaningless bug but slaying a mighty dragon (that just happened to be Jews).

The postwar German judiciary identified SS officers who had run amok in Jewish forced labor camps in Estonia as sadists, individuals acting on base motives. Thus a jury court in Ulm explained the brutality of Helmut Schnabel through his immense empowerment. A regional court in Stade, some ten years later, charged Erich Scharfetter with first-degree murder. Scharfetter was alleged in twenty-eight cases to have killed human beings cruelly. He did so "out of lust for murder or for other low motives, namely racial hatred and contempt for human life."[46]

Can it also be true of the Estonians? Did members of the Estonian Security Police and Omakaitse kill out of sadistic lust; did they take joy in human suffering, Jewish suffering? Rather not. In spite of the factor of negative selection, sadists they were not. One only needs to look at police investigation files to reach that conclusion. One thing that was notoriously missing in the police records was emotion. What comes most powerfully fore in the individual case files is political determination to see Jews responsible for the crimes committed by Communists.

Remember the Jewish girl Beile Ratut and her story that I described in chapter 6? Neither Oskar Angelus, nor Otto Leesement, nor any other leader of the Estonian Self-Government for that matter, wanted her dead. They just "worked on her case," shoveled it around, looked for better options. By so doing they proceeded as good bureaucrats, perfect collaborators—without much fuss yet efficiently. They had nothing against Ratut as an individual, a Jew, or a mentally ill person. Indeed, they did not care. It is just that at this particular hour, under these specific circumstances, for their superiors and for them personally, it was better if Beile Ratut were no longer around, locked up, or simply disappeared. The Estonians as a whole developed similar reasoning. They, too, did not have anything against Jews per se. Nevertheless, for their emotional well-being, for the sake of Estonian-German relations, for the good of the state that would be, it was better if Jews were no more.

The case study of Estonia further reinforces the thesis that Raul Hilberg put forward forty years ago: driven by an ideology, the decision-making process that led to the "Final Solution of the Jewish Question" developed only gradually. As regards the question of local collaboration, the driving force behind the persecution of the Jews in Estonia was an ideology of organic nationalism, of which anti-Semitism was just one component.[47] Conversely, the absence of violent anti-Semitism does not mean that ideology played no role at all in the mass murder—a mistake that some scholars have committed in the rush to defy Johan Goldhagen's misconceived thesis. Otherwise, the negation of an ideological explanation may easily slip into confusion between cause and effect. For example: Andres Kasekamp rejects the notion of Estonians as eager collaborators, which he said is derived from the fact that the Estonians had their own Waffen-SS division and that Estonia was the first country that Nazis declared free of Jews.[48] Actually, Estonians were granted substantial autonomy with regard to legal and military affairs because they *were* eager collaborators. The scope of autonomy was measured by the extent of services expected or already rendered—the principle *do ut des* in its purest form. In the Baltics, the Estonian Self-Government and the Estonian Security Police had much more leeway than their counterparts in Latvia and Lithuania. In effect, Estonians made perfect collaborators without holding any share in Nazi ideology.

The Estonian case demonstrates once again that there is no such thing as "good" or "bad" nationalism. Under extreme conditions, even moderate members of a community may resort to violence, or at least condone it. Nationalism by default contains unanticipated destructive power. Sometimes we do not even notice how we almost come to accept certain stereotypes, for example one that juxtaposes the savage, atavistic nationalism of the Ukrainians with the intellectual, "civilized" nationalism of the Estonians.[49] It is like arguing which means of execution is more "humane": the guillotine or the electric chair. In fact, the distance between the two is not that significant. Indeed, it is nonexistent: both are instruments of death. To explain complex issues, tautology at times suits better than definite theory: an ideology disguised as nonideology nevertheless remains one. What can be nobler than love toward one's country? Even more dignified is the thrust to defend one's country against brutal aggression. And that is what Estonians, Latvians, and Lithuanians did during World War II. Unfortunately, they did not realize that to overpower one dictatorship, they allied with another, and that while doing so they used the means of that other regime they had condemned.

However hard I have tried to avoid clichés, local collaboration in the Nazi murder of Jews in the Baltic States was a litmus test for a nation-state, a test that it failed. The participation of certain segments of the Estonian, Latvian, and Lithuanian populations in mass murder demonstrates most clearly the bankruptcy of nationalism in any form. Nationalism can be dormant for years, until a sudden change in structure generates a killer wave, as the tectonic plates, when shifted, cause a typhoon that destroys everything and everybody on its way, except that nationalism has nothing "natural" about it. This superstructure and what is beneath it is all man-made.

We can call it opportunism, though the term "political promiscuity" may better describe the psychological condition with which the majority of Estonians had lived since at least 1934. First Estonians almost gave themselves up to semi-Fascist rule, then acquiesced to an authoritarian regime, after that surrendered to a Communist dictatorship, and finally joined forces with Nazi tyranny. But it was more than just opportunism, because the idea of a national state had never died. Whatever Estonians had done, they did in the name of a greater-than-life ideal. Individual human life was too abstract an entity to make it into the shrine of national independence. When it came, in the summer and fall of 1941, to dealing with Jewish men, women, and children, one emotion was conspicuously missing, namely humanity. It was not the Soviets or the Nazis who robbed Estonians of that feature. Humanity simply was not in school textbooks, in university lectures, or in politicians' speeches. What was there, however, were the war of national liberation, suppression of the Communist putsch, and other sacrifices that the Estonian people had made in order to attain and preserve national independence.

APPENDIXES

NOTES

BIBLIOGRAPHY

INDEX

APPENDIX A
NUMERICAL STRENGTH OF ESTONIAN
SECURITY POLICE (SEPTEMBER 1942)

Central apparatus	208
Haapsalu	60
Kuressaare	75
Narva	144
Pärnu	93
Pechory	58
Rakvere	63
Tallinn-Harju	218
Tartu	184
Valga	48
Viljandi	61
Võru	49
Gatchina	155
Gdov	38
Kingisepp	58
Luga	73
Oranienbaum	38
Petergof	38
Porkhov	38
Pskov	215
Volosovo	38
Total:	1,952

Note: One-third of the rank and file deployed in Russia proper.

Source: Annual report of German Sipo in Estonia, 1941–42, ERA, 819/2/2.

APPENDIX B
DEATH TOLL IN NAZI-OCCUPIED ESTONIA, 1941–1944

Soviet POWs	15,000
Jews	8,614
Lithuanian (mainly) and Latvian Jews	5,572
Estonian Jews	963
Czech Jews	954
German Jews	917
French Jews	185
Russian Jews (POWs)	16
Finnish Jews	7
Ethnic Estonians	5,412
Ethnic Russians	1,185
Gypsies	800
Ethnic Latvians	17
Total:	31,028

Sources: Hiio, Maripuu, and Paavle, eds., *Estonia, 1940–1945,* 758; Paavle, *Eesti rahvastikukaotused,* 38, 43; numbers of Jewish and Gypsy victims are calculated on the basis of current research.

APPENDIX C
GERMAN PLACE NAMES AND THEIR EQUIVALENTS IN LOCAL LANGUAGES

Aegwid	Aegviidu
Aya	Ahja
Ahtme	Ahtme
Alexoten	Aleksotas
Ancupani	Ančupāni
Annia	Anja
Antoniusberg	Tõnismäe
Audrini	Audriņi
Hasenpoth	Aizpute
Ackmen	Akmene
Anzen	Antsla
Arensburg	Kuressaare
Asites	Asīte
Auwere	Auvere
Baltischport	Paldiski
Bauske	Bauska
Barsuki	Barsuki
Bickern	Biķernieki
Bistritz	Beszterce (Bistriţa)
Breslau	Wrocław
Bromberg	Bydgoszcz
Cherson	Kherson
Dagö	Hiiumaa
Danzig	Gdańsk

Dorpat	Tartu
Dünaburg	Daugavpils
Durben	Durbe
Elwa	Elva
Embach	Emajõgi
Ereda	Ereda
Fellin	Viljandi
Frauenburg	Saldus
Friedrichstadt	Jaunjelgava
Garsden	Gargždai
Gdow	Gdov
Goldfields	Kohtla
Gostyzi	Gostitsy
Gotenhafen	Gdynia
Gorodenka	Gorodenka
Grobin	Grobiņa
Gross-St. Johannes	Suure-Jaani
Gudmannsbach	Häädemeeste
Hanko	Hanko
Hapsal	Haapsalu
Hark	Harku
Harrien	Harju
Helsingfors	Helsinki
Hungerburg	Narva-Jõesuu
Illingen	Misso
Iwangorod	Ivangorod
Jaggowal	Jagala
Jakobstadt	Jēkabpils
Jamburg	Kingisepp
Jedelecht	Jõelähtme
Jerwakant	Järvakandi
Jerwen	Järva
Jewe	Jõhvi
Kabbal	Kabala
Kabberla	Kaberla
Kabbernömme	Kaberneeme
Kaiserwald	Mežaparks

Kabja	Kabja
Kalewi-Liiva	Kalevi-Liiva
Kapstfer	Torma
Kaschau	Kassa (Košice)
Katharinental	Kadriorg
Kauen	Kaunas (Kovno)
Käwa	Käva
Kegel	Keila
Kerstowa	Kerstovo
Kiviöli	Kiviõli
Klein-St. Marien	Väike-Maarja
Klooga	Klooga
Königsberg	Kaliningrad
Kostifer	Kostivere
Krasnogor	Kallaste
Krasnogwardeisk	Gatchina
Krottingen	Kretinga
Kuckers	Kukruse
Kudupe	Küdupe
Kurland	Courland
Kütte-Jöud	Kütte-Jõu
Laisholm	Jõgeva
Laksberg	Lasnamäe
Laakt	Lagedi
Laibach	Ljubljana
Laitz	Laitse
Laswa	Lasva
Lettgallen	Latgale
Libau	Liepāja
Loknja	Loknia
Ludse	Ludza
Marienburg	Malbork
Memel	Klaipėda
Männik	Männiku
Merreküll	Mereküla
Mitau	Jelgava
Mogilew	Mogilev

Moiseküll	Mõisaküla
Mon plaisir	Mummassaare
Murro	Murru
Narwa	Narva
Nasswa	Nasva
Naugard	Novgorod
Neuhausen	Vastseliina
Neu-Isenhof	Püssi
Nömme	Nõmme
Oberpahlen	Põltsamaa
Odenpäh	Otepää
Ore	Hiiu
Ösel	Saaremaa
Pankewitza	Panikovichi (Pankjavitsa)
Ponewesch	Panevéžys
Pernau	Pärnu
Peterhof	Petergof
Petschur	Pechory (Petseri)
Pilsen	Plzeń
Pleskau	Pskov
Polangen	Palanga
Pöllküll	Põlluküla
Ponary	Paneriai
Port-Kunda	Kunda
Posen	Poznań
Pravenischkis	Praveniškės
Prekuln	Priekule
Puschkin	Pushkin
Putki	Putke
Rasik	Raasiku
Rauna	Rauna
Reval	Tallinn
Rositten	Rēzekne
Robin	Grobina
Rujen	Rūjiena
Rumbuli	Rumbula
Ruthern	Dunte

Sackhof (Sakka)	Saka
Salismünde	Salacgrīva
Schaulen	Šiauliai
Sillamägi	Sillamäe
Schkeden	Šķēde
Slanzy	Slantsy
Soski	Soska
Stettin	Szczecin
Stutthof	Sztutowo
Taps	Tapa
Tarwast	Mustla
Tauroggen	Tauragė
Theresienstadt	Terezin
Tilsit	Sovetsk
Torgel	Tori
Törwa	Tõrva
Tschorna	Mustvee
Turgel	Türi
Ukmergi	Ukmergė
Ulenurme	Ülenurme
Ussaditsche	Usadishche
Waiwara	Vaivara
Walk	Valga (Valka)
Warschau	Warsaw
Wilo	Vilo
Weissenstein	Paide
Welikije Luki	Velikie Luki
Wenden	Cēsis
Werro	Võru
Wesenberg	Rakvere
Weimarn	Veimarn
Wiek	Läänemaa
Wierland	Virumaa
Wilna	Vilnius (Vilna)
Witebsk	Vitebsk
Wiwikond	Viivikonna
Wolmar	Valmiera

Wehma	Võhma
Worms	Vormsi
Zagorje	Zagorie
Zintenhof	Sindi

NOTES

AA	Auswärtiges Amt (German Foreign Office)
AEL	Arbeits- und Erziehungslager (labor education camp)
AK	Armeekorps (army corps)
AOK	Armeeoberkommando (army headquarters)
BAB	Bundesarchiv-Berlin (German Federal Archives, Berlin)
BAK	Bundesarchiv-Koblenz (German Federal Archives, Koblenz)
BAL	Bundesarchiv-Ludwigsburg (German Federal Archives, Ludwigsburg)
BA-MA	Bundesarchiv-Militärarchiv (German Federal Archives-Military Archives, Freiburg)
BDC	Berlin Documentation Center
BdrückwHGr	Befehlshaber des rückwärtigen Heeresgebietes (Commander of the Army Group Rear Areas)
BdS	Befehlshaber der Sicherheitspolizei und des SD (Commander in Chief of the Security Police and SD)
EAA	Eesti Ajalooarhiiv (Estonian Historical Archives, Tartu)
EAM	Eesti Ajaloomuuseum (Estonian History Museum, Tallinn)
EEC	Estonian SSR Extraordinary Commission for the Investigation of the Crimes Committed by German Fascists and their Collaborators on the Territory of Estonia
EM	Ereignismeldungen UdSSR (situational reports of the Sipo)
ERA	Eesti Riigiarhiiv (Estonian State Archives, Tallinn)
ERAF	Eesti Riigiarhiivi Filiaal (Estonian State Branch Archives, Tallinn)
ERR	Einsatzstab Reichsleiter Rosenberg (Operations Staff Rosenberg)
Est.	Estonian
EWZ	Einwandererzentralstelle (Central Immigration Office)
GBA	Generalbevollmächtiger für den Arbeitseinsatz (General Plenipotentiary for Labor Allocation)
Ger.	German
HGr	Heeresgruppe (army group)
IfZ	Institut für Zeitgeschichte (Institute of Contemporary History, Munich)

KL	Kaitseliit (Estonian Home Guard)
Kripo	Kriminalpolizei (criminal police)
KTB	*Kriegstagebuch* (war diary)
LCVA	Lietuvos centrinis valstybės archivas (Lithuanian Central State Archives, Vilnius)
LVVA	Latvijas Valsts vēstures arhīvs (Latvian State Historical Archives, Riga)
MbO	*Meldungen aus den besetzten Ostgebieten* (Reports from the Occupied Eastern Territories)
NARA	U.S. National Archives and Records Administration, Washington, D.C.
OK	Omakaitse (Estonian Auxiliary Police) (Self-Defense)
OKH	Oberkommando des Heeres (Army High Command)
OKM	Oberkommando der Kriegsmarine (Navy High Command)
OKW	Oberkommando der Wehrmacht (Armed Forces High Command)
O-VUROrg.	Ordnungspolizei-Verwaltung und Recht Organisation (Order Police Administration and Law Organization)
Pref.	Prefecture
RKFDV	Reichskommission für die Festigung des deutschen Volkstums (Reich Commission for the Strengthening of Germandom)
RSHA	Reichssicherheitshauptamt (Reich Security Main Office)
Sipo	Sicherheitspolizei (Security Police)
Tät.Ber.	*Tätigkeits- und Lagebericht des Chefs der Sipo und des SD* (activity report of the Commander of the Sipo)
TK	Teilkommando (partial detachment of SK)
USHMM	United States Holocaust Memorial Museum, Washington, D.C.
WiKo	Wirtschaftskommando (subunit of WiIn)
WiRü Amt	Wehrwirtschafts-Rüstungsamt des OKW (Economic and Armament Office of OKW)
WiStab Ost	*Wirtschaftsstab Ost* (Economic Staff East)
YIVO	YIVO Institute of Jewish History, New York City
YVA	Yad Vashem Archives, Jerusalem

1. ESTONIANS AND THEIR STATE

1. Jacob Robinson et al., *Were the Minorities Treaties a Failure?* (New York: Institute of Jewish Affairs, 1943), 165–67, 202–3. Finland was at once admitted to the League of Nations as a country that had met its obligations toward minorities.

2. Vahur Made, *Eesti ja Rahvaste Liit* (Estonia and the League of Nations) (Tartu: Tartu University Press, 1999), 110–14, 118–19; Rita Putins Peters, "Baltic State Diplomacy and the League of Nations Minorities System," in *The Baltic in International Relations Between the Two World Wars,* ed. John Hiden and Aleksander Loit (Stockholm: Studia Universitatis Stockholmiensis, 1988), 284–91.

3. Tiit Rosenberg, "Eesti 1919. aasta Maareform: Võrdlusjooni ida- ja kesk-Euroopa maadega" (The 1919 Land Reform in Estonia: A Comparative Study of East Central European Countries), in *Kaks algust: Eesti Vabariig—1920. ja 1990. aastad,* ed. Jüri Ant (Tallinn: Eesti Riigiarhiiv, 1998), 74, 77.

4. Michael Garleff, *Deutschbaltische Politik zwischen den Weltkriegen: Die parlamentarische Tätigkeit der deutschbaltischen Partein in Lettland und Estland* (Bad Godesberg: Verlag wissen-schaftliches Archiv Bonn, 1976), 16-18, 79.

5. Kopl Jokton, *Juutide ajaloost Eestis* (On the History of Jews in Estonia) (Tartu, 1992 [1926]), 4-9; Abe Liebmann, *Ajaloolised ja kultuurilised eeldused juudi koguduste tekkimiseks ja arenemiseks Eestis* (Historical and Cultural Preconditions for Establishment and Development of Jewish Com-munities in Estonia) (M.A. thesis, Tartu Univ., 1937), 25-27, 33, 35, 45, 60, 95-96.

6. Jokton, *Juutide ajaloost Eestis,* 12, 22; Elhonen Saks, *Kes on Juudid ja mis on holokaust?* (Who Are the Jews and What Is the Holocaust?) (Tallinn: Sild, 2003), 133.

7. *Evreiskaia Molodaia Mysl* (Reval), Apr. 1 and June 28, 1919.

8. Kari Alenius, "Under the Conflicting Pressures of the Ideals of the Era and the Burden of His-tory: Ethnic Relations in Estonia, 1918-1925," *Journal of Baltic Studies* 35, no. 1 (Spring 2004): 38.

9. Garleff, *Deutschbaltische Politik,* 158.

10. Jokton, *Juutide ajaloost Eestis,* 35-36, 39.

11. U.S. Legation in Estonia, "Survey of Conditions in Esthonia for the Month of February, 1925," Mar. 10, 1925; ibid. "for the Month of September 1925," Oct. 19, 1925, NARA, M-1170/2. The *h* in the word "Esthonia" was dropped upon a recommendation of the British Royal Geographical Society after September 1925.

12. Eugen Maddison, *Die nationalen Minderheiten Estlands und ihre Rechte* (Tallinn, 1930), 30-33; Ewald Ammende, *Die Nationalitäten in den Staaten Europas* (Vienna: Wilhelm Braumüller, 1931), 22.

13. For a different interpretation, see Kari Alenius, "The Birth of Cultural Autonomy in Esto-nia: How, Why, and for Whom?" *Journal of Baltic Studies* 38, no. 4 (Fall 2007): 445-62.

14. Werner Hasselblatt, "Hat sich die Kulturautonomie in Estland gewährt?" *Nation und Staat* 4 (1930-31): 443.

15. Helker Pflug, "Aspekte jüdischen Lebens in Estland bis 1940," in *Die vergessenen Juden in den baltischen Staaten* (Cologne: Verlag Wissenschaft und Politik, 1998), 54-55; Eugenia Gurin-Loov and Gennadi Gramberg, *Eesti Juudi Kogukond/The Jewish Community of Estonia* (Tallinn, 2001), 11.

16. For more details see Anton Weiss-Wendt, "Thanks to the Germans! Jewish Cultural Auton-omy in Interwar Estonia," *East-European Jewish Affairs* 38, no. 1 (Apr. 2008): 89-104.

17. AJDC (American Joint Distribution Committee), "Esthonia: Narva," no date [1926], YIVO, RG-335.2, box 1, folder 8.

18. American Jewish Committee, "Jews of Estonia," in *The Jewish Communities of Nazi-Occu-pied Europe* (New York: Howard Fertig, 1982 [1944]), 4-5.

19. Pflug, "Aspekte jüdischen Lebens," 55-56. At the same time, Jews spent more money on education per capita than any other ethnic group in the country.

20. American Jewish Committee, *The Jewish Communities,* 3.

21. Toomas Hiio, "Jewish Students and Jewish Student Organizations at the University of Tartu," *Tartu University Museum: Annual Report 1998* (Tartu: Tartu Univ. Museum, 1999), 151–72.

22. Ezra Mendelsohn, *The Jews of East Central Europe Between the World Wars* (Bloomington: Indiana Univ. Press, 1983), 227–33, 247–50.

23. Anton Weiss-Wendt, "The Soviet Occupation of Estonia in 1940–41 and the Jews," *Holocaust and Genocide Studies* 12, no. 2 (Fall 1998): 309.

24. Toomas Paul, "Eestlaste ja juutide suhetest" (On Estonian-Jewish Relations), *Looming,* no. 2 (1997): 244.

25. Paul Ariste, "Juut eesti rahvausus" (A Jew in Estonian Folklore), *Eesti Kirjandus,* nos. 1, 3, 4 (Jan., Mar., Apr. 1932): 1–11, 16, 132, 147–49, 226–28. Ariste's analysis is based on folkloristic material collected between 1880 and 1930.

26. *Põhja Kodu* (Narva), May 13, 1930.

27. "Estland: Einreise der Juden verboten," *Mitteilungen über die Judenfrage* 2, no. 26/27 (Sept. 1, 1938): 10.

28. German Consulate in Tallinn, Navy Attaché to Navy High Command, Dec. 14, 1938, BA-MA, RM 12 II/15.

29. *Päevaleht,* July 20, 1938.

30. *Uus-Eesti,* Aug. 24, 1938, quoted in Hannu Rautkallio, *Finland and the Holocaust: The Rescue of Finland's Jews* (New York: Holocaust Library, 1987), 54.

31. Alenius, "Under the Conflicting Pressures," 43, 44; Jokton, *Juutide ajaloost Eestis,* 41.

32. Saks, *Kes on Juudid,* 144–45.

33. Ibid., 145, 146.

34. *Rahvaleht,* Nov. 16, 1938.

35. German Consulate in Tallinn, Nov. 23, 1938, NARA, T-120/1005.

36. Toivo Raun, "Nineteenth- and Early Twentieth-Century Estonian Nationalism Revisited," *Nations and Nationalism* 9, no. 1 (2003): 142.

37. *Uus Eesti,* Jan. 11, 1936.

38. Jokton, *Juudi ajaloost Eestis,* 36; Leonid Lentsman, ed. *Estonskii Narod v Velikoi Otechestvennoi voine Sovetskogo Soiuza, 1941–1945* (Tallinn: Eesti Raamat, 1973), 1:452.

39. Andres Kasekamp, *The Radical Right in Interwar Estonia* (New York: St. Martin's Press, 2000), 73–77, 146–47.

40. Peter-Heinz Seraphim, *Das Judentum im osteuropäischen Raum* (Essen: Essener Verlagsanstalt, 1938).

41. K. W. Schade, "A Peasant Nation on Defense: Every Latvian Sets the Limits for the Jews," *Mitteilungen über die Judenfrage* 2, no. 2 (Mar. 3, 1938): 1–2.

42. Hans Hinkel, *Judenviertel Europas: Die Juden zwischen Ostsee und Schwarzem Meer* (Berlin: Volk und Reich Verlag, 1939), 52–53.

43. ERR, political report from Tallinn, Mar. 8, 1942, BAB, NS-30/152.

44. American Jewish Committee, "Jews of Estonia," in *The Jewish Communities of Nazi-Occupied Europe* (New York: Howard Fertig, 1982 [1944]), 6.

45. Raun, "Nineteenth- and Early Twentieth-Century Estonian Nationalism Revisited," 136–39.

46. Heino Arumäe, "Eesti Vabariigi välispoliitika üldised suundumused aastail 1920–1924" (General Trends in Estonian Foreign Policy, 1920–24), in *Kaks algust: Eesti Vabariig—1920. ja 1990. aastad,* ed. Jüri Ant (Tallinn: Eesti Riigiarhiiv, 1998), 33, 36.

47. Õie Elango et al., *Eesti maast ja rahvast: Maailmasõjast maailmasõjani* (On Estonia Land and Estonian People Between the World Wars) (Tallinn: Olion, 1998), 137–40, 145, 169, 204.

48. U.S. Consul in Tallinn, "Survey of Conditions in Esthonia for the Month of August 1923," NARA, M-1170/1.

49. U.S. Consul in Charge in Reval, Mar. 2 1921, NARA, M-1170/4.

50. U.S. Legation in Riga, Dec. 3, 10, 1924; U.S. Consul in Tallinn, Dec. 17, 1924, NARA, M-1170/1. In September 1923 a Communist putsch broke out in Bulgaria; in October, Communists attempted to seize power in Saxony, Thuringia, and Hamburg. In all four instances, the uprising was swiftly crushed.

51. U.S. Consul in Tallinn, Dec. 17, 1924; U.S. Consul in Tallinn, "Survey of Conditions in Esthonia for the Month of November, 1924"; "Survey of Conditions in Esthonia for the Month of December, 1924," NARA, M-1170/1.

52. *Law on the Defense of State Order, Riigi Teataja* (Governmental Gazette) 29–30, Feb. 19, 1925.

53. U.S. Legation in Tallinn to the Secretary of State, Nov. 16, 1934, NARA, M-1170/10.

54. Elango et al., *Eesti maast ja rahvast,* 248.

55. U.S. Legation in Riga, Mar. 5, 1925, NARA, M-1170/2.

56. Elango et al., *Eesti maast ja rahvast,* 209–10, 304. Minister of the Interior Kaarel Eenpalu proclaimed martial law a "universal devise for governance" *(universaalne valitsemisvahend).*

57. Ago Pajur, *Eesti Riigikaitsepoliitika aastail 1918–1934* (Estonian Defense Policies, 1918–34) (Tartu: Estonian Historical Archives, 1999), 39, 48–49, 98–101, 111, 142–44.

58. Ibid., 159, 172–75, 180, 187, 193–96, 202, 208–9, 296–97.

59. U.S. Consul in Tallinn, "Survey of Conditions in Estonia for the Month of August 1926," Sept. 15, 1926, NARA, M-1170/2.

60. Hannes Walter, "Eesti ühiskonna hoiakutest 1920. aastate algul" (The Estonian Society's Attitudes in the Early 1920s) in *Kaks algust: Eesti Vabariik—1920. ja 1990. aastad,* ed. Jüri Ant (Tallinn: Eesti Riigiarhiiv, 1998), 11–13.

61. U.S. Legation in Estonia to the Secretary of State, Mar. 9, Mar. 20, May 28, 1935, NARA, M-1170/10.

62. German Consulate in Estonia, Sept. 9, 1936, NARA, T-120/3600.

63. U.S. Legation in Estonia, memo, Nov. 16, 1934, NARA, T-1170/10.

64. "Lage: Estland," *Nation und Staat* 8 (1934–35): 793; *Nation und Staat* 9 (1935–36): 518.

65. U.S. Legation in Estonia to the Secretary of State, Sept. 27, 1934, NARA, M-1170/10.

66. Elango et al., *Eesti maast ja rahvast,* 283–304.

67. Ernst v. Maydell, "Die estnische Nationalismus," *Nation und Staat* 9 (1935–36): 441, 442.

68. Raun, "Nineteenth- and Early Twentieth-Century Estonian Nationalism Revisited," 133–35.

69. Hans Tankler, "Die Universität *Tartu* nach dem ersten Weltkrieg," in *Die deutsche Volksgruppe in Estland während der Zwischenkriegszeit und aktuelle Fragen des deutsch-estnischen Verhältnisses,* ed. Boris Meissner, Dietrich Loeber, and Cornelius Hasselblatt (Hamburg: Bibliotheca Baltica, 1997), 119–24, 131–33.

70. Theodor Hasselblatt, "Der deutsche Anteil am estländischen Kirchenwesen in der Zwischenkriegszeit," Meissner, Loeber, and Hasselblatt, *Die deutsche Volksgruppe in Estland,* 139.

71. Karl-Heinz Grundmann, *Deutschtumspolitik zur Zeit der Weimarer Republik: Eine Studie am Beispiel der deutsch-baltischen Minderheit in Estland und Lettland* (Hannover: Harro v. Hirschheydt, 1977), 239, 240.

72. George von Rauch, *The Baltic States: The Years of Independence. Estonia, Latvia, Lithuania, 1917–1940* (Berkeley: Univ. of California Press, 1974), 125; John Hiden and Patrick Salmon, *The Baltic Nations and Europe: Estonia, Latvia, and Lithuania in the Twentieth Century* (London: Longman, 1994), 81–84.

73. Hans-Erich Volkmann, "Ökonomie und Machtpolitik Lettland und Estland im politisch-ökonomischen Kalkül des Dritten Reiches (1933–1940)," in *Geschichte und Gesellschaf* 2 (1976): 476–79, 483.

74. Uno Kaur, *Wirtschaftsstruktur und Wirtschaftspolitik des Freistaates Estland 1918–1940* (Bonn: Baltisches Forschungsinstitut, 1962), 68.

75. U.S. Legation in Stockholm, Arvo Horm, report, "The Estonian Shale Oil Industry," June 2, 1944, NARA, M-1170/23.

76. U.S. Legation in Stockholm, Arvo Horm, report, "The Estonian Shale Oil Industry," June 2, 1944, NARA, M-1170/23; Kaur, *Wirtschaftsstruktur,* 69.

77. David Crowe, "The History of the Oil Industry in Independent Estonia," *Nationalities Papers* 6, no. 1 (1978): 11.

78. Manfred Rasch, "Zur Mineralölpolitik der Kriegsmarine: Dokumente aus dem Jahre 1935," *Militärgeschichtliche Mitteilungen* 71, no. 1 (1985): 71–82.

79. Vesa Vasara, "Die deutschbaltische Minderheit in Estland in der Zwischenkriegszeit: Wirtschaft und Finanzen," *Zeitschrift für Ostmitteleuropa-Forschung* 44, no. 4 (1995): 583.

80. Rasch, "Zur Mineralölpolitik der Kriegsmarine," 83–85.

81. Volkmann, "Ökonomie und Machtpolitik," 486–91.

82. Anu Mai Köll and Jaak Valge, "Economic Nationalism and Industrial Growth: State and Industry in Estonia, 1934–39," (Stockholm: Acta Universitatis Stockholmiensis, 1998), 111.

83. Vasara, "Die deutschbaltische Minderheit," 587–88. Presence of Laidoner on the ESTAG board of directors helped to win concessions for the Estonian oil shale industry in the 1930s.

84. Hiden and Salmon, *The Baltic Nations,* 115–16.

85. Head of RSHA Heydrich to Foreign Minister v. Ribbentrop, Oct. 9, 1939 (document N106); German Consulate in Tallinn to provincial NSDAP groups in Estonia, Oct. 20, 1939 (document N110), both in Dietrich Loeber, ed., *Diktierte Option: Die Umsiedlung der Deutsch-Balten aus Estland und Lettland 1939–1941* (Neumünster: Karl Wachholtz, 1972), 129, 138.

86. OKW WiRü Office, monthly report re. mineral oil deliveries for German armament industry, Aug. 1940, BA-MA, RW19/202.

87. Rasch, "Zur Mineralölpolitik der Kriegsmarine," 83; Rasch, "Die Bedeutung des Bankhauses Mendelssohn and Co," 209-10; Volkmann, "Ökonomie und Machtpolitik," 496-500.

88. David M. Crowe, *The Baltic States and the Great Powers: Foreign Relations, 1938-1940* (Boulder, Colo.: Westview Press, 1993), 223 f.

89. German (Ger.) Consulate in Tallinn, cable, Dec. 7, 1933, NARA, T-120/3507.

90. "Die Lage: Estland," in *Nation und Staat* 8 (1934-35): 794.

91. Volkmann, "Ökonomie und Machtpolitik," 475.

92. Ger. Consulate in Tallinn, Dec. 2, 1933; Feb. 3, 1934; Dec. 6, 1934, reproduced in Jürgen von Hehn, "Zur Geschichte der deutschbaltischen nationalsozialistischen Bewegung in Estland," *Zeitschrift für Ostforschung* 26, no. 4 (1977): 620-30.

93. Magnus Ilmjärv, *Nõukogude Liidu ja Saksamaa vahel: Balti rigid ja Soome 1934-1940* (Between the Soviet Union and Germany: The Baltic States and Finland, 1934-40) (Tallinn: Estonian Academy of Science, 1993), 13-15, 28.

94. Auswärtiges Amt (AA), Reich Minister's Office, Records on Estonia, June 17, 1936, NARA, T-120/120.

95. Karlis Kangeris, "Kollaboration vor der Kollaboration? Die baltische Emigranten und ihre 'Befreiungskomitees' in Deutschland 1940/1941," in *Europa unterm Hakenkreuz: Okkupation und Kollaboration (1938-1945)*, ed. Werner Röhr (Berlin: Hüthig Verlagsgemeinschaft, 1994), 170. Colonel Saarsen accompanied Laidoner on an official visit to Moscow on December 7, 1939. At the reception in the Kremlin, Saarsen let his Soviet negotiators know that he, a humble person, felt honored sitting between two great military commanders—Klement Voroshilov and Semen Budennyi.

96. Ilmjärv, *Nõukogude Liidu ja Saksamaa vahel,* 12, 16-18, 31, 35, 40-43, 52-53, 60, 79.

97. *Deutsche Schutzbund* to AA, "The Estonians and Their Politics," Aug. 25, 1927, NARA, T-120/5768.

98. Ibid.

99. Ibid.

100. Eduard Laaman and Leonid Kahkra, *Tänapäeva Saksamaa: Peajooni rahvussotsialistliku 'Kolmanda Riigi' arengust, olustest ja sisekorrast* (Germany Today: Notes on Developments and Internal Situation in the Nazi "Third Reich") (Tartu: Eesti Kirjanduse Selts, 1938), passim.

101. Vasara, "Die deutschbaltische Minderheit," 579-81, 587.

102. Ibid., 580-82.

103. Grundmann, *Deutschtumspolitik,* 241-45, 256, 267-70.

104. Walther Darré, quoted in Wilhelm Lenz, "Erbhöfe für baltische Restgutbesitzer im Warthegau: Briefwechsel zwischen Darré und Himmler," *Jahrbuch des baltischen Deutschtums,* 1982, 124-25.

105. Niels von Redecker, "Victor von zur Mühlen und die nationalsozialistische Bewegung im estländischen Deutschtum: Eine biographische Annäherung," in *Deutschbalten, Weimarer Republik und Drittes Reich,* ed. Michael Garleff (Cologne: Böhlau Verlag, 2001), 90, 96.

106. Ger. Consulate in Tallinn, Sept. 20, 1934, NARA, T-120/4948. On the Baltic German influence within the Nazi Party, see Walter Laqueur, *Russia and Germany: A Century of Conflict* (Boston: Little Brown, 1965).

107. Valdis O. Lumans, *Himmler's Auxiliaries: The Volksdeutsche Mittelstelle and the German National Minorities of Europe, 1933–1945* (Chapel Hill: Univ. of North Carolina Press, 1993), 103–4.

108. Ger. Consulate in Tallinn, Jan. 29, 1937, in von Hehn, "Zur Geschichte," 644–45.

2. THE BREAKDOWN, 1939–1941

1. Karl Hoover, "The Baltic Resettlement of 1939 and National Socialist Racial Policy," in *Journal of Baltic Studies* 13, no. 1 (Spring 1977): 82, 88.

2. Documents N72, 73, 102 in Loeber, *Diktierte Option,* 80–82, 116–17.

3. Bernd Nielsen-Stokkeby, "Die Umsiedlung der Deutsch-balten aus estnischer Sicht," *Baltisches Jahrbuch* 6 (1989): 220–23.

4. Ilmjärv, *Nõukogude Liidu ja Saksamaa vahel,* 85.

5. Jürgen von Hehn, *Die Umsiedlung der baltischen Deutschen—das letzte Kapitel baltischdeutscher Geschichte* (Marburg: J. G. Herder-Institut, 1984), 95–100.

6. Dr. Csaki, "The Resettlement of the Balts," Nov. 27, 1939, NARA, T-81/374.

7. Hehn, *Die Umsiedlung,* 170. See also: Hoover, "The Baltic Resettlement of 1939," 87.

8. Documents N40, 43, 44, 47, 57, 61, 77, 111 in Loeber, *Diktierte Option,* 45, 47–48, 50–51, 60, 65, 86–87, 139.

9. RSHA Roem, report, Oct. 14, 1939, BAB, R-69/105.

10. Kangeris, "Kollaboration vor der Kollaboration?" 170.

11. Kõll and Valge, *Economic Nationalism,* 112.

12. *Päevaleht,* Feb. 6, 1940. Elias Brisk was among those murdered in 1941.

13. Helmuth Weiss, "Zur Umsiedlung der Deutschen aus Estland 1939–1941: Erinnerungsbericht," *Zeitschrift für Ostforschung* 39, no. 4 (1990): 486.

14. Margus Ilmjärv, "Alistumine 1939–1940" (Submission, 1939–40), paper presented at the S-Keskus Center for the Study of Modern Estonian History, Tallinn, Mar. 3, 2000, available online at <http://www.s-keskus.arhiiv.ee/next.htm> (accessed Jan. 3, 2005).

15. Ilmjärv, *Nõukogude Liidu ja Saksamaa vahel,* 81.

16. Ger. Consulate in Tallinn, Apr. 29, 1940, NARA, T-120/279.

17. Ger. Consulate in Tallinn, Oct. 17, 1939, NARA, T-120/1027.

18. Ger. Consulate in Tallinn, June 2, 1936, NARA, T-120/2797.

19. AA, Reich Minister's Office, Records on Estonia, Aug. 31, 1938; German Consulate in Tallinn, Apr. 26, 1939, NARA, T-120/120.

20. Ilmjärv, "Alistumine 1939–1940."

21. Saulius Sužiedėlis, "Foreign Saviors, Native Disciples: Perspectives on Collaboration in Lithuania, 1940–1945," in *Collaboration and Resistance During the Holocaust: Belarus, Estonia, Latvia, Lithuania,* ed. David Gaunt et al. (Bern: Peter Lang, 2004), 317.

22. Ger. Consulate in Tallinn, Feb. 15, 1940, NARA, T-120/R785.

23. Narva Omakaitse OK, overview of activities through Aug. 6 1942, including the period of Soviet occupation, ERA, R-358/1/4.

24. Viljandimaa OK, overview of activities through the end of 1941, ERA, R-358/1/12.

25. Virumaa OK, 1941, ERA, R-358/1/23.

26. Ben Cion Pinchuk, *Jews under Soviet Rule: Eastern Poland on the Eve of the Holocaust* (Oxford: Basil Blackwell, 1990), 38–39.

27. Jüri Ant, *Eesti 1939–1941: Rahvast, Valitsemisest, Saatusest* (Estonia, 1939–1941: People, Governing, Fate) (Tallinn, 1999), 169–70.

28. U.S. Legation in Helsinki, Dec. 11, 1941; U.S. Legation in Stockholm, memo, "Conditions in Estonia, December 1941," NARA, M-1170/21.

29. Karlis Kangeris, "Die nationalsozialistischen Pläne und Propagandamassnahmen im Generalbezirk Lettland 1941–1942," in Gaunt et al., *Collaboration and Resistance During the Holocaust,* 165, 184.

30. Kaupo Deemant, "Massimõrv Tallinnas 23. juunil 1941" (Mass Execution in Tallinn on 23 June 1941), *Akadeemia* 6 (2001): 1200–1211.

31. Herbert Lindmäe, *Suvesõda Tartumaal 1941* (The Summer War in Tartu Province, 1941) (Tartu, 1999), 287–94.

32. Heino Tõnismägi, *Ülekohtu toimikud* (The Files of Injustice) (Tallinn: BNS, 1998), 113–24. A total of ninety people had been executed in Kuressaare.

33. HGr North, *KTB,* July 7, 1941, BA-MA, RH 19 III/767.

34. HGr North, *KTB,* July 8–30, 1941, BA-MA, RH 19 III/767.

35. Werner Haupt, *Baltikum 1941: Die Geschichte eines ungelösten Problems* (Neckargemünd: Kurt Vowinckel Verlag, 1963), 96–120.

36. HGr North, memo, "Fight Against the Russian Navy in the Gulf of Finland," Aug. 5, 1941, BA-MA, RH 20-18/101.

37. HGr North, *KTB,* Aug. 27 and 28, 1941, BA-MA, RH 19 III/767.

38. AOK 18 v. Küchler, appeal, Aug. 28, 1941; AK 42, special report for the German news service, Aug. 28, 1941, BA-MA, RH 20 18/108.

39. *Tät.Ber.* N3, Aug. 15–31, 1941, in *Die Einsatzgruppen in der besetzten Sowjetunion 1941/42: Die Tätigkeits- und Lageberichte der Chefs der Sicherheitspolizei und des SD,* ed. Peter Klein (Berlin: Edition Hentrich, 1997), 172.

40. *Deutsche Zeitung im Ostland,* Aug. 31, 1941, Sept. 8, 1941.

41. Lindmäe, *Suvesõda,* 129, 146, 195 f.

42. Virumaa OK, overview of activities though the end of 1941, ERA, R-358/1/21, 27.

43. Angelus to v. Roques, Nov. 28, 1956, BA-MA, N-153/33.

44. Tõnu Parming, "The Holocaust in Estonia: Conceptual and Methodological Problems in Research. A Critical Review," *Meie Elu* (Toronto), Feb. 4–Sept. 30, 1998.

45. Sužiedėlis, "Foreign Saviors," 319.

46. Mäe, "Unconditional Cooperation," *Deutsche Zeitung im Ostland,* Oct. 22, 1942.

47. KdS-Estland Sandberger, annual report from July 1941 through June 30, 1942, ERA, R-819/1/12.

48. Head of Estonian Self-Government Mäe to Hitler, no date [fall 1942], ERA, R-65/1/32.

49. EM N99, Sept. 30, 1941, BAB, R-58/217; "Der Verwaltungsausbau des Reichskommissariats Ostland und seine Voraussetzungen," *Nation und Staat* 15 (1941–42): 265, 268.

50. *Deutsche Zeitung im Ostland,* May 18, 1942.

51. Rolf-Dieter Müller, *Die deutsche Wirtschaftspolitik in den besetzten sowjetischen Gebieten 1941-1943* (Boppard: Harald Boldt Verlag, 1991), 228.

52. Estonia: population figures by provinces as of Dec. 1, 1941, *Statistische Berichte für das Ostland,* nos. 1–2 (Jan.–Feb. 1942): 50.

53. Pärnumaa OK, overview of activities through Aug. 6, 1942, ERA, R-358/1/9.

54. For more on the Jewish experience in Estonia in 1940–41, see Weiss-Wendt, "The Soviet Occupation," 313–18.

55. Dov Levin, "Baltic Jews," 4.

56. Vello Salo, *Population Losses, 1940-1941: Citizens of Jewish Nationality* (Tallinn: Estonian State Commission on Examination of the Policies of Repression, 2002), 3–5.

57. Edith Sekules, *Surviving the Nazis, Exile, and Siberia* (London: Valentine Mitchell, 2000), 68–72.

58. Rachmiel Shadsunsky (name denotes respective case file of the Est Sipo), ERA, R-64/4/913.

59. Gurin-Loov, *Eesti juutide katastroof,* 235.

60. Levin, "Estonian Jews in the USSR," 280.

61. Levin, *The Lesser of Two Evils,* 287.

62. Valgamaa OK, overview of activities though Aug. 1, 1942, ERA, R-358/1/18.

63. Meyer Rogonsky, ERA, R-64/4/683; David Prensky, ERA, R-64/4/634; Jacob Kolektor, ERA, R-64/4/1075; Meier Rogonsky, ERA, R-64/4/683.

64. Eduard Eitelberg, ERA, R-64/4/186.

65. Virumaa OK, 1941, ERA, R-358/1/24.

66. Est. Sipo in Narva, list of Communist activists fled from 1st police precinct, Jan. 22, 1942, ERA, R-59/1/65.

67. German Archival Commission for Estonia and Latvia, from letters of Dr. Mommsen and Dr. v. Stritzky, "The Bolshevikization of the Baltic," Feb. 11, 1942, NARA, T-81/19.

68. Uluots, "On the Bolshevik Domination in Estonia, 1940–41," Oct. 11, 1941, Eesti Aja-looarhiiv EAA, 2100/15/65.

69. "Notes on the Period of Bolshevik Terror in Estonia," November 1941, ERA, R-64/1/180. Georg Leibbrandt emphasized the nexus between Jews and "Asiatics" in his book *Moskaus Aufmarsch gegen Europa* (Munich: Zentralverlag der NSDAP, 1938), a classical example of literature on Jude-obolshevik conspiracy.

70. Robert Raid, *When the Soviets Came. . . .* 2 vols. (Cardiff, N.Y.: Boreas Publishing House, 1985–86), 2:171.

71. Tartumaa OK, overview of activities through the end of 1941, ERA, R-358/1/17.

72. See, for example, *Alvin Isberg, Zu den Bedingungen des Befreiers: Kollaboration und Frei-heitsstreben in dem von Deutschland besetzten Estland 1941 bis 1944* (Stockholm: Acta Universitatis Stockholmiensis, 1992), 29–30.

73. Hannu Rautkallio, *Finland and the Holocaust: The Rescue of Finland's Jews* (New York: Holocaust Library, 1987), 135.

74. *Eesti rahva kannatuste aasta* (The Year of Suffering of the Estonian People) (Tallinn: Esto-nian Self-Government, 1943), 141–43, 145–46, 152–53. About 25,000 copies of the book were pub-lished. The Estonian Directorate of Education began collecting data for the book in early 1942. In his letter of May 20, 1942, RMO Rosenberg emphasized the importance of the forthcoming book from the perspective of propaganda. Rosenberg urged RKO Lohse to quickly publish the book, while reserving the translation rights exclusively for his own ministry in Berlin (LVVA, R-70/3/52). At the same time, the ERR criticized Estonian book editors for having failed to achieve the level of a compendium published in Latvia. The Latvian edition was said to have been a better tool of propa-ganda than the Estonian edition. Supplemented with rich visual material, the former contained a compelling narrative of the Soviet occupation, while the latter mainly discussed the destruction of Estonian culture and the anti-Soviet resistance of the summer of 1941 (Dr. Speer's memo from Jan. 7, 1944, BAB, NS-30/33.)

75. Dov Levin, "Estonian Jews in the USSR, 1941–1945," *Yad Vashem Studies* 11 (1976): 276–77.

76. Dov Levin, *The Lesser of Two Evils: Eastern European Jewry under Soviet Rule, 1939–1941* (Philadelphia: Jewish Publication Society, 1995), 46, 336 f.

77. EM N51, Aug. 13, 1941, BAB, R-58/216.

78. Glika Koblens and Agnes Räitsak, ERA, R-60/2/396.

79. AOK 16, Counterintelligence unit, July 30, 1941, BA-MA, RH-22/271.

80. Pflug, "Aspekte jüdischen Lebens," 57.

81. Alexander Pankseiev, *Na osnove leninskikh organisatsionnykh printsypov* (Tallinn: Eesti Riiklik Kirjastus, 1967), 82; Alexander Pankseiev and Madis Pesti, eds., *Ocherki istorii Kommunis-ticheskoi partii Estonii (1920–1940 gody),* pt. 2 (Tallinn: Eesti Riiklik Kirjastus, 1963), 323.

82. Eugenia Gurin-Loov and Gennadi Gramberg, *Eesti Juudi Kogukond/The Jewish Commu-nity of Estonia* (Tallinn, 2001), 11.

83. Mati Õun, ed., *Eesti ohvitserid ja sõjandustegelased* (Estonian Officers and Military Figures) (Tallinn: Sentinel, 2002), 20. The names in the book are arranged in alphabetical order, along with the military rank. Jakobson is the only individual next to whose name is written "war criminal."

84. Olaf Kuuli, *Sotsialistid ja kommunistid Eestis 1917–1991* (Socialists and Communists in Estonia, 1917–91) (Tallinn, 1999), 64–65.

85. Raid, *When the Soviets Came,* 1:105, 111, 161. Raid and other émigré authors portrayed Gutkin, who was killed in the summer of 1941, as a symbol of Jewish treachery in Estonia.

86. Kuuli, *Sotsialistid,* 85–87.

87. Hiio, "Jewish Students," table 3, Fate of the Members of TU Jewish Student Associations. Most Jewish students at TU came from Latvia. Taking into consideration that information on 144 (out of 373) students is failing, the percentage of college-educated Jews in the Soviet apparatus may increase to 3.9.

88. Raid, *When the Soviets Came,* 2:90. Half of the people listed in this particular monolog had been murdered. Robert Raid's (original name Maxim Shklovski) book was originally published in 1953 in German. Subsequently it has been translated into Estonian, Spanish, and Latvian. *When the Soviets Came* abounds with anti-Semitic and anti-Russian rhetoric, which posed a problem when it came to publishing an English edition of the book. As a compromise, Raid agreed to omit first names as well as any references to ethnicity of the individuals he mentioned in his book (see book review in *Mitteilungen aus baltischem Leben* 3 [1987]: 16–17).

89. [Page missing], report "Jewish influence on various aspects of life in the Ostland," [no date], LVVA, R-1026/1/3; RFSS Himmler to RMO Rosenberg, Aug. 13, 1943, LVVA, R-1026/1/3.

90. EM N96, Sept. 27, 1941, BAB, R-58/217.

91. Andrew Ezergailis, ed., *Stockholm Documents: The German Occupation of Latvia, 1941–1945. What Did America Know?* (Riga: Historical Institute of Latvia, 2002), xi.

92. Narva OK, overview of activities through Aug. 6, 1942, including the period of Soviet occupation, ERA, R-358/1/4.

93. BdrückwHGr North v. Roques, *Tät.Ber.,* Aug. 17–31, 1941, BA-MA, RH-22/254.

94. Amir Weiner wrote extensively about the Vinnitsa case in his book *Making Sense of War: The Second World War and the Fate of the Bolshevik Revolution* (Princeton, N.J.: Princeton Univ. Press, 2001), in particular 264–68.

95. Min. of Education and Propaganda, list of propaganda items for the East [1943], IfZ, MA-65. Goebbels instructed his staff to use the word *Bolshevism* instead of *Communism* when addressing East European publics.

3. THE COLLECTIVE EXPERIENCE OF NAZI OCCUPATION

1. Schaefer to RKFDV Hintze, July 17, 1941; KdS-Lettland Lange to RSHA Roem, Jan. 7, 1942, LVVA, R-1019/1/3. Werneck used to be one of the biggest mental institutions in South Germany. Shortly before the arrival of the refugees from the Baltic, most patients at Werneck were murdered.

2. Interview with Mäe, Aug. 2–3, 1958, IfZ, ZS-2366.

3. Transcript, Nov. 7, 1947, NARA, M-895/15.

4. Hjalmar Mäe, *Kuidas kõik teostus: Minu mälestusi* (How Everything Has Happened: My Memoirs) (Stockholm: EMP, 1993), 211.

5. Isberg, *Zu den Bedingungen des Befreiers,* 42–43.

6. EM N71, Sept. 2, 1941, BAB, R-58/216.

7. Isberg, *Zu den Bedingungen des Befreiers,* 155f.

8. Interview with Mäe, Aug. 2–3, 1958, IfZ, ZS-2366.

9. Commander of SK 1a Sandberger, report, "The Estonian Nazi movement," [Sept. 1941], BA-MA, RH-19 III/470.

10. BdS-Ostland Jost to RKO Lohse, Aug. 11, 1942, BAB, R-6/354. Jost served in the capacity of BdS-Ostland between March and September 1942.

11. RMO Office, personal characteristic of Angelus, Öpik, and Wendt, [1942?], BAB, R-6/278; GK-Estland Office, report, "Current Estonian Directors," Nov. 1, 1943, BAB, R-6/67.

12. Mäe, *Kuidas kõik teostus,* 187.

13. RKO Lohse to RMO Rosenberg, Apr. 10, 1943, USHMM, RG-11.001M/R-74.

14. RMO Rosenberg to RKO Lohse, Mar. 7, 1942, BAB, R-2/30564.

15. Mäe, *Kuidas kõik teostus,* 243.

16. Quoted in Andres Kasekamp, "The Ideological Roots of Estonian Collaboration During the Nazi Occupation," in *The Baltic Countries under Occupation: Soviet and Nazi Rule, 1939–1991,* ed. Anu Mai Kõll (Stockholm: Acta Universitatis Stockholmiensis, 2003), 92.

17. Hitler, cable, Nov. 29, 1941, ERA, R-65/1/27.

18. Franz von Roques, memoirs, *Befehlshaber im Heeresgebiet Nord,* 16.III.1941–31.III.1943, 43, BA-MA, N 153/1.

19. Seppo Myllyniemi, *Die Neuordnung der baltischen Länder 1941–1944: Zum nationalsozialistischen Inhalt der deutschen Besatzungspolitik* (Helsinki: Dissertationes Historicae II, 1973), 45 f.

20. Interview with Mäe, Aug. 2–3, 1958, IfZ, ZS-2366.

21. GK-Estland Office, Feb. 22, 1942, ERA, R-65/1/4.

22. Commandant of Tallinn Scultetus, order N35, June 16, 1943, ERA, R-82/1/3.

23. Local headquarters in Nõmme, situational report, Oct. 26, 1941, BA-MA, RW-30/56.

24. Business report of Danish delegation on its trip to the Ostland. Meeting with GK Litzmann on Apr. 24, 1942, BAB, R-6/443. During the first ten months of his tenure, Litzmann held thirty-five public speeches and ten addresses before Estonian industrial workers and farmers.

25. OKW Staff, Hoffmann to Head of the Party Chancellery Bormann, May 19, 1942, IfZ, Fa-91/4.

26. Report on propaganda in the Ostland, Sept. 17, 1942, IfZ, MA-26/1.

27. One German Mark was worth ten Soviet Rubles or about ten Euro in today's money.

28. EG A, Consolidated Report from Oct. 16, 1941, to Jan. 31, 1942, USHMM, RG-11.001M/14.

29. AA Grosskopf, memo, June 25, 1941, NARA, T-120/333. In spite of his hostility toward Baltic Germans during World War II, Mäe had developed friendly relations with some of them after the war.

30. Head of Est. Self-Government Mäe to GK-Estland Litzmann, Oct. 15, 1943; RKO Lohse, note, Feb. 21, 1944; RKO Lohse to RMO Rosenberg, Mar. 7, 1944, LVVA, R-70/5/78. See also Oskar Angelus, *Tuhande valitseja maa: Mälestusi Saksa okupatsiooni ajast 1941–1944* (Land of the Thousand Rulers: Memoirs of German Occupation, 1941–1944) (Tallinn: Olion, 1995 [1956]), 18–19.

31. Est. Sipo, report, Oct. 1, 1942, ERA, R-64/1/202.

32. Est. Sipo, BIII, report on the population's mood, Dec. 1943, ERA, R-64/1/19.

33. Texts of public speeches of Litzmann and Bombe, Feb.–Nov. 1942, ERA, R-65/1/21; "Lage: Estland," *Nation und Staat* 16 (1942–43): 101.

34. U.S. Legation in Stockholm, "Radio News Broadcasts from Tallinn in the Period 1–15 March 1942," Apr. 17, 1942, NARA, M-1170/23.

35. Texts of public speeches of Mäe, Feb.–Nov. 1942, ERA, R-65/1/21.

36. Mäe speech from Sept. 5, 1942, quoted verbatim in a report of Est. Sipo in Tallinn-Nõmme, ERA, R-64/1/202.

37. Alexander Kaelas, "Sotsiialpoliitikast saksa okupatsiooni ajal" (On Social Policy in Times of German Occupation), in *Eesti riik ja rahvas II. Maailmasõjas* (Stockholm: EMP, 1959), 8:125 f.

38. EM N40, Aug. 1, 1941; EM N53, Aug. 15, 1941, BAB, R-58/215, 216.

39. GK-Estland Litzmann to RMO Rosenberg, Oct. 30, 1941, NARA, T-454/19.

40. That line runs through numerous popular mood reports compiled by Est. Sipo between 1942 and 1944. See *Eesti Julgeolekupolitsei aruanded, 1941–1944* (Reports of the Estonian Security Police, 1941–44) (Tallinn: Riigiarhiiv, 2002), passim.

41. Ian Kershaw, *Popular Opinion and Political Dissent in the Third Reich: Bavaria, 1933–1945* (Oxford: Clarendon Press, 1983), 36, 47, 148–49, 314, 328. For the matter of comparison, see EM N135, Nov. 19, 1941, BAB, R-58/219.

42. Mäe, speech delivered in Tartu on Oct. 29, 1943; Uluots, speech delivered in Tartu on Feb. 24, 1942; *Postimees,* Feb. 24, 1943, cited verbatim in Tartu district commissar Meenen's memo, Dec. 1943, BAB, R-90/3.

43. EM N190, Apr. 8, 1942, BAB, R-58/221.

44. Est. Sipo in Pärnu, report on the population's mood, Jan. 1943; ibid. in Narva, Jan. 1943; ibid. in Kuressaare, Dec. 1942–Jan. 1943, ERA, R-64/1/14.

45. Business report of Danish delegation on its trip to the Ostland. Meeting with GK Litzmann on Apr. 24, 1942, BAB, R-6/443.

46. Est. Sipo in Tartu, report on the population's mood, Jan. 17, 1944, ERA, R-60/1/54.

47. RKO Office, Vialon to Eckhardt, Febr. 14, 1944, BAB, R-2/30565.

48. Est. Sipo, report on the population's mood, Oct. 1943, ERA, R-64/1/19.

49. Minölko Estonia, Group "Work," review of *KTB* for July 1–Sept. 30, 1943, BA-MA, RW-46/755.

50. Ger. Naval Attaché in Helsinki, *KTB,* Apr. 15, 1943, BA-MA, RM-12 II/13.

51. EM N176, Mar. 4, 1942, BAB, R-58/221.

52. Est. Sipo in Tallinn-Harju to Head of Police and OK, no date [Feb. 1942?], ERA, R-64/1/48.

53. GK-Estland Office, IIa Dept., interim report on propaganda in Estonia, Nov. 21, 1942, ERA, R-65/1/28.

54. Est. Sipo, report on the population's mood, no date [Jan. 1943], ERA, R-65/1/1. See also Angelus, *Tuhande valitseja maa,* 211.

55. EM N166, Feb. 9, 1942, BAB, R-58/220.

56. GK-Estland Litzmann to RKO Lohse, Nov. 25, 1942, ERA, R-65/1/28.

57. High Command of HGr North, study, "Characteristics of the Estonians: Dealing with Estonians," Apr. 12, 1944, BAB, R-6/78.

58. Ibid.

59. Ibid.

60. Ibid.

61. GK-Estland Office, IIa Dept. to Litzmann, July 24, 1942, ERA, R-65/1/28.

62. V. Roques to Hosang, Oct. 20, 1958, BA-MA, N-153/33.

63. AA, Grosskopf, Aug. 8 and 13, 1941, NARA, T-120/333.

64. U.S. Legation in Stockholm, "Conditions in Estonia, December 1941," Dec. 27, 1941, NARA, M-1170/21.

65. RMO Rosenberg to RKO Lohse, July 13, 1942, NARA, T-454/80.

66. *Dieses Volk, das in seiner Gesamtheit rassisch gesund und das weitaus beste im ganzen Osten ist, wesentlich besser als das lettische und litauische Volk.* RuSHA to Staf. Uhlig, Nov. 8, 1944, ERA, R-165/1/23.

67. Dr. Csaki, travel report, "The Baltic, Northern Front, and Petersburg Region, 26 August–17 September 1942," Oct. 9, 1942, NARA, T-81/374.

68. KdS-Estland Sandberger, annual report from July 1941 through June 30, 1942, ERA, R-819/1/12. Interestingly enough, Nazi racial experts considered Estonian Germans a better stock than Latvian Germans. (Report on racial composition of Baltic Germans, [1940], BAB, R-69/589.)

69. U.S. Legation in Stockholm to the Secretary of State, May 11, 1942, NARA, M-1178/19.

70. RMO Office, Dr. Lange, report on business trip to Estonia, Oct. 7, 1941, BAB, R-2/30563.

71. ERR, Dr. Wilhelm Brachmann, report on Latvia, Sept. 23, 1941, BAB, NS-30/80.

72. EM N135, Nov. 19, 1941, BAB, R-58/219.

73. Commander of EG A Stahlecker, notes on political and economic situation in the occupied territories, July 19, 1941, BA-MA, RH-19 III/669.

74. GK-Estland Litzmann to RMO Rosenberg, Apr. 5, 1943, LVVA, R-1018/1/83.

75. *Archiv der Gegenwart,* July 17, 1940.

76. Raun, "Nineteenth- and Early Twentieth-Century Estonian Nationalism Revisited," 131.

77. OKH, *KTB,* Feb. 25, 1944, BA-MA, RH-19 III/271; HGr North, report on the conversation with HSSPF Jeckeln re. conscription in the Ostland, Jan. 29, 1944, BA-MA, RH-19 III/3. A poster in the Lithuanian city of Šiauliai distributed during the mobilization campaign read: "Autonomy first, then Legion."

78. RFSS Himmler to Reich Food Deputy Minister Backe, Aug. 20, 1943, BAB, NS-19/54.

79. Arnold Purre, "Eesti sõda Nõuk. Liiduga" (Estonia's War Against the Soviet Union), *Eesti riik ja rahvas II. Maailmasõjas* (Stockholm: EMP, 1959), 7:30–31.

80. HGr North, *KTB,* Feb. 6, 1944, BA-MA, RH-19 III/270.

81. Franz von Roques, memoir, *Befehlshaber im Heeresgebiet Nord, 16.III.1941–31.III.1943,* 47, BA-MA, N-153/1; Angelus to v. Roques, Aug. 28, 1956, BA-MA, N-153/33; Field Police Director by HGr North to Commander of HGr North v. Küchler, Aug. 31, 1942, BA-MA, RH-22/263.

82. Roger Petersen, *Resistance and Rebellion: Lessons from Eastern Europe* (Cambridge: Cambridge Univ. Press, 2001), 155.

83. Myllyniemi, *Die Neuordnung der baltischen Länder,* 82–83, 106.

84. Gerhard Bassler, "The Collaborationist Agenda in Latvia, 1941–1943," in Kõll, *The Baltic Countries under Occupation,* 78–82.

85. Mäe, *Kuidas kõik teostus,* 196.

86. EM N135, Nov. 19, 1941, BAB, R-58/219.

87. *MbO* N6, June 5, 1942, BAB, R-58/697.

88. EM N40, Aug. 1, 1941, BAB, R-58/215.

89. *MbO* N15, Aug. 7, 1942, BAB, R-58/698.

90. Local headquarters in Nõmme, situational report, Oct. 26, 1941, BA-MA, RW-30/56.

91. Commander of EG A Stahlecker, consolidated report from Oct. 16, 1941 to Jan. 31, 1942, USHMM, RG-11.001M/R-14.

92. KdS-Estland Sandberger, annual report from July 1941 through June 30, 1942, ERA, R-819/1/12.

93. WiKo Tallinn, situational reports, Mar. 28–Apr. 27 and Apr. 28–May 27, 1944, BA-MA, RW-30/59.

94. *MbO* N15, Aug. 7, 1942, BAB, R-58/698.

95. Est. Sipo in Narva to BIV, Oct. 8, 1943, ERA, R-59/1/95.

96. RMO Office, Dülfer, report on business trip, Mar. 20, 1944, BAB, R-6/180.

97. Chief of Ger. Sipo Kaltenbrunner to RMO Office, Ogruf. Berger, June 24, 1944, BAB, R-6/187.

98. KdS-Estland Sandberger to BdS-Ostland Jost, July 22, 1942, ERA, R-4365/1/3.

99. BdS-Ostland Pifrader to RMO, Dept I, Trampedach, Aug. 16, 1943, LVVA, R-1026/1/7.

100. GK-Estland Office, report on the population's mood, Sept. 1944, BAB, R-91/Reval/1.

101. RFSS Himmler, report prepared for Hitler re. situation in RKO, Sept. 13, 1944, BAB, NS-19/1704.

102. HGr North, daily report, Sept. 21, 1944, BA-MA, RH-19 III/319.

103. RMO Office, report on the situation in Estonia following the evacuation, [September 1944,] BAB, R-6/78.

104. Vineta Rolmane, "The Resistance in Latvia During the Nazi Occupation (July 1941–May 1945)," in *The Anti-Soviet Resistance in the Baltic States,* ed. Arvydas Anušauskas (Vilnius: Du Ka, 1999), 132, 136–38, 141.

105. U.S. Legation in Stockholm to the Secretary of State, June 8, 1942, NARA, M-1178/19.

106. Petersen, *Resistance and Rebellion,* 164, 167.

107. The fullest description of the Audriņi/Marduki execution can be found in Eberhard Groesdonk et al., "Die Vernichtung von Audrini, seine justizförmige Bearbeitung (1944–1994) und die Öffentlichkeit," *Juristische Zeitgeschchte* 4 (1996): 1–205. The execution was carried out by the Latvians on a German order. Most victims were ethnic Russians.

108. EM N181, Mar. 16, 1942, BAB, R-58/221. See also Helmut Krausnick and Hans-Heinrich Wilhelm, *Die Truppe des Weltanschauungskrieges: Die Einsatzgruppen der Sicherheitspolizei und des SD, 1938–1942* (Stuttgart: Deutsche Verlags-Anstalt, 1981), 339.

109. Indrek Paavle, ed., *Eesti rahvastikukaotused II/1: Saksa okupatsioon 1941–1944/Population Losses in Estonia II/1: German Occupation, 1941–1944* (Tartu, 2002), 45.

110. RMO Office, Dr. Werner Hasselblatt, report, "Population-political reflections on the question of Germanization of the Ostland's peoples," Dec. 14, 1942, BAB, R-6/160.

111. RMO Office, Leibbrandt, report, "The question of Germanization of the Ostland's peoples," Nov. 7, 1942; RMO Office, Dr. Werner Hasselblatt to Dr. Erhard Wetzel, Dec. 14, 1942, BAB, R-6/160.

112. Commander of EG A Stahlecker, consolidated report from Oct. 16, 1941 to Jan. 31, 1942, USHMM, RG-11.001M/14.

113. RFSS Himmler to Gruf. Greifelt, June 12, 1942, BAB, NS-19/1739.

114. Interview with Mäe, Aug. 2–3, 1958, IfZ, ZS-2366.

115. Mäe, *Kuidas kõik teostus,* 166, 184, 190, 202.

116. Est. Sipo in Tallinn, report on the population's mood, [Dec. 1941?], ERA, R-64/1/48; EM N156, Jan. 16, 1942, BAB, R-58/220; EM N186, Mar. 27, 1942, BAB, R-58/221.

117. RüKo Tallinn, Narva Office, *KTB,* Dec. 6, 1941, BA-MA, RW-30/63.

118. GK-Estland Office to Est. Minister of Technology Radik, July 1942, ERA, R-65/1/4.

119. Testimony of Kalju Treufeld at Laak-Gerrets-Viik-Mere trial, Tallinn, Mar. 6–11, 1961, USHMM, RG-06.026/12.

120. Commander of SK 1a Sandberger, report, "Political thoughts in the leading Estonian circles," [September 1941,] BA-MA, RH-19 III/470.

121. EM N135, Nov. 19, 1941, BAB, R-58/219.

122. RFSS Himmler, memo, Jan. 13, 1943, BAB, NS-19/1736.

123. RMO Office, report, "The Ostland," no date, BAB, R-6/159.

124. Memo, discussion in Hitler's headquarters, no date, BAB, NS-19/1704. GK Litzmann had no doubts that "as far as the objective of Germanization of Estonia is concerned, everything is clear. The only question is the methods and the speed of the chosen course of action." (Business report of Danish delegation on its trip to the Ostland. Meeting with GK Litzmann on Apr. 24, 1942, BAB, R-6/443.)

125. RMO Office, report on conscription of RAD volunteers in Estonia and Lithuania, July 2 and Sept. 15, 1943, BAB, R-6/187.

126. *Das deutsche Reval: Dokumente* (Leipzig: S. Hirzel, 1942), 5.

127. RMO Office, Mentzel, memo, July 16, 1943, BAB, R-6/67.

128. O-VUROrg., report on business trip to Estonia btw. Oct. 24 and 29, 1941, Nov. 1, 1941, BAB, R-19/119.

129. RMO Office, Kleist to Leibbrandt, May 1, 1942, BAB, R-6/296.

130. Chief of Sipo, bulletin N4, June 24, 1942, IfZ, Fb-101/23. Estonia was supposed to get 40,000 square miles and 1.7 million people, Latvia 28,000 square miles and 1.5 million people, and Lithuania 2,500 square miles and 140,000 people.

131. Interrogation of Ants Lõhmus, Tagula, Oct. 29, 1960, USHMM, RG-06.026/11.

4. THE COMING OF TERROR

1. BDC: Sandberger, IfZ, Fa-226/39. For more personal information on Sandberger, see Michael Wildt, *Generation des Unbedingten: Das Führungskorps des Reichssicherheitshauptamtes* (Hamburg: Hamburger Edition, 2002), 98–104, 170–73.

2. RSHA, VI Dept., characteristic, BDC: Sandberger, IfZ, Fa-226/39.

3. F. W. Rübesamen to v. Roques, Jan. 31, 1955, BA-MA, N 153/33.

4. Angelus, *Tuhande valitseja maa*, 67, 112, 158, 164–65, 173.

5. Wolfram Wette, "SS-Standartenführer Karl Jäger, Kommandeur der Sicherheitspolizei (KdS) in Kaunas: Eine biographische Skizze," in *Holocaust in Litauen: Krieg, Judenmorde und Kollaboration im Jahre 1941*, ed. Vincas Bartusevičius et al. (Cologne: Böhlau Verlag, 2003), 79–81, 84–85.

6. Peter Klein, "Dr. Rudolf Lange als Kommandeur der Sicherheitspolizei und des SD in Lettland: Aspekte seines Dienstalltages," in *Täter im Vernichtungskrieg: Der Überfall auf die Sowjetunion und der Völkermord an den Juden*, ed. Wolf Kaiser (Berlin: Propyläen, 2002), 125, 133.

7. Est. Sipo, BI, circular letter, July 5, 1943, ERA, R-60/1/5.

8. Head of RSHA Heydrich to Foreign Minister v. Ribbentrop, Oct. 9, 1939 (document N106); RFSS Himmler's order, Nov. 3, 1939 (document N116) in Loeber, *Diktierte Option*, 127, 147–48.

9. Commander of SK 1a Sandberger to EWZ, Oct. 1 and 6, 1941, BAB, R-69/722.

10. EWZ Sandberger to RSHA Müller, Oct. 13, 14 and 25, 1939; EWZ Sandberger to BdS-Streckenbach, Oct. 24, 1939; EWZ Sandberger to RSHA Ohlendorf, Oct. 25, 1939, BAB, R-69/1221; EWZ Sandberger to RSHA Heydrich, Oct. 22, 1939, BAB, R-69/1141.

11. EWZ Sandberger to RSHA Heydrich, Oct. 19, 1939, BAB, R-69/980.

12. EWZ Sandberger to RSHA Heydrich, Jan. 16, 1940, BAB, R-69/1052.

13. Documents N37 and N323 in Tone Ferenc, ed., *Quellen zur nationalsozialistischen Entnationalisierungspolitik in Slowenien 1941–1945* (Maribor: Založba Obzorja, 1980), 73, 640, 650, 652, 654, 658–60.

14. Interrogation of Marga Kolodziejski, July 7, 1959, BAL, 207 AR-Z 246/59, V1.

15. Interrogation of Bruno Streckenbach, Hamburg, Dec. 7, 1966, BAL, 201 AR-Z 76/59, V2; interrogation of Bruno Streckenbach, Hamburg, Nov. 26, 1970, BAL, 201 AR-Z 76/59, V5.

16. Commander of EG A Stahlecker, consolidated report through Oct. 15, 1941, USHMM, RG-11.001/15. EG A statistics are also reproduced in Ezergailis, *The Holocaust in Latvia*, 392–94.

17. Interrogation of Werner Hersmann, Ulm, Oct. 30 and Nov. 22, 1956, BAL, 207 AR-Z 15/58, V6; interrogation of Werner Hersmann, Ulm, May 16, 1957, BAL, 207 AR-Z 15/58, V12. This and similar statements with regard to Hitler's explicit order authorizing physical destruction of the Jews as a group should be treated with caution. As research has shown, defendants at the Einsatzgruppen trial in Nuremberg conspired to demonstrate the existence of such an order so as to shift the responsibility for mass murder (see, for example, Ralf Ogorreck, *Die Einsatzgruppen und die "Genesis der Endlösung"* [Berlin: Metropol, 1996], 47–55).

18. Stapo Tilsit to RSHA Müller, July 1, 1941, USHMM, RG-11.001M/10. Jürgen Matthäus took a more cautious position regarding Sandberger's involvement in the killing of Jews in the Lithuanian border area (Jürgen Matthäus, "Jenseits der Grenze: Die ersten Massenerschiessungen von Juden in Litauen (Juni–August 1941)," *Zeitschrift für Geschichtswissenschaft* 44, no. 2 (1996): 102–3, 105).

19. EM N6, June 27, 1941; EM N9, July 1, 1941, BAB, R-58/214.

20. Preliminary proceedings against Wilhelm Kraus et al., Munich, May 20, 1970, BAL, I 207 AR 2687/64, V1; the Liepāja-proceedings, Munich, July 17, 1969, BAL, I 207 AR 2687/64, V2;

interrogation of Wilhelm Kraus, Munich, Aug. 10, 1960, BAL, 207 AR-Z 246/59, V2; interrogation of Harry Friedrichson, Ingolstadt, Nov. 8, 1963 and Jan. 7, 1965, BAL, II 207 AR 2687/64, V1.

21. Marġers Vestermanis, "Local Headquarters Liepaja: Two Months of German Occupation in the Summer of 1941," in *War of Extermination: The German Military in World War II, 1941–1944*, ed. Hannes Heer and Klaus Naumann (New York: Berghahn Books, 2000), 229.

22. Transcript, Nov. 7, 1947, NARA, M-895/15.

23. Interrogation of Sandberger, Ludwigsburg, Feb. 18, 1960, BAL, 408 AR-Z 233/59, V1.

24. Personal communication from Andrew Ezergailis. Ezergailis based his account on a testimony of Rudolf Hofmanis (letter of Mar. 15, 2001).

25. EM N24, July 16, 1941, BAB, R-58/214.

26. Transcript, Nov. 12, 1947, NARA, M-895/15; Affidavit of Feder, Nov. 21, 1947 and Jan. 14, 1948; Affidavit of George Buchner, Dec. 8, 1948, NARA, M-895/27.

27. Commander of EG A Stahlecker, consolidated report through Oct. 15, 1941, USHMM, RG-11.001M/15; KdS-Estland Sandberger, annual report from July 1941 to June 30, 1942, ERA, R-819/1/12; Erich Rogge, Neumünster, June 20, 1960, YVA, TR-10/1196.

28. TK Feder, report, July 15, 1941, ERA, R-64/1/821.

29. EG A Stahlecker to RSHA, Nov. 11, 1941, LVVA, R-1026/1/17.

30. KdS-Estland Sandberger, annual report from July 1941 to June 30, 1942, ERA, R-819/1/12. Sandberger was officially appointed commander of the German Security Police in Estonia on Dec. 3, 1941.

31. KdS-Estland Sandberger, memo, Jan. 14, 1942, ERA, R-65/1/28.

32. EM N40, Aug. 1, 1941, BAB, R-58/215.

33. Ibid.

34. GK-Estland Litzmann to RKO Lohse, Mar. 10, 1942, LVVA, R-70/5/8.

35. KdS-Estland Sandberger, memo, Jan. 14, 1942, ERA, R-65/1/28.

36. KdS-Estland Sandberger, circular letter N11, Aug. 28, 1943, ERA, R-819/1/11.

37. Argo Kuusik, "Security Police and SD in Estonia in 1941–1944," in *Estonia, 1940–1945: Reports of the Estonian International Commission for the Investigation of Crimes Against Humanity*, ed. Toomas Hiio, Meelis Maripuu, and Indrek Paavle (Tallinn, 2006), 589.

38. Knut Stang, *Kollaboration und Massenmord: Die litauische Hilfspolizei, das Rollkommando Hamann und die Ermordung der litauischen Juden* (Frankfurt: Peter Lang, 1996), 64–65.

39. Michael MacQueen, "Einheimische Gehilfin der Gestapo: Die litauische Sicherheitspolizei in Vilnius 1941–1944," in Bartusevičius et al., *Holocaust in Litauen*, 104–8, 113f.

40. KdS-Estland Baatz, note on organization and method of KdS-Lettland, Jan. 18, 1944, ERA, R-819/1/11.

41. Interrogation of Balthasar Baron von Buxhöveden, Bad Schwartau, June 13, 1961, BAL, 207 AR-Z 246/59, V3.

42. Interrogation of Hinrich Möller, Kiel, Feb. 18, 1960, BAL, I 110 AR 162/75.

43. See, for example, interrogation of Peter Hipp, Munich, Dec. 3, 1968, BAL, 207 AR-Z 246/59, V7.

44. Mäe, *Kuidas kõik teostus*, 232, 242, 284; Angelus, *Tuhande valitseja maa*, photo. Posing next to Angelus: Mäe, Estonian mayor of Tallinn, Artur Terras, and wife of GK Litzmann; Sandberger is the only one genuinely smiling.

45. Interrogation of Erich Rogge, Neumünster, Mar. 26, 1968, BAL, 207 AR-Z 246/59, V7. According to the entry that Erich Rogge made in his pay book, Feder TK reached Gostitsy on July 26. (Excerpt from Rogge's interrogation records reproduced in Hans-Heinrich Wilhelm, *Rassenpolitik und Kriegsführung: Sicherheitspolizei und Wehrmacht in Polen und der Sowjetunion* [Passau: Richard Rothe, 1991], 202.)

46. GK-Estland Litzmann, report on the situation in Estonia, May 18, 1942, LVVA, R-1018/1/43.

47. Interview with Mäe, Aug. 2-3, 1958, IfZ, ZS-2366.

48. HGr North v. Küchler to GK-Estland Litzmann, Mar. 2, 1943, BA-MA, RH 19 III/492.

49. Minister of the Interior Angelus to OK commanders, Jan. 22, 1942, ERA, R-358/1/33; Overview of the History of OK, archival note on the OK collection (R-358) at ERA. The rank and file usually wore civilian cloths, but also military, KL, and even fire brigade uniforms.

50. AOK 18, v. Küchler, July 9, 1941, BA-MA, RH-20 18/91.

51. Overview of OK formation from July 1941 to Jan. 1, 1943, ERA, R-358/1/34.

52. EM N53, Aug. 15, 1941, BAB, R-58/216.

53. Police and OK Admin. to Head of Pärnu OK, June 12, 1942, ERA, R-210/1/1.

54. Commander of EG A Stahlecker, consolidated report through Oct. 15, 1941, USHMM, RG-11.001M/14.

55. Police and OK Admin. to Head of Pärnu OK, June 17, 1942, ERA, R-210/1/1.

56. Pärnumaa OK, overview of activities through Aug. 12, 1942, ERA, R-358/1/9.

57. Minölk. Estonia, Group "IV Wi," activity report, July 12–23, 1941, BA-MA, RW-46/759.

58. Tartumaa OK, overview of activities through the end of 1941, ERA, R-358/1/16, 17. In his order of July 9, 1943, the head of Tartumaa OK called upon members of OK to destroy at any cost Jewish plutocratic Bolshevism. Otherwise, he prophesized, not only the Estonian people but also all cultural nations *(kultuurrahvad)* of Europe would be exterminated (ERA, R-1607/1/3).

59. Petserimaa OK, overview of activities through Aug. 10, 1942, ERA, R-358/1/6.

60. Petserimaa OK, overview of activities during the year of Soviet occupation, 1942, ERA, R-358/1/8.

61. Viljandimaa OK, overview of activities through the end of 1941, ERA, R-358/1/12.

62. Viljandimaa OK to Viljandi County OK, Sept. 30, 1941, ERA, R-1680/1/1.

63. Valgamaa OK, overview of activities through Aug. 1, 1942, ERA, R-358/1/18, 19.

64. Võrumaa OK, overview of activities through Aug. 6, 1942, ERA, R-358/1/30.

65. Virumaa OK, overview of activities through the end of 1941, ERA, R-358/1/27.

66. Narva OK, overview of activities through Aug. 6, 1942, including the period of Soviet occupation, ERA, R-358/1/4, 5.

67. Järvamaa OK, overview of activities through Aug. 6, 1942, ERA, R-358/1/2.

68. Harjumaa OK, overview of activities through Aug. 6, 1942, ERA, R-358/1/1.

69. Läänemaa OK, overview of activities through Aug. 12, 1942, ERA, R-358/1/3.

70. Tallinn-Nõmme OK, overview of activities through the end of 1941, ERA, R-358/1/13, 15.

71. EM N71, Sept. 2, 1941, BAB, R-58/216.

72. Head of Tartumaa OK, Order N29, Oct. 29, 1941, ERA, R-1914/1/6.

73. Virumaa OK, overview of activities through the end of 1941, ERA, R-358/1/27, 28.

74. Viljandimaa OK, overview of activities through the end of 1941, ERA, R-358/1/12.

75. Herbert Lindmäe, *Suvesõda Tartumaal 1941* (The Summer War in Tartumaa Province, 1941) (Tartu, 1999), 74–76.

76. *Eesti rahva kannatuste aasta,* 6, 7.

77. Ibid., 92.

78. Paavle, *Eesti rahvastikukaotused,* 40.

79. Pärnumaa OK, overview of activities through Aug. 12, 1942, ERA, R-358/1/9.

80. "Who Were the People Who Took up Arms?" *Postimees,* July 27, 1942.

81. Võrumaa OK, overview of activities through Aug. 6, 1942, ERA, R-358/1/30.

82. Torma Parish OK, Dec. 31, 1942, ERA, R-1914/1/39.

83. Virumaa OK, overview of activities through the end of 1941, ERA, R-358/1/27.

84. Tallinn-Harju OK, list of officers and rank and file, Sept. 13–17, 1941, ERA, R-358/1/37.

85. Overview of OK formation from July 1941 to Jan. 1, 1943, ERA, R-358/1/34.

86. Saaremaa OK, overview of activities through the end of 1941, ERA, R-358/1/11.

87. RFSS Himmler to HSSPF Jeckeln, Prützmann, von Bach-Zelewski, and Globochnik, July 25 and 31, 1941, BAB, R-19/326.

88. AOK 18, Higher Quartermaster, July 23, 1941, BA-MA, RH-20 18/96.

89. Viljandimaa OK, overview of activities through the end of 1941, ERA, R-358/1/12.

90. RMO Office, Staff Ost, Dr. Nickel, memo, Oct. 22, 1941, BAB, R-2/30575.

91. Est. Police Admin, OK Division, letter book, Oct. 1, 1942; Dec. 1, 1942; Dec. 20, 1942, ERA, R-358/2/8. Originally, seven police battalions, numbered from 287 to 293, had been formed.

92. Commander of HGr North v. Küchler, monthly report, Sept. 8, 1942, BA-MA, RH-22/288.

93. Indrek Paavle, "Soviet Investigations Concerning the Activities of Estonian Defence Battalions and Police Battalions of the German Armed Forces in 1941–1944," in Hiio, Maripuu, and Paavle, *Estonia, 1940–1945,* 878–79. See also Toomas Hiio, "Eesti üksused Kolmanda Reich'I relvajõududes" (Estonian Units in the Armed Forces of the Third Reich), *Vikerkaar,* nos. 8–9 (Aug.–Sept. 2001): 156–79. The selective nature of available sources (mainly KGB trial records) regarding the daily activities of the Estonian Schuma had prevented scholars from writing a comprehensive study of the police battalions.

94. Est. Sipo, BII, memo, June 25, 1942, ERA, R-59/1/3.

95. Mäe, *Kuidas kõik teostus,* 291.

96. RKO Lohse, memo, Feb. 4, 1944, LVVA, R-70/5/58.

97. OK, list of major events, 1942–1943, ERA, R-358/2/8.

98. Interrogation of Harry Sturm, Frankfurt, Nov. 21, 1966, BAL, 207 AR-Z 246/59, V6. Some commissions had already come into existence in the summer 1941.

99. KdS-Estland Sandberger to Ger. Sipo branch offices, May 18, 1943, ERA, R-59/1/8.

100. Interrogation of Karl Tschierschky, Bad Homburg, Nov. 22, 1966, BAL, 207 AR-Z 246/59, V6.

101. EM N150, Jan. 2, 1942, BAB, R-58/219.

102. Viljandimaa OK, overview of activities through the end of 1941, ERA, R-358/1/12.

103. KdS-Estland Sandberger, annual report from July 1941 to June 30, 1942, ERA, R-819/1/12.

104. Head of Est. Sipo Ennok, memo, July 27, 1943, ERA, R-60/1/4.

105. Head of Est. Sipo Ennok, memo, Apr. 29, 1943, ERA, R-59/1/8.

106. Undated report of EG A [after Dec. 22, 1941], IfZ, Fb-101/18.

107. Angelus, *Tuhande valitsejate maa,* 174; Mäe, *Kuidas kõik teostub,* 291–93.

108. Hans-Heinrich Wilhelm, *Die Einsatzgruppe A der Sicherheitspolizei und des SD 1941/42* (Frankfurt: Peter Lang, 1996), 220–21.

109. Est. Sipo, letter books, ERA, R-294/1/167, 169; KdS-Estland Sandberger, memo, Sept. 24, 1942, ERA, R-294/1/152; interrogation of Osvald Mets, Tartu, Dec. 27, 1960, USHMM, RG-06.026/11.

110. Commander of HGr North v. Küchler, monthly report, Oct. 15, 1942, BA-MA, RH-22/288.

111. KdS-Estland Sandberger, guidelines N5, Apr. 30, 1943, ERA, R-64/1/190.

112. Audit of Est. Sipo in Narva, July 21, 1943, ERA, R-59/1/70.

113. Est. Sipo in Narva, membership list, [Apr. 1942], ERA, R-59/1/14.

114. Est. Sipo in Tallinn, 2 precinct, investigation team weekly reports, Feb.–May 1942, ERA, R-64/1/64.

115. Ibid.

116. Audit of Est. Sipo in Narva, July 21, 1943; Audit of Est. Sipo in Kiviõli, Nov. 11 1943, ERA, R-59/1/70.

117. Head of Est. Sipo in Järva province to Türi police commissar, Sept. 1941, ERA, R-89/1/1.

118. Est. Sipo, BIV to Est. Sipo in Tartu, July 21, 1943, ERA, R-60/1/4.

119. Ruth Bettina Birn, "Collaboration with Nazi Germany in Eastern Europe: The Case of the Estonian Security Police," *Contemporary European History* 10, no. 2 (2001): 193.

120. Interrogation of Marta Klement, Tallinn, June 9, 1961, USHMM, RG-06.026/11.

121. Reet Türno case file, USHMM, RG-06.026/11.

122. EM N96, Sept. 27, 1941, BAB, R-58/217.

123. SS- und Polizeiführer SSPF Estonia Möller, notice, Dec. 9, 1941, ERA, R-62/1/1; Est. Sipo School, Sept. 24, 1942, ERA, R-64/1/1.

124. Note on Riho Sammalkivi, Nov. 28, 1941, ERA, R-64/1/183.

125. Interrogation of Riho Sammalkivi, Tallinn, Oct. 3, 1960, USHMM, RG-06.026/12.

126. Paperwork in the case of Ellen-Erika Allik, Mar. 23–Apr. 8, 1943, ERA, R-59/1/70.

127. Est. Sipo in Petseri, Nov. 13, 1941, ERA, R-63/1/45.

128. Narva OK, overview of activities through Aug. 6, 1942, including the period of Soviet occupation, ERA, R-358/1/4.

129. Viljandimaa OK, overview of activities through the end of 1941, ERA, R-358/1/12.

130. Pärnu OK, overview of activities through Aug. 6, 1942, ERA, R-358/1/9; Tallinn-Nõmme OK, overview of activities through the end of 1941, ERA, R-358/1/13.

131. Paavle, *Eesti rahvastikukaotused,* 76, 121, 124, 148, 176, 232, 241.

132. Jaak Pihlau, "Aleksander Viidiku varjatud elu: Vabadussõjalasest NKVD tippagendiks" (The Hidden Life of Alexander Viidik: A Vabs into an NKVD Top Agent), *Akadeemia* 4 (2002), 726–34.

133. Verdict in the Case of Hans Laats and Elmar Ardla, Tallinn, Jan. 17, 1945, USHMM, RG-06.026.05.

134. Meelis Maripuu, "Faktide ja propaganda vahel: KGB ja kompartei inimsusevastaseid kuritegusid uurimas (1960.–1980. aastad)" (Between Facts and Propaganda: KGB and Communist Party and the Investigation of Crimes Against Humanities, 1960s–1980s), paper delivered at the conference *Modern History in Baltic and European Context,* Tallinn, Mar. 30, 2005.

135. Indrek Jürjo, *Pagulus ja Nõukogude Eesti* (Exiles and the Soviet Estonia) (Tallinn: Umara, 1996), 55–57.

136. Interrogation of Valdur Tullnola [phonetic], Tallinn, Oct. 5, 1960, USHMM, RG-06.026/12. In December 1943, Mere began harassing one of the Jägala concentration camp guards, whom he accused of sympathizing with Communists. Even though the allegations were baseless, the latter played it safe, having gone into hiding (interrogation of Kalju Treufeld, Tallinn, Dec. 26, 1960, USHMM, RG-06.026/12).

137. Est. Sipo, "Secret Collaborators and Police Surveillance," no date, ERA, R-60/1/4.

138. Interrogation of Francis Viipsi, Haapsalu, Nov. 2, 4, and 5, 1944, USHMM, RG-06.026/13.

139. Recently, Jan Gross discussed that trend in his book on Jedwabne. Thus Gross observed that among the individuals who participated in a Jewish pogrom there were some nationalistic Poles who started working for the Soviets, then allied themselves with the Germans, and finally went over to the Soviet side once again (Jan Gross, *Neighbors: The Destruction of the Jewish Community in Jedwabne, Poland* (Princeton, N.J.: Princeton Univ. Press, 2001), 155–57, 162–67).

140. RSHA to Commander of EG A Stahlecker, Sept. 1, 1941, USHMM, RG-11.001M/R-74.

141. RMO office, Nottbeck, report: "Some observations from the trip to the Ostland between 14 and 27 August 1941," NARA, T-454/26.

142. It is true, though, that the majority of people who had been executed during the Nazi occupation were ethnic Estonians.

143. RMO Office, short report on the political situation in Estonia, [after October 1943], BAB, R-6/78.

144. Virumaa OK, overview of activities through the end of 1941, ERA, R-358/1/28.

145. Viljandi Pref. Kutsar to Mustla police commissar, Aug. 9, 1941, ERA, R-93/1/1.

146. EM N99, Sept. 30, 1941, BAB, R-58/217.

147. KdS-Estland Sandberger, annual report from July 1941 to June 30, 1942, ERA, R-819/1/12.

148. GK-Estland Litzmann to district commissars, Dec. 9, 1941, ERA, R-65/1/38.

149. BdS-Ostland Pifrader, circular letter to KdS-Estland, Lettland, and Estonia, Apr. 27, 1943, IfZ, Fb-101/18.

150. Est. Sipo in Narva, report, Jan. 8–18, 1942; Narva Police Prefect, Mar. 8–18, 1942, ERA, R-59/1/88; Est. Sipo, BIV, memo, July 19, 1942, ERA, R-59/1/4.

151. KdS-Lettland Lange to BdS-Ostland Pifrader, Apr. 22, 1943, USHMM, RG-11.001M/R-75. The difference between the two countries was that owing to the lack of anti-German opposition in Estonia, Germans had by and large refrained from jailing nationalistically minded Estonians. Thus, all those who had been imprisoned might as well pass as "Communists" who fully deserved their lot.

152. Arno Mayer, *Why Did the Heavens Not Darken? The "Final Solution" in History* (New York: Pantheon Books, 1988), 106–8, 146–52, 173–74, 200–201, 208, 212, 226.

153. Ezergailis, *Stockholm Documents,* 459.

154. Wilhelm, *Die Einsatzgruppe A,* 143.

155. Ezergailis, *The Holocaust in Latvia,* 173–77, 184, 188.

156. Knut Stang, *Kollaboration und Massenmord: Die litauische Hilfspolizei, das Rollkommando Hamann und die Ermordung der litauischen Juden* (Frankfurt: Peter Lang, 1996), 122–23, 141, 157, 161–63, 167–71.

157. Stang, *Kollaboration und Massenmord,* 178–80.

158. Knut Stang, "Das Fussvolk und seine Eliten: Der Beginn der Kollaboration in Litauen 1941," in *Judenmord in Litauen: Studien und Dokumente,* ed. Wolfgang Benz and Marion Neiss (Berlin: Metropol, 1999), 85–87.

159. Dzintars Ērgils, "A Few Holocaust Episodes in Krustpils: Beila Bella Weide Case," in *Holocausta izpētes problēmas Latvijā/The Issues of the Holocaust Research in Latvia* (Riga: Historical Institute of Latvia, 2001), 2:291.

160. Rudīte Vīksne, "The Arājs Commando Member as Seen in the KGB Trial Files: Social Standing, Education, Motives for Joining It, and Sentences Received," in *Holocausta izpētes problēmas Latvijā/The Issues of the Holocaust Research in Latvia* (Riga: Historical Institute of Latvia, 2001), 2:350–75.

5. "ESTLAND IST JUDENREIN!"

1. See, for example, Dieter Pohl, "Der Krieg gegen die Sowjetunion—ein rassen-ideologisch begründeter Vernichtungskrieg," in *Täter im Vernichtungskrieg: Der Überfall auf die Sowjetunion und der Völkermord an den Juden,* ed. Wolf Kaiser (Berlin: Propyläen, 2002), 44–48; Kim Priemel, "Sommer 1941: Die Wehrmacht in Litauen," in Bartusevičius et al., *Holocaust in Litauen,* 29–36.

2. AOK 18 v. Küchler, orders, Aug. 7 and 9, 1941, BA-MA, RH-20 18/77; AOK 18 to HGr North, daily reports, Aug. 6–10 and 16, 1941, BA-MA, RH-20 18/79.

3. Counterintelligence Office in Königsberg to Army Group C, Apr. 23, 1941, BA-MA, RH-19 III/470.

4. Security Division 207, guidelines re. carrying out security tasks, July 4 and 5, 1941, BA-MA, RH-20 18/89.

5. AOK 18 Higher quartermaster, July 23, 1941, BA-MA, RH-20 18/96.

6. HGr North v. Leeb to AOK 18 and BdrückwHGr North, July 15, 1941, BA-MA, RH-19 III/470.

7. BdrückwHGr North v. Roques, memo, July 24, 1941, LVVA, R-1026/1/3.

8. Lohse's testimony, May 28, 1948, BAK, Z-42 III/1732.

9. Christoph Dieckmann, "Der Krieg und die Ermordung der litauischen Juden," in *National-sozialistische Vernichtungspolitik 1939–1945: Neue Forschungen und Kontroversen,* ed. Ulrich Herbert (Frankfurt: Fischer, 1997), 304–5.

10. EM N111, Oct. 12, 1941, BAB, R-58/218.

11. RSHA, Dept IV Müller to EG A, B, C, D, Aug. 30, 1941, IfZ, Fb-101/32.

12. Ger. Sipo to Police pref. in Rakvere, Sept. 11, 1941, in *Pruun Katk: Saksa fašistlik okupatsioon Eestis 1941–1944. Dokumente ja materjale* (Brown Plague: German Fascist Occupation of Estonia, 1941–44. Documents and Materials), ed. Anni Matsulevitš (Tallinn: Eesti Raamat, 1988), 121–23.

13. Tallinn concentration camp [Central prison], letter book, Sept.–Oct. 1941, ERA, R-294/1/166.

14. Interrogation of Pavel Kurovskii, Tallinn, Sept. 19, 1960, USHMM, RG-06.026/12.

15. Interrogation of Heinrich Möller, Kiel, Feb. 18, 1960, BAL, 7 AR-Z 233/59, V1.

16. Peter Witte et al., eds., *Der Dienstkalender Heinrich Himmlers 1941–42* (Hamburg: Christians, 1999), 214.

17. Est. Sipo, IV B, list of Jews executed through Oct. 6, 1941, ERA, R-64/1/100. Also reproduced in Gurin-Loov, *Eesti juutide katastroof,* 199–203.

18. EM N111, Oct. 12, 1941, BAB, R-58/218.

19. IRR personal file, XE000855, Sandberger, NARA, RG-319/box 191.

20. Ibid.

21. Rebecca Sule, ERA, R-64/1/842.

22. Angelus, *Tuhande valitseja maa,* 175.

23. Mark Dworzecki, *Vaise Nekht un Shvartse Teg: Yidn-Lagern in Estonie* (Tel Aviv: Tishlia, 1970), 36; Peter Longerich, *Politik der Vernichtung: Eine Gesamtdarstellung der nationalsozialis-tischen Judenverfolgung* (Munich: Piper, 1998), 399, 418.

24. Transcript, Nov. 12, 1947, NARA, M-895/15; Transcript, Nov. 14, 1947; Transcript, Nov. 17, 1947, NARA, M-895/16.

25. Breitman, *The Architect of Genocide,* 214. In fact, the question of transfer was discussed in Himmler's headquarters as early as September 25, 1941. The reason for Jeckeln's replacement was not so much his expertise in mass murder of Jews, but his bad relations with Erich Koch, Reich commissioner for the Ukraine. Some Nazi officials believed that Prützmann might have had a better rapport with the latter (Witte et al., *Der Dienstkalender Heinrich Himmlers,* 219.)

26. Ruth Bettina Birn, *Die Höheren SS- und Polizeiführer: Himmlers Vertreter im Reich und in den besetzten Gebieten* (Düsseldorf: Droste Verlag, 1986), 375, 392–95; Transcript, Oct. 22, 1947, NARA, M-895/14; Affidavit of Herbert Degenhardt, Jan. 22, 1948, NARA, M-895/27.

27. Interrogation of Friedrich Jeckeln, Dec. 14, 1945, quoted in Gerald Flemming, *Hitler and the Final Solution* (Berkeley: Univ. of California Press, 1984), 98.

28. Interrogation of Gustav Reitz, Hannover, June 1, 1960, BAL, 408 AR-Z 233/59, V2.

29. Interrogation of Gustav Reitz, Hannover, June 1, 1960; interrogation of Martin Heymuth, June 13, 1960, BAL, 408 AR-Z 233/59, V2.

30. Interrogation of Gustav Reitz, Hannover, June 1, 1960; interrogation of Martin Heymuth, June 13, 1960, BAL, 408 AR-Z 233/59, V2; interrogation of Rudolf Edelmann, Hannover, Nov. 15, 1960, BAL, 207 AR-Z 246/59, V 2.

31. Interrogation of Sandberger, Ludwigsburg, Feb. 18, 1960, BAL, 408 AR-Z 233/59, V1.

32. Mayer, *Why Did the Heavens not Darken?*, 300. Mayer's book has numerous shortcomings and is altogether a less reliable source.

33. "Numbers of Executions Carried Out by EG A Through 1 February 1942," in Krausnick and Wilhelm, *Die Truppe des Weltanschauungskrieges,* 607.

34. Est. Sipo in Tallinn-Harju, letter book, entries from Sept. 8 to Oct. 9, 1941, ERA, R-64/1/718.

35. EG A, consolidated report from June 21 to Oct. 15, 1941, USHMM, RG-11.001M/14.

36. Paavle, *Eesti rahvastikukaotused,* 40.

37. Kuusik, "Security Police," 594–95.

38. Testimony of Rudolf Sirge, EEC records: Tallinn, fall 1944, USHMM, RG-22.002M/25.

39. Meelis Maripuu, "Eesti juutide holocaust ja eestlased" (Estonians and the Holocaust of the Estonian Jews), in *Vikerkaar* 15, no. 8–9 (2001): 142.

40. Interrogation of Nikolai Jehe [phonetic], Oct. 10, 1960; interrogation of Jaak Lääts, Dec. 8, 1960; interrogation of Jurii Viidoja, Dec. 3, 1960 (all three in Tallinn), USHMM, RG-06.026/12.

41. Interrogation of Julius Mihkelsoo, Tallinn, Sept. 19, 1949, and Oct. 2, 1950, USHMM, RG-06.026/12.

42. Interrogation of Eduard Kaunsaar, Tallinn, Sept. 25, 1960, USHMM, RG-06.026/12.

43. Rautkallio, *Finland and the Holocaust,* 149. See also Maripuu, "Eesti juutide holocaust ja eestlased," 141.

44. Testimony of Hjalmar Mäe, Wiesbaden, Jan. 21, 1953, IfZ, ZS-2366. More precisely, executions usually took place around 4 A.M. (interrogation of Gerhard Isup, Tallinn, Apr. 5, 1945, USHMM, RG-06.026/12).

45. Est. Sipo, BIV, letter book, entry from May 1, 1942, ERA, R-64/1/740.

46. Est. Sipo in Tallinn-Harju, letter book, entry from Mar. 18, 1942, ERA, R-64/1/732.

47. Est. Sipo in Narva to Head of Narva prison, February 6, 1942, ERA, R-59/1/40; KdS-Estland Sandberger to Head of BIV Dept. Ennok, Aug. 29, 1942, ERA, R-59/1/4; AIV Bergmann to BIV Dept., Jan. 18, 1943, ERA, R-64/1/190.

48. EG A, consolidated report from June 21 to Oct. 15, 1941, USHMM, RG-11.001M/14.

49. ZEV, Tambek, circular letter, Oct. 10, 1941, ERA, R-93/1/1.

50. ZEV, Tambek, report on Estonian deportees, Dec. 2, 1942, ERA, R-64/1/7. A total of 1,587 victims were identified. The largest number of executed was reported in Tartu—407, followed by Tallinn—323, and Virumaa Province—262 (*Deutsche Zeitung im Ostland,* Dec. 14, 1942).

51. Head of Police and OK admin Soodla, circular letter, Nov. 7, 1941, ERA, R-93/1/1; Mäe, *Kuidas kõik teostus,* 245.

52. ZEV in Tallinn to ZEV regional offices, Oct. 7, 1941, ERA, R-62/1/7.

53. Lindmäe, *Suvesõda,* 293–94.

54. RFSS Himmler to RMO Rosenberg, Aug. 13, 1943, LVVA, R-1026/1/3; EM N 111, Oct. 12, 1941, BAB, R-58/218.

55. Est. Sipo in Tallinn-Harju, statistical chart, Dec. 31, 1941; BIV, "special treatment" table, Aug. 21, 1944, ERA, R-64/1/48.

56. Gruf. Harald Turner, chief of the military administration of Serbia, announced in August 1942 that Serbia was the only country in which both Jewish and Gypsy Questions were solved.

57. President of TU Kant to German field commandant, Aug. 18, 1941; Hans Kauri to H. Norman, Nov. 5, 1941, EAA, 2100/15/59. Kant, who formerly worked as a geography professor at TU, was also a member of the Tartu OK. The local headquarters approved Kant's appointment as president of TU.

58. Gurin-Loov, *Eesti juutide katastroof,* 222–23.

59. Correspondence among RSHA, KdS-Estland Sandberger, BdS-Ostland Stahlecker, and ERR, Nov. 27, 1941–June 25, 1942, USHMM, RG-15.007/11. There is no consensus as to how and when Simon Dubnov was murdered. Some authors argue that Dubnov died of infectious disease in the Riga ghetto while others think that he was executed on December 8, 1941, during the ghetto liquidation.

60. KdS-Estland Sandberger, memo, May 20, 1942, ERA, R-59/1/3.

61. GK-Estland Office, Dept. II, Mar. 2, 1942, ERA, R-65/1/4.

62. Ida Gelb, ERA, R-64/4/147; Isaac Freidin, ERA, R-64/4/1170.

63. Johan Parts, deposition taken at the U.S. Embassy in Stockholm, no date [1962?]. Parts did not give the names, which nevertheless are easy to derive from the context (YVA, 04/52).

64. Haim Rubin, ERA, R-64/4/1142.

65. Ruth Rubin, ERA, R-64/4/665; Ervin Martinson, *Slugi svastiki* (Tallinn: Estonian State Publishing House, 1962), 164–70. Information that Martinson presented in his book should be treated with caution, for the Soviets tended to embellish the evidence.

66. Elisabeth White, "Estonia's Gestapo: The Estonian Political Police in Tallinn, 1941–42," paper presented at the German Studies Association conference, Atlanta, Oct. 10, 1999.

67. Est. Sipo in Viljandi, Sept. 29, 1941, ERA, R-62/1/1.

68. *Postimees,* Sept. 11, 1941, in Gurin-Loov, *Eesti juutide katastroof,* 43.

69. List of confiscated property in Viljandi, 1941, ERA, R-62/1/7.

70. Ger. Sipo to Police pref. in Rakvere, Sept. 11, 1941, in *Pruun Katk,* 122.

71. Correspondence between Est. Self-Government and Viljandi Province admin, Feb. 16 and 19, 1942, in Gurin-Loov, *Eesti juutide katastroof,* 41–42.

72. Ber Kirschbaum, ERA, R-64/4/338; Rochelle Riva Brenner, ERA, R-64/4/86.

73. GK-Estland, Trustee Office, situational report, Apr. 12, 1942, LVVA, R-70/2/37; Gurin-Loov, *Eesti juutide katastroof,* 228.

74. Pärnu district commissar, appeal, July 28, 1942, ERA, R-65/1/2176.

75. RKO Lohse to GK-Estland Litzmann, Mar. 22, 1943, LVVA, R-70/5/24.

76. GK-Estland Office, press release, Nov. 6, 1942, ERA, R-65/1/1918.

77. Trusteeship by GK-Estland to Trusteeship by RKO, May 13, 1942, ERA, R-65/1/2176.

78. Narva Gk Jenetzky to Trusteeship by GK-Estland, July 21, 1942, ERA, R-65/1/2176.

79. Tartu GK Meenen to Trusteeship by GK-Estland, Apr. 10, 1943, ERA, R-65/1/1918; ibid. July 30, 1942, ERA, R-65/1/2176. It was not uncommon for the institutions of higher learning throughout Europe to acquire Jewish property. The University of Latvia, for example, laid claim to medical instruments in the Riga ghetto infirmary.

80. Pskov GK to Trusteeship by GK-Estland, May 22, 1942, ERA, R-65/1/2176.

81. List: monetary value of Jewish property, no date [spring 1942], ERA, R-65/1/2176.

82. Correspondence between KdS-Estland Baatz and GK-Estland Litzmann, Jan. 28 and 31, 1944, ERA, R-65/1/1918. Baatz replaced Sandberger as KdS-Estland in September 1943.

83. RSHA to BdS-Ostland Pifrader, June 29, 1943, USHMM, RG-11.001M/75.

84. Correspondence re. Allikvee, Dorbek, Kornel, and Ehajärv's cases, Dec. 1942–May 1944, ERA, R-65/1/1918; ERA, R-65/1/2176.

85. Ger. Sipo in Tallinn, minutes, May 31, 1943, ERA, R-65/1/1918.

86. Est. Sipo, BIV, lists of arrested individuals, Feb. 23 and 26, 1943, ERA, R-64/1/109.

87. Katrin Reichelt, "Der Anteil von Letten an der Enteignung der Juden ihres Landes zwischen 1941 und 1943," in Kooperation und Verbrechen: Formen der 'Kollaboration' im östlichen Europa 1939–1945, ed. Christoph Dieckmann (Göttingen: Wallstein Verlag, 2003), 234–36, 240–242.

88. Ezergailis, Stockholm Documents, 116.

89. Valentinas Brandišauskas, "Neue Dokumente aus der Zeit der Provisorischen Regierung Litauens," in Bartusevičius et al., Holocaust in Litauen, 57–59.

90. GK-Estland Office, memo, Apr. 20, 1942, ERA, R-65/1/2176. The former Jewish Club on Väike-Karja Street in Tallinn served as a storage facility for cultural treasures temporarily removed from one of the former manor houses (ERR, memo, Oct. 16, 1941, BAB, NS-30/146).

91. P. Ivask, report, Apr. 12, 1943, ERA, R-65/1/144.

92. List of archival records handed over by Haapsalu Kripo to Tallinn Central Archives, May 26, 1943, ERA, R-56/2/4.

93. GK-Estland, Statistics Office, Mar. 30, 1942, ERA, R-65/1/68.

94. Anton Weiss-Wendt, "Extermination of the Gypsies in Estonia During World War II: Popular Images and Official Policies," Holocaust and Genocide Studies 17, no. 1 (Spring 2003): 31–61.

95. AOK 18, IV Wi, to WiKo, Tallinn, Aug. 27, 1941, BA-MA, RW-46/299.

96. BdrückwHGr North v. Roques, Sept. 18, 1941, BA-MA, RH-22/254.

97. Viljandi pref., circular letter, Sept. 1941, ERA, R-62/1/1.

98. Local headquarters in Paide, order, Dec. 1, 1941, ERA, R-89/1/1.

99. Local headquarters in Nõmme, situational report, Oct. 26, 1941, BA-MA, RW-30/56.

100. Ger. Sipo in Tartu to Est. Sipo in Pechory, Nov. 11, 1942, ERA, R-60/1/11.

101. BIV Viks to AIV Bergmann, Oct. 31, 1942, ERA, R-64/1/101.

102. Testimony of Andrei Kurol, Oct. 19, 1960; testimony of Georgii Rents, Jan. 9, 1961 (both in Tallinn), USHMM, RG-06.026/12.

103. Est. Sipo in Narva, memo, Feb. 2, 1943, ERA, R-59/1/69.

104. Commandant of Tallinn AEL to Head of BIV, Feb. 10–24, 1943, ERA, R-64/1/106.

105. Interrogation of Johannes Palm, Sept. 13, 1960; interrogation of Victor Udam (both in Tallinn), Nov. 30, 1960, USHMM, RG-06.026/12.

106. Interrogation of Jan Viik, Tallinn, Sept. 23 and 29, 1960; Jan. 6, 1961, USHMM, RG-06.026/12.

107. Ibid., Dec. 29, 1960.

108. Weiss-Wendt, "Extermination of the Gypsies in Estonia," 49.

109. Ger. Sipo, AV to Est. Sipo, BV, Jan. 22, 1943; transfer deeds of property belonging to Anton Koslovski and Viilep Indus, Feb. 6, 1943, ERA, R-59/1/69; transfer deeds of property belonging to Nikolai Koslovski, Nikandr Koslovski, Eugenia Ivanov, Konstantin Ivanov, Feb. 7, 1943, ERA, R-63/1/8.

110. Ezergailis, *The Holocaust in Latvia*, 200 f.

111. Documents NN 122 and 123 in *My obviniaem* (Riga: Liesma, 1967), 195–98.

112. Marģers Vestermanis as quoted in Ezergailis, *The Holocaust in Latvia*, 288, 329 f.

113. Interrogation of Donat Bukovski, Mar. 4, 1965; Afanasi Aglish, Jan. 11, 1965; Kuprian Volkov (all in Riga), July 15, 1965, USHMM, RG-06.027 (case N45038).

114. BdO Lettland to SSPF Lettland, Mar. 11, 1942, in Wolfgang Benz et al., eds., *Einsatz im "Reichskommissariat Ostland": Dokumente zum Völkermord im Baltikum und in Weissrussland 1941–1944* (Berlin: Metropol, 1998), 98.

115. Guntis Dišlers, "The Attitude of Latvia's Lutheran Church Toward the Holocaust in World War II," *Holocausta izpētes problēmas Latvijā/The Issues of the Holocaust Research in Latvia* (Riga: Latvijas vēstures institūts, 2001), 2:247.

116. Interrogation of Jānis Jezens, Riga, Oct. 1962, USHMM, RG-06.027 (case N44899).

117. Liepāja pref. to commander of municipal police, Jan. 13, 1942, USHMM, RG-06.025/1.

118. Vytautas Toleikis, "Lithuanian Roma During the Years of the Nazi Occupation," in *Karo belaisvių ir civilių gyventojų žudynės Lietuvoje, 1941–1944* (Murder of Prisoners of War and Civilian Population in Lithuania, 1941–1944), ed. Christoph Dieckmann et al. (Vilnius: Margi raštai, 2005), 267–85; Documents NN 124, 126–28 in *Documents Accuse* (Vilnius: Gintaras, 1970), 259, 260, 262–65.

119. Michael Burleigh and Wolfgang Wippermann, *The Racial State: Germany, 1933–1945* (Cambridge, UK: Cambridge Univ. Press, 1991), 136–53.

120. EM N88, Sept. 19, 1941; EM N96, Sept. 27, 1941, BAB, R-58/217.

121. Documents NN 128 and 129 in *My obviniaem*, 213, 214.

122. Interrogation of Emilia Intenberg, Riga, Jan.–Apr. 1945, USHMM, RG-06.027 (case N16274).

123. Interrogation of Albert Belinis, July 1947; interrogation of Juris Šumskis (both in Riga), June 1945, USHMM, RG-06.027 (cases N695 and N42500).

124. Ezergailis, *The Holocaust in Latvia,* 188–89, 194. Ezergalis quotes from Šumskis's deposition selectively, failing to mention that the Arājs commando participated in the actual killing of the mentally ill.

125. *My obviniaem,* 213 f.

126. Testimony of Jānis Vilde, Riga, Dec. 24, 1945, USHMM, RG-06.025.01.

127. Interrogation of Friedrich Jeckeln, Riga, Dec. 21, 1945, USHMM, RG-06.026/12.

128. Krausnick and Wilhelm, *Die Truppe des Weltanschauungskrieges,* 607. The numbers differ from those presented in earlier EMs.

129. Hilberg, *The Destruction of the European Jews,* 217–18.

130. GK-Estland Office, Dept I to SSPF Möller, Dec. 27, 1941, ERA, R-65/1/124.

131. Statistics on executions in Tallinn-Harju pref. through Aug. 1944, ERA, R-64/1/48.

132. GK-Estland Litzmann to Minister of Justice Öpik, Apr. 1942, ERA, R-294/1/8.

133. Ken Kalling, "Estonian Psychiatric Hospitals During the German Occupation, 1941–1944," unpublished paper (2006).

134. Michael Burleigh, *Death and Deliverance: "Euthanasia" in Germany, 1900–1945* (Cambridge, Mass.: Harvard Univ. Press, 1994), 240–42.

135. Anna Metsaleid and Abutalip Abiasov, ERA, R-131/1/8.

136. Rahmiel Schadsunsky, ERA, R-64/4/913; David and Isak Rusinov, ERA, R-64/4/739, 740; Anna and Ella Klein (Paavle, *Eesti rahvastikukaotused,* 129).

137. Head of Ger. Kripo Bergmann, presentation, May 27, 1942, ERA, R-819/1/11.

138. Tallinn AEL, guidelines [1942?], ERA, R-64/1/46.

139. I am grateful to Christopher Browning, who pointed out that nuance to me.

6. "JEWISH" FILES: TALLINN

1. Sofia Isatchik (name denotes respective case file of the Est. Sipo), ERA, R-64/4/230.

2. Jacob Epstein, ERA, R-64/4/204; Ephraim Olei, ERA, R-64/4/550.

3. "Juden in Narwa," no date [Aug. 1941], ERA, R-59/1/23a. The list was compiled in Estonian and subsequently forwarded to the Ger. Sipo.

4. Rafael Goldmann, ERA, R-64/1/338.

5. Ger. Sipo, "Individuals, subject to arrest in Tallinn: The Search List *Ost,*" Tartu, July 23, 1941, ERA, R-60/1/11.

6. Est. Sipo, BIV, memo, Sept. 21, 1942, ERA, R-59/1/3.

7. Jossel Abramson, ERA, R-64/4/36; Gershon Herzenberg, ERA, R-64/4/902; Meier Pevsner, ERA, R-64/4/580.

8. Gurin-Loov, *Eesti juutide katastroof,* 224.

9. Basse Majofis, ERA, R-64/4/489.

10. Mordhe Majofis, ERA, R-64/4/528; Leib Majofis, ERA, R-64/4/529.

11. Shapshe Permand, ERA, R-64/4/1120; Samuel Permand, ERA, R-64/4/1119; Josef Permand, ERA, R-64/4/1118; Simon Rudnik, ERA, R-64/4/1129; Haim Rattud, ERA, R-64/4/1134; Jury Pliner,

ERA, R-64/4/610; Jonas Bobkovich, ERA, R-64/4/1053; Meyer Bam, ERA, R-64/4/1044; Samuel Levin, ERA, R-64/4/465; Abram Matskin, ERA, R-64/4/483; Abram Hecht, ERA, R-64/4/1172; Selik Haitin, ERA, R-64/4/1175; Joshua Haifon, ERA, R-64/4/1176; Ely Hoff, ERA, R-64/4/1178; David Noachas, ERA, R-64/4/533; Isaiah Dubrovkin, ERA, R-64/4/164.

12. Interrogation of Oskar Parvei, Tallinn, Dec. 1, 1944, USHMM, RG-06.026.09.

13. Paavle, *Eesti rahvastikukaotused,* 102.

14. Leo Klaus, ERA, R-64/4/374.

15. Koppel Koslovsky, ERA, R-64/4/322.

16. Gurin-Loov, *Eesti juutide katastroof,* 233–34.

17. Martin Gilbert, *The Righteous: The Unsung Heroes of the Holocaust* (New York: Henry Holt, 2003), 31–32; Gurin-Loov, *Eesti juutide katastroof,* 233; Stéphane Bruchfeld and Paul Levine, *Jutustage sellest oma lastele: Raamat holokaustist Euroopas aastatel 1933–1945* (Tell Your Children about It: A Book about the Holocaust in Europe, 1933–1945) (Tartu: Israeli Sõbrad, 2003), 93.

18. Benjamin Patov, ERA, R-64/4/578.

19. David Ginsburg, ERA, R-64/4/161; Deborah Alperovich, ERA, R-64/4/39; Peter Abraham, ERA, R-64/4/35; Zilla Arnovich-Jankel, ERA, R-64/4/33; Sarah Arnovich-Jankel, ERA, R-64/4/34; Lazar Arnovich-Jankel, ERA, R-64/4/37.

20. Jossel Abramson, ERA, R-64/4/36; Bella and Leo Kletzky, ERA, R-64/4/373.

21. Documents from the case file of Simon Rubinstein in Gurin-Loov, *Eesti juutide katastroof,* 129–31.

22. Hannah Brin, ERA, R-64/4/51; Esther Jakobson, ERA, R-64/4/929; Miron Brodsky, ERA, R-64/4/63; Isaac Freidin, ERA, R-64/4/1170.

23. Hain Herzfeldt, ERA, R-64/4/901; Eli Haitin, ERA, R-64/4/906; Jacob Bam, ERA, R-64/4/137; Rubin Racheltchik, ERA, R-64/4/1136.

24. Hirsh Ballak, ERA, R-64/4/136; Abram Abe Bass, ERA, R-64/4/1045; Markus Dubrovkin, ERA, R-64/4/179.

25. David Ginsburg, ERA, R-64/4/161; Moses Blechman, ERA, R-64/4/61; Gershon Herzenberg, ERA, R-64/4/902; Elias Hoff, ERA, R-64/4/1178; Joseph Girskovits, ERA, R-64/4/162; Gottfried Firk, ERA, R-64/4/868; Schenny Katsev, ERA, R-64/4/326.

26. Lazar Gershanovich, ERA, R-64/4/1055; Harry Itskovich, ERA, R-64/4/248; Moses Goldstein, ERA, R-64/4/1056.

27. Valentine Klompus, ERA, R-64/4/1069.

28. Salomon Lury, ERA, R-64/4/432.

29. Salomon Epstein, ERA, R-64/4/185.

30. Est. Sipo in Narva, Nov. 10–25 1941, ERA, R-59/1/40.

31. Hessel Aronovich, ERA, R-64/4/23; Jacob Kolektor, ERA, R-64/4/1075; Isaac Lopavok, ERA, R-64/4/1093; David Levin, ERA, R-64/4/1089; Aron Krenshinsky, ERA, R-64/4/1084; Rubin Racheltchik, ERA, R-64/4/1136.

32. Salomon Lury, ERA, R-64/4/432.

33. Est. Sipo in Narva, annual report through July 1, 1942, ERA, R-59/1/17.

34. Elias Elian, ERA, R-64/4/212.

35. Ephraim Olei, ERA, R-64/4/550. Birn came to the same conclusion in her article on the Estonian Security Police (Birn, "Collaboration," 189–90).

36. Salomon Epstein, ERA, R-64/4/185; Mikhail Sheer, ERA, R-64/4/914; Abe Bass, ERA, R-64/4/1048; Abram Iliashev, ERA, R-64/4/220; Härmo Pant, ERA, R-64/4/600.

37. Gurin-Loov, *Eesti juutide katastroof,* 225.

38. Israel Baskin, ERS, R-64/4/135; Salomon Epstein, ERA, R-64/4/185.

39. Rebecca Salome, ERA, R-64/4/800.

40. Anna Kalmanson, ERA, R-64/4/957.

41. KdS-Estland Sandberger, annual report from July 1941 to June 30, 1942, ERA, R-819/1/12.

42. Sonia Gasman, ERA, R-64/4/146; Ginda Rosenberg, ERA, R-64/4/1140. Rosenberg's story appeared also in Bruchfeld and Levine, *Jutustage sellest oma lastele,* 89.

43. Gisela Diewald-Kerkmann has recently challenged the view that women are more prone to informing than men. According to Diewald-Kerkmann, women accounted for 11 percent of all political denunciations in Nazi Germany. Gisela Diewald-Kerkmann, "Politische Denunziation im NS-Regime: Die kleine Macht der 'Volksgenossen,'" in *Denunziation: Historische, juristische und psychologische Aspekte,* ed. Günter Jerouschek et al. (Tübingen: Edition Diskord, 1997), 150.

44. Hanna Kronik, ERA, R-64/4/288.

45. Robert Gellately, "Denunciations in Twentieth-Century Germany: Aspects of Self-Policing in the Third Reich and the German Democratic Republic," in *Accusatory Practices: Denunciation in Modern European History, 1789–1989,* ed. Sheila Fitzpatrick and Robert Gellately (Univ. of Chicago Press, 1996), 193, 196.

46. KdS-Estland Sandberger to Est. Sipo Mere, Jan. 10, 1942, ERA, R-819/2/7. The signs of annoyance with the sheer amount of denunciations had already appeared in November (EM N135, Nov. 19, 1941, BAB, R-58/219).

47. Interview with Ain-Ervin Mere in *Postimees,* Sept. 3, 1942.

48. Virumaa OK, overview of activities through the end of 1941, ERA, R-358/1/27. See also interrogation of Arnold Mihkli, Tallinn, Nov. 19, 1960, USHMM, RG-06.026/12.

49. Anna Lind to Est. Sipo in Narva, Nov. 13, 1941, ERA, R-59/1/55.

50. U.S. Legation in Stockholm, "Digest of Radio News Bulletins from Tallinn and Helsinki for the Period 15 January–1 February 1942," Mar. 2, 1942, NARA, M-1170/23. The broadcast reiterated Angelus's order N40 of Jan. 22, 1942, that dealt specifically with informing (ERA, R-1197/1/1). The head of the Latvian civil administration, Oskars Dankers, broadcast a similar appeal condemning denouncers.

51. Hessel Aronovich, ERA, R-64/4/23; Hirsh Ballak, ERA, R-64/4/136.

52. Jossel Abramson, ERA, R-64/4/36; Abram Saltsmann, ERA, R-64/4/778; Leib Lipelis, ERA, R-64/4/458.

53. Maksim Kagan, ERA, R-64/4/281; Härmo Pant, ERA, R-64/4/600; Gottfried Firk, ERA, R-64/4/868; Gershon Herzenberg, ERA, R-64/4/902.

54. Harry Itskovich, ERA, R-64/4/248; Salomon Epstein, ERA, R-64/4/185; Rachmiel Shadsunsky, ERA, R-64/4/913.

55. Ella Brodsky, ERA, R-64/4/87.

56. Eduard Eitelberg, ERA, R-64/4/186.

57. Abram Sachar-Schocher, ERA, R-64/4/775.

58. Rochelle Hanin, ERA, R-64/4/905.

59. *U.S. v Karl Linnas,* Raul Hilberg-cross examination, Westbury, Long Island, New York, June 16, 1981, 164.

60. Miriam Lepp, ERA, R-64/4/424.

61. Ibid.

62. Ibid.

63. Birn, "Collaboration with Nazi Germany," 186.

64. Rebecca Salome, ERA, R-64/4/800.

65. Ibid.

66. Est. Sipo in Tartu, wanted list, Feb. 20, 1941, ERA, R-62/1/24.

67. Viljandi Pref. Kutsar, circular letter N184, July 25, 1941, ERA, R-93/1/1.

68. Excerpts from Miina Kuusik's case file, indictment of Jüriste, Linnas, and Viks, Tallinn, July 31, 1961, USHMM, RG-06.026/11.

69. Testimony of Hans Laats at Jüriste-Linnas-Viks trial, Tartu, Jan. 16, 1962, USHMM, RG-06.026/11.

70. Birn, "Collaboration with Nazi Germany," 191–96.

71. Raul Hilberg, *The Destruction of the European Jews* (Chicago: Quadrangle Books, 1961), 242–43.

72. Longerich, *Politik der Vernichtung,* 360, 390–92, 414–15, 680 f. See also Eric Heine, "Algemeine Ermächtigung und konkrete Eigendynamik: Die Ermordung der Juden in den ländlichen Gebieten Litauens," in Bartusevičius et al., *Holocaust in Litauen,* 94–95.

73. Interrogation of Felix Rühl, Opladen, Apr. 15, 1971, BAL, 201 AR-Z 76/59, V7. See also Breitman, *The Architect of Genocide,* 213.

74. Meier Pevsner, ERA, R-64/4/580; Basse Majofis, ERA, R-64/4/489; Härmo Pant, ERA, R-64/4/600; Abram Sachar-Schocher, ERA, R-64/4/775; Hirsh Harchat, ERA, R-64/4/907; Paul Klompus, ERA, R-64/4/283; Aron Krenchinsky, ERA, R-64/4/1084.

75. Rautkallio, *Finland and the Holocaust,* 135. The officer was visiting Tallinn between Oct. 1 and 12, 1941.

76. Testimony of Pavel Kurovskii at Laak-Gerrets-Viik-Mere trial, Tallinn, Mar. 6, 1961, USHMM, RG-06.016/12.

77. Minoche Idelson, ERA, R-64/4/226; Jente Harchat, ERA, R-64/4/884; Ida Bruck, ERA, R-64/4/77; Sima Brashinsky, ERA, R-64/4/49.

78. Gita Talaievsky and Anna Kalmanson, R-64/4/957.

79. Sarah Lipavsky, ERA, R-64/1/160.

80. Raisa Ostrovsky, ERA, R-64/4/551; Bella and Leo Kletzky, ERA, R-64/4/373; Paavle, *Eesti rahvastikukaotused,* 129.

81. Valentinas Brandišauskas, "Neue Dokumente aus der Zeit der Provisorischen Regierung Litauens," in Bartusevičius et al., *Holocaust in Litauen,* 52–53.

82. Documents from the case file of Beile Ratut in Gurin-Loov, *Eesti juutide katastroof,* 161–67. Swedish translation of the documents reprinted in Peeter Puide, *Samuil Braschinskys försvunna vrede. Dokumentärroman* (Stockholm: Norstedts, 1997), 24–29.

83. Jury Pliner, ERA, R-64/4/610. Swedish translation of the documents reprinted in Puide, *Samuil Braschinskys försvunna vrede,* 117–32.

84. Gurin-Loov, *Eesti juutide katastroof,* 229; Paavle, *Eesti rahvastikukaotused,* 144, 247, 254.

85. Yehuda Bauer, *Rethinking the Holocaust* (New Haven, Conn.: Yale Univ. Press, 2001), 51–52.

86. I acknowledge the difficulties in obtaining such evidence.

87. Erika Puis, Oct. 17, 1944, ERA, R-292/1/1; Pulkheria Tsakukhina, July 10, 1961, Jüriste-Linnas-Viks trial records, USHMM, RG-06.026.11.

7. THE END COMPLETE: JEWS IN PROVINCIAL CITIES

1. Interrogations of Rudolf Nüüd, Feb. 9 and June 19, 1968; Leonhard Pindis, Feb. 13, 1968; Alexander Janson, Mar. 13, 1968; Harald Plaado, Apr. 10, 1968 (all in Tallinn), USHMM, RG-06.026/14.

2. Rebecca Judelovich, ERA, R-52/2/18.

3. Est. Sipo in Paide, Eelnurm to Est. Sipo in Tallinn, Mere, Dec. 1941, in *Pruun Katk,* 138.

4. List of prisoners in Narva prison, Aug. 28–30, 1941; Benjamin Beilinson, ERA, R-59/1/30; Indrek Paavle, "Soviet Investigations Concerning the Executions in Estonia During the German Occupation in 1941-1944," in Hiio, Maripuu, and Paavle, *Estonia, 1940–1945,* 664.

5. Est. Sipo in Narva, Oct. 21, 1941, ERA, R-59/1/25.

6. Vera Panova, "Metelitsa," *Sobranie sochinenii v piati tomakh* (Leningrad, 1970), 5:67–70, 96, 102. Panova was the first author who produced a semifictional account that alluded to the murder of Jews in Estonia. Panova drafted this particular play in 1942.

7. Est. Sipo in Narva, statistics through June 15, 1942, in *Pruun Katk,* doc N120, 134.

8. Est. Sipo in Rakvere, list of individuals sentenced in Rakvere, ERA, R-64/1/90. See also Paavle, *Eesti rahvastikukaotused,* 62, 73, 85, 87, 107, 193, 224, 243, 269.

9. Saaremaa OK, overview of activities through the end of 1941, ERA, R-358/1/11.

10. Est. Sipo in Kuressaare to Registry Office, ERA, R-64/1/841.

11. Est. Sipo in Haapsalu to Registry Office, ERA, R-64/1/842.

12. Berra Smoliansky, ERA, R-56/3/46.

13. Pärnu prison composition, Sept. 1, 1941; Petitions of Pärnu Jewesses, Sept. 5 and 18, 1941; Commandant of Pärnu KZ to Head of OK, Oct. 4, 1941; Inspector of Pärnu penitentiaries to Head of Pärnu Police, Sept. 25, 1941; Inspector of Pärnu penitentiaries to Commandant of Pärnu KZ, Sept. 25, 1941; Head of Pärnu OK to Head of OK, Sept. 11, 1941, ERA, R-932/1/1.

14. List of Jews executed in Pärnu, Jan. 16, 1942 in Gurin-Loov, *Eesti juutide katastroof*, 204–6, 227, 230.

15. Interrogation of Konstantin Lehe, Tallinn, Oct. 19, 1960, USHMM, RG-06.026/12.

16. Head of Pärnu OK, Order N30, Oct. 31, 1941, ERA, R-207/1/3.

17. Interrogation of Hermann Riecken, Bergedorf, May 1948, BAK, Z-42 III/1732.

18. Martin Jüris, application in the name of Pärnu City Mayor, Sept. 1, 1941, ERA, R-932/1/1.

19. *Sirp ja Vasar*, Sept. 13, 1963; interrogation of Karl Leetsi, Pärnu, Apr. 3, 1950, ERAF, 23788.

20. Paavle, *Eesti rahvastikukaotused*, 72, 73, 77, 88, 89, 92, 97, 106, 118, 144, 160, 209, 244, 311–16.

21. Est. Sipo in Tartu, wanted list, Feb. 20, 1942, ERA, R-62/1/24.

22. It is possible that some Tartu Jews made it as far as Tallinn, where they were later arrested and executed.

23. Lindmäe, *Suvesõda*, 205, 209–11, 225, 326–27.

24. Tartumaa OK, overview of activities through the end of 1941, ERA, R-358/1/17.

25. AOK 18, Aug. 2, 1941, BA-MA, RH-20 18/99.

26. Paavle, *Eesti rahvastikukaotused*, 67, 73, 87, 95, 105, 118, 186, 236, 249, 280.

27. Isaac Mogilkin, ERA, R-60/2/200.

28. Moses Kaplan, ERA, R-60/2/139; interrogation of Eduard Hilpus, Tartu, Jan. 23, 1961, USHMM, RG-06.026/11.

29. EM N88, Sept. 19, 1941, BAB, R-58/217. Apparently male Jews were meant.

30. Interrogation of Voldemar Rajaloo, Tartu, Apr. 27, 1961, USHMM, RG-06.026/11.

31. Interrogation of Hans Laats, Tallinn, Feb. 23 and 27, 1961, USHMM, RG-06.026/11.

32. Interrogation of Voldemar Rajaloo, Tartu, Apr. 27, 1961, USHMM, RG-06.026/11.

33. Interrogation of Juhan Jüriste, Tallinn, Nov. 30, 1960, USHMM, RG-06.026/11.

34. Interrogation of Harald Kolberg, Mar. 31, 1961; Arnold Looman, Mar. 25, 1961 (both in Tartu), USHMM, RG-06.026/11.

35. Interrogation of Aksel Piir, Tartu, Mar. 28, 1961, USHMM, RG-06.026/11.

36. Interrogation of Juhan Jüriste, Tallinn, Dec. 2, 1960, USHMM, RG-06.026/11. Ironically, the street name, Õnne, means "happiness" in Estonian.

37. Interrogation of Alexander Kroon, Tallinn, Mar. 14, 1961, USHMM, RG-06.026/11.

38. Interrogation of Juhan Jüriste, Tallinn, Feb. 21, 1961, USHMM, RG-06.026/11.

39. Interrogation of Osvald Mets, Tartu, Dec. 27, 1960, USHMM, RG-06.026/11.

40. Interrogation of Juhan Jüriste, Tallinn, Dec. 13, 1960, USHMM, RG-06.026/11.

41. Interrogation of Rosalie Eres, Tallinn, Feb. 2, 1961, USHMM, RG-06.026/11.

42. Testimony of Jenny Nõu, Tartu, Dec. 23, 1960, USHMM, RG-06.026/11.

43. Interrogation of Juhan Jüriste, Tallinn, Dec. 12, 1960, USHMM, RG-06.026/11.

44. Interrogation of Hans Laats, Tallinn, Dec. 6, 1952, USHMM, RG-06.026/5; interrogation of Juhan Jüriste, Tallinn, Dec. 12, 1960; testimony of Irene Reinhold, Pärnu, Apr. 20, 1961, USHMM, RG-06.026/11.

45. Interrogation of Herbert Hinzer, Apr. 7, 1961; interrogation of Johannes Melder, Apr. 27, 1961 (both in Tartu), USHMM, RG-06.026/11.

46. Testimonies of Salme Rull and Lilly Lõoke, Tartu, Apr. 19, 1961, USHMM, RG-06.026/11.

47. Interrogation of Elmar Ardla, Tallinn, Dec. 10, 1945, USHMM, RG-06.026/5.

48. Interrogation of Juhan Jüriste, Tallinn, Mar. 2, 1961, USHMM, RG-06.026/11.

49. Interrogation of Harald Kolberg, Tartu, Mar. 31, 1961, USHMM, RG-06.026/11.

50. Interrogation of Hans Laats, Tallinn, Feb. 24, 1961; testimony of Hans Laats at Jüriste-Linnas-Viks trial, Tartu, Jan. 16, 1962, USHMM, RG-06.026/11.

51. Confrontation between Jüriste and Laats, Tallinn, Mar. 4, 1961; interrogation of Osvald Mets, Tartu, Dec. 27, 1960, USHMM, RG-06.026/11.

52. Interrogation of Hans Laats, Tallinn, Feb. 22, 1961, USHMM, RG-06.026/11.

53. Interrogation of Hans Laats, Dec. 10, 1952, USHMM, RG-06.026/5; interrogation of Karl Elk, Apr. 5, 1961; interrogation of Harald Kolberg, Oct. 29, 1960; interrogation of Manivald Muuli, Apr. 3, 1961 (all in Tartu); testimony of Irene Reinhold, Pärnu, Apr. 20, 1961; excerpts from various investigation files, USHMM, RG-06.026/11; interrogation of Herman Ehrlich, Mar. 3 and 10, 1948; interrogation of Evald Eelmets (both in Tartu), Mar. 10, 1948, ERAF, 1243/I; Paavle, "Soviet Investigations," 674–75. Some of the defendants who received prison sentences in the late 1940s later argued that the investigative officers forced them to confess to crimes they had never committed. Circumstantial evidence, as well as the testimonies collected in the 1960s, however, for the most part corroborates earlier findings.

54. To get cigarettes and vodka was a big deal; some of the perpetrators bitterly remarked that the officers had always had plenty of alcohol on their table.

55. Interrogation of Hans Laats, Tallinn, Feb. 27, 1961; testimony of Mikhail Afanasiev, Tartu, Mar. 24, 1961; interrogation of Juhan Jüriste, Tallinn, Nov. 30, 1960, USHMM, RG-06.026/11.

56. Interrogation of August Malts, Tartu, Mar. 29, 1961, USHMM, RG-06.026/11.

57. Interrogation of Olav Karikosk, Jan. 13, 1961; interrogation of Alexander Kroon, Mar. 15, 1961 (both in Tallinn), USHMM, RG-06.026/11.

58. Interrogation of Karl Elk, Apr. 5, 1961; confrontation between Jüriste and Elk, Apr. 5, 1961 (both in Tartu); interrogation of Ingrid Aksel, Tallinn, Jan. 9, 1961, USHMM, RG-06.026/11. See also Paavle, *Eesti rahvastikukaotused,* 183.

59. Testimony of August Tõnismaa, Tartu, Mar. 30, 1961, USHMM, RG-06.026/11.

60. Testimony of Elmar Puusepp, Tartu, Apr. 5, 1961, USHMM, RG-06.026/11.

61. Interrogation of Oskar Art, Tartu, Nov. 1, 1960, USHMM, RG-06.026/11.

62. Interrogation of Hans Laats, Tallinn, Feb. 27, 1961, USHMM, RG-06.026/11.

63. Gerhard Schoenberner, ed., *House of the Wannsee Conference: Permanent Exhibit. Guide and Reader* (Berlin: Hentrich, 2000), 128–29.

64. EEC records: Tartumaa and Tartu, fall 1944, USHMM, RG-22.002M/25; testimony of Irene Reinhold, Pärnu, Apr. 20, 1961; testimony of August Koort, Tartu, Apr. 26, 1961, USHMM, RG-06.026/11.

65. Riho Västrik, "Tartu koonduslaager" (Tartu Concentration Camp), *Ajalooline Ajakiri* 3–4 (1999): 78–80. As a result of a painstaking analysis of the available sources, Västrik came to the conclusion that the official Soviet figure of 12,000 is grossly exaggerated.

66. Salomon Lury, ERA, R-64/4/432; Salomon Epstein, ERA, R-64/4/185; Vera Rubanovich, ERA, R-64/4/711.

67. Case files, ERA, R-64/1/172.

68. Kalman Kliachko, ERA, R-64/4/284; Elias Elian, ERA, R-64/4/212; Mikhail Scher, ERA, R-64/4/914; Salomon Katz, ERA, R-64/4/370; Aron Rogovsky, ERA, R-64/4/1137.

69. Testimony of Victor Alaots, Tartu, Apr. 7, 1961, USHMM, RG-06.026/11.

70. RKO Lohse, note, June 21, 1942, LVVA, R-70/5/34; BdS-Ostland Jost to RKO Lohse, June 15, 1943, LVVA, R-70/3/112.

71. Narva pref. to Est. Sipo in Narva, Feb. 19, 1942, ERA, R-59/1/65.

72. Ger. Sipo, AIV to Est. Sipo, BIV, Nov. 15, 1943, ERA, R-64/1/44.

73. Est. Sipo, "List of Foreign Nationals from Enemy States in Tallinn, June 1942–Jan. 1943," ERA, R-64/1/62.

74. Leopold Silberstein, ERA, R-64/4/787; Leopold Levanovich, ERA, R-64/4/428; Paavle, *Eesti rahvastikukaotused,* 97, 181.

75. Rochelle Riva Brenner, ERA, R-64/4/86; Dora Ratner, ERA, R-64/4/1143.

76. Christopher Browning, *The Final Solution and the German Foreign Office: A Study of Referat D III of Abteilung Deutschland, 1940–43* (New York: Holmes and Meier, 1978), 50, 69, 70, 236 f.

77. Inspector of Est. Sipo and OK, letter book, entry from Dec. 16, 1941, ERA, R-64/1/719; inspector of Est. Sipo and OK, letter book, entry from Jan. 26, 1942, ERA, R-64/1/717; Est. Sipo, "List of Foreign Nationals from Enemy States in Tallinn, June 1942–Jan. 1943," ERA, R-64/1/62.

78. Ezra Pressman, ERA, R-64/4/640; Mikhail Kissis, ERA, R-64/4/332; Stalag 381 to KdS-Estland Sandberger, Feb. 18, 1942, ERA, R-64/4/976.

79. David Katz, ERA, R-64/4/341; Miron Birmann, ERA, R-64/4/47. The names of other Jewish Soviet citizens who had been executed in Estonia in 1942 and 1943 are listed in Paavle, *Eesti rahvastikukaotused,* 173, 312, 314–15.

80. Alter Meyer Kopel, ERA, R-64/4/392; Moses Levi, ERA, R-64/4/408; Boris Levi, ERA, R-64/4/431; Isaac Schatz, ERA, R-64/4/910. One other Jewish POW, Abram Frischer, was executed on the same day (Paavle, *Eesti rahvastikukaotused,* 87.)

81. Rautkallio, *Finland and the Holocaust,* 195, 205, 225–26, 231, 247, 261–62; William B. Cohen and Jürgen Svensson, "Finland," in *The Holocaust Encyclopedia,* ed. Walter Laqueur (New Haven, Conn.: Yale Univ. Press, 2001), 205.

82. Rautkallio, *Finland and the Holocaust,* 226, 235; Commandant of Tallinn TKL to Head of BIV Dept, Nov. [9], 1942, ERA, R-64/1/104.

83. Elias Kopelovsky, ERA, R-64/4/324.

84. *Kansan Uutiset,* Mar. 12, 1961, quoted in Martinson, *Slugi svastiki,* 63.

85. Kollmann mentioned Auschwitz-Birkenau in his testimony at Anthoni's trial in Turku in 1947. In fact, Kollmann had never been to Auschwitz; he was liberated from one of the camps in Austria. He invented the story of the heroic death of Hans Szubilsky—another Jew deported from Finland—at Auschwitz to console the brother-in-law of the departed (Georg Kollmann to Head of Helsinki Jewish congregation, Abraham Stiller, June 20, 1946, USHMM, RG-29.002/1). Taking into account that all Jewish refugees from Central European countries were executed *in* Estonia, it made no sense for the Security Police to transport the eight Jews it received in the fall of 1942 from Finland all the way to Poland.

86. Est. Sipo, B. Meret, critical report, "Axis: Anti-Commintern Pact. The Concept of National Territory," Mar. 11, 1943, ERA, R-64/1/202. See also Argo Kuusik, "Die deutsche Vernichtungspolitik in Estland 1941–1944," in *Vom Hitler-Stalin-Pakt biz zu Stalins Tod: Estland 1939–1953,* ed. Olaf Mertelsmann (Hamburg: Bibliotheca Baltica, 2005), 150.

87. Ger. Sipo, BIII, Biweekly report, May 25–27 1943, ERA, R-64/1/21.

88. Flyer, "Võitlev Eestlane," Aug. 28, 1943, ERA, R-64/1/828.

89. Anonymous letter to GK-Estland Litzmann, July 1943, ERA, R-65/2/1.

90. U.S. Legation in Stockholm, "Conditions in Estonia, December 1941," Dec. 27, 1941, NARA, M-1170/21.

91. Press Bureau of the Latvian Legation in Washington, D.C., "Latvia under German Occupation" (1943), 89, NARA, M-1177/16.

92. Karlis Kangeris, "Die baltischen Völker und die deutschen Pläne für die Räumung des Baltikums 1944," *Baltisches Jahrbuch* 5 (1988): 183, 194 f. Kangeris quotes from a communication to the U.S. Foreign Secretary from June 28, 1944, deposited at Roosevelt Library.

93. Monty Noam Penkower, *The Jews Were Expendable: Free World Diplomacy and the Holocaust* (Chicago: Univ. of Illinois Press, 1983), 268–70; Ezergailis, *Stockholm Documents,* 486.

94. *The American Jewish Year Book 5703,* vol. 44 (Philadelphia: Jewish Publication Society of America, 1942), 240–43; ibid., vol. 45 (1943), 312–14; ibid., vol. 46 (1944), 251–52. Conspicuously, Oct. 26, 1941, corresponds with a date in late October when the remaining Jewish women were arrested in Tallinn.

95. U.S. Legation in Stockholm, "Conversation with recent visitor from Riga," Oct. 26, 1943, NARA, M-1177/16.

96. U.S. Legation in Stockholm, *Ny Dag,* "The Germans in Latvia," Aug. 26, 1943, NARA, M-1177/16.

97. U.S. Legation in Stockholm, *NU,* "The War of Extermination Against the Lithuanian Intellectuals," July 16–22, 1943, NARA, M-1178/19.

98. U.S. Legation in Stockholm, May 5, 1944, NARA, M-1178/19.

99. U.S. Legation in Stockholm to the Secretary of State, Mar. 20, 1943, NARA, M-1178/21.

100. Foreign Nationalities Branch Office of Strategic Services, miscellaneous notes from the Lithuanian-American press, *Maujienos,* July 12, 1944, NARA, M-1178/22.

101. U.S. Legation in Stockholm, "The German Colonization of Lithuania," Dec. 19, 1942, NARA, M-1178/20.

8. JEWISH TRANSPORTS FROM CZECHOSLOVAKIA AND GERMANY, FALL 1942

1. List of special trains that departed from Frankfurt between Aug. 8 and Oct. 30, 1942; Fa, La, and Da train schedule for the period between Aug. 8 and Oct. 30, 1942, IfZ, Fb-85/11.

2. List of transports that departed Berlin "for the east" between June 2, 1942, and Febr. 26, 1943, YVA, TR-10/662 II.

3. Interrogation of Ralf Gerrets, Tallinn, June 14, 1960, USHMM, RG-06.026/12.

4. In the 1961 trial, Jaan Viik tried to defend himself by portraying Gerrets as a Baltic German footman of the Nazis who had manipulated common people like him, Viik.

5. Interrogation of Ralf Gerrets, Tartu, June 10 and 14, 1960, USHMM, RG-06.026/12.

6. Interrogation of Ralf Gerrets, Tallinn, June 11 and Dec. 23, 1960, USHMM, RG-06.026/12.

7. Lukáš Přibyl, "Die Geschichte des Theresienstädter Transports 'Be' nach Estland." In *Theresienstädter Studien und Dokumente* (Institut Theresienstädter Initiative, 2001), 174, 181.

8. Interrogation of Ralf Gerrets, Tallinn, June 14, 1960, USHMM, RG-06.026/12.

9. Interrogation of Ralf Gerrets, Tallinn, Oct. 21, 1960, USHMM, RG-06.026/12.

10. Interrogation of Ralf Gerrets, Tallinn, Dec. 23, 1960, USHMM, RG-06.026/12.

11. Testimony of Friedrich Anijalg at Laak-Gerrets-Viik-Mere trial, Tallinn, Mar. 6–11, 1961, USHMM, RG-06.026/12.

12. Interrogation of Ralf Gerrets, Tallinn, Sept. 14, 1960, USHMM, RG-06.026/12.

13. Testimony of Rein Järvine, Tallinn, Sept. 22, 1960, USHMM, RG-06.026/12.

14. Interrogation of Friedrich Anijalg, Tallinn, July 5 and Dec. 1, 1960, USHMM, RG-06.026/12.

15. Wolfgang Scheffler and Diana Schulle, eds. *Book of Remembrance: The German, Austrian and Czechoslovakian Jews Deported to the Baltic States* (Munich: G. Saur, 2003), 2:865.

16. Přibyl, "Die Geschichte," 148–49.

17. Testimonies of Hanna Klenkova, Jan. 23, 1969; Martha Brichta, Jan. 27, 1969; and Helena Freundova, Jan. 28, 1969 (all three in Kassel), BAL, 408 AR-Z 233/59, V25.

18. Přibyl, "Die Geschichte," 155.

19. Trial records of Heinrich Bergmann, Wiesbaden, Apr. 4, 1967, BAL, 408 AR-Z 233/59, V4.

20. Testimony of Martha Brichta, Kassel, Jan. 27, 1969, BAL, 408, AR-Z 233/59, V25.

21. The case of mass murder of the Jews who arrived in Estonia in September 1942, BAL, 207 AR-Z 246/59, V8. The Jewish desk within the German Security Police in Estonia was designated as AIV–B3 and later AIV–B4.

22. Testimony of Hanna Klenkova, Kassel, Jan. 23, 1969, BAL, 408 AR-Z 233/59, V25; testimonies of Flora Friedmanova, Praha, Oct. 7, 1960, and Eliška Munkova, Olomouc, Oct. 6, 1960, USHMM, RG-06.026/12.

23. Testimony of Hana Klenkova, Praha, Oct. 13, 1960, USHMM, RG-06.026/12.

24. Interrogation of Ralf Gerrets, June 14 and 18, 1960 USHMM, RG-06.026/12. The reserve detachment of the Estonian Security Police was stationed on the corner of Narva Avenue and Kreutzwaldi Street in Tallinn. The detachment supplied recruits for pursuit units *(Jagdkommandos)*, which had occasionally been dispatched to Russia proper to fight Soviet partisans.

25. Interrogation of Ralf Gerrets, Tallinn, June 14, 1960, USHMM, RG-06.026/12.

26. Interrogation of Ralf Gerrets, Tallinn, June 20 and Oct. 24, 1960 USHMM, RG-06.026/12.

27. Interrogations of Ralf Gerrets, Oct. 24, 1960, and Peeter Mälk (both in Tallinn), Sept. 6, 1960, USHMM, RG-06.026/12.

28. Interrogation of Ralf Gerrets, June 16 and Oct. 24, 1960, USHMM, RG-06.026/12.

29. Interrogation of Ralf Gerrets, July 8, 1960, USHMM, RG-06.026/12.

30. Interrogation of Ralf Gerrets, Aug. 22, 1960, USHMM, RG-06.026/12.

31. Testimonies of Teffer Laasik, Sept. 9, 1960, and Julius Repnau, June 3, 1960 (both in Kaberla), USHMM, RG-06.026/12.

32. Testimony of Raimond Peskman, Tallinn, Sept. 27, 1960, USHMM, RG-06.026/12.

33. Interview with Doris Rauch, Washington, July 7, 1995, USHMM, RG-50.106.15.

34. Testimony of Martha Brichta, Kassel, Jan. 27, 1969, BAL, 408 AR-Z 233/59, V25.

35. Testimony of Arnoštka Frischmanova, Gudlitsa (?), Oct. 10, 1960, USHMM, RG-06.026/12.

36. Testimony of Martha Brichta, Kassel, Jan. 27, 1969, BAL, 408 AR-Z 233/59, V25; testimony of Fanny Lederer, Frankfurt, Mar. 9, 1967, BAL, 207 AR-Z 246/59, V6; interrogation of Ralf Gerrets, Tallinn, June 20 and July 29, 1960, USHMM, RG-06.026/12.

37. Interrogation of Axel Auer, Frankfurt, Apr. 30, 1968; interrogation of Josef Schmid, Stuttgart, July 3, 1968; interrogation of Wilhelm Suttor, Munich, Dec. 4, 1968, BAL, 207 AR-Z 246/59, V7.

38. Interrogation of Ralf Gerrets, June 20, 1960; interrogation of Peter Oissaar, Oct. 11, 1960; interrogation of Jaan Ranne, Nov. 30, 1960; interrogation of Jaan Atka, Oct. 10, 1960 (all in Tallinn), USHMM, RG-06.026/12.

39. Testimony of Helena Freundova, Kassel, Jan. 28, 1969, BAL, 408 AR-Z 233/59, V25; testimony of Helena Freundova, Praha, Oct. 11, 1960, USHMM, RG-06.026/12.

40. RKO Lohse to GK-Estland Litzmann, July 25, 1942, ERA, R-65/1/4.

41. Testimony of Hanna Klenkova, Kassel, Jan. 23, 1969, BAL, 408 AR-Z 233/59, V25.

42. Monica Kingreen, "Gewaltsam verschleppt aus Frankfurt: Die Deportationen der Juden in den Jahren 1941–1945," *Nach der Kristallnacht: Jüdisches Leben und antijüdische Politik in Frankfurt am Main 1938–1945* (Frankfurt: Campus Verlag, 1999), 358–80.

43. Testimony of Selma Sundheimer, Frankfurt, Jan. 11, 1967; interrogation of Heinrich Baab, Butzbach, Jan. 24, 1967, BAL, 207 AR-Z 246/59, V5.

44. Fanny Lederer, "Meine Deportierung von Anfang bis Ende," Jan. 17, 1967, BAL, 207 AR-Z 246/59, V6.

45. *Book of Remembrance,* 865.

46. Deportations of Berlin Jews, investigation records, YVA, TR-10/662 III.

47. Testimony of Helga Verleger, Ravensburg, Feb. 19, 1968, BAL, 207 AR-Z 246/59, V7.

48. Testimony of Selma Sundheimer, Frankfurt, Jan. 11, 1967, BAL, 207 AR-Z 246/59, V5.

49. Testimony of Sally Herlitz, Frankfurt, Jan. 17, 1967, BAL, 207 AR-Z 246/59, V5. According to Gerrets, those Jews were further deported to Kiviõli area.

50. Interrogations of Ralf Gerrets, June 16, 1960; Jaan Viik, Nov. 18, 1960; Friedrich Anijalg, Oct. 5, 1960 (all in Tallinn), USHMM, RG-06.026/12.

51. Interrogation of Eino Liiv, Kadijärve, June 8, 1960, USHMM, RG-06.026/12. No date of the actual execution was explicitly mentioned. It must have taken place on Sept. 30, Oct. 1, or Oct. 2, 1942.

52. On social relations in Riga ghetto, see Ezergailis, *The Holocaust in Latvia,* 352–60.

53. Interrogation of Ralf Gerrets, Tallinn, Sept. 12, 1960, USHMM, RG-06.026/12.

54. Testimony of Rein Oiso at Laak-Gerrets-Viik-Mere trial, Tallinn, Mar. 6–11, 1961, USHMM, RG-06.026/12.

55. Testimony of Hanna Panyrkova, Kassel, Feb. 6, 1969, BAL, 408 AR-Z 233/59, V25.

56. Interrogation of Jaan Viik, Tallinn, July 7, 1960, USHMM, RG-06.026/12.

57. Testimony of Hanna Klenkova at Laak-Gerrets-Viik-Mere trial, Tallinn, Mar. 6, 1961, USHMM, RG-06.026/12.

58. Interrogation of Ralf Gerrets, Tallinn, Aug. 22 and Sept. 30, 1960, USHMM, RG-06.026/12.

59. KdS-Estland, I.A. Bergmann, to BdS-Ostland, I.A. Jagusch, Nov. 19, 1942, LVVA, R-1026/1/3.

60. Interrogation of Ralf Gerrets, Tallinn, June 16, 1960, USHMM, RG-06.026/12.

61. Testimony of Jarmila Adamova, Kassel, Jan. 24, 1969, BAL, 408 AR-Z 233/59, V25.

62. Testimony of Helena Freundova, Kassel, Jan. 28, 1969, BAL, 408 AR-Z 233/59, V25.

63. Interrogation of Albert Tärno, Tallinn, June 25, 1960, USHMM, RG-06.026/12.

64. Přibyl, "Die Geschichte," 171, 172.

65. Lederer, "Meine Deportierung," BAL, 207 AR-Z 246/59, V6.

66. Interrogation of Ralf Gerrets, Tallinn, Dec. 23, 1960, USHMM, RG-06.026/12. On one occasion in February 1943, several guards left their posts and went drinking in a nearby village.

67. Testimony of Jarmila Adamova, Abertany, Oct. 25, 1960, USHMM, RG-06.026/12.

68. Commandant of Tallinn AEL to Head of BIV, Dec. 17, 18, and 19, 1942, ERA, R-64/1/104.

69. Commandant of Tallinn AEL to Head of BIV, June 30, and Aug. 21, 1943, ERA, R-64/1/106.

70. Lederer, "Meine Deportierung," BAL, 207 AR-Z 246/59, V6.

71. Interrogation of Ralf Gerrets, Tallinn, July 29, 1960, USHMM, RG-06.026/12. The number 1,754 can be obtained by subtracting the number of Jews who were dispatched to Jaunjelgava and Tallinn Central prison (96 and 201 respectively) from the total number of Jews on the two transports, that is, 2,051.

72. Tallinn Central prison (postal address: 2 Kalda Street) was finally closed down in 2005.

73. Ronald Seth, *A Spy Has No Friends* (London: Andre Deutsch, 1952), 55.

74. KdS-Estland Sandberger to BdS-Ostland Pifrader, Jan. 30, 1943, IfZ, Fb-101/31.

75. Seth, *A Spy Has No Friends,* 56.

76. KdS-Estland Sandberger to RSHA, Jan. 30, 1943, USHMM, RG-11.001M/75.

77. KdS-Estland Sandberger, situational report "Estonia B," N34, May 3, 1943, USHMM, RG-15.007M/9.

78. Interrogation of Friedrich Hohmann, Frankfurt, Jan. 26, 1967, BAL, 408 AR-Z 233/59, V20.

79. Lederer, "Meine Deportierung," BAL, 207 AR-Z 246/59, V6.

80. Přibyl, "Die Geschichte," 186, 192–93.

81. Testimony of Hilda Levy, Hechingen, July 13, 1965, BAL, 408 AR-Z 233/59, V14.

82. Correspondence between KdS-Estland Sandberger and Tallinn AEL, June 24 and July 8, 1943, ERA, R-294/1/15.

83. Testimony of Helga Verleger, Ravensburg, Feb. 19, 1968, BAL, 207 AR-Z 246/59, V7.

84. Testimony of Ruth Hönke, Haifa, Jan. 16, 1968, BAL, 408 AR-Z 233/59, V23.

85. Testimony of Hanna Klenkova, Kassel, Jan. 23, 1969, BAL, 408 AR-Z 233/59, V25.

86. Lederer, "Meine Deportierung," BAL, 207 AR-Z 246/59, V6; testimony of Helga Verleger, Ravensburg, Feb. 19, 1968, BAL, 207 AR-Z 246/59, V7.

87. Wiln Ostland, Armament Dept., *KTB,* Oct. 11–17, 1943, BA-MA, RW-30/9.

88. Lederer, "Meine Deportierung," BAL, 207 AR-Z 246/59, V6.

89. *Book of Remembrance,* 867.

90. For a concise description of the experiments, see Christopher Browning, *Reserve Police Battalion 101 and the Final Solution in Poland* (New York: Harper Perennial, 1993), 167–74.

91. Interrogation of Rein Oiso, Tallinn, July 4, 1960, USHMM, RG-06.026/12.

92. Testimony of Harald Kolberg at Jüriste-Linnas-Viks trial, Tartu, Jan. 17, 1962, USHMM, RG-06.026/11.

93. Testimony of Pulkheria Tsakukhina, Tartu, July 10, 1961, USHMM, RG-06.026/11.

94. Testimony of Irene Reinhold, Pärnu, Apr. 20, 1961; testimony of Luisa Frei, Tartu, Apr. 21, 1961; testimony of Luisa Frei at Jüriste-Linnas-Viks trial, Tartu, Jan. 17, 1962, USHMM, RG-06.026/11.

95. Interrogation of Harald Kolberg, Mar. 31, 1961; testimony of Jan Tiits, Oct. 25, 1960; (both in Tartu), USHMM, RG-06.026/11.

96. Testimony of Hilda Jalakas, Mar. 27, 1961; testimony of Anna Punder, Mar. 22, 1961 (both in Tartu), USHMM, RG-06.026/11.

97. Testimony of August Tõnismaa, Mar. 30, 1961; testimony of Mikhail Afanasiev, Mar. 24, 1961 (both in Tartu), USHMM, RG-06.026/11.

98. Interrogation of Kalju Treufeld, Tallinn, Dec. 26, 1960, USHMM, RG-06.026/12.

99. Testimony of Oskar Kudu at Jüriste-Linnas-Viks trial, Tartu, Jan. 17, 1962, USHMM, RG-06.026/11.

100. Interrogation of Rein Oiso, Tallinn, July 4, 1960, USHMM, RG-06.026/12.

101. Ruth Bettina Birn, "Heinrich Bergmann—eine deutsche Kriminalstenkarriere," in *Karrieren der Gewalt: Nationalsozialistische Täterbiographien,* ed. Klaus Michael Mallmann and Gerhard Paul (Darmstadt: Wissenschaftliche Buchgesellschaft, 2004), 49, 54 f.

9. JEWISH SLAVE LABOR FOR THE BALTÖL EMPIRE

1. Göring, memo, Mar. 16, 1943, BAB, R-6/286.

2. Letter forwarded to Baltöl, June 19, 1943, ERA, R-187/1/7.

3. GK-Estland Office, notes on master plan for the Estonian oil shale region, Jan. 27, 1943, BAB, R-91/Reval/4.

4. Report: "Activities of Continental Oil in the Occupied Eastern Territories" [August 1941], NARA, T-454/91; OT Todt to Admiral Raeder, Aug. 29, 1941, NARA, T-454/78.

5. AOK 18, IV Wi to Minölko North, July 9, 1941, BA-MA, RW-46/298; AOK 18, IV Wi, to Minölko North, Aug. 10, 1941; AOK 18, IV Wi, to WiIn North, Aug. 18, 1941; WiIn North to WiStab Ost, Aug. 27, 1941, BA-MA, RW-46/299.

6. GK-Estland Office, note, May 15, 1942, ERA, R-65/1/4.

7. Naval Group Command North, *KTB,* Aug. 8, 1941, BA-MA, RM-35 I/137.

8. OKW WiRü Amt, *KTB,* May 16 and Dec. 5 and 12, 1941, BA-MA, RW-19/202.

9. OKW, WiRü Amt, Wartime supplies of fuel to Germany, Feb. 16, 1942, BA-MA, RW-19/202.

10. *Berliner Börsen-Zeitung,* Mar. 30, 1941; RMO Office, memo, Nov. 15, 1943, BAB, R-6/5.

11. Continental Oil to Baltöl, Oct. 1, 1942, ERA, R-187/1/7.

12. Director of Baltöl Mathy to NSDAP district leader Trefz in Tallinn, Mar. 4, 1944, ERA, R-187/1/3.

13. Roswitha Czollek, *Faschismus und Okkupation: Wirtschaftspolitische Zielsetzung und Praxis des faschistischen deutschen Besatzungsregimes in den baltischen Sowjetrepubliken während des zweiten Weltkrieges* (Berlin: Akademie-Verlag, 1974), 89.

14. Baltöl, memo, Sept. 8, 1943, ERA, R-187/1/3. The contract was signed on Feb. 12, 1944.

15. Minölko Estonia Krauch to WiStab Ost Stapf, Apr. 15, 1943; OT North-Russia, memo, Dec. 24, 1943, ERA, R-187/1/7.

16. *Revaler Zeitung,* Feb. 14, 1942.

17. Rolf-Dieter Müller, *Die deutsche Wirtschaftspolitik in den besetzten sowjetischen Gebieten 1941–1943* (Boppard: Harald Boldt Verlag, 1991), 210, 225.

18. U.S. Legation in Stockholm, Arvo Horm, report, "The Estonian Shale Oil Industry," June 2, 1944, NARA, M-1170/23.

19. Statistics: Current Condition of Baltöl, Jan. 15, 1944, ERA, R-187/1/3; WiStab Ost, transcript of a discussion, Mar. 17, 1944, ERA, R-187/1/7.

20. Baltöl, weekly report N4, Dec. 31, 1941, ERA, R-187/1/10; Baltöl to GK-Estland Litzmann, Apr. 20, 1942, ERA, R-65/1/4; GK-Estland Office, notes on the master plan for the Estonian oil shale region, Jan. 27, 1943, BAB, R-91/Reval/4. The total number of workers in Estonia decreased from 54,700 in 1937 to 31,400 in early 1942.

21. GK-Estland Office, Dept. III to Gruf. Aster, Jan. 20, 1943, ERA, R-65/1/113.

22. GK-Litauen v. Renteln to RKO Lohse, Oct. 29, 1942, BAB, R-91/Kauen-Land/1.

23. Baltöl, memo N704, June 30, 1943, ERA, R-187/1/3; Baltöl, note on conversation with Krauch, July 1, 1943, ERA, R-187/1/6.

24. Director of Baltöl Mathy, report, Jan. 6, 1943, ERA, R-187/1/3. As of Mar. 30, 1943, there were more than one thousand Latvians working in Estonia. One-third of the workforce was deployed at Kiviõli. The workers came from three townships: Riga, Jelgava, and Daugavpils (GK-Lettland Office, memo, Apr. 1, 1943, BAB, R-92/1153).

25. WiStab Ost, memo on employment conditions in Estonia, May 19, 1943, ERA, R-187/1/3.

26. Meelis Maripuu, "Soviet Prisoners of War in Estonia in 1941–1944," in Hiio, Maripuu, and Paavle, *Estonia, 1940–1945,* 744.

27. OKH, memo, Mar. 27, 1943, ERA, R-187/1/7.

28. Minölko Estonia, *KTB,* Apr. 6 and May 11, 1943, BA-MA, RW-46/754.

29. Statistics: Current Condition of Baltöl, Jan. 15, 1944, ERA, R-187/1/3; WiStab Ost, transcript of a discussion, Mar. 17, 1944, ERA, R-187/1/7.

30. Rose Lerer Cohen and Saul Issroff, *The Holocaust in Lithuania, 1941–1945: A Book of Remembrance* (Jerusalem: Gefen, 2002), 30.

31. Christian Streit, *Keine Kameraden: Die Wehrmacht und die sowjetische Kriegsgefangenen 1941–1945* (Bonn: Verlag J. H. W. Dietz Nachf., 1997), 275–79.

32. WiIn Ostland, *KTB,* July 19, 25, and 26, and Aug. 7, 1943; WiIn Ostland, Raw Materials Dept., weekly report, July 18–24, 1943; WiIn Ostland, report for the month of July 1943, Aug. 5, 1943, BA-MA, RW-30/8.

33. Franz Seidler, *Die Organisation Todt: Bauen für Staat und Wehrmacht 1938–1945* (Stuttgart: Bernard and Graefe Verlag, 1987), 101.

34. KdS-Estland Sandberger, situational report "Estonia B" N30, Jan. 4, 1943, USHMM, RG-15.007M/9.

35. Baltöl, memo, Oct. 25, 1943, ERA, R-187/1/6.

36. OKH to HGr North, Aug. 12, 1943, BA-MA, RH-19 III/293. The "Eastern Wall" started in Kerch and ran along the Dnepr River, through Dnepropetrovsk, Kiev, Gomel, and Orsha, to Vitebsk and Nevel. From Pskov, the defense line went farther north, along Lake Peipus and the Narva River.

37. Transcript of a conversation between Commander of HGr North v. Kühler, General Braemer, and RKO Lohse, Sept. 19, 1943, BAB, 45/TL.

38. OKM, Dönitz, memo, Mar. 27, 1944, BA-MA, RH-19 III/15.

39. HGr North v. Küchler to OKH Staff, Aug. 19, 1943; HGr North, points of reference for the discussion re "Panther Position," Sept. 1, 1943, BA-MA, RH-19 III/293.

40. Head of OT North-Russia Giesler to Head of OT Central Office Dorsch, Sept. 20, 1943; OT, Baltöl Gimple to RKO Lohse, Nov. 4, 1943, ERA, R-187/1/7.

41. WiIn Ostland, *KTB,* Aug. 9, 1943, BA-MA, RW-30/8.

42. GK-Estland Litzmann to RKO Office, Sept. 15, 1943, LVVA, R-70/5/72.

43. Baltöl, Wossagk to v. Kursell, July 21, 1943, ERA, R-187/1/33.

44. WiIn Ostland, *KTB,* Sept. 15, 1943, BA-MA, RW-30/8.

45. WiKo Tallinn, situational report, July 30–Aug. 28, 1943, BA-MA, RW-30/59.

46. WiIn Ostland, workshop, Sept. 13–14 1943, BA-MA, RW-30/8.

47. Interrogation of Hermann Riecken, Bergedorf, May 1948, BAK, Z-42 III/1732.

48. Sample letters from Vaivara, LCVA, R-1390/1/22.

49. Yitzhak Arad, *Ghetto in Flames: The Struggle and Destruction of the Jews in Vilna in the Holocaust* (Jerusalem: Yad Vashem, 1980), 402–7.

50. Marc Dvorjetski, *La victoire du ghetto* (Paris: Editions France—Empire, 1962), 272–73.

51. Testimony of Alexander Rindzunski, Dec. 21, 1945, USHMM, RG-06.025.01. Several excerpts from the letters reproduced in Herman Kruk, *The Last Days of the Jerusalem of Lithuania: Chronicles from the Vilna Ghetto and the Camps, 1939–1944* (New Haven, Conn.: Yale Univ. Press, 2002), 659–61.

52. Vladimir Porudominski, ed., *Die Juden von Wilna: Die Aufzeichnungen des Grigorij Schur, 1941–1944* (Munich: Deutscher Taschenbuch Verlag, 1999), 172, 175.

53. Arad, *Ghetto in Flames*, 408–15.

54. Ibid., 420, 429–32.

55. Arūnas Bubnys, "The Holocaust in Lithuania: An Outline of the Major Stages and Their Results," in *The Vanished World of Lithuanian Jews,* ed. Alvydas Nikžentaitis et al. (Amsterdam: Rodopi, 2004), 217.

56. Willem Mishell, *Kaddish for Kovno: Life and Death in a Lithuanian Ghetto, 1941–1945* (Chicago Review Press, 1988), 160, 165, 167–72; Avraham Tory, *Surviving the Holocaust: The Kovno Ghetto Diary* (Cambridge, Mass.: Harvard Univ. Press, 1990), 420, 456, 463, 474–75, 507.

57. Boris Kacel, *From Hell to Redemption: A Memoir of the Holocaust* (Niwot: Univ. Press of Colorado, 1998), 117–22. In fact, Kacel argues that the deportation to Estonia took place in late October 1943. A German document, however, mentions five hundred Jews who arrived in Estonia on November 21. Those could only be Jews dispatched from the Kaiserwald concentration camp (Minölko Estonia, Group "Work," Nov. 21, 1943, BA-MA, RW-46/756).

58. RSHA, IV C, Müller, circular letter, Oct. 2, 1943, BAB, R-58/1027.

59. Alfred Streim, "Konzentrationslager auf dem Gebiet der Sowjetunion," *Dachauer Hefte* 5, no. 5 (Nov. 1989): 174–76.

60. Indictment of Helmut Schnabel and Rudolf Klicker, Hannover, July 21, 1975, BAL, 408 AR-Z 233/59, V30.

61. Von Bodman complained about a female guard who was sent to Vaivara from Ravensbrück in her fifth month of pregnancy. Referring to poorer conditions and harsher rules of engagement at Vaivara, von Bodman requested the person in question to be sent back to Ravensbrück. Vaivara KZ Bodman to WVHA, Nov. 25, 1943, EAM, D 152/2/40. The English translation of all ten reports is available at USHMM.

62. Indictment of Helmut Schnabel and Rudolf Klicker, Hannover, July 21, 1975, BAL, 408 AR-Z 233/59, V30.

63. Indictment of Helmut Schnabel et al., Hechingen, Mar. 18, 1966, IfZ, Gh-06.03.

64. Steven Paskuly, ed., *Death Dealer: The Memoirs of the SS Commandant at Auschwitz Rudolf Höss* (New York: Da Capo Press, 1996), 230–32.

65. BDC: Aumeier, YVA, 068/382.

66. Verdict in the case of Hans Aumeier et al., Krakow, Dec. 16, 1947, IfZ, G-20/1.

67. Protocol re. Dr. Bodman, Linz, June 17, 1947, YVA, M-9/559. In his monthly report to WVHA of Nov. 25, 1943, von Bodman said literally that "their [old people] elimination is a relief for the entire Vaivara concentration camp." Von Bodman committed suicide on April 25, 1945;

Brenneis was killed in combat in 1944; Aumeier was sentenced to death and executed in Poland in early 1948.

68. Statistics derived from von Bodman's reports.

69. Interrogation of Engelbert Zweck, Günzburg, Jan. 13, 1961, YVA, TR-10/1196.

70. Minölko Estonia, Group "Work," Nov. 24, 1943, BA-MA, RW-46/756. Apparently by mistake, the document mentions Sillamäe. In all likelihood, Minölko Estonia meant Vaivara.

71. Mark Dworzecki, *Vaise Nekht un Shvartse Teg: Yidn-Lagern in Estonie* (Tel Aviv: Tishlia, 1970), 167–68, 187.

72. BdS-Ostland Panziger to EK 2 Traut, Feb. 19, 1944, IfZ, Fb-101/18.

73. Dworzecki, *Vaise Nekht,* 115.

74. WiIn Ostland, report for August 1943, Sept. 5, 1943; WiIn Ostland, workshop, Sept. 13–14, 1943, BA-MA, RW-30/8.

75. Minölko Estonia, Group "Z," *KTB,* Jan. 12, 1944, BA-MA, RW-46/757.

76. RKO, table, workforce demand in the Ostland as of Nov. 1, 1943, LVVA, R-70/5/8.

77. WiIn Ostland, Armament Dept., overview of developments in armament industry in the 4th quarter of 1943, Jan. 15, 1944, BA-MA, RW-30/9.

78. Minölko Estonia, Group "Work," review of KTB for July 1–Sept. 30, 1943, BA-MA, RW-46/755.

79. Minölko Estonia, *KTB,* Sept. 1–10, 1943, BA-MA, RW-46/755.

80. Baltöl to WiStab Ost, Aug. 8, 1943, ERA, R-187/1/6.

81. WiIn Ostland, report for the month of October 1943, Nov. 4, 1943, BA-MA, RW-30/9; ibid. for Jan. 1944, Feb. 3, 1944, BA-MA, RW-30/10; Minölko Estonia, Group "Work," review of KTB for Oct. 1– Dec. 31, 1943, BA-MA, RW-46/756. Efficiency rate indicates average amount of oil shale (in tons) mined daily.

82. WiIn Ostland, addendum to *KTB,* Jan. 18, 1944, BA-MA, RW-30/10.

83. Baltöl, transcript of a discussion, Nov. 8, 1943, ERA, R-187/1/26.

84. WiIn Ostland, Armament industry in the Ostland, report for Sept. 1, 1941–Aug. 8, 1944, BA-MA, RW-30/203.

85. Baltöl, employment statistics as of Jan. 31, 1944, ERA, R-187/1/24.

86. Baltöl, memo, Feb. 2, 1944; OT North-Russia, memo, Feb. 20, 1944, ERA, R-187/1/24.

87. Minölko Estonia, transcript of a phone conversation with Baltöl, Schön, Mar. 1, 1944, ERA, R-187/1/24.

88. Baltöl, transcript of a discussion, Oct. 28, 1943, ERA, R-187/1/5.

89. Baltöl, transcript of a discussion, Feb. 18, 1944, ERA, R-187/1/7.

90. Baltöl, construction employment statistics, [Feb. 1944], ERA, R-187/1/24.

91. AOK 16, KTB draft, Feb. 14 and 27, 1944, BA-MA, RH 20-16/351.

92. Minölko Estonia, Group "Z," *KTB,* Jan. 30, Feb. 2 and 4, 1944, BA-MA, RW-46/757.

93. WiStab Ost Mussert to Commander of Minölko Estonia, Feb. 5, 1944, ERA, R-187/1/7.

94. Minölko Estonia Stein to GBA Boening, Feb. 1, 1944, ERA, R-187/1/24.

95. Baltöl to Ministry of Defense, Feb. 7, 1944, ERA, R-187/1/7.

96. Minölko Estonia, general overview of the 1st quarter of 1944, Jan. 1-Mar. 31, 1944, BA-MA, RW-46/757.

97. Minölko Estonia, Group "Z," *KTB*, Feb. 13 and 14, 1944, BA-MA, RW-46/757.

98. Minölko Estonia, Group "Work," *KTB*, Feb. 14, 1944, BA-MA, RW-46/757. It is unclear whether the Dutch city of Breda was meant and not, for example, Polish Brdów or Ukrainian Brody.

99. Minölko Estonia, Group "Work," to HGr North, Mar. 5, 1944, ERA, R-187/1/67.

100. Minölko Estonia, Group "Work," *KTB*, Feb. 15-Mar. 25, 1944, BA-MA, RW-46/757.

101. KdS-Estland Baatz to BdS-Ostland Panziger, Feb. 26, 1944, IfZ, Fb-101/30.

102. Minölko Estonia, Group "Work," *KTB*, Apr. 24-30, 1944, BA-MA, RW-46/758.

103. WiStab Ost, monthly report, appendix 3, Aug. 23, 1944, NARA, T-454/98.

104. Baltöl Stapf to OKH, May 26, 1944, ERA, R-187/1/7.

105. GBA Ostland to Baltöl, Schön, Aug. 1, 1944, ERA, R-187/1/7.

106. Minölko Estonia, Group "Work," *KTB*, May 29-June 4, 1944, BA-MA, RW-46/758.

107. Seidler, *Die Organisation Todt*, 145, 146. In February 1943 ten thousand Hungarian Jews were dispatched to Serbia.

108. Testimony of Lea Meiri, Ber Sheva, Feb. 16, 1967, BAL, 408 AR-Z 233/59, V22.

109. Baltöl, memo, June 2, 1944, ERA, R-187/1/33.

110. Minölko Estonia, Group "Work," *KTB*, June 5-25, 1944, BA-MA, RW-46/758.

111. Christian Gerlach and Götz Aly, *Das letzte Kapitel: Realpolitik, Ideologie und der Mord an den ungarischen Juden 1944/1945* (Stuttgart: DVA, 2002), 382-83.

112. Commandant of Tallinn AEL Laak to Est. Sipo, Mar. 24, 1944, ERA, R-294/1/8; Ger. Sipo, June 8, 1944, ERA, R-64/1/69.

113. Saks, *Kes on Juudid*, 125, 126; Martin Gilbert, *Endlösung: Die Vertreibung und Vernichtung der Juden. Ein Atlas* (Hamburg: Rowohlt, 1995), 188-89.

114. Head of Lasnamäe camp to Commandant of Tallinn AEL Laak, Aug. 23, 1944, ERA, R-294/1/15.

115. Baltöl, memo, July 19, 1944, ERA, R-187/1/24.

116. RKO Office, III Dept., Martin Matthiesen, note for RKO, July 7, 1944, IfZ, MA-793.

117. Minölko Estonia, transcript of a discussion, July 28, 1944; Baltöl, conference report, Aug. 2, 1944, ERA, R-187/1/24.

118. WiIn Ostland, Armament Dept., addendum to *KTB*, May 1-7, 1944, BA-MA, RW-30/11.

119. Minölko Estonia, cable, Aug. 8, 1944, ERA, R-187/1/67.

120. WiRü Amt, *KTB*, Aug. 4, 5, and 10, 1944, BA-MA, RW-19/203. Hitler introduced the Geilenberg Program (named after the general manager of Braunschweig steelworks, Edmund Geilenberg) on May 30, 1944, with the purpose of protecting the ever-shrinking fuel production against the Allies' bombing raids.

121. Minölko Estonia, phone conversation N1798, Aug. 8, 1944; Baltöl, memo, Aug. 9, 1944; instructions re relocation of workers for/from the construction program, July 17-Aug. 13, 1944, ERA, R-187/1/24; Baltöl, Schön to WiStab Ost, Aug. 12, 1944, ERA, R-187/1/7.

122. Minölko Estonia, Group "Work," *KTB*, Aug. 6–13, 1944, BA-MA, RW-46/759.

123. OKM, Dönitz, memo, Mar. 27, 1944, BA-MA, RH-19 III/15.

124. Fischer to Baltöl, Schön, Aug. 30, 1944, ERA, R-187/1/7.

125. Přibyl, "Die Geschichte," 210.

126. Minölko Estonia, Group "Z," *KTB*, Aug. 21–Sept. 10, 1944, BA-MA, RW-46/759.

127. WiKo Tallinn, Group Rü, weekly report, Sept. 4–10, 1944, BAB, R-91/Reval/2.

128. OT North-Russia to Baltöl, Sept. 12, 1944, ERA, R-187/1/24.

129. Testimony of Riva Raichel, Hechingen, Oct. 13, 1965, BAL, 408 AR-Z 233/59, V14.

130. Interrogation of August Laasu, Nov. 8, 1948; Olev Koitla, Nov. 8, 1948; Jüri Taaramäe, Nov. 20, 1948 (all in Viljandi), ERAF, 3042.

131. Dworzecki, *Vaise Nekht*, 260–63.

132. Testimony of Molly Ingster, Tel Aviv, May 29, 1974, BAL, 408 AR-Z 233/59, V29.

133. Kacel, *From Hell to Redemption*, 143–47.

134. Minölko Estonia, *KTB*, Oct. 1–Dec. 31, 1943, BA-MA, RW-46/756.

135. Information received from Boris Lipkin, 1993. In the late 1980s and early 1990s, Lipkin, an amateur historian from Sillamäe, conducted a series of interviews with Estonian farmers who lived in the vicinity of the camps. According to one informant, A. E. wanted to get rid of Jews' dresses that she had acquired, by offering them to the locals 20 Rbl. apiece: "I have quite a few Jewish dresses: blue and black, made of silk and wool. Those are all expensive dresses, which you cannot get any more. Jews would not have taken any crap with them, or would they?"

136. Dworzecki, *Vaise Nekht*, 264, 360.

137. Interview with Karin J., Narva, June 15, 1997.

138. Maripuu, "Soviet Prisoners of War," 761.

139. BdrückwHGr North v. Roques to GK-Estland Litzmann, Mar. 12, 1942, BA-MA, RH-22/277; Minölko Estonia, Group "Work," review of KTB for July 1–Sept. 30, 1943, BA-MA, RW-46/755.

140. Ger. Sipo in Narva to Mayor of Narva, Sept. 23, 1943, ERA, R-59/1/95.

141. Case files, ERA, R-64/1/160, 161, 166, 168–72, 174, 175.

142. Interrogation of Mihkel Raudsepp, Tallinn, Dec. 6, 1950, USHMM, RG-06.026.07.

143. Kruk, *The Last Days of the Jerusalem of Lithuania*, 677, 679–80, 687.

144. John Hersey, "Prisoner 339, Klooga: Pole Who Escaped Labor Camp Tells How the Nazis Tortured, Butchered and Burned Their Captives," *Life*, Oct. 30, 1944, 76, 78.

145. Interview with Martti Soosaar, Tallinn, Dec. 7, 2002, USHMM, RG-50.559.1.

146. Elhonen Saks, "Kloogat peeti heaks Laagriks!" (Klooga Was Considered a Good Camp!), *Horisont*, no. 6 (1991).

147. Eugenia Gurin-Loov, "Verfolgung der Juden in Estland (1941–1944): Rettungsversuche und Hilfe," in *Solidarität und Hilfe für Juden während der NS-Zeit*, ed. Wolfgang Benz and Juliane Wetzel (Berlin: Metropol, 1996), 2:307.

148. Dworzecki, *Vaise Nekht*, 264–66.

149. Testimony of Hanna Panyrkova, Kassel, Feb. 6, 1969, BAL, 408 AR-Z 233/59, V25.

10. JEWISH FORCED LABOR CAMPS, 1943–1944

1. Nicholas Lane analyzed von Bodman's reports in connection with his work in the Estonian Historical Commission, which was established in 1998.

2. Indictment of Oskar Helbig, Cologne, 1974? BAL, 408 AR-Z 233/59, supV.

3. EEC final report on the mass execution of prisoners at Klooga KZ, Oct. 12, 1944, USHMM, RG-22.002M/25.

4. Dworzecki, *Vaise Nekht,* 201.

5. Kruk, *The Last Days of the Jerusalem of Lithuania,* 673; Vaivara KZ Bodman to WVHA, Sept. 25, 1943; Nov. 25, 1943; Dec. 29, 1943, EAM, D 152/2/40.

6. Indictment against Helmut Schnabel et al., Hechingen, Mar. 18, 1966, IfZ, Gh-06.03.

7. Testimony of Ben-Zion Zak, Jerusalem, Sept. 23, 1962, BAL, 408 AR-Z 233/59, V11.

8. Kacel, *From Hell to Redemption,* 123, 130.

9. Interrogation of Anton Birnmann, Nov. 26, 1960, BAL, 407 AR 91/65, V3; interrogation of Otto Schmid, Amberg, Apr. 6, 1961, YVA, TR-10/1196. The witness mistook Sillamäe for Kiviõli.

10. Indictment of Oskar Helbig, Cologne, 1974? BAL, 408 AR-Z 233/59, supp. V. At the beginning of November 1943, the death rate at Vaivara exceeded 12 percent.

11. Kacel, *From Hell to Redemption,* 126, 129, 131.

12. Indictment against Helmut Schnabel et al., Hechingen, Mar. 18, 1966, IfZ, Gh-06.03.

13. Testimony of Mordechai Rosenberg, Tel Aviv, Aug. 20, 1961, YVA, 04/383; interrogation of Josef Glöckle, Günzburg, Jan. 13, 1960, YVA, TR-10/1196; testimony of Moshe Danziger, Tel Aviv, Aug. 13, 1968, BAL, 408 AR-Z 233/59, V24.

14. Testimony of Mordechai Rosenberg, Tel Aviv, Aug. 20, 1961, YVA, 04/383.

15. Testimony of Mira Brojdo, [?], May 12, 1977, YVA, 04/413 I.

16. According to Dworzecki's estimate, close to 900 Jews lost their lives in Vaivara, while von Bodman reported only 111 deaths.

17. Vaivara KZ Bodman to WVHA, Feb. 20, 1944, EAM, D 152/2/40.

18. Report for Baltöl dir. Schön, Oct. 1, 1943; Baltöl, transcript of a discussion, Oct. 4, 1943, ERA, R-187/1/33.

19. Dworzecki, *Vaise Nekht,* 216.

20. Testimony of Sara Dimantstein, Tel Aviv, Aug. 30, 1964, YVA, 04/400

21. Nissan Anolik, testimony at Friedrich Jeckeln's trial, Riga, Feb. 1, 1946, LCVA, R-1390/2/68; testimony of Bunia Perelstein, Tel-Aviv, May 22, 1967, BAL, 408 AR-Z 233/59, V24.

22. Indictment against Helmut Schnabel et al., Hechingen, Mar. 18, 1966, IfZ, Gh-06.03; verdict against Helmut Schnabel et al., Ulm, Sept. 8, 1969, IfZ, Gh-01.04.

23. Interim report N18 of the Israeli Police (based on witness testimonies), Tel Aviv, Sept. 3, 1967, YVA, 04/52.

24. Minölko Estonia, transcript of a discussion, Feb. 14, 1944, ERA, R-187/1/68.

25. Minölko Estonia, *KTB,* Oct. 1–Dec. 31, 1943, BA-MA, RW-46/756.

26. Interrogation of Wilhelm Genth, Helmstadt, May 19, 1961, BAL, 408 AR-Z 233/59, V5.

27. AOK 18, IV Wi, to Minölko North, July 23, 1941, BA-MA, RW-46/298.

28. HGr North to HSSPF North-Russia Jeckeln, July 8, 1942; BdS-Ostland Jost to KdS-Estland Sandberger, July 21, 1942; BdS-Ostland to HGr North, July 28, 1942, IfZ, Fb-101/18.

29. Minölko Estonia, *KTB,* Sept. 21–30, 1943; WiKo Gdov, Slantsy Office, Oct. 2, 1943, BA-MA, RW-46/755; Minölko Estonia, Group "Work," Oct. 4, 1943, BA-MA, RW-46/756.

30. Vaivara KZ Bodman to WVHA, Oct. 25, 1943; Nov. 25, 1943; Dec. 29, 1943, Feb. 20, 1944, EAM, D 152/2/40.

31. Vaivara KZ Bodman to WVHA, Nov. 25, 1943; Dec. 29, 1943, Jan. 26, 1944; Mar. 25, 1944, EAM, D 152/2/40.

32. Testimony of Isaac Zak, Apr. 30, 1979, YVA, 04/414.

33. Vaivara KZ Bodman to WVHA, Nov. 25, 1943, EAM, D 152/2/40.

34. Testimony of Abraham Krein, Heidelberg, June 7, 1961, BAL, 408 AR-Z 233/59, V5.

35. Vaivara KZ Bodman to WVHA, Oct. 25, 1943; Nov. 25, 1943, Dec. 29, 1943, EAM, D 152/2/40.

36. Testimony of Mordechai Gordon, Bet Dagan, Mar. 6, 1967, BAL, 408 AR-Z 233/59, V6.

37. Interrogation of Wilhelm Genth, Helmstadt, May 19, 1961, BAL, 408 AR-Z 233/59, V5.

38. Vaivara KZ Bodman to WVHA, Feb. 20, 1944, EAM, D 152/2/40.

39. Indictment against Helmut Schnabel and Rudolf Klicker, Hannover, July 21, 1975, BAL, 408 AR-Z 233/59, V30.

40. Dworzecki, *Vaise Nekht,* 166.

41. Vaivara KZ Bodman to WVHA, Nov. 25, 1943; Feb. 20, 1944, EAM, D 152/2/40.

42. Testimony of Mordechai Gordon, Bet Dagan, Mar. 6, 1967, BAL, 408 AR-Z 233/59, V6.

43. Indictment against Erich Scharfetter, Stade, Aug. 2, 1978, YVA, 04/413 I; testimony of Harry Kagan, Hechingen, Aug. 25, 1965, BAL, 408 AR-Z 233/59, V14.

44. Interrogation of Fedor Room, Tallinn, Apr. 21, 1947, USHMM, RG-06.026/15.

45. Testimony of Iser Zak, June 13, 1979, YVA, 04/414.

46. Vaivara KZ Bodman to WVHA, Mar. 25, 1944, EAM, D 152/2/40.

47. Testimony of Yitzhak Kaufman, Bet Dagan, Feb. 13, 1967, BAL, 408 AR-Z 233/59, V22; interrogation of Otto Hefele, Hurlach, Mar. 5, 1961, YVA, TR-10/1196.

48. Interrogation of Erna Hornung, [?], Oct. 20, 1960, BAL, 7 AR-Z 233/59, V3.

49. Indictment against Erich Scharfetter, Stade, Aug. 2, 1978, YVA, 04/413 I.

50. Vaivara KZ, YVA, TR-10/1313.

51. Vaivara KZ Bodman to WVHA, Oct. 25, 1943; Nov. 25, 1943; Dec. 29, 1943; Jan. 26, 1944, EAM, D 152/2/40.

52. Testimony of Nissan Anolik, Riga, Feb. 1, 1946, LCVA, R-1390/2/68.

53. Ibid.; testimony of Nissan Anolik, Ludwigsburg, July 15, 1965, BAL, 408 AR-Z 233/59, V14.

54. Testimony of Aron Shuster, Chedera, Mar. 14, 1971, BAL, 408 AR-Z 233/59, V27; Vaivara KZ Bodman to WVHA, Feb. 20, 1944, EAM, D 152/2/40.

55. Vaivara KZ Bodman to WVHA, Nov. 25, 1943, EAM, D 152/2/40.

56. Dworzecki, *Vaise Nekht,* 215.

57. Est. Sipo in Narva-Jõesuu to police assistant, Nov. 10, 1943, ERA, R-59/1/95.

58. Vaivara KZ I. A. Bodman to WVHA, Dec. 29, 1943; Jan. 26, 1944, EAM, D 152/2/40.

59. Between the two world wars Ivangorod was officially part of Estonia.

60. Vaivara KZ Bodman to WVHA, Oct. 25, 1943, EAM, D 152/2/40.

61. Kruk, *The Last Days of the Jerusalem of Lithuania,* 663.

62. Testimony of Sima Skurkowicz, Jerusalem, June 26, 1962, BAL, 408 AR-Z 233/59, V11.

63. Interrogation of Baruch Gurwitz, Dec. 1943, ERA, R-966/1/1.

64. Interrogation of Isaac Zukermann, Dec. 1943, ERA, R-966/1/1.

65. Verdict against Helmut Schnabel et al., Ulm, Sept. 8, 1969, IfZ, Gh-01.04.

66. Testimony of Isaac Zohar, Tel Aviv, June 15, 1962, BAL, 408 AR-Z 233/59, V11.

67. Data from Dr. von Bodman's reports, EEC records: Harjumaa, fall 1944, USHMM, RG-22.002M/25.

68. Kruk, *The Last Days of the Jerusalem of Lithuania,* 664.

69. Testimony of Wolf Weisstein, Munich, Apr. 26, 1960, BAL, 407 AR 91/65, V3.

70. Testimony of Sara Dimantstein, Tel Aviv, Aug. 30, 1964, YVA, 04/400.

71. Indictment against Helmut Schnabel et al., Hechingen, Mar. 18, 1966, IfZ, Gh-06.03. Runde was charged with strangling five prisoners in January 1944.

72. Vaivara KZ Bodman to WVHA, Feb. 20, 1944, EAM, D 152/2/40.

73. Indictment against Helmut Schnabel et al., Hechingen, Mar. 18, 1966, IfZ, Gh-06.03. Some of the Estonian guards who convoyed Jews from Narva to Ereda argued that the number of inmates who were killed or died on the march was anywhere between thirty and fifty.

74. Testimony of Yitzhak Zohar, Bet Dagan, Oct. 6, 1968, BAL, 408 AR-Z 233/59, V24.

75. Report prepared for Baltöl dir. Schön, Oct. 1, 1943, ERA, R-187/1/33.

76. Interrogation of Wilhelm Werle, Worms, May 9, 1961, BAL, 207 AR-Z 246/59, V3.

77. Indictment against Oskar Helbig, Cologne, 1974? BAL, 408 AR-Z 233/59, supV.

78. Interrogation of Paul Hanke, Augsburg, Jan. 20, 1961, YVA, TR-10/1196.

79. EEC final report on the mass execution of prisoners at Klooga KZ, Oct. 12, 1944, USHMM, RG-22.002M/25.

80. Baltöl, report on the construction sites, Mar. 20, 1944, ERA, R-187/1/6.

81. Minölko Estonia, conversation with Gen. Stapf, Mar. 9, 1944, ERA, R-187/1/68.

82. Testimony of Isaac Zohar, Tel Aviv, June 15, 1962, BAL, 408 AR-Z 233/59, V11.

83. Interim report N36 of the Israeli Police (based on witness testimonies), Tel Aviv, July 19, 1970, YVA, 04/52.

84. Interrogation of Paul Hanke, Augsburg, Jan. 20, 1961, YVA, TR-10/1196.

85. Testimony of Moshe Danziger, Ludwigsburg, July 20, 1965, BAL, 408 AR-Z 233/59, V14.

86. Testimonies of Harry Berlin, Natania, Dec. 27, 1966; Szymon Gitelson, Jerusalem, Dec. 25, 1966, BAL, AR-Z 233/59, V22.

87. Indictment against Helmut Schnabel et al., Hechingen, Mar. 18, 1966, IfZ, Gh-06.03; interim report N12 of the Israeli Police (based on witness testimonies), Tel Aviv, June 23, 1966, YVA, 04/52.

88. Testimony of Fanny Pitum, Munich, July 2, 1959, BAL, 408 AR-Z 233/59, V12.

89. Interrogation of Heinrich Reintz [phonetic], Horn, Aug. 20, 1945, BAL, 408 AR-Z 233/59, V27. In spite of the contradictory nature of Reintz's statement, it does not appear that the defendant was deliberately trying to mislead investigators.

90. Interrogation of Heinrich Reintz, Horn, Aug. 20 and Sept. 4, 1945, BAL, 408 AR-Z 233/59, V27. See also Paavle, "Soviet Investigations," 881.

91. Interrogation of Heinrich Reintz, Horn, Aug. 20, 1945, BAL, 408 AR-Z 233/59, V27.

92. Interrogation of Oskar Parvei, Tallinn, Dec. 1, 1944, USHMM, RG-06.026.09.

93. Verdict against Helmut Schnabel and Rudolf Klicker, Hannover, May 13, 1977, BAL, 408 AR-Z 233/59, V31. Prisoners used to call Lower and Upper Ereda "summer" and "winter" camp respectively.

94. Ibid.

95. Interrogation of Franz Leichter, Wyhlen, Apr. 17, 1963, BAL, 408 AR-Z 233/59, V11.

96. Testimony of Isaac Zak, Apr. 30, 1979, YVA, 04/414; testimony of Szymon Tubiasiewicz, Tel Aviv, Apr. 5, 1963, YVA, 04/400.

97. Testimony of Franz Leichter, Wyhlen, Apr. 17, 1963, BAL, 408 AR-Z 233/59, V11; testimony of Rosa Mersel, Tel Aviv, May 30, 1974, BAL, 408 AR-Z 233/59, V28.

98. Verdict against Helmut Schnabel and Rudolf Klicker, Hannover, May 13, 1977, BAL, 408 AR-Z 233/59, V31. Drohsin was married and had two children.

99. Testimony of Franz Leichter, Wyhlen, Apr. 17, 1963, BAL, 408 AR-Z 233/59, V11.

100. Data from Dr. von Bodmann's reports, EEC records: Harjumaa, fall 1944, USHMM, RG-22.002M/25.

101. Testimony of Baruch Goldstein, Tel Aviv, July 19, 1973, BAL, 408 AR-Z 233/59, V28. According to Dworzecki, these people were deported to Auschwitz-Birkenau, where they arrived on February 22 (Dworzecki, *Vaise Nekht*, 146, 158, 165). However, the available evidence is inconclusive.

102. Vaivara KZ Bodman to WHVA, Feb. 20, 1944; Apr. 25, 1944, EAM D 152/2/40.

103. Indictment of Erich Scharfetter, Stade, Aug. 2, 1978, YVA, 04/413 I.

104. Indictment against Helmut Schnabel et al., Hechingen, Mar. 18, 1966, IfZ, Gh-06.03; Nissan Anolik, testimony in Friedrich Jeckeln's trial, Riga, Feb. 1, 1946, LCVA, R-1390/2/68.

105. Přibyl, "Die Geschichte," 199.

106. Testimony of Franz Leichter, Wyhlen, Apr. 17, 1963, BAL, 408 AR-Z 233/59, V11. In 1944, July 24 fell on a Saturday and not on a Friday as the witness told the investigation.

107. Report: mass execution of Jews at Ereda KZ, EEC records, Sept. 21, 1944, USHMM, RG-22.002M/25.

108. Testimony of Franz Leichter, Wyhlen, Apr. 17, 1963, BAL, 408 AR-Z 233/59, V11.

109. Ibid.

110. Testimony of Shlomo Baranovski, Bet Dagan, Jan. 24, 1967, BAL, 408 AR-Z 233/59, V22.

111. Vaivara KZ Bodman to WVHA, Oct. 25, 1943; May 26, 1944, EAM, D 152/2/40; testimony of Tzipora Golsman, Bet Dagan, Jan. 21, 1967, BAL, 408 AR-Z 233/59, V22.

112. Dworzecki, *Vaise Nekht*, 139–40.

113. Vaivara KZ Bodman to WVHA, Oct. 25, 1943, EAM, D 152/2/40.

114. Testimony of Wolf Koiaranski, Bet Shaan, Feb. 26, 1967, BAL, 408 AR-Z 233/59, V22.

115. Interim report N1 of the Israeli Police (based on witness testimonies), Tel Aviv, Aug. 29, 1962, YVA, 04/52.

116. Testimony of Alan Weiler, Hechingen, Aug. 17, 1965, BAL, 408 AR-Z 233/59, V14.

117. Testimony of Sima Skurkowicz, Jerusalem, Oct. 22, 1968, BAL, 408 AR-Z 233/59, V24.

118. Testimony of Sima Skurkowicz, Jerusalem, June 26, 1962, BAL, 408 AR-Z 233/59, V11.

119. Interim report [no number] of the Israeli Police (based on witness testimonies), Tel Aviv, Nov. 24, 1968, YVA, 04/52.

120. Kacel, *From Hell to Redemption*, 151–67.

121. Testimony of Herta Madlova, Hannover, June 19, 1979, BAL, 408 AR-Z 233/59, V28; testimony of Helena Freundova, Kassel, Jan. 28, 1969, BAL, 408 AR-Z 233/59, V25.

122. Lederer, "Meine Deportierung," Jan. 17, 1967, BAL, 207 AR-Z 246/59, V6.

123. Testimony of Anna Bauer, Bet Dagan, May 13, 1968, BAL, 408 AR-Z 233/59, V25; testimony of Anna Freiman, Bet Dagan, Feb. 24, 1967, BAL, 408 AR-Z 233/59, draft volume.

124. Interrogation of Johannes Tuudelepp, Tallinn, Nov. 10, 1948, ERAF, 3042.

125. Testimony of Alan Weiler, Hechingen, Aug. 17, 1965, BAL, 408 AR-Z 233/59, V14.

11. KLOOGA

1. Ironically, in Yiddish the name "Klooga" *(kloge)* rhymes with "lament" *(klog)* and "miserable" *(klogedik)*.

2. GK-Estland to RKO Lohse, Apr. 14, 1943; RKO, Dept. II, note, Aug. 23, 1943; number of refugees in Põllküla and Klooga camps as of Sept. 14, 1943, LVVA, R-70/5/72; note on Klooga KZ, Dec. 20, 1965, USHMM, RG-06.026/16.

3. BdrückwHGr North v. Roques, monthly report, Aug. 1942, BA-MA, RH-22/263.

4. Testimonies of Mytl Genzel, EEC records, RG-22.002M/25.

5. Testimony of Mendel Balberinski, EEC records, Sept. 29, 1944, USHMM, RG-22.002M/25.

6. Hersey, "Prisoner 339," 74. According to Weintraub, the transport from Vilna arrived in Klooga on Sept. 23, which is apparently incorrect.

7. EEC final report on mass execution of prisoners at Klooga KZ, Oct. 12, 1944, USHMM, RG-22.002M/25.

8. The list of Jewish prisoners reproduced in Zvika Dror, ed., *Klooga on the North: Testimonies of Survivors of a Concentration Camp in Estonia* (Kibutz Dalia: Ma'arechet, 1997), 65–126.

9. Riho Västrik, "Klooga koonduslaager—Vaivara süsteemi koletu lõpp" (Klooga Concentration Camp: An Ugly End to the Vaivara Camp System), *Vikerkaar* 15, no. 8–9 (2001): 149. Statistics based on the total of 2,156 prisoners; mathematical inaccuracies in text.

10. Kruk, *The Last Days of the Jerusalem of Lithuania*, 675, 676.

11. Testimony of Benjamin Anolik, Riga, Feb. 1, 1946, LCVA, R-1390/2/69.

12. Hersey, "Prisoner 339," 74.

13. Prisoner employment statistics at Klooga, May 1–10, 1944, ERA, R-170/1/1.

14. Kruk, *The Last Days of the Jerusalem of Lithuania*, 674, 681.

15. WiKo Talinn, weekly report for Aug. 6–12, 1944, Aug. 10, 1944, BAB, R-91/Reval/1.

16. Interrogation of Wilhelm Föhles, Hüls, June 25, 1960, BAL, 408 AR-Z 233/59, V3.

17. Testimony of Isaac Ratner, EEC records, Oct. 2, 1944, USHMM, RG-22.002M/25.

18. Testimony of Mendel Balberinski, EEC records, Sept. 29, 1944, USHMM, RG-22.002M/25.

19. Interview with Martti Soosaar, Tallinn, Dec. 7, 2002, USHMM, RG-50.559.1.

20. Interim report no. 18 of the Israeli Police (based on witness testimonies), Tel Aviv, Sept. 3, 1967, YVA, 04/52.

21. Interrogation of August Sinipalu, EEC records, Oct. 3, 1944, USHMM, RG-22.002M/25.

22. Testimony of Peisah Rubanovich, EEC records, Oct. 3, 1944, USHMM, RG-22.002M/25. According to other sources, A.I.K. ran a sawmill at Klooga. The company's sixteen workers commuted to Klooga from Tallinn.

23. Interrogation of Harald Saarberg, Tallinn, May 19, 1951, USHMM, RG-06.026.07.

24. Interrogation of Oskar Parvei, Tallinn, Dec. 4, 1944, USHMM, RG-06.026.09.

25. A. Krimm, report to BIV, July 29, 1944, ERA, R-64/1/197.

26. Medical certificates of individual prisoners at Klooga, Dec. 1943–June 1944, ERA, R-170/1/1.

27. Testimony of Isaac Ratner, EEC records, Oct. 2, 1944, USHMM, RG-22.002M/25. See also *Sovetskaia Estonia*, Oct. 3, 1944.

28. Interrogation of Wilhelm Föhles, Hüls, July 12, 1966, BAL, 408 AR-Z 233/59, V17.

29. Kruk, *The Last Days of the Jerusalem of Lithuania*, 703.

30. Interrogation of Wilhelm Genth, Helmstadt, May 19, 1961, YVA, TR-10/1196.

31. Testimony of Lazar Buzhanski, EEC records, Sept. 30, 1944, USHMM, RG-22.002M/25.

32. Preliminary proceedings against Wilhelm Genth and Wilhelm Werle, Heidelberg, July 18, 1962, BAL, 408 AR-Z 233/59, V7. The numbers seem inflated, considering that witnesses based their information on hearsay.

33. Hersey, "Prisoner 339," 76.

34. Report on the mass execution of Jews at Klooga camp, EEC records, fall 1944, USHMM, RG-22.002M/25.

35. Testimony of Isaac Ratner, EEC records, Oct. 2, 1944, USHMM, RG-22.002M/25.

36. WiKo Tallinn, weekly report for July 23–31, 1944, July 29, 1944, BAB, R-91/Reval/1; testimony of Hilda Levy, Hechingen, July 13, 1965, BAL, 408 AR-Z 233/59, V14.

37. Interview with Doris Rauch, Washington, July 7, 1995, USHMM, RG-50.106.15.

38. Přibyl, "Die Geschichte," 208.

39. Testimony of Nissan Anolik, Ludwigsburg, July 15, 1965, BAL, 408 AR-Z 233/59, V14.

40. Testimony of Rudolf Kalde, Raasiku, Oct. 18, 1960, USHMM, RG-06.026/12.

41. Seth, *A Spy Has No Friends*, 14–17.

42. Indictment against Helmut Schnabel et al., Hechingen, Mar. 18, 1966, IfZ, Gh-06.03.

43. Dworzecki, *Vaise Nekht*, 170.

44. Testimony of Josef Rabinovich, EEC records, Sept. 30, 1944, USHMM, RG-22.002M/25.

45. Est. Sipo, BIII, daily report, Aug. 21, 1944, *Pruun Katk,* doc N108, 125.

46. Hersey, "Prisoner 339," 78.

47. Testimony of Mendel Balberinski, EEC records, Sept. 29, 1944, USHMM, RG-22.002M/25.

48. Testimony of Benjamin Anolik, Feb. 1, 1946, LCVA, R-1390/2/69. Anolik's testimony also reproduced in *Neizvestnaia Chernaia Kniga* (Jerusalem: Yad Vashem, 1993), 337–42.

49. Ibid.; Dworzecki, *Vaise Nekht,* 377–78.

50. Testimony of Uriah Simanovich, EEC records, Oct. 7, 1944, USHMM, RG-22.002M/25.

51. Dworzecki, *Vaise Nekht,* 378–79. Dworzecki misspelled the name "Helbig."

52. Interrogation of Wilhelm Föhles, Hüls, July 12, 1966, BAL, 408 AR-Z 233/59, V17.

53. HGr North, daily report, Sept. 4, 1944, BA-MA, RH-19 III/318. Jeckeln proposed the evacuation of the Russian population from Estonia, based on the availability of ship-space and potential employment in the Reich.

54. OKH, Dept Rü, *KTB,* Sept. 5, 1944, BA-MA, RW-46/28.

55. KdS-Estland Baatz to Special Commandos Hasselbach, Prellberg, and Buchner, Sept. 10, 1944, ERA, R-59/1/69.

56. HGr North, daily reports, Sept. 16–18, 1944, BA-MA, RH-19 III/318, 319; WiIn Ostland, Armament industry in the Ostland, report for Sept. 1, 1941–Aug. 8, 1944, BA-MA, RW-30/203.

57. OKH to OKM, Sept. 18, 1944, BA-MA, RH-19 III/15.

58. HGr North, daily report, Sept. 27, 1944, BA-MA, RH-19 III/319.

59. HGr North, daily reports, Sept. 21–23, 1944, BA-MA, RH-19 III/319.

60. WiKo Tallinn, situational report, July 30–Aug. 28, 1944, BA-MA, RW-30/59. For a complete list of industry lines at Klooga, see RKO Lohse to GK-Estland Litzmann, Aug. 28, 1944, NARA, T-454/21.

61. HGr North, daily report, Sept. 6, 1944, BA-MA, RH-19 III/318.

62. Kruk, *The Last Days of the Jerusalem of Lithuania,* 694–99.

63. Interrogation of Walter Schwarze, Berlin, Apr. 8, 1947, BAL, 408 AR-Z 233/59, V27.

64. Testimony of Isaac Ratner, EEC records, Oct. 2, 1944, USHMM, RG-22.002M/25.

65. Testimony of Lisa Berchin, EEC records, Sept. 30, 1944, USHMM, RG-22.002M/25.

66. Hersey, "Prisoner 339," 78.

67. Testimony of Nissan Anolik, Ludwigsburg, July 15, 1965, BAL, 408 AR-Z 233/59, V14.

68. Hersey, "Prisoner 339," 81.

69. Interrogation of Wilhelm Föhles, Hüls, July 12, 1966, BAL, 408 AR-Z 233/59, V17.

70. Hersey, "Prisoner 339," 81.

71. Testimonies of Meier Trinapolski and Henryk Anfelbaum, EEC records, Oct. 1, 1944, USHMM, RG-22.002M/25.

72. Dworzecki, *Vaise Nekht,* 380.

73. Hersey, "Prisoner 339," 81.

74. Hersey, "Prisoner 339," 82.

75. Testimony of Mendel Balberinski, EEC records, Sept. 29, 1944, USHMM, RG-22.002M/25.

76. Testimony of Eugenia Olnepiskaia, EEC records, Sept. 30, 1944, USHMM, RG-22.002M/25.

77. Testimony of Mendel Balberinski, EEC records, Sept. 29, 1944, USHMM, RG-22.002M/25.

78. Report on mass execution at Klooga camp, EEC records, fall 1944, USHMM, RG-22.002M/25.

79. Memo re the case of Wilhelm Genth, Ludwigsburg, May 5, 1961, YVA, TR-10/1196.

80. According to other sources, the SS commando was composed of fifty people.

81. Testimonies of Josef Rabinovich and David Broch, EEC records, Sept. 30, 1944, USHMM, RG-22.002M/25.

82. Interrogation of Wilhelm Genth, Helmstadt, May 19, 1961, BAL, 408 AR-Z 233/59, V5.

83. Testimonies of Benjamin Weintraub and Meier Trinapolski, EEC records, Oct. 1, 1944, USHMM, RG-22.002M/25. Weintraub's testimony also reproduced in Vasili Grossman and Ilia Ehrenburg, eds., *Chernaia Kniga* (Jerusalem: Yad Vashem, 1980), 343–46.

84. Testimony of Isaac Ratner, EEC records, Oct. 2, 1944, USHMM, RG-22.002M/25.

85. Interrogation of August Sinipalu, EEC records, Oct. 3, 1944, USHMM, RG-22.002M/25.

86. Testimony of Isaiah Klatchko, Ramat Gan, Feb. 24, 1971, BAL, 408 AR-Z 233/59, V27. See also Dror, *Klooga on the North,* 126.

87. Indictment against Georg Ahlemann, Cologne, July 9, 1974, BAL, 408 AR-Z 233/59, V29.

88. Testimony of Aron Shuster, Chedera, Mar. 14, 1971, BAL, 408 AR-Z 233/59, V27.

89. Interrogation of Mihkel Raudsepp, Tallinn, Dec. 6, 1950, USHMM, RG-06.026.07.

90. List of survivors at Klooga KZ, EEC records, fall 1944, ERA, R-364/1/204.

91. Västrik, "Klooga koonduslaager," 155.

92. In the late 1980s and early 1990s Lipkin conducted a series of interviews with local Estonian farmers who had lived in the vicinity of the Vaivara and Viivikonna camps. Lipkin published his findings in a Sillamäe Russian-language newspaper. Currently his materials are deposited at Sillamäe City Museum.

93. *Eesti Express,* Sept. 13, 1996.

94. Minölko Estonia, Group "TB," *KTB,* Feb. 16, 1944, BA-MA, RW-46/757.

12. CONCLUSIONS: EXPLAINING COLLABORATION

1. John Armstrong, "Collaborationism in World War II: The Integral Nationalist Variant in Eastern Europe," *Journal of Modern History* 40, no. 3 (1968): 396.

2. Levin, *Baltic Jews,* 375.

3. Saulius Sužiedėlis, "The Historical Sources for Antisemitism in Lithuania and Jewish-Lithuanian Relations During the 1930s," in *The Vanished World of Lithuanian Jews,* ed. Alvydas Nikžentaitis et al. (Amsterdam: Rodopi, 2004), 145.

4. Ezergailis, "Collaboration in German Occupied Latvia." Jeffrey Burds is currently working on a book that looks comparatively at anti-Jewish pogroms in the western Soviet borderlands in the summer of 1941.

5. Martin Dean, *Collaboration in the Holocaust: Crimes of the Local Police in Belorussia and Ukraine, 1941–44* (New York: St. Martin's Press, 2000), 74.

6. Ezergailis, "Collaboration in German Occupied Latvia."

7. Gerhard Bassler, "The Collaborationist Agenda in Latvia, 1941–1943," in Kõll, *The Baltic Countries under Occupation*, 78.

8. Ezergailis, *Stockholm Documents*, xi.

9. Maripuu, "Eesti juutide holocaust ja eestlased," 146.

10. Stanley Milgram, "The Compulsion to Do Evil: Obedience to Criminal Orders," *Patterns of Prejudice* 1, no. 6 (Nov.–Dec. 1967): 3–7.

11. Browning, *Ordinary Men,* 171–76, 184–87.

12. Ervin Staub, *The Roots of Evil: The Origins of Genocide and Other Group Violence* (Cambridge, UK: Cambridge Univ. Press, 1989), 29.

13. Christoph Dieckmann, "Deutsche und litauische Interessen: Grundlinien der besatzungspolitik in Litauen 1941 bis 1944," in Bartusevičius et al., *Holocaust in Litauen,* 71.

14. Ezergailis made this comment at the conference *Collaboration and Resistance in "Reichskommissariat Ostland,"* Stockholm, Apr. 2002.

15. Ezergailis, *The Holocaust in Latvia,* 375–76.

16. Stang, "Das Fussvolk und seine Eliten," 69–89.

17. Michael MacQueen, "Nazi Policy Toward the Jews in the 'Reichskommissariat Ostland,' June–December 1941: From White Terror to Holocaust in Lithuania," in *Bitter Legacy: Confronting the Holocaust in the USSR,* ed. Zvi Gitelman (Bloomington: Indiana Univ. Press, 1997), 92, 98.

18. Eric Haberer, "Intention and Feasibility: Reflections on Collaboration and the Final Solution," *East European Jewish Affairs* 31, no. 2 (2001): 65–77.

19. Roger D. Petersen, *Understanding Ethnic Violence: Fear, Hatred, and Resentment in Twentieth-Century Europe* (Cambridge: Cambridge Univ. Press, 2002), xii, 1, 4, 21–22, 25, 29–30.

20. Ibid., 40–43, 48–52, 104–10, 112, 115.

21. Ibid., 111.

22. Ibid., 113.

23. Staub, *The Roots of Evil,* 14–18, 55–56, 88.

24. Ibid., 16, 19, 36–43, 48, 70, 252, 267.

25. Judith L. Herman, *Trauma and Recovery: The Aftermath of Violence—From Domestic Abuse to Political Terror* (New York: Basic Books, 1992), 33–39, 47, 56–58.

26. Ibid., 61–63, 70–73, 189–90, 208–11.

27. Ibid., 133–37, 142–43, 147–49, 159–60, 197.

28. Parming, "The Holocaust in Estonia."

29. White, "Estonia's Gestapo."

30. Staub, *The Roots of Evil,* 25, 33, 35.

31. Petersen, *Resistance and Rebellion,* 81, 129, 130. Petersen lists at least twelve underground groups that operated in Lithuania during the Soviet occupation. An umbrella organization, the Lithuanian Activist Front, had 35,000 members. For a country of about three million, Petersen argues, the scale of underground activity in Lithuania was striking. Petersen indicates two factors

that made clandestine resistance organization in Latvia and Estonia less efficient than that in Lithuania: the higher level of urbanization and the lack of a unifying religious force.

32. Christopher Browning, *The Path to Genocide* (Cambridge, UK: Cambridge Univ. Press, 1992), 7, 27. Robert Gellately provides a good summary of Nazi plans for Eastern Europe in his article "The Third Reich, the Holocaust, and Visions of Serial Genocide," in *The Specter of Genocide: Mass Murder in Historical Perspective,* ed. Robert Gellately and Ben Kiernan (Cambridge, UK: Cambridge Univ. Press, 2003), 252–63.)

33. Götz Aly and Susanne Heim, *Vordenker der Vernichtung: Auschwitz und die deutschen Pläne für eine neue europäische Ordnung* (Frankfurt: Fischer, 1993), 122–23, 278, 299, 364, 422, 439–40.

34. Bubnys, "The Holocaust in Lithuania," 214.

35. Interview with Mäe, Aug. 2–3, 1958, IfZ, ZS-2366.

36. Commander of SK 1a Sandberger, report, "Political Thoughts in the Leading Estonian Circles," [September 1941], BA-MA, RH-19 III/470.

37. Partisan commander of the liberated Estonian areas Kurg, order N5, July 29, 1941, in *Eesti riik ja rahvas II. Maailmasõjas* (Stockholm: EMP, 1958), 6:177.

38. RMO office, Maurach, report on exhibition "Vital Struggle of the Estonian People," [1943], NARA, T-454/21.

39. EM N96, Sept. 27, 1941, BAB, R-58/217; *MbO* N15, Aug. 7, 1942, BAB, R-58/698.

40. Interview with Mäe, Aug. 2–3, 1958, IfZ, ZS-2366.

41. EM N135, Nov. 19, 1941, BAB, R-58/219.

42. Quoted in Juhan Kokla, "Eesti ajakirjandus ja saksa okupatsioon" (Estonian Press and the German Occupation), in *Eesti riik ja rahvas II. Maailmasõjas* (Stockholm: EMP, 1959), 8:146.

43. Kasekamp, "The Ideological Roots of Estonian Collaboration," 91

44. RMO Office, Hasselblatt to Wetzel, Dec. 14, 1942, BAB, R-6/160.

45. Sužiedėlis, "Foreign Saviors," 359.

46. Verdict against Helmut Schnabel et al., Ulm, Sept. 8, 1969, IfZ, Gh-01.04; indictment against Erich Scharfetter, Stade, Aug. 2, 1978, YVA, 04/413 I.

47. Because of the marginality of the Estonian case, Hilberg only scantily mentioned Estonia in his book (in both 1963 and 1985 editions). Hilberg demonstrated the mastery of analysis when testifying as an expert witness in Karl Linnas's denaturalization trial in Westbury, New York, on June 16, 1981.

48. Andres Kasekamp, "The Ideological Roots of Estonian Collaboration During the Nazi Occupation," in Kõll, *The Baltic Countries under Occupation,* 85.

49. In response, some authors engaged in a senseless exercise of calculating the "evil index," which, unsurprisingly, favors the country of their origin. See, for example, Yaroslaw Bilinsky, "Methodological Problems and Philosophical Issues in the Studies of Jewish-Ukrainian Relations During the Second World War," in *Ukrainian-Jewish Relations in Historical Perspective,* ed. Howard Aster and Peter Potichnyj (Edmonton: Univ. of Alberta, 1990), 381.

BIBLIOGRAPHY

ARCHIVES

Bundesarchiv-Militärarchiv (German Federal Archives-Military Archives), Freiburg.

Bundesarchiv-Berlin (German Federal Archives), Berlin.

Bundesarchiv-Koblenz (German Federal Archives), Koblenz.

Bundesarchiv-Ludwigsburg (German Federal Archives), Ludwigsburg.

Eesti Ajalooarhiiv (Estonian Historical Archives), Tartu.

Eesti Ajaloomuuseum (Estonian History Museum), Tallinn.

Eesti Riigiarhiiv (Estonian State Archives), Tallinn.

Eesti Riigiarhiivi Filiaal (Estonian State Branch Archives), Tallinn.

Herder Institut (Herder Institute), Marburg.

Institut für Zeitgeschichte (Institute of Contemporary History), Munich.

Lietuvos centrinis valstybės archivas (Lithuanian Central State Archives), Vilnius.

Latvijas Valsts vēstures arhīvs (Latvian State Historical Archives), Riga.

U.S. National Archives and Records Administration, Washington, D.C.

United States Holocaust Memorial Museum, Washington, D.C.

YIVO Institute of Jewish History, New York City.

Yad Vashem Archives, Jerusalem.

UNPUBLISHED SOURCES

Birn, Ruth Bettina. "Collaboration in the Baltic States: Estonia." Paper presented at the symposium *Perspectives on Indigenous Collaboration in the Baltic States During the German Occupation,* United States Holocaust Memorial Museum, Washington, D.C., Mar. 23, 1999.

Hilberg, Raul. Deposition at Karl Linnas's denaturalization trial, *U.S. v. Karl Linnas.* Westbury, Long Island, N.Y., June 16, 1981.

Ilmjärv, Margus. "Alistumine 1939–1940" (Submission, 1939–40). Paper presented at the S-Keskus Center for the Study of Modern Estonian History, Tallinn, Mar. 3, 2000. Available online at <http://www.s-keskus.arhiiv.ee/next.htm> (accessed Jan. 3, 2005).

Kalling, Ken. "Estonian Psychiatric Hospitals During the German Occupation, 1941–1944." Unpublished paper, 2006.

Lederer, Fanny. *Meine Deportierung von Anfang bis Ende,* Jan. 17, 1967, Bundesarchiv-Ludwigsburg (German Federal Archives), Ludwigsburg, 207 AR-Z 246/59, vol. 6.

Liebmann, Abe. *Ajaloolised ja kultuurilised eeldused juudi koguduste tekkimiseks ja arenemiseks Eestis* (Historical and Cultural Preconditions for Establishment and Development of Jewish Congregations in Estonia). M.A. thesis, Tartu Univ., 1937.

Maripuu, Meelis. "Faktide ja propaganda vahel: KGB ja kompartei inimsusevastaseid kuritegusid uurimas (1960.–1980. aastad)" (Between Facts and Propaganda: The KGB and the Communist Party Investigating Crimes Against Humanity, 1960s–1980s). Paper presented at the conference *Modern History in Baltic and European Context,* Tallinn, Mar. 30, 2005.

Mäe, Hjalmar. Interview with, Graz, Aug. 2–3, 1958, Institut für Zeitgeschichte (Institute of Contemporary History), Munich, ZS-2366.

Roques, von Franz. Memoirs, *Befehlshaber im Heeresgebiet Nord,* 16.III.1941–31.III.1943, Bundesarchiv-Militärarchiv (German Federal Archives-Military Archives), Freiburg, N-153/1.

White, Elisabeth. "Estonia's Gestapo: The Estonian Political Police in Tallinn, 1941–42." Paper presented at the German Studies Association conference, Atlanta, Ga., Oct. 10, 1999.

PUBLISHED SOURCES

Alenius, Kari. "Under the Conflicting Pressures of the Ideals of the Era and the Burden of History: Ethnic Relations in Estonia, 1918–1925." *Journal of Baltic Studies* 35, no. 1 (Spring 2004): 32–49.

Aly, Götz, and Susanne Heim. *Vordenker der Vernichtung: Auschwitz und die deutschen Pläne für eine neue europäische Ordnung.* Frankfurt: Fischer, 1993.

American Jewish Committee. *The Jewish Communities of Nazi-Occupied Europe.* New York: Howard Fertig, 1982 [1944].

Ammende, Ewald. *Die Nationalitäten in den Staaten Europas.* Vienna: Wilhelm Braumüller, 1931.

Amitan-Wilensky, Ella. "Esthonian Jewry: A Historical Summary." In *The Jews in Latvia,* ed. Mendel Bobe, 336–47. Tel Aviv: Association of Latvian and Esthonian Jews in Israel, 1971.

Angelus, Oskar. *Tuhande valitseja maa: Mälestusi Saksa okupatsiooni ajast 1941–1944* (Land of the Thousand Rulers: Memoirs of German Occupation, 1941–1944). Tallinn: Olion, 1995 [1956].

Ant, Jüri. *Eesti 1939–1941: Rahvast, Valitsemisest, Saatusest* (Estonia, 1939–1941: The People, the Governing, the Fate). Tallinn, 1999.

———, ed. *Kaks algust: Eesti Vabariig—1920. ja 1990. aastad* (Two Beginnings: Estonia in the 1920s and 1990s). Tallinn: Eesti Riigiarhiiv, 1998.

Anušauskas, Arvydas, ed. *The Anti-Soviet Resistance in the Baltic States.* Vilnius: Du Ka, 1999.

Arad, Yitzhak. *Ghetto in Flames: The Struggle and Destruction of the Jews in Vilna in the Holocaust.* Jerusalem: Yad Vashem, 1980.

Ariste, Paul. "Juut eesti rahvausus" (A Jew in Estonian Folklore). *Eesti Kirjandus,* nos. 1, 3, 4 (Jan., Mar., Apr. 1932): 1–17, 132–49, 219–28.

Armstrong, John. "Collaborationism in World War II: The Integral Nationalist Variant in Eastern Europe." *Journal of Modern History* 40, no. 3 (1968): 396–410.

Aule, Olgred. "Juden und Esten." *Mitteilungen aus baltischem Leben* (Munich), no. 4 (Dec. 1987): 6–12.

Bassler, Gerhard. "The Collaborationist Agenda in Latvia, 1941–1943." In *The Baltic Countries under Occupation: Soviet and Nazi Rule, 1939–1991,* ed. Anu Mai Kõll, 85–95. Stockholm: Acta Universitatis Stockholmiensis, 2003.

Bauer, Yehuda. *Rethinking the Holocaust.* New Haven, Conn.: Yale Univ. Press, 2001.

Benz, Wolfgang, et al., eds. *Einsatz im "Reichskommissariat Ostland": Dokumente zum Völkermord im Baltikum und in Weissrussland 1941–1944.* Berlin: Metropol, 1998.

Berg, Eiki. "Juudi asustuse iseärasusi Eestis" (Peculiarities of Jewish Settlement in Estonia). *Akadeemia* 6, no. 4 (1994): 816–29.

Birn, Ruth Bettina. "Collaboration with Nazi Germany in Eastern Europe: The Case of the Estonian Security Police." *Contemporary European History* 10, no. 2 (2001): 181–98.

———. "Heinrich Bergmann—eine deutsche Kriminalstenkarriere." In *Karrieren der Gewalt: Nationalsozialistische Täterbiographien,* ed. Klaus Michael Mallmann and Gerhard Paul, 47–55. Darmstadt: Wissenschaftliche Buchgesellschaft, 2004.

———. *Die Höheren SS-und Polizeiführer: Himmlers Vertreter im Reich und in den besetzten Gebieten.* Düsseldorf: Droste Verlag, 1986.

Brandišauskas, Valentinas. "Neue Dokumente aus der Zeit der Provisorischen Regierung Litauens." In *Holocaust in Litauen: Krieg, Judenmorde und Kollaboration im Jahre 1941,* ed. Vincas Bartusevičius et al., 51–62. Cologne: Böhlau Verlag, 2003.

Breitman, Richard. *The Architect of Genocide: Himmler and the Final Solution.* Hanover, N.H.: Brandeis Univ. Press, 1991.

Browning, Christopher. *The Final Solution and the German Foreign Office: A Study of Referat D III of Abteilung Deutschland, 1940–43*. New York: Holmes and Meier, 1978.

―――. *Ordinary Men: Reserve Police Battalion 101 and the Final Solution in Poland*. New York: Harper Perennial, 1992.

―――. *The Path to Genocide*. Cambridge, UK: Cambridge Univ. Press, 1992.

Bruchfeld, Stéphane, and Paul Levine. *Jutustage sellest oma lastele: Raamat holokaustist Euroopas aastatel 1933–1945* (Tell Your Children About It: A Book About the Holocaust in Europe, 1933–1945). Tartu: Israeli Sõbrad, 2003.

Bubnys, Arūnas. "The Holocaust in Lithuania: An Outline of the Major Stages and Their Results." In *The Vanished World of Lithuanian Jews,* ed. Alvydas Nikžentaitis et al., 205–21. Amsterdam: Rodopi, 2004.

Burleigh, Michael. *Death and Deliverance: 'Euthanasia' in Germany, 1900–1945*. Cambridge, Mass.: Harvard Univ. Press, 1994.

Burleigh, Michael, and Wolfgang Wippermann. *The Racial State: Germany, 1933–1945*. Cambridge, UK: Cambridge Univ. Press, 1991.

Cohen, Rose, and Saul Issroff. *The Holocaust in Lithuania, 1941–1945: A Book of Remembrance*. Jerusalem: Gefen, 2002.

Crampton, R. J. *Eastern Europe in the Twentieth Century and After*. London: Routledge, 1997.

Crowe, David. *The Baltic States and the Great Powers: Foreign Relations, 1938–1940*. Boulder, Colo.: Westview Press, 1993.

―――. "The History of the Oil Industry in Independent Estonia." *Nationalities Papers* 6, no. 1 (1978): 9–17.

Czollek, Roswitha. *Faschismus und Okkupation: Wirtschafts-politische Zielsetzung und Praxis des faschistischen deutschen Besatzungsregimes in den baltischen Sowjetrepubliken während des zweiten Weltkrieges*. Berlin: Akademie-Verlag, 1974.

―――. "Zum Raub estnischer Ölschiefervorkommen für die deutsche Kriegswirtschaft." *Jahrbuch für Wirtschaftsgeschichte,* no. 2 (1969).

Dean, Martin. *Collaboration in the Holocaust: Crimes of the Local Police in Belorussia and Ukraine, 1941–44*. New York: St. Martin's Press, 2000.

Deemant, Kaupo. "Massimõrv Tallinnas 23. juunil 1941" (Mass Murder in Tallinn on 23 June 1941). *Akadeemia* 6 (2001): 1200–1211.

Das deutsche Reval: Dokumente. Leipzig: S. Hirzel, 1942.

Dieckmann, Christoph. "Deutsche und litauische Interessen: Grundlinien der besatzungspolitik in Litauen 1941 bis 1944." In *Holocaust in Litauen: Krieg, Judenmorde und Kollaboration im Jahre 1941,* ed. Vincas Bartusevičius et al., 63–76. Cologne: Böhlau Verlag, 2003.

————. "Der Krieg und die Ermordung der litauischen Juden." In *Nationalsozialistische Vernichtungspolitik 1939–1945: Neue Forschungen und Kontroversen,* ed. Ulrich Herbert, 292–329. Frankfurt: Fischer, 1997.

Dišlers, Guntis. "The Attitude of Latvia's Lutheran Church Towards the Holocaust in World War II." In *Holocausta izpētes problēmas Latvijā/The Issues of the Holocaust Research in Latvia,* 232–47. Riga: Historical Institute of Latvia, 2001.

Documents Accuse. Vilnius: Gintaras, 1970.

Dror, Zvika, ed. *Klooga on the North: Testimonies of Survivors of a Concentration Camp in Estonia.* Kibutz Dalia: Ma'arechet, 1997.

Drywa, Danuta. *Zagłada żydów w obozie koncentracyjnym Stutthof (wrzesień 1939–maj 1945).* Gdańsk: Museum Stutthof, 2001.

Dvorjetski, Marc. *La victoire du ghetto.* Paris: Editions France— Empire, 1962.

Dworzecki, Mark. *Vaise Nekht un Shvartse Teg: Yidn-Lagern in Estonie.* Tel Aviv: Tishlia, 1970.

Eesti rahva kannatuste aasta (The Year of Suffering of the Estonian People). Tallinn: Estonian Self-Government, 1943.

Elango, Õie, et al. *Eesti maast ja rahvast: Maailmasõjast maailmasõjani* (On Estonia Land and Estonian People Between the World Wars). Tallinn: Olion, 1998.

Ērgils, Dzintars. "A Few Holocaust Episodes in Krustpils: Beila Bella Weide Case." In *Holocausta izpētes problēmas Latvijā/The Issues of the Holocaust Research in Latvia,* 2:269–98. Riga: Historical Institute of Latvia, 2001.

Ezergailis, Andrew. "Collaboration in German Occupied Latvia: Offered and Rejected." In *Latvija nacistiskās vācijas okupācijas varā, 1941–1945/Latvia under Nazi German Occupation, 1941–1945,* 7:119–39. Riga: Historical Institute of Latvia, 2004.

————. *The Holocaust in Latvia, 1941–1944: The Missing Center.* Riga: The Historical Institute of Latvia, 1996.

————, ed. *Stockholm Documents: The German Occupation of Latvia, 1941–1945. What Did America Know?* Riga: Historical Institute of Latvia, 2002.

Ferenc, Tone, ed. *Quellen zur nationalsozialistischen Entnationalisierungspolitik in Slowenien 1941–1945.* Maribor: Založba Obzorja, 1980.

Fink, Carole. "Defender of Minorities: Germany in the League of Nations, 1926–1933." *Central European History* 5, no. 3 (Sept. 1972): 330–57.

Fitzpatrick, Sheila, and Robert Gellately, eds. *Accusatory Practices: Denunciation in Modern European History, 1789–1989.* Chicago: Univ. of Chicago Press, 1996.

Flemming, Gerald. *Hitler and the Final Solution.* Berkeley: Univ. of California Press, 1984.

Garleff, Michael. *Deutschbaltische Politik zwischen den Weltkriegen: Die parlamentarische Tätigkeit der deutschbaltischen Partein in Lettland und Estland.* Bad Godesberg: Verlag wissenschaftliches Archiv Bonn, 1976.

Gerlach, Christian, and Götz Aly. *Das letzte Kapitel: Realpolitik, Ideologie und der Mord an den ungarischen Juden 1944/1945.* Stuttgart: DVA, 2002.

Gilbert, Martin. *Endlösung: Die Vertreibung und Vernichtung der Juden. Ein Atlas.* Hamburg: Rowohlt, 1995.

———. *The Righteous: The Unsung Heroes of the Holocaust.* New York: Henry Holt, 2003.

Gross, Jan. *Neighbors: The Destruction of the Jewish Community in Jedwabne, Poland.* Princeton, N.J.: Princeton Univ. Press, 2001.

Grossman, Vasili, and Ilia Ehrenburg, eds. *Chernaia Kniga.* Jerusalem: Yad Vashem, 1980.

Grundmann, Karl-Heinz. *Deutschtumspolitik zur Zeit der Weimarer Republik: Eine Studie am Beispiel der deutsch-baltischen Minderheit in Estland und Lettland.* Hannover: Harro v. Hirschheydt, 1977.

Gurin-Loov, Eugenia. *Eesti juutide katastroof 1941/Holocaust of the Estonian Jews, 1941.* Tallinn: Estonian Jewish Community, 1994.

———. "Verfolgung der Juden in Estland (1941–1944): Rettungsversuche und Hilfe." In *Solidarität und Hilfe für Juden während der NS-Zeit,* ed. Wolfgang Benz and Juliane Wetzel, 295–308. Berlin: Metropol, 1996.

Gurin-Loov, Eugenia, and Gennadi Gramberg. *Eesti Juudi Kogukond/The Jewish Community of Estonia.* Tallinn, 2001.

Haberer, Eric. "Intention and Feasibility: Reflections on Collaboration and the Final Solution." *East European Jewish Affairs* 31, no. 2 (2001): 64–81.

Haupt, Werner. *Baltikum 1941: Die Geschichte eines ungelösten Problems.* Neckargemünd: Kurt Vowinckel Verlag, 1963.

Herman, Judith L. *Trauma and Recovery: The Aftermath of Violence—from Domestic Abuse to Political Terror.* New York: Basic Books, 1992.

Hersey, John. "Prisoner 339, Klooga: Pole Who Escaped Labor Camp Tells How the Nazis Tortured, Butchered and Burned Their Captives." *Life,* Oct. 30, 1944, 71–84.

Hiden, John, and Aleksander Loit, eds. *The Baltic in International Relations Between the Two World Wars.* Stockholm: Studia Universitatis Stockholmiensis, 1988.

Hiden, John, and Patrick Salmon. *The Baltic Nations and Europe: Estonia, Latvia, and Lithuania in the Twentieth Century.* London: Longman, 1994.

Hiio, Toomas. "Jewish Students and Jewish Student Organizations at the University of Tartu." *Tartu University Museum: Annual Report 1998,* 119–72. Tartu: Tartu Univ. Museum, 1999.

Hiio, Toomas, Meelis Maripuu, and Indrek Paavle, eds. *Estonia, 1940–1945: Reports of the Estonian International Commission for the Investigation of Crimes Against Humanity.* Tallinn, 2006.

Hilberg, Raul. *The Destruction of the European Jews.* Chicago: Quadrangle Books, 1967.

Hinkel, Hans. *Judenviertel Europas: Die Juden zwischen Ostsee und Schwarzem Meer.* Berlin: Volk und Reich Verlag, 1939.

Hoover, Karl. "The Baltic Resettlement of 1939 and National Socialist Racial Policy." *Journal of Baltic Studies* 13, no. 1 (Spring 1977): 79–89.

Ilmjärv, Magnus. *Nõukogude Liidu ja Saksamaa vahel: Balti rigid ja Soome 1934–1940* (Between the Soviet Union and Germany: The Baltic States and Finland, 1934–40). Tallinn: Estonian Academy of Science, 1993.

Isberg, Alvin. *Zu den Bedingungen des Befreiers: Kollaboration und Freiheitsstreben in dem von Deutschland besetzten Estland 1941 bis 1944.* Stockholm: Almqvist and Wiksell International, 1992.

Jerousche, Günter, et al., eds. *Denunziation: Historische, juristische und psychologische Aspekte.* Tübingen: Edition Diskord, 1997.

Jokton, Kopl. *Juutide ajaloost Eestis* (On the History of Jews in Estonia). Tartu, 1992 [1926].

Junghann, Otto. *National Minorities in Europe.* New York: Covici-Friede, 1932.

Jürjo, Indrek. *Pagulus ja Nõukogude Eesti* (Exiles and the Soviet Estonia). Tallinn: Umara, 1996.

Kacel, Boris. *From Hell to Redemption: A Memoir of the Holocaust.* Niwot: Univ. Press of Colorado, 1998.

Kaelas, Alexander. "Sotsiialpoliitikast saksa okupatsiooni ajal" (On Social Policy in Times of German Occupation). In *Eesti riik ja rahvas II. Maailmasõjas,* 8:123–41. Stockholm: EMP, 1959.

Kangeris, Karlis. "Die baltischen Völker und die deutschen Pläne für die Räumung des Baltikums 1944." *Baltisches Jahrbuch,* 1988, 177–96.

———. "Kollaboration vor der Kollaboration? Die baltische Emigranten und ihre 'Befreiungskomitees' in Deutschland 1940/1941." In *Europa unterm Hakenkreuz: Okkupation und Kollaboration (1938–1945),* ed. Werner Röhr, 165–90. Berlin: Hüthig Verlagsgemeinschaft, 1994.

———. "Die nationalsozialistischen Pläne und Propagandamassnahmen im Generalbezirk Lettland 1941–1942." In *Collaboration and Resistance During the Holocaust: Belarus, Estonia, Latvia, Lithuania,* ed. David Gaunt et al., 161–86. Bern: Peter Lang, 2004.

Kasekamp, Andres. "The Ideological Roots of Estonian Collaboration During the Nazi Occupation." In *The Baltic Countries under Occupation: Soviet and Nazi Rule, 1939–1991,* ed. Anu Mai Köll. Stockholm: Acta Universitatis Stockholmiensis, 2003.

————. *The Radical Right in Interwar Estonia*. New York: St. Martin's Press, 2000.

————. "Vapsid ja vähemusrahvused" (Vabs and Ethnic Minorities). *Ajaloo Ajakiri,* no. 1 (1997): 11–14.

Kaur, Uno. *Wirtschaftsstruktur und Wirtschaftspolitik des Freistaates Estland 1918–1940.* Bonn: Baltisches Forschungsinstitut, 1962.

Kershaw, Ian. *Popular Opinion and Political Dissent in the Third Reich: Bavaria, 1933–1945.* Oxford, UK: Clarendon Press, 1983.

Kingreen, Monica. "Gewaltsam verschleppt aus Frankfurt: Die Deportationen der Juden in den Jahren 1941–1945." In *Nach der Kristallnacht: Jüdisches Leben und antijüdische Politik in Frankfurt am Main 1938–1945,* 357–401. Frankfurt: Campus Verlag, 1999.

Klein, Peter. "Dr. Rudolf Lange als Kommandeur der Sicherheitspolizei und des SD in Lettland: Aspekte seines Dienstalltages." In *Täter im Vernichtungskrieg: Der Überfall auf die Sowjetunion und der Völkermord an den Juden,* ed. Wolf Kaiser, 125–36. Berlin: Propyläen, 2002.

————, ed. *Die Einsatzgruppen in der besetzten Sowjetunion 1941/42: Die Tätigkeits-und Lageberichte der Chefs der Sicherheitspolizei und des SD.* Berlin: Edition Hentrich, 1997.

Kokla, Juhan. "Eesti ajakirjandus ja saksa okupatsioon" (Estonian Press and the German Occupation). In *Eesti riik ja rahvas II. Maailmasõjas,* 8:144–66. Stockholm: EMP, 1959.

Kõll, Anu Mai, and Jaak Valge. *Economic Nationalism and Industrial Growth: State and Industry in Estonia, 1934–39.* Stockholm: Acta Universitatis Stockholmiensis, 1998.

Krausnick, Helmut, and Hans-Heinrich Wilhelm. *Die Truppe des Weltanschauungskrieges: Die Einsatzgruppen der Sicherheitspolizei und des SD, 1938–1942.* Stuttgart: Deutsche Verlags-Anstalt, 1981.

Kruk, Herman. *The Last Days of the Jerusalem of Lithuania: Chronicles from the Vilna Ghetto and the Camps, 1939–1944.* New Haven, Conn.: Yale Univ. Press, 2002.

Kuusik, Argo. "Die deutsche Vernichtungspolitik in Estland 1941–1944." In *Vom Hitler-Stalin-Pakt biz zu Stalins Tod: Estland 1939–1953,* ed. Olaf Mertelsmann, 130–50. Hamburg: Bibliotheca Baltica, 2005.

Laqueur, Walter, ed. *The Holocaust Encyclopedia.* New Haven, Conn.: Yale Univ. Press, 2001.

Lentsman, Leonid, ed. *Estonskii narod v Velikoi Otechestvennoi voine Sovetskogo Soiuza, 1941–1945.* Tallinn: Eesti Raamat, 1973.

Lenz, Wilhelm. "Erbhöfe für baltische Restgutbesitzer im Warthegau: Briefwechsel zwischen Darré und Himmler." *Jahrbuch des baltischen Deutschtums,* 1982, 124–34.

Leszczynskski, Kazimierz, ed. *Fall 9: Das Urteil im SS-Einsatzgruppenprozess, gefällt am 10. April 1948 in Nürnberg vom Militärgerichtshof II der Vereinigten Staaten von Amerika.* Berlin: Rütten and Loening, 1963.

Levin, Dov. *Baltic Jews under the Soviets, 1940–1946.* Jerusalem: Hebrew Univ. Press, 1994.

———. "Estonian Jews in the USSR, 1941–1945." *Yad Vashem Studies* 7 (1976): 273–97.

———. *The Lesser of Two Evils: Eastern European Jewry under Soviet Rule, 1939–1941.* Philadelphia: Jewish Publication Society, 1995.

Linck, Stephan. *Der Ordnung verpflichtet: Deutsche Polizei 1933–1949. Der Fall Flensburg.* Paderborn: Ferdinand Schöningh, 2000.

Lindmäe. *Suvesõda Tartumaal 1941* (The Summer War in Tartu Province, 1941). (Tartu, 1999).

Lindroos, Katri. "Judaistika õppetool Tartu Ülikoolis 1930. aastatel" (Chair in Judaic Studies at Tartu University in the 1930s). *Akadeemia* 6, no. 11 (1994): 2136–49.

Loeber, Dietrich, ed. *Diktierte Option: Die Umsiedlung der Deutsch-Balten aus Estland und Lettland 1939–1941.* Neumünster: Karl Wachholtz, 1972.

Longerich, Peter. *Politik der Vernichtung: Eine Gesamtdarstellung der nationalsozialistischen Judenverfolgung.* Munich: Piper, 1998.

Lumans, Valdis. *Himmler's Auxiliaries: The Volksdeutsche Mittelstelle and the German National Minorities of Europe, 1933–1945.* Chapel Hill: Univ. of North Carolina Press, 1993.

MacQueen, Michael. "Einheimische Gehilfin der Gestapo: Die litauische Sicherheitspolizei in Vilnius 1941–1944." In *Holocaust in Litauen: Krieg, Judenmorde und Kollaboration im Jahre 1941,* ed. Vincas Bartusevičius et al., 103–16. Cologne: Böhlau Verlag, 2003.

———. "Nazi Policy Toward the Jews in the 'Reichskommissariat Ostland,' June–December 1941: From White Terror to Holocaust in Lithuania." In *Bitter Legacy: Confronting the Holocaust in the USSR,* ed. Zvi Gitelman, 91–103. Bloomington: Indiana Univ. Press, 1997.

Maddison, Eugen. *Die nationalen Minderheiten Estlands und ihre Rechte.* Tallinn, 1930.

Made, Vahur. *Eesti ja Rahvaste Liit* (Estonia and the League of Nations). Tartu: Tartu Univ. Press, 1999.

Mäe, Hjalmar. *Kuidas kõik teostus: Minu mälestusi* (How Everything Has Happened: My Memoirs). Stockholm: EMP, 1993.

Maripuu, Meelis. "Eesti juutide holocaust ja eestlased" (Estonians and the Holocaust of the Estonian Jews). *Vikerkaar* 15, no. 8–9 (2001): 135–46.

Martinson, Ervin. *Slugi svastiki.* Tallinn: Estonian State Publishing House, 1962.

Matsulevich, Anna, ed. *Vähemusrahvuste kultuurielu Eesti Vabariigis, 1918–1940* (Cultural Life of the Ethnic Minorities in Estonia, 1918–40). Tallinn: Olion, 1993.

Matsulevitš, Anni, ed. *Pruun Katk: Saksa fašistlik okupatsioon Eestis 1941–1944. Dokumente ja materjale* (Brown Plague: German Fascist Occupation of Estonia, 1941–44. Documents and Materials). Tallinn: Eesti Raamat, 1988.

Matthäus, Jürgen. "Jenseits der Grenze: Die ersten Massen-erschiessungen von Juden in Litauen (Juni–August 1941)." *Zeitschrift für Geschichtswissenschaft* 44, no. 2 (1996): 101–17.

Mayer, Arno. *Why Did the Heavens Not Darken? The Final Solution in History.* New York: Pantheon Books, 1988.

Medijainen, Eero. *Saadiku saatus: Välisministeerium ja saatkonnad 1918–1940* (Fate of an Envoy: Foreign Ministry and Consulates, 1918–1940). Tallinn: Eesti Entsüklopeediakirjastus, 1997.

Meissner, Boris, Dietrich Loeber, and Cornelius Hasselblatt, eds. *Die deutsche Volksgruppe in Estland während der Zwischenkriegszeit und aktuelle Fragen des deutschestnischen Verhältnisses.* Hamburg: Bibliotheca Baltica, 1997.

Mendelsohn, Ezra. *The Jews of East Central Europe Between the World Wars.* Bloomington: Indiana Univ. Press, 1983.

———. *On Modern Jewish Politics.* Oxford, UK: Oxford Univ. Press, 1993.

Meriste, R. "Noorimana Julg.-grupp 185-ndas" (As the Youngest in the 185th Police Battalion). *Eesti riik ja rahvas II. Maailmasõjas,* 7:102–22. Stockholm: EMP, 1959.

Milgram, Stanley. "The Compulsion to Do Evil: Obedience to Criminal Orders." *Patterns of Prejudice* 1, no. 6 (Nov.–Dec. 1967): 3–7.

Mishell, Willem. *Kaddish for Kovno: Life and Death in a Lithuanian Ghetto, 1941–1945.* Chicago: Review Press, 1988.

Misiunas, J. Romuald, and Rein Taagepera. *The Baltic States. Years of Dependence, 1940–1980.* Berkeley: Univ. of California Press, 1983.

Müller, Rolf-Dieter. *Die deutsche Wirtschaftspolitik in den besetzten sowjetischen Gebieten 1941–1943.* Boppard: Harald Boldt Verlag, 1991.

My obviniaem. Riga: Liesma, 1967.

Myllyniemi, Seppo. *Die Neuordnung der baltischen Länder 1941–1944: Zum nationalsozialistischen Inhalt der deutschen Besatzungspolitik.* Helsinki: Dissertationes Historicae II, 1973.

Neizvestnaia Chernaia Kniga. Jerusalem: Yad Vashem, 1993.

Nielsen-Stokkeby, Bernd. "Die Umsiedlung der Deutschbalten aus estnischer Sicht." *Baltisches Jahrbuch* 6 (1989): 220–33.

Noormets, Tiit, ed. *Eesti julgeolekupolitsei aruanded, 1941–1944* (Reports of the Estonian Security Police, 1941–44). Tallinn: Riigiarhiiv, 2002.

Ogorreck, Ralf. *Die Einsatzgruppen und die 'Genesis der Endlösung.'* Berlin: Metropol, 1996.

Õun, Mati, ed. *Eesti ohvitserid ja sõjandustegelased* (Estonian Officers and Military Figures). Tallinn: Sentinel, 2002.

Pajur, Ago. *Eesti Riigikaitsepoliitika aastail 1918–1934* (Estonian Defense Policies, 1918–34). Tartu: Estonian Historical Archives, 1999.

Pankseiev, Alexander, and Madis Pesti, eds. *Ocherki istorii Kommunisticheskoi partii Estonii (1920–1940 gody).* Part 2. Tallinn: Eesti Riiklik Kirjastus, 1963.

Panova, Vera. "Metelitsa." *Sobranie sochinenii v piati tomakh.* Vol. 5. Leningrad, 1970.

Parming, Tönu. "The Holocaust in Estonia: Conceptual and Methodological Problems in Research. A Critical Review." *Meie Elu* (Toronto), Feb. 4–Sept. 30, 1998.

———. "The Jewish Community and Inter-Ethnic Relations in Estonia, 1918–1940." *Journal of Baltic Studies* 10, no. 3 (1979): 241–62.

Paskuly, Steven, ed. *Death Dealer: The Memoirs of the SS Commandant at Auschwitz, Rudolf Höss.* New York: Da Capo Press, 1996.

Paul, Toomas. "Eestlaste ja juutide suhetest" (On Estonian-Jewish Relations). *Looming,* no. 2 (1997): 244–53.

Pavle, Indrek, ed. *Eesti rahvastikukaotused II/1: Saksa okupatsioon 1941–1944* (Population Losses in Estonia II/1: German Occupation, 1941–1944). Tartu, 2002.

Penkower, Monty Noam. *The Jews Were Expendable: Free World Diplomacy and the Holocaust.* Chicago: Univ. of Illinois Press, 1983.

Petersen, D. Roger. *Resistance and Rebellion: Lessons from Eastern Europe.* Cambridge, UK: Cambridge Univ. Press, 2001.

———. *Understanding Ethnic Violence: Fear, Hatred, and Resentment in Twentieth-Century Europe.* Cambridge, UK: Cambridge Univ. Press, 2002.

Pflug, Helker. "Aspekte jüdischen Lebens in Estland bis 1940." In *Die vergessenen Juden in den baltischen Staaten,* 51–60. Cologne: Verlag Wissenschaft und Politik, 1998.

Pihlau, Jaak. "Aleksander Viidiku varjatud elu: Vabadussõjalasest NKVD tippagendiks" (The Hidden Life of Alexander Viidik: A Vabs into an NKVD Top Agent). *Akadeemia* 4 (2002): 726–34.

Pinchuk, Ben Cion. *Jews under Soviet Rule: Eastern Poland on the Eve of the Holocaust.* Oxford: Basil Blackwell, 1990.

Porudominski, Vladimir, ed. *Die Juden von Wilna: Die Aufzeichnungen des Grigorij Schur, 1941–1944.* Munich: Deutscher Taschenbuch Verlag, 1999.

Přibyl, Lukáš. "Die Geschichte des Theresienstädter Transports 'Be' nach Estland." In *Theresienstädter Studien und Dokumente*, 148–229. Prague: Institut Theresienstädter Initiative, 2001.

Puide, Peeter. *Samuil Braschinskys försvunna vrede. Dokumentär-roman.* Stockholm: Norstedts, 1997.

Purre, Arnold. "Eesti sõda Nõuk. Liiduga" (Estonia's War Against the Soviet Union). In *Eesti riik ja rahvas II. Maailmasõjas*, 7:22–55. Stockholm: EMP, 1959.

Putins Peters, Rita. "Baltic State Diplomacy and the League of Nations Minorities System." In *The Baltic in International Relations Between the Two World Wars*, ed. John Hiden and Aleksander Loit, 281–99. Stockholm: Studia Universitatis Stockholmiensis, 1988.

Raid, Robert. *When the Soviets Came. . . .* 2 vols. Cardiff: Boreas Publishing House, 1985 and 1986.

Rasch, Manfred. "Die Bedeutung des Bankhauses Mendelssohn & Co. für die Industrialisierung Estlands." *Mendelssohn Studien* 6 (1986): 183–213.

———. "Zur Mineralölpolitik der Kriegsmarine: Dokumente aus dem Jahre 1935." *Militärgeschichtliche Mitteilungen* 71, no. 1 (1985): 71–101.

Rauch, Georg von. *The Baltic States: The Years of Independence. Estonia, Latvia, Lithuania, 1917–1940.* Berkeley: Univ. of California Press, 1974.

Raun, Toivo. "Nineteenth-and Early Twentieth-Century Estonian Nationalism Revisited." *Nations and Nationalism* 9, no. 1 (2003): 129–47.

Rautkallio, Hannu. *Finland and the Holocaust: The Rescue of Finland's Jews.* New York: Holocaust Library, 1987.

Redecker, Niels von. "Victor von zur Mühlen und die national-sozialistische Bewegung im estländischen Deutschtum: Eine biographische Annäherung." In *Deutschbalten, Weimarer Republik und Drittes Reich*, ed. Michael Garleff, 77–117. Cologne: Böhlau Verlag, 2001.

Reichelt, Katrin. "Der Anteil von Letten an der Enteignung der Juden ihres Landes zwischen 1941 und 1943." In *Kooperation und Verbrechen: Formen der 'Kollaboration' im östlichen Europa 1939–1945*, ed. Christoph Dieckmann, 224–42. Göttingen: Wallstein Verlag, 2003.

Robinson, Jacob, et al. *Were the Minorities Treaties a Failure?* New York: Institute of Jewish Affairs, 1943.

Saks, Elhonen. *Kes on Juudid ja mis on holokaust?* (Who Are the Jews and What Is the Holocaust?). Tallinn: Sild, 2003.

———. "Kloogat peeti heaks Laagriks!" (Klooga Was Considered a Good Camp!). *Horisont*, no. 6 (1991): 12–13.

Salo, Vello. *Population Losses, 1940–1941: Citizens of Jewish Nationality.* Tallinn: Estonian State Commission on Examination of the Policies of Repression, 2002.

Scheffler, Wolfgang, and Diana Schulle, eds. *Book of Remembrance: The German, Austrian and Czechoslovakian Jews Deported to the Baltic States.* Vol. 2. Munich: G. Saur, 2003.

Schoenberner, Gerhard, ed. *House of the Wannsee Conference: Permanent Exhibit. Guide and Reader.* Berlin: Hentrich, 2000.

Seidler, Franz. *Die Organisation Todt: Bauen für Staat und Wehrmacht 1938–1945.* Stuttgart: Bernard and Graefe Verlag, 1987.

Sekules, Edith. *Surviving the Nazis, Exile, and Siberia.* London: Valentine Mitchell, 2000.

Seth, Ronald. *A Spy Has No Friends.* London: Andre Deutsch, 1952.

Smith, Graham, ed. *The Baltic States: The National Self-Determination of Estonia, Latvia, and Lithuania.* New York: St. Martin's Press, 1994.

Stang, Knut. "Das Fussvolk und seine Eliten: Der Beginn der Kollaboration in Litauen 1941." In *Judenmord in Litauen: Studien und Dokumente,* ed. Wolfgang Benz and Marion Neiss, 69–89. Berlin: Metropol, 1999.

———. *Kollaboration und Massenmord: Die litauische Hilfspolizei, das Rollkommando Hamann und die Ermordung der litauischen Juden.* Frankfurt: Peter Lang, 1996.

Staub, Ervin. *The Roots of Evil: The Origins of Genocide and Other Group Violence.* Cambridge, UK: Cambridge Univ. Press, 1989.

Streim, Alfred. "Konzentrationslager auf dem Gebiet der Sowjetunion." *Dachauer Hefte* 5, no. 5 (Nov. 1989): 174–87.

Streit, Christian. *Keine Kameraden: Die Wehrmacht und die sowjetische Kriegsgefangenen 1941–1945.* Bonn: Verlag J. H. W. Dietz Nachf., 1997.

Sužiedėlis, Saulius. "Foreign Saviors, Native Disciples: Perspectives on Collaboration in Lithuania, 1940–1945." In *Collaboration and Resistance During the Holocaust: Belarus, Estonia, Latvia, Lithuania,* ed. David Gaunt et al., 313–59. Bern: Peter Lang, 2004.

———. "The Historical Sources for Antisemitism in Lithuania and Jewish-Lithuanian Relations During the 1930s." In *The Vanished World of Lithuanian Jews,* ed. Alvydas Nikžentaitis et al., 119–54. Amsterdam: Rodopi, 2004.

Toleikis, Vytautas. "Lithuanian Roma During the Years of the Nazi Occupation." In *Karo belaisvių ir civilių gyventojų žudynės Lietuvoje, 1941–1944* (Murder of Prisoners of War and Civilian Population in Lithuania, 1941–1944), ed. Christoph Dieckmann et al., 267–85. Vilnius: Margi raštai, 2005.

Tory, Avraham. *Surviving the Holocaust: The Kovno Ghetto Diary.* Cambridge, Mass.: Harvard Univ. Press, 1990.

Truhart, von Herbert. *Völkerbund und Minderheitenpetitionen.* Vienna: Wilhelm Braumüller, 1931.

Tõnismägi, Heino. *Ülekohtu toimikud* (The Files of Injustice). Tallinn: BNS, 1998.

Ungern-Sternberg, Roderich. *Die Bevölkerungsverhältnisse in Estland, Lettland, Litauen und Polen: Eine demographisch-statistische Studie.* Berlin: Verlagsbuchhandlung von Richard Schoetz, 1939.

Vaatz, Alexander. *Baltikum und Weissruthenien in ihren landwirtschaftlichen Grundlagen.* Berlin: C. V. Engelhard, 1942.

Vasara, Vesa. "Die deutschbaltische Minderheit in Estland in der Zwischenkriegszeit: Wirtschaft und Finanzen." *Zeitschrift für Ostmitteleuropa-Forschung* 44, no. 4 (1995): 578–89.

Västrik, Riho. "Klooga koonduslaager—Vaivara süsteemi koletu lõpp" (Klooga Concentration Camp: An Ugly End to the Vaivara Camp System). *Vikerkaar* 15, no. 8–9 (2001): 147–55.

———. "Tartu koonduslaager" (Tartu Concentration Camp). *Ajalooline Ajakiri* 3–4 (1999): 71–80.

Verschik, Anna. *Estonian Yiddish and Its Contacts with Co-territorial Languages.* Tartu: Tartu Univ. Press, 2000.

Vestermanis, Marġers. "Local Headquarters Liepaja: Two Months of German Occupation in the Summer of 1941." In *War of Extermination: The German Military in World War II, 1941–1944,* ed. Hannes Heer and Klaus Naumann, 219–36. New York: Berghahn Books, 2000.

Vīksne, Rudīte. "The Arājs Commando Member as Seen in the KGB Trial Files: Social Standing, Education, Motives for Joining It, and Sentences Received." *Holocausta izpētes problēmas Latvijā* (The Issues of the Holocaust Research in Latvia), 2:350–80. Riga: Historical Institute of Latvia, 2001.

Volkmann, Hans-Erich. "Ökonomie und Machtpolitik Lettland und Estland im politisch-ökonomischen Kalkül des Dritten Reiches (1933–1940)." In *Geschichte und Gesellschaft* 2 (1976): 471–500.

Weiss, Helmuth. "Zur Umsiedlung der Deutschen aus Estland 1939–1941: Erinnerungsbericht." *Zeitschrift für Ostforschung* 39, no. 4 (1990): 481–502.

Weiss-Wendt, Anton. "Extermination of the Gypsies in Estonia During World War II: Popular Images and Official Policies." *Holocaust and Genocide Studies* 17, no. 1 (Spring 2003): 31–61.

———. "The Soviet Occupation of Estonia in 1940–41 and the Jews." *Holocaust and Genocide Studies* 12, no. 2 (Fall 1998): 308–25.

———. "Thanks to the Germans! Jewish Cultural Autonomy in Interwar Estonia." *East-European Jewish Affairs* 38, no. 1 (Apr. 2008): 89–104.

Wette, Wolfram. "SS-Standartenführer Karl Jäger, Kommandeur der Sicherheitspolizei (KdS) in Kaunas: Eine biographische Skizze." In *Holocaust in Litauen: Krieg, Judenmorde und Kollaboration im Jahre 1941,* ed. Vincas Bartusevičius et al., 77–90. Cologne: Böhlau Verlag, 2003.

Wildt, Michael. *Generation des Unbedingten: Das Führungskorps des Reichssicherheitshauptamtes.* Hamburg: Hamburger Edition, 2002.

Wilhelm, Hans-Heinrich. *Die Einsatzgruppe A der Sicherheits-polizei und des SD 1941/42.* Frankfurt: Peter Lang, 1996.

———. *Rassenpolitik und Kriegsführung: Sicherheitspolizei und Wehrmacht in Polen und der Sowjetunion.* Passau: Richard Rothe, 1991.

Witte, Peter, et al., eds. *Der Dienstkalender Heinrich Himmlers 1941/42.* Hamburg: Christians, 1999.

Wrangell, Wilhelm. "Zur Situation der Deutschbalten in Estland bis zur Umsiedlung." In *Zwischen Reval und St. Petersburg: Erinnerungen von Estländern aus zwei Jahrhundert,* 399–420. Weissenhorn: Anton H. Konrad Verlag, 1993.

INDEX

confessions. *See* forced confessions

Continental Oil, 247, 261. *See also* Estonian shale oil industry

conversion of Jews to Christianity, 3, 174

cooperatives, 139, 164, 170

Cornelius, Heinrich, 90

corpses, burning of, 207, 238, 260, 276, 283, 286–87, 292–93, 297, 306–7, 309, 314–19

courts, 105, 341

crematoria, 260, 276, 306

Crimea. *See* Crimean Peninsula

Crimean Peninsula, 247

Criminal Police, 92, 105, 144, 151, 182

criminals, habitual, 115, 155, 179

Croatia, 251

cultural autonomy, 1, 2–3, 5, 24, 26, 32, 73

culture: "Asiatic," 38, 341; Estonian, 6, 19, 67, 72–73, 81, 338–41; German, 3, 6, 19–20, 38, 68; Latvian, 6, 72–73; Russian, 3, 6, 38; shared, 65; Western, 65

Czechoslovakia, 49, 226, 230, 234, 240, 242, 245, 295. *See also* Jews, Czech; Protectorate of Bohemia and Moravia

Czechs, 3, 73, 216, 243

Dachau concentration camp, 75, 258–59

Dahlmann, Max, 279, 316

Danish and Icelandic Vice Consul in Estonia, 297

Danzig, 35, 86–87, 268, 300

Daugava River, 88

Daugavpils, 148, 253, 255

death certificates, 133, 152, 209

death penalty. *See* death sentences

death sentences, 15, 40, 103, 105, 140, 155, 186, 189, 193, 195, 268

death squads, 121–22, 313, 327, 332, 341

defendants, 108, 122, 161, 243, 273, 325

dehumanization, 186, 342

Denmark, 324

denunciations, 37, 100, 112, 114–15, 156, 158, 165–69, 177, 182, 187, 211, 333. *See also* informers

deportation of summer 1941, 35, 40–42, 50–51, 64, 108, 165, 341; Hitler briefed on, 42; Jews allegedly involved in, 158, 191, 194, 212; Jews as victims of, 48–49, 160, 171, 209; Mäe on, 46; numbers of deportees, 47–48, 134; Tambek on, 134; targeted Russian immigrants and Estonian officials, 42, 168; triggers for, 41; and war with Nazi Germany, 49, 94. *See also* Soviet terror

deportations of Jews: from Berlin, 220–21, 233–34, 242, 245; to Estonia, 251, 253, 321; from France, 266–67; from Frankfurt on Main, 220, 232–33, 242, 245; from Hungary, 266; from Kaiserwald camp, 275, 321; from Kovno ghetto, 253, 255–56, 282, 297, 302, 321; from Latvia, 321; from Lithuania, 318, 321; to Stutthof camp, 242, 265, 267–68, 275, 292, 298–300; from Theresienstadt ghetto, 223–25, 228, 230, 234, 242, 245; from Vilna ghetto, 253–55, 261, 269, 286, 293, 297, 302, 321. *See also* Jewish transports

Deportee Registration Office (ZEV), 133–34. *See also* deportation of summer 1941; Soviet terror

deserters, 116, 175, 338

Deutsche Schutzbund (Grenz- und Auslandsdeutschtum), 28

Deutsche Zeitung im Ostland, 217, 333. *See also* newspapers

diabetes, 281. *See also* diseases

diarrhea, 286. *See also* diseases

Dieckmann, Christoph, 326

diplomats: American, 5, 14–15, 41, 216, 218; British, 35, 320; foreign, 37; Latvian, 216

263, 288, 309–10; and von Roques, 60, 71,
337; Security Division 207, 60, 123; set to
capture Pskov, 43; shale oil region secured,
43–44; and shock battalions, 52, 90; 16th
Army, 263; 61st Infantry Division, 44;
SS training and replacement unit no. 20,
317; struggle against, 162; 38th Army
Corps, 43; troops committed to "Russian
campaign"; 26th Army Corps, 43–44, 246;
254th Infantry Division, 44; 291st Infan-
try Division, 95; 217th Infantry Division,
44; welcomed in Valga, Elva, Otepää, 45.
See also Waffen-SS; Wehrmacht
German civil administration, 59, 60–61, 63,
80, 128, 253; and Jewish property, 139–40,
143
German colonization, 31, 61, 82, 335. See also
Germanization; Lebensraum
German Criminal Police in Estonia, 144, 151
German Cultural Council, 24, 209
German Economic Office (WiKo), 76
German Empire, 29
Germanen, 79
German Foreign Office, 25–26, 28–29, 38, 212
Germanization policy, 67, 78–83, 339, 341
German League for the Defense of Ethnic
Germans Abroad, 28–30
German Ministry of Education and Propa-
ganda, 55
German occupation, 13, 25, 43, 64, 69–70, 78,
83–84, 105, 108, 115, 119–21, 135, 147, 148,
150, 155, 167–68, 179, 218, 239, 301, 324,
326, 330, 333–34, 336
German Order Police, 107
German Postal Service, 140
Germans: and Estonians, 3, 11, 36, 45, 59,
69–73, 75, 77, 79, 91, 106, 158, 164, 175,
207, 235, 243, 249, 271, 285, 297, 339
German Security Police, 58, 59, 90, 127;
and deportations from Vilna ghetto,

255; Heydrich as head of, 86; and Jewish
Mischlinge, 211; and Kostivere estate, 232;
officers of, 90, 127, 140, 154, 222, 245,
251, 258; outposts of, 103; and pogroms,
124; school in Berlin-Charlottenburg, 85;
school in Pretzsch, 87; and shooting of
mentally ill patients, 149; and Wehrmacht, 88, 124
German Security Police in Estonia: Baltic
Germans in, 108; carried out arrests
of intelligentsia, 76; decided against
pogroms, 124–25; and denunciations,
167; and deportees, 47; depot of, 231, 237;
and Estonians, 68, 119, 332; and Estonian
shale oil industry, 250; and executions of
Jews, 132, 176, 183, 209, 213–14, 227, 268,
316; and expropriation of Jewish property,
136, 139, 141, 231; female employees of,
231; and foreign Jews, 212; and Gypsies,
144; headquarters of, 87, 108, 125, 154,
181, 311; at Jägala camp, 225, 231, 235,
237, 240–41; and Jewish forced labor
camps, 279, 308; and Lepp case, 174–77;
members of, 231; office in Kiviõli, 92;
officials of, 225; and Omakaitse, 90, 99;
and Punishment Planning Commissions,
113; and Reichswehr, 340; relations with
Estonian Security Police, 90, 92, 108, 113,
245, 337; reports of, 50, 52, 54–55, 91; and
Tartu concentration camp, 200–201; and
Viidik, 115
German Security Police in Latvia, 120, 130,
148, 237
German Security Police in Lithuania, 147, 255
Germany, 1, 7, 13, 20, 57, 116, 146, 235, 259,
306, 308–9, 311, 335; crude oil production
in, 22; deportation of Jews from, 220–21,
234, 240, 242, 245; Estonia and, 27, 66;
and Gypsies, 148; Jewish emigration
from, 8, 9, 49, 211–12, 214; murder of

275, 277, 293, 302, 305, 313, 322; mur-
dered, 128, 130, 180–86, 190–91, 206–7,
227–28, 242–44, 260, 275, 277–78, 295,
299, 307, 342
Jewish consuls general, 8. *See also* Frankfurt
on Main; Hamburg
Jewish Councils, 277
Jewish Cultural Council. *See* Jewish Cultural
Self-Government
Jewish Cultural Self-Government, 5, 6, 54
Jewish elders, 126, 189, 230, 235, 237, 258,
283, 299
Jewish forced labor, 245, 250
Jewish forced labor camps, 217, 251, 254,
256–321, 342. *See also individual camps*
Jewish pale of settlement, 2, 4
Jewish police, 230, 235, 255, 258
Jewish politics, 7
Jewish property: and archives, 137; and
assets, 137; and Baatz, 141; BBC reported
on, 141; and Bergmann, 230–31; books,
135–36, 140, 143; and Economic and
Administrative Office, 140; and Estonian
Art Museum, 136; and Estonian police
officials, 231, 245; and Estonian Relief
Agency, 185; and Estonian Security
Police, 137, 141, 155, 245; and Estonian
Self-Government, 63, 139; and Estonian
Trusteeship Office, 139–40; expropriation of, 135–43, 184–85, 227–28,
254; and forced labor camps, 306, 317;
furniture, 140, 142–43; and German civil
administration, 139–40; and German
Security Police, 136, 139–41, 185, 245;
and Himmler, 136; at Jägala concentration camp, 227–32; in Latvia, 136–38,
142–43; and Lepik, 137; libraries, 136–37,
143; lists of, 138; in Lithuania, 138, 143;
and Litzmann, 139, 141; and Lohse, 139;
and Mäe, 136; and Mikson, 137–38; and

Möller, 141; in Narva, 140; in Nõmme,
142; and Omakaitse, 140; and Operations
Staff Rosenberg, 136; in Pärnu, 139; in
Pechory, 140, 188; in Põltsamaa, 139; in
Rakvere, 140; and Red Cross, 140; and
Reich Commissioner for Estonia, 137,
139–40; and Reich Security Main Office,
136–37; and Sandberger, 136; sold, 140;
in Tallinn, 125, 139, 141; in Tartu, 136,
140–41, 197–98, 204; and Tartu University, 135–36, 140; in Viljandi, 139, 141–42;
in Võru, 141; and Wehrmacht, 139–40
"Jewish Question," 8, 11, 50, 166; importance
of, 12, 56, 215, 341; in Latvia and Lithuania, 11; Möller on, 93; Sandberger on, 86,
91. *See also* "Final Solution of the Jewish
Question"
Jewish refugees, 49
Jewish survivors, 152, 156, 220–21, 226, 237,
241–42, 258, 262, 269, 273, 277–78, 291,
300, 304, 306, 308, 317–18, 321
Jewish transports, 216, 220–21, 223–24, 228,
230, 232–33, 245, 254–55, 265–66, 275,
277, 286, 289, 292, 300–302, 307. *See also*
deportations of Jews
Jewish women, 174–85, 233, 345; arrested,
155, 157, 216; denounced, 166–67;
executed at Kalevi-Liiva, 227, 234, 242;
in forced labor camps, 262–63, 266,
270, 276–78, 283–84, 286, 289, 295,
297, 299–300, 302–4, 306, 308, 312–13;
at Jägala concentration camp, 230–32,
236–38; from mixed marriages, 210;
murdered, 128, 130, 181, 189–91, 242–43,
277, 299, 305–6, 314, 342; in Narva, 161,
163, 189; in Pärnu, 132, 190–91; saved,
156; in Tallinn, 125–26, 132, 138, 181; in
Tallinn Central prison, 181, 240–42; at
Tartu concentration camp, 206–7, 244; in
Thresienstadt transport, 225